Every

MIRACLE

AND WONDER

in the Bible

Every

MIRACLE

AND WONDER

in the Bible

LARRY RICHARDS

Illustrated by

Paul Richards

THOMAS NELSON PUBLISHERS

Nashville

Library of Congress Cataloging-in-Publication Data

Richards, Larry, 1931–
    Every miracle and wonder in the Bible / Larry Richards ;
  illustrated by Paul Richards.
      p.   cm.
  Includes indexes.
  ISBN 0-7852-1264-7
    1. Miracles—Biblical teaching.   2. Bible—Criticism,
  interpretation, etc.   I. Title.
  BS680.M5R53   1997
  231.7′3—dc21   97-39584
                                        CIP

Printed in the United States of America

1 2 3 4 5 6 7 8—02 01 00 99 98

CONTENTS

See Expository and Scripture Indexes for Complete Topic and Scripture Listings

Every

MIRACLE

AND WONDER

in the Bible

CAN MIRACLES HAPPEN?

THE GRAND MIRACLES OF SCRIPTURE

Genesis 1—2; John 1:1–3; Romans 1:1–4

A suspicious Gideon said it well. "O my lord, if the LORD is with us, why then has all this happened to us? And where are all His miracles which our fathers told us about, saying, 'Did not the LORD bring us up from Egypt?' "

At times we wonder too. Where are all the miracles we read about in the Bible? At such times we need to hear the testimony of Scripture, which affirms, "You are the God who does wonders" (Psalm 77:14). The more clearly we see God as the God who does wonders, the more confident we will be when we face troubled times.

I. THE GRAND MIRACLES OF SCRIPTURE

Three "grand miracles" described in Scripture shape the Christian understanding of God. These grand miracles are defining events—happenings which stamp the Christian faith as unique. These three miracle are so central to our faith that, if any one of them were taken away, our faith could no longer be called "biblical" or "Christian."

The three grand miracles of Scripture are:

- the miracle of Creation,
- the miracle of the Incarnation, and
- the miracle of the Resurrection.

THE MIRACLE OF CREATION

Any person who sets out to understand the meaning of life realizes that his or her inquiry must begin with the question of origins. Where did this universe in which we live come from? And, how did human beings originate?

The reason our quest has to begin here is simply because the answer we give to these two most basic questions will shape the answers we give to every other question about life.

VARIOUS BELIEFS ABOUT ORIGINS AND THEIR IMPLICATIONS

Ancient Middle Eastern beliefs were expressed in religious terms. The people of the ancient world understood that the issue of origins was vital, and they struggled to suggest answers. Their answers were given religious form, in that they invented myths to explain where the world came from and to explain man's role in the world.

A popular myth in Mesopotamia portrayed the universe as the body of a god who had been killed in a cosmic struggle. Human beings had sprung from his drops of blood and they had been forced to work for all time for the victorious deity.

The Egyptians had at least five creation myths. These myths featured gods giving birth to other gods, with the universe an almost accidental by-product. In one of the myths, human beings sprang from the lewd sex act of one of their pagan gods.

In another ancient tradition, human beings were made after a rebellion by lower gods forced the higher gods to create man to do the labor which these lower gods refused to do.

In each of these belief systems, man's role was to toil and then to die, with little or no hope of an afterlife.

Today, of course, these ancient myths are rejected as naïve. They belong to the realm of superstition, surviving only as academic curiosities. Yet the questions the people of the ancient world sought to answer still remain with us. And the answers we give still shape our basic attitudes toward life and death.

Ancient Western beliefs were expressed in philosophical terms. In the West, the Greeks saw matter as co-eternal with the gods. Human beings were part of the material creation. Philosophers probed to find ways that men might live in harmony with an essentially impersonal universe, in which fate ruled the destiny of gods and men alike.

As elements of that impersonal universe, men and women were thought to live for a brief time before they slipped away into the realm of the dead. Wisdom demanded that human beings learn the limits imposed on them as creatures in the natural world. Their lives should be marked by moderation. The common belief was that if any part of man remained after death, it was doomed to wander endlessly in a dark and shadowy realm filled with misery.

In each world, Eastern and Western, beliefs about the origin of the universe and man's relationship to the material universe shaped the culture's basic attitudes toward life and death.

Modern beliefs about origins are stated in "scientific" terms. In the modern world, the ancient religious answers and philosophic approaches to the question of origins have been set aside in favor of the claim to "scientific" certainty. Those who hold the contemporary view of origins admit that the universe had a beginning, in some unexplained cosmic "big bang" explosion. But contemporary theory goes on to affirm that the matter and energy unleashed in this cataclysmic event is the only reality. Everything that exists today was formed by processes that operate in the material universe in conformity with known or as-yet-unknown natural laws.

According to this view, simple one-celled living creatures were generated spontaneously by the interaction of chemicals which existed in primordial seas. Gradually, over millions of years, these simple one-celled living things became more and more complex. Ultimately, life developed into the vast array of plants and animals that exists today. Human beings, like other members of the animal kingdom—so this theory goes—are no more than accidents, coming into existence by chance. In essence, mankind is no different from the apes, horses, or dogs which evolved through this same process.

This contemporary "scientific" view of the origin of the universe—and especially its explanation of the origin of human beings—has serious implications.

First, if human beings are nothing more than the products of a purposeless process, it is foolish to speak of life after death. If the material universe is in fact the only reality, then when the body dies the "person" no longer exists.

Second, if the material universe is the only reality, there can be no ethical or moral absolutes. Each society and individual is free to work out whatever system he wishes, and none can stand in judgment, saying one way is "right" and the other "wrong" Ethics and morality are merely matters of whether one way or another is "better," in that it provides a society or an individual with more benefits [pleasures?] than harm [pain?].

The biblical view of origins. The biblical view of origins stands in bold contrast to each of the theories outlined above. Scripture presents one God, who has existed eternally. It affirms that this God chose to create the material universe, and that it came into existence by his agency.

Genesis 1 tells the story of the creation of living things, again by God's will and design. Genesis 2 then goes into detail about the separate, special creation of human beings as creatures made in God's image and likeness and assigned dominion over the earth by the Creator Himself.

As the biblical story unfolds, it provides answers for our most basic questions about life. The Bible portrays human beings as the continuing objects of God's love. It promises that biological death is not the end. Each person, self-conscious and aware, will survive death to meet a destiny shaped by his or her response during this lifetime to the God who loves each one completely.

What is perhaps most striking about the Bible's answer to the question of origins is that it has no roots in any belief system of the ancient world. Each attempt to portray Scripture's vision of one supreme Creator God as a derivative of ancient faith fails totally. The Bible's explanation of origins burst as a striking revelation into a world which had forgotten the one true God. And it stands today as the only account of origins which offers an adequate explanation of life as we experience it as well as a foundation for hope beyond our earthly existence.

AN EVALUATION OF THE CONTEMPORARY "SCIENTIFIC" VIEW OF ORIGINS

There are really only two viable modern views concerning origins. The dominant view—that all that exists "evolved"—is presented as truth proven by "science." To most people in our culture, evolutionary theory is thought to provide an accurate, factual, and true explanation of origins. Yet, this materialistic explanation is not as reliable as most assume.

In a recent novel, Michael Crichton, who believes that evolution offers the only realistic explanation of origins, has one of his characters explain some of the problems with that theory which trouble scientists today:

"After Watson and Crick in 1953, we knew that genes were nucleotides arranged in a double helix. Great. And we knew about mutation. So by the late twentieth century, we have a theory of natural selection which says that mutations arise spontaneously in genes, that the environment favors the mutations that are beneficial, and out of this selection process evolution occurs. It's simple and straightforward. God is not at work. No higher organizing principle involved. In the end, evolution is just the result of a bunch of mutations that either survive or die. Right?"

"Right," Arby said.

"But there are problems with that idea," Malcolm said. "First of all, there's a time problem. A single bacterium—the earliest form of life—has two thousand enzymes. Scientists have estimated how long it would take to randomly assemble those enzymes from a primordial soup. Estimates run from forty billion years to one hundred billion years. But the earth is only four billion years old! So, chance alone can't account for it, particularly since we know bacteria actually appeared at least four hundred million years after the earth began. That's very fast—which is why some scientists have declared life on earth must be of extraterrestrial origin. Although I think that's just evading the issue."

"Okay . . ."

"Second, there's the coordination problem. If you believe the current theory, then all the wonderful complexity of life is nothing but the accumulation of chance events—a bunch of genetic accidents strung together. Yet when we look closely at animals, it appears as if many elements must have evolved simultaneously. Take bats, which have echolocation—they navigate by sound. To do that, many things must evolve. Bats need a specialized apparatus to make sounds, they need specialized ears to hear echoes, they need specialized brains to interpret the sounds, and they need specialized bodies to dive and swoop and catch insects. If all these things don't evolve simultaneously, there's no advantage. And to imagine all these things happen purely by chance is like imagining that a tornado can hit a junkyard and assemble the parts into a working 747 airplane. It's very hard to believe" (*The Lost World*, 1996, 226–227).

Irreducibly complex systems and evolution. The problem Crichton is referring to is developed in a 1996 book by biochemist Michael J. Behe, *Darwin's Black Box*. Aside from the fact that there is no existing scientific evidence of any such changes as evolutionists postulate, Behe points out that many biological systems are *irreducibly complex*.

By irreducibly complex, he means that most biological systems are integrated units. You cannot take away one element of the system and still have the system work. For instance, a mousetrap has a platform, a spring, a holding bar, a catch, and a hammer. It is designed to do one thing: to kill a mouse. If you take away any part of the trap—the spring, for example—the mousetrap simply will not work as designed and is therefore useless.

If we go back to Crichton's illustration of the bat, the system that enables it to fly and catch insects fits the criterion of an *irreducible complexity*. Take away the bat's ability to make specialized sounds, and its entire system is useless. Or take away the ability to hear echoes. Or any of the other elements. Take away *any* element—and the system fails. Each element must be present at the same time for the biological system to give the bat any advantage.

How then can evolution take place by a system of small changes—each of which provides some advantage to the creature—if no advantage exists unless all the elements of a complex system are present and working at the same time?

Irreducibly complex systems and design. What is even more disturbing to evolutionary theory is the fact that nature's irreducibly complex systems seem to be *designed to accomplish*

a specific purpose. That is, *there is a purposeful arrangement of the parts.*

No one coming across a mousetrap would imagine that it had been put together without a specific purpose in mind. In the same way, irreducibly complex systems by their nature *imply a design.*

How then can an evolutionist, looking at the multitudes of irreducibly complex systems in living creatures, even imagine that these systems are the product of chance? Every living thing bears the unmistakable stamp of design, and this implies a Designer.

Some have tried to get around this problem by assuming that evolution took place not by gradual changes but by giant leaps, or quantum changes in entire systems. There is an obvious problem with this notion. Such leaps would have to take place not in one individual creature, but in at least one male and one female of the species at the same time and same place if the change were to be transmitted to offspring. But even aside from this, University of Georgia geneticist John McDonald has noted a serious problem. He writes,

The results of the last 20 years of research on the genetic basis of adaptation has led us to a great Darwinian paradox. *Those [genes] that are obviously variable within natural populations do not seem to lie at the basis of many major adaptive changes, while those genes that seemingly do constitute the foundation of many, if not most, major adaptive changes apparently are not variable within natural populations* (Quoted in Behe, *Darwin's Black Box*, 37).

For example, genes that control the length of a bat's wings are variable in natural populations. Changes in length can and do take place. But genes that control the bat's ability to generate sounds, hear echoes, and interpret them, etc., do not exhibit variability. The irreducibly complex systems of living creatures simply do not change, and thus their existence is unexplainable by evolutionary theory.

The "intelligent design" movement. The January 6, 1997, issue of *Christianity Today* noted that challenges to Darwin are rooted in the growing awareness that the high level of complexity found in life forms could not have resulted from chance occurrences, as Darwinists believe. This, plus the fact that these complex systems display all the characteristics of purposive design, has led to the emergence of an "intelligent design" movement in the scientific community. This movement has aroused vigorous opposition, and has even been labeled "scientific heresy" by some.

Interestingly, the reason for the opposition is *not* that the facts and observations on which the movement is based are flawed. Law professor Phillip Johnson, author of *Darwin on Trial,* observed that "materialists do not challenge his [Behe's] facts. They just dismiss the logical inference from the facts as philosophically unacceptable" (*Christianity Today,* Jan. 6, 1997, 64).

Is evolutionary theory really "scientific?" The common assumption that the evolutionists' account of origins is scientific while the biblical account is a matter of faith is seriously flawed. Evolution proposes that the origin of all things, from our earth to the various living forms found on it, can be explained by the operation of natural processes which operate consistently throughout the universe and for all time.

Evolutionary theory was proposed by Darwin, who suggested possible mechanisms by which changes in living creatures might take place. His ideas, extended by his disciples, were quickly accepted by the scientific world. Initial arguments favoring the theory seemed impressive, and evidence to support it was quickly provided by partisans in many scientific disciplines. Paleontologists presented fossils; biologists traced similarities in animal forms.

But the early promise of proof of the theory remains unfulfilled. No fossil evidence has been provided that shows transition from one distinct life form to another. When superficial similarities were looked beyond, evidence pointed *away from* rather than toward direct-line evolution with family and genus. Today

our growing knowledge of microbiology and of complex biological structures is rapidly demonstrating more and more flaws in basic evolutionary assumptions. And now proponents of the growing "intelligent design" movement are providing more and more evidence which points to the likelihood that living creatures have a Designer.

Even the older references to "simple, one-celled animals" has been debunked, as microbiologists learn how complex single-cell creatures really are. When scientists are confronted with the facts about origins but refuse to question their commitment to the evolutionary view, it is clear that evolution is as much a "faith" for the materialist as is creation for the theist.

Eugenie Scott, executive director of the National Center for Science Education, made this very clear when she labeled intelligent design theorists as heretics, and declared, "You can't call it science if you allow in supernatural explanations" (*Christianity Today,* Jan. 6, 1997, 65).

In essence, the materialist argues that it is valid to reason from evidence provided by science . . . if you accept only conclusions that support materialist assumptions. Any evidence which points toward God and the supernatural is ruled out as "unscientific."

A flawed faith. There are many additional lines of scientific evidence to which we might appeal to demonstrate that the evolutionary explanation of origins by the materialists is fatally flawed. The line of evidence above is intended to show two things: (1) that we need not accept evolution as a "scientific fact," and (2) that evolutionary assumptions are actually rooted in faith rather than science.

The tragedy is that while many modern scientists are beginning to question evolutionary assumptions, most people assume that the evolutionary account of origins is a fact rather than a dubious theory. As a result, many even in our churches operate with a flawed God-concept. Rather than seeing God through the lens of creation's grand miracle, as the One who acts freely in our world of space and time, many limit God to a distant and shadowy "spiritual" realm where he has little impact on daily life. How different such a God is from the God of creation. For the God of creation is powerful, active in our world, unlimited in his freedom, able to help and heal us NOW.

GOD AS CREATOR: OUR RESPONSE TO THE FIRST GRAND MIRACLE

Psalm 77:14 reminds us, "You are the God who does wonders; / You have declared Your strength among the peoples." The psalmists go on to remind us often that we are to nurture our awareness that our God is One who does wonders.

- "I will praise You, O Lord, with my whole heart; / I will tell of all Your marvelous works" (Ps. 9:1).
- "Come and see the works of God; / He is awesome in His doing toward the sons of men" (Ps. 66:5).
- "We give thanks to You, O God, we give thanks!/ For Your wondrous works declare that Your name is near" (Ps. 75:1).
- "We will not hide them from their children, / Telling to the generation to come the praises of the LORD, / And His strength and His wonderful works that He has done" (Ps. 78:4).
- "That they may set their hope in God, / And not forget the works of God, / But keep His commandments" (Ps. 78:7).
- "Remember His marvelous works which He has done, / His wonders, and the judgments of His mouth" (Ps. 105:5).
- "He has made His wonderful works to be remembered" (Ps. 111:4).

How are we to "remember" this first of his grand miracles, creation, and how will nurturing an awareness of it affect our lives?

Creation described (Genesis 1, 2). Theologians describe the creation of the material universe as taking place *ex nihilo.* In the beginning, nothing existed except God. Then God spoke, and the entire material universe came into being. The myriads of stars, the earth, the moon, were all designed by God and brought into being by his power. The varied forms of life that exist on our earth's surface were also designed by God, and brought into being by him.

Some have interpreted the Genesis story to affirm that God directly created each breed of dog or cat, every strain of wheat, each different color of tulip. What the creation story actually teaches is that God created every "kind" of living creature, enabling them to reproduce only with others of the same "kind" (Gen. 1:21, 24, 25). Within the genetic code of each "kind" that God created there existed from the beginning the possibility of wonderful variations of size, shape, and color. The many breeds of animals and strains of vegetation that exist today developed from and within these original "kinds."

The emphasis within the theory of evolution on natural selection can and does account for this kind of variation in the natural universe. But it was God who created the original kinds from which the variety has sprung. There has been no "evolution" of the original kinds, nor has there been reproduction across kinds, as if a mammal mated with a bird or reptile.

But most important, Scripture's creation story sets the creation of human beings apart from the creation of all other animal life. Only human beings are made, as Genesis 1:26 declares, "in Our image, according to Our likeness." While sharing our physical nature with the animal creation, human beings possess a unique spiritual nature that has its origin in God's gift of his own image-likeness. Like God, human beings are persons. And Scripture's clear testimony is that each person, like God, is destined to exist as a self-aware individual, with his or her own personal identity, on into eternity.

The biblical account of creation thus makes unique claims about origins which have dramatic impact on our view of the world and life's meaning.

"In the beginning, God . . . . "

Some implications of the biblical account of creation. The material universe was created by God. According to Scripture, God is distinct from, and greater than, the universe he created. It follows that the material universe is subject to him, and that God is not limited in his ability to act by any "natural laws" that operate in the universe. Given a God who created and shaped all that exists, there is no reason to suppose that this all-powerful being cannot act in any way that he chooses within his own creation.

The existence of "natural law" within the material universe is no barrier to God's performing miracles which seem to us to "violate" natural law. God is free to act in any way he chooses, for he is sovereign over all he has made.

Human beings, as a special creation of God, are special to him. The sacred history recorded in Scripture is actually salvation history—an account of what God has done to bring salvation from sin and sin's consequences to humanity. The love of God for human beings, demonstrated over and over again in his Word, helps us to understand why God *should* perform miracles. Miracles are not random expressions of God's power, performed simply because God can do them. Miracles are an integral part of salvation history, linked to God's purposes and serving as vivid expressions of his love.

Thus, belief in the grand miracle of creation provides a solid basis for belief in the lesser miracles and wonders that Scripture reports. If we see God as the God of creation, sovereign over all he has made—and understand that all he does is linked with his salvation purpose—we will not shrink from belief in the "little" miracles the Bible records.

Why doubt that the God who brought into being all that exists should find it difficult to divide the waters of the Red Sea? Why question whether the God who formed the eye should be able to give sight to a man who was born blind? Or that the God whose sovereignty is clearly affirmed by his creation can act as he chooses in his world today?

If we approach the question of miracles and wonders with the assumption of the materialists—that all that exists can be accounted for without reference to the supernatural—we will rule out the possibility of miracles. But if we approach them in the firm conviction that God created and rules the universe, we will at least be open to the possibility of miracles. As we examine the miracles of Scripture, we should recognize that each is linked with God's deep love for humanity and his salvation purpose. Then we will come to under-

stand the distinctives that set biblical miracles apart from "magic" signs and pagan superstitions.

THE MIRACLE OF THE INCARNATION

Christian faith is centered in the person of Jesus Christ. Jesus is considered special by most people. Even Muslims acknowledge him as a prophet. And he is given a place on every list of humankind's great religious leaders. In his own time, Jesus was acknowledged to have special powers and to perform miracles. But in the world in which he spent his earthly ministry, Jesus' miracles would not have been viewed as absolute proof of his divinity.

FIRST-CENTURY MAGIC AND MAGICIANS

In the hellenistic world, distinctions between magic and religion were not very clear. The words *magos, magicus,* and *mageia* were used with a variety of meanings, ranging from

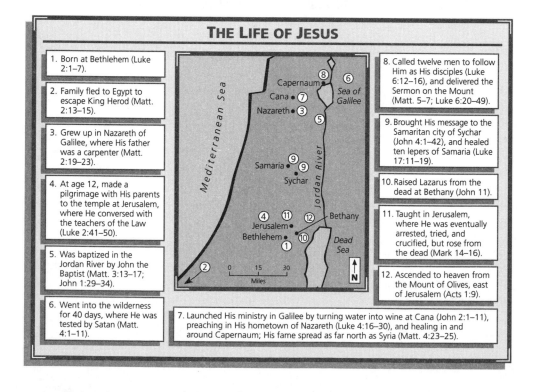

THE LIFE OF JESUS

1. Born at Bethlehem (Luke 2:1–7).

2. Family fled to Egypt to escape King Herod (Matt. 2:13–15).

3. Grew up in Nazareth of Galilee, where His father was a carpenter (Matt. 2:19–23).

4. At age 12, made a pilgrimage with His parents to the temple at Jerusalem, where He conversed with the teachers of the Law (Luke 2:41–50).

5. Was baptized in the Jordan River by John the Baptist (Matt. 3:13–17; John 1:29–34).

6. Went into the wilderness for 40 days, where He was tested by Satan (Matt. 4:1–11).

8. Called twelve men to follow Him as His disciples (Luke 6:12–16), and delivered the Sermon on the Mount (Matt. 5–7; Luke 6:20–49).

9. Brought His message to the Samaritan city of Sychar (John 4:1–42), and healed ten lepers of Samaria (Luke 17:11–19).

10. Raised Lazarus from the dead at Bethany (John 11).

11. Taught in Jerusalem, where He was eventually arrested, tried, and crucified, but rose from the dead (Mark 14–16).

12. Ascended to heaven from the Mount of Olives, east of Jerusalem (Acts 1:9).

7. Launched His ministry in Galilee by turning water into wine at Cana (John 2:1–11), preaching in His hometown of Nazareth (Luke 4:16–30), and healing in and around Capernaum; His fame spread as far north as Syria (Matt. 4:23–25).

the religious to witchcraft. In Rome, magic was viewed as subversive. Chaldean astrologers were driven from Rome in 33 B.C. on the grounds that they were magicians, and in 13 B.C. Augustus ordered all books on occult subjects burned. In A.D. 16 magicians and astrologers were expelled from Italy, an edict reinforced in A.D. 69 and 89.

These facts remind us that in the first century magic was taken seriously, or it would not have been outlawed. The repeated edicts against magic tell us that it was widely practiced. It is no surprise that in the world of the first century persons might present themselves to others as magoi, possessors of special powers.

How magi worked their magic. Magicians generally used spells to aid or attack others. An example is this spell, included by Lewis and Reinhold in their *Roman Civilization Sourcebook II* (New York: 1955), evoked against a charioteer named Eucherius:

I conjure you up, holy beings and holy names; join in aiding this spell and bind, enchant, thwart, strike, overturn, conspire against, destroy, kill, and break Eucherius, the charioteer and all his horses tomorrow in the circus at Rome. May he not leave the barriers well, may he not be quick in the contest, may he not outstrip anyone; may he not make the turns well; may he not win any prizes; and, if he has pressed someone hard, may he not come off the victor; and, if he follows someone from behind, may he not overtake him; but may he meet with an accident, may he be bound, may he be broken, may he be dragged along by your power in the morning and afternoon races. Now! Now! Quickly! Quickly!

Marlene LeFever, a senior editor at Cook Communications, teaches a Sunday school class in a little town outside Colorado Springs known for its covens of witches. One Easter Sunday when she told the story of the Resurrection, a nine-year-old girl in her class said in awe, "He must have been a really powerful warlock." Her immediate reaction to the miracle story was to assume that it was accomplished by magic.

In the first century, stories of Jesus' miracles might have suggested to many people just what the resurrection story implied for the nine-year-old in Marlene's class: Jesus must be a powerful sorcerer or magician.

FIRST-CENTURY CONCEPTS OF THE "DIVINE MAN"

The overlap of magic and religion in the first-century world allowed for another explanation for the miraculous. An individual might possibly be a true miracle worker, whose acts depended not on his mastery of occult practice but on true superiority of being. One example of the significance of this distinction is found in Porphyry's *Life of Plotinus*. Before mentioning Plotinus's feats, the author took care to establish his subject as a "divine man" who possessed a divine guiding spirit. Porphyry wrote,

Plotinus possessed by birth something more than is accorded to other men. An Egyptian priest who had arrived in Rome and, through some friend, had been presented to the philosopher, became desirous of displaying his powers to him, and he offered to evoke a visible manifestation of Plotinus's presiding spirit. Plotinus readily consented and the evocation was made in the Temple of Isis, the only place, they say, which the Egyptian could find pure in Rome.

At the summons, a divinity appeared, not a being of the spirit ranks, and the Egyptian exclaimed, "You are singularly blessed; the guiding-spirit within you is none of the lower degree, but a God." It was not possible, however, to interrogate or even to contemplate this God any further, for the priest's assistant, who had been holding the birds to prevent them from flying away, strangled them, whether through jealousy or in terror. Thus, Plotinus had for indwelling spirit a being of the more divine degree, and he kept his own divine spirit unceasingly intent upon that inner presence. (Cited in Plotinus, *The Enneads*, tr. Stephen MacKenna, London: 1965, p. 8.)

Porphyry then went on to describe several feats which he argued must be viewed as miracles rather than as magical manipulations because of Plotinus's obvious superiority to ordinary men.

The world of the first century was well acquainted with the idea that a person with a special relationship to a deity might perform miracles. To the first-century mind, one did not have to *be* God to do the kind of works ascribed to Jesus by the early Christians.

JEWISH CONCEPTS OF THE SPIRIT WORLD

It is notable that the Old Testament does not describe the kinds of miracles that Jesus performed with regularity. For example, there is no mention in the Old Testament of a prophet restoring a cripple's legs, or giving sight to the blind, or walking on water, or casting out a demon. So it is clear that Jesus' miracles had to be explained in some way peculiar to Jewish culture and theology.

The authenticity of the miracles is attested by the reaction of Jesus' opponents. They didn't deny the reality of miracles that large crowds had witnessed. They couldn't deny what so many knew to be true from personal experience. So instead of trying to cast doubt on the miracles themselves, Christ's opponents attempted to create doubt about the *meaning of the miracles.*

The Jewish leaders didn't accuse Jesus of magic. Christ used none of the incantations or materials associated with magic in the ancient world. And the Jewish leaders couldn't account for the miracles on the basis that Jesus had a unique relationship with God without being forced to acknowledge his spiritual authority. So the leaders devised another tactic. They began to whisper that "this fellow does not cast out demons except by Beelzebub, the ruler of the demons" (Matt. 12:24).

In first-century Judaism, much religious literature focused on the supernatural world, which was populated by angels and demons (See *Every Good and Evil Angel in the Bible,* Nelson, 1997). So it was not far-fetched to imply that while Jesus' powers were supernatural, they originated in the dark side of the spiritual realm, and that Satan energized Jesus and enabled him to work his miracles.

Jesus quickly brought this charge into the open and refuted it. If Jesus cast out demons by the power of the prince of demons, he reasoned, Satan must be fighting against himself! This meant Satan's kingdom would surely fall apart from internal strife (Matt. 12:25, 26).

In fact, by casting out demons Jesus entered Satan's own "house" (realm) and *bound* Satan, so that even the devil could not successfully oppose Christ's actions (Matt. 12:29)! Jesus' opponents had to come up with a better explanation than this to explain the source of Jesus' powers.

This survey of beliefs about miracle workers in the first century helps us identify the compelling issue raised by Jesus' miracles. The issue was not, "Did they happen?" It was not, "Can the miracles be explained away as hallucinations or the product of mass hysteria?" The issue was, and is, '*Who can this miracle-working person be?"*

In the context of the first-century world, the miracles Jesus worked led Jew or pagan to focus on the person of Jesus. Could Jesus be a magician? Could he be someone like Plotinus, who had a special relationship with a deity? Could he be an emissary of Satan, empowered by demons?

In answer to this issue raised by Jesus' miracles, the Gospel writers and apostles offered a unique response. Jesus was none of these. Jesus was God the Creator come into his universe in the flesh. Jesus was God incarnate: truly human, fully God.

This answer, as uncomfortable as it was to the Jewish religious leaders of the first century, is plainly taught in the Old Testament as well as in the New!

JESUS' MIRACLES IDENTIFIED HIM AS THE MESSIAH

At one point in Jesus' ministry, the disciples of his cousin, John the Baptist, came to Christ and asked him if he were really the Messiah. John had been thrown into prison by Herod the tetrarch (Matt. 14:3–12) and had begun to wonder about Jesus. Like other Jews of his time, John had expected the Messiah to throw off the yoke of Roman oppression and establish an earthly kingdom. When Jesus failed to meet these expectations, even such a person of faith as John the Baptist began to doubt.

Jesus answered his cousin by telling John's disciples to "go and tell John the things which you hear and see" (Matt. 11:4). Christ then described what he was doing in terms linked in Isaiah 29:18, 35:4–6, and especially in Isaiah 61:1, to the ministry of the promised Messiah.

The blind see and the lame walk; the lepers are cleansed and the deaf hear; the dead are raised up and the poor have the gospel preached to them (Matt. 11:5).

No Old Testament man of God performed the kind of miracles which Jesus did regularly. These miracles clearly identified him as the Christ, the Messiah whom God had promised to send as a Savior for his people. No one who knew the Old Testament prophecies—no one who witnessed the miracles that Jesus performed—should have had any question about his identity as the Messiah. But there is even more than this.

❖

Healing miracles connected Jesus to Isaiah's description of the Messiah.

THE OLD TESTAMENT IDENTIFIED THE MESSIAH AS GOD

The specific miracles that Jesus performed identified him as the Messiah. And the Old Testament identified the Messiah as God.

James Smith examined 73 key Old Testament prophecies about the Messiah. He identified 13 of these which teach the deity of the Messiah.

1. "For I know that my Redeemer lives, and he shall stand at last on the earth" (Job 19:25). The role of the Redeemer was clearly messianic. Here Job expressed confidence that the Redeemer "lives" even in Job's own time, and that he will "stand at last on the earth."

2. " 'Behold, I send My messenger, and he will prepare the way before Me. And the Lord, whom you seek, will suddenly come to His temple, even the Messenger of the covenant, in whom you delight. Behold, he is coming,' says the Lord of Hosts" (Mal. 3:1). The promised Messiah, the Messenger of the covenant, is to be the Lord himself, who will "suddenly come to His temple."

3. "Of old You laid the foundation of the earth, and the heavens are the work of Your hands" (Ps. 102:25). This verse, from the messianic Psalm 102, is quoted in Hebrews 1:10–12 as addressed by God to Jesus. The psalm goes on to affirm the eternity of the Messiah as well as his identity as the Creator himself.

4. "Your throne, O God, is forever and ever; a scepter of righteousness is the scepter of Your kingdom" (Ps. 45:6). This verse is from another messianic psalm. It is also applied to Jesus in Hebrews 1. Here the ruler of the messianic kingdom promised in the Old Testament is identified as God himself.

5. "For unto us a child is born, unto us a Son is given; And the government will be upon his shoulder. And his name will be called Wonderful, Counselor, Mighty

God, Everlasting Father, Prince of Peace" (Isa. 9:6). This pivotal Old Testament verse pointed out that the child born in fulfillment of the Messiah prophecies is to be "a Son . . . given." The fact that this son is God the Son is underlined by the titles given him in this verse. The one born as a human being is in reality the "Mighty God," the "Everlasting Father." This last term translated as "Father (source) of Eternity," placed the Messiah outside of time as the God who existed before Creation took place.

6. "Behold, the virgin shall conceive and bear a Son, and shall call his name Immanuel" (Isa. 7:14). Written about 700 years before Christ's birth, this verse described a conception that will take place without a human father, the offspring of which would be a son named Immanuel. In Hebrew the name Immanuel means "With us is God." Through a virgin birth, God will come in the flesh to be "with us" as a true human being.

7. "But you, Bethlehem Ephrathah, though you are little among the thousands of Judah, yet out of you shall come forth to Me the One to be Ruler in Israel, whose goings forth are from of old, from everlasting" (Mic. 5:2). This verse identified the Messiah's birthplace and affirmed his pre-existence.

8. "I will be his Father, and he shall be My son" (2 Sam. 7:14). This phrase from the Davidic covenant indicated that the Messiah, who is David's descendant, was also to be God's Son, a theme also addressed in the following several passages.

9. "I will declare the decree: the Lord has said to Me, You are My Son, today I have begotten You" (Ps. 2:7).

10. "I will make him My firstborn, the highest of the kings of the earth" (Ps. 89:27). Here the word "firstborn" is used in the technical sense of "heir."

11. "Out of Egypt I called My son" (Hos. 11:1). This verse is quoted in Matt. 2:15 and applied to the journey of Jesus and his family to and from Egypt when threatened by King Herod.

12. "Afterward the children of Israel shall return and seek the Lord their God and David their king" (Hos. 3:5). The Hebrew in this verse identified the Lord (here Yahweh, God's personal name) with the person of "David their king." Christ the descendant of David, who as Messiah fulfilled the promises given to David, is the Yahweh (Lord) of the Old Testament.

13. "Their king will pass before them, with the Lord at their head" (Mic. 2:13). Here again the Hebrew identified the messianic king with the Lord, Yahweh of the Old Testament. The messianic king and Yahweh are one and the same (James Smith, *What the Bible Teaches about the Promised Messiah,* Nelson, 1993).

Thus, hundreds of years before the birth of Jesus, the writers of the Old Testament predicted that a person would be born of a virgin. That person was to be God himself, yet at the same time the human descendant of King David. He and he alone would fulfill all the prophecies concerning Israel's Messiah. This person would be the Son of God—indeed, God the Son, who is the Yahweh of the Old Testament—who has existed forever and is himself the source of eternity.

In spite of the testimony of Jesus' miracles to his identity as the Messiah—and in spite of the testimony of Scripture to the Messiah's identity as God incarnate—Israel's leaders refused to accept Jesus Christ for who he is.

THE NEW TESTAMENT IDENTIFIED JESUS AS GOD THE SON

The New Testament, in complete harmony with the Old, gives a decisive answer to the issue raised by Jesus' miracles: "Who is he?" The answer is that Jesus is God come in the flesh. John's Gospel begins with this great affirmation:

In the beginning was the Word, and the Word was with God, and the Word was God. He was in the beginning with God. All things were made through Him, and without him nothing was made that was made. . . . And the Word became flesh and dwelt among us, and we beheld his glory, the glory as of the only begotten of the Father, full of grace and truth (John 1:1–3, 14).

This great affirmation is repeated throughout the Scriptures, which tell us that "God so loved the world that he gave his only begotten Son, that whoever believes in him should not perish but have everlasting life" (John 3:16). Colossians and Hebrews add their testimony to the first century's Hellenistic and Jewish populations that Jesus is indeed God in the flesh.

He is the image of the invisible God, the firstborn over all creation. For by him all things were created that are in heaven and that are on earth, visible and invisible. . . . All things were created through him and for him. And he is before all things, and in him all things consist (Col. 1:15–17).

God, who at various times and in various ways spoke in time past to the fathers by the prophets, has in these last days spoken to us by His Son, whom also He has appointed heir of all things, through whom He made the worlds; who being the brightness of His glory and the express image of His person, and upholding all things by the word of His power, when He had by Himself purged our sins, sat down at the right hand of the Majesty on high (Heb. 1:1–3).

Similar passages and references can be multiplied. Together they leave no doubt that the early Christians had a decisive and stunning answer to the issue posed by Jesus' miracles: "Who is this man?" The answer, found in the Old Testament and affirmed by Christ

In the miracle of the Incarnation, God entered into humanity.

himself and the apostles is, "Jesus Christ is God the Son; God come in human flesh."

Compared with the grand miracle of Incarnation—the miracle that IS Jesus Christ—the miracles performed by Jesus pale to relative insignificance. Why should we be surprised, if God the Creator walked among us as a human being, that he should be able to straighten bent limbs or give hearing to the deaf? Why doubt that, if God the Creator walked among us as a human being, he could still a storm with a gesture, walk on water as easily as on land, or expel the demons that tormented helpless victims?

If we accept this grand miracle, the Incarnation of Jesus, the credibility of all other miracles follows naturally and easily—especially when we link those miracles with salvation history and the purposes which God's Son came to accomplish.

Those who see Jesus as nothing more than a great religious teacher will be skeptical of the the miracle stories in the Gospels. Those who dismiss claims of his deity will tend to ignore the real issue which his miracles raise, concentrating instead on explaining them away. But anyone who looks to Scripture and accepts its testimony that Jesus is the Messiah—God the Son incarnate in human flesh—will focus on the meaning of the miracles rather than concentrate on whether or not they were real.

THE MIRACLE OF THE RESURRECTION

What happens to a person after death has been a concern of human beings from earliest times. No clearly defined beliefs emerged in East or West, other than the hope that after death a person might enter a realm in which he or she could experience some of the better things of earthly existence. Even this was a vague hope, by no means shared by all.

IMMORTALITY IN WESTERN THOUGHT

Homer's *Iliad* opens with a vision of souls being cast into Hades. For Homer the soul

(*psyche*) bore a resemblance to the physical body, but it was drained of all that made the individual vital and real. Death meant passage to a dreary world where shadows passed their time in weary, meaningless wanderings. The only meaningful immortality a person might gain was won by accomplishments that caused him or her to be remembered.

In the face of this grim expectation, some people feigned indifference. Many tombstones in the Roman world bore the initials NFFNSNC, standing for a Latin phrase which means, "I was not, I was, I am not, I care not."

In time, the belief that the afterlife involved reward and punishment emerged in the West. Its full development is seen in Virgil's *Aeneid*. The poet depicted the dead carried across the river Styx by the boatman Charon, to face a court which would send them either to the left, to Tartarus the place of punishment, or to the right, to the Elysian Fields where the pious were rewarded with a bright and beautiful existence. The philosophical school of the Pythagoreans adopted this view as a part of their doctrine.

In the first century, mystery religions from the East were adopted in the West. These promised their initiates a kind of salvation that guaranteed a blessed afterlife. Yet none of the religions of the first-century Roman world even imagined a resurrection. Most educated persons held little hope of any kind of survival of the individual after death.

RESURRECTION IN FIRST-CENTURY JUDAISM

Judaism in the first century experienced a significant division on this question. The majority of Jews, led by the Pharisees, believed firmly in the resurrection of the righteous. By contrast, the Sadducees denied the possibility of resurrection or survival of the individual after death.

When a group of Sadducees challenged Jesus with a riddle that had confounded the Pharisees, Jesus based his answer to them on the tense of a verb in the Old Testament. Jesus pointed out that God had said to Moses, "I am the God of Abraham. . . ." (Mark 12:26). Because God said "I am" rather than "I was" proves that the long-dead Abraham still was self-conscious and "alive" in Moses' time! Jesus also noted that any assumption that the resurrected would live the same kind of life people have now is unwarranted. "When they rise from the dead, they neither marry nor are given in marriage" (Mark 12:25).

Thus, while in Judaism there was no clear idea of what life after death would be like, there was at least a belief in resurrection. The awareness that God intended to raise human beings from the dead was not clearly defined until later in Old Testament times. On this point, one scholar commented:

The OT emphasizes the blessings of living on earth in obedient, intimate relationship with the Lord. In most cases, the "salvation" spoken of in the OT is deliverance from some present enemy or trouble. Yet it would be a mistake to conclude that the OT is a stranger to the doctrine of resurrection, or that OT saints enjoyed no such hope. In fact, saints who "died in faith" did look forward to a better country, to a city God would one day found (Heb. 11:8–16).

Many OT references may allude to the possibility of resurrection (cf. Gen. 3:22–24; Deut. 32:39; 2 Kings 2:11,12). Other statements, whose meaning may not be perfectly clear, still make sense only in the context of a belief in resurrection (cf. Job 19:25–27; Ps.16:9–11).

When we reach the prophets, we see this belief expressed clearly and confidently. One day death will be defeated (Isa. 25:8), and "your dead will live" as their bodies rise when "the earth gives birth to her dead" (Isa. 26:19). Daniel is very explicit. Those who "sleep in the dust of the earth will awake; some to everlasting life, others to shame and everlasting contempt" (Dan. 12:2, 3) (*Richards' Complete Bible Handbook*, 1987, 299).

Yet, belief in resurrection was focused in the distant future, when history reached God's appointed end. Resurrection was a hope. Then suddenly, in Christ, resurrection became an experienced reality!

THE RESURRECTION OF JESUS

This third of the grand miracles is so essential to Christian faith that the apostle Paul wrote, "If Christ is not risen, then our preaching is empty and your faith is also empty" (1 Cor. 15:14). It is striking that the teaching of every book of the New Testament is rooted in the firm conviction that Jesus Christ died a real death, and three days later was literally, physically raised from the dead.

In the opening verses of Romans, Paul linked the second and third of the grand miracles. Paul was an apostle of that gospel "which He [God] promised before through His prophets in the Holy Scriptures, concerning His Son Jesus Christ our Lord, who was born of the seed of David according to the flesh, and declared to be the Son of God with power according to the Spirit of holiness, by the resurrection from the dead" (Rom. 1:1–4). Jesus' resurrection from the dead was the final, decisive proof that He is Who He claimed to be: the human descendant of David and yet at the same time God the Son.

The resurrection of Jesus is also unmistakable confirmation of God's intention to raise believers in Jesus. Christ is the firstfruits—an image drawn from the Old Testament. Worshipers presented to the Lord the first crops to ripen in thankfulness for the harvest to follow (1 Cor. 15:20, 23). Jesus' resurrection is the guarantee that we too will rise.

This, the third of the three grand miracles of the Bible, was undoubtedly the most compelling to men and women of the first century. No one in the Roman Empire had even imagined a future resurrection. They had hoped for some kind of survival after death, but their hope was at best vague and uncertain. And then the Christian gospel broke through the darkness with its promise of full restoration to life!

The anguish of separation from loved ones could now be soothed by the expectation of seeing them once again. And death lost its most fearsome qualities in the promise that we will awake from it as from a sleep, restored and whole.

The resurrection of Jesus is perhaps the most disturbing of the grand miracles. To the materialist, who believes that this universe is the total reality, death is absolute finality. The materialist believes the person and his body are indistinguishable. Once the body dies, the person no longer exists.

Yet Jesus arose. And this forces us to make a choice.

- We can perceive reality as the materialist does. Or we can accept Scripture's perspective, and adopt a view of reality shaped by history's three grand miracles.
- We can accept Scripture's doctrine of creation and believe in a God who exists apart from and over the material universe.
- We can accept Scripture's report of the Incarnation, and put our faith in Jesus as God the Son, come among us as a human being.
- And we can accept Scripture's triumphant proclamation of Jesus' resurrection, believing God's promise that all who trust Jesus as Savior will share in the new life He has won.

So we see again as we begin our review of the miracles of Scripture that the real issue is not whether they happened. No one who approaches miracles with the materialist's as-sumption will accept miracle stories as true. And one who approaches miracles with his or her perspective shaped by belief in the three grand miracles of the Scriptures will have no doubt that God could do what the Bible records.

II. OBJECTIONS TO MIRACLES

The word *miracle* is not an easy term to define. This is especially true because we use the word so loosely. A baseball team that wins its last five games to reach the playoffs is likely to generate headlines about a "miracle finish." And many a sincere believer has asked God for "a miracle" when a loved one is seriously ill.

So before we look at objections that have been raised about miracles in general and especially about biblical miracles, we need to have at least a working definition of what a miracle is. For now, let's adopt the following general definition. Essentially, what we mean by a miracle—and what critics of miracles object to—is the idea that there have been or are . . .

extraordinary events
caused by God
which have religious significance.

The empty tomb affirms that Jesus was who He said He was, and believers can be assured they will be raised to eternal life.

HISTORIC ASSAULTS ON MIRACLES

Trench, in his *Notes on Miracles,* traced objections that have been raised to the stories of Jesus' miracles.

The Jewish leaders of Christ's own time attacked Jesus' miracles. They couldn't deny that what Jesus did constituted extraordinary events. There were too many witnesses. Nor could they doubt that the events had religious significance. So the Pharisees started a rumor that Jesus' miracles were not caused by God but by the devil (Matt. 12:24). If Satan were the source of his power to cast out demons, Jesus answered, Satan would be fighting against his own, and unable to maintain his authority (Matt. 12:26). Thus, the charge is foolish and inconsistent.

The heathen in the first centuries of the Christian era argued that similar wonders had been performed by men like Aesculapius and Apollonius. Hierocles, who was governor of Bythnia in the last decade of the first century, argued that "we do not account him who has done such things for a god, only for a man beloved of the gods: while the Christians, on the contrary, on the ground of a few insignificant wonder-works, proclaim their Jesus for a God."

This attack focused on the religious significance of the miracles as argued by early Christians. The critics did not doubt that such wonders had been done. They argued that others also performed such feats through powers bestowed by pagan gods.

This attack is not relevant today, since no contemporary miracles are being "played off" against Christ's.

The philosopher Spinoza in the 17th century argued that the idea of miracles was absurd. He believed the universe was uncreated, and that "God" is identical with the material universe. His attack was rooted in the conviction that the universe operates by fixed, immutable, natural laws. Miracles [i.e., extraordinary events] to Spinoza were violations of natural law and therefore impossible, and belief in them was irrational.

Spinoza's argument begs the question. He starts from the anti-supernaturalist premises that "God" and nature are identical and that the laws of nature are immutable. Anyone who begins with these assumptions will, of course, decide that belief in miracles is irrational. Spinoza's belief in a pantheistic universe, not the force of his arguments, determined his conclusions.

The skeptic philosopher David Hume in the 18th century agreed that as extraordinary events, miracles are violations of natural law. He also argued that natural laws are unalterably uniform. But rather than base his argument on a philosophical assumption as Spinoza did, Hume argued from experience.

Hume declared that what we call natural laws are defined by what we human beings observe to be regular occurrences. Because all of us experience events governed by natural laws as regular occurrences, we have to give great weight to the idea that they are unalterable.

Miracles, on the other hand, are by definition extraordinary events. As such, they could be experienced by very few persons. Thus, we have little evidence for miracles and should give little weight to miracle stories. What Hume argued is not that miracles are impossible, but that they are *incredible.*

The problem with Hume's argument is that he must *assume* uniformity of experience of natural laws. Suppose we were to live in a country where dogs are black. We set out to prove that *all* dogs are black, and so we survey everyone in the land. We ask them if they have seen dogs, and they say "Yes." We ask if they have seen anything other than a black dog, and they say "No." Finally, we add up our results. A total of 1,300,012 people have seen dogs. And all the dogs they have seen are black.

Can we conclude that all dogs are black? Not at all—only that no one we surveyed has ever seen anything other than a black dog.

Now suppose that we happen on a visitor from another country, and ask him if he has seen a dog. He answers, "Yes." Then we ask if all dogs he has seen are black, and he tells us, "No. In my country there are white dogs, black dogs, and spotted dogs."

If we were to use Hume's criteria, we would have to label this man's report incredible and unworthy of belief. Why? Because the weight of the evidence [1,300,012 to 1] is that all dogs are black. We must discount the one report of white and spotted dogs.

But what if we were to meet other people from that country who also report seeing white, black, and spotted dogs? How many witnesses would we need to consider the possibility that other than black dogs exist? Would we accept 1,300,012 to 10? Or 1,300,012 to 100? Or to 1000?

C. S. Lewis pointed out the fallacy of Hume's argument:

Now of course we must agree with Hume that if there is absolutely "uniform experience" against miracles, if in other words they have never happened, why then they never have. Unfortunately we know the experience against them to be uniform only if we know that all the reports of them are false. And we can know all the reports to be false only if we know already that miracles have never occurred. In fact, we are arguing in a circle (C. S. Lewis, *Miracles*, 102).

Hume never intended to survey every person who has ever lived. He only intended to count up those who had not witnessed a miracle and to use that number to insist that any miracle report was false. Hume had *decided beforehand* that reports of miracles found in Scripture and in other sources must be false.

The rationalist Paulus in the early 19th century focused his attention on the idea that Jesus' miracles were extraordinary events. He denied this, suggesting there was a rational explanation for what the Bible records. Rather than heal an impotent man at the pool of Bethesda, for instance, Jesus detected an imposter. Christ was not walking on the water but on the shore of Lake Galilee. It only appeared to the disciples that he was walking on the water.

This approach, which makes Jesus out to be the consummate trickster or the apostles to be unbelievably naïve, has few adherents today.

The theologian Bultmann in the 20th century recast miracle stories as myth. The third criterion of a miracle as defined earlier is that it has religious significance. The European theologian Bultmann argued that the miracle stories have significance that transcends history, and so serve as myths intended to convey deep spiritual truths. Such stories become articles of faith, and as such the issue of objective verification is irrelevant. All that can and, indeed, needs to be established is that the early disciples believed these stories and the spiritual truths they conveyed.

While Bultmann's argument seems to suggest that the historicity of miracles is irrelevant, he was actually determined to deny the miracle stories any possible claim to objective reality. This bias is shown by Geisler in his excellent book on miracles:

It is evident that the basis of Bultmann's antisupernaturalism is not evidential, nor even open to real discussion. It is something he holds no matter how many witnesses are cited. The dogmatism of his language is revealing. Miracles are "incredible," "irrational," "no longer possible," "meaningless," "utterly inconceivable," "simply impossible," "intolerable." Hence, the "only honest way" for modern people is to hold that miracles are "nothing else than spiritual" and that the physical world is "immune from interference" in a supernatural way. This is not the language of one open to historical evidence for a miracle. It looks more like a mind that does not wish to be "confused" with the facts! (Geisler, *Miracles and the Modern Mind*, 72).

How different Bultmann's approach to miracles is from that of the New Testament, which affirms that its writers have not conveyed "cunningly devised fables" (2 Pet. 1:16), but have spoken only of that to which they and many others were eyewitnesses (compare Acts 1:3; 1 John 1:3).

Contemporary philosophers have continued the attack on miracles, but their arguments tend to be refinements of those discussed above. Their arguments seem to reflect their assumptions rather than to prove their positions.

For some of the critics, miracles cannot happen because natural law cannot be violated. But this argument assumes that the material universe is all that exists or that, if there is a God, he is unable to act in the material realm.

Other critics argue that miracles need not be believed because it can never be proven that they have occurred. This argument rules out ahead of time the testimony of Scripture or any other witness to miracles. It is tantamount to saying, "Even if you see a miracle, I do not have to and will not believe your report."

Sophisticated statements of these two basic positions may sound compelling when couched in philosopher's words. But the fact remains that the issue of belief in miracles will be settled long before the arguments are addressed. We will either be committed to a concept of God that is defined by the three grand miracles of Creation, Incarnation, and Resurrection. Or we will adopt the evolutionist's materialistic view of reality.

If we are committed to the concept of God defined by the grand miracles, the idea that extraordinary events with religious significance should be caused by God will not surprise us. If we adopt the materialist's approach, we will deny this possibility, using those arguments which make us most comfortable with our choice.

If we believe in the God of Scripture, no compelling argument against miracles will force us to doubt their reality.

III. THE MEANING OF MIRACLES

We have already established the fact that the Gospel reports of Christ's miracles raise the issue of Jesus' identity. In a similar way, Old Testament miracle stories raise the issue of our concept of God.

MIRACLES AS A GROUP RAISE QUESTIONS ABOUT OUR CONCEPT OF GOD

Old Testament miracles force us to ask such questions as these: "Is it possible that God exists, or is the material universe the only reality?" "Is the material universe eternal or does it have a source?" "What is God's relationship with the material universe?" "What are the possibilities of God using events to punish or reward human beings?"

The testimony of the Old Testament's miracle stories supports Scripture's teaching that, as Creator, God is the source of the material universe, distinct from it, and totally free to act within it on behalf of his people.

Similarly, the Gospel miracle stories raise the issue of Jesus' identity. First-century men and women were forced to ask, "Is Jesus a magician or sorcerer? Is he a 'divine man,' whose superiority and closeness to God enable him to work wonders? Or is he God incarnate, as he claims?"

The miracles Jesus performed did not in themselves answer these questions. But they did impel those who heard the stories to make some decision about Jesus' identity. And in examining that issue, each person was confronted with Scripture's affirmation of all three grand miracles which shape the Christian's concept of God.

1. God created all things.
2. The Creator God became incarnate in Jesus.
3. God incarnate died, and was raised from the dead.

EACH INDIVIDUAL MIRACLE HAS ITS OWN RELIGIOUS SIGNIFICANCE

The story of Sodom and Gomorrah illustrates the priority of religious significance. At the same time that we affirm the larger significance to Scripture's miracle stories as a whole, we also have to affirm that there is intrinsic meaning to be found in every miracle reported in Scripture. We have already defined a "miracle" as "an extraordinary event caused by God which has religious significance." Now let's focus on this truth: *The religious significance of any miracle is of primary importance.*

Each miracle story in Scripture, studied in the context of its time and in view of God's salvation purpose, has its own special significance. In studying miracles, we might focus on the significance of the setting of Sodom and Gomorrah (Gen. 19). They lay in a valley formed by a major fault in the earth's crust. In that valley, deposits of bitumen and pitch abounded.

With this information, we could easily see how the two cities might be destroyed by fire falling from heaven. A massive shift along the fault line would cause an earthquake, filling the air with inflammable materials. Thunderstorms generated by the dust hurled into the sky would generate lightning and ignite that material, causing the entire valley to be scorched in a great firestorm.

But if we emphasized only their geologic setting in an attempt to make the event more credible to the modern mind, we would miss the meaning of Sodom and Gomorrah. The event was extraordinary not because it involved a violation of natural law, but because the Lord predicted it to Abraham (Gen. 18)

❖

Fire destroyed Sodom and Gomorrah.

and explained that he was about to cause it because of the sins of the men of those cities. The religious significance of the miracle is that God is the moral judge of our universe and that he will punish sins.

Biblical terms for miracles help us identify their religious significance. One thing that will help us determine the significance of miracles is the vocabulary used to describe them.

OLD AND NEW TESTAMENT WORDS FOR MIRACLES

Each testament has specialized vocabulary for identifying miracles. It is important to know what each of these words tells us about the miracles they describe.

Pala'. This word is used about 70 times in the Old Testament. It means "to be marvelous or wonderful." The root usually refers to God's acts, either in shaping the universe or acting in history on behalf of his people. The word focuses our attention on people's reaction when they are confronted by a miracle. The believer sees the awesome power of the God who has invaded time and space to do something too wonderful for humans to duplicate (*Expository Dictionary of Bible Words,* Zondervan, 444).

One authority says of *pala'*,

Preponderantly, both the verb and substantive refer to the acts of God, designating either cosmic wonders or historical achievements on behalf of Israel. That is, in the Bible the root *pl'* refers to things that are unusual, beyond human capacity. As such, it awakes astonishment (*pl'*) in man. Thus, the "real importance of the miraculous for faith (is)—not in its material factuality, but in its evidential character . . . it is not, generally speaking, the especially abnormal character of the event which makes it a miracle; what strikes men forcibly is a clear impression of God's care or retribution within it" (Eichrodt). We may add that it is essential that the miracle is so abnormal as to be unexplainable except as showing God's care or retribution (*Theological Wordbook of the Old Testament,* Moody, 1980, 723).

A number of English words are used to render *pala'*, including "wonder," "miracle," "wondrous works," "wonderful works," and "wonderful things."

Mopet. This Hebrew word occurs only 36 times in the Old Testament. It also means "wonder" or "miracle." It is used especially to recall God's mighty acts in Egypt performed to free his people from slavery. *Mopet* is also used of the punishments and the provision that show God's continuing care of Israel throughout history.

The *Theological Wordbook of the Old Testament* points out that *mopet* is frequently used with a third Hebrew word for miracle, `ot. The two together are typically translated "signs and wonders."

In Deuteronomy 13, *mopet* refers to a prediction required from anyone claiming to be a prophet. Depending on whether the `ot (sign) or *mopet* (wonder) actually happens, the would-be prophet is either authenticated or shown up as a false prophet.

Mopet standing alone is normally rendered as "wonder" or "wonders" in English versions of the Bible.

`ot. This Hebrew word means "miraculous sign." It has a wide range of meanings. The word is used to designate the heavenly bodies as "signs" which distinguish the seasons (Gen. 1:14) and to designate a signboard or standard (Num. 2:2). However, nearly all of its 80 occurrences in the Hebrew Old Testament carry the meaning of a miraculous sign, indicating a clear and unmistakable act of God. As noted above, `ot is frequently used with *mopet,* and the two together are rendered "signs and wonders."

Several other Hebrew words are used to describe miracles. For example, miracles are "mighty things" (*yalla*), or "mighty deeds" (*giborah*) which are the unmistakable works (*maasheh*) of God. We will examine these Hebrew words in more detail as we go on to look at every miracle in the Bible.

Dunamis. A number of Greek words are associated with miracles in the New Testament. Of the three major New Testament terms, *dunamis* identifies a miracle as a spontaneous expression of God's power. Like the other two primary miracle terms in the New Testament,

this word portrays a miracle as a clear violation of what first-century people understood of natural law. God's acts of power were so unmistakably extraordinary that none who observed a miracle could mistake it.

Semeion. This Greek word means "a sign, wonder, or miracle." The basic meaning of the word indicates a sign by which one recognizes a particular person or thing. When the *semeion* has a marvelous or extraordinary dimension, it is generally translated "miraculous sign." The *Expository Dictionary of Bible Words* notes that this word "emphasizes the authenticating aspect of the miracle as an indication that supernatural power is involved."

Teras. This word, translated "wonder," or "wonders," is found only 16 times in the NT, in each case connected with *semeion* as "signs and wonders." In Greek literature, *teras* denoted some terrible appearance which evoked fright and horror, and which contradicted the order of the universe. The Septuagint [a Greek translation of the Hebrew Old Testament completed in the second century B.C.] uses *teras* to translate *mopet,* thus indicating a token, sign, or miracle. Both the Old Testament word and its New Testament equivalent are linked with God's revelation of himself to human beings.

In addition to these three basic New Testament terms for miracles or wonders, the apostle John especially refers to Jesus' miracles as "works" (*ergon*), emphasizing that a particular event occurred through the active agency of God.

The biblical vocabulary of miracles helps us to define more sharply what a miracle is.

A miracle is an extraordinary event (*pala´, teras*). This event may involve violation of what we consider natural laws, as did the parting of the Red Sea and Jesus' raising of Lazarus. But an event doesn't have to violate natural law in order to be extraordinary. The ancient Middle East was familiar with swarms of locusts. But the swarm which appeared in Egypt in the time of Moses came at the exact time Moses predicted. A clear judgment on

Pharaoh, this was one of a series of devastating plagues (Ex. 10:1f). These factors marked this swarm of locusts and several of the other plagues on Egypt as extraordinary.

A miracle is an event caused by God (*pala´, dunamis, ergon*). The nature and timing of the event, along with its religious significance or an associated revelation, make it unmistakably clear that God has acted in our world of space and time.

A miracle is an event with religious significance (*`ot, semeion*). It is not a random but a purposeful act of God. For instance, the series of miraculous plagues God imposed on Egypt had at least four distinctive religious functions:

First, the plagues focused Israel's faith, for from that time on God was identified with these acts performed on behalf of his people (Ex. 6:7). God exercised his power to fulfill his ancient covenant promises to the children of Abraham.

Two other purposes are seen in the fact that it would be through the plagues that the Egyptians not only would be confronted with the knowledge of who Yahweh is but also would allow Israel to leave Egypt (Ex. 7:5).

Fourth, the plagues served as a judgment on the gods of Egypt (Ex. 12:12). The powerlessness of human religious invention would be displayed as the living God exercised his power.

Each of these purposes is clearly linked with God's revelation of his nature. The false images of believer and unbeliever alike are shattered as God steps from the mysterious beyond to enter our here and now. The God of miracle must be responded to and not ignored, for the God of Scripture is no being of tenuous spirituality whose influence is limited to a mystic, immaterial setting.

For believers, this affirmation of God's reality and power is comforting, and the psalms constantly call on worshippers to remember and tell of his works. As David expressed it, "Tell of all his wonderful acts. . . . Remember the wonders he has done, his miracle" and "declare . . . his marvelous deeds among all peoples" (1 Ch. 16:9, 12, 24). God can be counted on by his people (*Expository Dictionary of Bible Words,* 444).

IV. DO MIRACLES HAPPEN TODAY?

In an interview, Kim Kwong Chan, co-author of *Protestantism in Contemporary China*

(1994), gave his explanation of why the Chinese church is growing so rapidly. His first reason was the ideological vacuum in China. His second was the intimate love, caring, and concern that Christianity provides. And then he said, "There are the miracles." Kim went on to add,

When I travel to the interior of China, the Christian communities all claim they've seen and experienced miracles.

One typical example: An old Christian woman in one village decided, after her eightieth birthday, to start preaching the gospel. She went to the village where her daughter lived and began to preach there. Some villagers who had been afflicted with various incurable diseases, like cancer, came to this woman. When she prayed for them, many were suddenly healed.

Then two more people came to ask for healing, and she prayed, and they were healed. Then three more families. After this woman left, these villagers decided her God was very good. So they abandoned their idols and decided to believe in this Jesus.

But they didn't know how to believe. So they sent one person to nearby towns to look for a place where people worshiped Jesus. When they finally found such a church, they told the pastor, "We have nearly 80 people in our village who want to believe in Jesus. But we don't know how to believe in Jesus."

After that a new church was started. I hear such stories all the time in my travels (*Christian History,* Vol. XV, No. 4, 44).

To many Christians, such a report would be occasion for rejoicing. "How wonderful that God is still at work," they might exclaim. But other Christians would look on grimly, convinced that the miracles recorded in the Gospels and in Acts are not to be expected—or believed—in our day.

WHY SOME DOUBT THAT REPORTS OF CONTEMPORARY MIRACLES ARE CREDIBLE

The Christian skeptic's position is stated carefully by Benjamin B. Warfield. Warfield did not doubt the biblical miracle stories.

What he argued was that such wonders "belonged exclusively to the Apostolic age." Warfield wrote,

These gifts were not the possession of the primitive Christian as such; nor for that matter of the Apostolic Church or the Apostolic age for themselves; they were distinctively the authentication of the Apostles. They were part of the credentials of the Apostles as the authoritative agents of God in founding the church. Their function thus confined them to distinctively the Apostolic Church, and they necessarily passed away with it (B. B. Warfield, *Counterfeit Miracles,* 1918, 6).

Warfield argued his case on two grounds. First, he affirmed that the New Testament teaching as to the origin and nature of miracles supported his position, and second, he cited testimony from later ages that the miraculous gifts had ceased.

We must be careful in developing our arguments on either ground. First, those who accept Scripture's testimony as true may differ in their understanding of it. Many would argue that while the New Testament miracles did serve to authenticate Christ and the apostles as God's messengers, this was not their *only* function.

One major function of the miracle stories in the Gospels—and thus one of Christ's purposes in performing them—was to compel the hearer to deal with the issue of Jesus' identity. We might also argue that another role of Gospel miracles was to unveil the compassionate character of God as one who deeply loves those who suffer and who are oppressed by sickness or Satan.

Surely, there is no basis to argue that this latter function of miracles "confined them distinctively to the apostolic age." In every age, human beings need reminders that God cares. Through our fallible exegesis of the Scriptures, we should not place limits on God's freedom to act.

Second, the argument that the testimony of later ages shows that miraculous gifts no longer operate is patently false. Kim Kwon Chan's report is just one of thousands of reports of extraordinary events with religious significance that believers have credited to God. Whether these reports are true and factual may be questioned. But the existence of the reports themselves certainly may not be.

It seems unwise to begin any exploration of miracles with the assumption that the biblical reports are true, but that all other reports are false. Those who believe firmly in the God who reveals himself in Creation, Incarnation, and Resurrection should never place limits on his freedom to do extraordinary things anywhere in the world—or in our own experience.

BIBLICAL INSIGHTS ON THE QUESTION OF MODERN MIRACLES

The Gospel of Mark closes with the following passage.

And He said to them, "Go into all the world and preach the gospel to every creature. He who believes and is baptized will be saved; but he who does not believe will be condemned. And these signs will follow those who believe: In My name they will cast out demons; they will speak with new tongues; they will take up serpents; and if they drink anything deadly, it will by no means hurt them; they will lay hands on the sick, and they will recover."

So then, after the Lord had spoken to them, He was received up into heaven, and sat down at the right hand of God. And they went out and preached everywhere, the Lord working with them and confirming the word through the accompanying signs. Amen (Mark 16:15–20).

Those who challenge the idea of modern miracles point out that verses 9–20 in this chapter are not found in the two Greek manuscripts generally considered the most reliable. They argue that these verses were added later by someone other than Mark, and thus should not be considered Scripture.

Whatever the case, these verses do help us identify the events which proponents of modern miracles are likely to point to as supernatural events—casting out demons, speaking with "new tongues," and healings.

No one seems to argue that the kind of miracles that marked the Exodus period or the time of Elijah are being performed today. But many, like Kim Kwon Chan, do report miraculous healings. In fact, it is healing which, over the past 150 years, has often been the focus of the debate over contemporary miracles.

But before we look more closely at the question of miraculous healing, there are a few things that we should consider.

MIRACLES HAVE NEVER BEEN COMMONPLACE OCCURRENCES

Miracles have not been evenly distributed throughout sacred history. In fact, nearly all recorded miracles took place during two relatively brief periods.

The first of these periods was the time of the Exodus from Egypt and the conquest of Canaan. A flurry of devastating miracle-judgments forced Pharaoh to release his Hebrew slaves. The travels of Israel to Canaan and their conquest of the land was also supported by miraculous interventions. These miracles made such an impression that throughout the Old Testament God is frequently identified as the wonder-working Redeemer of his people.

These miracles made a great impression on Israel, and they are referred to many times in Israel's history. It's hard to believe that all these miracles took place within a span of about fifty years!

A second flurry of miracles was associated with the ministries of Elijah and Elisha. Some 21 miracles which God performed through these two prophets are recorded in the books of 1 and 2 Kings. These events also occurred in a span of just a few decades!

The time from Abraham to Christ covered about two thousand years. It's clear that most followers of the Lord who lived during these centuries did not witness miracles.

The third period of miracles recorded in Scripture extended from the time when Christ began his public ministry through the book of Acts. The miracles reported during this time were limited to a span of just three to four decades! While some of the early church fathers reported miracles, these reports were rare. They do not constitute a major emphasis in the writings of Christians who argued for Christianity against pagan critics.

It is helpful to remember that, whatever we may believe about contemporary miracles, Scripture does not support the notion that miracles are a necessary or even frequent supplement to faith.

MIRACLES SHOULD NOT BE CONFUSED WITH GOD'S ANSWERS TO PRAYER OR WITH DIVINE PROVIDENCE

We've defined a miracle as an extraordinary event caused by God which has religious significance. It's important to limit our concept of miracles to the truly extraordinary.

Christians believe that God answers prayer. But answers to prayer aren't miracles. A person with cancer for whom the church gathers to pray, and who experiences a sudden remission, has not experienced a miracle. Yes, we can credit God with the healing. But to the extent that God worked through the body's own resources or medical treatment, the recovery was not a miracle.

The Catholic church, which traditionally has been more open to contemporary miracles than Protestants, realized that it was necessary to define conditions under which a healing could be termed miraculous. Those conditions were defined in the 18th century by Pope Benedict XIV.

1. The sickness or disability must be serious.
2. At the time of the healing, the patient should not be improving or suffering from a condition that might be expected to improve.
3. The patient should not be taking orthodox medical treatment at the time.

4. The healing should be sudden and instantaneous.
5. The cure must be perfect and complete.
6. The cure should not occur at a time when a crisis due to natural causes has affected the patient or the illness.
7. The cure must be permanent.

One example of a cure that meets these standards is the documented case of Vittorio Michelli. In 1962 Michelli suffered from a cancerous tumor on his left hip. The hip bone disintegrated, and the bone of his upper left leg was left floating in tissue. During a visit to the shrine at Lourdes, Michelli felt a sensation of heat moving through his body, and he began to improve.

Back at home, he went to his doctors and insisted that his hip be x-rayed. The tumor had shrunk. Over the next several months the tumor disappeared. But what was unheard of in medical history was that the hip bone had regenerated—something considered impossible! That we can call a miracle.

John Wimber, the founder of the Vineyard movement and a leading proponent of modern miracles, told of a woman he met in South Africa whom cancer had reduced to 85 pounds. He and a friend prayed for her, but with little confidence. As he reported in *Christianity Today* (Oct. 7, 1996, 51),

That night she woke up with a vibrant, tingling feeling throughout her body. For the next four hours her body was full of intense heat. She tried to call out to her husband in the next room but couldn't raise her voice loud enough for him to hear.

Alone and frightened, she crawled into the bathroom, her body racked with pain. At the time she thought, "O my God. My body is coming apart and I'm dying." Without knowing it, she eliminated from her body a number of large tumors. Finally, exhausted, she fell back asleep. She didn't know if she'd wake up.

But a half an hour later she woke up incredibly refreshed. Later her husband woke up to the smell of freshly brewed coffee. "What are you doing!" he asked, astonished to see his wife on her feet and preparing breakfast.

She replied with sudden understanding: "God has healed me."

Two days later she reported to her doctors, who gave her a clean bill of health. They couldn't find a cancer in her body. God had completely delivered her of it.

Extraordinary events like these two can be considered miracles. But many recoveries we experience as answers to prayer should not be placed in the "miracle" category.

We can say the same about providential occurrences. The book of Esther provides a clear example of God's providential care of his people. The existence of the Jewish people was threatened. A high official in the Persian court decided to avenge a supposed insult by a Jewish bureaucrat by wiping out the Jewish people. He cast lots to determine just the right day to approach the king. Finally every omen was positive, and he talked the king into ordering the execution of all Jews in the Persian Empire.

But that night the king was unable to sleep, so he had a secretary read to him from the royal archives. The secretary happened to read about a time when the very Jew who provoked the official's wrath exposed a plot against the king's life. When the king discovered this man had not yet been rewarded, he determined to correct the oversight immediately. And it also happened that the niece of the man who provoked the official had recently become queen, her race unrevealed! In the end, these events conspired to bring about the deaths of the scheming official and other enemies of the Jews, while the Jewish people were saved.

No one reading the book of Esther can fail to notice how every circumstance "just happened" to fit together neatly to provide for the Jews' deliverance. Yet not one of those circumstances was, in itself, extraordinary. Not one required an open or unmistakable intervention by God. The believer looks at the sequence of events and sees God's hand behind the scenes, arranging what happened to lead to his desired end. The unbeliever scoffs,

pointing out that each event, however fortu-
itous, took place naturally. Each follows the
other in a chain of cause and effect which
doesn't require "God" to explain.

Thus, we need to be careful in speaking
of biblical or contemporary miracles. Answers
to prayer which come through seemingly normal processes and unlikely chains of event
which lead to fortunate outcomes may be
credited to God's providential care. But they
should not be called miracles.

Only extraordinary events which cannot
be explained in any way other than by divine
intervention merit consideration as miraculous.

PRACTICAL CONSIDERATIONS IN EVALUATING CLAIMS OF CONTEMPORARY MIRACLES

The Christian who believes in the God
who has defined himself in the three grand
miracles will not doubt that God is able to
cause extraordinary events in the material universe. This does not mean that Christians
naïvely accept every report of miraculous
events as gospel. A belief in the possibility of
contemporary miracles does not commit us to
accept the validity of any modern miracle tales.

What should we consider in dealing with
reports of modern miracles?

THERE ARE MIRACLE REPORTS WHICH ARE FALSE

The book of Acts tells of "a certain man
called Simon, who previously practiced sorcery in the city and astonished the people of
Samaria, claiming that he was someone great,
to whom they all gave heed, from the least to
the greatest, saying 'This man is the great
power of God' " (Acts 8:9, 10). These verses
remind us of several realities about miracle reports.

The reported miracle may be a counterfeit.
Simon was not performing miracles but using
"sorcery" to produce certain effects. As the
term was used in the first century, "sorcery"

may have involved what we call "magic" or "illusion" today. Or "sorcery" might refer to
events cause by a supernatural, demonic being. In neither case would the acts of Simon fit
our definition of a miracle—an extraordinary
event caused by God which has religious significance.

*Those reporting the miracle might be de-
ceived.* It is possible to believe an event is a
miracle—and to be totally deceived. Simon
had deceived the entire population of Samaria,
and thus was accorded a respect he didn't deserve. It's possible to believe sincerely in a miracle that we have supposedly observed, and
still be wrong.

*The motive of the supposed miracle-worker
may be questionable.* Simon used the so-
called miracles that he performed to support
his claim that "he was someone great." The
more stridently a person claims miracle-
working powers, the more likely it is that his
motives and thus his claims should be questioned.

It's especially important to weigh miracle
reports carefully and to apply the criterion established by Benedict XIV when "faith healers"
come to town. God can heal, and he can give
special gifts of healing to individuals. But faith
healers who are unwilling to provide information which would allow their claims of healing
miracles to be substantiated should not be respected as a "great power of God."

THE PRESENCE OR ABSENCE OF CONTEMPORARY MIRACLES NEITHER VALIDATES NOR INVALIDATES CHRISTIAN FAITH

It is important to keep the question of
miracles in perspective. The grand miracles of
Creation, Incarnation, and Resurrection are
central to Christian faith. They define our understanding of who God is, and thus who it is
in whom we believe.

But our faith in a God who is both our
Creator and Redeemer does not rest on
whether God performs miracles for us today.

We need to adopt the attitude of the three Hebrew officials in the Babylonian Empire who, when threatened with death in Nebuchadnezzar's fiery furnace, replied "Our God whom we serve is able to deliver us from the burning fiery furnace . . . But if not, let it be known to you, O King, that we do not serve your gods, nor will we worship the gold image which you have set up" (Dan. 3:17, 18).

God is able to perform miracles for us.

But if He chooses not to do so, we will still trust Him to the end.

MIRACLES ARE PERFORMED BY A SOVEREIGN GOD

John Wimber is a leading figure in the call for Christians to expect God to perform miracles today. In a moving article in *Christianity Today* (Oct. 7, 1996, 50), Wimber reflected on his own experience with life-threatening cancer:

When I began radiation treatments for my cancer, I discovered what it was like to walk through the valley of the shadow of death. As I spent weeks without eating solid food, I began to realize that the physical and emotional trauma coming my way could only be met by taking the hand of the Lord and walking with him.

. . .

Some Christians believe that we should never struggle with doubt, fear, anxiety, disillusionment, depression, sorrow, or agony. And when Christians do, it is because they're not exercising the quality of faith they ought to; periods of disillusionment and despair are sin.

If these ideas are true, then I'm not a good Christian. Not only have I suffered physically with health problems, but I also spent a great deal of time struggling with depression during my battle with cancer.

But I also found that the view from the valley gave me a focus on Christ that I wouldn't have gained any other way. Stars shine brighter in the desert. There are no obstructions, no distractions, no competing lights. The view from the valley isn't so bad because Jesus shines so clearly. I knew he was there even when I didn't always feel him close to me.

Wimber has now recovered from his cancer. And he realizes that God has healed him, even though through medical means. He also recognizes that others with just as much faith have died from a cancer like his. His conclusion provides a helpful reminder.

Two wonderful men from our Anaheim, California, congregation were diagnosed with cancer within weeks of my diagnosis. Harold Looney and Lynn Marang were both active servants in the church and very passionate in their worship of the Lord Jesus. We earnestly prayed in faith for their healings over the course of weeks and months, and in Lynn's case, well over a year. They had families that needed them and lives worth living. Yet in God's sovereign choice, he took each of them home to be with him. He chose to let me remain. I can't explain that. It's impossible to explain. The mystery of God's sovereign choice is the only answer.

As we come now to our study of biblical miracles, we want to affirm what Wimber calls "the mystery of God's sovereign choice."

- God does not perform miracles on demand.
- God may not perform miracles even when we believe they are most called for.
- But God, who created the world and who entered it to redeem us, performs miracles when to do so has served His sovereign purpose.

In examining the miracles of Scripture, we will discover something of what those purposes are. And we will develop a deeper trust in the God whose actions in our world display the unimaginable depth of His love for His people.

CHAPTER 2

MIRACLES THAT SHAPED OUR LIVES

RELATIONSHIPS OF GOD AND MAN

Genesis 1—19

Some miracles touch our lives. Other miracles shape them. In fact, wonders reported in Genesis have molded our most basic understanding of the nature and meaning of our lives. Even more, Creation, the first of the cosmic miracles reported in Genesis, established the very nature of the universe in which we live. The miracle of humanity's origin defined human nature and mankind's relationship with God. The miracle of the Genesis Flood established forever the truth that ours is a moral universe, and God is its moral Judge.

When we compare the cosmic miracles reported in Genesis with pagan notions of how the world began and how human life originated, we are stunned to discover how completely the Genesis miracle reports have shaped Western civilization, and our own most basic beliefs.

I. MIRACLES IN THE BOOK OF GENESIS

The following events reported in Genesis fit the criterion of a miracle as "an extraordinary event caused by God which has religious significance."

1. The miracle of material creation—p. 28
2. The miracle of God's creation of Adam—p. 32
3. The miracle of God's creation of Eve—p. 36
4. The miracle of Enoch's translation—p. 38
5. The miracle of the Flood—p. 40
6. The miracle of Babel—p. 45
7. The miracle of the plagued Pharaoh—p. 48
8. The miracle of Sarah's conception—p. 50
9. The miracle of the blinded Sodomites—p. 52
10. The miracle of Sodom's destruction—p. 54
11. The miracle of Lot's wife—p. 55

THE MIRACLE OF MATERIAL CREATION   *Genesis 1*

In chapter 1, we identified the Creation as one of three grand miracles which are critical in defining the nature of God as he is revealed in Scripture. The main concern of this chapter was to show that the only alternative to creationism—the materialist view as presented in the theory of evolution—cannot be given credibility. The evolution theory claims to explain how the universe could have taken its present shape and how the many forms and varieties of life could have emerged. But its explanation is not merely unproven; it is fatally flawed. This leaves us with only one intellectually honest option: what exists has been designed and brought into being by an intelligent Creator.

This is exactly what Genesis 1 affirms.

THE DESCRIPTION OF CREATION IN GENESIS 1

Creation arose from an original state of nothingness. Most English versions of the Bible translate Genesis 1:1, "In the beginning God created the heavens and the earth. The earth was without form, and void, and darkness was on the face of the deep." It's clear from Scripture that the phrase "heaven and earth" is the usual biblical term for the universe. This meaning is clear from the use of the phrase in such verses as Genesis 14:19 and Psalm 121:2.

Unfortunately, most English renderings make it seem that God created the heavens and earth and then went about adding light, etc.

A notable exception to the translation of Genesis 1 found in typical English versions occurs in modern Jewish versions of Genesis. These read, "When God began to create . . ." and "In the beginning of God's creating the heavens and the earth. . . ." Nine hundred years ago the great Jewish commentator Rashi wrote,

The passage does not intend to teach the order of creation, to say that these [namely, the heaven and the earth] came first; because if it had intended to teach this, it would have been necessary to use the form *barishonha.*

What Genesis 1:1–3 actually does is to make a statement. When God set about creating the heavens and earth—the earth being unformed and void and space dark and empty—the Spirit was hovering over its vast expanse. *Then* God said, "Let there be light."

The means of creation (Genesis 1:3–25). The Genesis account repeats a pattern seen first in 1:3. "Then God said, 'Let there be light,' and there was light." This same formula, at times with the variation "and it was so," is found in verse 6, 9, 11, 14, 20, and 24. Without the need for any other agency, God simply spoke the material universe into existence! Psalm 33:6 declared, "By the word of the Lord the heavens were made, and all the host of them by the breath of his mouth." No wonder the psalmist added,

> Let all the earth fear the Lord;
> Let all the inhabitants of the world
>   stand in awe of him.
> For he spoke and it was done;
> he commanded, and it stood fast
>   (Ps. 33:8).

The sequence of creation (Genesis 1:3–27). One fascinating feature of the Genesis account is the sequence in which creation is described. Several things about the sequence are of interest.

1. There is a clear pattern in the sequence. This can be shown as follows:

Framework	Detail
Day 1 Light and dark	**Day 5** Creatures of water, air
Day 2 Sea and sky	
Day 3 Fertile earth	**Day 6** Creatures of the land
Day 4 Lights of day, night	Human beings

2. The sequence is "scientific." That is, the sequence in the Genesis account agrees with the stages for earth's development proposed by scientists on the basis of geologic and fossil evidence. The materialist supposes that natural causes account for the shape of the universe and for life in all its varied forms. But the materialist cannot define the mechanisms which caused their evolution. Yet all the evidence scientists have gathered has led materialists to adopt a sequence for creation which Moses wrote some 3,500 years ago, thousands of years before "science" even addressed the question!

Edwwyn Bevan, an evolutionist, has commented on Genesis 1, "The stages by which earth comes to be what it is cannot indeed be precisely fitted to the account which modern science would give of the process, but in principle they seem to anticipate the modern scientific account by a remarkable flash of imagination, which a Christian may also call inspiration."

The framework of creation: the "days" of Genesis 1. Bible scholars disagree as to how the six "days" in which Genesis 1 describes creation should be understood. At least six different theories have been put forward. (1) Creation took place in six, sequential 24-hour periods. (2) "Day" is figurative, probably representing what we call a geologic age. (3) "Day" is literal, but an age intervened between each of the Genesis 1 days. Thus God introduced vegetation in a 24-hour period, but He waited thousands of years for its varieties to develop before the next creative day. (4) God created in seven literal days a few thousand years ago, with coal, fossils, etc. created in place to give the appearance of age. (5) The six days are not days of creation at all. They are revelatory days, in which God revealed His works to Moses. (6) The six-day structure is a literary device used by the author to organize his material.

The repeated references in the Genesis text to morning and evening make some of these theories difficult to sustain. Yet Origen, and St. Augustine after him, argued that the days of God need have no human analogy (compare Ps. 90:4; Isa. 4:2). Whatever our personal convictions about the nature of the days, their use in Genesis 1 emphasizes the fact that God's creation took place in planned, logical stages. This reinforces the main truth that our universe has its origin in a being who carefully designed it and our earth, and then implemented that design.

THE UNIQUENESS OF THE GENESIS ACCOUNT

When archaeologists first discovered documents in the ancient Near East which recorded Babylonian and Egyptian creation myths, critics hurriedly counted the supposed similarities to the biblical account. Their assumption was that the writers of Scripture relied on earlier myths when "inventing" the Hebrew creation story.

However, the more these Middle Eastern creation accounts have been studied, the clearer it has become that the biblical account is unique. In fact, many elements of pagan cosmologies are directly confronted by the Genesis account.

A unique vision of God. In Genesis, God stands as the one and only true God. Other Near Eastern accounts are cluttered with gods and goddesses, who often are rivals of the high god of the pantheon.

A unique vision of emptiness. In Genesis, only God has being before He acts to create. Creation takes place in a void where nothing "is." The heavens and earth are formed by God's Word, coming into existence from nothing.

In the ancient Babylonian creation epic known as *Enuma elish,* the heavens and earth are formed from the body of a defeated rival god by a victorious deity. In Egyptian creation myths, an original deity is on earth when he creates three subordinate gods from his semen, who then exist in uncreated primordial waters.

A unique view of human beings. Most significant, in these other Near Eastern creation accounts, human beings are formed accidentally or as an afterthought. In Scripture, the creation of human beings is God's culminating act of creation. Humankind is special, made in God's image, created to inherit and care for the world which God has made.

Any similarities between the Genesis account and the creation myths of the ancient world are superficial at best. They do not show harmony with the sequence of life's appearance on earth which is evident in the Genesis account. Neither do they match the Bible's exalted presentation of God as unique and all-powerful.

BIBLE BACKGROUND:

NEAR EASTERN CREATION MYTHS

In the Babylonian creation account known as *Enuma elish,* the material universe is formed by Marduk from the body of the slain goddess Tiamat. Tablet IV provides this description.

> he . . .
> turned back to Tiamat whom he had bound.
> The lord trod on the legs of Tiamat,
> With his unsparing mace he crushed her skull.
> When the arteries of her blood he had severed,
> The North Wind bore (it) to places undisclosed.
> On seeing this, his fathers were joyful and jubilant,
> They brought gifts of homage, they to him.
> Then the lord paused to view her dead body,
> That he might divide the monster and do artful works.
> He split her like a shellfish into two parts:
> Half of her he set up and ceiled it as sky,
> Pulled down the bar and posted guards.
> He bad them to allow not her waters to escape.

An Egyptian creation myth that reflects a motif going back to at least 3,000 B.C. is detailed in the Pyramid Texts. An excerpt describing the creations of Ra pictures this superior deity as coming into being "in this earth" and then creating subsidiary deities.

> I conceived in my own heart; there came into being a vast number of forms of divine beings, as the forms of children and the forms of their children.
> [The text then mentions the sexual act by which the beings Shur and Tefnut were "spat" and "spewed" from Ra's mouth.] By my father Nun, the Primordial Waters, were they brought up, my Eye watching after them since the eaons when they were distant from me.
> After I had come into being as the only god, there were three gods aside from me. I came into being in this earth, but Shue and

Tenut rejoiced in Nun, the Primordial Waters, in which they existed.

The contrast between the gods of ancient myths and the God of Scripture is strikingly clear.

THE RELIGIOUS IMPLICATIONS OF THE MIRACLE OF CREATION

Miracles are extraordinary events caused by God which have religious significance. Certainly creation fits the first two of these standards. But what are the implications of creation for faith?

Creation assures us that the universe is personal. There are really only two options: (1) Either the universe in which we live has been designed and brought into being by a supreme being, or (2) it has emerged randomly as the product of mere chance. If the first premise is true, existence has meaning beyond itself, and we can look to the Creator to discover what that meaning is. If the second assumption is true, existence is meaningless and we live in a universe that grinds on aimlessly toward an uncertain fate. If the universe is personal, there is hope that we might survive beyond the dissolution of our bodies. If the universe is impersonal, there is no hope for survival after death.

The Bible's affirmation of the miracle of creation assures us that the universe is personal rather than impersonal; that existence is meaningful rather than meaningless; that we can find this meaning by seeking to know the Creator; and that the possibility of life after death exists.

Creation portrays a trustworthy, caring God. Romans 1:20 asserts that God's invisible attributes are "clearly seen, being understood by the things that are made, even his eternal power and Godhead." The testimony of the creation is so overwhelming that every person intuitively recognizes God's existence. To deny God involves a suppression of known truth, and this act of denial is in itself a demonstration of human sinfulness (Rom. 1:18).

But the eye of faith learns much more about God from creation than his existence.

1. *Creation reveals a dependable God.* The creation—through its regular alternation of day and night, with season following season—reveals a God who is consistent in His works.

2. *Creation reveals a concerned God.* The vast complexity and multiple forms of animate and inanimate life are revealing. From the uniqueness of each snowflake to the individuality shown in the animal world, God's delight in creative expression and His concern for the individual are clearly displayed.

3. *Creation reveals a caring God.* Throughout Genesis 1 we read God's response to what He has done: "It is good." In the beauty and infinite variety of the universe, we catch a glimpse of a God who values the beautiful and the good. Surely our Creator is a God who *cares.*

Creation is one of the three grand miracles of Scripture. Together, these three miracles significantly define who God is. The Genesis account of creation stands as a unique vision of how our world came into being. Its striking contrast with ancient creation myths and with contemporary evolutionary theory challenges all to examine the implications of belief and disbelief, and to make a decision for or against God.

THE MIRACLE OF ADAM'S CREATION   *Genesis 1:26–31; Genesis 2:1–17*

While the creation of human beings is part of the Genesis creation account, it deserves to be treated as a distinct, separate, and extraordinary act of God. This account is given briefly in Genesis 1, and then in greater detail in Genesis 2.

THE TEXTUAL CHALLENGE TO EARLY GENESIS

In chapter 1 we looked briefly at the materialists' challenge to the Genesis account of creation, based on the theory of evolution. There we saw that evolution is hardly the "fact" which most people assume it to be. We also pointed out one of the fatal flaws which undermine its credibility.

Before we look at the Genesis account of mankind's creation, we need to note another challenge to Genesis. This challenge emerged in the 19th century as scholars began to argue against Mosaic authorship of the Pentateuch. They saw Genesis not as a revelation from God given through Moses, but as the patchwork creation of a religious document by human beings, completed centuries after its supposed date of composition. Rabbi Shlomo Riskin, dean of Israel's Ohr Torah institutions and chief rabbi of Efrat, commented on this attack:

> What would eventually receive recognition as the Wellhausen School of Biblical Criticism plunged its teeth deep into the flesh of Jewish tradition. Its major hypothesis is that no fewer than four separate documents have contributed to the Torah [i.e., the Pentateuch]—commonly called J,E,P,D.
>
> J stands for the first letter of God's four-letter name, and thus the sections where God appears with that appellation. E is for Elokim, the sections where God's name is Elokim. P is for the Priestly Code, and D for the Deuteronomist—author or editor of the last of the Five Books.
>
> Based on a system of comparing the names of God as well as selected verses that sound redundant or dissimilar with other sections, and combined with conjectures about contemporaneous historical events, such biblical critics are direct heirs of the attempt to whittle the Bible down to human size that was originally called the Wissenschaft des Judentums (science of Judaism)
>
> . . .
>
> Now, long before the critics appeared, rabbinic tradition explained the distinctions between the two names. *Elokim* represents the universal God of nature, law and justice, while the four letter name represents the more personal God of compassion and human involvement. As to the narrative accounts, the supposed difference disappears if only we read the total narrative (*Jerusalem Post,* October 1, 1994).

Riskin went on to point out that the first chapter of Genesis sets the creation of human beings within the framework of the creation of the universe.

The second chapter of Genesis returns to the creation of human beings for a closer look at this special creature God has made. It looks in detail at what God has done, and in this, Genesis 2 helps us define original human nature. The shift from use of the name Elohim in Genesis 1 to Yahweh in Genesis 2 does not indicate a patchwork of two separate and different creation accounts. Rather, as Rabbi Riskin pointed out, this shift emphasizes the personal involvement of God in the creation of human beings.

All the major *assumptions* of the Wellhausen school—that writing did not exist in Moses' time, that Israelite religion evolved from polytheism to monotheism, that repetition and duplication prove separate authorship—have been discredited by the discovery of ancient Semitic literary documents. Yet the *conclusions* reached by that school, including the J,E,P,D documentary hypotheses on which Riskin comments, are still uncritically accepted by many contemporary scholars!

It is bizarre that such groundless methodologies are still used by many who reject Scripture's own affirmation that it is the revealed Word of God. We must take our stand with Rabbi Riskin, who concluded his article,

> The Bible critics make a fatal error. They divest the Torah of context and subtext, examining the mechanics of the words while disregarding the majesty and the fire, the vision and the message.

> What we must remember is that the Bible is not a book written by man. It emanates from God—a description not only of what humanity is, but what it must strive to become.

THE GENESIS 1 ACCOUNT OF THE CREATION OF MAN

The Genesis 1 account of man's creation begins with the statement of God's intention, "Let Us make man in our Image, according to Our likeness" (Gen. 1:26). The verse then goes on to express God's intention to "let him have dominion." Verse 27 tells us, "So God created man in his own image; in the image of God he created him; male and female he created them."

These verses are particularly significant.

1. *The use of the name Elohim* makes it clear that the one who created humankind is the same supreme being who created the universe.
2. *The name Elohim* is a plural noun. Together with plural pronouns, it indicates the personal nature of God and also suggests the trinitarian nature of God, which is fully revealed later.
3. *The terms image and likeness,* when used together, serve as a technical theological term. Only human beings are said in Scripture to be created in the image-likeness of God. This means that when trying to understand human nature, we cannot look to the animals to discern man's essence. We must look to God and evaluate humankind on the basis of man's resemblance to Him.
4. *The phrase "have dominion"* further sets humanity apart from the animal creation, which was created in the same Genesis "day" (the sixth). Mankind is not only different from earth's animals, but he is also set apart from them by his likeness to God and by the mission which mankind is assigned by the Lord.
5. *The phrase "male and female"* underlines the essential equality of man and woman. Each shares equally in the image of God. Each shares responsibility to care for the earth and its creatures.

The insights in Scripture's first overview of the extraordinary creation of man is further developed in the expanded description which occurs in Genesis 2.

THE GENESIS 2 ACCOUNT OF THE CREATION OF MAN

Genesis 2 comes back to the story of man's creation to provide a close-up look which develops additional details. Genesis 2:7 says,

And the Lord God formed man of the dust of the ground, and breathed into his nostrils the breath of life; and man became a living being.

The next section of Genesis, 2:8–17, describes a garden in which the Lord placed the first man, Adam. These verses also reveal much about the nature of God and the significance of man's creation in the image-likeness of God.

We especially note the following about Genesis 2:7:

1. *The text adds the personal name of Yahweh (the Lord)* to that of Elohim (God) in describing how God created man. Man was created by "the Lord God" (Yahweh Elohim). This addition emphasizes a personal investment in the miracle of man's creation which is not present in the creation of the material universe or the creation of other living things.

2. *God used pre-existing material,* the "dust of the ground," to make man's body. This shows that man is one with the universe in which we live.

3. *God breathed life into Adam* to make him a living being. This indicates that human nature is shaped by more than what can be accounted for physically. Human nature has a spiritual dimension. This dimension of being is not ascribed to any other creature in the animal kingdom.

4. *God planted a garden eastward in Eden* in which Adam was to live. The word *planted* focuses attention on God's design of Eden. The description of Eden provides clues as to the meaning of man's creation in the image-likeness of God. Each element of the garden's design provided Adam an opportunity to exercise capacities which he had received from God. These capacities remind us that human beings are persons who share with God all the attributes of personhood.

Some have interpreted the original image and likeness which God shared with Adam to be holiness. However Genesis 9:6 and James 3:9 base significant teaching on the assumption that even fallen human beings retain at

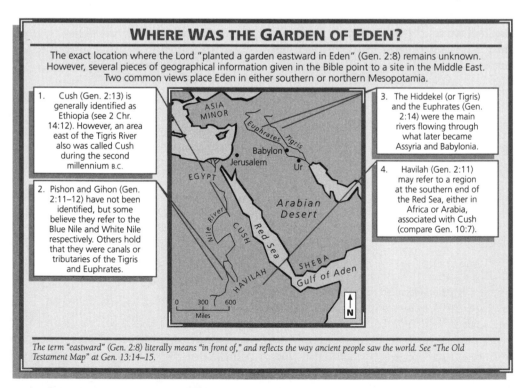

WHERE WAS THE GARDEN OF EDEN?

The exact location where the Lord "planted a garden eastward in Eden" (Gen. 2:8) remains unknown. However, several pieces of geographical information given in the Bible point to a site in the Middle East. Two common views place Eden in either southern or northern Mesopotamia.

1. Cush (Gen. 2:13) is generally identified as Ethiopia (see 2 Chr. 14:12). However, an area east of the Tigris River also was called Cush during the second millennium B.C.

2. Pishon and Gihon (Gen. 2:11–12) have not been identified, but some believe they refer to the Blue Nile and White Nile respectively. Others hold that they were canals or tributaries of the Tigris and Euphrates.

3. The Hiddekel (or Tigris) and the Euphrates (Gen. 2:14) were the main rivers flowing through what later became Assyria and Babylonia.

4. Havilah (Gen. 2:11) may refer to a region at the southern end of the Red Sea, either in Africa or Arabia, associated with Cush (compare Gen. 10:7).

The term "eastward" (Gen. 2:8) literally means "in front of," and reflects the way ancient people saw the world. See "The Old Testament Map" at Gen. 13:14–15.

least a reflection of God's image-likeness. It is better to understand image-likeness in terms of those things which make a human being a person: our reason, will, appreciation of beauty, ability to feel and to love, etc.

The *Teachers Bible Commentary* observes,

Remember that God's own personality was mirrored in Adam. Adam shared a capacity to appreciate. So the plantings of Eden included every tree "that is pleasant to the sight" (v. 9). God knew that man would be dissatisfied without work, so in the garden God let Adam "till it and keep it" (v. 15). God knew man's need for opportunity to use his intellectual capacities, so God brought the animals to the man "to see what he would call them; and whatever the man called every living creature, that was its name" (v. 19). God knew man's need for freedom to choose, so he placed a forbidden tree in the garden and commanded man not to eat fruit from it. This action once for all set man apart from creatures who live by instinct and demanded that he use his capacity to value and to choose.

In all these ways, then, the miracle of man's creation establishes a distinction between human beings and the rest of animal creation. The creation account lifts human beings up, setting them apart as special. Mankind is not only special within the created universe; he is special to God, as shown in the unique way in which the miracle of man's creation took place.

BIBLE BACKGROUND:

MAN'S CREATION IN NEAR EASTERN MYTHS

Ancient Near Eastern creation myths assign a very different place to human beings than does Genesis. Tablet VI of the *Enuma Elish* gives this account.

When Marduk hears the words of the gods,
His heart prompts (him) to fashion artful works.
Opening his mouth, he addresses Ea
To impart the plan he had conceived in his heart:
"Blood will I mass and cause bones to be,
I will establish a savage, 'man' shall be his

name. Verily, savage-man I will create.
he shall be charged with the service of the gods
That they might be at ease!
The ways of the gods I will artfully alter.

The Egyptian Pyramid Texts tell of Ra's loss of his eye. Fellow deities return Ra's lost eye. Man is derived from this incident in an unplanned and almost accidental manner. The text reads:

After I had united my members, I wept over them, and that was the coming into being of mankind, from the tears which came forth from my Eye.

What a difference from the origin of humankind which Scripture describes and the exalted place that Scripture assigns to human beings.

IMPLICATIONS OF THE MIRACLE CREATION OF MANKIND

God's miraculous creation of Adam establishes Scripture's view of humankind. If we believe that human beings are nothing more than evolved animals, we will have a very different view of people and society than if we subscribe to the miracle of man's creation. In a materialistic society, the state and the "many" have clear priority over the individual, who exists to serve the collective. In this scheme of things, individuals are unimportant. The state or collective society has priority.

But if human beings are made in God's image, individuals are far more significant. Individual human beings have a worth and value that cannot be measured by the contribution they make to the state—or on the basis of race, education, or economic status. Only if human beings are God's direct and special creation is there a basis for the kind of respect and love each human being truly deserves.

One writer observed:

So what's at stake in the interpretation of Genesis is not merely the historicity of ancient narratives, or the doctrine of biblical inerrancy, or even the systems of theology based on an inerrant historical record of Creation, Fall, and Deluge. . . . From the perspective of a critical hermeneutics, what's ultimately at stake in the interpretation of Genesis is nothing less than the social order, its character and sanctions, as dependent on human nature, created and corrupt (James R. Moore, *Interpreting the New Creationism,* 113).

The way we view ourselves and other human beings will shape the way we relate to others. This will also affect the kind of society we build.

THE MIRACLE OF GOD'S CREATION OF WOMAN   *Genesis 2:18–25*

Genesis 1:27 states that God created man as male and female. Genesis 2 describes that creative work as taking place in two distinct steps. God first created Adam, giving him time to explore the Garden of Eden. At a later time God created Eve. Genesis reports,

And the Lord God said, "It is not good that man should be alone. I will make him a helper comparable to him." Out of the ground the Lord God formed every beast of the field and every bird of the air; and brought them to Adam to see what he would call them. And whatever Adam called each living creature, that was its name. So Adam gave names to all cattle, to the birds of the air, and to every beast of the field. But for Adam there was not found a helper comparable to him.

And the Lord God caused a deep sleep to fall on Adam, and he slept; and he took one of his ribs, and closed up the flesh in its place. Then the rib which the Lord God had taken from man he made into a woman, and he brought her to the man. And Adam said:

"This is now bone of my bones
And flesh of my flesh;
She shall be called Woman,
Because she was taken out of Man."

PREPARATION FOR THE CREATION OF WOMAN

After God stated His intention to create a "helper comparable to" Adam, Genesis describes God bringing every kind of animal and bird to Adam. The great Jewish commentator Rashi observed that this verse does not describe a new creation, but it elaborates on the making of animals referred to in Genesis 1:28.

The text should read, "Out of the ground God had formed every beast, and [now] He brought them to Adam."

Why is Adam's naming of the animals described in this text, following the statement of God's intention to create woman? To understand the reason for this insertion, we need to consider three things.

The revelation that God created animals "out of the ground" emphasizes further the distinction of all other members of the animal kingdom from humanity. Animals are of the earth only. They lack the God-given "breath of life" which transmitted God's image-likeness to man alone.

The naming of the animals has great significance. In Hebrew thought, a "name" was descriptive, intended to communicate something of the essential nature or character of the thing named. For Adam to name the animals implied a long process of study of each animal's habits and behavior. Adam became a careful observer of each creature's ways; then he chose a name which expressed its uniqueness.

Adam could find no "comparable helper" in spite of his careful research into the animal kingdom (Gen. 2:20). God had said it was not good for the man to be alone. The process of naming the animals taught Adam what God already knew: Adam could find among them no suitable companion to whom he could relate physically, intellectually, emotionally, or spiritually.

THE FULL EQUALITY OF MEN AND WOMEN

Full equality is seen in the statement of God's intent (Genesis 2:18). The verse expresses God's intention to make a "helper comparable to" Adam. Other English translations of the Hebrew phrase `etzr kenegdo` render it "a fitting helper for him" (RSV), an "aid fit for him" (Anchor Bible), "suitable helper" (NIV), and "a helper who is right for him" (God's Word). Unfortunately, each of these translations seems to suggest that woman was created *for the ben-*

God brought each creature before Adam, for him to name them.

efit of man. Understood in this way, the text would support the assumption of many that females are by nature and by God's intent subordinate to males.

But this is *not* implied in the Hebrew phrase. In fact, this phrase guards against just this sort of misinterpretation of male-female relationships! Psalm 33:20 uses the exact word translated "helper" here in Genesis to describe God. The psalmist declared, "Our soul waits for the Lord; he is our help and our shield." Likewise, God is identified as man's helper (`*etzer*) in Exodus 18:4 and Psalm 70:5. Being a "helper" does not indicate subordination or that the person who helps exists for the benefit of the one being helped.

What Genesis 2:18 emphasizes is that only one who is fully a person—completely human as Adam was human and thus "comparable to him"—could meet the needs of Adam or any other human being.

Full equality is implied in the means God used to create woman (Genesis 2:22). God took a rib from Adam and used it as the basis for forming Eve. If God had made Eve as He formed Adam—from the dust of the earth—

there would have been no *essential connection* between man and woman. Woman would have been a separate and subsequent creation. By using Adam's rib, God further affirmed the identity of man and woman as humans who were equally possessors of the divine image-likeness.

Full equality was expressed in Adam's response to Eve (Genesis 2:23). Gordon Wenham, in the *Word Biblical Commentary,* noted that this verse scans as Hebrew poetry. He captured its essence when he described Adam as "in ecstasy," bursting into poetry on meeting his perfect helpmeet. Adam understood fully the fact that in Eve God had created a person who was "flesh of my flesh"—a person who shared with him all that it means to be human.

In the deepest sense, Adam and Eve—and the men and women who have descended from them—are not "different" but one.

IMPLICATIONS OF THE MIRACLE OF WOMAN'S CREATION

Materialists who adopt an evolutionary view of men and women tend to define male and female by their physical characteristics [men are stronger] and supposed evolutionary roles [women are nurturers, men hunters].

Christians who have misunderstood the message of woman's creation in Genesis 2 have tended to *limit* women's roles. Women are supposed to stay at home, rear children, and care for their husbands because God created them to be "helpers." For generations, this religiously based bias kept women in Western society from studying to be doctors or scientists.

Yet rightly understood, this miracle of God's creation of woman as a "helper comparable" to man emphasizes the equality of the sexes. God has gifted each sex with every capacity provided to humanity as a whole. Women do not come behind men in intellectual, emotional, or spiritual gifts. And only when we affirm, as Adam did, "This is now bone of my bones and flesh of my flesh," will we experience to the full all the wonderful ways in which God intends us to be helpers of one another.

THE MIRACLE OF ENOCH'S TRANSLATION   *Genesis 5:19–24; Hebrews 11:5*

This event is reported in a single verse nestled in the lengthy genealogy which traces Seth's descendants to Noah. The list names individuals and their offspring, indicating how long they lived. The entry for Enoch reads

Enoch lived sixty-five years, and begot Methuselah. After he begot Methuselah, Enoch walked with God three hundred years, and had sons and daughters. So all the days of Enoch were three hundred and sixty-five years. And Enoch walked with God; and he was not, for God took him (Gen. 5:21–24).

The Jewish rabbis have understood the phrase "and he was not" to mean that Enoch died. Noting the long lives of men before the Flood, some rabbis have suggested that the description of Enoch as one who "walked with God" is included to keep us from concluding that his relatively short life was ended as a divine judgment. The *Midrash* suggests that Enoch, although righteous, was likely to go

astray. So God cut his life short to avert that possibility.

However, the writer of the New Testament book of Hebrews has a very different explanation for the phrase "and he was not":

By faith Enoch was taken away so that he did not see death, "and was not found, because God had taken him," for before he was taken he had this testimony, that he pleased God (Heb. 11:5).

Thus, we have it on the authority of God's inspired Word that what Genesis actually describes is a miracle. Enoch was taken to be with the Lord without experiencing physical death.

ONE OTHER REFERENCE TO "ENOCH"

Another reference is made to "Enoch" in Jude 14, 15. This text speaks of "Enoch the seventh from Adam" prophesying. It also quotes Enoch's prophecy.

The difficulty is that the words quoted as those of Enoch are from a pseudepigraphic book, 1 Enoch, a Jewish religious treatise dating from the second or first century B.C. Some have assumed, because Jude quotes 1 Enoch, that Scripture authenticates this book—or at the least the content of the quote. However, other authorities have a different explanation:

The quotations are to be explained as necessary to the author's [the author of Jude] argument against the false teachers. . . . The author demonstrates that even these texts were misused by the heretics and he seeks to demonstrate that even the legends, when rightly interpreted, supported the orthodox view of the OT (Zondervan *Pictorial Encyclopedia of the Bible,* vol. 3, 734).

For this reason, we should not attempt to draw from Jude 14, 15 the kind of insights we can discern in the canonical texts which mention Enoch.

THE GENEALOGICAL SETTING OF THE MIRACLE STORY

The miracle of Enoch's translation is mentioned in a longer genealogy in Genesis 5.

This genealogy traces the family line of Adam's son Seth. It is notable for several reasons.

Long lives were ascribed to pre-Flood human beings. According to the text, it was not unusual for human beings before the Genesis flood to live eight or nine hundred years. There is no indication here that the numbers are meant to be figurative.

How could such lengthy lives be possible? Research has revealed that most diseases are linked to damage to various genes. This damage is transmitted from generation to generation. It does not seem unreasonable that the closer persons were to the perfect human gene pool in Adam and Eve, the less damage they would have experienced and the longer they would have lived. Another theory is that before the Flood a water vapor layer protected the earth from cosmic radiation, which has been linked to aging (compare Gen. 2:5 with Gen. 6:11, 12).

The Sumerian King List, an ancient Near Eastern document, names eight kings who ruled before "the Flood swept over (the earth)." The shortest length of rule cited for one of these kings is 18,600 years, and the longest 43,200! The document witnesses to a common tradition, showing that the life spans mentioned in Genesis 5 are conservative rather than exaggerated.

The length of lives cannot be "added up" to derive a date for creation. An attempt to do so by Bishop Usher in the 18th century led many people to believe the Bible teaches that creation took place in 4004 B.C. However, Hebrew genealogies typically do not list every person in a family line. And the Hebrew term translated as "son of" or "begat" is used of more distant descendants as well as one's children.

THE BIBLE'S DESCRIPTION OF ENOCH

It is clear from the comments about Enoch in Genesis and in Hebrews that his life and relationship with God was unusual.

He walked with God (Genesis 5:22, 24). Twice Genesis says that Enoch "walked with God." The same evaluation is given of Noah (Gen. 6:9). Malachi 2:6 indicates that priests were expected to walk with God, and Micah 6:8 indicates that what the Lord requires of His people is "to do justly, to love mercy, and to walk humbly with your God." The phrase in Genesis 5 clearly suggests Enoch's special intimacy with God and a life of piety.

The book of Hebrews adds that "before he was taken away, he had this testimony, that he pleased God."

THE BIBLE'S DESCRIPTION OF THE MIRACLE

Four phrases are used in Genesis and Hebrews to describe what happened to Enoch. The two accounts use phrases which stand in parallel:

Gen. 5	Heb. 11
he was not	he was not found
God took him	God had taken him

Each of these phrases is suggestive.

"He was not" (Genesis 5:24). Enoch ceased to exist as far as life on earth was concerned. He had spent about 365 years on earth. Then, suddenly, the life he had lived as a man came to an end.

For each of us, the time when we "are not" is fast approaching. We may leave our earthly life through the door of death or be caught up to join Jesus when he returns. But the one sure thing is that a day is coming when it will be said of us, "He was not."

When that time comes, how important it will be for the Lord to say of us that we "walked with God" during our days on earth.

"God took him" (Genesis 5:24). The phrase implies that God took Enoch *to be with Him*. The transition must have been an easy one for Enoch. He had spent his days living in fellowship with the Lord and walking with Him. Imagine how uncomfortable it would be to a person who is a stranger to the Lord to be suddenly brought into His presence. The more intimate our walk with the Lord here on earth, the more ready we will be to meet Him at the end of this life.

There is another implication of the phrase "God took him." Only God can make it possible for a human being to be with Him. It was only because of the promise of Christ's atoning death on Calvary that Enoch—a sinner like us—could be taken by God to be with Him.

"He was not found" (Hebrews 11:5). This phrase suggests that Enoch's contemporaries looked for him. He was not just gone; he was missed. A person who truly walks with God will be the kind of loving, caring individual whom others are drawn to and to whom they look for inspiration.

"God had taken him" (Hebrews 11:5). Hebrews speaks of the translation in the past tense. For Enoch the struggles of life on earth were over. Now and forever, Enoch was destined to enjoy endless life in the presence of the God with whom he had walked during his time on earth. For us the journey continues. But one day the journey will be over for us too. However great our trials and tragedies, they will be forgotten. Life will be past tense for us, as we enter an endless eternity.

We live in a day when we at last understand how God is able to forgive us so freely and to invite us into His presence. The death of Jesus lies in our past. The full benefits of His work lies ahead. Like Enoch, we lay hold of Him and all He has for us "by faith" (Heb. 11:5).

THE RELIGIOUS SIGNIFICANCE OF THE MIRACLE

There is much to consider in Scripture's description of Enoch and what God did for him. But there is also great significance in the miracle of translation itself.

After relating the story of creation (Gen. 1, 2), this first book of the Old Testament immediately tells the story of the Fall (Gen. 3). Adam and Eve sinned, and although they did not lose the image-likeness of God, their natures were twisted and corrupted. Genesis 4 goes on to display the impact of the Fall in the stories of Cain—who murdered his brother Able in a fit of jealous anger—and of Lamech—who rejected the divine ideal for marriage by taking two wives. Lamech also tried to justify his killing of a young man who had injured him. These stories demonstrated clearly that Adam's offspring had inherited the first couple's sin nature and had wandered far from God.

If early Genesis left us there, with images of sin burned into our eyes, we might conclude that there is no hope. But Genesis 5 relates the miracle of Enoch's translation. Enoch, a human being like us—a sinner living in a sinful world—chose to walk with God. And God took Enoch to be with Him.

What a message of hope this miracle conveys! Yes, we have sinned. But God is loving and gracious. If we choose to walk with Him, He will accept us and take us to be with Him one day as well.

THE MIRACLE OF THE FLOOD
Genesis 6—8

Genesis 6—8 describes a cataclysmic Flood which God used to purge the earth of a humanity totally corrupted by sin. Only one man, Noah, had not given in to this immorality. Noah, like Enoch, "walked with God." This just man, "perfect in his generations" (Gen. 6:9), "found grace in the eyes of the Lord" (Gen. 6:8). Noah was given instructions for building a great floating ship, an ark. He and his sons were also given 120 years to complete its construction (Gen. 6:3).

When the ark was built and provisions had been stored aboard, God caused pairs of animals to enter the vessel. Noah, with his three sons and their wives, joined the animals aboard the ark. God then brought a devastating flood which wiped out humanity and "all flesh in which is the breath of life" (Gen. 6:17).

A year later the flood waters receded. Noah and his family left the ark to reenter a refreshed earth. According to Genesis, all earth's living things are descended from the life forms preserved on Noah's ark.

IS THERE SCIENTIFIC EVIDENCE OF SUCH A FLOOD?

In March 1929 Sir Leonard Wooley, who excavated Ur, published a report in the *London Times* that the expedition had discovered unmistakable evidence of the Flood. He wrote, "We were loath to believe that we had obtained confirmation of the Deluge of Genesis, but there is no doubt about it now."

Wooley was wrong. Although he is still quoted by some in support of the flood story, what Wooley found was evidence of a local flood with an impact far less than would have been created by the Flood described in Genesis.

Geologists today are committed to the doctrine of uniformitarianism. This theory insists that every feature on the earth's surface can be explained by natural processes which are at work even today. They ridicule the notion of the watery cataclysm. Some theologians have responded by arguing for a local flood. They argue that if the human race was limited to populating a relatively small area in Mesopotamia, God's intent of wiping out the race could have been achieved without a flood that covered the surface of the earth. This comment on the debate is typical of that reasoning:

Few biblical events have stirred more interest. Is the story a myth, or is it historical? Was the Flood universal, or local? When did it happen? How does it fit into the historic or prehistoric record? We know that:

1. No other story is so widely repeated in traditions of ancient peoples all over the globe as that of a judgmental flood.
2. Detailed tradition from the Mesopotamian Valley, where the Scripture locates Noah, has revealed striking supportive evidence (*Enuma elish*).
3. Some argue the Flood was world-wide (universal) with "all the high mountains under the entire heaven" (Gen. 7:19) covered to a depth of 20 feet (Gen. 7:20). Others argue this is phenomenological language, implying only that the high ground in the writer's part of the world was inundated. Local Flood proponents argue that God's purpose, to judge a civilization which was likely localized in the great valleys of the Fertile Crescent, could be accomplished without universality.
4. Universalists see the Flood as a great catastrophe, with continental changes. The water vapor canopy of Genesis 2 fell to earth; quakes released subterranean waters on which the continents floated. The great weight of released waters resculptured the surface of the globe, thrusting up mountain ranges and depressing sea beds. This view is well presented in *The Genesis Flood,* by Whitcomb and Morris.
5. Local Flood proponents argue that a catastrophic flood would leave different evidence in the fossil record and rock strata. They interpret the words of Genesis 7 phenomenologically.
6. Neither group has solid evidence for dating the Flood, though suggestions range from 10 to 60 thousand years ago (*Richards Complete Bible Handbook* (Word), 38, 39).

If we leave aside the scientific debate and focus on the biblical text, there is much to learn from the miracle of the great Flood.

THE BIBLE'S DESCRIPTION OF THE GREAT FLOOD

The causes of the Flood (Genesis 6:5, 11). Genesis describes a corrupt civilization in which sin was institutionalized to the extent that "every intent of the thoughts of his [mankind's] heart was only evil continually" (Gen. 6:5). In this pre-Flood civilization, people freely acted on their intent and thoughts. Thus "the earth was corrupt before God, and the earth was filled with violence" (Gen. 6:11).

These conditions led God to determine "I will destroy man whom I have created from the face of the earth" (Gen. 6:7). There is no doubt that Genesis portrays the Flood as an act of divine judgment.

Coming at the point where it does in the sacred history, the Flood is a compelling witness to the moral character of God and His commitment to serve as the moral Judge of His universe. God may withhold His judgment out of love, to give us an opportunity to repent (Rom. 2:3, 4). But as the Genesis Flood reminds us, God *will* judge sin. And His judgments are severe.

(NOTE: The much debated identity of the "sons of God" referred to in Genesis 6:1–4 is thoroughly discussed in the companion volume, *Every Good and Evil Angel in the Bible,* also from Nelson.)

The choice of Noah (Genesis 6:8, 9). The description of Noah as a "just man, perfect in his generations" should not be taken to imply that Noah was sinless. He was not. Noah had chosen to walk with God (Gen. 6:9). To call him "just" indicates that he conducted himself in a righteous way. To call him "perfect in his generations" indicates that *in every respect* he tried to live a godly life.

Even so, God's choice of Noah was rooted in grace. The Jewish rabbis tend to interpret the phrase "Noah found grace in the eyes of the Lord" to indicate that God's favor was extended because Noah had earned it. It is far better to see Noah's godly character as *a result of God's grace.* Why did Noah live the kind of life described in verse 9? It was because Noah had "found grace" (verse 8)! Or perhaps we should say that God in grace had found Noah.

The ark Noah constructed (Genesis 6:14–16). The Genesis account gives very specific dimensions for the ark. It has been argued that the ark was too small to carry Noah's family, all the animals, and their food. Supposing the "cubit" (a unit of linear measure) Noah used was 24 inches rather than the more common 18-inch cubit, the ark, at 600 feet long, 100 feet wide, and 60 feet deep, would have a capacity of 3,600,000 cubic feet.

Through the ark, Noah and all creatures were saved from the Flood.

This would have been room for 2,000 cattle cars!

Earth today contains about 300 species (as distinct from sub-species) of land animals larger than sheep, about 750 species ranging in size from sheep to rats, and about 1,300 species smaller than rats. Two of each—plus seven pairs of ritually clean animals, with food for all—would have fit easily in the space available. Clearly, it would not have taken a miracle for the ark to hold the creatures and the necessary food to sustain life for the duration of the Flood.

The biblical description of the Flood itself (Genesis 7:11—8:14). There is no doubt, however, that the flood described in Genesis was a miracle. We can hardly imagine a more extraordinary act caused by God. No natural processes account for the things that happened.

According to Jewish exposition of the Hebrew text of Genesis 7:11, the "waters inundated the earth in a great seismic upheaval" while such torrential rains fell from heaven that they caused "complete havoc obscuring day and night." Genesis 7:19 indicates that the waters covered "all the high hills [Heb., mountains, *haharim*] under the whole heaven" to a depth of 15 cubits. The water level over all the earth's surface is thus said to have been at least 20 feet higher than the mountains!

This, of course, would have been possible only if before the Flood the earth's surface were smoother. The weight of the flood waters must have forced the upthrusting of earth's present mountain ranges and depressed the sea beds.

Another aspect of the Flood which emphasizes its miraculous nature is its length. It was five full months before waters receded enough for the ark to come to rest on the "mountains of Ararat" (compare Gen. 7:11 with 8:4).

The outcome of the Genesis Flood (Genesis 7:21–22; 8:20–22). The text indicates three results of the great Flood.

1. It accomplished God's intent of destroying the sinful civilization (Gen. 7:21–22). These verses assert that "every man" who was on the dry land died.

2. It moved Noah to worship (Gen. 8:20). When Noah finally led his family from the ark, he sacrificed one of each from the seven pairs of clean animals that had entered the ark (Gen. 7:2, 3).

3. It culminated in God's promise not to destroy the human race, no matter how corrupt civilizations might become (Gen. 8:21, 22). This promise, however, was limited to "while the earth remains." At history's end a day of final judgment will come.

THE FLOOD ACCORDING TO THE EPIC OF GILGAMISH

A Sumerian account of a flood which destroyed mankind is contained in the Epic of Gilgamish, which predates the Genesis account by perhaps a thousand years. As in the Genesis story, the hero was warned by a deity to build a great boat to save himself and the animals. While the framework of the flood story is very close to the Genesis account, the moral tone and the concept of the gods displayed in the epic is strikingly different from the Genesis account.

The causes of the flood. Like Genesis, the Gilgamish Epic interpreted the flood as divine punishment. But rather than being a response to man's sin, the gods in the Epic decided to destroy mankind because man's buzzing irritated them.

The warning to Gilgamish. One of the gods, Ea, violated the intent of the council of the gods and warned Gilgamish. When Gilgamish asked how he could explain his project to others, Ea told him to deceive them about the intent of the gods.

> "Thou shalt then thus speak unto
>   them:
> "I have learned that Enlil is hostile to
>   me,

So that I cannot reside in your city,
Nor set my foot in Enlil's territory.
To the Deep I will therefore go
    down,
   To dwell with my lord Ea.
But upon you he will shower down
    abundance,
The choicests birds, the rarest fishes.
The land shall have its fill of harvest
    riches.
he who at dust ordered the husk-
    greens,
Will shower down upon you a rain
    of wheat."

When the ark was prepared and boarded, a terrible storm broke out. The flood of waters was so devastating that the gods themselves were terrified. The Epic states,

The gods were frightened by the
    deluge,
And, shrinking back, they ascended
    to the
    heaven of Anu.
The gods cowered like dogs
Crouched against the outer wall.

Finally the flood ended, and the gods reconsidered. In their irritation at humanity, they forgot that by man's offerings they were fed! When Gilgamish offered a sacrifice, the gods crowded greedily around. The gods promised never to destroy mankind again, but their motive was purely from self-interest and not of grace. The epic states,

The gods smelled the sweet savor,
The gods crowded like flies around
    the sacrificer.
When at length as the great goddess
    arrived,
She lifted up the great jewels which
    Anu had
    fashioned to her liking:
"Ye gods here, as surely as this lapis
Upon my neck I shall not forget,
I shall be mindful of these days,
    forgetting never."

FLOOD STORIES FROM AROUND THE WORLD

Some might argue it is not surprising that the Hebrews, Sumerians, Assyrians, and Babylonians shared a tradition of a great, destructive deluge. It is much harder to explain the fact that similar stories are found in the legends of peoples from around the world.

A comprehensive list of flood legends can be found in James Frazier's *Folklore in the Old Testament* (vol. 1, 1918). He discovered similar traditions in the Egyptian story of Toth, and the Greek tradition of Deucalion and Phyrrha. The Hindu legend of Manu relates how eight were saved from a worldwide flood, a story paralleled by the Chinese legend of Fah-he. Among the Hawaiians, the flood hero is called Nu-u; among the Mexican Indians, he is called Tezpi. Among our own Algonquin Indians, the hero is Manabozho.

Similar traditions are found in Sumatra, Figi, New Zealand, the Sudan, Greenland, and among the Kurnai tribe of Australian aborigines, and many others.

In these stories, the common theme is that the human race, with the exception of a few survivors, was wiped out at one time by a great flood. In these stories, the reason mankind was purged from the earth was divine displeasure over human sin.

The universality of these legends suggests that the miracle of the Genesis Flood made a deep impression on the human beings who descended, as all have, from Noah's sons and daughters-in-law. Through this racial memory, God declares that He rules a moral universe and that He most surely will judge man's sin.

THE RELIGIOUS SIGNIFICANCE OF THE MIRACLE OF THE GENESIS FLOOD

Probably no other miracle except for Creation itself has made such an impact on humanity, as demonstrated by the traditions of a world-wide flood which exist in many cultures. The story of this miracle serves as a present warning. God is a God of love. But God is also a God of justice. If we do not accept the love of God, we will surely experience His justice.

As Peter wrote in his second epistle, scoffers will say, "Where is the promise of his coming?" and continue in their sin, confident that "all things continue as they were from the beginning of creation" (2 Pet. 3:4). But all things have not continued the same! Peter wrote, "For this they willfully forget: that by the word of God the heavens were of old, and the earth standing out of water and in the water, by which the world that then existed perished, being flooded with water" (2 Pet. 3:5–6).

Today this world is reserved for another judgment—a judgment by fire. And the miracle of the Flood reminds all mankind that the day of God's judgment will appear.

THE MIRACLE OF BABEL   *Genesis 11:1–9*

The story of the Tower of Babel [Babylon] is told in a few brief verses. Yet it relates the last great judgment on mankind before the time of Abraham. The story reminds us that while God had destroyed sinful human civilization in the Flood, He had not put an end to sin. We can change the environment in which people live. But we cannot change fallen human nature. The stain of sin lies within us, not in outward circumstances.

After the Flood, the human family had "one language and one speech." When people multiplied, they determined to build a city and a tower "whose top is in heaven" as a symbol of human accomplishment and unity. This enterprise was contrary to God's earlier command to "fill the earth and subdue it" (Gen. 1:28). Rather than punish these builders, God "confused the language" they spoke and understood. Then those groups which did speak a common language were scattered "abroad over the face of all the earth."

This miracle had a universal impact, just like the others recorded in early Genesis. It affected all humankind and the development of peoples and nations. The miracle account also has great spiritual significance.

THE MOTIVES OF THE TOWER BUILDERS   *(Genesis 11:4)*

Genesis 11:4 reports the revealing words of the tower builders.

"Come, let us build ourselves a city, and a tower whose top is in the heavens; let us make a name for ourselves, lest we be scattered abroad over the face of the whole earth."

"Build ourselves a city." Hebrews 11:16 praised the Old Testament heroes of faith because they desired "a better, that is, a heavenly country. Therefore God is not ashamed to be called their God, for He has prepared a city for them." By contrast, the tower builders' concern was entirely focused on life in this world and what human effort could accomplish.

The society that developed after the Flood did not display the violence and intent to do evil described in Genesis 6:5 and 6:11. But man's proud and sinful nature had found a new form of expression.

"A tower whose top is in the heavens." Many scholars have noted that this tower was undoubtedly a ziggurat, a stepped tower similar to a pyramid with a temple on the top. Towers like this were found in all major Mesopotamian cities. The ziggurat of the temple of Marduk at Babylon was named Esaglia, meaning "whose top is [in] heaven." It measured 295 square feet at the base and rose to an equal height.

The name *Esaglia* tells us that the tower builders of Babel intended their structure to be a place of worship. In planning the building, they revealed a universal assumption. Human beings suppose that man by his own efforts can find God. This is contrary to the Bible's teaching that God must take the initiative. It is He who has reached down to reveal Himself to us.

There is really only one choice—to worship the gods of human invention or to worship the God of revelation. The men of Babel chose human religion.

"Let us make a name for ourselves." The tower was to be a spectacular achievement by which the builders would "make a name for" themselves. Their goal was not to glorify God in creating their religious structure but to gain fame and glory for themselves. Isaiah 2:17 commented on motives like those that drove the men of Babel:

> The loftiness of man shall be
>   bowed down,
> and the haughtiness of men shall
>   be brought low;
> the Lord alone will be exalted in that
>   day.

The day is coming when we will be ashamed of everything we did to exalt ourselves and to make a name for ourselves. How much better to devote ourselves to exalting the Lord, in preparation for that great day.

"Lest we be scattered abroad over the face of the whole earth." The tower builders expected their achievement to provide a basis for social unity. They could look with pride at the structure towering over the plains and find their identity in what they had done.

People today still struggle to find their own identity and relational bonds in their accomplishments. We define ourselves by our jobs. We feel closer to those who share the same work and have the same education, or who have gained enough wealth to live in the same neighborhood with us. But God calls us to find our identity and a basis for unity with others in who we are as persons created in His image and likeness (Gen. 1:26). We are also directed to find an even greater identity in a personal relationship with Jesus. Through Him we become children of God and brothers and sisters of other believers (Gal. 3:26–28).

GOD'S GRACIOUS RESPONSE TO THE TOWER BUILDERS
(Genesis 11:5–8)

In response to the tower builders, God planted a number of different languages in the minds of the inhabitants of the area. This led to total confusion, ultimately separating the peoples who spoke the different languages from one another. In one sense, this miracle was a judgment on the tower builders, who had rejected God's command to fill and subdue the earth. But in many ways, this "judgment" was a great blessing for humankind.

God examined the builders' work (11:5). There is more than a little irony in the phrase, "God came down" to see the tower. The skyscraper—in spite of all the claims of the builders that its top reached heaven—fell so far short that the Lord could hardly see it. He had to "come down" to look at it.

On one hand, the Genesis account is a sharp attack on the theology and mythology of Mesopotamia, a region which featured the mythical tower of Esagil. This miracle also refuted the notion that God could be reached in the temples atop the ziggurats. The greatest of the ancient Near Eastern temple towers were beneath the true God's notice.

More significantly, the phrase "come down" reminds us how futile is to try to im-

The tower builders sought to reach up to heaven by their efforts.

press God through human effort. Titus 3:5 states, it is "not by works of righteousness which we have done, but according to his mercy he saved us." Our attempts to gain heaven must surely fail. Only by faith in the God who came down from heaven in Christ can we establish a personal relationship with Him.

God expressed concern for humankind's future (11:6). The verse reads, "indeed the people are one and they all have one language, and this is what they begin to do; now nothing that they propose to do will be withheld from them."

"The people are one and they all have one language." The builders had expressed concern that they might be scattered (11:4). They had failed to realize that the common language they spoke provided a bond that would hold them together. God, however, reminds us of the significance of language in facilitating unity of thought and intent.

"And this is what they begin to do." The plan to build the Tower of Babel revealed the direction in which the race was moving. Noah's descendants had focused on life in this world. In their arrogance, they thought they could reach any goal by self-effort. They were intent on making a name for themselves. Without God's intervention, they would have continued in the path they had chosen, moving further away from what God knew was best for them.

"Now nothing that they propose to do will be withheld from them." Human beings have wonderful abilities. It seems that nothing can interrupt the explosion of mankind's technological progress. We can build great cities, put libraries of information on a single silicon chip, and travel through space. It is this kind of progress that seemed to be in God's mind as he made this statement.

The key to interpretation of the passage is the phrase, "That they propose to do." The tower builders' focus was technological. They used the raw materials nature provided, made bricks and "bake(d) them thoroughly." Surely

with the tower finished, man's natural curiosity would have led to more and more inventions and discoveries.

But our generation demonstrates clearly that technological advances do not necessarily improve quality of life. In spite of all that man has created, the issues of injustice and crime have not been resolved. In every society, times of advance and prosperity are often followed by periods of decline and moral decay.

What might have been accomplished if our race, unified by a common language, had directed all its energies to building and making a name for itself? We cannot know for sure. But God's wise evaluation was that "nothing that they propose to do will be withheld from them." And that would not have been good for humankind.

GOD ACTED AND CONFUSED MAN'S LANGUAGE   *(Genesis 11:7)*

God's solution was simple. He impressed a number of different languages on the minds of the builders. One evening all went to bed speaking the same tongue; they awoke the next day speaking languages their neighbors no longer understood.

THE PRACTICAL CONSEQUENCES OF THE MIRACLE   *(Genesis 11:7, 8)*

The people were "scattered . . . abroad from there, over the face of the whole earth" (11:8). Through this miracle, God's intent for mankind to populate the earth was implemented. The different language groups chose willingly to separate from each other.

It would be a mistake to interpret the actions of the builders of the Tower of Babel as *intentional rebellion* against the desire which God expressed at the creation of Adam and Eve. Many of our most serious sins do not grow out of intentional rebellion. Proverbs 21:2 reminds us that "Every way of a man is right in his own eyes, but the Lord weighs the heart." Rather than an act of rebellion, the intent of Noah's descendants to build the tower of Babel revealed a basic corruption of heart and motive which the Lord clearly discerned.

Men could no longer "understand one another's speech" (Genesis 11:7). This result of the miracle is more subtle but more far reaching that the scattering of the population. Language is more than a means of communicating. It determines the way we perceive and organize experiences—the way we think. English tenses carefully locate actions in the past, present, and future. Greek tenses emphasized the nature of the action—whether it was to be seen as continuing, as completed, as extending into the future—or whether a completed action had an impact on our present. Such a simple thing as this variation in the emphasis of tenses causes one language group to think differently than another group in society. And this difference can be multiplied by dozens of differences and hundreds of languages!

In confusing man's tongues, the Lord introduced a unique capacity for human beings to think about the world in a variety of different ways, expanding the possibilities for our race.

At the same time, the introduction of such significant differences makes clear communication difficult. Throughout history, human beings have focused on their differences as a cause for hostility and war. But the Lord determined that it would be better for the future of mankind to be divided by different languages than to be united by a common language. This would be better than all of mankind focusing on a common goal which could cause irreparable harm.

THE MIRACLE OF THE PLAGUED RULERS   *Genesis 12:14–20; 20:1–18*

Abraham is known in Scripture as a man of faith. Yet the Bible records two incidents in which Abraham failed to display trust in God, resorting to deceit to avoid imagined dangers. In each case, God himself intervened to protect Sarah from the consequences of Abra-

ham's failures. These two stories remind us that even the greatest of Scripture's heroes was marred by sin, as we are. Each also reminds us that God in grace will often, although not always, protect us from the consequences of our failures to trust Him.

ABRAHAM'S SIN AND ITS CAUSES *(Genesis 12:11, 12; 20:10, 11)*

When these miracles occurred, Abraham was living a nomadic life in Canaan, now called Palestine. Genesis 12 tells of a visit by Abraham to Egypt caused by a severe famine. Genesis 20 simply states that Abraham "stayed in Gerar," without explaining the reason. In each place, Abraham begged his wife and half-sister, Sarah, to pretend that they were not married. He was afraid the strangers among whom they had settled would kill him in order to take his beautiful wife.

In each case, the deceit led to a foreign ruler taking Sarah into his harem. In his action and his failure to speak up for his wife, Abraham sank to a low level of moral degradation. Why did Abraham lie and put his wife—and indeed the future which God had promised them—at such risk?

He let circumstances dictate his choice (Genesis 12:10). The circumstance that brought Abraham to Egypt was a famine in Canaan. God had led Abraham to Canaan and promised the land to his descendants (Gen. 12:7). There is no hint in the text that Abraham consulted the Lord when the famine struck Canaan. Apparently, Abraham let the circumstances dictate his actions, and he made the move to Egypt without seeking God's leading.

It is true that circumstances sometimes play a role in God's leading. But like Abraham, when we are divinely guided to a certain place in our lives, we should not be panicked by circumstances into hasty action.

He imagined what might happen (12:12). When Abraham and his party approached Egypt, he began to imagine the worst. Abraham knew Sarah was beautiful. And he imagined that "when the Egyptians see you . . . they will say, 'This is his wife,' and they will kill me, but they will let you live."

Abraham could neither predict nor control the future. But he based his request that Sarah lie on the basis of what he *imagined* the future might hold. How important it is to remember that our sovereign God controls the future. He remains free to make choices that are right rather than decisions which seem expedient.

He selfishly failed to consider others (12:13). Abraham begged his wife to consider him and to join in the lie "for my sake." But Abraham did not do himself what he asked from her. Abraham did not consider what it would mean to Sarah to be torn from her husband and taken into a strange man's harem.

When we are faced with difficult choices, we need to examine carefully not only our own motives but the impact of our decisions on others as well.

He acted in fear rather than in faith (20:10–11). In the second incident at Gerar, Abraham was asked "Why?" by Abimelech. "What did you have in view, that you have done this thing?" Abraham's answer was revealing. He replied, "I thought, surely the fear of God is not in this place; and they will kill me on account of my wife."

Two fallacies lie at the root of this kind of thinking. One is the notion that those who lack faith in God must be immoral. This simply is not true. There are many "good" people who try to do what's right by their own lights. To say that "all have sinned" does not mean that all people sin continually, or that all will do as much evil as they possibly can.

The second fallacy is to assume that because others do not believe in God, the Lord cannot influence their behavior. Abraham's God is a sovereign God, who is able to preserve His people in any circumstance. When fear keeps us from doing what we know is right, the problem is not in the circumstances but in our lack of faith.

GOD'S MIRACLES OF INTERVENTION *(Genesis 12:17–20; 20:17–18)*

These miracles were not the spectacular type in which everyone recognized the hand of God. They were so ordinary that they would hardly have been recognized had not most people in the time of Abraham ascribed physical ills to supernatural sources.

Plagues struck Pharaoh and his court (Genesis 12:17–20). The Lord plagued Pharaoh with "great plagues because of Sarai, Abram's wife." Deuteronomy 28:59 identifies "extraordinary plagues—great and prolonged" as disciplinary punishments that God may use.

The Egyptians typically used some sort of magic to identify the source of such plagues. Perhaps God spoke to Pharaoh in a dream as he did some 20 years later to Abimelech. However he found out, Pharaoh fixed on Abraham as the reason he and his court were suffering. Abraham and Sarah were then sent away with all their possessions.

Abimelech's wife and servants became barren (20:17–18). Childlessness in the ancient world was not unusual. But in this case, *no women* in Abimelech's household could become pregnant. After a time, God revealed the cause of this curse to Abimelech in a dream.

Sarah and the kings were protected from committing adultery (12:19; 20:6). Although Sarah was taken into the harems of two kings, in neither case was she forced to have sex with the rulers. As God said to Abimelech, "I also withheld you from sinning against Me; therefore I did not let you touch her."

THE RELIGIOUS MESSAGE OF THE MIRACLE OF THE PLAGUED RULERS

There is much for us to learn by analyzing Abraham's mistakes and determining to avoid them. But there are additional messages for us in the account of these quiet, almost whispered miracles.

God's grace extends to sinners. Abraham's behavior in each case was inexcusable. Yet Abraham's failures did not cause God to withdraw His love or to rescind the covenant promises He had made to Abraham.

This is especially driven home by the promise given to Abraham that he would "be a blessing" to others (Gen. 12:2). In his attempts to deceive Pharaoh and Abimelech, Abraham had actually become a curse to each ruling house! Only God's intervention protected the two rulers and their subjects from greater suffering.

Miracles are evidence of God's grace, not of the holiness of any human being. One of the major theological dividing lines between Catholics and Protestants is the view of Catholics that miracles witness to the saintliness of persons associated with them. In the Catholic view, miracles authenticate one's faith. Thus John Milner argued that "the Catholic church, being always the beloved *spouse of Christ,* Rev. xxi.4, and continuing at all times to bring forth children of heroic sanctity, God fails not in this, anymore than in past ages, to illustrate her and them by unquestionable miracles." In order to be certified a "saint" by the Catholic church, definite evidence of miracles performed by the candidate or associated with him or her after death must be presented.

These two incidents involving Abraham remind us that association with miracles is not a guarantee of saintly character or spiritual superiority. Such miracles reaffirm God's grace to sinners, awakening thanksgiving for the Lord's kindness and mercy.

THE MIRACLE OF SARAH'S CONCEPTION   *Genesis 17:15–19; 18:10–14; 21:1–7*

God made great covenant promises to Abraham and his descendants. Yet as the years rolled on, Abraham's wife Sarah remained childless. Then, long after Sarah was past the child-bearing age, she became pregnant and gave birth to a son.

EVIDENCE THAT SARAH'S CONCEPTION WAS A MIRACLE

In the biblical world, barrenness was one of the greatest curses a woman could experience. Yet, six prominent Old Testament women were childless for much of their lives. Rebekah (Gen. 25:21) conceived after her husband Isaac prayed for her. Rachel (Gen. 29:31f) so despaired over her childlessness that she followed an ancient custom and had her maid Bilhah serve as a surrogate mother. Rachel eventually bore Joseph, whom God used to save His people from a terrible famine.

Manoah's wife (Judg. 13) was childless until told by God she would bear a son who would be named Samson. Hannah (1 Sam. 1) prayed desperately for a son. She later gave birth to Israel's last judge, the prophet Samuel. In the New Testament Elizabeth, who is described as "well advanced in years," bore John the Baptist after his birth was announced by an angel to her husband, Zacharias (Luke 1:5–25).

The common thread that runs through these stories of barren women is that each son they finally bore played a significant role in the spiritual history of God's people.

What sets the conception of Sarah apart as a miracle is more than the pre-announcement by the Lord (Gen. 17:16; 18:10) or the fact that Isaac was born "at the set time of which God had spoken" (Gen. 21:2). The truly miraculous part is revealed in the statement that "Sarah had passed the age of childbearing" (18:11). The Hebrew text says, literally, "the manner of women had ceased to be with Sarah." This delicate circumlocution meant that Sarah had stopped having her menstrual cycle. She had gone through menopause, and her womb had dried up. It was physically impossible for Sarah to have a child.

Sarah's conception of Isaac, while he was produced from her egg and Abraham's seed, was a truly extraordinary event. The Hebrew text implies that God was the cause of this miracle (compare Gen. 17:16; 18:14). "The Lord did for Sarah as He had spoken" (Gen. 21:1), and performed a miracle.

REACTIONS TO GOD'S ANNOUNCEMENT OF THE MIRACLE

Commentators have been fascinated by one aspect of this miracle story. When God told Abraham that he would become the father of a son by Sarah, "Abraham fell on his face and laughed, and said in his heart, 'Shall a child be born to a man who is one hundred years old? And shall Sarah, who is ninety years old, bear a child?' " (Gen. 17:17). Later, when Sarah heard the Lord in the guise of a human visitor make the same promise, the text reminds us of Sarah's sterile condition and says, "Therefore Sarah laughed within herself, saying, 'After I have grown old, shall I have pleasure?' " (Gen. 18:12).

In each of these two cases, the same Hebrew word is used for "laughed." Yet the Lord rebuked Sarah for her laughter but did not rebuke Abraham. Why?

The view of the Jewish sages. Jewish biblical scholars, many from the first and second centuries, argued that God rebuked Sarah because her laugh was "incredulous" (*Rashi*), indicating utter disbelief (*Midrash Aggadah*). In contrast, Abraham's laughter was a jubilant outburst, which according to Rashi, showed that he was "gratefully overjoyed."

This interpretation is rooted in the tremendous respect accorded to Abraham in Judaism. Although the word for "laugh" is the same in each verse, it is impossible to entertain the idea that this first of the patriarchs was flawed.

BIBLE BACKGROUND:

ABRAHAM'S MERITS

The common teaching indicated that all Israel participated in the merits of the patriarchs—of Abraham in particular. These merits made prayers acceptable, protected people from danger, helped them in war, were a substitute for each person's lack of merit, expiated sins, appeased the wrath of God, warded off God's punishment, saved people from *Gehinnom,* and assured them a share in God's eternal kingdom (Joachim Jeremias, *Jerusalem,* 300).

Given this doctrine, it is no wonder that the rabbis and sages were unwilling to criticize Abraham or ascribe any but the most gracious motives to his actions.

The evidence from Scripture. There is reason to believe that in spite of the use of the same word for laughter, Abraham's and Sarah's response to the announcement truly was different.

Abraham's laughter was linked with worship (Genesis 17:17). When Abraham received God's promise he "fell on his face." This represented deep respect and worship in Old Testament times. The text places worship immediately before Abraham's laughter. Thus Abraham's joyful laughter should be understood as an act of worship rather than an expression of doubt.

Psalm 126:2 records a parallel to Abraham's reaction: "Then our mouth was filled with laughter, and our tongue with singing. Then they said among the nations, 'The Lord has done great things for them.' "

Sarah's laughter earned her a rebuke (Genesis 18:13, 14). Sarah's denial that she laughed along with God's pointed question, "Is anything too hard for the Lord?" make it clear that her reaction was different from Abraham's.

The New Testament emphasized Abraham's faith (Romans 4:20, 21). The New Testament declared that Abraham "did not waver at the promise of God through unbelief." Unlike Sarah, he was "fully convinced that what God had promised, he was also able to perform."

Before we are too hard on Sarah, however, we need to remember that Abraham knew he was speaking with the Lord when the promise was given to him. Sarah overheard Abraham talking with angels, who appeared to be human beings. While we know that nothing is too hard for the Lord, we would probably react like Sarah if mere mortals were to promise us miracles!

RELIGIOUS SIGNIFICANCE OF THE MIRACLE OF SARAH'S CONCEPTION

Genesis 1-11 describes miracles which emphasize God's control over the physical universe. These were cosmic miracles, with direct impact on all mankind. The miracle described here, like that of the closing of the womb of Abimelech's women, is a miracle on a far smaller scale. At first glance, it seems the miracle involved in Sarah's giving birth to Isaac was almost a private miracle and that only the aging couple were affected.

But this extraordinary event is far more significant than that. God had told Abraham that the covenant promises He had made to him would be transmitted through his offspring. God was intent on creating a covenant people who would be the agency through which he revealed himself to all humanity and through which the Savior would come. The

The birth of Isaac began the fulfillment of God's promise to Abraham.

miracle happened to be a great blessing to the childless Sarah. But God performed it to accomplish a grander purpose.

Miracles are performed to fulfill God's purposes; they don't usually happen simply because we "need" them. God is gracious and loving in meeting our needs. But He will normally do so through natural rather than supernatural means.

THE MIRACLE OF THE BLINDED SODOMITES   *Genesis 19:9–11*

For centuries the name *Sodom* has been associated with depravity and sexual perversion. The Bible describes the valley in which Sodom and its associated cities were located as "well watered" and "like the garden of the Lord, like the land of Egypt as you go toward Zoar." The beautiful and fertile Jordan valley would have provided the people of Sodom with plenty of food, perhaps even agricultural wealth.

But in spite of the ideal conditions in which they lived, the people of the plain were unusually corrupt. Genesis reveals that the Lord told Abraham that "the outcry against Sodom and Gomorrah is great, and . . . their sin is grave" (Gen. 18:20). Two investigating angels paid a visit to Sodom. The men of the city gathered, intent on homosexual gang rape of the two visitors. The implication is that the "outcry against Sodom" had been made by earlier travelers who were treated in similar fashion.

But the cloaked angels had been invited into the home of Lot, Abraham's nephew. When the crowd attempted to break into Lot's house, the angels blinded them so they couldn't find the door. This is the first of three miracles reported in the account of Sodom's destruction.

The angels brought Lot and his wife and daughters to safety, then sent a rain of fire on the cities. The fiery destruction of the cities of the plain is the second miracle.

As Lot and his family fled from Sodom, Lot's wife looked back and was turned into a pillar of salt. This is the third miracle. We need to look at each of these.

ANGELS INVESTIGATE THE OUTCRY AGAINST SODOM AND GOMORRAH (Genesis 18:20, 21; 19:1–22)

Angels are associated in Scripture with the divine moral law, and especially with the later giving of the Mosaic Law (Acts 7:53; Gal. 3:19, 20). Two angels were sent to investigate Sodom and Gomorrah. They did so by entering the city of Sodom dressed as ordinary travelers. The way they were treated provided evidence of the truth of complaints against the city and its sin.

Lot's righteousness was established by his hospitality (Genesis 19:1–4). Showing hospitality to strangers was a primary moral value in the biblical world. Lot's insistence that the two travelers stay with him along with his preparation of a special meal for them mirrored Abraham's treatment of strangers (Gen. 18:1–8). In the context of the times, Lot's welcome was evidence of his righteous character (compare Gen. 18:23–24).

The Sodomites' wickedness was established by their behavior (19:4–11). That night the men of Sodom gathered outside Lot's house, demanding that he turn the two travelers over to them. The phrase "that we may know them" means "to have sex with them." One Jewish commentary on Genesis quotes several sages on the matter, noting that "this interpretation is based on the fact that *yada,* know, is used in Scripture as a delicate term for carnal knowledge and marital intimacy. In this case the Sodomites wished to vent their lust upon the visitors" (*Bereishis,* Mesorah Publications, Vol. 1, 682).

Just as Lot's hospitality established his righteousness, the behavior of the "men of Sodom—both old and young, all the people from every quarter" (19:4)—established their

wickedness. Based on this evidence, God's subsequent destruction of the city is seen to be just.

BIBLE BACKGROUND:

WHAT WAS THE REAL SIN OF SODOM?

Jewish commentators have tended to downplay the behavior described in Genesis 19, suggesting that the Sodomites' real sin was their lack of hospitality. The great rabbi *Ramban* even suggested that their purpose in gang raping visitors was to prevent the impoverished from coming into their fertile valley. "Although they were notorious for every kind of wickedness their fate was sealed because of their persistent selfishness in not supporting the poor and needy (see Ezek. 16:49)."

While the sin of Sodom was not limited to illicit passion, most references in Scripture to Sodom's sin emphasize the sex sin (compare Jer. 23:14; 2 Pet. 2:6). Jude 1:7 cites "Sodom and Gomorrah, and the cities around them" which, "having given themselves over to sexual immorality and gone after strange flesh, are set forth as an example."

The weight of the evidence is that their attempted homosexual rape of the angels was the culminating sin which fully expressed the wickedness and corruption of the society. (For an unambiguous description of Scripture's attitude toward homosexuality, see Romans 1:21–26).

Lot's futile attempt to save his visitors (19:6–11). Typically, a miracle is unnecessary if its purposes can be achieved by ordinary means. In this case, Lot's efforts to protect his guests were useless.

Lot tried moral persuasion (19:7). He begged his neighbors not to "do so wickedly."

Lot offered his daughters in his guests' place (19:8). This shocking offer reflects both the sanctity of the host-guest relationship in biblical times and the devastating effect of living in a sinful society. Even Lot—who was "oppressed by the filthy conduct of the wicked," which "tormented his righteous soul from day to day by seeing and hearing their lawless deeds" (2 Pet. 2:7, 8)—was debased by his association with them.

Lot's wicked offer has troubled the sages. *Tanchuma* suggested Lot wanted to keep his daughters for himself (compare v. 36). The *Mishna Horayos* suggested that the prevention of perversion takes priority over the prevention of natural forms of immorality. Several rabbinic authorities suggested Lot's offer was insincere, for Lot knew that the men of Sodom would not accept, and he hoped only to gain time. Yet the horror of the offer itself, whatever Lot's intent, reminds us that we cannot make sinners our constant companions without being corrupted by them to some extent.

Lot tried to interpose his body (19:9). The crowd reviled Lot and "pressed hard against" him. The phrase suggests physical violence against Lot. When Lot's efforts proved futile and the Sodomites were about to break down his door, the angels acted.

The miracle and its nature (19:11). The text indicates the angels "struck the men . . . with blindness." The word translated "blindness" suggests a temporary disorientation or delusion, in which a person may "see" but not know what he sees. It seems the men of Sodom did not realize what had happened to them, for they "became weary trying to find the door."

With Lot and his family temporarily secure, the angels told him they were about to destroy the city and urged him to leave. When Lot lingered (Gen. 19:16), the angels transported the family outside the city and urged them to hurry to safety.

How good of God to intervene with miracles when all our efforts fail or when we hesitate to go His way.

THE MIRACLE OF SODOM'S DESTRUCTION   *Genesis 19:23–25*

At dawn, when Lot entered a nearby city named Zoar, "then the Lord rained brimstone and fire on Sodom and Gomorrah, from the Lord out of the heavens." In this rain of fire, the sinful cities and all their inhabitants were destroyed.

THE LOCATION OF SODOM AND THE OTHER SINFUL CITIES
(Genesis 13:11; 18:1, 28)

The biblical text locates Sodom and the other cities which were destroyed in the Jordan River valley, within sight of the heights of Mamre where Abraham lived. Early archaeologists suggested the ruins of these cities now lie under the southern basin of the Dead Sea. In recent years, Willem C. van Hatem and others have suggested the cities may be represented by fire-blackened ruins along wadis (dry riverbeds) in the foothills just south of the Dead Sea. There is no question, however, about the general location of these cities.

The area around Sodom and Gomorrah had natural deposits of asphalt, a flammable, semisolid mixture of bitumens (Gen. 14:10).

The destruction by fire and brimstone (19:24). There is no mystery about how the cities of the plain were destroyed. Archaeologist M. G. Kyle described it succinctly.

There is a stratum of marl mingled with free sulfur. It is a burned out region of oil and asphalt. A great

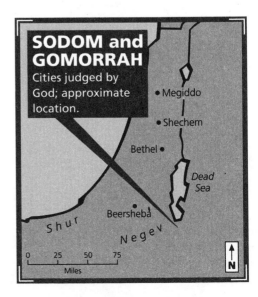

SODOM and GOMORRAH

Cities judged by God; approximate location.

• Megiddo

• Shechem

Bethel •

Dead Sea

Beersheba •

S h u r

N e g e v

0   25   50   75

Miles

N

rupture in the strata occurred. At the proper time God kindled the gases. A great explosion took place. The salt and the sulfur were thrown into the heavens red hot, so it did literally rain fire and brimstone from heaven.

Why should the destruction of these cities be considered a miracle? Like an earthquake in California, Sodom might have been destroyed at any time.

Its extraordinary nature. To say that an event is "extraordinary" does not mean that no natural agents can be used. What marked the destruction of Sodom as extraordinary was its occurrence as a judgment on sin (Gen. 18:20), its pre-announcement by God (Gen. 18:21–23), and its timing—immediately after Lot had safely left the city (Gen. 19:23, 24).

Its direct divine intervention. The angels told Lot the Lord had sent them to destroy the city (Gen. 19:13). The text also states that "then the Lord rained brimstone and fire" (Gen. 19:24). God apparently used the angels as instruments to carry out His will. As the one commanding the action, God was considered fully responsible for it.

Its lasting religious significance. The Bible refers back to the destruction of Sodom 28 times, 10 of them in the New Testament. Of these, four speak of the sins of Sodom. Six references in Ezekiel use "Sodom" as a caustic synonym for the northern Hebrew kingdom of Israel, while Revelation 11:8 refers to human civilization as "the great city which spiritually is called Sodom."

The other 17 specific biblical references point to Sodom as a grim reminder of the certainty of divine judgment on sin.

In addition, Luke 17:28–31 emphasizes the suddenness and unexpectedness of the day on which "it rained fire and brimstone from heaven and destroyed them all" (v. 29). Up until that day, the people of Sodom were completely focused on their life here on earth, eating and drinking, buying and selling, planting and building. In the same way, Jesus taught, people will be occupied with the af-

fairs of this world when he returns again to judge mankind as Sodom was judged.

Most significantly, Jesus said of the cities where He taught and performed His miracles and subsequently was rejected, "I say to you that it will be more tolerable in that Day for Sodom than for that city" (Luke 10:12; compare Matt. 10:15; 11:24; Mark 6:11).

This last statement, often repeated in the Gospels, is a healthy reminder. While homosexuality and other sins call for divine judgment, all sins are forgivable, and the saved sinner's life can be redirected to holy ways. Paul reminded the Corinthians that "neither fornicators, nor idolaters, nor adulterers, nor homosexuals, nor sodomites, nor thieves, nor covetous, nor drunkards, nor revilers, nor extortioners will inherit the kingdom of God." But Paul immediately went on to add, "And such were some of you. But you were washed, but you were sanctified, but you were justified in the name of the Lord Jesus and by the Spirit of our God (1 Cor. 6:9–11). The far greater sin is to be exposed to the Christ of the gospel—and to refuse to acknowledge Him as Lord.

As we deal with the question of homosexuality in our day, we should remember that *all* have sinned. The critical issue is not which sins are worse than others, but what will the sinner do with Christ. He will wash, sanctify, justify, and transform all who receive Him.

THE MIRACLE OF LOT'S WIFE
Genesis 19:26

As Lot and his family hurried toward the hills and away from doomed Sodom, according to the biblical account, "his wife looked back behind him, and she became a pillar of salt."

THE NATURE OF THE MIRACLE

There is a question about whether the fate of Lot's wife should be considered a miracle. The text gives no details, and many Bible students have speculated about the exact nature of this event. Deuteronomy 29:22 notes that this entire area around the Dead Sea was "sulfur and salt." The Jewish sage Ibn Ezra suggested the bones of Lot's wife were burned and then encrusted with salt that fell with the sulfur. Lockyer suggests she was probably "struck by lightning and covered and stifled by sulphurous matter and vapors, transforming her into a pillar of salt."

Another theory suggests that an earthquake thrust up a mound of salt from the underground deposits in the area and that Lot's wife was entombed in this pillar. Another possibility is that as Lot's wife looked back toward the cities, she fell into one of the slime pits in the area, where her body was encrusted with salt.

It is interesting that in the first century both the Jewish historian Josephus and the early church father Clement of Rome were shown a pillar identified by local guides as "Lot's wife."

Both Jewish and Christian teachers agree that the death of Lot's wife was an extraordinary event caused by God and that it had religious significance. In this sense, at least, it must be considered a minor miracle.

WAS THE DEATH OF LOT'S WIFE A DIVINE JUDGMENT?

The view that the death of Lot's wife was a divine judgment is deeply rooted in Judeo-Christian tradition.

Suggested reasons for the judgment. The problem for commentators has been to determine a *reason* for the judgment. The *Midrash,* reasoning much as did Job's friends, notes that if Lot's wife had been righteous she would not have come to harm. The sage *Ralbag* thought that her looking back showed compassion on the wicked, which was a sin. *Abarbanel* says she was in the rear trying to save the family wealth when the sulfur and fire overtook her. *Radak* says she had little faith and so looked back to see if the angel's words were true.

Lockyer explains why she was turned into a pillar of salt by arguing that the phrase "she looked back" indicates motive. He says, "God read the motive of her heart (19:26) and

knew of her regret on having to leave the sinful pleasures of Sodom." Looking back was an indication of "incurable rebellion."

In these explanations offered for why Lot's wife died, the commentators go far beyond anything indicated in the biblical text.

A biblical reason for the judgment. The one clear statement we have in Scripture is found in Genesis 19:17. The angels told the family, "Do not look back, or stay anywhere on the plain. Escape to the mountains, lest you be destroyed." So the one certain fact we have is that in looking back Lot's wife disobeyed the angels who were eager to save the family.

THE RELIGIOUS SIGNIFICANCE OF THE MIRACLE

The death of Lot's wife raises a significant question. Does such slight disobedience as merely looking back call for punishment so serious? The story of Lot's wife, intertwined as it is with the story of Sodom, serves as a solemn warning. We human beings are prone to make distinctions between "little" and "big," between "venal" and "mortal" sins. But the disobedience by Lot's wife of a clear command from God was no less a sin than the wicked behavior of the men of Sodom. And any sin, involving as it does rebellion against the will of God, is deserving of death.

So the story of Lot's wife is a helpful reminder. We need not search for arguments to prove that her sin was great and serious. We need simply to remember that in agreeing that Sodom's greater sins called for punishment, we condemn ourselves for our own lesser sins. It is only by the forgiving grace of God that any of us are enabled to stand, purified, in the presence of our Lord.

JESUS' APPLICATION OF THE STORY (LUKE 17:28–32)

Jesus spoke about the unexpected and sudden nature of His second coming, warning that His return would bring terrible judgments on the earth. He used both the Genesis

Flood (Gen. 6—8) and the destruction of Sodom as images of what will happen to a sinful humankind when He returns. So Jesus urged immediate flight from doomed civilization at the first signs of His coming. The need to flee will be so urgent that a person working in the field must not go home even to snatch up food or clothing. And in this context Jesus said, "remember Lot's wife."

The only way to escape the fate of sinners is to run to Christ, without looking back to check on what we have left behind.

CHAPTER 3

MIRACLE UPON MIRACLE!

FROM EGYPT TO SINAI

Exodus 3—20

No period in history has witnessed an outburst of miracles like those compressed into the span of a few brief years around 1400 B.C. During those few years miracles turned the wealthy land of Egypt into a wasted ruin, freed and commissioned a race of slaves as God's chosen people, and shook a flaming mountain as God delivered a Law which continues to shape mankind's moral vision more than three milleniums later.

Perhaps most significantly, the outburst of miracles that marked Israel's Exodus from Egypt indelibly identified God as One who is able to act in this world on behalf of His own.

The Exodus miracles provided Israel with unmistakable evidence of the reality of God. Today, too, the Exodus miracles remind us that God is real, that God is present, and that God has all power.

The impact of this brief period is reflected in both the opening and the conclusion of Psalm 105, the body of which traces the history of the patriarchs and celebrates the miracles by which the Lord redeemed Israel from slavery in Egypt.

Oh, give thanks to the LORD!
Call upon His name;

Make known His deeds among the
peoples!
Sing to Him, sing psalms to Him!
Talk of all His wondrous works!
Glory in His holy name;
Let the hearts of those rejoice who
seek the LORD!
Seek the LORD and His strength
Seek His face forevermore!
Remember His marvelous works
which He has done,
His wonders, and the judgments
of His mouth,
O seed of Abraham His servant,
You children of Jacob, His chosen
ones!
. . .
For he remembered His holy
promise,
And Abraham His servant.
He brought out His people with
joy,
His chosen ones with gladness (Ps.
105:1–6, 42, 43).

No other series of events stands out so vividly in the Old Testament. The Exodus and the miracles associated with it had an unparalleled impact on Israel's perception of God and their relationship with Him.

THE ROLE OF MOSES

The towering figure who served as both mediator of the miracles of this period and as Israel's law giver was Moses. He is one of history's most amazing characters. When Moses was born, the Pharaoh of Egypt had decreed death for every male child born to an Israelite. Yet Moses was brought up as a son in Egypt's royal family, where "he was learned in all the wisdom of the Egyptians, and was mighty in words and deeds" (Acts 7:22). In spite of his upbringing, Moses considered himself an Israelite and dreamed of freeing his people.

Moses' identification with the Israelite slaves was so great that, at age forty, he killed a taskmaster who was mistreating a Hebrew slave. When Moses realized the deed was known, he fled from Egypt. His next forty years were spent in the wilderness of the Sinai peninsula, where he herded his father-in-law's sheep. As the decades dragged on, Moses' dream died. But when Moses was eighty years old, God spoke to him from a burning bush, and everything changed.

Moses was called from herding sheep to become shepherd to God's people across the next forty critical years. Moses' first challenge was to win the freedom of his people. God used a series of ten devastating plagues, which struck at Moses' word, to bring Egypt's proud ruler to his knees and force the release of his slaves. God directed Moses and led the people into the Sinai Peninsula. On this journey the people faced a number of perils, each of which was overcome by God's personal, miraculous intervention. Again, Moses was the mediator of these miracles. When at last the people reached Mount Sinai, God Himself appeared atop the mountain, again in the guise of fire shrouded by clouds.

Moses, alone, climbed the mountain, where he was given the Ten Commandments and the rest of the Law which God intended to govern the life of His people. Thus Moses

gained his reputation as Israel's law giver as well as mediator of God's miracles. After Abraham, he was the most awesome and respected of sacred history's figures.

The book of Exodus leaves us at Sinai, as Moses established not only the moral code for Israel but also set out its religious practices.

The last three books of the Pentateuch continue the story of Moses' ministry as he—at last—brought Israel to the borders of Canaan. There Moses finally died.

MIRACLES IN THE BOOK OF EXODUS

The book of Exodus, which covers events of a one- to two-year period, relates the following extraordinary events caused by God which had religious significance.

Summary of Miracles in the Book of Exodus

Miracles of Preparation

The Ten Plagues

Miracles of the Journey to Sinai

THE MIRACLE OF THE BURNING BUSH *Exodus 3:2–6*

This first miracle in the book involves the appearance of God to Moses as a "flame of fire" (see Mark 12:26; Luke 20:37). Moses saw the fire raging inside a bush, but the bush was not consumed. When Moses approached to see why the bush wasn't burned up, the Lord called to him. Moses was told to take off his sandals for he was standing on ground made holy by the presence of God. God then identified Himself as the God of Abraham and the patriarchs, and Moses hid his face in awe, unwilling to look at God.

Many people in discussing this miracle have focused on the failure of the fire to burn the bush; but far more significant miracles are involved.

MIRACLES OF THE BURNING BUSH *(Exodus 3:2, 3)*

The miracle of the unburned bush. A flame which does not burn may seem to be a mira-

cle. In fact, the text emphasizes the flame no less than five times in verses 2 and 3. Moses was curious because there was a "flame of fire," the bush was "burning with fire" but "not burned up." It was certainly a "great [unusual] sight," and Moses wondered "why the bush does not burn." Moses was at first just curious, not frightened. He assumed there must be a natural cause, and he went closer to investigate it.

The description tells us much about Moses' state of mind. He was not superstitious, and he certainly didn't expect a miracle. Yet when Moses drew near, what he experienced was miraculous indeed.

The miracle of God's manifestation (Exodus 3:2). The Angel of the Lord (identified as God in 3:4) "appeared to him in a flame of fire."

Fire is frequently used in descriptions of manifestations of the divine presence (compare Gen. 15:17; Ex. 13:21f; 19:18; 24:17; Num. 9:15–16; 14:14; Deut. 1:33; 4:11–12; Ezek. 1:4, 13; 8:2; Ps. 78:14). Fire is formless, mysterious, nonmaterial. Humans draw back from raging fires, aware that fire is dangerous and destructive. Both the nature of God and His awesomeness are symbolized in His manifestations as fire.

At this appearance of the Lord to him, Moses hid his face in fear (Ex. 3:6). How striking that, as Moses came to know God more and more intimately, he lost his fear and begged to see more of God than he had been shown (see Ex. 33:18–23). It should be the same with us. It is right to be awed when we first sense God's presence. But as we grow in faith, it is appropriate to desire to draw closer and closer.

The miracle of God's conversation with Moses (3:7—4:17). The book of Genesis reports direct divine revelations to Abraham and others through dreams or in appearances as the Angel of the Lord. But this is the first report in the Bible of direct conversation with God. This appearance provided the context for a number of significant revelations. In this conversation with Moses, the Lord:

- identified Himself (3:6),
- announced His intent to free Israel (3:7–9),
- commissioned Moses as His agent (3:10–12),
- revealed His personal name to Moses (3:14–15),
- instructed Moses what to say to Israel's elders,
- described exactly what would happen when Moses confronted Pharaoh (3:18b–22),
- gave Moses three confirming signs, or miracles, and
- permitted Moses to have his brother Aaron as his spokesman (4:10–17)

Each element of this divine-human conversation authenticated the appearance of "Him who dwelt in the bush" as God (Deut. 33:16). Everything the Lord told Moses happened just as the Lord said, and Moses was able to do and to repeat the three signs he was given by the Lord.

THE RELIGIOUS SIGNIFICANCE OF THE MIRACLE APPEARANCE AND REVELATION OF GOD

This appearance of God is one of Scripture's pivotal events. It put sacred history on a different course. The appearance set in motion a series of events which led to the freeing of Israel from slavery, the giving of the Law on Sinai, the unifying of the people by a common religion and code of behavior, and their eventual settlement in the promised land. This miracle appearance of God to Moses was viewed from that point on as having the following religious significance.

The miracle appearance marked the revelation of God's personal name to Israel (Exodus 3:13–15). The title "God of your father . . ." was widely used in the ancient Near East. This was a title, not a name. In the biblical world, the "name" conveyed something of the essential nature of the person or thing named. When Moses asked the Lord how to respond if he were asked the name of the God he repre-

sented, Moses was seeking a deeper revelation of God's nature.

God responded by revealing the name *Yahweh,* or *Jehovah,* formed by the four consonants YHVH. Just what this name means, and what it reveals about God, has been discussed and debated. All agree that the name is constructed on the Hebrew verb "to be." Thus the translation in our text, "I AM." In Scripture, YHVH is associated with the Lord's personal involvement in the lives of his people and his intervention on their behalf. I AM emphasizes the ever-present nature of God, and it probably means something like "The God Who Is Always Present."

The Hebrews then enslaved in Egypt knew God as the One who had spoken in the past to their forefathers: Abraham, Isaac, and Jacob. They may have known God as the One who in the future would keep the covenant promises given to the patriarchs. But in all their decades of misery, they had never perceived God as present with them. In the next few months, they would come to know God as He *Who is Always Present,* as God made His presence known in miracle after miracle.

God told Moses, "This is my name forever, and this is my Memorial [how I am to be remembered] to all generations" (Ex. 3:15b). From this time onward, Israel was never to doubt the powerful presence of God, or His complete commitment to His people. From the Exodus onward, Israel was to remember that God would be with them always in His wonder-working power, meeting their needs as He had met the needs of His people long ago.

The miracle appearance marked God's commissioning of Moses (3:12). The appearance of God as fire within the bush launched Moses' career as God's agent. As the months passed, that commission would be unmistakably confirmed again and again. Yet an even more certain sign that Moses was God's man would follow.

God told Moses "this will be a sign [`ot, *miraculous confirmation*] that I have sent you:

When you have brought the people out of Egypt, you shall serve God on this mountain." The extraordinary event that would confirm for all time the divinely appointed nature of Moses' mission would be the assembly of Israel to serve God on Sinai—the very place where God was appearing to Moses in the burning bush.

The miracle appearance showed that the Lord is a covenant-keeping God (3:6–8). God announced Himself as the God of Abraham, then proceeded to state His intent to bring the Israelites into the land He had promised to Abraham's descendants. The series of events that brought about the redemption of Israel from slavery and led to the conquest of Canaan demonstrate how committed the Lord was to keeping His promises.

What reassurance this is for all believers. We can also rely on His promises to us.

The miracle appearance contained an implicit promise of life after death (Exodus 3:6; Matthew 22:30–32). Jesus pointed to God's first words to Moses when speaking with the Sadducees, who believed that death was the end. God told Moses, "I am the God of Abraham. . . ." God did not say, "I was the God of Abraham," as though Abraham were dead and gone. In saying "I am the God of Abraham," God indicated that Abraham existed even then, some 600 years after he had died.

In all these ways, God's appearance to Moses in the burning bush was one of history's most significant events.

THE MIRACLE OF MOSES' ROD
Exodus 4:2–5, 30–31; 7:9–13

When Moses expressed doubt that the elders of Israel would pay attention to a stranger from out of the Sinai, God gave Moses several miraculous signs to authenticate his mission.

The first sign was turning his rod into a serpent, and then back again into a rod. Later when Moses performed this sign for Pharaoh, the "magicians of Egypt" appeared to duplicate the feat.

THE TRANSFORMATION OF MOSES' ROD

Several features of this account make it clear that a real miracle was involved.

The use of Moses' own rod (4:2). God used the rod in Moses' hand. Moses knew this rod for what it was. It was no piece of specially prepared magic equipment designed to promote an illusion. Likewise, God will use what *we* have, transforming it as necessary to achieve his purposes.

Moses' reaction to the transformation (4:3, 4). God told Moses to throw the rod on the ground, where it became a serpent. The Hebrew language uses the general word for serpent but, since Moses "fled from it," it was probably a poisonous snake.

God then told Moses to take the serpent by the tail. The Hebrew word indicates that the still-fearful Moses "snatched at" or "grabbed" the serpent. It then became Moses' familiar rod once again.

The belief of the Israelites (4:30–31). When Moses performed the signs he had been given "in the sight of the people" of Israel, they believed. And when Moses indicated the Lord had promised to set them free from slavery, "they bowed their heads and worshiped."

Note that the miracle which confirmed the messenger also opened the hearts of the people to welcome his message. Like other miracles, this one had a deeper purpose than its surface appearance.

THE REACTION OF PHARAOH TO THE MIRACLE
(Exodus 7:9–13)

When Moses first spoke with Pharaoh, Egypt's ruler demanded he "show a miracle for yourselves." This was not a surprising demand.

Miracle stories in Egypt. The Egyptians enjoyed tales of magic and the supernatural. One popular work, known as *Tales of the Magicians,* tells of King Cheops (Khufu), who reigned about 2600 B.C., being entertained with tales of famous magicians by some of his sons. One story is about Waba-aner, whose wife was being unfaithful to him. Waba-aner molded a crocodile from wax and muttered a magic spell over the image. The next day, when his wife's lover left and stopped to wash nearby, Waba-aner's servant threw the wax figure into the water. It became a crocodile and killed the lover.

The Pharaoh of Moses' day would have known this and other tales of magic. It was natural for him to ask for magical proof of Moses' commission by God. And the story of Waba-aner would have prepared him for the specific sign that Moses was given!

The confrontation (7:10–13). When Pharaoh demanded Moses and Aaron "show a miracle [mophet] for yourselves," Aaron cast down his rod. The assumption is that as the spokesman for Moses, Aaron was bearing Moses' rod. Immediately it became a snake. But the feat was apparently duplicated by Egypt's magicians— until Aaron's rod "swallowed up" their rods. Several things are of note in this story.

The change of names (7:9–12). The Hebrew word for "serpent," *nahash,* is found in Exodus 4:2 and 7:15. In these verses, another word, *tannin,* is used. This word indicates *giant* reptiles, including crocodiles. The serpent Moses and Aaron produced was no garden snake!

Pharaoh's wise men (7:11). Pharaoh called for the very best Egypt could produce—its "wise men and the sorcerers" and its "magicians" with their enchantments. It took Egypt's best to compete with this stranger from the desert and his slave brother.

Trickery or magic? The wise men and magicians of Egypt duplicated Aaron's feat ("did in like manner," v. 11). Some have argued that the conflict was a pseudo-struggle between illusionists. By stroking the stomach of a reptile turned upside down, whether snake or crocodile, the creature can be placed in a listless trance. When thrown down, it becomes active again. So even if Aaron's staff-to-snake-to-staff transformation was a miracle, some scholars claim the Egyptians performed an illusion.

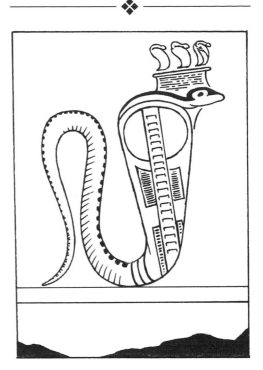

BIBLE BACKGROUND:

SNAKES IN EGYPTIAN RELIGION

In the ancient Near East, snakes were associated with wisdom, fertility, and healing. Not so in the Bible, where their association with temptation, sin, and Satan is established in the third chapter of Genesis. Nowhere in the Bible except during the Exodus period are snakes associated with miracles. Why did the Lord choose this miracle to give to Moses?

The answer lies in the role of snakes in Egyptian religion. While considered a source of evil and danger, the snake was the primary form of the god Apophis. The snake goddesses Renenutet and Meret-seger were worshiped so that snake-bite could be avoided or healed. The cobra-goddess Wadjyt was the patroness of lower Egypt, and the poised cobra was a symbol of Pharaoh's kingship and his title, *weret hekaw,* "great of magic."

When the serpent produced by Aaron's rod consumed the serpents produced by Egypt's magicians, it was a powerful sign of the impotence of the deities of Egypt before the God of Israel.

Others have pointed out that the serpent was worshiped as a God in Egypt, and that Scripture teaches that demons lie behind the pagan deities (compare Lev. 17:7; Deut. 32:17; Ps. 106:37).

Worship on Stele of Paneb, showing him worshiping the goddess Meret-seger in the form of a serpent

The events in Egypt represented a conflict between God and the dark powers that had bound his people. Perhaps we are to understand this initial confrontation as the beginning of a conflict of supernatural powers. Thus we can interpret the transformations performed by Egypt's sorcerers as real.

Proof of God's superiority (7:12). The magicians' triumph was temporary. Aaron's staff immediately consumed the great serpents produced by the magicians. God in his superior power was triumphant.

Pharaoh's response (7:13). Pharaoh refused to accept what his own eyes had seen. Since he had watched Aaron's rod devour the creatures produced by his own magicians and sorcerers, he had clearer evidence of God's presence with Moses than did the elders of Israel. A person who wills not to believe cannot be convinced, even by miracles.

It would take a series of devastating judgments to bring the proud ruler to his knees before the God of the Hebrew slaves.

THE MIRACLE OF MOSES' LEPROUS HAND   *Exodus 4:6–8, 30–31*

Moses had expressed concern that the elders of Israel might not accept him as God's messenger. God gave him a second authenticating sign, which he later showed to his people but not to Pharaoh.

THE SIGN EXPERIENCED BY MOSES   *(4:6, 7)*

The second authenticating sign given to Moses was a dual expression of the miracle-working power of God. Moses was to slip his hand inside his garment and touch his chest.

When he drew out the hand, it was leprous. Moses was then to touch his chest again, and when he drew the hand out it was restored. What can we say about this miracle?

It served as a "faith sign." Some have called it a faith sign, as it was intended to help relieve Moses' fears and resolve his doubts. As such, the miracle, called a "sign" in verse 8, was evidence to Moses of God's working in his life.

It was a traumatic experience for Moses. What horror Moses must have felt as he saw his hand covered with leprosy in its advanced stages. There was no known cure for this awful disease, which marked the victim as an outcast.

It was a test of faith for Moses. God told Moses to put his hand inside his clothing and hold the leprous hand next to his chest. The Hebrew word translated "leprosy" throughout the Old Testament means "infectious skin disease," and it is not limited to what we call leprosy today (Hansen's disease). Moses would have shuddered at the thought of placing his infected hand against his unprotected, healthy skin. Yet Moses obeyed, and when he drew out his hand it was fully restored.

It was a significant foreshadowing of God's saving power. In Scripture leprosy is often a mark of divine judgment (compare Lev. 13, 14; Num. 12; 2 Kings 5:1–14; 15:4–5; 2 Chron. 26:16–21). This sign may have suggested God's displeasure with Moses' hesitancy and his doubts. But the healing of the leprosy was far more significant than the discovery that the hand was infected. Whatever judgments God might inflict on His people, He would reverse them on evidence of repentance. In this miracle, the slaves would be able to see not only the power of God but the promise of the restoration of their freedom and the healing of their wounded hearts.

THE MIRACLE OF NILE WATER TURNED TO BLOOD   *Exodus 4:9*

God described a third miracle which Moses would be able to perform when he returned to Egypt. This was the ability to pour out clean water from the Nile River and see it turn into blood on the ground. The fascinating thing about this miracle is that it apparently was never performed!

An unperformed miracle. There is no evidence in the Exodus accounts that this miracle was needed to authenticate Moses and his mission. This miracle is similar to the turning of the waters of the Nile River into blood, which was the first of the ten plagues, but it is not the same—nor did it have the same purpose. This miracle, like the rod and the leprous hand, was intended to authenticate Moses as God's agent. The miracle of the Nile, along with the other nine, was intended to judge Egypt and its pagan gods (Ex. 12:12).

The significance of the unperformed miracle. It was apparently unnecessary for Moses to perform the third sign to convince Israel's leaders of his call from God. They were more ready to believe than Moses had feared. This provision of a third, unperformed miracle reminds us that God can do more than the necessary. His resources are endless. God has at hand whatever it takes to achieve His purposes.

THE TEN PLAGUES *Exodus 7—11*

THE TEN AS "PROVING ACTS"

These chapters describe a series of ten devastating plagues that struck Egypt. The ten have rightly been called "proving acts." The book of Exodus lists three reasons why God imposed this series of judgments on Egypt. Through them:

God proved His superiority to the gods of Egypt. Exodus 12:12 declares, "And against all the gods of Egypt I will execute judgment: I am the Lord." Each plague demonstrated the futility of relying on the deities of the Egyptians.

God proved His presence to Israel. Exodus 6:7 says, "I will take you as My people. . . . Then you shall know that I am the Lord your God who brings you out from under the burdens of the Egyptians." Forever after, Israel looked back to this series of events as unmistakable proof of God's commitment to His people, the descendants of the patriarchs.

God proved His power to the Egyptians. Exodus 7:5 declares, "The Egyptians will know that I am the Lord, when I stretch out My hand on Egypt and bring out the children of Israel from among them." The Egyptians had worshiped idols. Through the ten great "proving acts" of God, they were forced to acknowledge the power of the one true God.

THE RELIGION AND GODS OF EGYPT

Egyptian theology was complex and, in many ways, confusing. Ancient Egypt was divided into forty petty states, called *nomes*. Each of these had local deities. As various *nomes* gained or lost political power, their prominence was reflected in the importance given the gods of the *nomes'* major cities. Over the centuries, attributes and roles ascribed to one deity were added to the attributes and roles of others. Thus, more than one deity might be worshiped as creator, or spoken of as supreme in the underworld, or viewed as the goddess of fertility or healing.

While the system of gods worshiped by the Egyptians was confusing, they looked to their gods to maintain the harmony of the natural universe. The gods governed the passage of night and day, controlled the seasonal flooding of the life-giving Nile River, and governed every other feature of life in the land.

It was stunning to the Egyptians when the God of the Hebrew slaves imposed on Egypt ten great proving acts which destroyed the harmony of their lives, shattering the illusion that they could rely on their gods.

In the ten plagues, the very foundation of Egyptian religion—the belief that their gods existed and were in fact able to maintain nature's harmony—was exposed. Egypt's gods were judged, and all power was shown to reside in a God the Egyptians had scorned—the one true God of their slaves.

BIBLE BACKGROUND:

HOW ANCIENT PEOPLES RATED DEITIES

In the ancient world and throughout Old Testament times, the power ascribed to deities was a reflection of the military might of their worshipers. The Babylonian warrior assumed that his gods were the most powerful during the era of Babylonian empire-building.

In the same way, the Egyptians—one of the most powerful nations on earth at the time of Moses—credited their gods with their dominant position in the world. It is no wonder that Egypt's young Pharaoh initially scoffed at the God worshiped by the Hebrew slaves. To Pharaoh, the powerlessness of the Israelites was proof of the feebleness of their God! It took the devastating series of plagues which God brought on the land to convince the proud Egyptians to submit to the God of their slaves. His acts revealed that *their* gods—not the God of Israel—were weak.

THE MIRACLE OF THE NILE
TURNED TO BLOOD   *Exodus 7:14–24*

The Nile River was the source of Egypt's life. Each year its swelling waters deposited fresh soil in the fields along its shores, making the land fertile. Later in the year, its waters were channeled to irrigate the growing crops. The Nile also teemed with fish, which served as the basic source of protein for most Egyptians. It's no wonder that the Egyptians deified the Nile. The Nile god, known as Hopi, was portrayed as a vigorous but fat man. To strike at the Nile was to strike at Egypt's very life-source.

When Pharaoh scoffed at the signs Moses displayed (Ex. 7:9–13), Moses announced that God would strike the waters of the Nile and "they shall be turned to blood. And the fish that are in the river shall die, the river shall

stink, and the Egyptians will loathe to drink the water of the river" (Ex. 7:17–18).

Several things are significant about this first proving act.

It was clearly a miracle (Exodus 7:19–20). Some have tried to provide naturalistic explanations of the plagues of Exodus. To them, the "bloody Nile" was nothing more than a major outbreak of an algae which tinted the waters red. But the biblical text indicates that this curse included rivers, ponds, and pools of water throughout Egypt—and even water collected in buckets and cisterns (Ex. 7:19). This pre-announced event was a miracle indeed.

BIBLE BACKGROUND:

THE RELATIONSHIP OF EGYPTIAN MAGIC AND EGYPTIAN GODS

One standard title given the goddess Isis was *Weret Hekau,* "Great of Magic."

Egyptians had two names: a "real name" which was kept secret, and a public name. They believed that if an enemy learned the real name of a person, that enemy would have power over him. One Egyptian myth related how Isis created a serpent to sting the sun god, Ra. When its poison was killing this greatest of Egyptian deities, Isis promised to cure him if he would reveal to her his secret name. He did so, and she became "Great of Magic." By using Ra's name in incantations, she could force him to do whatever she demanded.

This story illustrates the link between Egyptian magic and the gods. To make any spell work, it was essential to call forth the spirit of deity *by name.* The Egyptians believed that the deity, when called upon by his or her real name, had to follow the desires of the magician who was casting the spell!

Since the magicians of Egypt turned water to blood "by their enchantments," they called on their gods to duplicate what God had done.

The miracle was "duplicated" by Egypt's magicians (7:22). The report that Egypt's sorcerers did the same thing "with their enchantments" reminds us that this was a conflict of supernatural powers. It was more than a demonstration of the power of the true God versus the figments of man's imagination. Behind the gods of Egypt lurked demons, exercising their powers to keep the peoples in spiritual bondage (Lev. 17:7; Ps. 106:37). Yet, how ironic the report that Egypt's magicians called on the powers of their deities to do by magic what God had done.

The miracle was duplicated, but not reversed! Here is the irony of the text. The demonic beings behind Egypt's deities could move only in the direction allowed by God! They could not reverse what he had done. And they didn't even *try!*

The gods of Egypt enabled the magicians to do on a tiny scale what God had done "throughout all Egypt." But this simply made matters worse!

Strikingly, this irony was not obvious to the Pharaoh. He took the work of his wise men, although it was tiny by comparison, as reassurance of the power of Egypt's gods. What empty comfort this must have been to the people of his land. They were forced to dig holes along the river bank so the sand could filter the water for drinking (Ex. 7:24).

The miracle was long remembered by the Egyptians. A catalog of catastrophes dating from 1350–1100 B.C. described terrible conditions in Egypt which occurred about a thousand years before. Among the listed disasters is one involving the Nile:

> Why really, the River is blood,
> If one drinks of it,
> One rejects (it) as human
> and thirsts for water.

It is fascinating to speculate about the source of this description, coming as it does so shortly after the Exodus events.

THE MIRACLE OF THE FROGS
Exodus 8:1–14

Egypt was familiar with frogs. Each year as the Nile began to recede from its flood stage, in September/October, frogs would breed in the pools of water left behind. In fact, one goddess of fertility, Heqt, was portrayed with the head of a frog. So there had always been frogs aplenty in Egypt. But before this

The Nile River and its water was the lifeblood of Egypt, and when it turned to blood they dug holes to let the sand filter the water for drinking.

miracle, there had never been frogs in such abundance.

The text tells us that frogs "covered the land," and Psalm 105:30 adds this detail: "Their land abounded with frogs, even in the chambers of their king."

There are several fascinating aspects to this second of the ten mighty acts that proved God's presence and power to both Israel and the Egyptians.

Heqt was goddess of fertility and childbirth. The fact that Heqt was linked with childbirth has led some to suppose that this plague was retribution for an earlier Pharaoh's demand that Egypt's midwives kill Hebrew male babies at birth (Ex. 1:15).

Egypt's magicians again made matters worse! (Exodus 8:7). Again Egypt's sorcerers duplicated Moses' miracle—and created more frogs! Perhaps these magicians intended to drive the frogs back into the river, but their magic was reversed by God. They actually multiplied rather than reduced the number of frogs.

Again, the irony is strong. "We can do that!" Egypt's sorcerers claimed. And in doing their best, they made the situation worse. With servants like these, Pharaoh didn't need any enemies!

Pharaoh at last asked Moses to entreat the Lord (8:8). For the first time, Pharaoh seemed to acknowledge the power of God. He begged Moses to entreat God to remove the frogs. But like many who call on God when in trouble, Pharaoh would quickly forget him when this trouble passed.

Moses permitted Pharaoh to say "when" (8:9–11). Moses gave Pharaoh the honor of saying when the frogs would go. In this way Moses, offered further proof of the power of Israel's God. There could be no trickery involved here. God would act on the timetable Pharaoh himself set.

It seems ironic that Pharaoh said "tomorrow." In effect, he asked for another night with frogs in his bedroom! How often we look to the Lord and hope that perhaps he will act in our lives "tomorrow." Let's claim our privileges as God's children, and in faith call on the Lord to act in our *today!*

BIBLE BACKGROUND:

PHARAOH'S HARD HEART

Throughout the description of the plagues, reference is made to Pharaoh's hardened attitude [heart] toward Moses and God. The stubborn ruler refused to bow and submit to the Lord, no matter how great the evidence of his power.

Some Exodus verses describe Pharaoh's heart as hard (Ex. 7:13, 22), while others speak of God hardening Pharaoh's heart (Ex. 7:3), and still others—as in this case—speak of Pharaoh hardening his own heart (Ex. 8:15). How could God blame or punish an individual whose heart he had hardened?

In Old Testament thought, God was seen as involved in everything. This idiom in no way diminishes the Pharaoh's personal responsibility for his choices. We also need to ask what God *did* to harden Pharaoh's heart. What God did was to reveal gradually more and more of himself. When the elders of Israel saw the signs God gave to Moses, they believed and worshiped (Ex. 4:31). When Pharaoh saw the same authenticating signs, "Pharaoh's heart grew hard" (Ex. 7:13). God did not play with Pharaoh, forcing him to act against his will. Each succeeding revelation led to a reaction which further demonstrated Pharaoh's pride and arrogance.

We see similar responses today. As the gospel is shared, some welcome its good news while others reject it. Just as the sun melts wax and hardens clay, so the light of revelation melts open hearts while causing closed hearts to harden.

Even the removal of the frogs proved to be a plague (8:13, 14). Moses promised that, just as Pharaoh had asked, the frogs would "depart from you, from your houses, from your servants; and from your people" (Ex. 8:11). But Pharaoh had not specified "how" he expected the frogs to go. The frogs that infested the land simply died—"out of the houses, out of the courtyards, and out of the fields. The people gathered them together in heaps, and the land stank."

When God answers the prayers of sinners, it may not be what they expected!

The plague was more than a nuisance (Exodus 8:3; Psalm 78:45). When we read the description of the infestation, we're likely to laugh. The frogs would "come into your house, into your bedroom, on your bed, into the houses of your servants, on your people, into your ovens, and into your kneading bowls." But these frogs were more than a nuisance. Psalm 78:45 speaks of "frogs which destroyed [devastated] them." Apparently, none of the Egyptian people died, but the piles of rotting frogs polluted the land, and their stench permeated the air.

THE MIRACLE OF THE LICE   *Exodus 8:16–19*

Only a few verses are devoted to this third plague, but it is still significant. The meaning of the Hebrew word *kinnim,* translated as "lice," is difficult to determine. Among the suggested translation, along with "lice," have been "gnats," "mosquitoes," "maggots," and the more general term "vermin." The description of these vermin being "on man and beast" suggests "lice" is as likely a possibility as any other.

Note that:

The miracle was unannounced. Previous wonders had been pre-announced by God. This one struck without warning. It also apparently followed immediately after Pharaoh's hardened response to the divine relief from the plague of frogs (Ex. 8:15).

In a sense, this timing may be seen as evidence of God's grace. The longer the consequences of our wrong actions are delayed, the more likely we are to repeat them. A parent is wise to impose consequences for the wrong

actions of his or her children immediately, rather than to delay in hope that no discipline will be required. God struck immediately after Pharaoh hardened his heart as a clear indication that Pharaoh had done wrong.

The miracle could not be duplicated (Exodus 8:16–18). When Aaron struck the ground with his rod, the dust of the land "became lice on man and beast." This was an act of creation; of bringing life from inanimate matter. The magicians "worked with their enchantments to bring forth lice," but they could not. Only the Creator God can cause what is dead to live.

Newspaper headlines proclaimed in 1953 that Stanley Miller, a college science student, had created "life in a test tube." In fact, Miller had mixed chemicals and tried to duplicate conditions which evolutionists thought had once existed on earth. What he actually produced were some amino acids and other simple compounds found in living things—and ounces of sludge. While amino acids are building blocks in living creatures, they are not life. It was as though a person found three or four blocks in the back yard, and newspaper headlines trumpeted, "Local man builds 50-story skyscraper!"

In spite of the excitement in 1953, scientists in the years since have not come close to creating life—and they never will.

The miracle's source was acknowledged by Egypt's sorcerers (8:19). The magicians of Egypt were finally impressed. This was one feat they couldn't duplicate, and they reported to Pharaoh, "This is the finger of God."

The word for God here is the general term, *elohim*—not the personal name of Israel's God, Yahweh. This confession should not be understood as a testimony to the Lord. It was simply a confession by the magicians that they had been defeated by a supernatural power that far outdistanced the powers they represented. This confession is significant. Egypt's best admitted they fell short of these two representatives of the Lord whom Pharaoh still refused to take seriously!

Egypt's wise men were not heard from again.
This is the last time the magicians or sorcerers
of the Pharaoh confronted Moses and Aaron.
They withdrew, defeated. But even more than
a simple defeat may be involved.

The Egyptians made a fetish of personal
cleanliness. Herodotus, the Greek historian,
reported that no one was allowed to enter a
temple in Egypt with vermin on his body and
that priests were to shave their bodies every
three days. And Egypt's wise men—drawn
from the priestly class—were now lice-
infested too. Not only were these opponents
of the Lord defeated; they were cut off from
the source of their powers. They had no doubt
that in this plague a great supernatural power
had been at work.

THE MIRACLE OF THE BITING FLIES
Exodus 8:20–32

Another miracle judgment struck immediately without any report of relief from the
previous plague. Moses was told to "rise early"
and wait for Pharaoh where he came down to
the waters to bathe. Moses was to demand
that the Israelites be permitted to go into the
desert to worship the Lord. If Pharaoh refused, God would send "swarms of flies on
you and your servants."

The Hebrew word translated "flies" is
`arov. It is found only here in the entire Old
Testament, making its meaning uncertain. It
may be a general term for insects or—as the
Septuagint renders it—it may refer specifically
to the dog fly [stable fly], with a vicious bite
which draws blood.

The prospect of Egypt filled with swarms
of these insects "on you and your servants, on
your people and into your houses" (Ex. 8:21)
would be terrifying indeed. Pharaoh was told
that this miraculous sign would be given "tomorrow." Then Moses and Aaron withdrew.

There are several distinctive elements in
the account of this miracle.

***The miracle plague was to strike the Egyp-
tians only (Exodus 8:22–24).*** God's people
were subject to the distress caused by earlier
plagues on Egypt. But from now on, only the
Egyptians would suffer under the hand of
God.

God declared, "I will make a difference
between My people and your people." When
we experience troubles, it may be hard for us
to realize that the Lord still makes a distinction
between his own and others. We have no idea
how many troubles we have been spared. But
we do know that in our trials, God provides a
strength and peace which no others can know.

***Pharaoh bore the brunt of this plague (8:21,
24).*** Both the announcement of this plague
and its description focused on Pharaoh himself. "Thick swarms of flies came into the
house of Pharaoh, into his servants' houses,
and into all the land . . . ."

In Egyptian thought, the pharaoh of the
land was the primary mediator between the
people and Egypt's gods. It was his responsibility to maintain the harmony of the land. It
is clear from the account of this plague that
what motivated Pharaoh was not the welfare

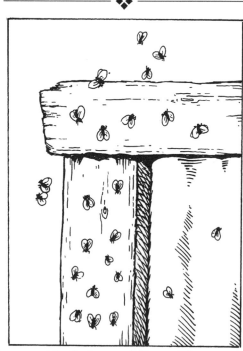

After the lice came swarms of flies.

of his people but his own well-being! It was his personal suffering that moved him to call quickly for Moses and Aaron!

Pharaoh appeared willing to compromise (8:25–30). From the beginning, Moses had demanded that Israel be permitted to travel three days' journey into the wilderness to sacrifice to the Lord (Ex. 3:18; 5:3). This request was another evidence of God's grace. If Moses had demanded initially that Pharaoh free his slaves, resistance would have been intense. By asking for less than the Lord intended to do, God made it easier for Pharaoh to agree to Moses' request.

But this approach actually made no difference as far as the pharaoh was concerned. Intent on oppressing Israel, he was unresponsive to Moses' request.

Even while tormented by the biting insects, Pharaoh tried to negotiate. He told Moses that the Israelites could sacrifice "in the land" (Ex. 8:25). Moses replied that his people's sacrifices would be "an abomination" to the Egyptians, so Pharaoh's solution was impractical. The same word translated "abomination" or "objectionable" is used in Genesis 43:32 and 46:34. There it relates to the Egyptian's attitude toward eating with Hebrews and to the Hebrews' vocation as shepherds.

Pharaoh recognized the force of the argument and gave in. He promised to let the Hebrew people go, if only Moses will "intercede for me." Once again, we see Pharaoh's basic concern. He did not ask Moses to intercede for his people, but "for me."

Pharaoh again went back on his agreement (8:31–32). Moses promised to pray to the Lord, indicating that the flies will "depart tomorrow." As quickly as the swarms of flies had arrived they would disappear. And Moses warned Pharaoh not to "deal deceitfully any more" in regard to letting Israel go.

In spite of this warning, when the swarms were removed "Pharaoh hardened his heart at this time also; neither would he let the people go" (Ex. 8:32).

How clearly Pharaoh in these accounts represents the sinfulness of the human heart.

Called to represent his people and serve them, Pharaoh's first concern was always himself. When under intense pressure, Pharaoh seemed ready to submit to God, but as soon as the pressure was relieved, his arrogant and cruel attitude revived. In these reactions to God's self-revelation, we see mirrored the flaws of all humankind.

THE MIRACLE OF THE ANIMAL EPIDEMIC *Exodus 9:1–7*

Anthrax has been suggested as the disease which caused this epidemic. It is clear from the text that it should be interpreted as a miracle, whatever the disease may have been. Its miraculous nature is seen in its prediction, its appearance at the designated time, and in the immunity of the Israelites' cattle.

The meaning of "all" in the text (Exodus 9:6). The text indicates that "all of the livestock of Egypt died" in the epidemic. How then could more cattle have been killed in hail storms, as described in Exodus 9:22f ? The answer is found in Exodus 9:3. The plague was limited to "your cattle in the field." So it was all the livestock of Egypt grazing on open range at the time of the plague that suffered in this epidemic. Those confined to stables or pens survived.

Pharaoh's skepticism displayed (9:7). Moses announced that the epidemic which killed the cattle of the Egyptians would not touch the cattle of the Israelites. This time Pharaoh sent servants to check, and he learned that not one head of Israelite livestock had died. Pharaoh ignored this evidence. Again, his heart "became hard, and he did not let the people go" (Ex. 9:7).

The plague had not harmed Pharaoh personally. He apparently didn't care that the wealth of his people was being destroyed.

THE MIRACLE OF THE BOILS *Exodus 9:8–11*

In this sixth proving act, God caused boils to erupt on the Egyptian people and their animals. The Hebrew word *shehin*, translated as "boils," suggests deep, painful, ulcerous boils. Deuteronomy 28:27 warned Israel against disobeying the Lord lest God punish them with "the boils of Egypt." Clearly, the fiery eruptions were no normal inflammations.

The boils were on "all the Egyptians" (Exodus 9:11). Again Israel was exempt from the effect of God's judgment on the oppressors. The Egyptians were guilty corporately as well as individually for their nation's treatment of the Hebrew slaves.

The magicians were singled out for extreme affliction (9:11). The sorcerers to whom Pharaoh had turned to oppose Moses were so covered with boils that they "could not stand before Moses because of the boils." While all members of a sinful society bear some guilt, some individuals are more guilty than others. When God judges, his punishments are proportionate and fair.

Only now did God harden the heart of Pharaoh (9:13). After each of the preceding miracles, Scripture indicated either that "Pharaoh's heart grew hard" (Ex. 7:13; 7:22; 8:19; 8:32; 9:7) or that Pharaoh "hardened his heart" (Ex. 8:15). The natural inclination of Pharaoh's heart, without any intervention by God, had been clearly displayed. Some have taken God's hardening of Pharaoh's heart to be a judicial act. That is, Pharaoh had resisted God's will so stubbornly that part of God's punishment was to cause him to remain stubborn.

THE MIRACLE OF DEVASTATING HAILSTORMS   *Exodus 9:13–25*

This confrontation between Moses and Pharaoh was unique. Moses warned Pharaoh that if he had wished, God could have wiped out all the Egyptians. The land had been spared only to serve as an arena in which the Lord could display his power and prove his presence. In spite of the evidence of God's greatness in the preceding plagues, Pharaoh

continued to tyrannize God's people (Ex. 9:17, "exalt yourself against").

The downpour of "very heavy hail" (Exodus 9:18, 23). Some commentators have made much of the fact that Egypt does have infrequent and light hailstorms, arguing that the miracle involved intensifying and controlling the timing of a natural phenomenon. This misses the point, which is that each of the proving acts was unmistakably a supernatural event. The hailstones struck throughout Egypt, destroying the barley and flax crops which had just come up (Ex. 9:31) killing any humans caught in the fields, and felling livestock. The hailstones were of tremendous size, and "fire [lightning] mingled with the hail." The text specifically says that never had there been such a storm in all [any part of] Egypt "since it became a nation" thousands of years before!

There is no need to argue that this or any other plague which struck Egypt "really could have happened" by pointing to similar natural happenings. The biblical text emphasizes the fact that these were *miracles, not like* similar natural events.

❖

"Never had there been such a storm" as the hail and lightning God sent on Egypt.

The first death-dealing judgment (9:19). The earlier miracles were either nuisances or caused some suffering. It was a bother to have to dig along the Nile for water, and the biting flies and boils were a painful inconvenience. But now, suddenly, one of God's proving acts threatened to take the lives of Egyptians. There is a definite escalation in the seriousness of the actions caused by God.

Psalm 32:8, 9 states God's promise to instruct and teach his people in the way we should go, and warns, "Do not be like the horse or like the mule, which have no understanding, which must be harnessed with bit and bridle." The harder we, like Pharaoh, pull away from the will of God, the harder he must pull to bring us back to the path he wants us to take.

The first opportunity to exercise faith (9:19, 20). When God announced the coming hail storm, he warned the Egyptians through Moses to "gather your livestock and all that you have in the field" and take them inside.

The Bible says "he who feared the word of the Lord among the servants of Pharaoh" rushed to bring man and beast inside. The preceding plagues had led some of the Egyptians to some level of trust in the reliability of God's Word as spoken by Moses. This is what "faith" is—reliance on the trustworthiness of God's Word which leads us to act on it.

What disasters we too can avoid if we trust God's Word fully and make it our rule and guide each day.

Pharaoh at last acknowledged God by name (9:27, 28). When Moses first went to Pharaoh, he had scorned, "Who is the Lord, that I should obey his voice to let Israel go? I do not know the Lord . . ." But now, as terrifying lightning flashes illuminated the massive hail stones that pummeled his land, Pharaoh sent for Moses and Aaron and confessed, "I have sinned this time." He begged Moses to "entreat the Lord that there may be no more mighty thundering and hail." In his terror, Pharaoh promised, "I will let you go."

"Sinned this time" (9:27). Pharaoh had not just sinned "this time"; he had sinned continually. The admission forced from him by his fear fell far short of heartfelt repentance and far short of a genuine acknowledgment of the extent of his sins.

Let's not mistake fear-driven confession for a true change of heart. Under stress, many are ready to admit fault, even though they do not feel guilt.

"The Lord is righteous. . . . Entreat the Lord" (Ex. 9:27, 28). This was the first time that Pharaoh seemed to deal directly with the Lord by name. Pharaoh had asked Moses to intercede for him (Ex. 8:28), but now he began to see that the issue was not between Pharaoh and Moses, but between Pharaoh and the Lord.

"I will let you go" (Ex. 9:28). Moses warned Pharaoh not to go back on this promise. But as soon as the thunder, lightning, and hail stopped, both Pharaoh and his servants hardened their hearts and refused to release the Israelites.

True repentance and conversion are measured by behavior. Like Pharaoh, the person who bargains with God when under stress without an awareness of guilt and need for forgiveness will—when the stress is removed—quickly return to his or her old ways.

THE MIRACLE OF THE LOCUSTS
Exodus 10:1–20

Locusts were a devastating reality in the ancient East. They multiplied at an astounding rate. At times they gathered in swarms so thick that they literally blotted out the sun. One swarm of locusts that crossed the Red Sea in 1899 was estimated to cover 2,000 square miles! One square kilometer can contain fifty million insects, which can devour one hundred thousand tons of vegetation in a single night!

The miraculous nature of this locust invasion (Exodus 10:4, 6, 19). While this proving act again used a "natural" means, it was clearly an extraordinary event caused by God. It came when the Lord announced it would; it was more devastating and extensive than any locust plague in history (Ex. 10:14); and every single locust was removed in response to Moses' prayer.

The dialogue with Pharaoh (10:3–11). The text reports in unusual detail Moses' meeting with Pharaoh before this plague struck.

A clear warning was given (10:3–6). Moses clearly described the consequences to Egypt if Pharaoh should still refuse to let the Israelites go.

Pharaoh's servants urged him to free Israel (10:7). Pharaoh's "servants" were the high officials who ran Egypt's bureaucracy. They were aware of the devastation caused by the earlier plagues, which wiped out Egypt's cattle and early crops. They urged Pharaoh to get rid of Moses at any cost.

Pharaoh continued to bargain (10:8–11). At first Pharaoh told Moses to "go serve the Lord." But then he wanted to limit those who went into the wilderness for worship to adult men only. Moses refused, indicating that every Israelite and all their cattle would go out to worship.

At this, Pharaoh warned Moses. He declared that God had better be with them, because he was more determined than ever to persecute the Hebrew slaves (Ex. 10:11).

The escalation of the miracles was matched by the increasing hardness of Pharaoh's heart.

The life-threatening nature of the locust invasion (10:15). The hail had wiped out the early crops of flax and barley (Ex. 9:31). Now the wheat and spelt had sprouted, and these basic food crops would also be destroyed. Starvation for the Egyptian people was a significant possibility. It was this danger which led Pharaoh's officials to urge him to let the Israelites go.

Pharaoh had to understand the consequences. But the pressure the Lord placed upon him only hardened him further. We can-

not expect increased pressure to motivate anyone to change his or her attitude toward God. Only love can motivate a heart-response to the Lord.

Pharaoh again confessed he had sinned (10:16–17). When the fields of Egypt had been stripped of everything green, Pharaoh called for Moses "in haste." This confession of sin was as insincere as his earlier admission (9:27), and it was driven by the same motives.

God hardened Pharaoh's heart (10:20). Again, we have an example of what is probably a judicial hardening of Pharaoh's already stubborn heart. A person who travels too far along the road of arrogant rejection of God may find it impossible to turn, however compelling the reasons to do so.

THE MIRACLE OF THICK DARKNESS
Exodus 10:21–29

The ninth proving act struck Egypt without any warning. The Lord told Moses to

If locusts ate their basic food crops, the Egyptian people faced starvation.

stretch out his hand toward heaven, and for three days there was "thick darkness" which could "be felt" over all of Egypt.

The nature of the darkness (Exodus 10:21–23).

Even Lockyer, who holds that the ten mighty acts which God performed against Egypt were true miracles, gives a naturalistic explanation for this miracle. He and others assume that the darkness was caused by sand from the desert carried by the *khamsin* winds that sometimes blow across Egypt.

But the darkness described in these verses is far different. It was a darkness which could "be felt"—so thick it caused people to grope their way about. It was an eerie darkness that no light from the sun or any lamp could penetrate. The darkness was so frightening that for the entire three days not one person dared to "rise from his place" (10:23).

A direct confrontation with Egypt's premier deity, Ra.

We noted earlier that Exodus 12:12 states that one purpose of the miracles God performed was to execute judgment "against all the gods of Egypt." Some have tried to identify specific gods against whom each mighty act was directed. This may be possible in the case of a few of the miracles. For instance, a case can be made for seeing the miracle of the frogs as directed against the goddess Heqt (see page 67).

However, to strain to identify minor deities against whom this or that plague might be directed is to miss the point. Exodus 12:12 indicates that the *series* of miracles is a judgment against *all the gods* of Egypt—and there were hundreds!

The Egyptians assumed it was the duty of their entire pantheon of gods to maintain the harmony of nature and the peace of Egypt, the "blessed land." God's acts not only disrupted the harmony of nature, but also desolated Egypt and threatened the every existence of the nation and its people. *All the gods of Egypt* were shown to be powerless before the God of the people which Pharaoh and his nation had oppressed. And now the God of these slaves was exacting full payment for that oppression,

displaying the weakness of the gods on whom the Egyptians had relied.

At the same time, the plague of darkness may be interpreted as a judgment against the king of Egypt's deities—Ra, the sun. A hymn to Amen-Ra, dating from about the time of the Exodus, praised him as

The sole king, unique among the gods,
    with multitudinous names,
    whose number is not known,
Who arises on the eastern horizon,
    and sets on the western horizon,
Who is born early every day,
    and every day overthrows his enemies.

But suddenly, without warning and at Moses' signal, Amen-Ra did not arise. This king of Egypt's gods was overthrown, and darkness ruled. How utterly terrifying this must have been to the Egyptians—and what unmistakable evidence that all their gods were defeated.

Pharaoh continued to bargain (10:24).

When the light returned, Pharaoh called Moses and told him to go and take all the Israelites into the desert. But again, Pharaoh demanded a concession. He insisted on keeping the livestock and herds of the Israelites, which had been exempt from the miracles that had destroyed the Egyptian cattle. Moses refused, demanding that all the Israelites' livestock go. The livestock were required for sacrifice, and "even we do not know with what [i.e., with how many] we must serve [sacrifice to] the Lord until we arrive there" (Ex. 10:26).

There's a principle here for us. We need to bring all to the Lord, for we never know ahead of time what the Lord may ask of us. Pharaoh's way was to hold back something; Moses' way was to give all.

Pharaoh threatened to kill Moses (10:27, 28).

Again, the text confirms a judicial hardening of Pharaoh's heart. In frustration and fury, Pharaoh expelled Moses and Aaron from the palace and threatened them. He declared that the next time he saw either of them, he would have them killed.

Moses would never see Pharaoh again. Soon Pharaoh would send messengers begging the Israelites to leave.

The pattern in Pharaoh's hardening (compare Revelation 9:19, 20).

It is tempting to read more into the phrase "the Lord hardened Pharaoh's heart" than we should. In view of the devastating judgments on Egypt, common sense suggests that Pharaoh simply *had* to give in to God. We may even go so far as to assume that God had to cause Pharaoh to act against his own better judgment. But this isn't true.

Revelation 9 describes a terrifying series of judgments that will strike the earth at history's end. These also bear the mark of miracles: they are extraordinary events caused by God for a religious purpose. Will these judgments bring about repentance and a change of heart? Revelation 9:20–21 relates,

But the rest of mankind, who were not killed by these plagues, did not repent of the works of their hands, that they should not worship demons, and idols of gold, silver, brass, stone, and wood, which can neither see nor hear nor walk. And they did

not repent of their murders or their sorceries or their sexual immorality or their thefts.

Divine judgment tends to make a heart which has been hardened by sin and arrogance even more stubborn and resistant. Pharaoh's apparent repentances were never heartfelt or lasting. All the Lord needed to do to harden Pharaoh's heart was to nudge him in the direction he was already determined to go.

THE MIRACLE OF THE DEATH OF EGYPT'S FIRSTBORN   *Exodus 11:1–10; 12:29–36*

Pharaoh threatened Moses and expelled him from the palace (10:27–29). Before he left, Moses announced one last terrible judgment on Egypt. God would strike the firstborn "from the firstborn of Pharaoh who sits on his throne, even to the firstborn of the female servant who is behind the handmill" (Ex. 11:5). From highest to lowest, every Egyptian family would lose a loved one. Even the firstborn of any remaining animals would die.

The Ten Miracles

#	Miracle	Hebrew term	Distinctives	Special deity judged
1.	Nile to blood	*dam*	Water undrinkable, fish died Duplicated by magicians	Hopi
2.	Frogs	*tsefardea'*	Frogs infest land, died and rotted Duplicated by magicians	Heqt
3.	Lice	*kinnim*	All infested by vermin Magicians rendered unclean	
4.	Biting flies	*'arov*	All Egyptians bitten Israelites exempt—from now on	
5.	Animal epidemic	*dever*	Egyptian livestock in the fields died	Hathor
6.	Ulcerous boils	*shehin*	Painful boils incapacitated the Egyptians. For the first time God hardened Pharaoh's heart.	
7.	Hail storms	*barad*	Gigantic stones killed men and beasts. Early crops destroyed. First killing plague	
8.	Locusts	*'arbeh*	Locusts destroyed remaining crops. Egypt threatened with starvation.	
9.	Darkness	*hoshekh*	Supernatural darkness isolated, im- mobilized Egyptians	Amon-Ra
10.	Death of firstborn		The firstborn in every Egyptian family was killed at midnight.	

Moses' angry threat hung in the air as he left the stunned Pharaoh and his court.

"At midnight the Lord struck" (Exodus 12:29). Attempts to ascribe the deaths to a particular disease again miss the point. This was a miracle. The Lord struck all those who died at the same time—midnight. The deaths were selective—only the firstborn died. The miracle was inclusive—no Egyptian family was spared. Yet at the same time, the miracle was exclusive—not one Israelite or a single animal belonging to the Israelites died.

"Rise, go out . . . go" (12:31). Pharaoh's response was immediate and desperate. Just as Moses had predicted (Ex. 11:8), Pharaoh sent his officials to Moses and begged him to get out. The urgency of the Egyptian request was expressed in three active verbs in Exodus 12:31, which use three different words in the imperative, each of which can be rendered "go." We might express the rising desperation by rendering Pharaoh's message, "go, Go, GO!"

The final proving act at last won Pharaoh's unconditional surrender.

"None of the children of Israel" (11:7). The means God used to preserve Israel foreshadowed later revelation. God commanded the Hebrew families to kill a lamb and sprinkle its blood on the door frames of their dwellings. Those inside homes marked by the blood of the lamb were spared.

It was not that the Israelites were sinless, or even morally superior to their oppressors. The testimony of Scripture is that all have

Blood on the doorpost was a sign for God to pass over an Israelite home.

sinned. It was the blood that God ordained should be shed which sheltered God's people from his wrath.

It is the same today and forever. Christ, the lamb of God, shed his blood that those who seek shelter in him might find forgiveness and be sheltered eternally from the wrath of God.

"They had asked . . . articles of silver, articles of gold" (12:35). Moses told the Israelites to ask [not "borrow"] the Egyptians for precious articles. The text suggests that the Egyptians were awed by Moses (cf. Ex. 11:3), and they readily gave their wealth away to any Hebrews who asked.

Much of this wealth would be freely given in later years by God's people to construct a portable worship center, which they carried with them in the wilderness. However great the accumulated wealth the Israelites gained, it was poor compensation for the years of harsh oppression they had endured.

The Passover recalled this tenth miracle (12:1–28). Between Moses' announcement of the tenth miracle in Exodus 11:1–10 and the description of its occurrence in 12:29–36, the book of Exodus established an annual celebration reenacting the experiences of that unforgettable night. Jewish families gathered and shared a meal featuring lamb and unleavened bread—bread made without yeast because there was no time for the bread to rise before the Israelites hurriedly left Egypt.

For all time, the Passover—Israel's festival of freedom—was to stand as a reminder of the ten proving acts by which God demonstrated his presence with the Israelites and his power over their enemies.

MIRACLES ALONG THE WAY
Exodus 13—17

The Israelites were freed from Egyptian slavery by ten miraculous "proving acts" which judged Egypt's gods and demonstrated the real presence of God to Egyptian and Israelite alike. Yet, release from Egypt was only

the beginning of Israel's challenges—challenges which could be overcome only by the continual exercise of God's wonder-working power.

Taken together, this cluster of miracles speaks of God's complete provision for the needs of his people.

1. The miracle of the cloudy-fiery pillar. P. 78
2. The miracle at the Reed Sea. p. 79
3. The miracle of the healed waters. p. 81
4. The miracle of the manna. p. 82
5. The miracle of the quail. p. 83
6. The miracle of the smitten rock. p. 84
7. The miracle victory over Amalek. p. 85

THE MIRACLE OF THE CLOUDY-FIERY PILLAR   *Exodus 13:21–22; 40:34–38*

Exodus 13 describes this miracle provision:

And the Lord went before them by day in a pillar of cloud to lead the way, and by night in a pillar of fire to give them light, so as to go by day and night. He did not take away the pillar of cloud by day or the pillar of fire by night from before the people (Ex. 13:21, 22).

The cloud has been described by some as a "luminous mist." Apparently, it changed, becoming a cloud by day and a source of light by night. This miraculous apparition had several functions during the travels of Israel from Egypt to Canaan.

It served as a visible reminder of God's presence with his people. There was no way that Israel in the wilderness could forget that God was with them. The majestic pillar in the sky was constant evidence of his nearness.

It served as a guide throughout Israel's travels (Exodus 13:21). Through the pillar of cloud, the Lord went before them "to lead the way." God did not stand back and tell Israel, "Go." Instead God went ahead, and said, "Come." It is the same in our experience today. The Lord never asks us to go on ahead of him or to travel alone. He stays with us. He who knows the way leads us to our personal promised land.

It served as a shield when Israel was endangered (14:19, 20). Egypt's Pharaoh did not remain content to let Israel go. His spies informed him that the Israelites were trapped on the shore of the "Red Sea." Pharaoh marshaled his army and set out to recapture the slaves. When the Egyptian forces approached, the cloudy-fiery pillar stood between Israel and the Egyptians, its dark side blinding the pursuers, and its bright side giving light to the escaping Israelites.

It marked Moses' conferences with God (33:9). This symbol of God's presence served to authenticate further Moses as God's confidant and the people's appointed leader by descending when God met with Moses.

It served as God's authoritative word of direction to Israel (40:36–38). The last chapter of Exodus sums up this aspect of the miracle cloud. When the cloud moved ahead, the people of Israel followed. And when the cloud hovered, the people did not move until the cloud led the way.

This also has a lesson for us. At times God leads us to wait—not to wait interminably, but to wait until he leads us on. Our times of waiting can be as significant as times for action.

Finally, Exodus 40:38 reminds us that the cloud was in sight of all the house of Israel "throughout all their journeys." In the same way, God remains close to us throughout our lives. All we need do is look to him.

THE MIRACLE AT THE REED SEA
Exodus 14:21–32

God led the Israelites away from the direct coastal route to Canaan, aware that this route would involve conflict with the inhabitants of that region (Ex. 13:17). Egyptian records use the same name for the route as this verse, "the way of the land of the Philistines," indicating that it was well fortified. Generations of slavery had not equipped the Israelites for warfare!

But God then proceeded to lead the Israelites into a trap, where they had no choice but to rely completely on him.

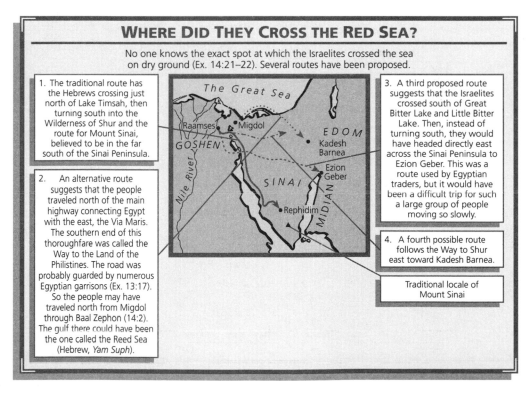

WHERE DID THEY CROSS THE RED SEA?

No one knows the exact spot at which the Israelites crossed the sea on dry ground (Ex. 14:21–22). Several routes have been proposed.

1. The traditional route has the Hebrews crossing just north of Lake Timsah, then turning south into the Wilderness of Shur and the route for Mount Sinai, believed to be in the far south of the Sinai Peninsula.

2. An alternative route suggests that the people traveled north of the main highway connecting Egypt with the east, the Via Maris. The southern end of this thoroughfare was called the Way to the Land of the Philistines. The road was probably guarded by numerous Egyptian garrisons (Ex. 13:17). So the people may have traveled north from Migdol through Baal Zephon (14:2). The gulf there could have been the one called the Reed Sea (Hebrew, *Yam Suph*).

3. A third proposed route suggests that the Israelites crossed south of Great Bitter Lake and Little Bitter Lake. Then, instead of turning south, they would have headed directly east across the Sinai Peninsula to Ezion Geber. This was a route used by Egyptian traders, but it would have been a difficult trip for such a large group of people moving so slowly.

4. A fourth possible route follows the Way to Shur east toward Kadesh Barnea.

Traditional locale of Mount Sinai

Map labels: The Great Sea · Raamses · Migdol · GOSHEN · Nile River · EDOM · Kadesh Barnea · Ezion Geber · SINAI · MIDIAN · Rephidim

***The identity of the "Red Sea" (Exodus
14:2, 9).*** Scholars have known for some time
that *yom suph* means "reed sea," not Red Sea.
The Sinai peninsula has several lakes. God led
the Israelites to the shore of one of these lakes.
Its shallows were filled with papyrus reeds.
The text of Exodus gives four reference points
(Ex. 14:1–2). While they cannot be identified
today, the names are suggestive. *Pi-hahiroth*
means the "mouth of Hirot," a river or canal.
Several fortified Egyptian towns were called
"Migdol." The point of these identifications
was to show that the Israelites were trapped,
with no way to turn.

The Egyptians pursued (14:5–9). When
Pharaoh heard that the Israelites were trapped
on the seashore, he assembled his army to
pursue. Their approach terrified the Israelites

(Ex. 14:10), who cried out to the Lord but
then complained bitterly to Moses (Ex.
14:11, 12).

Pharaoh seemed to have forgotten the terrible cost of conflict with Israel's God.

The waters of the Reed Sea divide (14:21).
Lockyer makes much of the fact that the waters of the Red Sea are six thousand feet deep
and miles broad at its narrowest point. But Israel crossed the Reed Sea, not the Red Sea. Yet
it is clear from the text that the actual crossing
was a miracle.

*The wind which drove the waters back "divided
the waters" (14:21, 22).* The waters were not
driven to one side of the sea, as with a normal
wind, but formed "a wall to them on the right
hand and on the left."

God divided the waters of the sea for the Israelites to cross.

The Israelites crossed "on dry ground" (14:22). Normally, the bed of such a sea would be thick mud. But the text specifically states the bed was dry ground for the Israelites' crossing.

The cloudy-fiery pillar spread darkness which held back the Egyptians (14:20). In contrast, the side of the pillar facing the Israelites provided light, so God's people could see to pass through the sea.

When the Egyptians pursued, they were "troubled" by God (14:24). Verse 25 seems to suggest that the seabed turned muddy again, bogging down the Egyptian chariots.

When the entire army had been committed, the waters returned (14:26–28). On God's command, Moses stretched his hand over the sea and the waters rushed back to drown the Egyptians. The text indicates that "not so much as one" soldier survived.

The "miracle at the Reed Sea" was actually a series of miracles, blended together to punish Egypt further and to demonstrate the unshaken commitment of God to his people Israel.

Messages in the Reed Sea miracles. What happened at the Reed Sea were undoubtedly extraordinary events caused by God for a religious purpose.

The miracles increased Israel's respect for the Lord (Exodus 14:30). Exodus indicates that Israel "saw the Egyptians dead on the seashore." The next verse again emphasizes the fact that Israel "saw the great work." Why this emphasis?

The most devastating of the plagues that struck Egypt *passed the Israelites by!* They were isolated in Goshen from the devastation which touched the rest of Egypt. They simply had not seen for themselves what the Lord could do.

At the Reed Sea, they *saw.* As the dead bodies of the army of their oppressors washed up on the shore, they could no longer question or doubt the power and presence of the Lord.

The miracles increased Israel's respect for Moses (14:31). This verse adds, "and [the Israelites] believed the Lord and his servant Moses." They had heard that plagues struck Egypt at Moses' command, but now they had seen Moses raise his hand and watched the waters recede and then return. For perhaps the first time, all Israel sensed the greatness of their leader, who had come to deliver them as their God's representative.

This cluster of miracles continued to instruct God's people. There are many lessons we can draw from the events described in Exodus 14.

- We're reminded that when God leads us into trouble, he will also provide a way out.
- We're reminded that God's presence provides protection from those who would harm us.
- We're reminded that God has devised ways to deal with every difficulty, however confusing or complex our present situation may be.
- We're reminded of the importance of complete reliance on the Lord. How many times Moses' word to Israel is God's word to us: "The Lord will fight for you, and you shall hold your peace."
- We're reminded that those who trouble God's people will suffer loss while those who serve him who will survive to rejoice and to praise.

THE MIRACLE OF THE HEALED WATERS *Exodus 15:22–26*

Following God's victory over the Egyptian army at the Reed Sea, the Israelites traveled on into the wilderness. They traveled only three days before they ran out of water. The response of the Israelites was immediate and striking. They "complained against Moses." Moses prayed, and God met the need. He showed Moses a tree which could be thrown into the "bitter" waters to make it sweet (drinkable).

Israel's lack of faith revealed (Exodus 15:23, 24). The first thing this incident reveals is Israel's lack of faith. Just three days before, the people had witnessed the miraculous destruction of the Egyptian army. All they needed to do was look into the sky to be reminded of God's presence in the cloudy-fiery pillar. Yet when they discovered undrinkable waters, their first response was unbelief rather than faith.

The grumbling introduced here would characterize Israel's relationship with Moses and God on the journey both to and away from Sinai. No matter what God did, it would never be enough to satisfy his discontented people. And no provision of God would ever convince Israel that the Lord could be trusted in the next crisis.

God's gracious provision revealed (15:25). In spite of Israel's ungratefulness and lack of faith, God purified the waters so his people could drink. How graciously God provides, even when we don't deserve his gifts.

God's ability to meet every need further revealed (15:25). This miracle was not as spectacular as the miracles performed at the Reed Sea. Yet it was an *essential* miracle. Water for drinking is one of life's basic needs—essential for life itself.

"The Lord who heals you" (15:26). The miraculous provision of water served as an occasion for the Lord to present a "test" to Israel. The verse does not imply that God is about to test Israel. We might say that God proposed that Israel try out being obedient. If they obeyed, God would "put none of the diseases on you which I have brought on the Egyptians." God can do this, because he is Yahweh-the-Healer.

In essence, God suggested that his people had nothing to lose. The one who healed the waters of Marah had displayed his ability to heal. Why not then try obedience, and see how the Lord would be their personal healer as well as healer of the waters?

The message of the miracle. The test that God proposed suggests the primary message of the miracle to the Exodus generation. God has demonstrated his healing powers. If Israel would be obedient, God would commit himself to protect Israel from all the diseases of the Egyptians.

It's tempting to apply this verse as an open promise to all of God's people. Certainly God continues to be our healer, and often intervenes for us. But before assuming this verse states an unchangeable divine commitment, we need to look at Deuteronomy 28.

In Deuteronomy, the promise of healing is notable because it does not occur in the list of blessings God declared he would provide for an obedient Israel (Deut. 28:1–13)! On the other hand, if Israel was disobedient, God declared he would "strike you with the boils of Egypt, with tumors, with the scab, and with the itch, from which you cannot be healed" (Deut. 28:27).

God is gracious, and he meets our most basic needs. God is merciful, and he is our Healer. But even the most obedient believer, such as the apostle Paul, has no guarantee of physical healing by the Lord (cf. 2 Cor. 12:5–12).

THE MIRACLE OF THE MANNA
Exodus 16:1–5, 14–35

A month and a half into the wilderness, the Israelites' food supplies ran out. Again, the "whole congregation" responded with complaint rather than faith. The complaint motif recurs seven times in Exodus 16:2, 7, 8, 9, and 12. In spite of Israel's lack of faith, God told Moses he would "rain bread from heaven."

The nature of the miracle (Exodus 16:4). Some have provided naturalistic explanations of the manna to make the biblical account "credible." Honey-like gums and Arabian lichens have been put forward as candidates for the miraculous food. But the text makes it clear that God provided the food miraculously.

- Manna appeared six days, but not on the Sabbath (Ex. 16:4, 5).
- Manna met the daily need, whether much or little had been gathered (Ex. 16:16).
- Manna kept overnight spoiled, so it had to be gathered daily (Ex. 16:19–20).
- Manna preserved by Moses as a memorial never spoiled (Ex. 16:33–34).
- Manna was provided all the years Israel traveled in the Sinai, and it stopped the day the people entered Canaan 40 years later (Ex.16:35).
- Enough manna was provided each day to feed the Israelites who followed Moses— estimated at nearly two million (compare Ex. 12:37).

There is no doubt that what the Bible describes was a miracle.

The significance of the manna miracle. What is the religious significance of this extraordinary event caused by God?

Manna was continuing evidence of God's presence with Israel and his commitment to them. God met their every need.

Manna was rationed in a way that taught dependence on God for daily bread. The familiar phrase in the Lord's prayer reminds us that we need to learn this lesson as well.

Manna was intended to instruct Israel to depend on God's word, not to live by bread alone (Deut. 8:3). Jesus returned to this verse when challenged by Satan to turn stones into bread (Luke 4:4).

Manna was a symbol of divine provision of life itself (John 8:31–58). Jesus spoke of himself as the true bread from heaven, who provides eternal life to all who partake of him.

God's provision of manna had a significance far beyond its ability to sustain the life of the wilderness travelers. In this notable miracle, the Lord instructed Israel as well as modern believers.

THE MIRACLE OF THE QUAIL
Exodus 16:3–13

The Israelites complained of more than lack of bread. They also wanted meat! The overstatement of their condition in Egypt is laughable: "we sat by the pots of meat and . . . ate bread to the full" [i.e., "until we were stuffed!"]. Egyptian records of food supplied to hired workers on government projects show how faulty Israel's memory was. The

God's provision of manna underscored their dependence on Him.

typical worker's menu included bread, vegetables, and beer—and fish or meat occasionally.

God's miracle provision of quail. In response to Israel's complaint, God provided quail to supplement the manna. The text simply says that "quails came up at evening and covered the camp" (Ex. 16:13). The low-flying birds were easy prey for the hungry Israelites.

We are not told how God brought enough quail to feed the multitude. A parallel passage in Numbers 11 indicates that at that time a wind brought a great flock of quail, which settled around the Israelites' camp.

The episodic nature of the miracle. The miracle of the manna was a *sustained* miracle. Every week for 40 years God faithfully supplied the bread that preserved life. The miracle of the quail was episodic. The Old Testament records only two instances of this provision of a supplementary food.

This episodic miracle has a valuable message. The God who provides all we *need* will sometimes provide things that we *want* but do not need. When this happens, we should certainly be more grateful than the Israelites were.

THE MIRACLE OF THE SMITTEN ROCK   *Exodus 17:1–7*

As the Israelites traveled, they again camped where there was no water. They began to complain.

The intensity of the Israelites' complaints (Exodus 17:3, 4). This time when they grew thirsty, they accused Moses of trying to kill them and their children. The term "accuse" is appropriate, for the Hebrew word *rib,* is used. This word in the Old Testament relates primarily to formal court proceedings. The people were ready to take Moses to court and charge him with attempted murder!

Even worse, they had already determined the verdict. Moses cried, "They are almost ready to stone me!"

The underlying lack of faith (17:7). This incident is recalled in both the Old and New Testaments. In spite of the proof of God's presence provided by the pillar of cloud which led them, and the manna which daily fed them, the people "tempted [tested] the Lord, saying, 'Is the Lord among us, or not!'"

Later in Deuteronomy, Moses warned the next generation of Israelites, "You shall not tempt the Lord your God, as you tempted him in Massah" (Deut. 6:16). Jesus quoted this verse when challenged by Satan to leap from the pinnacle of the temple (Luke 4:9–12). The believer is to live by faith, confident that the God who has promised to be with us *is* with us, even when we don't see evidence of his presence.

Another proof-of-presence miracle (17:5–6). God provided further proof of his presence. He sent Moses, with some of the elders as witnesses, to strike a rock with his staff. When Moses did so, water flowed.

John I. Durham, in his commentary on Exodus, made this penetrating comment.

God provided water out of a rock.

Once more, when a need arises, the Israelites do not wait for it to be met; indeed they do not even assume that it can be met. Rather they attack Yahweh and put him on trial by attacking Moses to put *him* on trial. Their thirst, of course, was real. But infinitely more real was the powerful Presence of Yahweh in their midst. The lesser reality they embraced; the more important reality they ignored and doubted: so once more, God dealt with the lesser reality by a demonstration of the greater, underlying reality (p. 232).

All the miracles of Scripture, like this one, unveil God as the great underlying reality in our universe. How wonderful to have a personal relationship with him. How gently he frees us from doubts and fears by an inner evidence of his presence that is more wonderful than the miracles of old.

Paul's application of the miracle (1 Corinthians 10:4–6). In the New Testament, the apostle Paul identified Jesus with the "Rock that followed them." Paul's point was that throughout history Christ himself cared for the nation from which he sprang.

It was Jesus who met every need of Israel in ancient times. And this same Jesus will meet our needs as we journey with him in the walk of faith.

THE MIRACLE VICTORY OVER AMALEK   *Exodus 17:8–13*

For the first time, the traveling Israelites were forced to fight. Joshua led on the battlefield; but the key to victory was Moses, standing on a hill top. Whenever Moses' arms were upraised, Israel prevailed. When his arms drooped, the Amalekites won. Finally, Moses' two companions held up his arms, and the victory went to Israel.

The miracle victory reminded Israel that their success depended on the Lord rather than their warriors and that Moses was God's chosen mediator.

THE MIRACLE PRESENCE AT SINAI
Exodus 19

Mount Sinai was a massive tower of rock thrust upward out of the surrounding plain. Known today as Jebel Musa, the 7,363-feet-high granite mountain dominates the surrounding countryside.

It was to this awe-inspiring mountain that God led Israel. There God would give Moses a law that spelled out the Lord's expectations of his people—a law which would regulate every detail of their lives and set Israel apart from surrounding peoples. At last, Israel would learn the lifestyle through which God's people could express their faith in Yahweh and through which succeeding generations could find blessing and peace.

The significance of the moment was underlined by further miraculous evidence of the divine presence.

More proofs of presence (Exodus 19:16–19). The evidence of God's miracle presence is described in these verses:

Then it came to pass on the third day, in the morning, that there were thunderings and lightnings, and a thick cloud on the mountain; and the sound

Lessons from the Miracles on the Way to Sinai

Miracle	Text	Lesson concerning God's presence
Pillar of cloud/fire	Ex. 13	God leads, guides, and protects his people.
Parting of Reed Sea	Ex. 14	God rescues from danger, protects his people from enemies.
Purifying bitter water	Ex. 15	God meets the basic life needs of his people.
Providing manna	Ex. 16	God continually meets the basic needs of his people on a daily basis.
Providing quail	Ex. 16	God may graciously provide what we want but do not need.
Bringing water from the rock	Ex. 17	God meets the needs even of the doubting and the ungrateful, but warns against testing him.
Victory over Amalek	Ex. 17	Success depends on God's presence and aid.

of the trumpet was very loud, so that all the people who were in the camp trembled. And Moses brought the people out of the camp to meet with God, and they stood at the foot of the mountain.

Now, Mount Sinai was completely in smoke, because the Lord descended upon it in fire. Its smoke ascended like the smoke of a furnace, and the whole mountain quaked greatly. And when the blast of the trumpet sounded long and became louder and louder, Moses spoke, and God answered him by voice.

Every sense of the Israelites was filled with evidence of God's presence. They saw the mountain shrouded in smoke and flame. They smelled and tasted the smoke. They felt the ground shake. They heard a loud trumpet-like

❖

Smoke and fire marked God's presence on Mount Sinai.

sound and actually heard God speak with Moses "by voice."

There could be no doubt. God was present on Mount Sinai. The evidence was overwhelming.

The purposes of the miracle (Exodus 20:18–20). These verses describe the reaction of the Israelites.

The people "trembled and stood afar off" (20:18). Both Psalms and Proverbs remind us that the fear of the Lord is the beginning of wisdom (Ps. 111:10; Prov. 9:10). The Israelites had doubted God, displaying a lack of faith and appreciation. As they stood before the mountain, the Israelites were at last awed and filled with a fearful respect for the One whose voice they now heard for themselves.

The people told Moses, "You speak with us, and we will hear" (20:19). The fear that God's miracle presence inspired created fresh respect for Moses. Israel accepted him as the authentic mediator of God's words to mankind. The conviction that God spoke to and through Moses has shaped Jewish as well as Christian thought from that moment.

Moses told the people that God intended the display to help them fear him (20:20). In the Old Testament, the "fear of God" does not indicate dread *of* God but rather awed respect *for* God. The reason that God wants us to fear him is explained in this verse: "so that you may not sin." A person filled with respect for God's power and his greatness will not doubt his presence or his ability to help. Rather than sin, as Israel had in doubting the Lord, the believer who respects God will follow him gladly.

CHAPTER 4

MIRACLES ALONG THE WAY

DISCIPLINE IN THE DESERT
Leviticus—Numbers

It's dangerous to make God promises which aren't kept.

At Sinai the Israelites had sworn, "All that the Lord has said, we will do, and be obedient" (Exodus 24:7). But as the books of Leviticus through Deuteronomy trace Israel's journey toward the Promised Land, time and time again the Israelites disobey! And God intervenes with miracles—but now they are miracles of judgment.

Does God perform disciplinary miracles today? Certainly God did in times past!

Miracles of Discipline in Leviticus & Numbers

1.	The miracle judgment of Nadab and Abihu	p. 87
2.	The miracle judgment by fire	p. 88
3.	The miracle judgment by quail	p. 89
4.	The miracle judgment of Miriam's leprosy	p. 90
5.	The miracle judgment of Korah's followers	p. 91
6.	The miracle judgment by serpents	p. 93
7.	The miracle of Balaam's donkey	p. 94

THE MIRACLE JUDGMENT OF NADAB AND ABIHU   Leviticus 10:1–7

The book of Leviticus focuses attention on worship and holiness. The word "holy" is used 87 times, while words for "sacrifice" occur approximately 300 times in this 27-chapter book. And "priest" or "priests" are found 152 times.

It is clear that priests and their ministry are significant in this book on the worship and lifestyle of God's people. This is why the only miracle in Leviticus involves two priests—Nadab and Abihu, sons of Aaron.

The nature and cause of the miracle judgment (Leviticus 10:1). Nadab and Abihu "each took his censer, put fire in it, put incense on it, and offered profane fire before the Lord." The Hebrew word `esh zarah,* means "alien fire." When the two approached the tabernacle worship center, fire flared from the Lord and killed them.

The text does not explain their sin. But the priestly prescriptions in Leviticus do. Leviticus 6:12, 13 instructed the priests to keep fire burning on Israel's altar. Leviticus 16:12 instructed the priests to use the altar fires to ignite incense offerings. The two young priests ignited their incense with alien fire, thus violating God's instructions for worship.

God's explanation (Leviticus 10:3). Moses offered this word of explanation to the bereaved father, Aaron. "By those who come near Me, I must be regarded as holy." It was especially important for the priests to pay close attention to God's instructions. In carrying out their duties, they came closer to the Lord than Israelites from any other tribe.

The priests, with the rest of the people, had committed themselves at Sinai by declaring, "All that the Lord has said we will do, and be obedient" (Ex. 24:7). Nadab and Abihu's disregard for God's worship instructions could not be tolerated if his people were to regard the Lord as holy and to obey him completely.

This miracle judgment established a pattern. While the people were on the way to Sinai, the Lord had overlooked their rebellion and disrespect. Now that the Law had been given and accepted, there would be no more divine indifference to sin. God would act to punish sin when it occurred in order to teach his people the necessity of trust and discipline.

God's miracle judgments may seem harsh. But his earlier leniency had failed to bring Israel to maturity or to deepen their faith. By the end of the journey from Sinai to Canaan, God's people had to learn to trust and obey the Lord. Then a disciplined and confident people would be ready to conquer Canaan and claim God's blessings.

THE MIRACLE JUDGMENT BY FIRE
Numbers 11:1–3

The book of Numbers describes the organization of the Israelite camp in preparation for the journey to Canaan. Beginning with Numbers 10:33, events on the journey to Canaan are described.

The first event (Numbers 11:1–3). The journey began in judgment. The first event was a familiar refrain: "the people complained." The Septuagint translates the Hebrew word for "complain" with the same term used to translate the many references to Israel's "murmuring" on the way to Sinai (see Ex. 16 and 17).

The Israelites still displayed the negative, untrusting, and hostile attitude they had shown earlier.

God was displeased, and acted. Now their behavior "displeased the Lord . . . and his anger was aroused."

The Law, which Israel had voluntarily accepted, provided a standard which the people had violated. Now a basis for judgment existed. God did not hesitate. "The fire of the Lord burned among them, and consumed some in the outskirts of the camp" (Num.

"The fire of the Lord burned among them, and consumed some in the outskirts."

1:3). The Lord would no longer put up with the rebellious behavior he had overlooked before.

The initial lesson taught by the miracle judgment. The nature of the miracle fire made it clear that God was the cause of this extraordinary event. It followed immediately upon the complaining of the people. Thus the link between cause and effect was clearly established, and Israel began to learn that obedience to the Lord meant blessing, while disobedience brought disaster.

This is a lesson each of us must learn. By God's grace, we are permitted to learn it from the experience of ancient Israel, recorded for us in God's book. If we will not learn this lesson from others, we may force God to teach us by our own personal experience.

How much better to take Scripture's lessons to heart, and to avoid so much suffering and pain.

THE MIRACLE JUDGMENT BY THE QUAIL   *Numbers 11:4–23, 31–34*

The next event on the journey immediately followed the first miracle judgment. The word for "mixed multitude," *asafsruf,* is best translated "rabble" or "riffraff." It should not be taken to refer to non-Israelites, as the root word means "to collect," indicating a gathering or group of people.

The cause of the judgment (Numbers 11:4–6). It was God's people—those who had been freed from slavery and given his Law—who surrendered to their craving for variety in their diet, rejecting God's provision of manna.

God's reaction (11:10). Again, the Lord's anger was "greatly aroused." Rather than be thankful for what God had provided, the Israelites wept and complained about what they didn't have.

The apostle Paul learned well the lesson Israel had not. In Philippians, Paul wrote, "In regard to need, I have learned in whatever state I am, to be content" (Phil. 4:11). Paul accepted what he received from the hand of God with thanksgiving, without focusing on what

he didn't have. When we understand that God is a loving Father who provides what is best for us, we will also be able to find contentment and peace.

Moses' frustration and despair (11:10–15). This complaining reaction of the people plunged Moses into despair. To him, leadership of Israel felt like an unbearable burden (Num. 11:11). Before we criticize Moses, let's remember that his emotions reflected the frustration and anger felt by God as well. There are times when others—even our own children—seem like an unbearable burden. Like Moses, we almost wish we could die (Num. 11:15).

In his frustration, even Moses forgot to trust in the Lord. He asked, "Where am I to get meat to give to all these people?" (Num. 11:13). When had Moses provided *anything* to meet Israel's needs? It had always been God, present with his people, who provided and preserved.

This is also an important truth to remember. When we are frustrated and we feel that we are at the end of our resources, we need to remember that God is the One who has provided. When we are full of ourselves, there is no room for God to store what he provides. When we are empty, there is space aplenty for him to fill us up.

God's gracious response to Moses (11:16–17). Before the Lord dealt with Israel, he promised to meet Moses' most pressing need. God would spread his spirit on the elders of Israel, enabling them to share some of the burden of leadership.

But why did God respond graciously when Moses complained while judging so severely the people who murmured against him? Moses had taken his complaint directly *to* God. But the people complained *about* God.

We honor the Lord when we acknowledge him as the cause of all things, expressing to him our fears and frustrations. The Israelites failed to honor God by recognizing his sovereignty in the situation. In fact, they "despised the Lord" by weeping and saying,

"Why did we ever come up out of Egypt" (11:20).

The miracle judgment (11:17–23; 31–34). As he had done on the journey to Sinai, the Lord provided quail to satisfy his people's craving for meat (see Ex. 16:11–13). But this time, "while the meat was still between their teeth, before it was chewed, the wrath of the Lord was aroused against the people, and the Lord struck the people with a very great plague" (Num. 11:33). And there they buried those who had yielded to their cravings.

Lessons in the miracle judgment of the quail. This experience was another lesson for Israel on how to live in relationship with the God who was present with them. Not only must Israel acknowledge his presence, but they must also accept his sovereignty in their lives relying on him to provide what was best for them.

This is the way that we must live if we are to be comfortable in our relationship with the Lord. God is sovereign, and he will supply what is best. May we learn to praise him for what we have, and may we find freedom from cravings for whatever he has not chosen to give.

THE MIRACLE JUDGMENT OF MIRIAM   *Numbers 12:1–16*

Aaron and Miriam, the brother and sister of Moses, "spoke against" Moses.

The brother's and sister's complaint (Numbers 12:1–2). The phrase "speak against" is used in Numbers 21:5, 7 and in other passages. It means "hostile speech." In this case, the two found fault with Moses for marrying an Ethiopian [a black]. Their complaint seemed to hinge on the notion of racial purity, so significant in ancient and rabbinic Judaism. God had spoken by Moses to Pharaoh, but through Aaron, and he had spoken by Miriam after the Reed Sea crossing (see Ex. 15). Their argument seems to have been that they—as "pure" Israelites—deserved more significant leadership roles.

Moses' reaction (12:3). The comment in this verse on Moses' humility is generally taken to have been added long after the original text was written. However, it has significance in context. The humbleness of Moses does not suggest that he didn't argue with his siblings. In fact, it suggests that Moses may have been swayed by their arguments! The truly humble person fails to recognize his or her unique gifts, and may be pushed aside by those less gifted who want the spotlight!

God intervened (12:4–8). God called the three together and confronted Aaron and Miriam. He affirmed the special relationship that Moses had with God, and asked "why then were you not afraid to speak against My servant Moses?"

The miracle judgment (12:9–13). When the Lord left, the three realized that Miriam had become leprous. Aaron pleaded with Moses to heal her, and Moses begged God to heal his sister.

The Lord condemned Miriam to seven days as a leper, during which she had to live outside the camp. Only after this public rebuke was Miriam healed.

Why not Aaron? Some have seen evidence of biblical chauvinism in the fact that only Miriam was stricken with leprosy. The reason why Aaron did not suffer the same fate is that he was Israel's high priest. And the Law specified that no person with a physical defect could come near the offerings made to the Lord (Lev. 21:21). If Aaron had been stricken with leprosy, he would not have been available to offer sacrifices for the sins of the Israelites.

The message of this miracle of judgment. It is tempting to suggest from this miracle that we are not to speak against our spiritual leaders. And this is probably an apt application. But it does not suggest the need for unquestioning agreement with all our leaders say. In Scripture, we have the standard by which all of us, leader and lay alike, are judged. We are to hew to that standard when any conflict between Scripture and leadership emerges.

What we can draw from this miracle is that leaders as well as the people whom they lead are accountable to God. No commission from God exempts us from the standards which Scripture holds up for all.

THE MIRACLE JUDGMENT OF KORAH'S FOLLOWERS *Numbers 16:1—17:12*

These chapters recount a rebellion against the authority of Moses and Aaron, led by a Levite named Korah and two others, Dathan and Abiram. The rebellion led to a series of miraculous events in which the rebels were judged and the authority of Moses and Aaron was confirmed by the Lord.

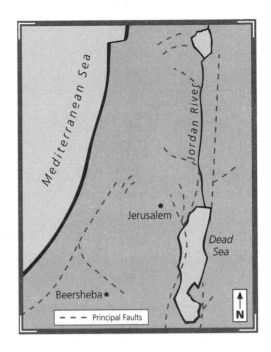

The rationale for the rebellion (16:1–3). Korah's rebellion grew out of an overemphasis on one facet of revealed truth. God had said that all of Israel was holy—that is, set apart to him (see Ex. 19:6). To Korah this meant that all God's people were equal, and so Moses' leadership was invalid. "Why," Korah asked Moses and Aaron, "do you exalt yourselves above the assembly of the Lord?"

Korah ignored unmistakable evidence that Moses was God's chosen leader for Israel. Moses was the one who had mediated the miracles that won Israel's freedom—the one who had trudged alone up Mount Sinai to meet with the Lord. By emphasizing one truth and ignoring another, Korah's reasoning led him into error and rebellion.

We must be careful lest we fall into the same error and fail to consider the whole counsel of God.

God's response to the rebellion (16:4–14). God through Moses commanded Korah and the two hundred and fifty leaders he had influenced to appear before the Tabernacle the next day, carrying censers. There they would see for themselves whom the Lord accepted, and whom he did not.

But Dathan and Abiram refused to appear. They would not dignify Moses by obeying *any* command of his. Instead they accused Moses of trying to exterminate the people and failing to bring Israel into the promised land.

The miracle of the opened chasm (16:24–34). God dealt first with Dathan and Abiram. As they and their families stood at the door of their tents, the earth opened and swallowed them up.

The nature of this miracle of divine judgment was important to Moses. He announced beforehand that this specific miracle would confirm that all the miracles he was associated with had been done by the Lord, and not "of my own will."

It happened just as Moses said. The earth opened and "they and all those with them went down alive into the pit; the earth closed over them, and they perished from among the assembly" (v. 33).

The miracle of the consuming fire (16:35). At about the same time "a fire came out from the Lord and consumed the two hundred and fifty men [with Korah] who were offering incense."

Because of their rebellion, Dathan and Abiram and their families were swallowed up by a crack in the earth.

The two miracle judgments made it clear that God had rejected the position taken by Korah and the more extreme position taken by Dathan and Abiram.

The miracle of the following plague (16:41–49). These judgments made it clear that it was God who had acted against the rebels. Yet the next day "all the congregation of the children of Israel" accused *Moses* of killing the Lord's people (Num. 16:41)! Clearly, Israel had not taken the judgments to heart or learned from them.

God reacted immediately with a plague which killed 14,700 people. Only Moses' hasty action in sending Aaron to stand between the dead and the living with a censer of incense kept the death toll this low.

Parallels with the plagues on Egypt. The trail of judgments that runs through Numbers has an interesting relationship to the plagues that struck Egypt.

In each case an increasing hardness was displayed. Pharaoh became more and more stubborn as judgment miracles followed one after the other. In the early chapters of Numbers, we see the Israelites become more and more stubborn as judgment miracle followed judgment miracle.

In each case the judgment miracles increased in severity. The miracles of Egypt show a gradual but definite escalation in severity. This same pattern is evident in Numbers.

In each case an ultimate resolution called for death. The miracles in Egypt culminated in the death of the firstborn. Even after this extreme judgment, Pharaoh marshaled his army to pursue Israel, and saw that force wiped out

(Ex. 14). The miracles in Numbers reveal such an intense stubbornness and unbelief that God's death sentence on the Exodus generation was fully justified.

For those who wouldn't respond to either grace (Exodus 16, 17) or discipline (Numbers), God exercised his option to set them aside, beginning anew with the next generation.

The miracle of Aaron's rod that budded (Num. 17:1–12). The final miracle in this sequence is not a miracle of judgment, but a miracle performed to *avoid* the necessity of future judgments.

Moses collected rods from the leaders of each of the twelve Israelite tribes and placed them in the tabernacle. The next morning, Aaron's rod had "sprouted, and put forth buds, had produced blossoms and yielded ripe almonds" (v. 8).

The miracle confirmed the role of the Aaronic priesthood, and the rod was preserved as a "sign against the rebels," to forestall future rebellions like that of Korah and the terrible judgments which must follow (Num. 17:10).

THE MIRACLE JUDGMENT BY SERPENTS   *Numbers 21:4–9*

Again, the people spoke "against God and Moses" (Num. 21:4). This faultfinding arose just after God had given Israel a victory over the Canaanites (Num. 21:1–3). Rather than be thankful, the Israelites reacted with hostility and complaints!

The miracle judgment itself (Numbers 21:6). Once again, God disciplined immediately, this time by sending "fiery [deadly] serpents" among the people. The Hebrew words in verse 6 say literally, "many biters and many bitten."

The Israelites responded (21:7). This time the Israelites quickly acknowledged their sin and begged Moses to ask God for relief. This was in stark contrast to their reaction the last time God disciplined them during Korah's rebellion. The people accepted responsibility for their actions and confessed their sin—a sign of spiritual growth.

God provided an unusual remedy (21:8–9). God instructed Moses to mold a bronze model of a deadly serpent and to place it on a pole in the middle of the camp. God promised that any person who had been bitten by the deadly snakes could survive the ordeal by looking at the bronze serpent.

There is no medicinal value in looking at a bronze image. God's promised healing is clearly miraculous in nature. The bronze serpent saved lives in Moses' time, but it was later misused by Israel.

Israel's misuse of the bronze serpent (2 Kings 18:4). When Israel traveled beyond the area of the fiery serpents, they carried the bronze image with them. It may have served at first as a reminder of the cost of sin and of the saving grace of God. But in time it became an object of worship and veneration. Later generations

Looking to the bronze serpent for healing was a call to faith in God.

burned incense to it, calling it the "Bronze Thing" (*Nehushtan*). Finally, about 700 years later, King Hezekiah had it broken in pieces. It was destroyed along with other idols that Israel was worshiping in place of the Lord.

The true symbolic significance of the bronze serpent. Nearly 1,500 years later, Christ referred to this incident reported in Numbers when speaking with Nicodemus. Jesus said, "And as Moses lifted up the serpent in the wilderness, even so must the Son of Man be lifted up, that whoever believes in him should not perish but have everlasting life" (John 3:14, 15).

There are several points of comparison between the bronze serpent and the cross. These establish the serpent's true symbolic significance.

Each symbolize both the curse and its cure. The cross in Roman times was reserved to punish the most heinous of crimes. It served as a symbol of deadly sin as well as punishment. The fiery serpent was also linked with sin and its punishment. It was through Jesus' death on the cross that eternal life was provided for humankind, and it was through the image of a death-dealing serpent that people who were bitten could be healed.

Each addressed man's helplessness. The Israelites who had been bitten by serpents were doomed. The spiritual condition of every human being is equally desperate. Sinners have no hope of avoiding what Scripture calls the "second death," or hell (Rev. 20:14; 21:8).

Each promised life. The Israelites who looked on the bronze serpent were promised life rather than death. Each human being who looks to the cross of Christ is promised eternal life.

Each offered deliverance only to those who believe. The Israelites who believed the promise of healing hurried to look at the bronze serpent when bitten. The Israelites who did not believe failed to make that journey and died. In the same way, only the person who believes

God's promise of forgiveness wrought at Calvary will respond by trusting Christ and receiving eternal life.

The bronze serpent was a matter of life and death to those who had been bitten. For later generations, the bronze serpent served as a reminder that only God can preserve life. A faith-response to him is the key to salvation.

THE MIRACLE OF BALAAM'S DONKEY   *Numbers 22:1—25:10*

Balaam was a pagan seer or prophet. He was called by a worried ruler to curse Israel as God's people approached the borders of his land. Most Bible students know the story of Balaam's donkey, who miraculously spoke to the amazed prophet. But there are actually three miracles in the story of Balaam's brief association with the people of God.

The miracle of the speaking donkey (Numbers 22:22–30). Balaam was offered riches by the anxious king if he would curse Israel. Although God warned Balaam in a dream not to go, the lure of riches was too great, and Balaam won God's reluctant permission. On the journey, God's angel stood in the path of Balaam "as an adversary."

Sensing the angel's presence, the donkey avoided the danger three times. Finally, the donkey lay down and refused to go on, saving Balaam's life. Furious, Balaam beat the donkey. Then "the Lord opened the mouth of the donkey," who told Balaam what had *really* happened, and Balaam was enabled to see the angel.

It's beside the point to argue that a donkey can't talk, or that the dialogue between the donkey and Balaam displayed reasoning beyond the capacity of any animal. What we have is a miracle—an extraordinary event caused by God with a distinct religious purpose. Balaam's experience with the donkey forced him to realize that even though he had been employed to curse Israel, he should not utter a word other than those which God commanded (see Num. 22:38).

It took a message from a donkey for Balaam to see the error of his ways.

The miraculous blessing of God's people (23:24). Three times Balaam ordered that sacrifices be made on heights from which he could see Israel's camp. Each time, rather than curse Israel, Balaam was commanded to bless them instead!

The wonder is not that God spoke through a pagan prophet. The significant thing is that in spite of Israel's constant rebellion, the Lord remained faithful in his commitment to them. That wonder is expressed in Balaam's first prophetic words:

God is not a man, that He should lie,
Nor a son of man, that He should
    repent.
Has He said, and will He not do?
Or has He spoken, and He will not
    make it good?
Behold, I have received a command
    to bless;
He has blessed, and I cannot reverse
    it.

He has not observed iniquity in
    Jacob,
Nor has He seen wickedness in Israel
    (Num. 23:19–21).

God's commitment to Israel remained unshakable. The Lord had chosen his people, and he would not change his mind ("repent"). In spite of their rebellion, God had not "observed" or "seen" it. This idiom means God has not taken Israel's iniquity into account in determining to remain faithful to his commitments. God's miracles of judgment were signs of his continuing love, not of rejection. As Scripture says,

My son, do not despise the
    chastening of the Lord,
Nor detest His correction;
For whom the Lord loves He
    corrects,
Just as a father the son in whom
    He delights (Prov. 3:11, 12).

What an important reminder to us. The discipline we experience is not an indication of divine rejection. It is a sign of God's loving commitment to us. God is determined to bless us, just as he was determined to bless ancient Israel. And God will do whatever is necessary to correct us and bring us to the place where he can truly bless.

The miracle plague on sinning Israel (Numbers 25:2–9). Balaam's blessings left the king who employed him angry and frustrated. But before leaving, Balaam suggested that the king employ young women to seduce Israelite men and draw them into idolatry (Num. 25:1, 2; compare Num. 31:16). Numbers 25:3 indicates, "So Israel was joined to Baal of Peor, and the anger of the Lord was aroused against Israel."

God again struck Israel with a plague, which killed twenty-four thousand (Num. 25:9). The plague was stopped only by the quick action of Moses. He told the leaders who served as judges within their clans to kill "every one of you his men who were joined to the Baal of Peor" (Num. 25:5).

Evidence of spiritual growth. As we review this sequence of judgment miracles, we find something lacking in the earlier miracle judgments against Israel. We find evidence of spiritual growth! God's program of discipline seemed to be working!

We noted some evidence of growth in Israel's reaction to the judgment involving fiery serpents. But in this judgment at Baal Peor—while God had to strike the people with a plague—*the people themselves took responsibility for punishing the guilty!*

In this episode, Phinehas was singled out. When he saw an Israelite man taking a Midianite woman into his tent, Phinehas entered the tent and drove his javelin through their joined bodies. For the first time, the Israelites expressed anger at the sinners who brought judgment on them. Their anger was not directed at God or Moses! What significant progress!

God had been wise in using miracles of judgment to discipline and purify his people. By the end of the 40 years of wandering, a new generation would be spiritually prepared to enter the promised land at God's command. There they would claim blessings which can be enjoyed only by those who are willing to walk hand in hand with the Lord.

MIRACLES IN DEUTERONOMY

The name *Deuteronomy* means "second law." In this great book, Moses speaks to the children of the Exodus generation, now matured and disciplined, and ready to conquer the promised land. Deuteronomy is an extended sermon, not a book of history, and it records no new miracles.

However, Deuteronomy does refer frequently to the miracles of the Exodus period. This shows how significant those miracles were in shaping Scripture's vivid picture of a God who acts on our behalf. The mighty acts God performed were stamped forever upon the memory of God's people.

For "did God ever try to go and take for himself a nation from the midst of another nation, by trials, by signs, by wonders, by war, by a mighty hand and an outstretched arm, and by great terrors, according to all that the Lord your God did for you in Egypt before your eyes? To you it was shown, that you might know that the Lord himself is God; there is none other besides him" (Deut. 4:34, 35).

CHAPTER 5

MIRACLES IN THE PROMISED LAND

DEMONSTRATIONS OF DIVINE PRESENCE

Joshua; 1 Samuel—2 Chronicles

When you are going through a dry spell spiritually, sometimes you would give anything to witness a miracle. Do we really need to see miracles to maintain our faith in God? Most of God's Old Testament people lived their entire lives without witnessing any miracles personally. Indeed, once the flurry of miracles associated with the Exodus subsided, miracles were rare.

But when the Bible hero Gideon asked an angel who visited him, "where are all His miracles which our fathers told us about," Gideon raised a question many of us want to ask.

In this chapter we check out the very few miracles which the Bible records from around 1390 B.C. to about 930 B.C. These miracles remind us that God is with His people, even when He seems silent or withdrawn.

MIRACLES IN THE BOOK OF JOSHUA

When Moses died, the Israelites were camped near the Jordan River, across from the territory that we know today as Israel. Joshua had been appointed as Moses' successor. He was to have the privilege of leading Israel in the conquest of that land promised by the Lord to Abraham and his descendants many years before (Gen. 12:7).

The main purpose of the miracles in the book of Joshua was to validate Joshua as God's new leader of Israel. They also fulfilled God's commitment to "fight for" his people (Deut. 1:30, 42; 20:4). The miracles described in Joshua are:

- The miracle crossing of the Jordan—p. 97
- The miracle fall of Jericho—p. 99
- The miracle hail—p. 100
- The miracle of the sun standing still—p. 101

THE MIRACLE CROSSING OF THE JORDAN *Joshua 3, 4*

This miracle is introduced with God's announcement to Joshua, "This day I will begin to exalt you in the sight of all Israel, that they may know that, as I was with Moses, so I will be with you" (Josh. 3:7). Joshua then called the people together, told them what was about to happen, and said "By this you shall know that the living God is among you, and that he will without fail drive out from before you the Canaanites . . . "(Josh. 3:10). The miracle crossing thus served to build the people's confidence in Joshua. But more importantly, it served notice of God's presence and his intention to assist in the conquest.

The nature of the miracle (Joshua 3:12–13). It was January, and the Jordan River was flooded by the early rains and snow melting from Mount Hermon to the north. The place where the Israelites had to cross was called the Zoar, a narrow depression about a mile wide, which was probably flourishing with plant life because of the annual floods. It would take a miracle for Israel to cross the swift river during this flood stage.

Joshua placed the priests carrying God's ark (see Ex. 25:10–33) about three thousand feet in front of the marching Israelites. When the priests' feet touched the waters, the flow from upstream stopped, while the downstream flow continued and drained the flooded river. The Israelites then safely crossed over into Canaan.

An unmistakable miracle. Some have sought a naturalistic explanation for the crossing. They have noted that several times in recorded history the Jordan's flow has been stopped when the river's high banks collapsed, damming its channel. For instance, in July 1927 a landslide near El-Damiyeh caused a stoppage of the Jordan's flow for about 21 hours. However, these stoppages did not occur during flood stage, when the river had overflowed its banks.

The biblical account makes it clear that we are to understand this as an extraordinary event caused by God for the religious purposes noted above.

- The flow stopped the instant the priests' feet touched the water (3:15, 16).
- The text emphasizes twice that Israel crossed "on dry ground" (3:17). The same word is used to describe conditions when Israel crossed the Reed Sea (Ex. 14:21).
- The water resumed its flow as soon as the priests' feet touched land on the other side of the river (Josh. 4:18).
- The inhabitants of the land recognized the event as a miracle (Josh. 5:1).

Only a miracle could have allowed the Israelites to cross over the flooded Jordan River.

The memorial heap of stones (Joshua 4:2–7). An unusual but significant feature of this miracle was a monument which Joshua ordered built from 12 stones taken from the river. The stones were to "be for a memorial to the children of Israel" (v. 7). The word for "memorial"

With the priests and the ark of the covenant leading the way, God stopped the waters of the Jordan River so Israel could cross.

is *zikkaron,* a special word used of objects or actions designed to help Israel identify with a particular truth. The Passover feast, reenacting Israel's last meal in Egypt, was also called a *zikkaron,* translated "memorial" or "remembrance." This memorial beside the Jordan River was intended to help future generations of Israelites realize that when God acted for their forefathers, he had acted for *them.*

Christian communion as observed by believers today is a *zikkaron.* This is why Jesus said "do this in *remembrance* of Me" (Luke 22:19). When we take the bread and the cup, we stand at the foot of the cross. In our mind's eye we are there, as Christ's sacrifice is made for us. Calvary is more than a historical event; it is a historical reality which echoes through the centuries. Celebrating communion is just as significant for our generation today as it was for the first followers of our Lord.

This kind of echo is what Joshua intended future generations to hear through the heap of stones. God's miracle for that generation, through which Israel entered the promised land, was performed for each succeeding generation as well.

THE MIRACLE FALL OF JERICHO
Joshua 6—8

The story of the fall of Jericho ranks with David's defeat of Goliath as one of the most familiar stories in Scripture. Jericho was a fortified city which controlled the passes leading into Canaan's central highlands. Its strategic position made its destruction essential to the conquest of Canaan.

Archaeological investigations at Jericho. Jericho has been the focus of both archaeological investigation and heated debate. An early archaeologist, Garstang, described its destruction:

The main defenses of Jericho in the Late Bronze Age (c. 1500–1200 B.C.) followed the upper bank of the city mound, and comprised two parallel walls, the outer six feet thick and the inner twelve feet thick. Investigations along the west side show continuous signs of destruction and conflagration. The outer wall suffered most, its remains falling down the slope. The inner wall is preserved only where it abuts upon the citadel, or tower, to a height of eighteen feet; elsewhere it is found largely to have fallen, together with the remains of the buildings upon it, into the space between the walls which was filled with ruins and debris. Traces of intense fire are plain to see, including reddened masses of brick, cracked stones, charred timbers and ashes. Houses alongside the wall are found burned to the ground, their roofs fallen upon the domestic pottery within.

This destruction of Jericho's tumbled walls fits the account in Joshua. But the debate has focused on the pottery found at the site. Kathleen Kenyon, a later archaeologist, argued from pottery remains that Jericho fell in the 1200's B.C. Her view was accepted for decades, and the date of the Exodus was shifted from the traditional 1400 B.C., which corresponds with biblical references to dates, to the 1200's. Bimson in recent years has reviewed the pottery data, arguing convincingly that the archaeological evidence fits the earlier date rather than the late date.

The most interesting data from archaeology, however, was summed up by Unger:

The walls were of a type which made direct assault practically impossible. An approaching enemy first encountered a stone abutment, eleven feet height, back and up from which sloped a thirty-five degree plastered scarp reaching to the main wall some 35 vertical feet above. The steep smooth slope prohibited battering the wall by any effective device or building fires to break it. An army trying to storm the wall found difficulty in climbing the slope, and ladders to scale it could find no satisfactory footing (*Archaeology and the Old Testament,* 174).

It would take a miracle to take Jericho quickly. And this is exactly what God provided.

The peculiar conditions of the miracle (Joshua 6:3–5). The Israelites were instructed by the Lord to circle the city once for six consecutive days, in complete silence. The seventh day they were to circle the city seven times, and then when the priests blew their trumpets, to shout. And, Joshua was told, when the people shout, the wall "will fall down flat" (v. 5). The Hebrew wording says "sink down to the ground."

The Israelites obeyed the strange command of Joshua, and it happened just as God had said (Josh. 6:12–16). When the wall collapsed, the Israelites rushed the city and "utterly destroyed all that was in the city" (Josh. 6:21).

Some have suggested naturalistic explanations, such as an earthquake, for the collapse of the wall. Such attempts to make the biblical account credible are unnecessary. The fall of the wall was pre-announced; it happened at the moment the people shouted; the walls fell outward—all these facts emphasize the miraculous. Jericho's wall fell because God caused it to do so; no earthquake was necessary.

An associated miracle: Rahab's deliverance (Joshua 2; 6:22–25).

Joshua had sent men earlier to scout the city. Two of them had been trapped in Jericho. Their lives had been saved by a prostitute innkeeper named Rahab. She hid them and then let them down over the city walls so they could make their escape. Rahab was convinced that God was with the Israelites, so she bargained with the two Israelites spies for her life. They promised that when Jericho fell, she and any family members found in her home would be spared.

When the walls fell, apparently that section against which Rahab's house was constructed (see Josh. 2:15) remained standing. The miracle was selective: God in his sovereignty spared Rahab's house, and she and her family were led safely out of the city (Josh. 6:22).

The book of Hebrews declares that "by faith the harlot Rahab did not perish with those who did not believe, when she had received the spies with peace" (Heb. 11:31). Even more striking is another New Testament reference to Rahab found in Matthew 3. Tracing the lineage of Jesus, Matthew reveals that "Salmon begot Boaz by Rahab, Boaz begot

Obed by Ruth, Obed begot Jesse, and Jesse begot David the king" (Matt. 1:5, 6). Rahab the prostitute, saved and transformed by her faith, was an ancestress of David, and thus of Jesus Christ.

Perhaps a greater miracle than the fall of city wall was the redemption and transformation of a human heart.

The meaning of the miracle at Jericho (Joshua 6–8).

This miracle reflects a major theme in the book of Joshua: obedience brings victory, while disobedience brings defeat.

What is striking about the events at Jericho is that there was no apparent relationship between what God told the Israelites to do and the fall of the city. No army in history has ever attacked a city by walking around it for several days. Israel might have questioned the strange command. But instead Israel obeyed—and the city fell.

We are not given the choice of which commands of God to obey, depending on whether they are reasonable or sensible. The God we have been called to serve expects us to trust him and to follow him always.

The importance of obedience is underlined by the story of Achan. When Jericho fell, Achan violated God's command. He took some of the city's treasures and hid them. When the Israelites attacked the smaller city of Ai, Israel was defeated and 38 lives were lost. God revealed to Joshua that Achan's disobedience was responsible for the defeat, and Achan was executed. With the disobedient Achan purged, God again blessed Israel with victory.

The book of Joshua is a testimony to the victories to be won by those who trust God enough to obey his Word. Our success depends on our responsiveness to the will of our God.

THE MIRACLE HAIL
Joshua 10:10, 11

In a battle with a coalition of Canaanite kings "the Lord routed them . . . with a great slaughter." As the Israelites pursued, "the Lord cast down large hailstones from heaven on them as far as Azekah, and they died. There were more who died from the hailstones than the children of Israel killed with the sword."

No natural event. The Jewish sage Malbim, paraphrased by Rabbi Reuven Drucker in his commentary on the book of Joshua, observed:

The fact that hailstones descended from heaven and killed people could be construed as a natural event. In this case, however, it was clearly miraculous, because the hailstones killed only Emorites, not the Israelites who were following in close pursuit (p. 247).

An interesting Jewish Midrash [interpretation], noting that the text has the definite article—*"the* hailstones"—suggests that these were hailstones left over from the killing hail which fell on Egypt (Ex. 9:33). The event was clearly a miracle, fulfilling God's promise in Deuteronomy 20:4, "the LORD your God is He who goes with you, to fight for you against your enemies, to save you."

THE MIRACLE OF THE SUN STANDING STILL   *Joshua 10:12–14*

This brief miracle report is unique in Scripture. It seems to describe a major suspension of natural law. As the Israelites pursued the fleeing enemy, it appeared night would fall before final victory could be achieved. Joshua called on the sun and moon to stand still until the enemy army was wiped out. The text says,

So the sun stood still in the midst of heaven, and did not hasten to go down for about a whole day. And there has been no day like that, before it or after it, that the Lord heeded the voice of a man; for the Lord fought for Israel (Josh. 10:13, 14).

The nature of the miracle. Many commentators have debated the nature of this miracle. Is the description phenomenological? That is, does the text describe what Joshua and the Israelites *saw?* If so, God may have performed a *local* miracle, causing the sun's light to shine on Israel while the rest of the world experienced normal day and night. Or does the text make a *scientific* statement? If so, God may

have halted the earth's rotation, with all the adjustments this would have required. In either case, the prolongation of daylight was a miracle.

The real uniqueness of the miracle (10:14). In commenting on this miracle, the text says, "There has been no day like that, before it or after it." But what made the day unique was not the extension of daylight. The true wonder is "that the LORD heeded the voice of a man."

Normally God informs human beings that a miracle will take place. But Joshua himself "invented" and asked for this miracle! And God did as Joshua asked.

Some have assumed that it takes faith to believe in miracles. But whatever faith belief in miracles may require is overshadowed by the faith that Joshua exhibited. Of all the unchangeable things we know, the motion of the earth around the sun is perhaps the most regular. Day follows night without interruption. All our experience leads us to expect that this cycle will go on unchanged through our lifetime and beyond. Yet Joshua called on the Lord to halt the sun and moon until final victory could be won. And God did.

We're sometimes told that God has gone out of the miracle business. Certainly the kind of miracles that God performed in the Exodus age have not been repeated. But there are private as well as public miracles. The God who answered Joshua's prayer can and does answer our prayers. And if the request we make is for an extraordinary intervention by God on our behalf, we need to have the faith that Joshua demonstrated.

MIRACLES IN THE BOOK OF JUDGES

The book of Judges sketches critical events during the 400-year period between the conquest of Canaan and the emergence of the Hebrew monarchy. As story follows story, a common pattern emerges.

The Israelites turned away from God to worship pagan deities. God then permitted a neighboring people to oppress them. In desperation, the Israelites returned and appealed to the Lord. God then raised up a judge—a military-political-religious leader—who defeated the enemy and initiated a time of peace. After the judge died, the people again turned to idolatry—and the cycle begins all over again.

Many stories from the book of Judges are well known. We're familiar with Deborah, the first woman judge; and with Samson, Israel's strong man. Some extraordinary events took place during these years, such as Samson's pushing down the support pillars of the Philistine temple at Gath. But most do not fit our definition of a miracle.

In fact, the miracles that occur in the book of Judges are what we might call "private miracles." They were given to strengthen individuals rather than sent as a public witness of God's presence to Israel and its enemies. Aside from the angel appearance to the parents of Samson (Judg 13:9–23; see *Every Good and Evil Angel in the Bible*), the one report of unmistakable miracles involves Gideon.

Gideon the skeptic (Judges 6:12–16).

An angel, apparently in the guise of an ordinary traveler, appeared to Gideon and announced, "The Lord is with you." Gideon was not impressed. "If the Lord is with us," he responded, "why then has all this happened to us? And where are all his miracles which our fathers told us about?"

The angel responded by informing Gideon that he was to be God's chosen instrument to defeat the Midianite raiders. These robbers or thieves appeared at harvest time, stripping the land of its crops. Although the angel promised Gideon "I will be with you, and you shall defeat the Midianites" (v. 16), Gideon remained skeptical.

Gideon asked for a "sign" (6:17).

The Hebrew word used by Gideon is *'ot*. This word, found only here in the book of Judges, means a "miraculous sign"—something that is unmistakably the work of God. The text goes on to relate three signs that the Lord provided. The first authenticated the original message,

and the second and third strengthened Gideon's budding faith.

The rock-fire (6:19–21). In the tradition of hospitality, Gideon prepared a meal for his visitor. The angel asked Gideon to place the food on a rock. When the angel touched the food with the end of his staff, "fire rose out of the rock" and burned the offering. Then the angel disappeared.

Gideon was convinced. When the Lord told him to tear down the community's idolatrous worship center, Gideon did so, in spite of his fears (Judg. 6:25–27). When the Midianites approached, Gideon also sent messengers throughout the nearby tribes to assemble an army.

But Gideon was still hesitant and afraid.

Putting out the fleece (6:36–38). Gideon asked God to reassure him by another private miracle. Gideon put out a fleece, a piece of wool cut from a sheep. If the ground was dry in the morning and the fleece was wet with dew, Gideon would know God was with him. It happened just as Gideon asked.

Gideon used a fleece to gain reassurance.

Putting out the fleece again (6:39–40). Gideon approached the Lord and begged for further confirmation. This time he asked that the fleece be dry and the ground all around wet with dew. Again it happened as Gideon asked.

Reassured, Gideon set out to battle the Midianites.

Should we ask for confirming miracles today?
Some have seen the experience of Gideon as a model for today. When faced with a significant decision, they think they should ask for a confirming "miracle," just to be sure that a specific choice is God's will. Typically the miracle requested is minor, and it's impossible to distinguish it from mere chance: "If I'm supposed to go, Lord, let my sister call me in the next ten minutes." While God can certainly influence one's sister, this "miracle" is hardly to be classed with the signs granted to Gideon. A phone call may be nothing but a coincidence; wet fleece on dry ground cannot.

Notice that Gideon's obedience to the will of God did not *depend on* the miracles of the fleece. As soon as Gideon realized that God was commanding him, he chose to obey. Long before setting out the fleece, Gideon tore down the local worship center and called for the men of Israel to assemble. He *acted before he was given the sign, not afterward.*

The miracle of the fleece was a gracious reassurance granted by God to a man who already trusted him enough to act on his word.

In living out our relationship with the Lord, we are not to try to find the will of God by "putting out the fleece." What we are to do is to seek God's will. Once we sense what his will is, we are to act on it. God has given us his Word, the Holy Spirit, and our fellow believers to help us find our way. We do not have to rely on "putting out the fleece" to determine what God wants us to do.

MIRACLES OF THE BOOKS OF 1, 2 SAMUEL; *1 Kings 1—13; 1 Chronicles; and 2 Chronicles 1—9*

These portions of the Old Testament tell the story of Israel's transformation from loosely associated tribes into a powerful and united monarchy under David and Solomon. The events reported in these books cover a period of about 120 years—between 1050 B.C. and 930 B.C. The chart below shows the relationship of the books to one another and to key figures.

Each miracle in these books is associated with worship. In the extraordinary events of this era, the Lord emphasized to Israel the importance of focusing on him.

It is perhaps no wonder then that Israel's greatest king, David—who forged the powerful and united nation that Israel became—was so deeply committed to worshiping the Lord. We see this reflected in the many stories which emphasize David's sensitivity to the Lord. This is also evident in the Psalms, Israel's prayer book. A total of 73 of the 150 psalms in this book bear the superscription, "a psalm of David."

c.1050	c.1010	970	930
1 Samuel	2 Samuel	1 Kings 1–13	
	1 Chronicles	2 Chronicles 1–9	
Samuel _____ .			
Saul _____ .			
	David _____ .		
		Solomon _____ .	

Miracle reports (chapters)

1 Sam. 5, 6	2 Sam. 6	1 Kings 8; 12;
	1 Chron. 13	2 Chron. 7

A warrior and military strategist, David was also a consummate politician. He was an organizational genius who created a system for the administration of the new nation as well as a gifted musician and poet. But perhaps more than anything else, David was a man who loved and worshiped God. He related every experience of life to the God whom he knew was present with him.

The message of the miracles of this era—that we must put God first and do so on his own terms—was enfleshed in David. The heart of this shepherd boy who became a king remained focused on the Lord in spite of his personal flaws.

The miracles reported in these Scriptures are:

1. The miracle of Dagon's fall.—p. 104
2. The miracle of the tumors.—p. 105
3. The miracle return of the ark.—p. 106
4. The miracle judgment on Israel.—p. 106
5. The miracle on the ark's journey to Jerusalem.—p. 107
6. The miracle of the shekinah.—p. 109
7. The miracle judgment on Jeroboam.—p. 110

THE MIRACLE OF DAGON'S FALL
1 Samuel 5:1–5

Young Samuel had just been recognized as a prophet when the Israelites chose to rebel against the dominating Philistine army. On the first day of battle the Israelites were defeated. In desperation, the despondent Israelites sent

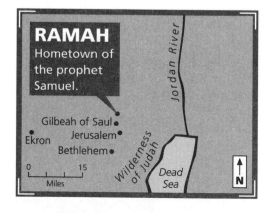

RAMAH
Hometown of the prophet Samuel.

Gilbeah of Saul
Ekron   Jerusalem
Bethlehem

Jordan River

Wilderness of Judah

Dead Sea

0   15
Miles

N

two corrupt priests to bring the ark of the covenant to their camp (1 Sam. 4:1–10).

The significance of the holy ark. The ark of the covenant had been constructed in the time of Moses. Considered the most holy object in Israel's religion (Ex. 25), the ark was a portable chest which contained the Ten Commandments God had engraved in stone, a jar of manna, and Aaron's rod. The lid featured the figures of two angels, bending over a spot where once a year on the Day of Atonement sacrificial blood was poured by the High Priest (Lev. 16).

Most significantly, the ark was the place where God and man met in restored harmony on the great Day of Atonement. Thus the ark symbolized the presence of God with his people.

Why the Israelites sent for the ark (1 Samuel 4:3). The thinking of the Israelites is clear in this verse. They said, "Let us bring the ark . . . that when it comes among us *it may save us* from the hand of our enemies."

The verse displays a corruption of Israel's faith by pagan notions. The peoples surrounding the Israelites thought of their pagan idols as *real*. To them, an idol was a nexus at which the deity was present. The Egyptians even "fed" their idols, gave them baths, changed their clothes, and treated them as if the god which the idol represented were present in the image.

What the Israelites had fallen into believing, according to this verse, was that God would *have* to be present if they had the ark. With the ark, they could expect God to fight for Israel against the Philistines. Bringing the ark into the camp was an attempt to manipulate God!

The Philistines shared the Israelites' magical view, and they were terrified when they realized the ark of the God who had struck the Egyptians was in Israel's camp. They determined to fight the next day, fully expecting to lose (1 Sam. 4:7–9).

But the next day the Philistines won the battle—and the ark of God was captured. The

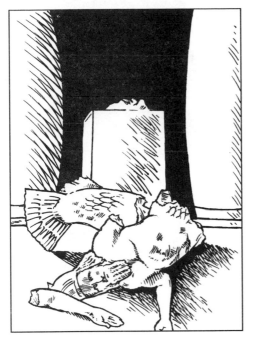

The Philistine statue of Dagon mysteriously fell down when the ark was placed beside it.

capture was the first in a series of events which would shift the eyes of Israel from the ark to the invisible God whom it represented.

A dangerous trophy (1 Samuel 5:1–5). Following ancient custom, the Philistines placed the ark of the Lord as a trophy in the temple of their god, Dagon. There it would represent the "capture" of Israel's God by their own deity, testifying to Dagon's superiority.

The morning after the ark was placed in the temple, the Philistine priests were shocked to find that the statue of Dagon had fallen on its face before the ark of God (1 Sam. 5:3). The priests propped up their deity and braced it so the idol couldn't fall. But the next morning they found the statue of Dagon again on its face, with its head and hands broken off! (1 Sam. 5:4).

The event was recognized as a miracle, indicating that Israel's God was greater than the Philistine god Dagon.

How strange that those who acknowledge the greatness of the Lord would think he can be manipulated to serve human ends. God is no magic lamp that we rub when we want a need met, nor is he a talisman that we affix to the dashboard of our cars. Our God is the Creator of the universe, the miracle-working God who is free to act in any situation as he wills.

This first of the miracles associated with the ark began a healthy shift of focus from objects representing God to the one supreme Lord behind the objects. This was a concept Israel would need desperately if the Lord was to build a nation which would reflect his glory to all the world.

THE MIRACLE OF THE TUMORS
1 Samuel 5:6—6:6

The story of the captured ark continues with the report of an epidemic. The ark was carried to the Philistine city of Ashdod. While it was there, the Lord "ravaged them and struck them with tumors, both Ashdod and its territory."

The nature of the miracle (1 Samuel 5:6). The tumors were probably inflamed swellings of the lymph glands that are characteristic of bubonic plague. This view is supported by two facts. The tumors brought "very great destruction" (1 Sam. 5:9, 11), and the outbreak was associated with rats—carriers of the plague in ancient as well as medieval times (1 Sam. 6:4).

The response of the Philistines (5:7–12). The people of Ashdod realized that the plague was God's judgment on them and their God (1 Sam. 5:7). The leaders decided to send the ark to Gath, another of the five principle Philistine cities. But when the ark reached Gath, the plague broke out there as well. The ark was then taken to Ekron, and again the plague followed. At this point, the people no longer asked their leaders what to do. They demanded, "Send away the ark of the God of Israel, and let it go back to its own place, so that it does not kill us and our people" (1 Sam. 5:11).

The marks of a miracle. We have defined miracles in this study as extraordinary events caused by God with a religious purpose. While bubonic plague has natural causes, this outbreak was extraordinary. It occurred only where the ark of God rested. When the ark was moved, the plague followed. The Philistines concluded from the evidence that Israel's God was the cause of their distress.

The purpose of this miracle is also clear: God was judging Dagon as he had judged the gods of Egypt (Ex. 12:12). Through these plagues, God was forcing the Philistines to return the ark to Israel so it could continue its vital role in the religion of God's people.

What Israel had seen as a terrible defeat for the Lord—the capture of the ark of the covenant—had become an occasion for the Lord to display his power. What an important truth this is to remember when we experience defeats. God can use our setbacks and weaknesses to display his power and remind us of his loving presence.

THE MIRACLE RETURN OF THE ARK   *1 Samuel 6:7–16*

The Philistine leaders were willing to return the ark to Israel, along with golden tumors and golden rats that represented a "trespass offering." They remembered how Pharaoh had hardened his heart, causing the entire land of Egypt to be ravaged. So the Philistines determined not to resist Israel's God (1 Sam. 6:6). At the same time, they wanted to be sure the Lord had been the cause of the plague. The next miracle was God's response to a test devised by the Philistines.

The nature of the miracle (1 Samuel 6:7, 12). Every farmer knows about the patterning behavior of cows. When brought in at night, a cow will go to its own stall. If placed in a strange stall, it will show extreme distress. Cows will also stay close to their calves when their offspring are young and still suckling.

The Philistines also recognized these traits. They placed the ark on a cart, with their trespass offering, and hitched two milk cows

which had young calves to the cart. Acting against their nature, and lowing in complaint all the way (1 Sam. 6:12), the cows left their calves and familiar territory and set out along the road to Beth Shemesh, in Israelite territory.

The Philistine leaders followed, watching as the ark was returned to Israelite hands. Then they returned home, no doubt in great relief.

THE MIRACLE JUDGMENT ON ISRAEL   *1 Samuel 6:19–21*

When the ark was returned to Beth-Shemesh, many of the curious Israelites peered at it and even looked inside. God struck the curious dead, creating terror among the people. They exclaimed, "Who is able to stand before this holy LORD God."

The nature of the miracle (1 Samuel 6:19). These sudden deaths were clearly caused by their gathering around the ark to look inside. The cause-and-effect link was so clearly established that the observers had no doubt the multiple deaths were a miracle—an extraordinary event caused by God himself.

The number of those who died was seventy—not 50,070, as translated by the King James Version. Hebrew numbers are difficult to read. Rather than use numbers, the Hebrews used letters of the alphabet. Thus *aleph* ["a"] was one, *bet* ["be"] was two, and so on. Tiny marks were then written above them to represent multiples of ten. As manuscripts aged or were copied, it was easy to mistake the original number. As the NKJV footnote indicates, it is best to understand the text to say that seventy men died because they looked into the ark of God.

Why God struck the Israelites dead. As the most holy object in Israel's religion, the ark represented the meeting of God with man. The cover of the ark was the place where sacrificial blood was poured on the annual Day of Atonement. The message was clear. Sinful man could meet with a holy God only through sacrifice. The ark may be interpreted as a symbol of the Cross of Christ, where Jesus shed his blood to make peace between mankind and God by offering himself as full payment for our sins.

Exodus 40:20–21 relates how the ark was placed in the tabernacle, concealed behind a curtain and partitioned off so that even the priests who ministered in the tabernacle would not be able to see it. When being carried by the Levites, the ark was to be covered by the veil that concealed it from the eyes of the priests (Num. 4:5). Numbers 4:20 warned that even the Levites, who carried the tabernacle and its contents during the wilderness journey, "shall not go in to watch while the holy things are being covered, lest they die." What the Israelites did at Beth-Shemesh was to show a lack of respect or reverence for God by treating the ark as a common object.

The results of the miracle (6:20). The impact of the miracle was immediate. The Israelites were awed and impressed at the power of "this holy LORD God." The disrespect they had shown for the things of the Lord was replaced by an awed realization that God is holy and that he must be approached with deep respect.

The people of Beth-Shemesh were also uncomfortable in the presence of such a God, so the ark was moved about nine miles away. It was sheltered at Kirjah Jearim for the next 20 years.

1 Samuel 7:2 indicates that during this time all Israel "lamented after God." The Hebrew words read, "Went into mourning toward God." The idiom means that, at last, Israel wept in repentance. At last the Israelites realized they needed a revitalized relationship with the Lord.

Then Samuel challenged Israel to put away every idol promising that a return to the Lord would mean deliverance from Philistine domination. Israel did return. After a great revival meeting at which the people fasted and confessed their sins, Israel won a decisive victory over the Philistines at Mizpah (1 Sam. 7:4–14).

The significance of the miracles of the captured ark. The four miracles reported in 1 Samuel 5—6 were not isolated incidents. Each contributed to a vital message which Israel needed to hear. The miracles in Philistia revealed the power of Israel's God and his superiority to the deities of Israel's oppressors. The miracle at Beth-Shemesh reaffirmed the holiness of Israel's God, and the importance of treating the Lord with appropriate respect.

Once Israel grasped these two vital messages—that Yahweh, the God who is present with his people, was both powerful and holy—a radical change was gradually worked in their hearts. When at last confession and recommitment restored their relationship with the Lord, Yahweh again acted for them. The enemy was defeated, and the land had peace throughout Samuel's judgeship.

It's the same for us today. Our God is present with us. He is powerful and holy. When by confession and recommitment we live in intimate relationship with the Lord, he will act for us. And we will also know peace.

THE MIRACLE ON THE WAY TO JERUSALEM   *2 Samuel 6*

The next miracle recorded in the historical books occured during the reign of David. This miracle also involved the ark of God.

David unified the nation, establishing Jerusalem as his capital. Deeply aware of the role God must play in the life of his people, he intended to make Jerusalem a center for the worship of Yahweh as well as the political center of the nation. David in later years would revitalize worship by organizing the priests and Levites to serve God, by reviving the religious festivals ordained in the Pentateuch, and by writing many of the songs and hymns used in public worship.

David realized that his first step must be to bring the ark of God to Jerusalem. But as the ark was being transported to Jerusalem, a young man named Uzzah reached out to steady it. The moment he touched the ark, Uzzah was struck dead.

When Uzzah touched the ark to steady it on the cart, he was struck dead.

Why did Uzzah die? (Exodus 25:10–14). According to instructions given to Moses, the ark was not to be touched by anyone. It was originally constructed with a ring at each of its four corners. Moses was told by the Lord that "you shall put the poles into the rings on the sides of the ark, that the ark may be *carried* by them" (Ex. 25:14).

But David had the ark placed on a cart for transport. When the cart tipped and Uzzah reached out to steady it, he accidentally touched the ark—and died.

David's initial reaction (2 Samuel 6:8, 9). The death of Uzzah both angered and terrified David. Why would the Lord do such a thing? Uzzah had only been trying to save the ark, and David's motives in transporting it to Jerusalem were pure.

But David had either ignored God's instructions for moving the ark, or he had failed to consult the Scriptures. In either case, the mode of transport conveyed a disrespect for the Lord that could not be tolerated if the new nation was to experience his blessing. The death of Uzzah again emphasized the holiness of Israel's God and the necessity of carefully seeking his will in every situation.

The ark arrived in Jerusalem at last (6:12–13). David left the ark at the house of a man named Obed-Edom, near the place where Uzzah had died. God uniquely blessed Obed-Edom during this period, so David concluded it was safe to bring the ark to Jerusalem as he had planned. This time David consulted Scripture to make sure he transported the ark according to its instructions (v. 13).

David and his people learned anew the lesson which Israel had experienced in Samuel's time. If we are to walk with God, we must treat him as holy and seek his will in every situation.

God was with David all the days of his life. In his 40-year reign, the territory controlled by Israel was multiplied ten times. For the first time, God's people possessed most of the land promised to Abraham's descendants (Gen. 12:7).

THE MIRACLE OF THE SHEKINAH   *1 Kings 6:19–21; 2 Chronicles 7:1–3*

David had dreamed of building a temple for the Lord in Jerusalem. But the Lord told David that his son Solomon would build the temple. David's last years were spend assembling materials for this great project, drawing plans and outlining the responsibilities of the priests and Levites who would serve at the temple (1 Chron. 22—29).

When David died and Solomon succeeded his father, the new king set about building the temple. It took seven years. Solomon himself led the service of dedication.

Solomon's dedicatory prayer (2 Chronicles 6:13). Pagan peoples viewed their temples as the "house" of their deities. This was where their gods lived. Solomon knew this would not be true of the Lord. He prayed,

But will God indeed dwell with men on the earth? Behold, heaven and the heaven of heavens cannot contain You. How much less this temple which I have built! (2 Chron. 6:18).

What Solomon asked was that God's "eyes may be open toward this temple," and that the Lord would answer prayers addressed to him by his people.

The miracle response (1 Kings 8:10, 11; 2 Chron. 7:1–3). Chronicles describes God's miracle response at the Temple's dedication.

When Solomon had finished praying, fire came down from heaven and consumed the burnt offering and the sacrifices; and the glory of the Lord filled the temple. And the priests could not enter the house of the Lord, because the glory of the Lord had filled the Lord's house (2 Chron. 7:1–3).

This "glory" of the Lord was the shekinah, a bright, visible expression of the very presence of God. This was an unmistakable miracle, an extraordinary event caused by God. But the appearance of the shekinah was not a unique event. It had happened before!

The glory of the Lord had appeared atop Mount Sinai in the time of Moses (Ex. 16:10; 24:16). It had filled the tabernacle when that worship center was dedicated (Ex. 40:34, 35). Ezekiel 43:4, 5 spoke of God's glory filling a yet-future Jerusalem temple. Both Isaiah 40:5 and Habakkuk 2:14 looked forward to history's end, when the whole world will be filled with his glory.

The meaning of this miracle was recognized immediately by all Israel. God was present with them. And he would answer their prayers.

The response of Israel to the miracle (2 Chronicles 7:3). Israel's response is described in this verse:

When all the children of Israel saw how the fire came down, and the glory of the Lord on the temple, they bowed their faces to the ground on the pavement, and worshiped and praised the LORD, saying:

"For He is good,
For His mercy endures forever."

Comparisons and contrasts with the miracles involving the ark of God. Like the other miracles in this sequence, this wonder drew attention to worship. When Solomon offered his prayer, the ark of the covenant rested in the temple, isolated in the Holy of Holies. Unlike the other miracles, which reflected Israel's failure to honor and respect the Lord, this miracle recognized Israel's commitment to him, demonstrated by construction of the temple. The earlier miracles, by which sins were judged and exposed, stimulated awe but also terror. This miracle, which recognized Israel's dedication to the Lord, also created awe. But now praise replaced fear, as all Israel realized that "He is good" and that "His mercy endures forever."

This is a good reminder for us. God intends to reveal himself to us. If we ignore him, his revelation may take the form of judgment. If we honor him and respond to his word as the ultimate reality, God will bless us and fill our lives with rejoicing.

THE MIRACLE JUDGMENT ON JEROBOAM   *1 Kings 12:25—13:6*

Solomon ruled Israel for forty years. Toward the end of his reign, he turned away from the Lord. The people had also begun to worship pagan deities (1 Kings 11:33). As a judgment, the united kingdom of David and Solomon was divided, into north and south.

The ruler of the new Northern Kingdom, which retained the name *Israel*, was Jeroboam. He was a competent man who had been one of Solomon's officials. God informed Jeroboam through the prophet Ahijah what he would do. He also promised Jeroboam that if he would be faithful to the Lord and keep his commandments, Jeroboam's dynasty would last (1 Kings 11:38).

But when Ahijah's prophecy came true, Jeroboam worried. He was afraid to let his people go up to Jerusalem each year to worship and celebrate the religious festivals which God had ordained. Jeroboam feared that shared worship would affirm the common bond between north and south, leading his people to demand reunification.

Jeroboam's sinful solution (1 Kings 12:25, 26). When he was confirmed as king, Jeroboam instituted a counterfeit religious system. This system was modeled on that revealed by Moses, but it was significantly different.

Jeroboam established two worship centers to serve as rivals to the temple in Jerusalem. He cast two metal bulls for these worship centers. The bulls did not represent Yahweh, but they replaced the ark. The bulls were intended to symbolize the presence of the Lord. The Israelites were to imagine God's presence as resting on the back of these idols.

Jeroboam also ordained ordinary men as priests rather than limit this office to the descendants of Aaron. He instituted a system of sacrifices. Jeroboam established religious festivals, but he directed that they be observed at different times than the Mosaic festivals.

We have already noted that God struck seventy men dead for peeking into the ark and struck Uzzah dead for touching it. This shows what a great sin Jeroboam's deliberate violation of God's Word truly was.

The miracle judgment (1 Kings 13:1–4). On the day Jeroboam dedicated his worship center at Bethel, God sent a young prophet to confront the king. The prophet cursed the altar and predicted its future destruction. The text indicates that the young prophet "gave a sign the same day."

The word for "sign" in this passage is *maasheh,* which is used to identify an unmistakable work of God (see p. 21). It might not have been miraculous for a newly constructed altar to split apart and for its ashes to pour out. But when this happened immediately following a prediction by a man who claimed to be speaking for God, it must be considered a miracle.

Jeroboam's reaction led to a further miracle (1 Kings 13:4). Furious, Jeroboam pointed at the young prophet and demanded, "Arrest him!" The text says, "Then his hand, which he stretched out toward him, withered, so that he could not pull it back to himself." Convinced now and frightened, Jeroboam begged the young prophet to pray that his hand be restored. In answer to this prayer, it was restored, "and became as before" (1 Kings 13:6). The humbled ruler offered to reward the prophet. But Jeroboam was not dissuaded from his intention to establish counterfeit worship in Israel.

The fate of the young prophet (1 Kings 13:11–30). The next event contributes to our understanding of the message of this miracle. God told the young prophet not to eat or drink while in the north. But an old prophet who lived nearby lied and said that the Lord had told *him* to give the younger man a meal. The young prophet took the older man's word and violated God's command. On leaving, he was met and killed by a lion.

When Jereboam set up an alternate worship center, God sent a prophet to confront him.

The implications are profound. The young prophet died because he accepted man's word, which contradicted what he knew to be God's word. Jeroboam had done far worse. If the Israelites adopted the worship system established by the king, they would also be honoring man's word and rejecting the clear Word of God. If the young prophet did not escape the consequences of his failure to honor the Lord's word, how much more severe would Israel's punishment be for participating in counterfeit worship?

The message of the miracle was taken to heart by some. Second Chronicles 11:16 indicates that the priests and Levites in Israel moved to the south, and that "those from all the tribes of Israel, such as set their heart to seek the LORD God of Israel, came to Jerusalem to sacrifice to the LORD God of their fathers." This shift of population weakened Israel, and made "the son of Solomon strong" as long as he honored God as David had.

The miracle sequence. The miracles in the books of Samuel and the first half of 1 Kings and 2 Chronicles are clustered around the ark of the covenant. They served to rebuke God's people for treating him lightly and to underline the twin themes of God's power and his holiness.

When Israel took these miracles to heart and honored God by obeying his Word, the nation prospered. It could be that the lessons learned in the time of Samuel and in David's early rule were the key to the rise of the united kingdom. Awareness of God's power and his holiness was also the foundation for Israel's prosperity during the early years of Solomon.

But God's people did not continue to live with an awareness of the Lord's power and holiness. In Solomon's later years, both king and people turned to idolatry. The united kingdom was torn in two, and the untrusting Jeroboam chose to ignore God's promise and to disobey his word. The last miracle in this sequence confirmed the message contained in the earlier miracles. God is both powerful and holy. And those who will not honor him will bear the consequences of their sins.

May we learn from the miracles of the ark to honor God in our own lives. And to act always in full awareness that our God is powerful. And that our God is holy. Such a God is to be held in awe. And to be obeyed.

CHAPTER 6

THE MIRACLE MINISTRY OF ELIJAH

GOD'S CHAMPION AGAINST BAAL

1 Kings 17—2 Kings 2

Some marriages seem made in heaven. The union of King Ahab of Israel and Jezebel of Phoenicia seemed made in hell.

The two set out together to exterminate God's prophets and brought hundreds of pagan prophets of Baal and his consort Asherah into the northern Hebrew kingdom, Israel. They intended to replace Yahweh with Baal as the official god of the nation.

A single, bold figure stood up against the evil king and his pagan queen. At this critical moment in sacred history, God raised up the prophet Elijah, and through Elijah God performed a series of miracles which demonstrated conclusively that the Lord, not Baal, was the true and only God.

The Recorded Miracles of Elijah

1. Elijah stops the rains.—p. 112
2. Elijah multiplies a widow's food.—p. 113
3. Elijah restores the widow's son.—p. 114
4. Elijah calls down fire at Carmel.—p. 115
5. Elijah restores the rains.—p. 118
6. Elijah calls down fire on soldiers.—p. 119
7. Elijah divides the Jordan's waters.—p. 120

ELIJAH STOPS THE RAINS *1 Kings 17:1–8*

King Ahab is introduced in 1 Kings 16. Verses 30–33 sum up his character and career.

Now Ahab the son of Omri did evil in the sight of the Lord, more than all who were before him. And it came to pass, as though it had been a trivial thing for him to walk in the sins of Jeroboam the son of Nebat, that he took as wife Jezebel the daughter of Ethbaal, king of the Sidonians; and he went and served Baal and worshiped him. Then he set up an altar for Baal in the temple of Baal, which he had built in Samaria. And Ahab made a wooden image. Ahab did more to provoke the Lord God of Israel to anger than all the kings of Israel who were before him.

Elijah the prophet. Elijah is one of the most striking figures in the Old Testament. Second Kings 1:8 describes him as a hairy man wearing a leather belt. The name *Elijah* means "Yahweh is God," so his name sums up his mission. Elijah was called to proclaim to Israel that Yahweh was the true God and to turn back the tide of Baalism that threatened to sweep the nation. All of Elijah's miracles demonstrated the truth that "Yahweh is God."

Elijah announced a drought (1 Kings 17:1). Elijah did not warn Ahab of the coming drought or give him a chance to repent. The king was committed to evil, and he was rapidly leading his people to a commitment to Baal. It would take a dramatic miracle to make Ahab pay attention to any prophet of the Lord.

So at God's leading Elijah sought out Ahab and announced, "As the Lord God of Israel lives, before whom I stand, there shall not be dew nor rain these years, except at my word."

"As the LORD *God of Israel lives."* To Ahab, the name *Yahweh* was an empty term, a word which he could safely ignore. It was "Baal" who seemed real to Ahab. Elijah announced the miracle as proof that "the Lord God of Israel lives." Only a God who was real could cause a drought at the word of one of his prophets—or bring rain at that prophet's word. Ahab and all Israel needed unmistakable evidence that Yahweh lived.

"Not be dew nor rain." This particular judgment was doubly significant. First, drought was to be one of the consequences of abandoning the Lord, a fact which Moses had spelled out for Israel in Deuteronomy 28. That passage warned, "Your heavens which are over your head shall be bronze, and the earth which is under you shall be iron. The LORD will change the rain of your land to powder and dust; from the heaven it shall come down on you until you are destroyed" (28:23–24).

Second, and more significantly, Baal was a nature god. He was viewed as god of the storm. One of his responsibilities was to provide rains and maintain the fertility of the land. The drought which would prove that God lives would also prove the impotence of Baal, challenging the king's claim that Baal was the deity on whom Israel could rely.

In New Testament times, Jesus revealed that this drought announced by Elijah lasted for three and a half years and that "there was a great famine throughout all the land" (Luke 4:25). God's power over the elements supposedly controlled by Baal was made plain.

"Except at my word." Droughts are natural happenings. But a drought that comes and goes at the command of a man is not natural. Such a drought is an extraordinary event, and Elijah declared it was caused by God. Its purpose was to demonstrate the power and presence of Israel's living God.

Miracles and the miraculous (1 Kings 17:2–7). After making his announcement, Elijah hid. God directed him to a brook that flowed into the Jordan River. In this location, "ravens brought him bread and meat in the morning, and bread and meat in the evening" (1 Kings 17:6). This was not a miracle performed *by* Elijah—but God's miraculous intervention *for* Elijah.

The drought affected the whole land and brought terrible suffering. But God took care of his faithful prophet.

ELIJAH MULTIPLIES A WIDOW'S FOOD   *1 Kings 17:8–16*

As the drought worsened, the brook where Elijah was staying dried up. God then sent him to the home of a widow in Zarephath.

The irony of the location (1 Kings 17:9). The city of Zarephath was in Sidon, a territory ruled by the father of Ahab's wife Jezebel. This was the land from which the pagan missionaries intent on turning Israel to the worship of Baal had been recruited!

While Israel suffered from the drought, Elijah would be safe in the homeland of his persecutors. What an echo of Psalm 23:5, "You prepare a table before me in the presence of my enemies." God had thrown his protective mantle over Elijah; he was safe in the land of his enemies.

The widow and her situation (17:10–12). When Elijah arrived in Zarephath, he found a widow who was about to prepare the last remaining food in her house. The drought which struck Israel had also affected surrounding nations. There was no one to whom she could appeal for food when the little amount she had was gone (see 1 Kings 17:14). The widow was destitute and on the verge of starvation.

It is interesting that the widow recognized Elijah as a prophet. But her words, "As the LORD your God lives," are best understood as a polite greeting rather than an indication that she believed in Yahweh (see 1 Kings 17:24).

The woman's amazing faith (17:13–15). When the widow told Elijah of her desperate situation, the prophet directed her to feed *him* first, and only then feed herself and her son. The prophet also promised in the name of the Lord God of Israel that "the bin of flour shall not be used up, nor shall the jar of oil run dry until the day the Lord sends rain on the earth" (1 Kings 17:14).

In one way, it is amazing that the woman did as Elijah asked. On the other hand, she really had little choice. If she kept the last of the food for herself, she and her son would surely starve. If she did as Elijah said and God *did* maintain their food supply, they would live. Facing the options of certain death versus possible life, the widow made the wisest choice.

❖

Elijah promised the widow's flour and oil supply would not run out.

It is strange how few people today show similar wisdom. Many who are introduced to the gospel, which promises eternal life, are unwilling to *listen.* How important in life-or-death issues to listen when someone speaks in the name of the Lord!

The widow made her choice, and "did according to the word of Elijah." Her risk of faith was rewarded, and "she and he and her household ate for many days."

Again, God demonstrated his power as well as his gracious provision for those who place their faith in him.

ELIJAH RESTORES THE WIDOW'S SON   *1 Kings 17:17–24*

While Elijah was staying with the widow, her son died. The widow confronted the prophet, who took him to the upper room where he was lodging and prayed for his restoration. The Lord answered Elijah's prayer, and the prophet took the living boy downstairs and presented him to his mother.

The widow's bitter words (1 Kings 17:17, 18). We can understand the widow's anguish. Had God preserved her family from the drought, only to take her son? Was God the kind of person who gives with one hand while taking away with the other?

But the widow also blamed herself as well as God. This is shown in her words, "Have you come to me to bring my sin to remembrance, and to kill my son?" The word "remember" has a distinct connotation in the Hebrew language. She impled that Elijah's presence drew God's attention to her as a sinner and that he remembered her sins and acted appropriately in taking her son.

People who do not know the Lord sometimes assume their tragedies are divine punishment. But the widow was about to learn that her tragedy would become an occasion for God to display his power and grace.

Elijah's prayer (17:19–21). Elijah questioned God's permitting the boy to die. But he also prayed that the child's life would be restored.

His prayer was answered and the child revived.

"Have You also brought tragedy?" Like the widow, Elijah struggled to understand the boy's death. Why would God do this? Did he intend to "bring tragedy"?

Elijah's reaction differed from that of the woman. She immediately concluded God was punishing her. But Elijah asked God about his intention. Did the Lord intend to bring tragedy, or was this event to be understood differently? In fact, the "tragedy" would soon become a cause for rejoicing, demonstrating that the widow needed to trust completely in the Lord and his spokesman (compare 1 Kings 17:24).

How often what we interpret as tragedy is intended by God as a blessing. How wise to adopt Elijah's stance—and look for the blessing that is hidden in the pain.

"He stretched himself out on the child three times." Elijah was truly a "man of God." An Israelite who touched a dead body was made unclean (Num. 19:11). Yet Elijah, out of his deep concern for the widow and her son, not only touched the child; he stretched out on his body. This was a symbolic act—an acted out way of praying, "Let this lifeless body be as my living body."

"Let this child's soul come back to him." The prayer, literally, was "let this child's life [*nephesh*] return."

Some people have called this miracle a "resurrection." It was not. History's only resurrection was that of Jesus. Raised, Jesus lives forever—his body transformed. The miracle described here, like the raising of Lazarus, was a resuscitation—a return to mortal life. The boy whose life was restored grew old and died again, just as Lazarus did. The restoration of mortal life is a miracle—but far less a miracle than the transformation we will experience in our resurrection when Jesus comes again.

God answered Elijah's prayer (17:22–23). The Lord answered Elijah's prayer and restored the child. Elijah brought the boy downstairs and presented him to his mother: "See, your son lives" (1 Kings 17:24).

The meaning of the miracle (17:24). The woman summed up the meaning of the miracle: "Now by this I know that you are a man of God, and that the word of the Lord in your mouth is the truth."

"You are a man of God." The miracle authenticated Elijah as God's spokesman. But the miracle did more. It also revealed Elijah as a caring, godly man. We need to keep this in mind as we read later accounts of what seem to be harsh acts of the prophet.

"The word of the LORD in your mouth." The miracle also authenticated the God whose word Elijah spoke. If there had been any doubt in her mind that the Lord is the living God, that doubt was erased. By giving life, Yahweh was revealed as living himself. There could be no doubt of his reality.

"The word of the LORD is truth." Truth as understood in the Bible has an unbreakable link to reality. What is true corresponds with what is real. What is false is unreal, and thus unreliable. The woman realized that the ultimate reality in our universe is God.

ELIJAH CALLS DOWN FIRE AT CARMEL   1 Kings 18:1–46

The most spectacular of Elijah's miracles was performed near the end of the three-and-one-half-year drought.

Ahab and Jezebel had massacred most of the prophets of the Lord (1 Kings 18:4). Yet the Lord told Elijah to go to Ahab, and that he would send rain. Before the return of the rains, however, Elijah proposed a contest with the prophets of Baal. The outcome would convince the people of Israel that the Lord is God.

Ahab's greeting (1 Kings 18:17–18). Ahab greeted Elijah as "troubler of Israel." The title was ironic, as Elijah pointed out. "I have not troubled Israel, but you and your father's house have, in that you have forsaken the commandments of the Lord and have fol-

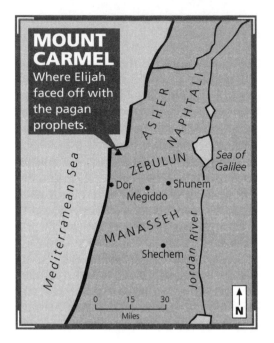

MOUNT CARMEL
Where Elijah faced off with the pagan prophets.

ASHER
NAPHTALI
ZEBULUN
Sea of Galilee
Mediterranean Sea
Dor
Shunem
Megiddo
MANASSEH
Jordan River
Shechem

0   15   30
Miles

N

lowed the Baals." How often the guilty person blames others for the consequences of his own sins.

The gathering on Mount Carmel (18:19, 20). Throughout this story, Elijah took the initiative. He proposed gathering all Israel at Mount Carmel and calling the 450 prophets of Baal whom Ahab had imported. Ahab quickly agreed. This suggests that he fully expected Baal to defeat Yahweh. We might call Ahab a "true believer," who was completely wrong, in spite of his sincerity!

Elijah also called for the "four hundred prophets of Asherah, who eat at Jezebel's table" to join the contest. Asherah was the female counterpart of Baal who served as his consort. The prophets "who eat at Jezebel's table," were under the queen's direct authority. Jezebel chose *not* to send them to Carmel! This may imply that Jezebel was not convinced of the power of her gods. The conversion of Israel to Baal worship may have been motivated by politics rather than the queen's religious convictions!

Elijah's challenge to the people of Israel (18:21). The Israelites were vacillating be-

tween the claims of the two deities, Yahweh and Baal. Elijah called for commitment. The people must make a choice. A literal translation of the verse reads, "If Yahweh is God, go after Him; if Baal is, go after Him." The commitment Elijah sought was not belief alone but action as well. The Israelites must live out their commitment, "going after" [obeying, walking in the path laid out by] either Yahweh or Baal.

At this point, the people remained silent. They were unsure and indecisive. They wanted proof that one of the competing deities truly was God.

The test (18:22–24). When Elijah explained the test, he emphasized how unequal it appeared—a lone prophet of the Lord, facing 450 prophets of Baal. Surely they had the advantage!

Then Elijah proposed that each side build an altar, cut a bull in pieces, and place the sacrifice on wood laid out on the altar. But neither side would light the fire. This had to be provided in the form of fire from heaven. Only the true God would be able to perform this miracle: "The God who answers by fire, He is God" (1 Kings 18:24).

The failure of the prophets of Baal (18:25–29). Elijah let the prophets of Baal go first. Their futile efforts provoked a series of sarcastic remarks from Elijah. From morning until noon, the pagan prophets cried out "O Baal, hear us." Finally Elijah began to offer suggestions.

> "Cry louder. After all, he's a god."
> "Maybe he's meditating?"
> "Maybe he's busy."
> "Maybe he's off on a journey."
> "Maybe he's sleeping, and you have to wake him up!"

Elijah's mockery stimulated Baal's prophets to greater efforts. The text indicates they "cut themselves . . . with knives and lances, until the blood gushed out on them." But at evening there was still "no voice; no one answered, no one paid attention."

BIBLE BACKGROUND:

WHY BAAL'S PROPHETS CUT THEMSELVES

The following is from one of six broken clay tablets called "Stories of Ba'al and Anat" from Ugarit. They reveal the bloodthirsty nature of these pagan deities. One tablet describes Anat destroying two armies and then, unsatisfied, building bleachers for massed warriors she engaged in deadly games. The text reads,

Once again Anat could fight with vigor,
    Slaughter everyone in sight.
Anat's body trembled with gladness,
    Her heart filled with joy
    Her soul gloated with triumph,
As, again, she waded knee deep in warrior's blood,
    Up to her thighs in their guts (l. li).

The prophets of Baal cut themselves because they believed their god was stimulated and excited by the scent of blood. And they were desperate to attract his attention!

Elijah's miracle victory (18:30–38). Elijah called the people to draw closer. He built his altar, made a trench around it, and prepared the wood and sacrifice. He also ordered that the offering and altar be saturated with water.

Some have ridiculed this account, arguing that if the drought was so severe, no water would be available. However, archaeologists have located wells below Mount Carmel which do not go dry even in droughts.

When all had been done, Elijah prayed aloud that God would "let it be known this day that You are God in Israel and I am your servant, and that I have done all these things at Your word" (1 Kings 18:36).

When Elijah prayed, fire fell. It consumed the sacrifice and burned up the altar stones and the pools of water in a trench Elijah had dug around the altar.

The people's response to the miracle (18:39–40). The people of Israel were convinced. They shouted, "The Lord, he is God! The Lord, he is God."

Wherever the word *Lord* appears in the Old Testament, the Hebrew reads "Yahweh." This decisive event on Mount Carmel tipped the scales against the deities of Ahab and Jezebel, convincing the population that Israel's ancestral God, Yahweh, was the one true God.

Elijah commanded the people to seize the prophets of Baal. There was not one survivor among those who had conspired with the king to corrupt the faith of Israel. Deuteronomy 13:5 explains the execution. God had commanded,

That prophet or that dreamer of dreams shall be put to death, because he has spoken in order to turn you away from the Lord your God, who brought you out of the land of Egypt and redeemed you from the house of bondage, to entice you from the way in which the Lord your God commanded you to walk. So you shall put away the evil from your midst.

The religious purpose of the miracle (18:36–37). There are few miracles in Scripture performed with clearer intent. Elijah summed it up in his prayer. He called for fire to "let it be known this day that You are God in Israel." The miracle proved decisively that the Lord is the one true God.

But Elijah's prayer expressed another purpose as well. Elijah asked God to act "that this people may know that You are the Lord God, and that You have turned their hearts back to You again" (1 Kings 18:37). The miracle was intended to turn Israel's hearts away from Baal-Malquart, and back to the Lord. And for a time—through the ministry of Elijah and his successor Elisha—Israel's hearts were turned.

The king and queen remained stubborn. But the ordinary people no longer hesitated between deities. They chose the Lord.

God can perform the most wondrous miracles. Jesus performed many that were unmistakably God's work. Yet he was eventually rejected by Israel and crucified. There is no such thing as *compelling* proof. Individuals who are determined *not* to believe will not believe—no matter what God does to demon-

After three and one-half years, Elijah prayed for God to restore the rains.

strate his power. For at least this moment in Israel's history—as a nation's destiny hung in the balance—the people of Israel were open and responsive to the Lord.

ELIJAH RESTORES THE RAINS
1 Kings 18:41–46

Three and one-half years earlier, Elijah had told King Ahab that there would be no rain in Israel "except at my word" (1 Kings 17:1). After the defeat and execution of the prophets of Baal, Elijah announced to Ahab "there is the sound of abundance of rain."

Elijah went to the top of Mount Carmel and prayed ["bowed down on the ground"]. At first only a tiny cloud appeared on the horizon over the Mediterranean. But soon the clouds filled the sky, and wind-driven rains

saturated the parched lands. Elijah warned Ahab to hurry home before the wheels of his chariot became bogged down in the mud!

Again, the miracle was in the timing, as well as in the abundance. God miraculously restored what he had miraculously taken away.

The extent of restoration. We can gauge how fully God restored the prosperity of the land from the biblical text and from history. First Kings 18:5 reports that Ahab had previously assigned one of his officials the task of identifying every spring and brook in the land which still had water that "perhaps we may find grass to keep the horses and mules alive." If the official was unsuccessful, the last of Ahab's livestock would have to be killed.

Why was Ahab so concerned about horses? Because these animal were needed to pull his military chariots, which might be described as the "tanks" of ancient warfare. How do we know the rains restored prosperity? We know because the records of Shalmanesser III of Assyria indicated that Ahab of Israel provided the most chariots—2,000—to the coalition of kings that defeated him in 853 B.C.

God sometimes uses his miracles to judge.

But God will also use his miracles to restore.

The miraculous in Elijah's life (1 Kings 19). The highest spiritual peaks sometimes lead directly to the darkest spiritual valleys. This was true for Elijah. When Ahab returned to his capital, he told Jezebel everything that had happened. Jezebel immediately sent a messenger to Elijah, threatening his life (1 Kings 19:2).

Jezebel's strategy. Jezebel could just as easily have sent soldiers to kill Elijah, but she didn't want to create a martyr. Her goal was to frighten the prophet and thus expose him to the charge of being a fraud. She could not fight God. But she might be able to discredit God's prophet.

Elijah's response to Jezebel's threat. Elijah fell into Jezebel's trap. Terrified, the prophet abandoned his ministry. The text indicates he "ran for his life" (1 Kings 19:3). Finally, after traveling for miles and growing exhausted, the prophet dropped to the ground and begged God to let him die.

God's response to Elijah's flight. Rather than speak harshly to Elijah, the Lord provided him with food that sustained him on a forty-day journey to Horeb [Mount Sinai]. There, where God had given Israel the Law accompanied by an awesome display of his presence (see Ex. 24:16–18), God spoke to Elijah in a whisper (1 Kings 19:11–12). The Lord reassured Elijah that other people in Israel also worshiped him. Elijah was not alone. The Lord also gave Elijah specific tasks to accomplish and provided him with a companion, Elisha.

The God who had judged the apostate King Ahab and his pagan prophets so harshly was gentle with his depressed prophet. With a series of quiet miracles—strengthening for the journey, a gentle revelation—the Lord ministered compassionately to the man of God.

Encouragement from the incident. Elijah had abandoned his ministry and run away. Even more, his disappearance provided Jezebel with a propaganda advantage. But the Lord neither criticized nor condemned. Instead, he showed great compassion for Elijah and eventually restored his ministry.

What an encouragement to us. We are also vulnerable to those deep valleys that lie beyond the spiritual and emotional peaks in our lives. At times, we will also give God's enemies occasion to criticize him. How important to remember the quiet miracles that God performed for Elijah. Our Lord will strengthen and restore us in our "down" times, as he did his prophet of old.

ELIJAH CALLS DOWN FIRE ON SOLDIERS   *2 Kings 1:1–17*

After Ahab died, his successor Ahaziah was seriously injured in a fall. Ahaziah sent messengers to a pagan deity to ask if he would recover. God sent Elijah to confront the messengers. Since Ahaziah had showed contempt for the Lord by not seeking information from him, Ahaziah would die, Elijah declared. When his messengers reported this to the king, he sent fifty soldiers to bring Elijah to him.

"Man of God, the king has said" (2 Kings 1:9). These words alert us to the significance of the coming miracle. Jezebel still lived, and her son Ahaziah had adopted her religion and her policies.

Jezebel had earlier won a propaganda victory by forcing Elijah to flee. In that confrontation between the political and spiritual powers, Elijah had surrendered to the state. Confronted once more with the power of the state—expressed in the soldiers standing before him— would he surrender again, admitting the authority of the state over God? Or would this confrontation have a different outcome?

"Come down" (1:9). The army officer was confident. He commanded, "Man of God, the king has said, 'Come down.'" He fully expected spiritual power, which he acknowledged by addressing Elijah as "Man of God," to bow to the secular power. To this officer, "the king has said" settled every matter.

"Let fire come down from heaven" (1:10). Elijah answered by announcing, "If I am a man of God, then let fire come down from heaven and consume you and your fifty men." In uttering the phrase "if I am a man of God," Elijah accepted his role as representative of the spiritual authority of God. When Elijah spoke, fire fell and consumed the soldiers.

The second fifty met the same fate (1:11–12). A second officer approached Elijah, arrogantly commanding him in the King's name, "Come down quickly." Again Elijah called down fire on the soldiers.

A third officer appealed for his life (1:13–14). A third officer approached Elijah with a totally different attitude. He never mentioned the king or his command. Instead, he appealed to Elijah as a man of God to "let my life and the life of these fifty servants of yours be precious in your sight."

"Let my life." The state is feared because it has the power of life or death. This officer had learned that the real power of life or death is God's, not the king's.

"These fifty servants of yours." The first two officers were committed to serve the state. But God requires our first allegiance. In any conflict between the two powers, the claims of the state must come last.

"Be precious in your sight." What a blessing that the Lord does have priority over the state. We can appeal to God because he *cares*. We cannot expect political powers to have any real concern for individuals.

This officer's appeal was heard, and his life was spared.

"Go down with him; do not be afraid" (1:15–17). It is unlikely that Elijah fully understood the issue involved in this confrontation. The angel's reassuring words, "Don't be afraid," suggested that Elijah himself feared the power of the king. But the angel's command, "Go down with him," reminds us of a vital truth. We live in a world in which believers must deal with the secular powers. We cannot and must not try to isolate ourselves from the society in which we live. Yet in our interaction with the powers of this world, we need not be afraid. God rules, and he is far greater than any secular power.

"Thus says the Lord" (1:16). When Elijah met the king, he spoke boldly. He announced God's judgment on the apostate ruler: "You shall surely die."

Elijah walked away unharmed.

And Ahaziah died.

The message of the miracle. A miracle is an extraordinary event caused by God for a religious purpose. It would be wrong to interpret the fire which killed a hundred soldiers as a petty act performed by a frightened prophet. God's purpose in performing this miracle was far more significant.

Because of this confrontation, all Israel would remember that in a direct conflict between the spiritual and political powers, the state was powerless. And we today are to take heart in this truth as well. As the palmist wrote in Psalm 56:11,

> In God I have put my trust,
> I will not be afraid;
> What can man do to me?

ELIJAH DIVIDES THE JORDAN'S WATERS   2 Kings 2:1–11

When Elijah's ministry was completed, God revealed that he and his companion Elisha would be carried to heaven without experiencing death. As the two walked together into the Jordan River valley, they were observed by a group of fifty prophets. When they got to the river, Elijah rolled up his cloak and struck the water. The river "was divided in this way and that, so that the two of them crossed over on dry ground."

BIBLE BACKGROUND:

THE "SONS OF THE PROPHETS"

The phrase "sons of the prophets" occurs only in 1 and 2 Kings, where it occurs 10 times in 11 different verses. Some take the phrase to mean "prophets in training," assuming that Elijah and Elisha set up a sort of seminary for prophets. Others interpret the phrase to mean "prophet," pointing out that "son of . . ." is idiomatic in Hebrew, indicating membership in a class or group. To say "sons of the prophets" indicates that the persons so identified are members of the group known as "prophets."

In either case, the fifty who witnessed the miracle performed by Elijah and later duplicated by Elisha were the future spiritual leaders of Israel.

The miracle by Elijah (2 Kings 2:8). The miracle of dividing the waters was clearly linked with two earlier miracles: the crossing of the Reed Sea and the dividing of the waters of the Jordan in the time of Joshua.

But why would Elijah perform this miracle now, at the end of his career? The answer was obvious when Elisha performed the same act a little later. This served as a sign that he had succeeded Elijah as Israel's premier prophet.

The miracle for Elijah (2:11–13). In earlier days, God had performed several miracles *for* Elijah. The Lord sent ravens to feed Elijah during the drought when he lived by the brook Cherith. God provided supernatural food that sustained Elijah for a forty-day jour-

ney to Mount Sinai. Now the Lord performed one other miracle for the prophet. As Elijah and Elisha walked in the Jordan valley, "suddenly a chariot of fire appeared with horses of fire, and separated the two of them; and Elijah went up by a whirlwind into heaven" (2 Kings 2:11). God took Elijah into heaven without sending him through the experience of death.

We often focus on the more spectacular miracles of Scripture: the crossing of the Reed Sea, the fall of Jericho's walls. But the more personal miracles God performed for his people are a rich source of encouragement and hope. God does the great things that a whole nation remembers. But the same God also does the small, compassionate things that we as individuals remember with wonder, thanksgiving, and praise.

God carried Elijah up into heaven.

CHAPTER 7

THE MIRACLE MINISTRY OF ELISHA

SHOWING GOD'S COMPASSION

2 Kings 2—13

Miracles can tell us a lot about God. Elijah's miracles proved to Israel that God is real, and all-powerful. But we need to know much more. How does God feel about us? Can we ever feel comfortable in the presence of a miracle-working God? These questions suddenly became important to the population of the northern Hebrew kingdom, which had been convinced by Elijah's miracles that the LORD is God.

To answer such questions God sent Israel another prophet, Elisha. Elisha's miracle ministry revealed the compassion of a God who loves individuals, and who yearns to be gracious to all who trust in Him.

Elisha's deepest desire (2 Kings 2:9–10). Elisha had been Elijah's companion and apprentice during the final years of Elijah's ministry. Scripture's transition from the ministry of Elijah to that of Elisha is reported in 2 Kings 2. As the two men walked together in the Jordan valley on Elijah's last day on earth, Elijah asked his friend Elisha, "What may I do for you, before I am taken away from you?"

Elisha's request was, "Please, let a double portion of your spirit be upon me." In Israel

the oldest son in a family was given a double portion of the family wealth as an inheritance (Deut. 21:17). Elisha asked to be Elijah's successor and to inherit his role as God's premier prophet in Israel.

The request was not for Elijah to grant. God himself calls his spokesmen. But Elijah promised that if Elisha witnessed Elijah's departure, God would grant what he desired. Elisha did see the angels who took Elijah to glory. (For a discussion of this angelic appearance, see the companion volume, *Every Good and Evil Angel in the Bible.*) Elisha did succeed Elijah. In fact, the recorded miracles of Elisha actually doubled those performed by Elijah himself. God granted even more than Elisha had asked.

Elisha the man. The earnest request of Elisha tells us much about the man. He had traveled with Elijah for some time, observing the kind of life Elijah lived. He was fully aware that the call to ministry was a summons to a life of challenge and difficulty, not a life of ease. But Elisha had a heart for God and a heart for God's people. Elisha was eager to serve.

How blessed we are when those in spiritual leadership are men and women who are

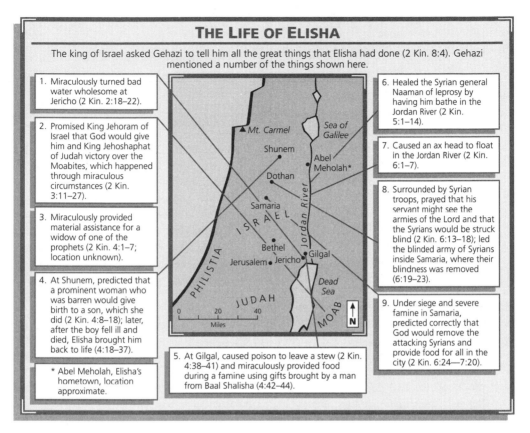

THE LIFE OF ELISHA

The king of Israel asked Gehazi to tell him all the great things that Elisha had done (2 Kin. 8:4). Gehazi mentioned a number of the things shown here.

1. Miraculously turned bad water wholesome at Jericho (2 Kin. 2:18–22).

2. Promised King Jehoram of Israel that God would give him and King Jehoshaphat of Judah victory over the Moabites, which happened through miraculous circumstances (2 Kin. 3:11–27).

3. Miraculously provided material assistance for a widow of one of the prophets (2 Kin. 4:1–7; location unknown).

4. At Shunem, predicted that a prominent woman who was barren would give birth to a son, which she did (2 Kin. 4:8–18); later, after the boy fell ill and died, Elisha brought him back to life (4:18–37).

* Abel Meholah, Elisha's hometown, location approximate.

5. At Gilgal, caused poison to leave a stew (2 Kin. 4:38–41) and miraculously provided food during a famine using gifts brought by a man from Baal Shalisha (4:42–44).

6. Healed the Syrian general Naaman of leprosy by having him bathe in the Jordan River (2 Kin. 5:1–14).

7. Caused an ax head to float in the Jordan River (2 Kin. 6:1–7).

8. Surrounded by Syrian troops, prayed that his servant might see the armies of the Lord and that the Syrians would be struck blind (2 Kin. 6:13–18); led the blinded army of Syrians inside Samaria, where their blindness was removed (6:19–23).

9. Under siege and severe famine in Samaria, predicted correctly that God would remove the attacking Syrians and provide food for all in the city (2 Kin. 6:24—7:20).

Map labels: Mt. Carmel; Sea of Galilee; Shunem; Abel Meholah*; Dothan; Samaria; Jordan River; ISRAEL; PHILISTIA; Bethel; Jerusalem; Jericho; Gilgal; Dead Sea; JUDAH; MOAB; 0 20 40 Miles; N

eager to serve—not because they want the limelight, but because they love God and care about his people. How important it is that our hearts be like Elisha's, if we should receive a call to leadership.

Elisha's miracles (2 Kings 2—7). The recorded miracles of Elisha are double the seven performed by Elijah. There is another difference as well. While the major miracles of Elijah were miracles of judgment, the major miracles of Elisha were miracles which focused on life rather than death. The thirteen miracles performed by God through Elisha are:

ELISHA DIVIDES THE JORDAN'S WATERS   *2 Kings 2:13–15*

Elisha knew that he had been chosen as Elijah's successor. He had seen Elijah caught up into heaven. Now it was time to demonstrate his commission from God.

The miracle (2 Kings 2:14). When Elijah was carried into heaven, his cloak had fallen to the ground. Elisha had picked it up. Arriving at the Jordan River, Elisha used the cloak to duplicate Elijah's earlier miracle (2 Kings 2:8). Elisha struck the water with the cloak, and the water divided so Elisha could cross over.

"Where is the Lord God of Elijah? This question was answered by the miracle. The God of Elijah was now with Elisha. Elisha's voice was raised in confidence, not doubt. Elisha had seen the miracle of Elijah's transformation, and this was confirmation enough for him. But there were others who needed to be convinced. Elisha raised his voice so the witnesses could hear and affirm the miracle of the divided water as the answer to his question.

"They . . . bowed to the ground before him" *(2:15).* The fifty prophets who had earlier seen Elijah divide the Jordan River recognized the significance of Elisha's act. They said, "The Spirit of Elijah rests on Elisha." And they showed Elisha the respect they had reserved earlier for Elijah as the recognized leader of God's prophets in Israel.

This was an authenticating miracle. Its purpose was made clear by the response of the witnesses. Elisha's position was now established.

ELISHA HEALS A SPRING'S WATERS
1 Kings 2:19–22

The men of Jericho appealed to Elisha to do something about the water in a nearby spring. They described the water as "bad," meaning toxic, or poison. Nothing would grow where these waters flowed.

"Put salt in it" *(2 Kings 2:20).* Elisha called for a new bowl filled with salt. Salt water is also toxic to man, animals, and land plants. Elisha was using a curse to cure a curse.

There is a fascinating foreshadowing here. The cure of the curse of sin was accomplished at Calvary, of which Deuteronomy 21:23 says, "He who is hanged [on a tree] is accursed of God." The curse that Jesus took upon himself became the cure for the curse that brought death to us, even as the salt which is toxic to humanity became a cure for the toxic waters of Jericho.

"Thus says the Lord" *(2:21).* Elisha spoke and acted in the name of the Lord. There was no suggestion that Elisha himself was special. It was the God represented by Elisha who was to be given the credit and glory for meeting the need of the people of Jericho.

❖

When Elisha struck the water with Elijah's cloak, the Jordan divided.

Elisha's earlier miracle at the Jordan River had convinced the prophets that he had been commissioned by God. The people of Jericho had obviously heard of the event, for they begged Elisha to perform a miracle for them. This miracle performed in the name of the Lord reminded all Israel that the Lord is real and that he aids his people.

The miracle also set the tone for future miracles by Elisha. Most would be like this one—miracles of compassion in which God showed his willingness to meet his people's needs.

"The water remains healed to this day" (2:22). The comment added by the compiler of the history of the kings also reflects the situation today. Springs of pure water still bubble up near modern Jericho. The fruits and vegetables of the area are valued throughout the land.

ELISHA CURSES JEERING YOUNG MEN   *2 Kings 2:23–24*

As Elisha left Jericho and set out toward Bethel, a group of youths came from the city and mocked him. They repeatedly cried out, "Go up, you baldhead!" Elisha turned and cursed them in the name of the Lord. A few minutes later two female bears came out of the woods and mauled forty-two of the youths.

This miracle curse has troubled many, particularly as the original King James Version rendered this phrase, "There came forth *little children* out of the city." How could a compassionate prophet curse little children? And how could a compassionate God turn wild beasts upon them?

"Some youths" (2 Kings 2:23). The New King James Version corrects the impression that these were harmless children set on ridiculing a bald man. They were young adults, and their ridicule was not of Elisha's hairless state.

"Go up, you baldhead!" (2:23). The ridicule was directed against the report of Elisha that the Lord had caught Elijah up into heaven.

These young people mocked the very notion. How could anyone be caught up by angels? And how could anyone be foolish enough to credit any god with such an action? And so the cry "go up!" was a challenge to Elisha to duplicate the feat to prove his claims of what God had done.

This situation was similar to the Israelites who murmured against Moses in the wilderness. The mockery of Elisha by the youths was not directed against the prophet, but against God. These young people had heard of Elisha's miracle at the Jordan River. If they were from Jericho rather than Bethel, they had also witnessed his healing of the waters. Yet, they refused to believe.

He "pronounced a curse on them in the name of the Lord" (2:24). Some have suggested that Elisha overreacted. Perhaps he was sensitive about his baldness. Or just tired. But Elisha knew exactly what he was doing. He did not react irritably. He did not curse the youths because he was offended. He pronounced a curse on them *in the name of the Lord.*

Again, it is important to remember the significance of the "name" in Old Testament thought. The name expressed *the essence of the person or thing named.* To speak in the name of the Lord was more than a claim to be an authorized spokesman. It was an affirmation that the words spoken were in complete harmony with the character and will of the person named. Cursing these young men "in the name of the Lord" showed that Elisha was acting in full awareness of God's will and in complete harmony with God's character.

If this was the case, why did God punish these mocking young men? For the same reason that he had struck the curious who peeked at the ark at Beth-Shemesh (p. 106) and the same reason he had struck Uzzah when he reached out to steady the ark of God (p. 107). Elisha's encounter with these youths was a critical moment in Israel's history. It demonstrated clearly that God's people must hold him in utmost respect if they are to receive his blessing.

The curse was immediately fulfilled (2:24). Perhaps it was even as Elisha spoke that two female bears emerged from the woods and mauled forty-two of the youths. The consequences of showing disrespect for God were immediate and severe.

The lesson learned (2 Kings 3:1–3). Any reader of the Bible needs to be aware that the organization of scriptural material is significant. This is sometimes disguised by the artificial separation of passages by chapter and verse divisions. These were added many centuries after the text was originally written. This passage is a good example of this point.

Elisha traveled on, eventually returning to Samaria (2 Kings 2:25). Samaria was the capital city of the Northern Kingdom, Israel. So the geographical notation directs our attention to Israel's royal house. The opening verses of chapter three indicate that King Ahab was dead. But his legacy continued! Jehoram, a second son of Ahab, was now king, and "he did evil in the sight of the Lord." While his evil was not "like his father and mother," Jehoram maintained the counterfeit religious system instituted by Jeroboam (see page 110–111). Whatever respect the new king had for the Lord, it was not enough to bring obedience or radical change.

Respect for the Lord is the key to personal and national prosperity. Elisha fully understood this truth. When Elisha's God was mocked and jeered, the prophet responded appropriately. The fate of the young men was a warning to the entire nation—and especially to its ruler—that God must be treated with utmost respect.

ELISHA WINS A BATTLE FOR ISRAEL
2 Kings 3:1–26)

Moab had been subdued some years before by an earlier ruler. The Moabites rebelled and refused to pay tribute. The king of Israel recruited help from the kings of Judah and Edom and set out to punish the Moabites. The army took a roundabout route that left them stranded without water.

Jehoram's interpretation of the imminent disaster (2 Kings 3:10). Jehoram immediately assumed the Lord had brought the allied army to its present state in order to destroy it. He had experienced the Lord's judgments before, and he must have known that the official religion which he supported was an abomination to God.

Jehoshaphat of Judah sought a prophet's help (3:11–12). Jehoshaphat was one of Judah's more godly kings. He insisted that all the kings in this alliance consult a prophet of the Lord. The king of Israel was silent, but one of his officials knew about Elisha. Jehoshaphat was familiar with Elisha's reputation as a prophet of the Lord, so the kings went to consult him.

Elisha confronted Jehoram (3:13–19). When the kings arrived, Elisha dismissed Jehoram with contempt, telling him to go the gods of his parents.

Jehoram's sin. The king of Israel's response was, "No, for the LORD has called these three kings together to deliver them into the hand of Moab." This was not an expression of faith, but blame. Jehoram was declaring it was the Lord's fault that the kings were in such danger. Not only did Jehoram blame God; he even presumed to explain God's motive.

Elisha's contempt for Jehoram. The king's reaction deepened Elisha's contempt for Jehoram. But because the godly king of Judah was there, Elisha decided to tell them what God had to say. Elisha apparently used music to focus his mind on the Lord and become more open to divine revelation (2 Kings 3:15).

God's Word to Elisha. God told Elisha that he was about to show Israel that it was "a simple matter in the eyes of the Lord" to turn disaster into triumph. God commanded the kings to "make this valley full of ditches." The next morning God would fill the ditches with water, and this would be the key to a great victory by the coalition of kings.

Note that the kings were told to make the valley full of ditches. They had to have enough faith in God's words to act on them if they wanted to have God act for them.

The predicted victory over Moab (2 Kings 3:20–25). The next morning, as sacrifices were made to the Lord, "suddenly water came" and filled the ditches. The Moabites saw the morning sun reflecting blood red off the water, and they assumed the kings of Israel, Judah, and Edom had turned on each other. They rushed headlong to collect the expected spoils—and were attacked by the allied army. The Moabites fled after they crumbled under the assault. The Israelite-led coalition army pursued them and devastated the land of the Moabites.

The war ended without victory (3:26–27). The description of the end of the war has puzzled commentators. The typical interpretation of this text is that the king of Moab sacrificed his own son on the city wall. Some have suggested that this act horrified the Israelites, or that it had some unknown magical meaning which terrified them.

The explanation is much simpler. Verse 26 mentions that the Moabites tried to break through to the king of Edom. If the Edomites had been forced into an earlier treaty with Moab, a counter-attack to punish them would have made sense in the warfare patterns of the ancient world. And why had the Edomitites joined the coalition? If Edom was threatened by a resurgent Moab, this would also make sense. It is likely that Edom had earlier been required by Moab to provide the heir to its throne as a hostage.

So the reference in verse 27 to "his eldest son" is not to the son of the king of Moab, but to the son of the king of Edom!

When the Moabites sacrificed the Edomite heir, "there was great indignation against Israel"—by the Edomites! The very thing that the Moabites had earlier assumed—that the allied kings fell to fighting among themselves—was now a very real danger. And so the Israelites "returned to their own land."

God won the battle, but Israel lost the war. The miracle God performed won the initial battle for the king of Israel and his allies. But Israel had set out to subdue Moab, forcing the king to begin paying the tribute exacted by an earlier ruler. This goal was not achieved.

An archaeological find known as the Moabite Stone celebrated the recovery of Moab's independence from Israel. The stone's inscription made it clear that the borders with Israel had been substantially strengthened. This explains why the coalition of kings took the long route to attack Moab: fortifications on the border with Israel were too strong.

This miracle demonstrated that when God fights for his people, they will be victorious. Israel's failure to reclaim dominion over the Moabites also revealed another truth: without the Lord, Israel could expect ultimate defeat.

The rest of Elisha's miracles were performed during the reign of Jehoram. This king never learned the lessons which the prophet's miracles clearly taught.

ELISHA MULTIPLIES A WIDOW'S OIL
2 Kings 4:1–7

The Old Testament shows a special compassion for widows and the fatherless (Deut. 24:20–21; Prov. 15:25). God has a special concern for the helpless. This miracle of Elisha reflects this concern.

The widow's need (2 Kings 4:1). The widow who appealed to Elijah had been married to one of the Lord's prophets. Her husband had died, leaving her and their two sons destitute and in debt. Her appeal was urgent, for the creditor was coming to take her two sons as slaves. The impending separation from her sons was almost more than she could bear.

"Nothing . . . but a jar of oil" (4:2). The oil was olive oil, used in cooking, burned in oil lamps, and eaten as a substance similar to butter.

The first question Elisha asked the widow was, "What do you have?" God is just as ready to perform miracles for us today as he was in the past. But when we ask for God's help, we must be willing to commit our own resources.

❖

BIBLE BACKGROUND:

SLAVERY IN THE OLD TESTAMENT

Children or adults could be sold into slavery to pay a debt. But a Hebrew slave could not be mistreated or held beyond seven years. At the end of seven years, the Hebrew slave was granted freedom and enough money and resources to launch an independent life. A man's motive in selling himself into slavery was sometimes to learn a trade or land management from his master. Young girls were often purchased as future brides for the buyer or his sons. Under Old Testament law, slavery thus had positive social intentions, unlike slavery as practiced in the pagan world or in modern nations. For a description of Old Testament laws governing slavery, see Exodus 21:1–10.

This does not mean that the law regarding slavery was always carried out. Even in the best of situations, a slave lost his right of self-determination. In the worst of situations, mistreatment occurred. At various times in Israel's history, the law's requirement that slaves be freed after seven years was ignored.

❖

"Go, borrow vessels" (4:3). Elisha told the woman to borrow several empty vessels. The limits to the miracle God would perform were not set by the Lord; they were determined by the widow's faith and obedience.

"Shut the door behind you and your sons" (4:4). Some miracles are meant to be public. Some are private, "family" miracles, whose workings aren't meant to be advertised. It is possible to confuse the two.

"Pour [the oil] into all those vessels" (4:4). The widow filled empty vessel after empty vessel until every one of the borrowed jars was full.

"Pay your debt; . . . and . . . live on the rest" (4:7). Preachers often make much of the fact that if the widow had had more faith, and borrowed more empty vessels, there would have been more oil. This is true. But let's remember that she had borrowed enough so that the oil paid her debt and she still had enough for her and her sons to live on.

There is no need to charge her with little faith. She had faith enough. And what God provided in this miracle was enough as well.

The message of the miracle. Again, this is an extraordinary event clearly caused by God. But what is the religious purpose of the miracle? On the one hand, it testifies to the compassionate love of God, and the concern of God's prophet. But more than that, it revealed clearly that faith was still a resource for the powerless. The God who could defeat armies could also meet the needs of the helpless who trusted in him.

❖

The miracle of the widow's oil demonstrated God's unlimited resources.

ELISHA PROMISES A PREGNANCY
2 Kings 4:8–17

Elisha wanted to do something for a woman who provided food and lodging for him when he visited her neighborhood. She herself had asked for nothing. But Elisha's servant Gehazi pointed out that her husband was old, and the woman had no son.

Elisha didn't hesitate. He called her and said "About this time next year you shall embrace a son" (v. 16).

The woman's reaction (2 Kings 4:16). The woman had become reconciled to her childlessness. It must have been a bitter process. Bearing children and especially sons was the dream of Hebrew women. Apparently, she had suppressed all hope of becoming a mother.

Elisha's announcement was painful, because the hope she had long since buried was aroused. The woman knew the anguish of hope disappointed again and again. Even hope offered by God's prophet seemed deceiving—a lie setting her up for another crushing disappointment.

The child's birth (4:17). The text indicates that "the woman conceived, and bore a son when the appointed time had come" (v. 17). In spite of the pain of disappointments, those who know God should never give up hope.

The meaning of the miracle. What marks this birth as a miracle is not the age of the husband but Elisha's pre-announcement. The miracle birth approaches the heart of the ministry of Elisha. He was called to demonstrate to Israel the life-giving and life-sustaining power of the God whom the royal family had abandoned.

ELISHA RAISES THE WIDOW'S SON
2 Kings 4:32–37

A few years later, this widow's son went into the fields with his father. He apparently suffered sun stroke and died. The unsolicited gift had been taken away!

The mother's reaction (2 Kings 4:21–25). Some have called the mother's reaction "cold."

She carried the boy to the room set aside for Elisha and closed the door. Then she politely asked for a donkey, brushed aside her husband's questions, and set out to find Elisha. Yet we can sense the urgency in her words, "Do not slacken the pace for me." She was trying to keep her boiling emotions under control.

The account also demonstrates her faith. She brought the body to Elisha's room, ready for his intervention. Rather than weep, she set out to reach the one person who could help.

"It is well" (4:25–27). As the woman approached, Elisha sent his servant to ask about her husband and son. Is something wrong? Her answer "It is well," may be taken as another expression of faith. Yet it seems more likely that the woman simply could not bear to speak of her son's death to Gehazi.

How often we respond the same way when someone asks, "How are you?" Although we may be aching inside, the answer we typically give, is "I'm fine. How are you?" There is a time for polite small talk. But when we truly hurt, we need someone with whom we can share our pain.

"Her soul is in deep distress" (4:27–28). When the woman saw Elisha, she fell down and grasped his feet. Elisha immediately sensed her deep distress and gave her his full attention.

How much we need a person like Elisha when we are in deep distress—a person who will be attuned to our emotions, willing to listen and to help.

The words "Did I ask a son?" spilled from the woman's lips. Before the prophet came, she had become reconciled to her life. There was no joy, but neither was there any deep pain. With the gift of the son, joy had been born. But with the deepening of her emotional life, there also came the potential for excruciating pain. Now the life she had lived before—suppressing her capacity for deep emotions—seemed so attractive. At least before, she had never known pain like this.

This truth speaks to us. Some are unwilling to take the risk of loving and being loved.

Some feel safer in the Christian community standing on the sidelines, not involved in the lives of fellow believers or needy people in the community. Such a life may feel empty. But at least there is no risk of being hurt.

The problem with this approach is that it doesn't allow us to see God working significantly in our lives, as the woman was about to experience.

"He arose and followed her" (4:29–32). Elisha sent Gehazi on ahead with his staff to try to restore the child. Then he hurried with the woman to cover the distance from Carmel to her home. When he arrived, he found the child "lying dead on his bed."

Elisha went into the room, shut the door, and prayed. Finally, Elisha stretched out on the child. [For a discussion of this act, see "Elijah Restores a Widow's Son," page 114–115.] And the boy's life was restored.

The mother's response (4:36–37). When Elisha called the woman into the room, he told her, "Pick up your son." At those words, she "fell at his feet, and bowed to the ground." The fall and the bowing should be separated. Suddenly all her suppressed emotions were released, and the woman collapsed. She then expressed her gratitude to Elisha and "picked up her son and went out."

The meaning of the miracle. This is the central miracle in the Bible's report of Elisha's ministry. [See the discussion of the literary form on page 106.] It is a miracle of the restoration of lost life. And this is the theme of Elisha's work. The God who punishes the wicked is the same God who can restore life to those who turn to him—just as the woman sought Elisha, his representative. How important it was that Israel turn to God, who alone can save.

ELISHA MAKES POISONED FOOD HARMLESS   *2 Kings 4:38–41*

During a time of famine, people ate wild seeds and plants to survive. At one gathering of prophets, poisonous wild gourds had been added to a stew. Elisha added flour, miraculously neutralizing the poison.

ELISHA MULTIPLIES LOAVES OF BREAD   *2 Kings 4:42–44*

When there was not enough bread to feed the prophets who had gathered, Elisha announced in the name of the Lord that "they shall eat and have some left over."

"Twenty loaves of barley bread" (4:42). This miracle seems insignificant. Twenty loaves of bread? Surely that was enough to feed one hundred hungry men—but only if we assume that the loaves in this story were the same size as the bread we buy at the store. In fact, these barley loaves were no larger than small dinner rolls. There was hardly enough for three or four hungry men.

"Some left over" (4:44). This miracle foreshadows even greater miracles performed by Jesus. With fewer pieces of bread than this, Jesus fed thousands of people. The people who shared that meal probably recalled this wonder worked by Elisha in the name of the Lord. Perhaps they understood that in Jesus Christ, someone far greater than Elisha was among them.

ELISHA HEALS NAAMAN THE LEPER
2 Kings 5:1–19

The healing of Naaman is a story most people know from their Sunday school days. Naaman was the commander of the Syrian army, and Syria was a traditional enemy of Israel. A young Israelite girl, undoubtedly captured in a raid on Israel, was a slave in Naaman's house. She told her mistress that there was a prophet in Samaria, Israel's capital, who could cure Naaman of his leprosy.

The report was passed from the wife to Naaman to the king of Syria, who wrote a letter to Jehoram, king of Israel.

The letter to Jehoram (2 Kings 5:6–7). The letter was brief and to the point. The Syrian ruler indicated he was sending Naaman to the king, "that you may heal him of his leprosy." Jehoram saw only one possible way to interpret the letter. Syria was looking for an excuse to launch a war against Israel. There was no way he could heal a leper. As a sign of his agitation and distress, the king tore his clothes.

In fact, the appeal to the king did not require *him* to do the healing. The Syrian ruler assumed that Jehoram would command the prophet to do the healing. But Jehoram did not even *think* of Elisha.

Elisha volunteers (2 Kings 5:8). Elisha sent a letter to Jehoram, asking him to send Naaman to him. The words "and he shall know that there is a prophet in Israel" are ironic. The Syrian, who worshiped a pagan god, would recognize Elisha as a prophet of God, even if the king of Israel did not!

Naaman's visit to Elisha (5:9–11). When Naaman arrived at Elisha's door, the prophet didn't even step outside. Elisha sent a messenger, who told Naaman to go wash seven times in the Jordan River. In this act, his flesh would be restored.

Naaman was insulted and "became furious." He was an important man! He had brought expensive gifts for the prophet (2 Kings 5:5). And besides, Elisha didn't act as Naaman thought a prophet should. A real prophet should be more like a magician: he should mutter an incantation in the name of his God, wave his hand, and heal the leprosy.

How like Naaman so many of us are. We have our own idea of how God should meet our needs. We assume that our needs are so important that the Lord himself should step outside to deal with us. Elisha's actions humbled and infuriated Naaman. But Naaman had to be humbled to the point where he would honor God and obey the prophet's command. How often humbling must occur before we are ready to receive God's help.

Naaman's healing (5:12–14). The angry Naaman left Elisha's home in a rage. The rivers of Damascus in Syria were cleaner and just as wet as the Jordan. If water would heal a leper,

he could have washed in them! But Naaman's servants respectfully suggested that if Elisha had asked him to do something really difficult, he would have done it. Why reject the prophet's prescription, they said, just because it is easy?

Again we have a reminder of the gospel message. "Only believe! Too easy." What a foolish reason to reject the good news of salvation in Christ.

Naaman's healing and his response (5:14–19). When Naaman did as the prophet said, "his flesh was restored like the flesh of a little child."

Naaman hurried back to Elisha and proclaimed his conversion: "Now I know that there is no God in all the earth, except in Israel." Naaman also asked for two mule loads of Israel's earth to take back to Syria with him.

He intended to spread it at the worship center where he sacrificed to symbolize that his worship was now directed to Israel's God. Namaan also asked for and was granted an exception to his promise to worship Yahweh.

Under protest, Naaman washed in the Jordan.

This was on state occasions, when he had to accompany the king of Syria to the temple of Rimmon, Syria's god.

The meaning of the miracle. God's grace calls for a faith response. The completeness of Naaman's conversion stands in sharp contrast to the reaction of Jehoram to Elisha's earlier miracle on his behalf (p. 126–127). The pagan general recognized God's hand and committed himself to worship the Lord only. The Israelite king failed to respond to God's gracious gift of victory. Ignoring the presence of God's prophet in Israel, he went his own way.

When we experience God's grace, it's important for us to recognize its source and to honor the Lord in our lives.

ELISHA CURSES GEHAZI WITH LEPROSY   2 Kings 5:20–27

When Naaman went to Israel, he took expensive gifts which he intended to give the prophet who healed him. After the leprosy was gone, Naaman tried to give Elisha a reward. Elisha refused. But after Naaman set out for home, Elisha's servant Gehazi hurried after him. Representing himself as a messenger of the prophet, Gehazi asked for a talent (about 75 pounds!) of silver and two sets of clothing. Naaman urged him to take 150 pounds of silver, which he did. Gehazi then hid the wealth in his home.

Elisha's judgment (2 Kings 5:25–27). When Elisha asked Gehazi where he had gone, Gehazi blandly said, "Nowhere." But Elisha knew exactly what had happened, and he described it for Gehazi. Elisha then announced the consequences: Gehazi and his descendants would be lepers "forever."

The meaning of the miracle. There are many lessons to be drawn from this miracle. The most important is that God's grace is free. We can never place a price tag on God's grace. We should not give others the impression that anything they can *do* or pay will bring God's gracious working in their lives.

In addition to this central message, there are others.

Ministry means putting others first (5:26). Elisha asked Gehazi if this was the time "to receive money . . . olive groves and vineyards. . . ." That is, is this the time to look out for ourselves and our material well-being? The answer, of course, is "No." Their mission was to look out for others and their spiritual well-being. Gehazi had been called to ministry. He had abandoned his calling for material gain.

"Your servant did not go anywhere" (5:25). How foolish to assume that we can hide our actions from God, or that what we do will never be found out by others. What we would not do if others were watching is something we should not do. Period.

"You and your descendants" (5:27). It is true that each person stands or falls before God on the basis of his or her own faith. But it is also true that what we do always affects others. Those most affected by our choices are our children and their children. We need to make choices that will bless future generations, not curse them.

ELISHA MAKES AN AX HEAD FLOAT 2 Kings 6:1–7

A dormitory occupied by a number of prophets needed to be expanded. One prophet who was working in the construction project lost an ax head in the Jordan River. The ax had been borrowed, and the young prophet was responsible for repaying what had been lost. Elisha met this need by cutting a stick and throwing it into the river, whereupon the ax head floated to the surface.

ELISHA BLINDS AND GIVES SIGHT 2 Kings 6:8—7:20

This passage contains an account of several miracles. Two of these are typically counted on lists of the fourteen miracles performed by Elisha. Because they have common features, these two miracles are treated together here.

The miracle context (2 Kings 6:8–12). The account begins with a report of Syrian raids on Israel. The Syrian high command would plan the attacks. But each time they raided, they were turned back by an Israelite force. The king of Syria concluded that one of his officers must be a spy, so he confronted them (2 Kings 6:11). One claimed the problem was the prophet Elisha, who "tells the king of Israel the words that you speak in your bedroom" (2 Kings 6:12). It was as if Elisha were present in the war room, watching and listening as the Syrians laid their plans.

The "first" miracle (6:13–17). When lists of Elisha's fourteen miracles are compiled, this next event is usually included. The king of Syria sent a force to capture Elisha, who was at Dothan. The Syrians arrived at night and surrounded the little cluster of homes.

Elisha's servant discovered the Syrian force and ran in terror to his master. Elisha told the servant not to worry, and asked God to open his eyes. The prayer was answered, and suddenly the servant saw a force of fiery angels deployed between Elisha and the Syrians. God had placed a hedge of protection around his prophet.

The "second" miracle (6:18–23). Elisha prayed that the Syrians would be struck with "blindness." The Hebrew word, found only here and in Genesis 19:11, doesn't indicate that the Syrians couldn't see. It means the Syrians were unable to *interpret* what they saw. They saw what God and the prophet intended them to see—a scene which didn't accord with reality.

Elisha boldly approached the Syrian commander and led his force inside the walls of Samaria, Israel's capital. Then the Lord "opened their eyes," and the Syrians realized where they were. The troops sent to take Elisha had been captured by Elisha!

The excited Jehoram wanted to kill the Syrians, but Elisha had a better plan. He would humiliate the Syrians by treating them as guests, then send them back to Syria. The strategy worked, and for a time no more raids were mounted against Israel.

The Syrians besiege Samaria (6:24—7:20). The Syrians later attacked Israel in force and besieged Samaria. Conditions inside the city became so desperate that some people resorted to cannibalism (2 Kings 6:26–31). The king blamed Elisha, God's representative, rather than acknowledging that it was a result of his own refusal to turn to the Lord.

In the name of the Lord, Elisha announced that food would be sold the next day at the gate of Samaria at bargain prices. One of the king's officers scoffed at Elisha's words. What Elisha announced was impossible, even for God (2 Kings 7:2). Elisha responded that the officer would see it, but he himself would never eat of the plenty provided by God.

That night the Syrian army heard noises that the soldiers interpreted as Hittite or Egyptian armies come to break their siege. Terrified, the entire Syrian force fled, leaving all its supplies behind. The next day, alerted by a few lepers who were crouched outside Samaria's walls, the people of the city poured out to gather the food the Syrians had left behind. The prophecy of Elisha came true. Food was sold to the hungry masses at bargain prices. And the officer who ridiculed God's ability to do as his prophet promised saw the food, but he was trampled to death in the peoples' rush to reach it.

The meaning of the miracles in this sequence. The common element in this section of 2 Kings is "revelation." God revealed the plans of the Syrians to Elisha. Elisha opened the eyes of his servant to reveal the angel army protecting them. Elisha confused the sight of the Syrian army so they completely lost touch with the reality of their situation; then he restored their ability to see and grasp reality. Finally, Elisha foresaw and predicted that the besieged and starving Israelites would be rescued and fed. This prophetic vision was rejected by Jehoram's officer, who died because of his doubts.

The message of these miracles is clear. God's revelation enables us to see the spiritual realities which must govern our actions in the material world.

THE LITERARY FORM OF THE ELISHA STORIES

The stories of Elisha's miracles are organized below in a literary form known as *chiasm*. Chiasm is the parallel arrangement of material, in which themes or thoughts are repeated in reverse order. That is,

    A. Expresses idea #1
        B. Expresses idea #2
        B. Expresses idea #2
    A. Expresses idea #1

When the chiasm has an odd number of elements, the single element standing at the center typically states the governing theme the author is developing.

If we review the recorded miracles of Elisha, we see that they have a chiasmic order. The single miracle standing at the center provides the key to understanding the underlying message not only of the whole, but also the unique contribution of each parallel pair.

The chart below so arranges fourteen miracles, counting miracles 13 and 14, which share the theme of blinding and restoring sight, as one.

Insights from the chiasmic organization of Elisha's miracles. There are many insights to gain from studying the order in which these miracle reports are organized.

Resurrection: life for the dead. This is the central theme of the miracle sequence expressed in G-7—Elisha's restoration of a child's life. Thus the miracles all express some vital truth about God's power to bring the spiritually dead to life and to restore what has been lost.

The message of these miracles is for Israel and for us. Israel abandoned the Lord and his word to follow a religion established by Jeroboam (see page 110–111). But if the nation would only turn back to the Lord, he would provide spiritual life and restore the nation's health.

God's good word to us is the same. However dead we have been to him in the past, however far we have strayed, his power has a resurrection quality that can revive and revitalize us.

Revelation (A-A): The first step toward new life. Miracles A-A are about revelation. In miracle A-1, prophets saw Elisha separate the Jordan's

  A. Elisha divides the Jordan. (1)
      B. Elisha heals a spring of water. (2)
          C. Elisha curses jeering youths. (3)
              D. Elisha wins a battle. (4)
                  E. Elisha multiplies a widow's oil. (5)
                      F. Elisha predicts a child's birth. (6)
                          G. Elisha restores the child's life. (7)
H.   F. Elisha makes poison harmless. (8)
I.   E. Elisha multiplies loaves. (9)
J.   D. Elisha heals General Naaman. (10)
K.   C. Elisha curses Gehazi. (11)
L.   B. Elisha makes an ax head float. (12)
M. A. Elisha blinds and gives sight. (13, 14)

waters, and they recognized him as God's spokesman. They will hear his words.

In miracle A-13, 14, God enabled Elisha to see reality and opened the eyes of Elisha's servant so he would also know the truth. But the Syrian army wandered in a world of illusion, until Elisha opened their eyes as well. And the official who doubted God's word was trampled to death by the crowd rushing to get to the food he had said God couldn't provide.

If we would have what God alone can provide, we must rely on revelation, the Word of God, which guides us to life. To reject his Word means death.

Redemption (B-B): God's power redeems and saves. In B-2, Elisha healed a spring of water which destroyed all the vegetation it touched. What mankind needs is a new heart, from which the pure and refreshing will flow. God is not concerned with moral whitewashing. He requires that our hearts, from which our actions flow, be cleansed and purified.

B-2 and B-12 are linked by the water. In B-12, the ax head was lost in the Jordan River. Elisha miraculously made the ax head float so what had been lost could be recovered.

Those who accept revelation discover that in God's eyes, they are corrupt and lost. Yet God can purify the heart and save the lost.

Relationship (C-C): to live with God we must hold him in awe as God. C-3 and C-11 are linked by the word *curse.* The youths who jeered at God's power (C-3) suffered death. If we come to God, we must be prepared to treat him with utmost respect.

The attempt of Gehazi to deceive Elisha (C-11) showed how little he respected the Lord. As a leper, Gehazi lost the privilege of intimate relationship with God, expressed in Old Testament times by participation in the life of the community. The leper was forced to live outside the community (Lev. 13:45, 46).

Reconciliation (D-D). God's new life means peace with God. D-4 and D-10 are linked by warfare. God provided victory for the three allied kings in their battle with Moab (D-4). Yet subse-

quently the war was lost, and there was no lasting peace.

In D-10, the Lord brought healing and peace to Naaman, the leper (D-10).

It is important to note the role of obedience in each of these miracle accounts. The kings obeyed God and dug the ditches which were the key to the victory God provided. Yet Jehoash's heart was unchanged by God's blessing, and he returned home unwilling to submit to God's will. Naaman obeyed God; when he washed in the river Jordan, he was healed. Naaman then returned to Elisha to express his commitment to the Lord. Naaman, unlike Israel's king, had peace with God.

Provision (E-E): God supplies what we need to sustain the life he provides. The link between these two stories is the multiplication of necessities. In E-5, Elisha multiplied a widow's supply of olive oil. This not only saved her sons from slavery but also gave the family enough to live on.

In E-9, Elisha multiplied a tiny store of bread so that it fed one hundred men, with some left over.

In each case, God used what the needy had and multiplied it. In each case, there was more than enough. The God who gives us new life surely will supply what we need to sustain that life and us as well.

Preservation (F-F): God preserves the life he gives. In F-6, Elisha predicted a son's birth. The miracle speaks of the preservation of a family line in Israel.

In F-8, Elisha neutralized poison in the prophets' meal. This miracle preserved God's prophets from death.

We can perhaps see in the preservation of the family in F-6 a suggestion of the continuation of our lives beyond time into eternity. And F-8 contains a parable promising that nothing can take away the eternal life that God provides.

Additional insights from the chiasm. The arrangement of the miracle stories yields to further analysis as well. There is an additional relationship between the miracles. This relationship can be diagrammed as follows:

A-1
B-2
C-3
D-4
    E-5
    F-6
      G-7
    F-8
    E-9
D-10
C-11
B-12
A 13, 14

Arranged in this way, the key is God's miracle gift of resurrection life (G-7).

The miracle stories EF-FE are promises which can be claimed only by true believers. This is shown by the repeated reference to closed doors behind which the miracles E-5 and F-6 were performed, and the fact that miracles F-8 and E-9 were performed in a private gathering of God's prophets.

Only a person who has received new life from God can experience the wonder of his provision and preservation. The message of these miracles can be understood and appropriated only by those who have put their trust in him.

The miracles in ABCD and DCBA are miracles of gospel invitation. They are messages the lost need to hear: messages of revelation, redemption, relationship and reconciliation. Through them, we learn how to approach God and to receive the spiritual life he offers freely to all.

THE MIRACLE OF A LIFE RESTORED
2 Kings 13:20–21

One last miracle was associated with Elisha, but it was not a miracle which the prophet performed. A group was about to bury a dead man when raiders from Moab appeared. The funeral party placed the body in Elisha's tomb. When the body touched Elisha's bones, the man revived and stood up.

The message of the miracle is clear. Elisha was dead. But the God of Elisha lived! The promise implicit in Elisha's miracles still stood. God's offer of life was still open. Israel could turn to him—and live.

The cycle complete. This final miracle completes the cycle of the miracles of Elijah and Elisha. The focus now shifts from Israel to Judah, where the three final miracles contained in the books of history are found.

CHAPTER 8

MORE MIRACLES IN HISTORY, POETRY, AND PROPHECY

Magnifying God's Presence

2 Kings—Daniel

Aggressive TV ads for the Psychic Hot Line promise to tell callers about themselves and their futures. But Old Testament prophets had to pass a far more rigorous test that any phone-line psychic. And pass the test they did!

God revealed the future to His prophets, instructed them to predict what would happen, and invariably their words came true. We see this phenomenon in miracle prophecies recorded in the Old Testament. And we see God celebrated for His miracle working power in Old Testament poetry.

THE MIRACLE OF UZZIAH'S LEPROSY *2 Kings 15:1–8; 2 Chronicles 26:1–21*

Uzziah (called Azariah in 2 Kings) was a man who "did what was right in the sight of the LORD" (2 Kings 15:3). Second Chronicles adds details. The king "sought God in the days of Zechariah. . . . And as long as he sought the Lord, God made him prosper" (2 Chron. 26:5). The same book reveals that Uzziah became "exceeding strong," developing a powerful military which won a wide reputation in the ancient world.

Uzziah's fall (2 Chronicles 26:16–19). When Uzziah became strong, "his heart was lifted up." The king arrogantly tried to usurp the privilege of burning incense in the temple, which God's Law reserved for priests alone. When the priests tried to stop him, Uzziah became furious. He was determined to offer that incense, no matter what the priests or God's Law said!

Uzziah's punishment (26:19–21). Before Uzziah could act, leprosy broke out on his forehead. The priests hurried him out of the temple, and indeed Uzziah was anxious to go! The Bible says that "Uzziah was a leper until the day of his death," and that he "dwelt in an isolated house, because he was a leper." The Hebrew phrase is "house of quarantine," and a similar phrase in Ugaritic suggests humiliation and disgrace. Uzziah's son, Jotham, became co-regent and ruled in Judah.

The message of the miracle. In Judah, the king was not an absolute monarch. He was to be responsive to God and to be guided by God's Law. As long as Uzziah was humble enough to seek God by submitting to God's revealed will, he and the nation prospered. But when Uzziah became too proud to submit to God's Law, the Lord struck him with leprosy and set him aside. What an important message for the people of Judah. If God would not stand for disrespect from a king, how much less will he tolerate disrespect from ordinary citizens! God is to be honored and held in awe.

THE MIRACLE OF THE ASSYRIAN SLAUGHTER   *2 Kings 18, 19; 2 Chronicles 32; Isaiah 37*

The fact that this story is repeated three times in Scripture underlines its importance. While the miracle itself is striking, its context provides clues to its lasting significance.

The setting (2 Kings 18:1–17). Some years before this account, an Assyrian army had taken Samaria and resettled the people of the Northern Kingdom in other lands. When Sennacherib of Assyria threatened Judah, King Hezekiah had stripped the land to pay a ransom. But the Assyrians were not satisfied. Some years later they returned, intent on subduing Judah and deporting its population. The Assyrians succeeded in destroying the fortified cities on Judah's borders and even threatened the capital city of Jerusalem.

But Hezekiah, one of Judah's most godly kings, had led a great revival in the land. When an Assyrian envoy called for Jerusalem's surrender, Hezekiah laid the envoy's insulting words before the Lord and begged for his intervention.

The Assyrian's insult to God (18:31–35). The Assyrian envoy stood outside the city walls and, speaking Hebrew, threatened and made promises, demanding the surrender of the city. In his diatribe, he warned, "Do not listen to Hezekiah, lest he persuade you, saying, 'The Lord will deliver us'" (1 Kings 18:32). The envoy then went on to compare Yahweh to the gods of the nations which Assyria had conquered. Had any of those gods delivered their people? Why then should they expect Yahweh to deliver them?

There was a direct challenge and an ironic one as well. At the founding of the nation Israel, God had done something no other god could do. He had taken for himself "a nation from the midst of another nation, by trials, by signs, by wonders, by war, by a mighty hand and an outstretched arm, and by great terrors" (Deut. 4:34). From the very beginning, God had set himself apart from all that others called "god!" Now the Assyrian envoy contemptuously lumped the Lord with the frivolous gods of the nations. What an insult to the one true God!

Hezekiah's prayer (19:14–19). When the Assyrian envoy later returned and again insulted the Lord, Hezekiah went to God in prayer. He affirmed his faith that "You are God, You alone," and asked the Lord to save Jerusalem that "all the kingdoms of the earth may know that You are the Lord God, You alone."

God answered Hezekiah's prayer (19:32–35). The prophet Isaiah conveyed God's answer to Hezekiah. The Lord would defend the city, and not even an arrow would fly over Jerusalem's walls.

A few nights later an angel killed 185,000 Assyrians, and Sennacherib returned to Nineveh, where he was assassinated by two of his sons. Because of the difficulty of translating numbers in Hebrew (see page 106), the number 185,000 has been challenged. But there is no doubt that a substantial number of the Assyrian force was devastated.

"That all the kingdoms of the earth may know" (19:19). There is a fascinating aspect to this request in Hezekiah's prayer. Herodotus, over two centuries later, told the story of Sennacherib's defeat after an unexplained military disaster. The memory of God's overthrow of

Thousands of Assyrians were killed by God's angel, without any fighting by Judah.

❖

the ruler who had ridiculed him was preserved by this Greek historian, that the nations might know.

THE MIRACLE SIGN TO HEZEKIAH *2 Kings 20:1–11; 2 Chronicles 32:24; Isaiah 38*

When Hezekiah became ill, Isaiah warned him that he would die. Hezekiah, who had been dedicated to the Lord, begged God for recovery. Isaiah returned with word that God would add fifteen years to Hezekiah's life. The king then asked for a sign ['ot] that he might be sure of God's intention.

The miraculous sign (2 Kings 20:8). In fact, a sign had already been given. Isaiah had told Hezekiah that in three days he would recover enough to go to the temple and worship (2 Kings 20:5). But Hezekiah could not wait for that sign. He had been facing death, and he wanted reassurance. This the Lord graciously provided. Isaiah asked whether Hezekiah wanted the shadow on some nearby stairs to move upward or downward ten "degrees."

The common notion that Hezekiah referred to a "sundial of Ahaz" (20:11) is not sup-

ported by the Hebrew text. The original simply calls them "steps of Ahaz." It is most likely these were a set of stairs on which the passage of time was roughly estimated by where the sun's shadow fell. Hezekiah chose to ask that the shadow move *backward,* and it did.

It is not necessary to suppose that the position of the earth and sun were affected. It was the *shadow* that moved.

Hezekiah was then healed. A poultice of figs was laid on his boils, and Hezekiah recovered to live for fifteen more years.

The timing of the miracle. Hezekiah died in 686 B.C. If we subtract fifteen years, his illness and recovery took place in 701 B.C., about the time of Sennacherib's invasion. It is fascinating to speculate what might have happened in Judah if the godly King Hezekiah had not lived to pray for Jerusalem and his people.

Hezekiah had been a godly ruler, dedicated to the Lord. But the healing which God provided was not simply for Hezekiah. It was also for the nation. God may be gracious to us when we are ill. When we recover, it is only appropriate to ask ourselves how we may serve him in the additional years he has granted.

SENNACHERIB'S OWN ACCOUNT

The military annals of Sennacherib have been recovered by archaeologists. Typically, the conqueror's report of this expedition into Judah failed to mention his defeat. For all Sennacherib's boasting, he failed to do to Judah what Shalmaneser had done to Israel a few decades before. He was unable to take Jerusalem and depopulate the Holy Land. Knowing the true story from Scripture, his boasting account sounds hollow indeed.

As for Hezekiah of Judah, he did not submit to my yoke, and I laid siege to forty-six of his strong cities, walled forts, and to the countless small villages in their vicinity, and conquered them using earth ramps and battering rams. These siege engines were aided by the use of foot soldiers who undermined the walls. I drove out of these places 200,150 people—young and old, male and female, horses, mules, donkeys, camels, large and small cattle beyond counting and considered them as booty. I made Hezekiah a prisoner in Jerusalem, like a bird in a cage. I erected siege works to prevent anyone escaping through the city gates. The towns in his territory which I captured I gave to Mitinti, King of Ashdod, Padi, King of Ekron, and Sillibel, King of Gaza. Thus I reduced his territory in this campaign, and I also increased Hezekiah's annual tribute payments.

Hezekiah, who was overwhelmed by my terror-inspiring splendor, was deserted by his elite troops, which he had brought into Jerusalem, and was forced to send me 30 talents of gold, eight hundred talents of silver, precious stones, couches and chairs inlaid with ivory, elephant hides, ebony wood, box wood, and all kinds of valuable treasures, his daughters, concubines, and male and female musicians. He sent his personal messenger to deliver this tribute and bow down to me.

MIRACLES IN THE POST-CAPTIVITY BOOKS

In 586 B.C. the kingdom of Judah finally fell—to the Babylonians. Its people were de-ported to Babylon and settled there. Three Old Testament books of history take up the story of what happened later.

THE BOOK OF ESTHER

In time the Persians replaced the Babylonians as the dominant power in the Middle East. The book of Esther tells the fascinating story of how a young Jewish girl became queen of Persia, and saved her people from extinction.

The book is noted for a series of "coincidences" which led to the Jews' deliverance. While God is not mentioned in Esther, it is clear that the Lord was at work through a series of unlikely coincidences to preserve his people.

God no longer would perform miracles to deliver Israel. But God had not abandoned his people. The Lord was at work behind the scenes of history to preserve the people he had chosen as his own.

EZRA AND NEHEMIAH

These two books tell the story of the small parties of Jews which returned to Judah after decades of captivity in Babylon. There they rebuilt the temple and later the defensive wall of Jerusalem. Although Judah was only a tiny district in one of the 128 provinces in an empire dominated by Persia, Jews once again lived in their homeland. There they awaited God's next step in fulfilling his ancient promises to Abraham.

There are no accounts of miracles in these books, although the praise song in Nehemiah 9 affirms that the Lord is a miracle-working God (Neh. 9:10, 17). Yet it is clear that God was again at work—settling the Jews in their land and preparing them for a new age of miracles which would occur when the Messiah came.

MIRACLES OF THE POETICAL BOOKS

The books of the Old Testament classified as poetry are Job, Psalms, Proverbs, Ecclesiastes, and Song of Solomon.

❖

JOB

Job is a work which tries to explain why bad things happen to good people. Job reported no miracles, but he did affirm the wonder-working power of God (Job 5:9). Job, the main character in the book, was challenged by God to consider his wondrous works (Job 37:14, 16).

PSALMS

Psalms is the hymn and praise book of Israel, filled with references to God's wonderful works, awesome deeds, signs, and wonders. While Psalms does not report any new miracles, the book sings a song of praise to God for his past wonders. The following passages in the Psalms refer to God's signs, miracles, and wonderful works.

PROVERBS

The book of Proverbs is a collection of sayings and practical advice intended to guide us to make wise choices in life. Because of the nature of this book, it contains no accounts of miracles.

ECCLESIASTES

The book of Ecclesiastes records one man's search for the meaning of life apart from God. Solomon, the traditional author of Ecclesiastes, limited himself to deductions he could make from personal experience and from observing life "under the sun." He refused to look to revelation or to consider miracles in his search. Solomon was forced to conclude that human life apart from God is meaningless.

The book stands as a powerful witness to the truth that humankind can find meaning only by establishing a personal relationship with God, who has revealed himself in his written Word and in miracle.

Bible Background: Verses in the Hebrew Psalms which Refer to Miracles

Psalm 9:1	Psalm 77:12	Psalm 104:25	Psalm 111:2
Psalm 28:5	Psalm 78:4	Psalm 105:1	Psalm 111:4
Psalm 40:5	Psalm 78:7	Psalm 105:2	Psalm 111:6
Psalm 44:1	Psalm 78:11	Psalm 105:5	Psalm 111:7
Psalm 46:8	Psalm 78:12	Psalm 105:27	Psalm 118:17
Psalm 65:5	Psalm 78:32	Psalm 106:2	Psalm 119:27
Psalm 65:8	Psalm 78:43	Psalm 106:7	Psalm 135:9
Psalm 66:3	Psalm 86:8	Psalm 106:22	Psalm 136:4
Psalm 66:5	Psalm 89:5	Psalm 107:8	Psalm 139:14
Psalm 71:17	Psalm 92:5	Psalm 107:15	Psalm 145:4
Psalm 73:28	Psalm 96:3	Psalm 107:21	Psalm 145:12
Psalm 75:1	Psalm 98:1	Psalm 107:24	Psalm 145:17
Psalm 77:11	Psalm 104:24	Psalm 107:31	Psalm 150:2

SONG OF SOLOMON

The Song is an extended love poem. Again, the author's subject matter means that he neither recounted nor referred to miracles.

MIRACLES IN THE BOOKS OF PROPHECY

PROPHECY AS MIRACLE

The *Revell Bible Dictionary* defines prophets and prophecy as follows. A prophet is

one who communicates or interprets messages from God. A prophet is a person authorized to speak for God. The prophet's message was called in Hebrew a *nebu'ah*, "prophecy;" sometimes it was also termed a vision, oracle, or burden, but most often it was identified as "the word of the Lord" (p. 822).

Recognizing the true prophet (Deuteronomy 13:1–5; 18:18–22). The Old Testament set up standards which a person who claimed to be a prophet had to meet. The tests are specific and clear:

- The prophet must be "from your midst, from your brethren" (Deut. 18:15). That is, the prophet must be a Hebrew, one of God's covenant people.
- The prophet must speak in the name of the Lord (Deut. 18:19). No true prophet will credit a pagan deity with his message.
- The prophet will be recognized by his ability to make accurate predictions about the future. "When a prophet speaks in the name of the Lord, if the thing does not happen or come to pass, that is the thing which the Lord has not spoken" (Deut. 18:22).
- Even if a prophet should make a prediction which comes true ["give a sign or a wonder"], but calls the hearer to abandon the Lord or his commandments, that "prophet" shall be put to death (Deut. 13:1–5).

Thus, a prophet of the Lord was determined by checking his message against God's revealed Word. He was also proven by his per-

formance of miracles or by making predictions which came true.

The miracle of predictive prophecy. The Old Testament makes it clear that predictive prophecy is in itself a sign or a miracle. Isaiah, giving God's words to a rebellious people, spoke of the fact that only God knows and can reveal the future.

> Remember this, fix it in mind,
>   take it to heart, you rebels.
> Remember the former things, those
>   of long ago;
>   I am God, and there is no other;
>   I am God, and there is none like
>   me.
> I make known the end from the
>   beginning,
>   from ancient times, what is still
>   to come.
> I say: My purpose will stand,
>   and I will do all that I please . . . .
> What I have said, that will I bring
>   about;
>   what I have planned, that will I do
>   (Isa. 46:8–11, NIV).

In this great affirmation, the Lord claims not only to know but also to control the future. He can predict what will happen the next day or in a thousand years, because God is sovereign and will cause what he says to happen.

When a person speaking in the name of the Lord accurately predicts future events—precisely and without mistakes—his claim to be God's messenger is authenticated. In harmony with our definition of miracles, such prediction can be classified as an extraordinary event—one caused by God, with a religious purpose.

Since no person in his or her own strength can accurately predict the future, such events are extraordinary. Consistent accuracy in these predictions is evidence that God is the source of the prophet's predictions. And such predictions have religious purpose, not only to reveal information but also to authenticate the prophet as God's spokesman.

he extent of predictive prophecy in the Old estament. Some have estimated that as much s a third of the Old Testament is predictive rophecy. The *Revell Bible Dictionary* observes hat "predictive prophecy falls into one of two ategories: near-term or far-term."

Iear-term predictions tell what is about to be expe.enced by those in the prophet's own generation. :remiah's announcement that Hananiah would die rithin a year is a near-term prediction, and within vo months Hananiah was dead. Habakkuk's preiction of a coming invasion of Judah by Babylon robably took place within two decades, even 1ough its fulfillment called for the unexpected verthrow of Assyria by the Babylonians and the nergence of a new, vast empire. The fulfillment of ear-term predictions served to authenticate the rophet as God's messenger (p. 826).

There are many examples in the Old Tesiment of far-term prophecy which has been 1lfilled. About 700 years before Jesus' birth, rophets predicted he would come from avid's line (Isa. 9:6, 7), be born of a virgin sa. 7:14) in Bethlehem (Micah 5:2), and)end his early years in Nazareth of Galilee sa. 9:1, 2). His death was described in detail, om his execution with criminals (Isa. 53:9, 2) and his burial with the rich (Isa. 53:9).

Several centuries before Jesus was born, salmists described the offer of vinegar made hile he hung on the cross (Ps. 69:21) as solers gambled for his clothing (Ps. 22:18). /en his dying words were recorded (Ps. 22:1; :5), as well as the fact that while his side ould be pierced (Zech. 12:10), not a bone of s body would be broken (Ps. 34:20).

There are many more incidents of fulfilled ‑term prophecy in Scripture, ranging from scriptions of coming world empires in Daniel powerful images of the fate of cities and nans which oppressed God's people, Israel.

While near-term prophecy authenticated e prophet in the eyes of his generation, farm prophecy which has been fulfilled auenticates the Bible itself as a miracle book. ch prophecies are powerful sources of obtive data that support Scripture's claim to be e revealed Word of God.

In a sense, all predictive prophecy is miracle. But our study of all the prophecies of the Bible must await another book in this series. For the present, we can only note that the Bible is rich in prophetic miracles—and limit our examination of the writings of the prophets to their reports of other miracles.

MIRACLES IN THE WRITINGS OF THE PROPHETS

MIRACLES IN THE BOOK OF ISAIAH

Isaiah has been called the "evangelist of the Old Testament." His ministry extended over about 50 years, through the reigns of Uzziah, Jotham, Ahaz and Hezekiah of Judah, and into the reign of Manasseh. Throughout the 66 chapters of this towering work, condemnation of Judah's sins is balanced by promises of God's coming redemption though his servant, the Messiah.

While the book is filled with near-term and far-term prophecies, it contains no accounts of the kind of miracles we are studying here.

MIRACLES IN JEREMIAH AND LAMENTATIONS

Jeremiah has been called the "weeping prophet." He ministered during the last four decades of Judah's existence as a nation, constantly warning God's people to submit to the pagan nation Babylon. Condemned as unpatriotic for his warnings, Jeremiah and his message were rejected by a generation rushing toward God's judgment.

Jeremiah's prophetic words truly were from the Lord. He lived to see the city captured and its people deported to Babylon, just as he had predicted.

The book of Jeremiah doesn't report any miracles. The reason why is made clear in Jeremiah 21 and 32. King Zedekiah sent officials to Jeremiah to see if God would "deal with us according to all his wonderful works" (21:2) when the king of Babylon invaded. Jeremiah answered in God's name, "I Myself will fight against you with an outstretched hand and with a strong arm, even in anger and fury and great wrath" (Jer. 21:5). God would not perform miracles for his sinning people; indeed, he would work against them!

The same thought is expressed in Jeremiah 32:20–23. Jeremiah praised God for the signs and wonders he had done in Egypt, but expressed regret that Israel had "not obeyed Your voice or walked in Your law." In such a land, at such a time, God would work no miracles.

Jerusalem did fall, and Solomon's temple was destroyed.

The book of Lamentations, which tradition claims was written by Jeremiah from Babylon, captures the feelings of the captives as the people of Judah finally realized how much they had lost.

MIRACLES IN THE BOOK OF EZEKIEL

While Jeremiah prophesied in Judah during its last days, the prophet Ezekiel ministered to the Jewish community in Babylon. This community was made up of persons who had been captured in the Babylonian expeditions to Judah in 605 B.C. and in 598 B.C. Ezekiel warned the captives of the coming destruction of Jerusalem, even as Jeremiah warned the Jews still living in their homeland.

Many wonderful visions were given to Ezekiel (see especially Ezek. 1—3 and 40—48). But only one vision in Ezekiel fits our standard for a miracle—and this primarily because it is the reverse of a miracle experienced by Israel centuries before.

The shekinah entered the temple (1 Kings 8:10–12). When King Solomon dedicated the Jerusalem temple in 963 B.C., the visible glory of God filled the structure and awed the people. The shekinah's presence was a visible sign that the Lord would hear prayers directed toward his temple and would protect his people. (See the discussion of this miracle on page 109.)

Even as the Babylonian army marched toward Judah, the people took comfort in the fact that the temple stood in their Holy City. God had placed his presence there. Whatever sins Israel committed, God would never permit an enemy to overrun his temple. The Ezekiel had a vision in which he served as the sole witness to a terrible event.

The shekinah left the temple (Ezekiel 8—11) Ezekiel was transported in a vision to Jerusalem. There he witnessed the people of Judah worshiping idols. Many of the elders of Judah had gathered in one of the rooms of the temple to worship images drawn on the wall. The vision made the extent of Judah's sin and idolatry clear, setting the scene for what Ezekiel witnessed next.

What Ezekiel saw was the shekinah glory of the Lord rising up from where it rested over the ark of the covenant in the innermost room of the temple. The shekinah slowly moved toward the door of the temple. It hovered for a moment as if reluctant to leave, then rose even higher. Finally, God's glory left the city and retreated over the eastern mountains.

The message of the miracle vision was clear. Judah's sins had caused God to withdraw his presence and protection. The city guarded now by a temple which was nothing but a heap of stones, was no protection at all Jerusalem and Judah were doomed.

Judgment—and hope (Ezekiel 11). As Ezekiel watched the shekinah withdraw, God gave him a message for the people of Judah. The city would surely fall, and his people would be scattered across the Babylonian Empire. But one day God would keep the promise had made to Abraham. One day, God said, will gather you from the peoples, assemble you from the countries where you have been scattered, and I will give you the land of Israel" (Ezek. 11:17).

God's withdrawal was temporary, not permanent. His people must be punished. But they would not be abandoned. What a wonderful reassurance this is for us. Our sins may block our fellowship with the Lord, leading

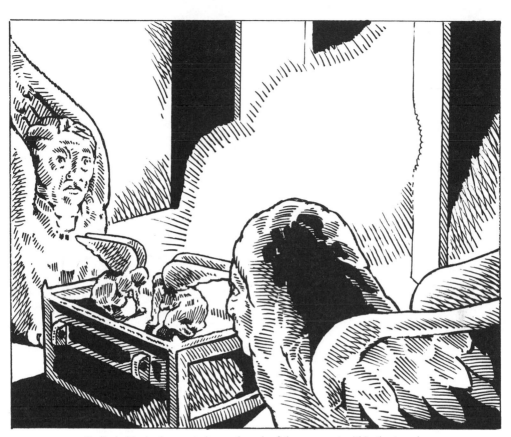

God's shekinah glory rested over the ark of the covenant within the temple.

even to painful consequences. But our God stands ready to forgive and restore.

THE MIRACLES OF THE BOOK OF DANIEL

The first part of the book of Daniel reads like a book of history rather than a book of prophecy. But Daniel alone, of all the prophets, described a series of miracles. Several miracles are reported in the book's first six chapters. These miracles played a role in Daniel's advancement and ultimately influenced the conversion of Nebuchadnezzar himself.

The story of Daniel. Daniel was a young man who was deported along with Judah's leading families after the Babylonian invasion of 605

B.C. Along with three other promising Jewish youths, Daniel was enrolled in a school which King Nebuchadnezzar of Babylon had established to train officials to run his empire.

The miracle of Nebuchadnezzar's first dream (Daniel 2). The Babylonian king had a dream that disturbed his sleep, but when he awoke he couldn't remember the content of the dream. He called all his counselors and advisors, demanding that they tell him the dream and its meaning. The demand was unreasonable, but the king threatened to kill all his advisors if they failed. When the wise men were unable to help, Nebuchadnezzar began the slaughter (Dan. 2:1–13)! Those threatened included Daniel and his three Jewish friends, who were graduates of the king's school!

Daniel promised to tell the dream and its meaning (Daniel 2:14–18). When the soldiers came to take Daniel, he asked for time. Daniel then joined his three friends in prayer, asking God to reveal Nebuchadnezzar's dream, "so that Daniel and his companions might not perish with the rest of the wise men of Babylon" (v. 18).

God revealed the dream and its meaning (Daniel 2:19–23). That night God revealed the dream to Daniel. His prayer of praise serves as a model for us when our prayers are answered.

Daniel explained the dream to the king (Daniel 2:23–45). When Daniel was taken to the king, he was careful to give God the credit for the revelation. Daniel told the king that his dream concerned a great image, and he provided the interpretation.

Nebuchadnezzar was impressed by Daniel and Daniel's God (Daniel 2:46–49). Nebuchadnezzar honored and promoted Daniel and his three friends. This was the king's first encounter with the God of Israel, and he was impressed. He declared, "Truly your God is the God of gods, the Lord of kings, and a revealer of secrets" (Dan. 2:47).

The religious purpose of the miracle. There is no doubt that in the dream, and through Daniel's explanation of it, God addressed Nebuchadnezzar. As the sequence of miracles recorded in Daniel continued, it was clear that the Lord intended to be gracious to this world conqueror.

The miracle of the fiery furnace (Daniel 3).

King Nebuchadnezzar was an arrogant man. He created a golden image, then commanded officials from throughout his empire to bow down and worship it. His reasoning may have been more political than religious: the worship of a ruler's gods was one way people in the ancient world expressed loyalty. But the three young Jewish men who came to Babylon with Daniel and who were at this great gathering refused to bow down. Some of the Babylonian officials were quick to accuse them!

The king's anger (3:13–15). Nebuchadnezzar was furious, and he confronted the three men. He gave them another chance to worship the idol, but they refused. The king couldn't understand their loyalty to their own God. He asked, "Who is the god who can deliver you from my hands?"

The faith of the young men (3:15–18). The three affirmed their belief that God, the supreme ruler of the universe, was able to deliver them. Yet they did not know that God would do so. No matter what God chooses to do, they declared, they would remain loyal.

This should be our attitude too. God can deliver us from cancer and any other illness or problem. But God may choose not to do so. Whatever God in his sovereignty chooses to do, we have the privilege of continuing to trust and honor him.

God delivered them (Daniel 3:19–27). Furious, Nebuchadnezzar ordered the three young men thrown into the firepit. Then the ruler

A burning fiery furnace.

and his officials saw four persons, walking unharmed in the flames.

Nebuchadnezzar's startled description of the fourth figure has caused confusion, leading some to believe the fourth figure was Christ. In Hebrew idiom the phrase "a son of God" simply means "a supernatural being" or "angel." Nebuchadnezzar realized immediately the fourth person was no mere human!

The king called the three out of the flames. To his amazement, not a hair on their heads was burned nor did their clothing smell of fire.

Nebuchadnezzar's confession (Daniel 3:28–30). This was the king's second experience with the God of Israel, and he realized the Lord was greater than he—a powerful king. Nebuchadnezzar issued a decree that no one should speak a word against the Lord, on penalty of death, "because there is no other God who can deliver like this" (v. 29).

The meaning of the miracle. On one hand, the miracle was a testimony to God's faithfulness toward those who are loyal to him. But again, the religious impact of the miracle was felt by Nebuchadnezzar. The arrogant ruler, who held the power of life and death over his subjects, was confronted by a power greater than him. Nebuchadnezzar decreed death, but God decreed life; and the earthly king's orders were set aside. God continued to show grace to Babylon's ruler by revealing more and more of himself. And Nebuchadnezzar, unlike Egypt's pharaoh in the time of the Exodus, acknowledged the powerful presence of the Lord.

Nebuchadnezzar's madness (Daniel 4). Chapter 4 of Daniel is in the form of a confession of faith, sent by the king to everyone in his empire.

The king's dream and its interpretation (Daniel 4:1–27). The king told of a dream which only Daniel could interpret. The dream was a warning. Nebuchadnezzar was directed to set aside his pride and to honor God as the one who had given him his power. The ruler was also to "break off your sins by being righteous,

and your iniquities by showing mercy to the poor" (Dan. 4:27).

The dream came true (Daniel 4:28–36). A year after the dream, God struck the arrogant ruler. Nebuchadnezzar became mad and lived in the fields like an animal for "seven times" (v. 32). This term may refer to days or weeks, although in a later prophecy of Daniel a "time" [literally just a "seven"] represented a year (Dan. 9:24–27).

After this period, Nebuchadnezzar recovered his senses and returned to the throne. His concluding words have been interpreted by some as the confession of a sincere and saving faith in the Lord.

Now I, Nebuchadnezzar, praise and extol and honor the King of heaven, all of whose works are truth, and his ways justice. And those who walk in pride he is able to abase (Dan. 4:37).

One meaning of the miracle sequence. In each of the first three miracles recorded in Daniel, there was a single central figure: Nebuchadnezzar. Each miracle recounted an extraordinary event caused by God. And each miracle brought a positive response from the great ruler! Gradually, Nebuchadnezzar was brought to see more and more of the power of heaven's King, until at last this earthly king praised, extolled, and honored the Lord as the one true God.

The sequence reminds us of many wonderful truths. God is truly gracious. He even showed grace to the pagan ruler Nebuchadnezzar, who devastated Judah and destroyed the temple in Jerusalem. God's concern for human beings is universal. The Lord reveals himself to all people, and this happened even in Old Testament times. Any person who responds to God's revelation as Nebuchadnezzar did can and will be saved.

The miracle of the writing hand (Daniel 5). After Nebuchadnezzar's death, Daniel continued to serve in the Babylonian Empire. When the event reported in chapter 5 of Daniel took place, a Persian force under Cyrus was assembled outside Babylon, a city considered impregnable because of its massive walls and defenses.

Inside the city, the current Babylonian ruler, Belshazzar, was giving a banquet. As the king and his guests partied, a hand appeared and wrote four words on the wall. Shaken by the supernatural event, the ruler called for an interpretation. But the king's wise men could neither read nor understand the message.

At last, someone suggested Daniel as an interpreter. The prophet, by this time an old man, reminded Belshazzar of Nebuchadnezzar's humbling by God many years before. Unlike Nebuchadnezzar, Belshazzar had shown contempt for God, even drinking from holy vessels taken from the Lord's temple in Jerusalem.

Daniel then explained that the words written on the wall represented descending values of currency. The meaning was that God had weighed Belshazzar and found him lacking. His kingdom would fall to the Persians.

That very night, the Persians diverted a river that flowed into Babylon to undermine the city walls. They captured the city, killed Belshazzar, and took over Babylon's empire.

Once again, a ruler of Babylon was the focus of the miracle. But this ruler, unlike Nebuchadnezzar, had ignored the Lord's revelation of himself and arrogantly dishonored the Lord.

The message of this miracle is that the fate of all peoples and nations hinges on their response to the one true God.

Daniel is delivered from a lion's den (Daniel 6). When Daniel was an old man, jealous officials manipulated the Persian ruler of Babylon, Darius, into issuing a decree against prayers and petitions which they knew Daniel would violate. Because of a peculiarity in Persian law, even the ruler couldn't change a decree once it had been issued. So Daniel was condemned to be thrown to the lions.

Even though he could not take back his command, Darius expressed his hope to Daniel that "your God, whom you serve continually, He will deliver you" (Dan. 6:16). The anxious king stayed awake all night. The next morning he hurried to the lion's den. Daniel was alive! God had sent an angel, who shut the lions' mouths.

Both relieved and angry, Darius ordered that those who had plotted against Daniel should suffer the fate they had intended for him.

Darius later wrote a testimony honoring "the living God," ordering that every person in his kingdom should "tremble and fear before the God of Daniel" (Dan. 6:26).

Again, a ruler was the focus of this miracle. This ruler, like Nebuchadnezzar and unlike Belshazzar, knew about God and his wonder-working power (Dan. 6:16). Like Nebuchadnezzar, Darius both believed and openly witnessed to the power of God.

The larger message of the miracle sequence in Daniel. In Daniel's time, the Jewish people had been torn from the land which God promised to Abraham's descendants. As captives in Babylon, the Jews recognized their deportation from their homeland was punishment for their

Belshazzar was frightened when a hand appeared and wrote on the palace wall.

unfaithfulness to God. But the Jews must have wondered if their sins had been so terrible that God had permanently set them aside. Would he ever bring them home again?

The second half of the book of Daniel is filled with prophecy. Daniel's predictions describe in amazing detail a series of future world empires—Babylonian, Persian, Greek, and Roman—which would for centuries dominate the biblical world. Israel's questions about God's plans would remain unanswered for more than 400 years!

This helps us see the main message of the first half of the book of Daniel. *Daniel described miracles in which God displayed his sovereignty over the Gentile rulers of the ancient world!* Throughout the coming centuries Israel would remember that, although gentile powers dominated their homeland, God remained in control! Israel's God could bring a Nebuchadnezzar to his knees, punish a Belshazzar, and replace him with a Darius who honored the Lord and carried out his will.

And, until God moved again to keep his ancient promises to Abraham, through all the ups and downs of the ages, the Daniels of God—his faithful servants—would be protected and promoted to places of power and influence.

How clearly the miracles of Daniel prepared the way for the predictive prophecy which followed. How wonderfully those miracles remind us that, no matter what happens, our God is the Lord of history. He rules, even through those who don't know him.

THE MINOR PROPHETS

The last dozen writings of the prophets are shorter books. The name of this collection, "Minor Prophets," refers to their length rather than to the significance of the books. Unlike the book of Daniel, the Minor Prophets contain no narrative account of divine miracles. It is true that they contain miracle predictions about near and distant events. But we hope to explore this type of miracle thoroughly in a future book in this series.

The last book in the Old Testament, Malachi, was written about 400 years before the birth of Jesus. During those four centuries, God seemingly remained silent. We have no written record or documentation of any divine miracles during this long period. And so God's people waited for a new flurry of miracles. These would show clearly that God was about to reveal the next stage of his eternal plan.

JESUS: A MAN MARKED BY MIRACLES

GOD WITH US

Matthew—John

No one in first century Judea thought of Jesus as an ordinary man. Some today attempt to cast Jesus as a simple visionary or a misunderstood but good man. But one phenomenon forced even contemporaries who were hostile to Jesus to hesitate. Jesus was a Man marked by miracles!

The people who witnessed the healings performed by Jesus had no doubt that they were seeing miracles. Some reacted with fear. Others responded with faith. The miracles made one thing perfectly clear. Jesus could not simply be dismissed as insignificant. Every person, now as then, must make a decision about the claims of this Man marked by miracles.

INTRODUCTION

For centuries Israel had experienced divine silence. After Malachi delivered his message around 450 B.C., no prophet spoke to Israel with God's voice for nearly five centuries. Israel lived in a great void, anchored to the past by the Scriptures, struggling to deal with changing conditions as sages and rabbis sought to determine how God's Law should be applied in an age when Gentiles ruled and ten times as many Jews lived outside the holy land as within it.

Yet Israel's hope was never extinguished. One day God *would* send the Messiah, the Anointed One promised by the prophets. Then the entire promised land would be occupied by a new Jewish state, and Israel rather than Rome would dominate the world. "The Lord will make you the head and not the tail; you shall be above only and not be beneath," Moses had promised (Deut. 28:13). In the coming messianic age, Israel would once again be obedient to the Lord, and the Lawgiver's ancient promise would be fulfilled.

GOD'S SILENCE IS BROKEN

Then the silence of God was broken. Rumors of angel annunciations kindled Jewish expectations, and these simmered for nearly thirty years. Then a prophet whose dress and lifestyle reminded Israel of Elijah appeared out of the desert. He preached repentance, called for public baptism as a sign of confession and recommitment, and warned Israel to get ready—the promised Messiah was about to appear.

For the first time in nearly 500 years, a prophet's voice was heard again in the Holy Land. John the Baptist had begun his ministry, preparing the way for Jesus, the Christ.

John's ministry reached its peak one day by the Jordan River. He had preached his fiery message of moral renewal, warning that judgment would follow hard on Messiah's heels. But that day John's cousin, Jesus, came to him for baptism.

John refused at first (Matt. 3:13–15). He knew his cousin Jesus well, and John's message was addressed to those who had strayed from the Law. "I need to be baptized by You, and are You coming to me?" John objected (v. 14). There was nothing in Jesus' life to confess—nothing that required the radical change of heart that John preached. Indeed, Jesus' life was more pure than John's!

❖

Jesus came to be baptized by John.

Jesus insisted that he be baptized. "It is fitting for us to fulfill all righteousness," he said, meaning that it was only right for him to be baptized and take a stand with John to affirm the prophet's message. So John agreed. And on that day, John witnessed a miracle seen only by himself and Jesus (compare Matt. 3:16–17; John 1:29–34).

Earlier God had revealed to John that one day he would see the Spirit descend and rest on someone—and that this person would be the Messiah (John 1:33). "I didn't know him," John later confessed, perhaps distressed that he had not realized that his own cousin was the One. But as Jesus came up from the Jordan's waters, John saw the Spirit descending as a dove. He heard a voice from heaven announce, "This is My beloved Son, in whom I am well pleased" (Matt. 3:17). And John bore witness to what he had seen. "I have seen and testified that this is the Son of God" (John 1:34).

Then the truly unexpected jolted religious leaders and commoners alike. As Jesus began his public ministry, a new age of miracles came. Within the span of about three years, miracle after miracle was witnessed by thousands. Like Elijah and Elisha, Jesus multiplied resources. But while Elisha had fed a hundred with twenty loaves, Jesus fed thousands on far less! Like the two ancient prophets, Jesus raised a child who had just died. But then Jesus raised Lazarus, an adult who had been in the grave for three days!

Unlike any prophet in sacred history, Jesus even healed the sick. He restored withered limbs, gave sight to men born blind, and even expelled demons. The miracles of Jesus surpassed the miracles of the prophets of old. Even those most hostile to Christ and his message were forced to confess that he actually did work wonders.

MIRACLES MARK JESUS' BIRTH

The mark of miracles, which set Jesus apart, surrounded His birth as well as His public ministry. Both Matthew and Luke record several such wonders. Blending the two accounts, we can identify no less than thirteen miraculous signs associated with Jesus' birth and early years.

Gabriel appeared to Zacharias (Luke 1:11–22).

While an aged priest named Zacharias was offering incense in the temple, the angel Gabriel appeared to him and announced that he and his wife would have a son. The son was to be named John, and the angel announced that he would be the forerunner of the promised Messiah. Many things about this incident bear the mark of the miraculous.

He was chosen to offer incense by lot (Luke 1:8). The ordinary priests who ministered in the temple were divided into twenty-four orders, or groups. Each order served for just two weeks a year in Jerusalem. There were so many priests in each order that only once in a man's lifetime might he have the privilege of offering incense at the time of morning or evening prayer. God saw to it that Zacharias was chosen by lot that one special time.

Elizabeth, his wife, was barren (Luke 1:7). The text emphasizes the fact that both Zacharias and his wife were old (Luke 1:7, 18). The implication is that both were too old to have children normally. As in the case of Abraham and Sarah, it took a special work of God to quicken Elizabeth's womb so that John could be born.

The birth would fulfill prophecy (Luke 1:17). The last words of Malachi, the final book of the Old Testament, predicted the coming of an "Elijah" who would turn the hearts of God's people to the Lord, in preparation for the coming of the Messiah. The angel announced that John, the child to be born to Zacharias and Elizabeth, would fulfill this promise-prediction.

Zacharias was struck temporarily dumb (Luke 1:20). Zacharias doubted the angel's promise, and as a consequence he was struck dumb until the child was born and named. When he

left the temple, observers realized that he had seen a vision which had literally left him speechless.

Gabriel appeared to Mary (Luke 1:26–38).

Six months after Elizabeth conceived, Gabriel appeared to Mary. At the time Mary was probably a teenager, since in New Testament times most Jewish girls were married between ages 13 and 15.

The angel announced that Mary had been chosen by God to bear a son who would be the "son of the Highest" and the "Son of God." Mary was also told that her son would be the Messiah [the son of David] and that "of His kingdom there will be no end."

When Mary asked how this was possible, since she had never had sex with a man, Gabriel told her that God the Holy Spirit would overshadow her. The "father" of her son would be God Himself.

Unlike Zacharias, Mary expressed no doubt at this amazing announcement, but instead expressed her submission to God's will

❖

"Do not be afraid, Mary."

(Luke 1:38). The touching faith of this Jewish teen-ager in response to the announcement of history's greatest miracle stands as an example for us today. As a woman of great and wonderful faith, Mary merits our appreciation and deepest respect.

Mary is "with child" by the Holy Spirit (Matthew 1:18).

The announcement to Mary that she would become pregnant even though a virgin came true. Matthew looks back to the Old Testament prophet Isaiah and notes that God had promised that His Messiah would be virgin born. While some have noted that the Hebrew word *almah,* found in Isaiah 7:14, can be translated a "young unmarried woman," Matthew in translating the ancient prophecy into Greek uses the word *parthenos,* which can only mean a virgin. The "young unmarried woman" of the prophecy was always intended to be understood as an unmarried woman who was a virgin.

There can be no doubt that the virgin birth is one of the premier miracles of Scripture. If it were possible to create a viable fetus using only a woman's egg, that child would be a daughter, never a son. Only a male can provide the chromosome that, along with the woman's, makes possible the birth of a son. That chromosome, with the others that formed the theanthropic person Jesus (fully God as well as truly human), was provided by the Holy Spirit.

The virgin birth, predicted in the Old Testament and described in the New, marks Jesus as utterly unique. Like His miracles, as we will see, this beginning set Him apart from sacred history's prophets and clearly identified Him to Israel both as Messiah and as Son of God.

An angel appears to Joseph in a dream (Matthew 1:19–25).

The text of Matthew describes Joseph both as "betrothed" to Mary (Matt. 1:18) and as her "husband" (Matt. 1:19). In New Testament times Jewish marriages were contracted in two stages. During the first stage a binding contract was entered into by the bride and groom. This was typically negotiated by the families, and executing it meant that the couple was fully committed to each other. The second stage was the wedding itself, in which the husband took the bride into his own home, to live with him as his wife. The phrase "before they came together" in Matthew 1:18 makes it clear that, while Joseph and Mary were contracted to each other, they were not yet living together.

In this case Joseph learned that Mary was pregnant and naturally assumed that she had been unfaithful to her commitment to him. Her pregnancy was grounds for public divorce and disgrace. Yet Joseph cared for Mary, and while he felt he could not go through with the marriage, he planned to protect her reputation by putting her away "secretly."

Before this could happen an angel came to Joseph in a dream and told him what Gabriel had told Mary. Mary was pregnant by the Holy Spirit. Joseph was to marry her, and when the son was born acknowledge him by naming him—a father's privilege in Israel. The name Joseph was to give Mary's child was Jesus, the Greek spelling of the Hebrew name Joshua, which in each language meant "Savior." This Jesus would "save His people from their sins."

The child in Elizabeth's womb recognized Mary (Luke 1:41).

Mary was herself pregnant when she went to visit her relative Elizabeth, who was carrying the child who would grow up to become John the Baptist. When Mary greeted Elizabeth, the child in Elizabeth's womb leaped in recognition.

Elizabeth was filled with the Spirit and blessed Mary (Luke 1:41–44).

Elizabeth, without hearing the story of Gabriel's appearance to Mary, blessed Mary and acknowledged her as "the mother of my Lord." This wonder must have comforted and encouraged Mary. She was not alone in understanding what God had done within her.

Zacharias predicts John's ministry (Luke 1:59–80).

When Elizabeth's child was born, Zacharias spoke and confirmed that he was to be named John. The loosening of Zacharias' tongue was viewed as a miracle by onlookers. More significantly, Zacharias was then filled with the Spirit and prophesied concerning John's ministry. John was destined to "go before the face of the Lord" as one preparing the way for the Messiah.

Caesar called for a census that brought Mary and Joseph to Bethlehem (Luke 2:1–7; Matthew 2:6). On its surface, the Roman call for a census hardly seems to qualify as a miracle or wonder. The Emperor Augustus had instituted a policy of having citizens throughout the empire return to their home town to be counted, as a basis for assessing taxes. First century census documents from Egypt show that this policy was followed in lands besides Palestine and Syria.

Yet this census decree was instrumental in the fulfillment of a prophecy made by Micah some 700 years before Jesus' birth. The decree brought Joseph and Mary to Bethlehem just in time for the Christ-child to be born in the home town of King David! When events fall together in such a way that prophecy is fulfilled, we surely can call them miracles of Providence. God, behind the scenes, is ordering and timing what happens to fulfill His own purposes and plan.

Angels announced Jesus' birth to shepherds (Luke 2:8–20). The night Jesus was born angels announced His birth to shepherds in the fields near Jerusalem. The wonderful news was that "there is born to you this day in the city of David a Savior, who is Christ the Lord" (Luke 1:11).

This familiar part of the Christmas story is far more significant than we normally imagine. Today Christians tend to romanticize shepherds, seeing them as selfless individuals who are symbols of God's own care for His human flock. We do not realize that in the first century shepherds were viewed with suspicion and contempt. They were generally considered to be thieves, and in fact were not even allowed to testify in Jewish courts because their testimony could not be trusted! How appropri-

ate then that the angel appeared to shepherds, first century "sinners," with the good news that a Savior was born that very night.

What wonderful news that was, for them and for us, for like the shepherds we too need a Savior desperately.

Simeon identified baby Jesus as the Christ (Luke 2:21–35). Jewish ritual law called for the offering of a sacrifice by the mother after bearing a child. When Mary and Joseph traveled to the Jerusalem temple to offer the sacrifice, they were approached by an aged man named Simeon. God had told Simeon that he would not die until he had seen the Christ, the promised Messiah. Simeon was led to the temple by the Holy Spirit, who identified the infant Jesus as the Savior. Simeon held Jesus, and praised God for permitting him to see the one who would save God's people.

Anna the prophetess acknowledged Jesus as the Messiah (Luke 2:36–38). Anna joined Simeon in identifying Jesus as the promised redeemer.

A star brought wise men from the East to Judea to find Jesus (Matthew 2:1–12). When the wise men appeared in Jerusalem Jesus was probably about two years old (cf. Matt. 2:7, 16). Their familiar story is filled with wonders.

The wonder of the star (Matt. 2:2, 7). People today debate the nature of the star the wise men saw. Was it a super-nova, which appeared suddenly in the night sky? Was there a juxtaposition of planets, which gave the appearance of a bright and unexpected star in the heavens? Or was it simply a miracle-star, a bright new light shining above? We have no clear answer as to the nature of the star. But clearly there was an unusual light in the heavens, which the wise men not only recognized but which appeared to move and which in the end led them to the very home where Jesus lived (Matt. 2:9).

The wonder of the star's identification (Matt. 2:2). When the wise men entered Jerusalem they asked for the newborn king of the Jews, and stated that they had seen "his star" and had come to honor him. People have wondered what led the wise men to identify the new light in the sky with a Jewish ruler?

We know that Magi—the word rendered "wise men" in our English versions—were a special class of persons in the Persian Empire noted for their encyclopedic knowledge. We also know that a major center of Jewish learning existed from the sixth through first centuries in Babylon, where some of the Magi lived and worked. Most commentators suggest that the Magi of Matthew's Gospel linked the new star with a rather obscure prediction in Numbers 24:17, which reads "A Star shall come out of Jacob; a Scepter shall rise out of Israel."

While this theory is possible, we simply do not know how the Magi recognized the star as a symbol of the birth of the Messiah, the descendant of David, destined to rule Israel and the world. The appearance of the Magi is one of the wonders associated with the story of Jesus' birth and childhood.

Matthew makes it clear that they did come. They worshiped Jesus and gave him expensive gifts. And then, warned in a dream, they went home without telling Herod where Jesus could be found.

Joseph was warned in a dream to flee to Egypt (Matt. 2:13–15). This wonder too is associated with Jesus' birth and earliest years. King Herod the Great, noted for his fierce attacks on any who seemed to threaten his throne, determined to kill this "king of the Jews" the Magi had spoken of.

The dream warning is not the only wonder associated with the flight to Egypt. In addition there is the prophecy the flight fulfilled (Matt. 2:15), and God's provision for the journey.

Luke 2:24 tells us that when Mary came to the temple to offer the required sacrifice after childbirth, she offered "a pair of turtledoves or two young pigeons." According to Old Testament law, the normal offering was a lamb (Levitcus 12:6–8). Only if the family was too poor to afford a lamb could the woman offer a pair of birds. Joseph and Mary, then, were poor people. Yet it would be expensive to travel to Egypt and live there for any length of time.

Wise men from the east brought gifts to the young Jesus.

The answer, of course, is the gifts given Jesus by the Magi. Each of their expensive gifts could be, and undoubtedly were, sold and the proceeds used to finance the flight to Egypt that saved the Christ child from Herod's executioners. In this we clearly have yet another wonder of divine providence—striking evidence that God was personally involved in the birth and early life of our Lord.

Jesus was indeed marked by miracles, and His birth and early life were accompanied by wonders that set Him apart from all.

The underlying wonder of the Logos (John 1). We cannot understand Jesus if we simply treat the events surrounding His birth. The reason for this is simple. While conception and birth mark the beginning of existence for normal human beings, neither conception nor birth were a beginning for the Son of God.

John in his Gospel launches the story of Jesus where his story truly begins. In the first verses of the Gospel of John, Christ is called the "Word," our English rendering of the Greek word *logos*. That Greek term might also be rendered as the "expression" or "revelation." John takes us back into eternity, and asserts that in the beginning there was God. And that the Word was with God, and in fact was God. In fact the Word, the eternal expression of God, was the Creator of all, and the source of life and light. It was the Word, the One who has always expressed and revealed God, who came into our world as a human being. It was the Word, the One we know as the Son of God, the second Person of the Trinity, who bonded with humanity in Mary's womb, and who was born as a baby, grew into manhood, and began a miracle ministry in which He expressed God's compassion and love for humankind.

Ultimately it was the Word, the eternal Son of God, who in Jesus Christ found expression in the grand miracle of the Incarnation, who died on Calvary as a sacrifice for our sins, and who was raised again in the grand miracle of resurrection.

It is no wonder that Jesus' birth and early life were marked by miracles, for He Himself is the greatest miracle of all: God, come in the flesh; God, come to save us; God, calling us to find forgiveness and eternal life in Him.

THE MIRACLES OF JESUS FORCE US TO SAY YES OR NO TO HIM

Studies of Jesus' miracles often descend into debate about the credibility of individual wonders. The skeptic argues that the miracles weren't all that special. The sick were about to recover anyhow. The illnesses were psychosomatic—and moderns know how suggestion can bring about amazing cures in such cases. Jesus only seemed to be walking on water; really he was on the shore and the disciples were far enough away so that he *appeared* to walk on the surface of the sea. And besides, the critics claim, the miracle stories were written years later by disciples who were intent on making Jesus into someone he had never been—a deity rather than a Jewish rabbi whose teachings were within the traditions of Judaism.

Even believers sometimes argue the case for Jesus' miracles on the skeptic's grounds. The sicknesses described were serious. But no matter how responsive the victim was to suggestion, they reason, no cure of this malady could have been effected by such means. Many modern "faith healers" have been exposed as frauds because they pre-selected those they permitted on the stage and did not permit follow-up studies of their supposed "healings." Jesus' healings were different. The Gospel accounts were written so close to these miracle events that there were living witnesses who could have contradicted any lies or exaggerations. And so the debate rages on.

This kind of argument confuses the real issue. Miracle accounts are intrinsic to the message of the Gospels, growing out of the theology of the Old Testament. This theology affirms the existence of a Creator who lives and acts in the world he made on behalf of the people whom he has chosen. The miracles are consistent with the nature of the God of the Bible. A. Richardson states this position strongly:

The history which the Evangelists write is their good news, their gospel. They believed that in Jesus of Nazareth God had spoken his saving Word to the world. If we accept their gospel, we accept the history which they record, and we do not find it difficult to believe with them that the *form* of the revelation which God made in Christ included the working of the "signs" which proclaimed to opened eyes the fulfillment of the age-long hope of the prophets of Israel, the promise that God would visit and redeem his people. If we reject that gospel, we shall inevitably reject the view that Jesus performed miracles, or we shall seek to explain them away by means of the hypothesis of "faith healing" or other modern theories equally removed from the standpoint of the biblical theology. The truth is that, as we have all along maintained, the miracle-stories are a part of the gospel itself; Christ is to the New Testament writers the manifestation of the power of God in the world, and his mighty deeds are the signs of the effectual working of that power. But in this age the power of God is veiled; revelation is by the gift of faith. It is possible for us to fail to see Christ as the manifestation of the power and the purpose of God; then we shall be content with an explanation of the miracle-stories in terms of modern psychology or folk-mythology. The miracle-stories, as an essential part of the preaching of apostolic Christianity, confront us with the question whether the power of God was or was not revealed in the person and work of Jesus Christ. They compel us to say Yes or No (p. 126).

THE AUTHENTICATING FUNCTION OF MIRACLE CLUSTERS

As we examine each of the recorded miracles of Jesus, we will see that each had wonderful messages for those who observed it as well as for us today. But it would be a mistake to look at each miracle as an isolated event without considering the significance of the whole. In fact, the one unmistakable impression we gain from reading the Gospels is not that Jesus performed a miracle here and there, but that Jesus' whole ministry was marked by a concentrated cluster of miracles. And it is the significance of the several concentrated clusters of miracles recorded in Scripture that we must consider first.

The Exodus miracles. The first of these concentrated clusters occurred at the time of the Exodus. These miracles authenticated Moses as God's spokesman, essential because Moses was commissioned to introduce a new stage in God's eternal plan. Israel was to be formed into a nation. God's chosen people were to be governed by a Law revealed to Moses at Mount Sinai.

It was vital that Moses be firmly established as God's spokesman so the revelation he mediated would be accepted by all. This was accomplished by the ten proving acts—the ten plagues on Egypt.

Note that these ten establishing miracles were followed by a series of supportive miracles. These were performed on the journey to Sinai, and they continued on the journey to Caanan. The establishing miracles, acknowledged by Israel, were followed by supportive miracles which showed the Lord's presence with his people.

The miracles of Elijah/Elisha. The next cluster of miracles took place in the eighth century B.C. King Ahab had launched an intense campaign to make Baal worship the official religion of Israel. God's revelation was under attack.

At this critical stage in Israel's history, Elijah's miracles—especially the miracle at Mount Carmel—authenticated Elijah as God's spokesman and re-established the fact that "the Lord, He is God" (1 Kings 18:39). The earlier revelation given through Moses was reaffirmed, and the wavering population was called back to God.

The miracles performed by Elisha were supportive miracles. Like the miracles on the journey to Canaan, Elisha's miracles demonstrated the continuing presence of God with the people who would acknowledge him and his word.

The miracles of Jesus. The third concentrated cluster of biblical miracles occurred during Jesus' public ministry, which spanned only three years. Jesus, like Moses, was the mediator of a new revelation, which unveiled more elements of God's eternal plan. The miracles of Jesus also established him as God's spokesman, whose words were to be heard and whose teachings were to be accepted. His establishing miracles had to be significant; they authenticated a messenger whose revelation supplanted and superseded the Law given by Moses.

It was also essential that Jesus' establishing miracles authenticating the new revelation be followed by supporting miracles. These were necessary to demonstrate the presence of God with those who accepted the new revelation.

Just as the miracles of the journey served as supporting miracles for the establishing miracles of the ten plagues on Egypt; just as the miracles of Elisha served as supporting miracles for the establishing miracles of Elijah—so the miracles of the apostles recorded in the book of Acts served as supportive miracles for the establishing miracles of Jesus. The miracles of Acts demonstrated the presence of God with those who accepted Jesus and the revelation which came through him.

Miracle Clusters as Authenticating Acts

The Exodus Cluster
 Establishing Miracles: The Ten Plagues
 Moses is God's spokesman.
 The revelation given by Moses is God's Word.
 Supporting Miracles: The Journey Miracles
 God is present with those who receive his revelation.

The Elijah/Elisha Cluster
 Establishing Miracles: The Miracles of Elijah
 Elijah is God's spokesman.
 The revelation given by Moses is God's Word.
 Supporting Miracles: The Miracles of Elisha
 God is present with those who honor his revelation.

The Jesus Cluster
 Establishing Miracles: The Miracles of Jesus
 Jesus is God's spokesman.
 The revelation given by Jesus is God's Word.
 Supporting Miracles: The Apostles' Miracles
 God is present with those who receive Jesus and his revelation.

MIRACLE CLUSTERS AND GOD'S SELF-REVELATION

The miracle clusters in Scripture vouch for God's messenger, authenticating the revelation they mediate. But there is another important function of the miracle clusters in Scripture. This function is seen clearly when we separate the miracles of Jesus and the apostles, and include a cluster of miracles which is the subject of unfulfilled prophecy.

The Exodus miracles. The Exodus miracles established Moses as God's spokesman. But they had an even more significant function. This function was stated by the Lord in Exodus, when he explained the purpose of the devastating plagues he brought on Egypt. On the one hand, the plagues were a judgment on Egypt's gods (Ex. 12:12). More importantly, the miracles were performed so the Egyptians might know that Yahweh is God (Ex. 7:5) and so Israel might realize that "I am the Lord your God, who brings you out from under the burdens of the Egyptians" (Ex. 6:7).

Israel had known God as the God of Abraham, Isaac, and Jacob. But the revelation of his personal name, Yahweh, "I AM," was given through Moses at this critical point in sacred history [see pages 176–178]. The Exodus miracles, both establishment and support, affirmed a central truth of Scripture: The Lord is God.

The Elijah/Elisha miracles. When the Elijah-Elisha miracles took place, the people of the Northern Kingdom, Israel, were wavering between Yahweh and Baal. Who was the real God? Whose ways should the Israelites follow?

Elijah the prophet was thrust into this gap. On Mount Carmel he performed a miracle which convinced Israel that "the Lord, he is God" (1 Kings 18:39). The establishing miracles of Elijah and the supporting miracles of Elisha served as a reaffirmation of the truth that the Lord truly is God and is present with his people.

The miracles of Jesus. The third cluster of miracles was concentrated in the three years that Jesus taught and healed in Judea and

Galilee. These miracles established Jesus as God's spokesman and authenticated his message. At the core of Christ's message was the stunning affirmation, "I and My Father are One" (John 10:30). Jesus had spelled out the meaning of this statement in a controversy with some Pharisees.

After being ridiculed for his claim of having seen Abraham, Jesus responded, "Most assuredly, I say to you, before Abraham was, I AM" (John 8:58).

Christ's listeners understood this claim, and they tried to stone him for blasphemy. Jesus was identifying himself with the Yahweh of the Old Testament! Christ was claiming to be God!

The apostolic miracles. If we treat Christ's miracles and the apostolic miracles as separate clusters, we make a fascinating discovery. The message of the apostles was that Jesus Christ is Lord (cf. Acts 2:36). Their miracles were performed in the name of Jesus Christ (cf. Acts 3:6; 16:18). The doctrine that Jesus Christ is Lord was supported by the miracles performed in his name—miracles which proved his continuing presence with his followers.

The end-time miracles. Old and New Testament writers foresaw a concentrated cluster of judgment miracles destined to take place at the end of history. Many of these awesome judgment miracles, which far overshadow the plagues on Egypt, are described in the book of Revelation. Second Thessalonians sums up the impact of this period of righteous retribution. It will be a time when "the Lord Jesus is revealed from heaven with his mighty angels, in flaming fire taking vengeance on those who do not know God, and on those who do not obey the gospel of our Lord Jesus Christ" (2 Thess. 1:7–9).

The self-revelatory aspect of miracle clusters. If we look at these miracle clusters as self-revealing acts of God, we find a fascinating pattern, shown in the chart above. Each cluster of miracles makes a decisive statement about who the God of Scripture is. These

statements can be expressed in the form of a chiasm (see page 134).

Miracle Clusters and God's Self-revelation	
A. <u>The Exodus Miracles</u>:	The Lord is God.
B. <u>Elijah/Elisha Miracles</u>:	The Lord is God.
C. <u>Jesus' Miracles</u>:	Jesus is God.
B. <u>Apostolic Miracles</u>:	Jesus is Lord.
A. <u>End-time Miracles</u>:	Jesus is Lord.

In this arrangement, the central self-revelation is that of Jesus Christ as God. The other self-revelations support the central affirmation.

The first "A" miracle cluster introduces Yahweh to humankind as God. The second "A" miracle cluster forces all humankind to acknowledge Jesus as Lord and God. Each of the "A" miracles—the ten plagues and the end-time plagues—are miracles of judgment.

The first "B" miracle cluster resolves doubts by offering evidence that Yahweh truly is God, while the second "B" miracle cluster settles doubts by offering evidence that Jesus is Lord. The "B" miracles are miracles of provision.

The central "C" miracle cluster affirms the truth that the God of the Scriptures is Jesus—and that Jesus is the God of the Scriptures.

Viewed in these ways, as both authenticating and as self-revelatory acts, the miracle clusters of Scripture make important theological statements about the Bible's teaching about God. We cannot treat miracles apart from this theology. If we are to be biblical in our approach to the miracles of Scripture, we must accept them as they are described. If we are asked whether these miracles actually took place, we must answer a confident "Yes."

The miracles of the Bible are so tightly linked to what Scripture teaches about God that the only way to reject the miracles of the Bible is to reject the God of the Bible.

JEWISH RELIGIOUS LEADERS' RESPONSE TO JESUS' MIRACLES

The leaders' hostility. As we look at the Gospel accounts of Jesus' miracles, we are struck by the fact that the leaders of the Jews remained hostile to Christ in spite of his miracles. How could they be so blind? Were the miracles of Jesus nothing but rumors that an enlightened religious establishment could easily ignore? The answer to that question is evident throughout the Gospels. Christ's opponents could not and did not dispute that he performed miracles (John 3:2; 9:15–16). How then did they justify their rejection of Jesus as God's spokesman and his message as God's Word?

The leaders' strategy (Matthew 12:22–24). One day Jesus healed a man who was demon-possessed, blind, and mute. The healing was spectacular. Christ healed him "so that the blind and mute man both spoke and saw" (v. 22).

Many of the onlookers drew a logical conclusion from this event. The religious significance of this miracle might be that Jesus was the "Son of David," the promised Messiah!

But the Pharisees and other religious leaders responded by making this accusation: "This fellow does not cast out demons except by Beelzebub, the ruler of the demons" (Matt. 12:24). We see the logic of the strategy when we remember our working definition of a miracle. A miracle is an extraordinary event caused by God with religious purpose or significance.

An extraordinary event. The healing of this demon-possessed man was certainly extraordinary. Not one witness, whether leader or commoner, could challenge the fact of the miracle.

Pharisees and other Jewish leaders were hostile to Jesus and His ministry.

There were too many witnesses, undoubtedly including some leaders.

Caused by God. The people who witnessed this miracle naturally assumed that God was the source of Jesus' power. Who else but God could perform such miracles? Even the religious leaders had not challenged this assumption at first. When Nicodemus, a member of the ruling Jewish council, came to Jesus earlier, he confessed, "We know that You are a teacher come from God, for no one can do these signs that You do unless God is with him" (John 3:2). The "we" undoubtedly included Nicodemus' fellow leaders.

With religious significance. Nicodemus had spoken of Jesus' miracles as "signs." In the Old and New Testaments, this word indicates a miracle which authenticates the person who performed it as God's spokesman. The miracles were God's stamp of approval on Jesus and his message. God's people were bound by Scripture to listen and respond to such a person (compare Deut. 18:19).

From what Jesus taught and did, it was logical for the Jews to conclude that he was who he claimed to be—the promised Son of David, the Messiah, as well as the Son of God.

The leaders' problem and its solution. The leaders couldn't attack Jesus' miracles on the grounds that no miracles had taken place. Everyone agreed that Jesus performed miracles. The leaders could not attack the conviction that Jesus' miracles had religious significance. Such miracles required that the Jew who spoke in the name of the Lord must be heard (Deut. 18:19).

But the leaders could attack the assumption that the miracles of Jesus were caused by God! And this they did attack—both directly and through a campaign of rumors. They had to admit that Jesus performed miracles, but they charged the source of his miracles was Satan, not God!

If this notion were accepted, the religious implications were reversed. Rather than listen to Jesus, it would be the duty of the Jewish people to reject him and his teachings.

In the confrontation reported in Matthew 12, Jesus refuted this accusation. If Satan were casting out Satan, Jesus reasoned, he was fighting himself. No kingdom wracked by civil war—war against itself—could possibly stand. And besides, if Jesus were casting out demons by Satan's power, was it possible that Jewish exorcists were drawing on the demonic when *they* cast out demons?

The fact that the demons were subject to Jesus showed that even Satan was powerless before him. In reality, the miracles of Jesus demonstrated that God's kingdom was once again breaking into the world, as God's power was exercised for all to see.

The leaders did not hesitate. They had not launched their attack on Jesus' miracles to convince others, but to raise doubts and to give themselves an excuse for their hatred of the Lord. If Jesus were God, they would have to bow to him and surrender their privileged position as interpreters of God's will. And this they would not do.

As for the people, they hesitated too long. They were ready to exalt Jesus as a prophet as great as any Old Testament figure other than Moses. But they would not acknowledge Jesus as the Savior sent from God or entertain the possibility that he might be who he claimed.

And so the miracles of Jesus led not to acclamation but to a cross and a barren tomb. But that tomb witnessed the greatest miracle of all: the resurrection. This event proved without a doubt that Jesus was the Son of God with power (Rom. 1:4).

And since that moment the world has never been the same.

THE SOURCES WHICH REPORT JESUS' MIRACLES

How the Gospels differ from one another. The miracles of Jesus are reported in the four Gospels. Each of the Gospels draws a word portrait of Jesus, designed to present him to a different audience. The Gospel of Matthew was written for the Jews. It sought to prove that Jesus was indeed the Messiah prophesied in the Old Testament. The Gospel of Mark was written for the Romans, portraying Jesus as God's agent who carried out the Father's will. The Gospel of Luke was written for the Hellenistic [Greek] mind. It portrays Jesus as the fulfillment of the Greek ideal of excellence—as the perfect man. The Gospel of John was written to demonstrate to all that Jesus undoubtedly was the living Son of God.

Implications of the Gospel differences. Each of these authors arranged his material to fit his audience and theme. Each selected from among Jesus' miracles those which best advanced his Gospel's argument. Each shaped the emphasis of the miracle story to contribute to reaching his goal. Thus the sequence in which various miracle stories were recounted, as well as details emphasized by the Gospel writers, are sometimes different. When details differ, it doesn't mean the accounts *conflict*, but that the authors emphasized elements of the events that best suited his purpose.

This means that we need to be aware of how the same miracle story may be used in different Gospels to make different points. A sequence of miraculous events may be ordered differently to emphasize a particular author's point.

The Gospel writers selected from a range of miracles that Jesus performed. Some miracles are reported in all the Gospels, while others occur in only one. Such a selection process was natural, considering the different emphasis of each Gospel writer. This means a miracle reported in a single Gospel is no less true or important than a miracle reported in all four.

The miracles of Jesus. It is somewhat deceptive to speak of the miracles of Jesus. The biblical text often refers to miracles which are not described in any Gospel. These references make it clear that Jesus performed many more miracles than the 35 which the Gospels treat in some detail. Healing miracles in particular were performed by Jesus throughout his ministry, even during his last week in Jerusalem.

GENERAL REFERENCES TO JESUS' MIRACLES IN THE GOSPELS

The following general references to miracles in Matthew alone make it clear that Christ performed many more miracles than are described in the Gospels.

Jesus went about all Galilee, teaching in their synagogues, preaching the gospel of the kingdom, and healing all kinds of sickness and all kinds of disease among the people. Then his fame went throughout all Syria; and they brought to him all sick people who were afflicted with various diseases and torments, and those who were demon-possessed, epileptics, and paralytics; and he healed them (Matt. 4:23, 24).

When evening had come, they brought to him many who were demon-possessed, and he cast out the spirits with a word, and healed all who were sick (Matt. 8:16).

Then Jesus went about all the cities and villages . . . healing every sickness and every disease among the people (Matt. 9:35).

Great multitudes followed him, and he healed them all (Matt. 12:15).

When Jesus went out he saw a great multitude; and he was moved with compassion for them, and healed their sick (Matt. 14:14).

They sent out into all that surrounding region, brought to him all who were sick, and begged him that they might only touch the hem of his garment. And as many as touched it were made perfectly well (Matt. 14:35).

And great multitudes followed him, and he healed them there (Matt. 19:2).

Then the blind and the lame came to him in the temple, and he healed them (Matt. 21:14).

Similar lists can be constructed from each of the other Gospels. In Mark: Mark 1:32–34, 39; 3:10,11; 6:2, 5; 6:55, 56. In Luke: Luke 4:40, 41; 6:17–19; 7:21, 22; 8:2; 9:11. In John: John 2:23; 6:2.

Jesus' Miracles in the Gospels

Ch	Matthew	Mark	Luke	John
1		Catch of fish Synagogue demoniac Peter's mother-in-law Leper cleansed		
2		Paralytic healed		Water to wine
3		Withered hand		
4	Catch of fish	Stilling the storm	Synagogue demoniac Peter's mother-in-law	Nobleman's son
5		Demoniac of Gadara Woman healed Jairus' daughter	Catch of fish Leper cleansed Paralytic healed	
6		Feeding 5,000 Walking on water	Withered hand	Feeding 5,000 Walking on water
7		Syro-Phonecian woman's daughter Deaf/dumb man		Centurion's servant
8	Peter's mother-in-law Leper cleansed Centurion's servant Stilling the storm Demoniac of Gadara	Feeding 4,000 Blind man	Widow's son Stilling the storm Demoniac of Gadara Woman healed Jairus' daughter	
9	Paralytic healed Woman healed Jairus' daughter Two blind men healed Dumb demoniac healed	Demonized boy	Feeding 5,000 Demonized boy	Man born blind
10		Blind Bartimaeus		
11		Fig tree cursed		Raising Lazarus
12	Withered hand			
13			Infirm woman	
14	Feeding 5,000 Walking on water	Malchus's ear	Man with dropsy	
15	Syro-Phonecian woman's daughter Feeding 4,000			
16		END OF BOOK		
17	Demonized boy Coin in fish		Ten lepers	
18			Blind Bartimaeus	Malchus's ear
19				
20	Blind Bartimaeus			
21	Fig tree cursed			Catch of fish END OF BOOK
22			Malchus's ear	
23				
24			END OF BOOK	
25				
26	Malchus's ear			
27				
28	END OF BOOK			

The 35 described miracles. The Gospels describe in detail only 35 of Jesus' many miracles. The Gospel writers wove these miracles into their accounts in the order and with the details that best contributed to the distinct theme and purpose of their respective books.

The chart on page 163 lists the 35 described miracles of Jesus as they appear, chapter by chapter, in each Gospel. We can see quickly these important facts:

- No Gospel writer included all 35.
- Some miracles are included in all four Gospels and some in only one.
- The miracle accounts may occur in different order in different Gospels.
- In the Synoptics [Matthew, Mark, Luke], the writers tended to cluster miracles to establish something important about Jesus.

The framework of Jesus' miracles. Before we go on to look in detail at the miracles of Jesus, it's important to note that the entire ministry of Jesus was encompassed within a miracle framework. Matthew and Luke began with accounts of Jesus' virgin birth, and John began with an affirmation of Jesus' pre-existence. The grand miracle of Incarnation [page 8–14] set the stage for the signs and wonders Jesus' performed. Looking ahead, the miracles of Jesus were to be expected, for Jesus was God come among us in human flesh.

As Jesus' miracle-working days drew to a close, the grand miracle of Resurrection [page 15–17] marked their end as a new beginning. Again, looking back, the miracles of Jesus were to be expected, for in the resurrection Jesus was declared to be the Son of God with power (Rom. 1:4).

Viewed from either direction, looking ahead from the viewpoint of the Incarnation or looking back from the viewpoint of Resurrection, Jesus' miracles were in one sense not extraordinary at all, for the mighty works of Jesus were performed by history's most extraordinary personality.

Most of Jesus' ministry focused on individuals with special needs.

THE MIRACLES OF JESUS CHRIST

We are now ready to look at the 35 recorded miracles of Jesus. The order we will follow is the actual historical order—as best we can tell—in which these miracles took place, although they may be sequenced differently in the different Gospels.

1. Jesus turns water to wine.—p. 165
2. Jesus heals a nobleman's son.—p. 169
3. Jesus provides a great catch of fish.—p. 176
4. Jesus heals a demoniac in a synagogue—p. 171
5. Jesus heals Peter's wife's mother.—p. 174
6. Jesus cleanses a leper.—p. 181
7. Jesus heals a paralytic.—p. 183
8. Jesus heals a cripple at Bethesda.—p. 186
9. Jesus heals a withered hand.—p. 190
10. Jesus heals a centurion's servant.—p. 191
11. Jesus raises a widow's son.—p. 194
12. Jesus stills a storm.—p. 196
13. Jesus delivers a demoniac in Gedara.—p. 198

JESUS TURNS WATER TO WINE *John 2:1–11*

Jesus went to a wedding in Cana. When the supply of wine ran out, he turned more than 100 gallons of water into wine.

Weddings in New Testament times (John 2:1). Jewish marriages were two-stage affairs. Betrothal involved the signing of a binding agreement between two families. A couple who had been betrothed to each other was considered husband and wife. The actual union took place a year later, when the groom went to the home of the bride with his friends and brought her to their new home. Festivities might continue for a week, with the bride and groom treated as queen and king.

Jesus attended one such wedding in Cana of Galilee, a small town about four miles from Nazareth. His mother Mary was there, and we can assume that friends and relatives from all around gathered to rejoice with the newlyweds. The wedding was the site of Jesus' first recorded miracle.

Jesus and his disciples (John 2:2). Just three days before this wedding event, Jesus had been baptized by John and identified by the Holy Spirit as the Son of God (John 1:33–34). Four of the men who later became his disciples stayed with Jesus—Andrew, Peter, Philip, and Nathaniel. Quite possibly John was at the wedding too, although his name is not mentioned. Jesus and these disciples may have been passing through Cana on the way to Nazareth when all "were invited to the wedding."

Most commentators tend to see the wedding as a significant setting for Jesus' first miracle (John 2:11). They also see Christ's presence as blessing and confirming the institution of marriage. But Christ's presence at this event may have been more prophetic.

Weddings were joyous occasions. For perhaps the only time in what was a difficult life, the bride and groom were treated as queen and king. Married life in first-century Palestine began with joy, but for most couples it was marked by toil as the couple struggled just to survive.

What is fascinating is that Jesus' earthly ministry began with a wedding—and human history will end with a wedding. At history's end God's people will celebrate what Revelation 19:9 calls the "marriage supper of the Lamb." For Jesus, many trials lay between the beginning of his ministry at that wedding in Cana and the fulfillment of his ministry at the marriage supper of the Lamb.

Trials are also a reality for us between our discovery of Christ and the fulfillment of faith's promise. But for Jesus and for us, the beginning and the end are set aside for joy!

The hosts ran out of wine (John 2:3a). Wedding feasts often lasted a week. The hospitality shown to Jesus and his friends helps explain a possible reason for the shortage of wine. More people than were expected joined the festivities.

The shortage happened in spite of the fact that wine was generally diluted with water. Most rabbinic prescriptions called for three parts of water to one part wine; others called for seven parts water to one part wine. Wine in the Old Testament was viewed somewhat ambivalently. In its undiluted form wine was a "strong drink," and was condemned as a source of drunkenness (Prov. 20; 21:17; 23:20) and associated sins (Amos 2:8, 12; 5:11; 6:6). Yet wine was also a symbol of joy and feasting (Amos 9:13–14). Wine was given as gifts (1 Sam. 25:18; 2 Sam. 16:1), and was included among offerings made to the Lord (Ex. 29:40; Lev. 23:13; Num. 15:7).

To argue that Jesus would neither drink nor create a fermented beverage not only fails to fit the Scriptures; it is unnecessary to establish Scripture's position that drunkenness is a foolish sin.

The exhaustion of the supply of wine at the wedding in no way suggests the guests had drunk to excess.

Mary appealed to her son Jesus (John 2:3b–5). The exchange between Mary and her son Jesus is puzzling. Questions that have been raised include:

Why did Mary tell Jesus "they have no wine"? (John 2:3b). The implication is that Mary expected Jesus to do something about the shortage. But what did she expect? For some thirty years Jesus had lived a rather ordinary life in Nazareth. There was no reason for Mary to look to him for a miracle.

One possibility is that she hoped Jesus would contribute toward the purchase of additional wine. It was not unusual for guests to do so. Another possibility is suggested by the practice of mentioning a guest's name as a round of wine was poured. Mary may have been upset that the hosts ran out before Jesus could be honored.

Why did Jesus respond to Mary as he did? (John 2:4). Several things are puzzling about this verse. The NKJV reads, "Jesus said to her, 'Woman, what does your concern have to do with Me? My hour has not yet come.' "

1. "Woman," a polite form of address, was in no way harsh (compare John 19:26). Yet it was not the way grown sons generally addressed their mothers in the first century. It shows a distinct distancing of Jesus from his mother. Jesus was about to set out on the mission for which he came. One phase of his life on earth ended at his baptism— when the Spirit identified him as the Son of God—and another phase began. From now on his "family" would be composed of those who trust him as the Messiah (compare Matt. 12:48).

2. A literal translation of the Greek phrase is, "What to me and to you?" This was generally a harsh rather than polite phrase in the first century. It may have meant little more than "why involve Me?" Yet it further increases the distance between Mary and Jesus implied in his choice of the term *woman*.

3. The most difficult phrase is the last one Jesus uttered: "My hour has not yet come." If Mary was upset over a possible slight to Jesus by not mentioning his name when a round of wine was mixed and poured, Christ's remark may mean little more than "it isn't my turn [to be so honored] anyway."

However, most interpreters see far more implied. In the New Testament, Jesus' "hour" most often refers to his crucifixion (Matt. 26:45; John 7:30). What Jesus may have been saying was, "Once I act and reveal who I am, my course is fixed, and I have set out for the cross."

Jesus did act. A few minutes later he turned water into wine. This first miracle marked him: it revealed his glory and led his disciples to believe in him. With this miracle, performed to protect his hosts from the embarrassment of running out of wine, Jesus took the first step along a path which would bring healing to many, the agony of the cross for him, and salvation to us.

Why did Mary tell the servants to do whatever Jesus said? (John 2:5). Mary's words recall those of other saints who did not take "No" for an answer to their prayers (compare Gen. 32:26–30; 1 Kings 18:36–37; 2 Kings 4:14–28). Jewish readers would have taken her words as an expression of deep faith and confidence that Jesus would be able to do *something*.

Mary's confidence in Jesus was not misplaced. In spite of the fact that Jesus seemed to rebuke her, we must never lose sight of the fact that Mary was a woman of great faith.

BIBLE BACKGROUND:

SUPPOSED EARLY MIRACLES OF JESUS

After the church was established, a number of pseudo-Gospels were written. Several of these described miracles supposedly performed by Jesus as a boy. Lockyer recounted a few. "When the holy family was threatened by a number of dragons emerging from a cave, Jesus leapt from his mother's lap and dispersed the dragons, saying, 'Fear not, for although I am only an infant, it must needs be that all the wild beasts should grow tame in My presence.' Another miracle was that of the Child Jesus shortening a thirty-day journey into one day, and as the family entered Egypt 355 idols in a heathen temple there fell prostrate on the ground. Then there is the weird story about Jesus making twelve sparrows out of mud, clapping his hands and commanding them to fly."

These fables bear no resemblance to the miracles of Jesus recorded in the Gospels. And all are ruled out by the affirmation of John 2:11 that the changing of water into wine was the "beginning of" the miraculous signs which Jesus performed.

Water changed into wine (John 2:6–11). The large stone jars contained water to be used for ceremonial washing of the hands, and perhaps to fill the ritual bath, the *mikva*. Rabbinic law specified the water for this bath had to be "living water"—i.e., running water. However, collected rain water would do in Galilee, which was far less rigid about such matters than Judea. Jesus' choice of these jars was an early indication of Christ's hostility to the constant addition to God's written law made by the rabbis in New Testament times (see Matt. 15:9).

What occurred next was an unmistakable miracle. There was no way that the miracle Jesus performed could involve trickery. It was servants who followed Jesus' instructions and filled water pots from the larger jars. Servants followed Jesus' instructions and carried the filled pots to the master of the feast, who was responsible for mixing and distributing the wine. Jesus' future disciples stood by and observed all that happened. When the master of the feast pronounced the drink a far better wine than had been served earlier in the week, the servants knew. And the disciples knew. Jesus had turned the water into wine.

There are several things to note about this miracle.

The miracle was of the "old creation." There is a harmony between Jesus' miracle and what happens in nature. It is natural for water to fall from the heavens, to be absorbed by the roots of a grape vine, to be drawn up into the grapes, and then to be pressed out of the ripe grapes as "new wine." What Jesus did was not contrary to this natural process but in harmony with it.

The difference is that Jesus changed the water into wine without the agency of the vine—and that he did so immediately without the time required by the normal transformation.

We so easily take for granted the "natural processes" of this world that we fail to see the hand of God in what are actually wonders. Surely the God who designed nature to produce wine from water by such a complex process as we observe in the grape vine was not tested by producing wine that day in Cana.

The miracle was a sign (2:11). The Greek word used here for "sign" is *semeion*, which occurs 77 times in the New Testament. It is used to identify an act which calls for the exercise of supernatural power. Biblical signs are recognized as supernatural by observers. They au-

Jesus gave instructions for large jars to be filled with water, but what the servants drew from the jars was wine for the wedding.

❖

thenticate the person who performs the sign as someone sent by God.

The miracle was performed without incantations or spells. The people of the biblical world turned to magic to exercise some control over their environment. A "magician" would have made a great show of his attempt to turn water into wine. He would have uttered the names of angels and demons, and called them to do his will. In contrast, Jesus stood by quietly as the servants carried out his instructions, and then simply waited as the master of the feast took a first taste. Jesus' power to perform miracles did not lie in his mastery of magic but within his own person.

The miracle manifested Jesus' glory (2:11). In Scripture, God's "glory" is associated with his self-revelation. And the display of God's glory throughout Scripture is linked closely to God's acts in our universe.

John, in the introduction to his Gospel, wrote that "the Word became flesh and dwelt among us, and we beheld His glory, the glory as of the only begotten of the Father, full of grace and truth" (John 1:14). The miracles of Jesus made it clear that God was again acting in this world. The reality of who Jesus was began to shine through in this very first miracle. With each succeeding wonder, Christ's deity beamed brighter and brighter, until the resurrection set to rest any shadow of doubt. Jesus is God incarnate as a human being.

The miracle developed the disciples' trust in Jesus (2:11). Two disciples had heard John identify Jesus as the Son of God (John 1:34). They found the others and excitedly reported, "We have found the Messiah [the Christ]!" (John 1:41). Another, Nathaniel, had been convinced by speaking to Jesus himself (John 1:47–51). These men *already* believed in Jesus, at least to the extent to which they knew him. What the miracle at Cana did for them was to deepen their existing faith rather than create a non-existent faith.

Personal applications of the miracle at Cana.
Mary, Jesus' mother, seemed certain that Jesus could do something about the failure of the wine supply. She didn't know what he might do, but she appealed to him anyway. Even his strange response did not quench her confidence. Mary surely did not expect the solution that Jesus provided. Christ solved the problem in his own way, by performing the first of a number of miracles recorded in the Gospels.

It's important for us, when we're faced with a situation that seems hopeless, to follow Mary's lead and turn to Jesus. We may not receive an immediate reply; we may even feel put off. But like Mary, we need to have confidence in his ability to come to our aid.

We can never predict what Jesus will do to help us. But we can know that our God is a miracle-working God and that his solution to our problem will be far better than our own. As Christ answers our prayers, he continues to display his glory. And our faith in him continues to grow.

JESUS HEALS A NOBLEMAN'S SON
John 4:46–54

An anxious father traveled twenty miles to beg Jesus to heal his dying son.

The background of the miracle. This miracle, like Jesus' first, also occurred at Cana of Galilee. But time has passed. In the interim, Jesus had performed miracles in Jerusalem during Passover week (John 2:23) which impressed the religious leaders so much that they concluded at first that God must be with him (John 3:2). When Jesus returned home, he was welcomed by his fellow citizens of Galilee. Many had witnessed the miracles He had performed in Jerusalem.

Stories about Jesus had spread rapidly. When "a certain nobleman whose son was sick at Capernaum" heard that Jesus was in Galilee, he immediately went to him (John 4:46, 47).

The parties to the miracle. More people were involved in this miracle than is generally true of Jesus' miracles. The participants or parties to the miracle were Jesus, the anxious father, the dying son, bystanders, and the nobleman's household. Significantly, Jesus' disciples are not mentioned by John. The text says "Jesus came again to . . . Galilee," not when *they* came. Jesus was apparently traveling alone.

Jesus. Jesus had now performed miracles which had set him apart. Tales of his wonders spread rapidly. The Passover was a religious festival which every Jewish man in Judah and Galilee was supposed to attend. Many other Jews came from across Eastern and Western worlds. But at this point in his ministry, the people were unclear just who Jesus was. They knew only that God had worked wonders through him, indicating that he must at least be a prophet.

The nobleman. The word translated "nobleman" means "royal official." The fact that he lived in Capernaum indicates he was an officer in the service of Herod Antipas, tetrarch of Galilee and Perea. Herod was addressed by the courtesy title of "king."

When we meet the royal official, however, we don't see an important man; we see an anxious father. All the externals such as social position meant nothing; all he could think of was the son who appeared to be dying. When he heard that Jesus was in Cana, he didn't hesitate. He set out immediately and in person to beg Christ to heal his son.

The dying son. Twice the text emphasizes the fact that the son was "at the point of death" and dying (John 4:47, 49). A true emergency existed. The fear that drove the father was well-founded.

The bystanders. The reference to bystanders is almost an aside in the text, but it is clear that many people witnessed the exchange between Jesus and the anxious father. We see this in John 4:48. Jesus addressed the crowd and said, "Unless you *people* see signs and wonders, you will by no means believe." The word *people* was supplied by the translators of this text, because the "you" is plural. Jesus was not rebuking the father. He was commenting on the attitude of the crowd. They trailed after Jesus not because they were eager to hear and believe what he might say, but because they wanted to see a miracle!

The nobleman's "whole household." In biblical times, the household of an important man included not only his wife and children and other relatives but also his servants and, in many cases, others who depended on his generosity (known in Rome as "clients").

The servants clearly shared the official's concern for his son. When the child suddenly recovered, several set out from Capernaum to report the wonderful news.

It is significant that as a result of the miracle, "he himself believed, and his whole household (John 4:53). Each person made his or her own choice of faith. Yet they had seen proof of Jesus' power and his compassion. It was natural for them to join their master, placing their trust in Jesus Christ as well.

How the story unfolds. The official heard that Jesus was in Cana and immediately set out to reach him. When he found Jesus, he implored Christ to "come down and heal his son" (John 4:47).

We can imagine the onlookers drawing closer, waiting to see what Jesus would do. Will they get to see another miracle? This was when Jesus looked at them and rebuked them. All they were concerned about was seeing "signs and wonders."

At this, the father burst out, "Sir, come down before my child dies" (John 4:49). The royal official could care less about witnessing a miracle. It was his desperate need, not curiosity, that drove him to Jesus.

How important to distinguish the curious from the needy today. God has not called us to debate theology or pander to the interests of those who love to speculate about religion. There are men and women all around us who hurt and for whom only a relationship with Jesus can heal. These are the people to whom we are to give our time and show Christ's compassion. These are the people whose hearts God is preparing to open.

Jesus then spoke to the father who had begged him to go to Capernaum. "Go your way; your son lives" (John 4:50). We might paraphrase this, "Go on home. Your son is all right." This comment from anyone else might have been considered a cold, heartless remark. But the official did not see it as such. He took it as a binding promise. Believing, he started back to Capernaum.

On the way "down"—Cana lies in the highlands well above Capernaum—servants met him and told him the boy was all right. Apparently the father had expected a gradual recovery, for the Greek wording is better translated, "He asked them the hour when he *began to get better*" (John 4:51). The servants' answer revealed that at the very moment Jesus had said "Your son lives," the boy had recovered completely and instantly!

The text indicates that the father and his whole household—including no doubt the son—put their trust in Jesus.

And so John concluded, "This again is the second sign Jesus did when He had come out of Judea into Galilee" (v. 54). This was Jesus' second sign in Galilee.

Jesus' unbounded power. This miracle of Jesus did more than authenticate him as God's spokesman. It demonstrated that Jesus' power is unbounded. The space of twenty miles between Jesus and the dying boy was no barrier to our Lord. He spoke, "He lives," and the son's recovery was instantaneous and complete.

In the same way, no boundaries exist for Jesus today. Christ is in heaven, but he is also here with us. Any word he speaks will be obeyed, to the outer limits of the universe. No matter what our emergency, we can reach him instantly as well. He hears our prayers today, just as he heard the pleadings of the anxious father so long ago. As Christ in compassion reached across the miles to meet that father's need, so he will reach out today to meet ours.

Faith that grows. It is always important in looking at a miracle story to be alert for repeated words and themes. In this story "faith" is a repeated theme. The word *believe* occurs in John 4:48, 50, 53. Faith is also implicit in the anxious father's efforts to reach Jesus. He would not have set out unless he had some hope, some budding belief that Jesus could help.

In the account, faith was contrasted with curiosity. The crowds that observed the miracles were there because they wanted to see a miracle. There is no indication in the text that the miracle, to which only the father and his household were actually witnesses, had any impact on the curious. The cry, "Show us a miracle," was not an indication of faith, but unbelief.

In the account, faith was interpreted as growing. The theme of faith is clearly developed in the miracle account.

1. The father had some faith initially, as demonstrated by the fact that he set out to find Jesus. It may have been little faith, fanned by desperation. But faith it was.
2. His faith was then tested by Jesus' command and promise. It is significant that the command, "Go your way," was uttered first. But the promise *accompanied* the command: "Your child lives."

How often we delay obeying God, hoping that he will act or that he will at least give us more faith. But the only way our faith can grow is by exercising it. To exercise our faith, we must obey the commands of God, however strange they may seem.

This miracle reminds us that with every command there is a promise. With every step of obedience, we move further into the circle of God's richest blessings.

3. Faith that is exercised grows and spreads. The official's faith not only matured; it was reflected in his "whole household" (John 4:53). It is not that the household believed *because of* the father's faith. The father's faith—focused as it was on Jesus and his word—*directed the attention* of the members of his household to the Lord.

They believed because they saw Jesus for themselves. But they looked to Jesus in the first place because the official directed their gaze toward him.

Faith in John's Gospel. One of the main themes of John's Gospel is trust, or faith. Near the end of his Gospel, John wrote, "Truly Jesus did many other signs in the presence of his disciples, which are not written in this book; but these are written that you may believe that Jesus is the Christ, the Son of God, and that believing you may have life in His name" (John 20:30, 31). How clearly the healing of the nobleman's son illustrated John's theme.

In the face of death, a hopeful faith drove the anxious father to Jesus. Christ gave him a command and a promise. In faith the father obeyed and claimed the promise. And the result was life. The son recovered, and new faith was born in the hearts of all in that household who witnessed the healing.

Today, looking into the Scriptures, we also place our trust and faith in Jesus. As we do, we are given eternal life in his name.

JESUS HEALS A DEMONIAC IN A SYNAGOGUE   *Mark 1:21–28; Luke 4:31–37*

When a demon-possessed man interrupted a synagogue service where Jesus was teaching, Christ commanded the demon to leave.

Background of the miracle. Jesus was already established as a wonder-worker when he went to the synagogue outside Capernaum one Sabbath. After performing notable signs in Jerusalem during Passover, Jesus had moved his primary residence from Nazareth to Capernaum (Matt. 17:24), where he stayed with a successful fisherman named Peter (Mark 1:2–31).

That morning in the synagogue, Jesus was teaching the Scriptures. His exposition of the Old Testament was different from what the worshipers expected. The text indicates they were astonished "for he taught them as one having authority, and not as the scribes" (Mark 1:22).

By Jesus' time, what is known as rabbinic Judaism was already well established. A long oral tradition regarding their faith and beliefs had been built up, consisting of the rulings of earlier rabbis. This body of interpretations would continue to build during the first century. Thus, those who taught in the synagogues usually cited the words and sayings of earlier sages or contemporaries like Hillel or Shammai. But when Jesus spoke, he did not cite the rabbis. He taught as if he himself was Scripture's interpreter—as "one having authority."

It was in the context of Jesus' authoritative exposition of the Word of God that a striking miracle took place.

Parties to the miracle. The parties to this miracle were Jesus, the demonized man, the demon, and the assembled congregation.

Jesus. This miracle was placed early in Jesus' ministry by both Mark and Luke. It is interesting that immediately before relating this story, Luke described in some detail what Jesus taught in his home synagogue in Nazareth.

It was traditional during synagogue services to honor an important visitor by inviting him to read and comment on the Scriptures. In Nazareth, Jesus was handed the scroll containing the prophecies of Isaiah. He turned to a messianic passage, Isaiah 61:1, 2, read it, and then announced, "Today this Scripture is fulfilled in your hearing" (Luke 4:21).

The demon-possessed man. The text describes this man as one "who had a spirit of an unclean demon" (Luke 4:33). Demons are just as real as angels. Like angels, they are personal beings created holy by God, who chose to follow Satan in a great rebellion which occurred before the creation of Adam and Eve. (See the companion volume, *Every Good and Evil Angel in the Bible.*)

Typically, the people who are described as demon-possessed in the Gospels display various symptoms, ranging from apparent madness and unusual strength to a variety of physical infirmities. But this man appeared normal. He attended synagogue with his neighbors, acting no differently than they. He apparently lived according to Moses' laws and was outwardly "clean," while within he was in the grip of corruption.

This demon-possessed man is a healthy reminder to us. We judge by appearances. The well-dressed man or woman sitting beside us in the pew may seem completely respectable. But it is not appearance that counts with God. God considers what is in the heart.

The demon. What a commentary on the spiritual state of Israel—the demon felt comfortable in the synagogue! The people had gathered to worship God. Yet there was no sense of the reality of God to make the demon uncomfortable—until Jesus joined that company.

There are spiritually powerless churches today. And there are spiritually powerful churches. The difference is Jesus. Where Christ is loved and honored—where hearts are lifted in praise and his Word is lived—no unclean person or demon can be comfortable.

The congregation. The congregation gathered that Sabbath heard Jesus teach. They witnessed the deliverance of the demonized man. They were not passive witnesses. But neither were they convinced, for they did not understand what they saw that day.

How the story unfolds. The accounts in Mark and Luke agree in every detail about this miracle. Jesus was teaching in the synagogue. The congregation was amazed because he taught as a person having authority, not as a person relying on established rabbinic authorities.

As Jesus was teaching, one man in the congregation interrupted with an anguished shout. It was a man with an unclean spirit, a demon. It was the demon and not the man who shouted, "Let us alone! What have we to do with You, Jesus of Nazareth? Did You come to destroy us? I know who You are—the Holy One of God!" (Luke 4:34).

Jesus immediately rebuked the evil spirit, commanding it to be quiet and to come out of the man.

At Jesus' command, the demon uttered a shriek, convulsed the man he possessed, and left. The congregation witnessed the whole thing in amazement. They couldn't grasp what was happening. They knew that Jesus commanded the unclean spirit and that it obeyed him. But what did it all mean?

The story was told "throughout all the region around Galilee," and Jesus' fame spread (Mark 1:28).

In the story, the event unfolded rapidly— the confrontation with the demon took place in moments. Yet so much of what happened in those moments is significant.

The demon's reaction to Jesus (Mark 1:24).

The Greek verb used to describe Jesus' teaching suggests that he expounded the Scriptures for some time. The congregation quickly realized that Jesus' teaching was different.

But while the congregation wondered, one man in the synagogue had been growing more and more agitated. He was responding to the emotions that surged in an evil being who had taken up residence in his life—a demon.

The demon was not concerned with Jesus' teaching but was reacting to Christ himself. Finally the demon could stand it no longer. Gripped by terror and revulsion, the demon forced his host to stand and shouted at Jesus.

Let us alone! This first cry shows how painful it was for the demon to be in Jesus' presence. To demons, who conceal themselves in darkness, it is agonizing to be in the presence of light. And Jesus was and is the Light of the World (John 8:12).

What have we to do with You, Jesus of Nazareth? The phrase means "What have we in common?" In the first century it was typically spoken by an inferior to a superior. The demon recognized the authority of Jesus and that Christ would be responsible for whatever would follow.

There is perhaps more here for us. The cry reminds us that demons have nothing in common with Christ. When Satan rebelled, he and his followers turned their back on God. They became the enemies of their Creator, hostile to all whom he loves. Whatever means the demon used to gain access to the man he possessed, his intent was to do harm—while Jesus came to help and to redeem.

Did You come to destroy us? The demon was aware that God had decreed punishment for the devil and his angels (Matt. 25:41). What troubled the demon was "when?" The query torn from the demon was, "Are you here to judge us *now*?"

Likewise, there is no uncertainty about the fate of human beings. The only question is, "How soon will the day of judgment dawn?" How important it is to respond to the gospel today, while the door of salvation remains open.

I know who You are—the Holy One of God! While Jesus' humanity concealed his essential deity from human beings, his identity was known to demons. His shining essence was evident to the demon, who was not limited to physical sight. Mark frequently described encounters with demons who identified Jesus as the Son of God (see Mark 3:11; 5:7).

The demon's reaction to Jesus displayed both terror and doubt. The demon was afraid of what Jesus might do to him, but at the same time he was forced to acknowledge Jesus' authority over him.

Jesus' response to the demon (Mark 1:25).

The Greek word translated "rebuked" has a technical meaning. It refers to a commanding word spoken by God or his spokesman. By this word, evil powers are forced to submit.

Jesus' first command: "Be quiet." The literal meaning of the word is "be muzzled." While the demon was able to shriek, he did not utter another word.

Why was Jesus unwilling to receive the testimony of this and other demons (see Mark 1:34)? Some suggest Jesus had not yet laid a foundation in teaching and wonder-working to be ready to state his claim. Others wonder if Jesus was guarding himself against the charge made later by the Pharisees that he derived his power from Satan (see Matt. 12:24). A better explanation may be the general conviction in first-century Judaism that any testimony from certain sources was suspect.

For instance, in Jesus' time a shepherd was not allowed to give testimony in court. The reputation of first-century shepherds as vagabonds and thieves made whatever they might say suspect in the eyes of the rabbis! If the testimony of a shepherd was automatically discounted, how much more the testimony of a demon?

Jesus needed no such testimony to establish his deity. His words and his miracles spoke for themselves.

Jesus' next command: "Come out of him." The demon had no choice but to obey. He uttered a shriek, threw his host into a convulsion, and left the man.

The reaction of the congregation (Mark 1:22, 27). This story appears to focus on the confrontation between Jesus and the demon. Certainly this is its most dramatic element. Yet the greater significance of the miracle is seen in two words which bracket the miracle—words which describe the reaction of the congregation to Jesus.

"They were astonished at his teaching" (Mark 1:22). The Greek word used here is *ekplesso*. It is usually used to describe the reaction of uncommitted listeners to Jesus' teaching. It suggests an amazement which so stunned the listener that he was unable to grasp the meaning of what has happened. Jesus taught as a person having authority, but the congregation could not imagine what this implied about him.

"Then they were all amazed" (Mark 1:27). This describes the congregations' reaction to the miracle. The word used is *thambeo*, which emphasizes the fright caused by an amazing event.

The *Expository Dictionary of Bible Words* notes, "This family of words helps to remind us that Jesus' acts and words were 'amazing' primarily to those who did not believe in him" (p. 38). The phrase, "So that they questioned among themselves" further describes the congregation's reaction. It implies their intense argument and dispute. Jesus was clearly special. His teaching was unique. But what did it mean? Even demons obeyed him. But who was he?

Today, looking back from the perspective of the Cross and the Resurrection, we have no doubts about Jesus' identity or his authority. Yet even in his own day this miracle, and others recorded in the Gospels, began to forge a chain of evidence that left those who ultimately rejected him without excuse.

JESUS HEALS PETER'S WIFE'S MOTHER   *Luke 4:38, 39; Matthew 8:14–15; Mark 1:29–31*

Jesus returned to Peter's house from the synagogue and healed Peter's mother-in-law of a fever.

Background of the miracle. Jesus had just cast out a demon from a man in the synagogue at Capernaum (p. 171). He and four fishermen friends went to Peter's house, where Jesus probably stayed while in Capernaum. There Jesus was told that Peter's mother-in-law was suffering from a severe fever. What follows is recounted in each of the synoptic Gospels, but it is the briefest account of any miracle recorded there.

Parties to the miracle. The central figures were Jesus and Peter's mother-in-law. Mark made an oblique reference to members of the household, simply saying that "they" told Jesus about the sick woman, while Luke indicated "they" made request of him concerning her.

Jesus. The picture of Jesus in this miracle contrasts with that in the miracle account which immediately preceded it. There, Jesus was described as a figure with immense authority, displayed both in his teaching and in his casting out of a demon. In this miracle, Jesus seems more of an ordinary man. He walked home from the synagogue with his friends. He went into the house where he was staying, ready to eat a meal. When Jesus learned that Peter's mother-in-law was sick, he went in to see her.

These are all ordinary acts—the acts of a common man. And they remind us that while Jesus was truly God, he was also fully human.

The mother-in-law. None of the evangelists do more than identify the sick woman by her relationship to Peter. She lived in Peter's house (Luke 4:38), which suggests she was a widow. She was sick with what Luke—a physician interested in medical details—described as a "high" fever.

The household. No one in the household was named. The ruins of a larger home in Capernaum have been excavated and tentatively identified as Peter's residence. The "they" in this text probably included Peter's wife, any children, and perhaps servants.

How the story unfolds. Returning from the synagogue, Jesus found Peter's mother-in-law was sick. He went into the sick room. Each Gospel writer adds a detail to what happened in that room. Jesus rebuked the fever, and it left immediately. Jesus also touched the woman, then took her hand to help her up from the bed. Completely restored, Peter's mother-in-law then served the men the meal which she had prepared the previous day, before the Sabbath.

Jesus "rebuked" the fever (Luke 4:39). The Greek word for "rebuked"—*epetimesen*—is the same word Jesus used when he cast out the

Jesus healed Peter's mother-in-law of a fever.

demon in the synagogue (Luke 4:35). This word had a technical meaning. It indicated a commanding word spoken by God or his spokesman, by which evil powers were forced to submit.

Just as the demon was an evil power bent on harming humankind, so sickness was an evil power. Christ came to break the grip of every evil that holds down humanity. This mission will ultimately be fulfilled at our resurrection. In the meantime, Jesus' ability to heal was clearly demonstrated in this and many other miracles described in the Gospels.

The outcome of the miracle (Luke 4:39). Each Gospel's account of this miracle relates that "she arose and served *them.*"

How neatly we could apply this miracle if only the text read, "She arose and served *him.*" Then we could point out the symmetry of salvation. Jesus served us by making us spiritually whole, and in response we commit our lives to serving him. But each of the three accounts agrees—that she got up and served *them.* It was as though nothing out of the ordinary had happened. The men returned home. The mother-in-law, who had laid out the table and the food the previous afternoon, had them sit down and then she served them— just like any other Sabbath.

It is almost as if the miracle were too small a thing to interrupt the pattern of the family's life. We can almost imagine a later conversation:

"Anything special happen after synagogue?"
"No, nothing much. Oh, wait. Jesus healed Peter's mother-in-law."
"That was nice. What did she serve for Sabbath dinner?"

What a difference there had been in the synagogue after Jesus expelled a demon. In the synagogue there had been anxiety, uncertainty, and confusion as the congregation pondered the meaning of what it had heard and seen. But in Peter's house, everything continued on in its ordinary way.

In a sense, this "unexceptional" miracle of Jesus at Peter's house reflects something of our own experience with the Lord. His miracles for us are often quiet and ordinary. Yet it is his presence in our home that averts so many tragedies, maintaining the peace that we enjoy. Perhaps the little miracles of Jesus, performed behind closed doors so that ordinary people can continue on in their ordinary ways, are the most significant miracles of all.

JESUS PROVIDES A GREAT CATCH OF FISH *Luke 5:1–11*

Jesus' miracle at the Sea of Galilee illustrated the mission to which he called his disciples.

Background of the miracle. Each of the synoptic Gospels gives an account of Jesus' call of a closely knit group of fishermen to become his disciples. Each writer portrayed a few fisherman on the shore of the Sea of Galilee [called Lake Gennesaret by Luke]. Some were mending drag nets, while others listlessly threw cast nets (Matt. 5:18–21). Only Luke's

Gospel went into detail about what happened there that day, and only Luke described the miracle of the great catch of fish.

According to Luke and Mark, the call of the disciples followed miracles Jesus performed in the synagogue at Capernaum in the home of Peter. It's important to remember this. Otherwise, we might get the impression that Jesus just happened to be at the seaside, where he invited four strangers to become his disciples. It wasn't like that at all.

Jesus' relationship with the fishermen. The four fishermen were Peter, Andrew, James, and John; and Jesus knew each of them well. Peter and Andrew had met Jesus the day he was baptized by John the Baptist several weeks or months before (John 1:35–42). James and John were partners with Peter in a successful fishing business. Several of these fishermen, perhaps all four, had been with Jesus in Cana of Galilee, where they witnessed his first miracle (John 2:2).

The four had undoubtedly been witnesses to miracles Jesus performed in Jerusalem before returning to Galilee. They had been together in the Capernaum synagogue when Jesus cast a demon out of a man in the congregation. It is clear that the four were already very close to Jesus. After this miracle,

they went with Jesus to eat together at Peter's house (Mark 1:29).

So Jesus' call to discipleship was no spontaneous invitation issued to strangers. Jesus had invested significant time in their relationship before calling these four to become his disciples.

It's good to remember this. At times we try to rush others into a decision about Jesus. We need to invest time as Jesus did, building a relationship in which others can come to know and trust us. Then through us, they can come to know and trust Christ.

The call to become disciples. Sometimes the word *disciple* is used in the Gospels to describe the curious who became loose adherents of his movement. But when *disciple* is applied to the Twelve, it has a different, more technical meaning.

In the first century, those intent on becoming religious leaders attached themselves to a man who was already recognized as a rabbi, an expert in written and oral Law. They became "disciples" and lived with their teacher for a period of years, intent on mastering all that the teacher knew and becoming as much like him as possible (see Luke 6:40). This training, a rigorous spiritual apprenticeship, was the only way a person could gain a position of religious authority in Judaism.

It was to this rigorous spiritual apprenticeship that Jesus called the four fishermen that day. They would have to leave their business behind, abandoning all to be with Jesus night and day. In coming years, Jesus' disciples would gradually learn from his example and from his public and private teaching, until they were fully equipped to become leaders in the movement Jesus founded. It was no light thing to be a teacher's disciple in New Testament times. Discipleship called for informed commitment.

This is why Jesus spent so much time with these men who formed the core group of the Twelve, whom he ultimately assembled. They had to know and trust him, so that when he called them to discipleship, they would make the choice with eyes wide open.

The parties to the miracle. Luke 5 provides the sharpest and most detailed description of the setting of the miracle. The central parties to the miracle were Jesus and Peter, a great crowd, and Peter's fishing partners.

Jesus. Jesus was teaching crowds that had gathered in response to his spreading fame. Yet he paid primary attention not to the multitudes but to individuals—and particularly Simon Peter.

Peter. In spite of his closeness to Jesus, Peter was still busy working as a fisherman. Every hint in Scripture indicates that he was a very successful fisherman. Although originally from the small town of Bethsaida (John 1:44), Peter had purchased a large home in Capernaum, the political center of the district, and he and his partners fished and marketed their catch from there. He was clearly the most influential in the partnership, as he continued to be after becoming a disciple of Jesus.

In almost every dialogue between Jesus and the disciples, Peter's is the first voice we hear, opinionated but not always right (see Matt. 16:22–23; 26:33–34). In this account, Peter expressed not only his own feelings, but the unspoken feelings of his partners.

The multitudes. Aside from providing the occasion for the miracle and the call of Jesus' first disciples, the crowds that had come to Capernaum to see Jesus had no role in the miracle report.

Andrew, James, and John. These three of the four who were called by Jesus to be his disciples that day are almost ignored. We are told of their reaction to the miracle (they were astonished), and of their response to Jesus (they "forsook all and followed him"; Luke 5:11). But otherwise, they stood outside the spotlight, letting Peter speak what they may have been feeling as well.

How the story unfolds (Luke 5:1–11). The crowds that had gathered to hear Jesus pressed so close that Christ, standing on the shore of Galilee, was almost pushed into the water. So Jesus got into Peter's boat and asked his friend to push him out from the shore. There, isolated from the crowd, Jesus taught from the boat.

When he finished teaching, Jesus told Peter to row out to deeper water and let down his nets. Peter, an experienced fisherman, knew there were no fish. Most fishing on Galilee was done at night, and the schools of fish the fisherman pursued were never found where Jesus told Peter to let down his nets.

Peter, complaining a bit ("We have toiled all night and caught nothing"), did as Jesus said. But Peter let down only one net rather than the "nets" Jesus had called for (compare Luke 5:4 and 5:5). Even this partial obedience was rewarded overwhelmingly. So many fish were caught in the net that it began to break!

It took all the partners working in two boats to bring in the catch. The two boats were so full of fish that they began to take on water.

The miracle had a peculiar effect on Peter. He fell on his knees and begged Jesus, "Depart from me, for I am a sinful man, O Lord!" (Luke 5:8). Instead of leaving, Jesus reassured Peter. He was not to fear, for God had something more important for Peter to do than catch fish: "From now on you will catch men."

The story ended with the partners pulling their boats on the shore, leaving everything behind—boats and fish as well—to set out after Jesus.

Reluctant obedience (Luke 5:5). Peter was clearly reluctant to launch out into deeper water and let down a net. After all, Peter was an experienced fishermen. He knew the ways of fish, and where they could be found. Peter knew there was no way any fish would be in the spot where Jesus told him to let down the net. In spite of all this, Peter respected Jesus. He obeyed not because he expected a miracle, but out of respect.

But respect only carried Peter so far. Peter couldn't see the sense in letting down "nets." Reluctantly, Peter did push out and let down one net.

Jesus had told Peter to let down his nets *"for a catch"* (Luke 5:4). But Peter was unprepared when suddenly the net bulged with fish. When Jesus tells us to obey and get ready for results, it's best that we be prepared!

❖

Jesus told Peter, "Let down your nets for a catch."

Peter's use of "master" and "Lord" (Luke 5:5; 5:8). At the beginning of the story, the reluctant Peter addressed Jesus as *epistata.* The word is typically translated "master," even though "boss" perhaps better captures its flavor. Although it was a blue-collar word, no disrespect was implied. The use of *epistata* still implied recognition of Jesus' authority.

Even so, *epistata* was not as significant a word as the one Peter chose after the great catch of fish. Stunned as only an experienced fisherman would be, Peter fell on his knees before Jesus and cried out, *Kurie,* which has the force of "supreme Lord" (Luke 5:8). Peter was overwhelmed with the realization that God was present in this Jesus, whom he had been treating only as a respected friend!

It is good for us to be on familiar terms with Jesus. We can go to him as *epistata,* or even as a brother and friend. But we can never forget that Jesus is at the same time the supreme Lord of the universe, whom we are to view with respect and awe.

Peter's request (Luke 5:8). At first, Peter's response to the miracle amazes us. Why did Peter ask Jesus to go away, using the excuse that he was a sinful human being? Why wasn't Peter excited about the miraculous catch? Why wasn't he thankful?

Not the miracle, but the miracle worker. Peter's reaction is rooted in the fact that he was no longer concerned with the miracle. The miracle had forced Peter to look at Jesus in a new way. It was one thing to see Jesus perform miracles for others. But it was another thing entirely for Peter to experience the miracle *personally.* This time he felt the net's ropes ripped out of his hand. He struggled to lift the surging net. He hurriedly transferred fish from the net to the boats. He saw the loaded boats sink deeper into the water until the waves began to sweep over their sides. Peter had felt and smelled and tasted this miracle for himself. And suddenly he was forced to look at Jesus with fresh eyes and to see him for the awesome person he was.

In that moment of personal discovery, Peter fell to his knees and cried out, *Kurie,* "O Supreme Lord."

Not the fisherman, but the sinner (Luke 5:8). Just as the miracle forced Peter to look at Jesus with fresh eyes, the sudden realization of who Jesus was triggered self-discovery. Peter had thought of himself primarily as a master of his trade. Now he was overwhelmed by the realization that "I am a sinful man."

We cannot stand in the presence of Jesus and see him clearly as the Holy One of God without becoming sensitive to the fact that we are sinners. A person who compares himself to other people can take some comfort in the fact that many are worse than he. But if we compare ourselves to Jesus Christ, we take no comfort at all. We know how far short we fall.

When this happens, our first reaction may be that of Peter, who felt both guilt and shame. Peter's impulsive solution was to beg Jesus to withdraw. But if Jesus were to withdraw from us, we would be left with our problem of guilt and shame unresolved.

"He and all who were with him were astonished" (Luke 5:9). The word translated "astonished" is *thambeo,* which is also used in Luke 4:36. In each case, it depicted fright caused by an amazing event. Peter and the others were uncertain of the meaning of the great catch of fish. They knew it was a miracle. They felt a sudden awe of Jesus. But what did this demonstration of Jesus' power *mean?*

Their initial reaction of fear was only natural. Like Peter, the others had experienced Jesus in a new way. Their recognition of his deity and their own sinfulness made them anxious. This holds a lesson for us. God may seem a frightening specter as long as his intentions remain a mystery. But when Jesus speaks, he makes his intentions clear.

"Do not be afraid" (Luke 5:9). Jesus' first words reassured the fishermen. In making himself known to Peter and his friends, Jesus intended no harm. There is no need to be afraid of Jesus Christ.

"From now on you will catch men" (Luke 5:10). Jesus knew that Peter and his partners were sinners. But Jesus wanted them as his own nonetheless. By choosing to follow Jesus, their lives would be reoriented. The partners who had once invested their lives in catching fish would soon invest their lives in a far more significant task. They would share in Jesus' ministry, investing their lives in capturing human hearts and turning them to the Lord.

"They forsook all and followed him" (Luke 5:11). The miracle had its desired effect. Peter and his partners looked not at what Jesus had done, but at Jesus himself. They bowed to the ground, confessing Jesus as supreme Lord.

Now when their supreme Lord commanded them to follow him, they were ready. What a stunning discovery. In coming to earth, the Son of God had not come to punish or to condemn, but to recruit followers who would make his mission their own. Captured by this vision, the four fishermen left everything behind and with joy and wonder set out to follow him.

May we make the same discovery, as his miracles refocus our attention, challenging us to follow Jesus as well.

CHAPTER 10

JESUS: MIRACLES
OF THE MESSIAH

GOD'S SAVIOR HAS COME
Matthew—John

What do Jesus' miracles tell us about Him? What did the miracles Jesus performed tell the people of His own day?

Centuries before Christ's birth the prophet Isaiah described the kind of miraculous healings that would mark the introduction of the messianic age. The recorded miracles of Jesus fulfilled this 700-year-old prophecy exactly!

The kind of miracles that Jesus performed—miracles done by no prophet before His appearance—were proof positive that Christ was the promised Messiah, the Savior of Israel!

JESUS CLEANSES A LEPER   *Mark 1:40–45; Luke 5:12–15*

Jesus touched and healed a leper who appealed to him for help.

Background of the miracle. The leprosy of the Old and New Testament was any infectious skin disease. The social impact of the disease was even greater than its physical problems. While suffering from such a disease, a person was to be isolated from the community. To touch a leper made a person ritually unclean. Leviticus 13:45 says, "His clothes shall be torn and his head bare, and he shall cover his mustache, and cry, 'Unclean! Unclean!' " Other people were to be warned of the leper's unclean state so they could avoid contact.

Because this disease made a person ritually unclean, priests were given the duty of examining rashes to see if they should be classified as leprosy. Detailed instructions for making this diagnosis are included in the book of Leviticus. A person who recovered from leprosy was to go to a priest, who would examine him and pronounce him ritually clean again.

Parties to the miracle. In each report of this incident, the text mentions only Jesus and the leper. This was apparently a private miracle. Mark notes that it was the leper rather than others who "went out and began to proclaim" his cure freely (v. 45).

Jesus. Mark emphasized Jesus' compassion for the leper who appealed to him for healing (Mark 1:41). Jesus healed the leper, not as a sign, but simply because he cared.

The leper. Luke described the man as "full of leprosy" (Luke 5:12). His case was severe, and he had probably been a leper for a long time. Yet this leper expressed confidence that Jesus could heal his disease if he chose to do so. The leper was right. Jesus could heal him—and he did.

How the story unfolds. The story is told abruptly, with only Matthew providing anything like a transition statement (Matt. 8:1). The leper saw Jesus, and fell down before him, begging for healing. Jesus responded by reaching out to touch the leper while saying "be cleansed." Instantly the leprosy was gone.

Jesus told the man to go to a priest, as the Old Testament required, so he could be certified as ritually clean. And, although Jesus warned the leper to tell no one, the leper was so excited by his cure that he couldn't help telling everyone he met what Jesus had done for him.

"Lord, if you are willing" (Luke 5:12). The leper had no doubt about Jesus' ability to cure him. But he was uncertain as to whether Jesus would be willing to do so. The rabbis thought leprosy was God's punishment for slander, one of the most wicked sins in rabbinic eyes. The leper's hesitant request may reflect his question, "Will Jesus help so great a sinner?"

Many people are burdened by guilt, and they wonder if God could possibly care for them. But Jesus' response to the leper offers wonderful assurance and relief.

"Moved with compassion" (Mark 1:41). Mark takes us into the heart of Jesus and reveals what moved him to act. The Greek word for "compassion" is *splanchnizomai,* which depicts the emotions of pity, compassion, and love. Jesus *did* care, no matter what the leper's past sins.

This word is not used often in the New Testament. But when the Gospels portray Jesus as being moved by compassion, his subsequent action usually marks the turning point in a person's life. This was the case with the leper. And it can be true for us.

Whatever our past, whatever our failings or needs, Jesus does have compassion for us. And when we come to him for help, he will change our lives.

"He put out His hand and touched him" (Luke 5:13). The act was doubly significant.

It was a true expression of compassion. As much as the leper needed healing, his heart must have ached for the touch of another human hand. How terrible it must have been to see everyone draw back as he approached, lest they be contaminated by brushing against him. Jesus responded to the man's heartache, giving him not only what he asked for—healing—but what he longed for as well—a human touch.

It was a stunning demonstration of spiritual power. According to the law, anything which touched an object or person who was ritually unclean became unclean itself. But Jesus' touch had the opposite effect! It removed the disease which had made the man unclean.

"Go and show yourself to the priest" (5:14). Jesus instructed the cleansed leper to do what God's Law required. Jesus' conflicts with the Pharisees and others over "the law" was over their additions to the Old Testament, not over the Law itself.

"He charged him to tell no one" (5:14). It would be easy to criticize the healed leper for disobeying Jesus. Yet we can understand how he couldn't keep silent. The joy he felt simply overflowed.

How strange it is—when Scripture urges us to tell others of the cleansing we have experienced through Jesus—that so many Christians keep silent. The leper was healed of a disease which cut him off from fellowship with other human beings. Christians have been cleansed from sins which once cut us off from personal relationship with God. How powerfully the joy of that cleansing should move us to share Christ's love with others.

JESUS HEALS A PARALYTIC   *Luke 5:18–26; Matthew 9:2–7; Mark 2:3–12*

Four friends carried a paralyzed man to Jesus. Jesus shocked onlookers by forgiving the man's sins and then curing the paralysis.

Background of the miracle. Luke noted that as more and more people heard about Jesus, multitudes gathered to hear him and be healed (Luke 5:15). The furor apparently brought to Capernaum a delegation of "Pharisees and teachers of the Law," made up of rabbis from Galilee, Judea, and Jerusalem. Their mission was to evaluate Jesus' teaching.

On this particular day great crowds had gathered, and the delegation had seen Jesus heal many people (Luke 5:17). The delegation later met with Jesus inside a home, most likely Peter's (Luke 4:38). These men represented the spiritual leaders of Judaism, and they were listening critically. They needed to decide how to deal with this young preacher who was working miracles and drawing such great crowds.

It was while Jesus was dealing with them that this interruption described in three of the Gospels took place.

The parties to the miracle. This miracle account carefully described the interaction between several parties. There was Jesus, who was presenting his teaching to the delegation sent to examine him. There was the delegation made up of Pharisees and teachers of the law. There was a paralyzed man and the friends who carried him to Jesus.

Jesus. Jesus was clearly the focus of attention. Crowds had come to hear him, and he had healed many. In all this, he had been carefully observed by the delegation of religious leaders. When this miracle happened, he was in a room with his examiners. There is no hint that Jesus was making a defense of his teaching. Rather, he was actively instructing those who assumed they had the authority to evaluate him!

The Pharisees and teachers of the law. These were men who had undergone the rigorous training required of anyone in Judaism who wanted to become a spiritual leader. The term *Pharisee* was used to describe a small, dedicated core of people, mostly laymen, who were totally committed to keeping God's law as interpreted by the rabbis.

These men honored what was called the oral law—memorized interpretations of the written Law of Moses and legal rulings of earlier rabbis—as if it were the very word of God. Later they would become the enemies of Jesus. He ignored the oral Law and criticized the Pharisees for following precepts which canceled out the written Word of God.

At this point, these influential men had not made up their minds. Yet, like the teachers of the Law who were there with them, the Pharisees had come to judge Jesus by their standards. It had never occured to them that their standards might be judged by Jesus' teachings!

The paralyzed man and his friends. These men are portrayed as individuals of persistent faith. They were determined to reach Jesus, because they firmly believed he could heal their friend.

There is a powerful contrast here. The Pharisees and law teachers came to Jesus to evaluate him. The paralytic and his friends came to Jesus for help. Faith recognizes its need for the things that only Jesus can provide. Unbelief assumes the right to judge God himself.

How the story unfolds. Jesus was inside a home teaching the investigating committee. The crowd had pressed around the house outside, hoping to overhear. When the paralytic was brought by his friends, there was no way to get through the crowds packed around the door and windows.

But the paralytic's friends were not about to give up. They climbed the outside staircase that led to the flat roof. These were typical features of Palestinian homes. They broke through the roof, letting the paralyzed man down into the room where Jesus was teaching. Mark pictured this graphically: they "dug through" (*apestgasan*) the layers of plaster, sticks, and mud used to construct the roof.

Jesus recognized their faith and responded to it. He declared, "Man, your sins are forgiven" (Luke 5:20). This shocked the delegation of religious leaders. Only God could forgive sins! Sensing their thoughts, Jesus challenged them. Was it easier to say, "your sins are forgiven" or to say "rise up and walk?" Then, to show that his words were authoritative, Jesus told the paralyzed man to get up, pick up the pallet on which he had been carried to the house, and walk home.

The man got up and carried his bed home. No one who comes to Jesus with faith goes away the same.

Luke concluded, "They were all amazed, and they glorified God and were filled with fear, saying, "We have seen strange things today" (5:26).

"When He saw their faith" (Luke 5:20). This is the first direct reference to faith in Luke's Gospel, although the issue of belief versus unbelief has already been raised (compare Luke 1:20, 45). But what does Luke mean by "faith"? In his Gospel and in Acts, faith is ascribed to persons who act decisively on the conviction that God's help is to be found in Jesus.

The persistence of the paralytic's friends demonstrated the reality of their faith. Biblical faith is more than wishful thinking. It is a confidence that Jesus can help which moves us to act according to his Word.

"Man, your sins are forgiven you" (5:20). The paralytic came for physical healing. Jesus first provided spiritual healing. Jesus would give the man what he wanted—but first he would give him what he *needed*. We can live with physical infirmities. But we cannot survive without God's forgiveness.

A man lowered through a roof received healing from Jesus.

"Who is this who speaks blasphemies?" *(5:21).* We can almost hear the investigating committee breathe a sigh of astonishment. Now they could categorize Jesus!

"Who is this?" This was the question they had been sent to answer. Was Jesus really a messenger sent by God? Might he even be the Messiah? Or was he another of those fraudulent figures who often appeared on the religious scene, gained a few moments of notoriety, and then disappeared? How should the religious establishment react to him?

The wonder is that they needed to raise the question at all. All that day the delegation had seen Jesus heal. Later a man who had been given sight by Jesus would state the obvious: "Why, this is a marvelous thing, that you do not know where he is from. . . . If this man were not from God, he could do nothing" (John 9:30, 33).

The teachers of the law and Pharisees who were so reluctant to acknowledge Jesus' authority simply *had to know* that the miracle worker had come from God.

"Who speaks blasphemies." Unwilling to accept the testimony of Jesus' miracles about his identity, the delegation was quick to fasten on his words. Jesus had pronounced the paralytic's sins forgiven.

In first-century Judaism, the forgiveness of sins was thought to be something God would announce only in the final day. Jesus spoke as if he had divine authority to forgive sins, although the scribes and Pharisees observed, "Who can forgive sins but God alone?" (Luke 5:21; compare Ps. 103:3; Isa. 45:25). What's more, Jesus' pronouncement also brought forgiveness into the realm of the present. To the Jewish leaders, this was blasphemy indeed.

Although the leaders did not announce then that Jesus was a blasphemer, this conclusion had been fixed in their mind. Although Jesus went on to prove that he had the authority to make such a pronouncement, the investigating commission had made up their minds. By their standards, what Jesus had said

was blasphemous. This was enough to settle their attitude toward him.

Many people think it presumptuous for human beings to claim they know their sins are forgiven, and that they are assured of heaven. They consider this pride, as though we had confidence in our own goodness. But those who realize that Christ died for our sins so we might be forgiven do know the joy of redemption. Our forgiveness rests entirely on what Jesus did for us—not on what we do for ourselves.

"Which is easier, to say?" *(5:23)* Jesus was not asking whether it is easier to forgive sins or to heal paralysis. He was asking about *words.*

Do Jesus' words have meaning? Jesus asked which is easier *to say.* The obvious answer is that it is easier to say sins are forgiven. It is easier because there is no way to tell whether such words have meaning. Forgiveness is a transaction that takes place between an individual and God. No one can peer into the heart to witness that inner transaction.

But if a person says to a paralytic, "Get up, pick up your pallet and go home," there is an immediate and sure way to tell whether his words are empty. If the paralytic gets up and goes home, the words of the speaker are authoritative indeed. If the paralytic continues to lie there, the words of the speaker are meaningless.

"That you may know" *(Luke 5:24).* Jesus healed the paralytic as a witness to the investigating committee. Are the words of Jesus authoritative? Does he have the right *(exousia)* to forgive sins? To show how powerful his words were, Christ turned to the paralytic and told him to get up and go home.

"And they were all amazed" *(5:26).* An unusual Greek word is translated "amazed" in this passage. The word is *ekstasis,* from which our word *ecstasy* comes. In classical Greek, the word implied an intense but passing excitement. Here it conveyed a sense of astonishment. Luke filled in the portrait of the delega-

tion's reaction, for the "all" is best to be taken as referring primarily to the delegation in the room where Jesus taught.

"They were all amazed." The miracle astonished the onlookers. What irony this is. These men, who claimed spiritual authority in Judaism because they had mastered the words of the written and oral law, had come to pass judgment on Jesus. But with a few brief statements, Jesus proved that the words he spoke were infused with an authority and power they could not match, or imagine.

The religious leaders spent their lives arguing about words. But not one of them could heal a paralytic. Yet they dared to assume they had the right to judge the teaching of a man whose words had miracle-working power!

"They glorified God." Some take this statement as a positive assessment of the investigating committee's reaction to Jesus' miracle. It is not. The phrase more likely reflects the delegation's unwillingness to give Jesus any credit at all!

Later the religious leaders of Judaism would tell a blind man Jesus had healed, "Give God the glory! We know that this man [Jesus] is a sinner" (John 9:24). No miracle ever changed a closed heart. And this miracle didn't change the conviction of the Pharisees or teachers of the Law that Jesus had committed blasphemy.

"They were filled with fear" (v. 26). The Greek word used here is the most common term for fear—*phobos.* Frequently in the Gospels, when the religious leaders are described as being afraid, the fear makes them resist an impulse to attack Jesus (compare Matt. 21:46; Mark 12:12). In the face of such a notable miracle, the delegation was afraid to take a stand against Jesus.

"We have seen strange things today" (v. 26). We cannot imagine a more noncommittal expression. The delegation walked away, its members shaking their heads.

The healing of the paralytic proved that Jesus' words rang with God's authority, but the Pharisees withheld their stamp of approval.

They were convinced that a teacher whose words did not agree with their understanding of God's plan must be wrong. But not one had the courage to pronounce *anathema* on those who listened to what Jesus said. They would not risk exercising the religious authority they claimed, because the miracle had filled them with uncertainty and fear.

And so they shook their heads and went away. All anyone heard them say was, "Strange. Really strange."

And strange indeed it is—strange not that Jesus should forgive or heal, but that human beings still tend to cling to wrong ideas about God in spite of the authoritative words spoken by Jesus. As we study miracle after miracle in the Gospels, may we have the faith to recognize Jesus for who he is and—like the paralytic—come to him.

JESUS HEALS AN INVALID AT BETHESDA   *John 5:1–18*

Jesus healed a man who had been an invalid for 38 years.

Background of the miracle. Jesus walked through a crowd of disabled people gathered around an open-air pool. Verse 4, which is not found in the more reliable Greek manuscripts, explains that they gathered there because they believed an angel stirred the waters occasionally. After this stirring, the first person into the pool would be healed.

This miracle took place on the Sabbath. The Old Testament decreed that a person should do no work on the Sabbath (Ex. 20:8–10). By Jesus' time, the rabbis had expanded this simple command by going into great detail about what constituted "work."

For instance, it was permissible to have a fire which kept water hot if the fire was built before the Sabbath. But cold water could not be added to the hot water, lest the cold be warmed. Heating water would constitute work. However, it was permissible to add hot water to cold water in a cup, on the theory that the cold would cool off the hot, and this would not be work (*Mishna,* Shabbat 3:5). It is not surprising that the religious leaders with such a mindset were shocked and angered at what Jesus did on the Sabbath.

Parties to the miracle. The text focuses on Jesus, the invalid, and "the Jews." When John uses the phrase "the Jews," he is referring to the religious leaders, not to the general population and certainly not to the Jewish people as a race.

Jesus. Jesus initiated a conversation with the invalid. People generally approached Jesus for healing, and they usually began the conversation. In this case, Jesus selected one from the many in need and initiated the conversation. It is also striking that Jesus walked through the crowd of the infirm unrecognized. While most would have heard of Jesus, there was nothing out of the ordinary about his appearance.

The invalid. The man had been bedridden for 38 years, and he was without hope of being cured. He had no idea who Jesus was. Even after his healing, when questioned by the religious leaders, the text says "the one who was healed did not know who it was" (John 5:13). There is no question about one thing: faith was not a condition of this healing.

The Jews. The Jewish leaders were scandalized that the man, after being healed, was carrying his bed (a cloth pallet). When they learned the miracle had been performed by Jesus, all they could think of was making an accusation against him "because he had done these things on the Sabbath" (John 5:16).

How the story unfolds. John organized his report of this miracle story into five vivid scenes.

Scene 1. John sketched the setting, telling about the crowds of "sick people, blind, lame, paralyzed" lying near the pool. These were people we would classify as "incurable." Their only hope was for a miracle. John then drew attention to a single individual: a man who had been an invalid for nearly four decades.

Scene 2. Jesus entered, walking through the crowd. He stopped before the invalid and asked him a question. The man's answer revealed his hopelessness. After 38 years, he had lost not only the ability to move but also all hope. Without further comment, Jesus told the man to get up, pick up his bed, and walk. The invalid must have felt the strength flow back into his limbs, for he immediately got up

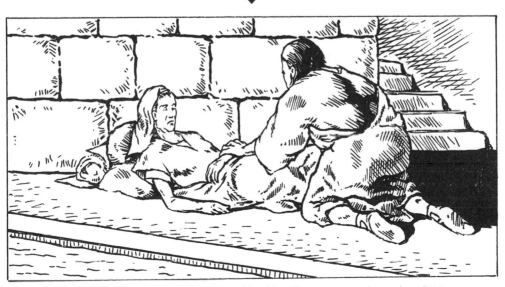

"When Jesus saw him lying there, He said to him, 'Do you want to be made well?' "

and did as Jesus said. Jesus walked away and was lost in the crowds (John 5:13).

Scene 3. The man was spotted by "the Jews," members of the religious establishment. They confronted him for carrying his pallet on the Sabbath. When the healed invalid told what had happened, the religious leaders interrogated him about who had instructed him to violate the Sabbath. The man replied that he didn't know who he was.

Scene 4. Jesus found the man he had healed in the temple. He identified himself and warned the man to "sin no more, lest a worse thing come upon you" (v. 14). The man then hurried to the religious leaders and reported that it was Jesus who had made him well.

John commented on the leaders' reaction: "The Jews persecuted Jesus" because he had done these things on the Sabbath (John 5:16). The phrase "and sought to kill him" is not in the best Greek texts, but it accurately reflects the intent of the religious leaders as described in other passages.

Scene 5. Later, the incident led to an open confrontation between Jesus and the religious leaders, which featured an extended teaching by Jesus. This is a basic pattern in the Gospel of John—a miracle precedes a message. In this particular message, Jesus pointed out that his miracles demonstrated his intimate relationship with God the Father, and that he was to be honored as God. If the religious leaders truly believed the Old Testament, they would acknowledge Jesus, for the Scriptures testified to him.

"A certain man" (John 5:5). The characteristics of this man are significant. He had been an invalid for a long time. He didn't expect to recover. He didn't recognize Jesus or know who he was; thus, he was without faith. Even after being healed, he didn't know Jesus. But later, when Christ found him, the man recognized the One who healed him.

This gives insight into God's gracious working for the unsaved of every age. Are God's miracles reserved only for the believer who knows the Lord and exercises faith in him? No, because Jesus showed his grace to an invalid who neither knew nor believed in him. God is free in his sovereignty to show grace to any human being, as he often does in unexplained healings and in other ways. How often an anonymous providence raises up those who do not know or acknowledge God.

Yet it is significant that the healing prepared the beneficiary in this story for a later meeting with Jesus. Jesus Christ was ultimately recognized as the source of blessing.

"Do you want to be made well?" (John 5:6). Jesus' question was penetrating. It's true that the invalid had lost much because of his illness. His limbs atrophied, and he lost the ability to move. He declared, "I have no man" to help. He lost the network of friends which those with a normal life typically build.

Yet for nearly four decades, the invalid had looked to others for alms. If he were healed, he would have to become responsible for himself. He would have to find work, to reenter a social world to which he is a stranger. "Do you want to be made well" is a valid question indeed.

How many today don't really want to be well! How many who live on welfare fear the idea of assuming responsibility for themselves? How many invalids want to be dependent on their caregivers? How many who are spiritual invalids fear spiritual growth and commitment?

The sick man didn't answer Jesus' question. He offered an excuse, explaining why he couldn't be made well. But note that Jesus didn't wait for his answer. He said to him "Rise, take up your bed and walk" (John 5:8).

Perhaps the question, "Do you want to be well?" was raised to force us to face our own inner hesitancy. Maybe the command, "Rise, take up your bed and walk," was uttered to remind us that we *are* to be responsible; that with God's help we can walk—and carry our own load.

"The Jews therefore said to him ..." (5:10–12). When the invalid told them about his cure, the religious leaders gave not a single thought to the man or what the cure must have meant to him. They didn't rejoice with him or seem to care. All they wanted was to find the person who had violated their rules on Sabbath behavior so they could confront him!

When in the name of religion we lose our capacity to care about others, there is something wrong with our religion.

"The one who was healed did not know" **(5:13).** The healing of the invalid was an act of sovereign grace. There was no appeal by the invalid to Jesus; he exercised no faith—he didn't even know who Jesus was.

"Jesus found him in the temple" (John 5:14). The healed man didn't go looking for Jesus. Perhaps this would have been an impossible task, because Jerusalem was crowded during religious festivals (compare John 5:1). But Jesus did go looking for the man.

It's significant that Jesus found the man in the temple. He may have gone there to thank God for his healing. Or perhaps the religious leaders had taken him there to be questioned about the incident.

In any case, Jesus found him—and warned him. "You have been made well. Sin no more" (John 5:14). A literal translation of the Greek is "don't keep on sinning." Some interpreters point out that the phrase suggests that when Jesus healed the man's body, he also forgave his sins. Others emphasize the connection between sickness and sin in the Bible. But it is more likely that when Jesus warned "lest a worse thing come upon you," he was speaking of the spiritual consequences of sin.

"The man departed and told the Jews that it was Jesus" (5:15). The man has been criticized for "betraying" Jesus. Yet Christ didn't try to hide his miracles, nor is there any indication that Jesus told the healed invalid not to tell anyone what had happened. In fact, when the leaders hurried to accuse Jesus, he used the occasion to state his true identity and to press his claim for Israel's allegiance.

While we as believers are commissioned to tell others about Jesus, we are not responsible for their response. Perhaps we should grant this man who was healed the same consideration.

"Because he had done these things on the Sabbath" (5:16). We have already noted the extreme emphasis on Sabbath-keeping that characterized the Pharisees and experts in biblical Law. The Gospels record seven Sabbath healings. Several of them led to serious confrontations with the religious establishment. The seven are:

1. Jesus healed the demoniac in the synagogue at Capernaum. See page 171.
2. Jesus healed Peter's mother-in-law. See page 174.
3. Jesus healed the cripple at Bethesda. See page 186.
4. Jesus healed a man with a withered hand. See page 190.
5. Jesus healed a man born blind. See page 222.
6. Jesus healed a woman bound by Satan. See page 225.
7. Jesus healed a man with dropsy. See page 227.

"But Jesus answered them" (5:17). The incident gave Jesus an opportunity to confront the assumptions of the religious leaders and to state his claims openly. The text indicates that Christ's claims were clearly understood. "The Jews sought all the more to kill him, because he not only broke the Sabbath, but also said that God was his Father, making himself equal with God" (v. 18).

The religious leaders didn't reject Christ out of some misunderstanding of who he claimed to be. They understood his claims perfectly, and they rejected him *because of these claims.*

The larger meaning of the miracle. The miracle displayed the power of God to act in sovereign grace on behalf of anyone whom he chooses. Miracles don't depend on our faith: God is free to work with or without our cooperation.

The miracle also showed that God is willing to touch the lives of those who do not know him. His compassion is not limited to members of his spiritual family.

More significantly, the miracle Jesus performed on the Sabbath supported his claim to be One with the Father. He acted as sovereign Lord, choosing to show grace to whomever he wished. He acted on the Sabbath, asserting his Lordship over that holy day. And the nature of his miracle—restoring a hopeless invalid—suggests what Christ's power can do if we heed the gospel call to arise and walk with him throughout life.

JESUS HEALS A MAN WITH A WITHERED HAND   Luke 6:6–10; Matthew 12:9–14; Mark 3:1–6

Jesus healed a man with a withered hand on the Sabbath, infuriating the Pharisees and scribes [experts in Mosaic Law].

Background of the miracle. This is another of Jesus' Sabbath miracles (see the list on page 189). Jesus' performance of miracles on the Sabbath angered the religious establishment, which had defined in minute fashion every action a person could perform on the holy day. They had gone far beyond the simple Old Testament prescription for observance of the Sabbath. The charge that Jesus was a Sabbath-breaker was one of the most serious the Jewish leaders lodged against Jesus.

Parties to the miracle. The individuals who interacted in this miracle account were Jesus, the man with the withered hand, and "the scribes and Pharisees."

Jesus. In this account Jesus was the central figure, confronting the religious leaders whose efforts to discredit him were constantly frustrated. Jesus is also portrayed as a truly godly person who, unlike the leaders, had a deep concern for disabled man.

The man with the withered hand. He was the silent beneficiary of Jesus' compassion and power. We know little about this man except that he was there and Jesus healed him.

The scribes and Pharisees. The Pharisees were committed to strict observance of Israel's Law. The "scribes" were men whose status was based on a knowledge of the Old Testament and what was known as the oral law—the rulings of earlier and contemporary rabbis. In the Gospels they are also called "lawyers," and "experts in the Law."

This passage shows these men in a bad light. They gathered in the synagogue not to worship but to find some charge against Jesus. They watched intently to see what Jesus would do for the man with the withered hand, not because they cared about his suffering, but so they could criticize and condemn if Jesus healed him. They are displayed as vindictive and heartless, more concerned about themselves and their privileged position than the people they led.

How the story unfolds. Jesus was teaching in a synagogue. In the congregation was a man with a withered hand. Scribes and Pharisees were also there, hoping Jesus would heal the man so they could accuse him of Sabbath-breaking.

Jesus interrupted his teaching and told the man with the withered hand to stand. As all eyes shifted toward the disabled man, Jesus challenged the religious leaders. He asked them "Is it lawful on the Sabbath to do good or to do evil, to save life or destroy?"

Jesus glared angrily at each scribe and Pharisee (Mark 3:5), but they remained silent. Jesus then told the man to stretch out his withered hand, and Christ restored it. The scribes and Pharisees remained silent, but they seethed with internal anger at this healing. Later they discussed "what they might do to Jesus" (Luke 6:11).

"A man was there" (Luke 6:6). Many have suggested that the scribes and Pharisees *arranged* for the man to be in the synagogue that morning. Their own presence—and the intentness with which they watched—does seem to suggest a trap!

"That they might find an accusation against him" (6:7). These men were completely closed to what Jesus was teaching. Their only concern was finding evidence on which they might accuse him of lawbreaking.

"Is it lawful on the Sabbath to do good or to do evil, to save life or to destroy?" (6:9). The rabbis did make exceptions to the Sabbath laws on work in order to "do good." For instance, giving alms was considered a major good work in Judaism. Yet, to give alms required carrying a coin or some food and transferring it from one person to another. On the Sabbath, it was unlawful to put something in the beggar's bowl, or to carry something outside the house to give to him. But the Mishna said,

> [If] the beggar stuck his hand inside, and the
> householder [took something] from it,
> or if [the householder] put something in it and he [the beggar] removed it,
> both of them are exempt (SHABBAT, III. J-L).

Again, the Mishna dealt with exceptions to putting out an oil lamp. If this were done to save the wick, it would be work—because to put out a wick was considered an action which turned it into charcoal. However,

> he who puts out a lamp because he is afraid of
> gentiles, thugs, a bad spirit,
> or if it is so that a sick person might sleep,
> is exempt [from punishment] (SHABBAT V 2:5 A-C).

It is clear, then, that even the scribes and Pharisees recognized in principle that it was lawful to do good on the Sabbath. In the synagogue that morning, Jesus' unanswered question showed up these scribes and Pharisees as hypocritical and heartless.

No wonder they raged inside (Luke 6:11). With a few words and a miracle of compassion, Jesus exposed their wickedness. They had no sense of guilt, but they were very sensitive to shame. And Jesus shamed them in front of everyone.

"He . . . looked around at them with anger" (Mark 3:4). Jesus felt compassion for the man with the withered hand. But he was angered by the heartlessness of the scribes and Pharisees. By having such disregard for another human being in need, these men who claimed to set the standard of piety in Israel had actually betrayed the God they claimed to honor.

Orthodoxy of the head without orthodoxy of the heart is an insult to God.

The meaning of the miracle. In addition to revealing the power of Jesus, this miracle contrasted the attitude of Jesus and the religious leaders of his time toward human beings. To Jesus, people were precious and their needs were paramount. To the Pharisees, ordinary people were nothing but *am ha-eretz,* "people of the land," commoners whose lack of dedication to the details of the law made them contemptible.

How amazing that to God each of us is of immeasurable worth, no matter what others may think of us. Those who dismiss any person with contempt reveal how far they are from the heart of God.

JESUS HEALS A CENTURION'S SERVANT   *Matthew 8:5–13; Luke 7:1–10*

A Roman army officer appealed to Jesus to heal his servant, displaying an amazing faith in Christ's power.

Background of the miracle. Centurions were the working officers of the Roman army. The title comes from the fact that they originally led one hundred men [from a term for a "century"]. They were intelligent and well-paid, typically staying in the military beyond the normal twenty-year enlistment. When discharged, centurions received a large bonus and generally became influential citizens of the cities in which they settled. In every mention of centurions in the New Testament, they are presented in a positive light (see also Mark 15:39; Acts 10:2; 27:43).

We do not know whether this centurion was retired or on active duty in Capernaum. We do know that the elders of the Jews interceded on his behalf—an unusual thing for a Jew to do for a Gentile. But their description of the centurion was also unusual. Most people in the Roman forces occupying Palestine were antagonistic toward the Jews. But this centurion was described by Jews as one who "loves our nation, and has built us a synagogue" (Luke 7:5).

The story appears in both Matthew and Luke. The details differ in the two accounts, but these are easily reconciled. The heart of the story is the same in each Gospel.

Parties to the miracle. Combining the two accounts, we see the following persons interacting in this miracle account: Jesus, the Jewish elders of Capernaum, the centurion, the sick servant, and friends whom the centurion sent to meet Jesus.

Jesus. In this story, Jesus is portrayed as the reliable object of an unusual faith. The centurion counted on Jesus far more than did the Jews to whom Jesus was sent. This is perhaps a foreshadowing of the church. In the book of Acts, far more Gentiles than Jews responded in faith to the message of the gospel.

The centurion. Several things about the centurion are attractive. He had a deep concern for a servant. The Greek word is *doulos,* "slave." In the hellenistic world, slaves were property. It was unusual for an important person to be concerned over a slave's well-being. In addition, the centurion had made an effort to understand the people among whom he was assigned. Rather than hold the Jews and their religion in contempt, this army officer had come to love the people and to honor their God. He was apparently a person of faith as well.

The centurion's slave. The only thing we know about this slave is that he was "lying at home paralyzed, dreadfully tormented" (Matt. 8:6). This is all we need to know about another person. If someone is hurting and we can help, it is our duty to respond.

The Jewish elders. These were the leading men or civil rulers of Capernaum rather than the scribes and Pharisees who made up the religious establishment. They interceded for the centurion to let Jesus know they considered him worthy of help, even though he was a Gentile who had no real claim to mercy from a Jewish prophet.

The centurion's friends. Luke 7:6 indicates that at one point the centurion sent friends to meet Jesus and to express the centurion's awareness that he was unworthy of welcoming Jesus into his home. This showed the centurion's sensitivity, for a strict Jew would consider himself defiled if he entered the house of a Gentile.

How the story unfolds. A centurion who lived in Capernaum, where Jesus had performed many miracles, had a sick slave about whom he was deeply worried. When the centurion heard that Jesus had returned to the city, he asked the Jewish elders of the city to intercede for his servant (Luke 7:3–5). Jesus heard them and started off with them toward the centurion's house.

The group was not far from the centurion's home when several of his friends meet Jesus with a message: the centurion realized he was "not worthy that You should enter under my roof." The centurion did not feel worthy to approach Christ in person (Luke 7:6, 7). But the centurion, as an army officer, understood how authority worked. So if Jesus would just say the word, he knew that his slave would be healed.

But the centurion was so concerned about the torment experienced by his slave that he couldn't wait. A few moments later, he himself arrived to plead for his slave (Matt. 8:6), personally expressing his confidence that Jesus need only say the word and his slave would be healed.

"Say the word, and my servant will be healed."

Both Gospel writers indicate that Jesus "marveled," and told the crowds that "I have not found such great faith, not even in Israel" (Luke 7:9; Matt. 8:10).

Matthew followed up by quoting Jesus' warning to Israel. People from all over the world would respond with faith to Jesus as the centurion has and have a share in the kingdom promised to Abraham. But the "sons of the kingdom" would be cast into outer darkness (Matt. 8:11, 12).

Then Jesus dismissed the centurion. "As you have believed, so let it be done for you." And the slave was healed "that same hour" (Matt. 8:13).

The two accounts. Many interpreters have seen "errors" in these two Gospel accounts, arguing that the discrepancies disprove the doctrine of inspiration. But are the differences really errors? The narrative above integrates the two accounts easily, showing how the details in one Gospel supplement rather than contradict the details in the other.

But why the differences? Each Gospel writer had his own theme and audience in mind as he selected details to include in his account. Matthew's account doesn't mention the centurion's relationship with Jews. Matthew's account contrasts the faith-response of this Gentile with the lack of faith exhibited by Jesus' own people. The story is not only a miracle account but also an acted-out parable. Israel must respond with a faith like this Gentile's, or it will lose any privileges it counted on through physical descent from Abraham.

Luke, on the other hand, emphasizes the human dimension of Jesus' ministry. He, the elders, and the centurion are all part of a community. The Gentile centurion respects the Jews and their religion; the Jewish elders intercede for this Gentile with Jesus; Jesus willingly goes with them to the centurion's home. In Luke the thing that binds all the parties to the miracle together is a common faith in Jesus.

The elders appeal to Jesus for healing; the centurion exhibits an even greater faith than theirs. There is no warning to Israel in Luke, because Luke is intent on showing that through a common faith in Jesus the barriers that separate people can be broken down.

Luke, writing to the Hellenistic world that idealized harmony between peoples, shows that such harmony is possible when people have a common faith in Jesus Christ. Matthew, writing to Jews, is intent on showing his Jewish brothers and sisters that faith in Jesus is a matter of life and death.

In each Gospel, the focus is on faith in Jesus and an understanding of the source of his authority. But the details selected by each writer explore the implications of faith in a way that is appropriate to his audience.

"I also am a man placed under authority" (Luke 7:8; Matthew 8:9). The centurion explained what he meant with an illustration. He has soldiers under him. When he says "go," they go. As one "under authority," his right to command is rooted in his connection with the Roman emperor—the source of all authority in the Roman Empire. The soldiers

did not obey him as a person but as a representative of the emperor.

Under whose authority then was Jesus? The answer is that Jesus' connection was with God—the source of all authority in his universe. It follows that Jesus need not come to see the slave to heal him. Jesus only had to speak the word. Because Christ spoke with God's authority, the centurion knew that if Jesus commanded it, his servant would be healed. This is faith indeed.

While the Jewish people witnessed Jesus' miracles and wondered, the centurion saw them and believed. How ironic. The meaning of Christ's miracles was clear to a Gentile military man, while God's chosen people hesitated and held back.

"The sons of the kingdom will be cast out" (Matthew 8:12). The Jews of the first century believed that in addition to any personal merit they might gain from keeping the Law and from good works, they also accrued merit from the patriarchs Abraham, Isaac, and Jacob. Thus, not only was the nation God's chosen people; individuals were also given a boost in their efforts to earn salvation by their descent from Abraham.

Jesus' warning cut against this belief which was entrenched in rabbinic Judaism. What won the centurion Jesus' commendation was not his ancestry but his "great faith." Jesus went on to say that many people outside the Jewish nation [the meaning of "from east and west"] would have a place in the kingdom of heaven. Ancestry has nothing to do with salvation. The kingdom of heaven is for those who, like Abraham (Gen. 15:7) and the centurion, have faith in Christ.

This is true for us today. It's not what we do for God that wins us a place in his kingdom. It is faith in what God through Jesus has done for us.

JESUS RAISES A WIDOW'S SON   *Luke 7:11–17*

Jesus stopped a funeral procession and raised the only son of a widow.

Background of the miracle. Jesus had an itinerant ministry, traveling especially throughout the province of Galilee (compare Matt. 4:23). Luke places one of these journeys the day after the healing of the centurion's slave (see p. 191). Jesus came to the city of Nain, which was not far from Nazareth. As Jesus arrived, a large crowd was following a funeral procession.

Jewish custom required that a person be buried the day he or she died. The body was carried not in a coffin, as our text suggests, but in an open wicker bier. It was considered important for people to join a funeral procession as it passed by, so the mourners could be accompanied as a loved one was laid to rest. Thus, the raising of the widow's son was witnessed by many.

Parties to the miracle. The central figures in the drama were Jesus, the widow, her son, and the crowd accompanying the bier.

Jesus. Although Luke emphasizes the human side of Jesus, this is the only miracle report in which Luke mentions Jesus' compassion. In contrast, Christ's compassion for the hurting is mentioned three times in Matthew (14:14; 15:32; 20:34) and three times in Mark (1:41; 6:34; 8:2). No one in this report either asked for or expected the miracle which Jesus performed.

The widow. Luke indicates that Jesus had compassion "on her" (Luke 7:13). While Luke portrays her tears, he also introduces two special reasons for Jesus' emotional response. First, the dead man was her only son. And second, the woman was a widow.

The plight of a widow in biblical times is expressed in this saying of Rabbi Eliezer, "A slave gains when he acquires freedom from his master, but for a woman it is a liability, for she becomes disqualified from receiving *terumah* and loses her maintenance" (bGitt. 12:b). A wife was vulnerable in the ancient world. While her husband lived, he assumed the responsibility of her support. When he died, she was left on her own.

The problem was complicated in this case by the fact that in first-century Judaism, women could not inherit property from their husbands. Family property passed to the sons or, in exceptional cases, to a daughter. While there were systems by which wealthy husbands could provide support for their wives after death, the typical Galilean family had little. So it fell to the oldest son to care for his mother, in accord with the commandment, "Honor your father and your mother" (Ex. 20:12).

But the widow of Nain was truly a tragic figure. She had lost her husband, and now their only son, so that she herself was left destitute. No wonder Jesus had compassion on her!

The dead son. When Jesus raised the widow's son, he addressed him as "young man" (v. 14). The term suggests he was unmarried and had no children.

The crowd. The reaction of this crowd to Jesus' miracle contrasted starkly with the healing of a paralyzed man (Luke 5:26). In that healing, the religious leaders glorified God *instead of* giving Jesus any credit. In this case, the crowd glorified God because "a great prophet has risen up among us" (Luke 5:16).

How the story unfolds. Jesus "happened" to reach Nain just as a funeral procession was leaving. Jesus felt compassion on the widow. He told the widow not to weep and placed his hand on the bier to stop the procession. He then addressed the young man, commanding him, "Arise." Restored to life, the young man sat up, began to speak, and was presented by Jesus to the widowed mother. The crowd was awed, and they glorified God for raising up a prophet in Israel once again.

"Young man, I say to you, arise" (Luke 7:14). Several of the miracles of Jesus have been compared to those performed by Elijah and Elisha in the eighth century B.C. Like these two prophets, each of whom restored a dead person to life, Jesus also raised the dead. But there is a significant difference in the description of the process. Elijah and Elisha prayed, waited, and even stretched themselves out on the dead bodies before their return to life. Jesus did not appeal to God. He simply spoke to the dead, and the young man revived.

Christ had power *in himself* to raise the dead, for he *was* God.

The comparison between Jesus and the earlier prophets was not lost on the witnesses. Their happy cry, "A great prophet has risen up among us," reflects their immediate association of Jesus with Elijah and Elisha.

"God has visited his people" (7:16). The phrase is idiomatic, meaning "God is again acting for us!" The miracles that had marked God's intervention for Israel in the past were now being performed by Jesus. Surely history had again reached a major turning point!

"When the Lord saw her" (Luke 7:13). Luke earlier reported conversations in which others called Jesus "Lord" (Luke 5:8, 12; 7:6). But this is the first time Luke referred to Jesus as "the Lord." With this miracle, Luke expected his readers to recognize who Jesus was.

The meaning of the miracle. The miracle at Nain had great religious significance. First, it revealed Jesus' compassion. Second, it established the unlimited extent of Jesus' power. He exercised control over demons (Luke 4:33–36, 41), disease (Luke 5:12–15; 5:17–26), and now even death (Luke 7:11–17). Third, its correspondence to miracles performed by Elijah and Elisha marked Jesus unmistakably as a prophet in the eyes of the people.

But there is perhaps an even more important message. In this miracle of restored life, Jesus took the initiative. He saw the need, felt compassion, reached out to touch the dead man, and restored him to life. What a clear picture this is of our salvation. We did not seek God. As lost sinners, we were hostile to God and counted among his enemies because of our wicked works (Col. 1:21). But God had compassion on us. God took the initiative. He sent his Son to earth, and in his death on Calvary Jesus reached out to touch us. In this act, he did more than restore physical life. The crucified and risen Christ provided forgiveness and eternal life.

Jesus took the initiative. All we can do is to accept by faith the wonderful gift of life that he alone can give.

JESUS STILLS A STORM   *Mark 4:35–41; Luke 8:22–25; Matthew 8:23–27*

Jesus was asleep in a small boat when a sudden squall threatened to sink it. The terrified disciples awoke Jesus, who calmed the storm and used the incident to teach them about faith.

Background to the miracle. The Sea of Galilee lies between high hills. Sudden winds funneled between these hills can whip up the waters and create waves that endanger small boats. However, even the fishermen who were in the boat with Jesus were terrified by this storm, convinced they were about to die.

This miracle account is a favorite of most believers. Nearly every sentence in the brief story has immediate application to our lives.

Parties to the miracle. This is one of several "private miracles" performed for the benefit of Jesus' disciples. This miracle not only saved them but instructed them as well. The parties to this miracle were Jesus and an unspecified number of his disciples.

Jesus. Jesus was exhausted after a full day of ministry, and was asleep in the boat. The image of Jesus asleep while the storm raged around them is a vivid portrait of his calm confidence in God.

When Jesus was awakened by his terrified disciples, he immediately took charge, commanding the churning waters to "be still" (Mark 4:39). Jesus then used the experience to teach the disciples about faith by challenging them to evaluate their reaction during the storm.

The disciples. When the storm struck, the disciples were navigating the boat while Jesus slept. As the storm grew worse, they became terrified. Finally they woke Jesus up. When Christ commanded the storm to stop and the waters immediately become calm, the disciples were fearful and amazed. They asked each other, "Who can this be, that even the wind and the sea obey him?" (Mark 4:41).

How the story unfolds. Jesus slept as the disciples sailed a fishing boat toward the opposite

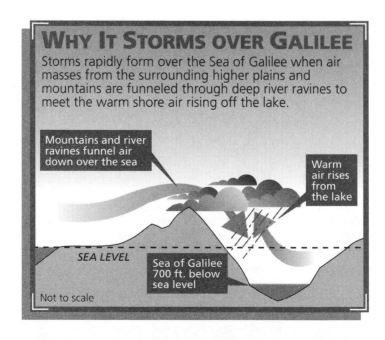

WHY IT STORMS OVER GALILEE

Storms rapidly form over the Sea of Galilee when air masses from the surrounding higher plains and mountains are funneled through deep river ravines to meet the warm shore air rising off the lake.

Mountains and river ravines funnel air down over the sea

Warm air rises from the lake

SEA LEVEL

Sea of Galilee 700 ft. below sea level

Not to scale

In the midst of a storm, Jesus rebuked the wind and sea—and they became calm.

shore of the Sea of Galilee. A terrible storm struck suddenly. The terrified fisherman, certain the boat was about to sink, awakened Jesus. He stopped the storm and rebuked the disciples for their lack of faith. The amazed disciples voiced the question Mark wanted his readers to consider: "Who can this be?"

"He . . . rebuked the wind" (Mark 4:39). We have seen this term *rebuked* used by Jesus when casting out a demon (page 174) and when healing sickness (page 171). It is a word which indicates the subduing of an evil power. Some have taken its use here to indicate that Satan was behind the strong storm that struck while Jesus slept. In this view, Jesus' "rebuke" was of the demonic beings behind the storm.

This suggestion is unlikely. Ever since the Fall, nature itself has been turned against hu-manity (Gen. 3:17, 18) and mankind has become vulnerable to all sorts of natural disasters. The miracle is intended to show Jesus' power over nature itself, and so to suggest his deity. The Creator alone can control material creation. Jesus' action that day recalled the words of Psalm 89:8, 9.

> O Lord God of hosts,
> Who is mighty like You, O Lord?
> Your faithfulness also surrounds You.
> You rule the raging of the sea;
> When its waves rise, You still them.

The answer to the disciples' question, "Who can this be?" had been provided long ago in the Word of God.

Personal application of the miracle account. This miracle account is a favorite of believers perhaps because it speaks so clearly and directly to each of us in our own lives.

- The great windstorm represents the storms we face in our lives.
- The boat represents our security, which is threatened by the waves beating into it.
- Jesus asleep in the boat represents the apparent silence of God when we are overcome by stress or fear.
- The cry "do You not care that we are perishing" (Mark 4:38) expresses our own deep feelings of abandonment by God when life overwhelms us.
- Jesus' rebuke of the wind and sea remind us of Christ's sovereign control over every circumstance in our lives.
- The calm that followed immediately after the storm symbolizes the inner calm we can experience when we rely on Jesus' love and his Word.
- Jesus' rebuke, "Why are you so fearful?" (Mark 4:40), reminds us that when Jesus is in our lives, we must trust him, even when life's storms intensify.
- Jesus' question, "How is it that you have no faith?" invites us to remember all that Christ has done for us in the past. Remembering yesterday's goodness strengthens the faith we need to face today and tomorrow.
- The disciples' fear reminds us always to hold Jesus in awe, remembering that he truly is God.
- The question, "Who can this be?" is answered by the miracle and the Scriptures. We are to concentrate on him, and not let life's circumstances confuse or distract us.

JESUS DELIVERS A DEMONIAC IN GEDARA   *Luke 8:27–39; Matthew 8:28–34; Mark 5:1–20*

Jesus met a violent man who terrorized the region of Gedara, and cast many demons out of him.

Background of the miracle. Demon possession was a reality in New Testament times, as

it is in our own day. For a fascinating exploration of this subject, see *Every Good and Evil Angel in the Bible.*

Mark and Luke give lengthy reports of this miracle, and each writer mentions only one demonized man. Matthew mentions two men and identifies the area where the miracle took place as Gergesa rather than Gerasa (Mark; see the NKJV footnote to Luke 8:26). The variants in the names are not a major problem, because one refers to a town and the other to a district in the general area of Decapolis [the "ten cities"], which was Gentile territory.

The discrepancy between the number of demonized men has led some interpreters to argue that one of the Gospel accounts must be in error. But one authority makes this point:

Suppose you told a friend, "Jim was at the party but came late," while another person told the same friend, "Jim and Carl came late to the party." Should you be charged with an error because you failed to mention Carl when telling about Jim? Of course not. Why then should the New Testament be charged with an error because Matthew mentions two demon-possessed men while Mark and Luke tell about only one? (*Bible Difficulties Solved,* Baker, 237).

The fact is that the basic elements in each Gospel are the same, and there is no major conflict among these three different accounts. For the sake of simplicity, our discussion will draw from the accounts in Mark and Luke. They are longer and more detailed than Matthew's version.

Parties to the miracle. The interaction in the story focuses our attention on Jesus, the demonized man, the demon, and the people of the region.

Jesus. Again, Jesus is shown to be in complete control in a confrontation with a demon. Although the many demons exercised control of an individual, Jesus' power over the demons was undiminished.

The demonized man. The contrast between the condition of the man while dominated by demons and after Jesus expelled them is sharply drawn.

The symptoms of extreme demon possession seen in this man include the following:

- Disregard for personal dignity (nakedness, Luke 8:27).
- Withdrawal from society (Luke 8:27).
- Disregard for normal comforts (lived in the tombs, Luke 8:27).
- Affinity for unclean, isolated locations (lived in tombs, Luke 8:27).
- Violence against others (Luke 8:29).
- Unusual physical strength (Luke 8:29).
- Inarticulate speech (Mark 5:5).
- Self mutilation (Mark 5:5).

Perhaps the decisive demonstration of possession was the recognition by the demon of Jesus (Luke 8:30) and forced submission to him (Luke 8:31).

What a contrast we see in Luke 8:35, which describes the man who had been freed from the control of demons as "sitting at the feet of Jesus, clothed and in his right mind." The evil powers which had dominated him were gone, and the transformation was evident to all.

The demon. The demon had complete control of the man, and spoke through his voice. The name "Legion" was descriptive rather than personal. The name was appropriate because many demons had taken up residence in the victim's personality. But it is also clear from each account that the demons had to acknowledge the sovereignty of Jesus and to do whatever Christ commanded.

The people of the region. The people of the region reacted strangely to the miracle. Rather than see the possibilities for healing of their own sick by Jesus, they felt only a terror of the unknown, and they begged Jesus to leave the region.

How the story unfolds. Jesus sailed with his disciples across the Sea of Galilee to Gentile territory. As soon as he landed, he was met by a demon-possessed man. The demon was forced

to his knees before Jesus, for he recognized Christ as the "Son of the Most High God," and begged Jesus not to "torment me." The demon confessed that his name was Legion, "because many demons had entered him."

The demons, fully exposed, begged Jesus to let them enter a nearby herd of pigs. Jesus permitted them to do so, but the pigs ran into the sea and drowned.

The demonized man was fully restored and listening to Jesus when people from the area hurried to this location to find out what had happened. They were so terrified by the supernatural events that they begged Jesus to leave their territory.

When the restored man asked permission to go with Jesus, Christ sent him home, encouraging him to "tell what great things God had done for you."

"He lived in the tombs" *(Luke 8:27).* Tombs as the resting place of the dead were ritually unclean for Jews. It is fascinating to note that the demons in this man begged to enter pigs,

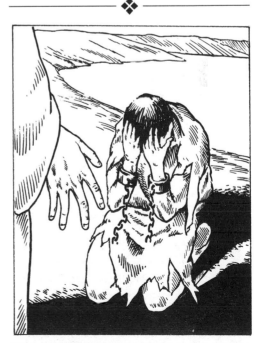

"There met Him a certain man who had demons for a long time."

who were also ritually unclean. The account is thus bracketed by references to the unclean places preferred by demons. This underlines their own corrupt and corrupting nature (see Luke 8:29, which calls the demon an "unclean spirit").

"What have I to do with you" (8:28). The Greek saying, "What to me and to you," is both an admission of Jesus' superiority and an expression of the demon's desire to distance himself from Christ.

"I beg You, do not torment me" (8:28). The demon's cry may sound pitiful. But that demon had no pity on the man whom he tormented. Although Jesus had commanded the demon to leave the man, and the demon had to obey, he begged Jesus for a concession.

"Legion, because many demons had entered him" (8:30). There were 6,000 men in a fully staffed Roman legion. This name doesn't necessarily mean there were 6,000 demons infecting this victim. It does indicate what the text states: that "many demons had entered him."

We know little about how a demon settles into the personality and gains control over a person. This passage reminds us that more than one demon can express itself through individuals who become vulnerable to possession. Satanism and demon possession are often depicted by movie producers who know nothing of the terrible reality. This encourages the foolish to seek out such experiences.

"Into the abyss" (8:31). The "abyss" is a place in which some of the angels who fell with Satan are currently confined, awaiting God's final judgment (see 2 Pet. 2:4; Jude 6).

"He permitted them" (8:32). Christ's control over the demons was so complete that they could not act of their own volition. They could do only what Jesus permitted them to do. It is ironic that the demons begged to be permitted to enter other living beings, even animals. Yet as soon as they entered the pigs, they dashed into the sea and were drowned.

What God permits the evil spirits to do always proves to be their undoing.

"The whole multitude . . . asked him to depart" (8:37). The interesting thing about this request is that it was made after the people of the region had carefully examined what had happened. They "heard" reports of what had happened (Luke 8:34), and then "went out to see what had happened" (Luke 8:35). When they saw the demonized man fully restored, they inquired and learned "by what means he who had been demon possessed was healed" (Luke 8:36). Yet, after going through this process and learning the facts, the "whole multitude" asked Jesus to leave.

How amazing! Were they afraid Jesus' powers would be turned against them? Were they worried about the possible fate of other herds of pigs? Couldn't they see what Jesus' powerful, healing presence might mean to them and their loved ones?

We can't understand how these people, after such careful examination, could turn Jesus away! This is a powerful reminder to us that while the facts call for full commitment to Jesus, commitment remains a matter of faith.

"Jesus sent him" (8:38, 39). The man Jesus had restored wanted to go with Jesus. Instead, Jesus sent him to his "own house" to "tell what great things God has done for you." Christ still has a mission for those who make the commitment of faith to him. And it is the same mission on which the man freed from demons was sent. We are to go to our "own house"—our own family, our own coworkers, our own neighborhood—and tell what God has done for us.

The message of the miracle. The miracle accounts emphasize the total control the demons had gained over their victim. Yet that control was easily broken by Jesus. He easily expelled not one but many demons. The response of the Gerasenes and the freed victim portray the two possible responses we can make to Jesus. The miracle itself emphasizes the absolute and total authority of Jesus over all in the spiritual realm that might harm us.

JESUS HEALS A HEMORRHAGING WOMAN   *Luke 8:43–48; Matthew 9:20–22; Mark 5:25-34*

While Jesus was on his way to respond to a father's desperate appeal for help, he was touched by a woman with an unstoppable menstrual flow. She touched the hem of his clothing and was healed.

Background to the miracle. The condition of the woman with the flow of blood is far more serious than we might imagine. The medical complications are significant enough, for the constant loss of blood drains the victim of iron and other vital minerals. But in Judaism, such a flow of blood also made the woman ritually unclean.

The menstruant was *niddah*, and prohibited from having sexual relations. Rabbi Yoshaayah taught that a man should separate from his wife when she even *neared* her period. Rabbi Shimeon bar Yohai, in commenting on Leviticus 15:31, announced that "he who does not separate from his wife near her period, even if he has sons like the sons of Aaron, they will die."

The problem for the woman who sought out Jesus was even more acute. Menstruant women transferred their impurity to whatever they touched, including household implements and their contents. The rabbis decreed that even the corpse of a woman who died during her period had to undergo a special purification with water *(tNidd.9.16)*. Thus the woman in this miracle account was not only cut off from her husband but also disqualified from the contribution she would normally have made to the family. And this had been the woman's experience for twelve long years (Luke 8:43)!

It is no wonder that, as Luke relates, she had "spent all her livelihood on physicians" (Luke 8:43). The tragedy was that although she had spent all she had, she "could not be healed by any."

Parties to the miracle. There seem to be only two parties to this miracle—Jesus, and the woman—although Peter has a small speaking part. Yet there is one other person who is not mentioned in this story of a miracle within a miracle. And that is Jairus, the anxious father of a dying daughter who had asked Jesus to treat her.

Jesus. Jesus had set out on an urgent mission, but he stopped when he felt "power going out from Me" (Luke 8:46). Christ was so filled with healing power that it was unnecessary for him to direct it. The miracle emphasizes the intrinsic power that resides in Christ.

The woman. Mark makes a point of this woman's reaction when Jesus stopped in the middle of the crowd and asked who touched him. She was "fearing and trembling, knowing what had happened to her" (Mark 5:33). The fear and trembling she felt may have been anxiety over Christ's reaction to being touched by an "unclean" woman. Any of the religious leaders of the time would have been horrified and angry, for her touch would have made *them* unclean. What the woman did not yet realize was that Christ had such a vitalizing holiness that a simple touch from him cleansed the unclean.

Peter. Mark describes "the disciples" reaction to Jesus' question about who touched him, while Luke casts Peter as the spokesman. Peter couldn't understand why Jesus would ask this question. How could anyone possibly identify a single touch while pushing his way through a crowd of people?

Peter failed to understand that Jesus was speaking of a special kind of touch—a touch which tapped into Jesus' unlimited source of power.

Jairus. This anxious father is not mentioned in this account, but his presence can be sensed. He had urged Jesus to come to his home because his only daughter was dying. It must have been hard enough for Jairus as the multitudes that thronged Jesus slowed their progress. But when Jesus actually stopped—to listen closely to this woman's story and then to encourage her—Jairus must have been frantic.

Didn't Jesus realize that his mission was *urgent*? How could the Lord dawdle when Jairus's little girl was dying?

And then as soon as Jesus finished speaking with the woman, word arrived that the daughter had died. We can only imagine the father's emotions, but from Jesus' words to him, fear seemed to predominate (Luke 8:50).

How the story unfolds. As Jesus followed Jairus to his home, a woman who had suffered from a continual menstrual flow for a dozen years came up behind him. Convinced that she would be made whole if only she could touch Jesus, she reached out and made contact with the hem of his garment. And her flow of blood miraculously stopped!

Jesus stopped too and asked who had touched him. The disciples did not realize that Jesus was speaking of a special touch. They expressed surprise that Jesus should ask such a question.

Finally the woman came forward, trembling. She fell down in the position of a supplicant and told her story, relating that she was healed the moment she touched Jesus. Christ not only showed no anger over being touched by a woman who was *niddah*, but explained,

"Your faith has made you well." Then he dismissed her with a blessing, "Go in peace" (Luke 8:48).

"Somebody touched Me" (Luke 8:46). What was so special about the touch of the woman?

It was intentional. The woman did not simply brush against Jesus accidentally. She intended to touch him.

It was purposeful. The woman was intent on being healed from the flow of blood that had made her an outcast for so many years.

It was faith-driven. The woman believed that Jesus had power in himself to heal her. It was this faith that drove her to find Jesus and to touch him.

It was efficacious. When the woman touched Jesus, she was healed immediately, and she felt the difference. She did not have to wait to see if the bleeding had really stopped. She knew immediately.

"Your faith has made you well" (Luke 8:48). The Greek word translated "made you well" is *sesoken*, from *sozo*, "to save." The primary focus is on deliverance from her medical condi-

A woman came up behind Jesus and touched His garment to receive healing.

tion. But in view of the implications of this woman's conditions in rabbinic Judaism, a broader meaning is implied.

- *The flow of blood* drained her physically.
- *The flow of blood* made her socially unclean and isolated her from others in the community.
- *The flow of blood* made her religiously unclean, and cut her off from worship at the temple.

Jesus' touch, however, *saved her physically* by restoring her health; saved her socially by restoring her fellowship with others in the community; and *saved her spiritually* by enabling her to join again those who worshiped God at the temple and on Israel's religious holidays.

What a picture this is of our salvation. When we approach Jesus with this woman's kind of faith, he saves us physically (a promise to be fulfilled completely in our resurrection). He saves us socially, as the Holy Spirit bonds us to others in the body of Christ to form a new and loving community. He saves us spiritually, forgiving us and making us children of God with access to the Father.

The tense of the Greek verb translated as "healed" in verse 48 emphasizes that the woman's healing had taken place, and that her deliverance would continue to affect her life. It is the same for us. We are saved once for all when we trust Jesus as Savior. And the saving impact of Jesus in our lives will continue to affect us for time and eternity.

"Your faith has made you well" (Luke 8:48). When the woman had told her story to Jesus, Jesus announced it was her faith that had made her well.

This statement is significant, for it is another clear expression of the gospel principle of grace. The woman was healed not because of any merit of hers, but because she exercised faith in Jesus. In the same way, people today can reach out to touch Jesus. How? Our approach to Jesus must be:

- *Intentional.* We consciously choose to come to Jesus Christ.

- *Purposeful.* We come to Jesus with the awareness that we are spiritually sick and need healing.
- *Faith-driven.* We come to Jesus because we believe that he and he alone can save.
- *Efficacious.* We sense within ourselves the Holy Spirit's testimony that we have been truly saved and made well.

"Go in peace" (Luke 8:48). The blessing with which Jesus dismissed the woman is also ours to claim. Christ had met her need on every level, bringing peace. When we come to Jesus with this woman's kind of faith, he meets our every need, and we also find peace.

JESUS RAISES JAIRUS'S DAUGHTER
Luke 8:41–56; Matthew 9:18–26; Mark 5:22–43

Jesus responded to the pleas of Jairus to help his daughter. The girl died while Jesus was on the way to her home, but Christ restored her to life.

Background of the miracle. The man who came to Jesus for help, Jairus, is identified in Luke 8:41 as a "ruler of the synagogue" (*archon tes synagoges*). This was an important position in Judaism. Three men represented the synagogue in local government. The president of this group of three was the "ruler of the synagogue." He was also was considered an archon of the local community ("rulers" in Matt. 9:18).

The head of the synagogue was not necessarily a rabbi, but he was an educated man who could evaluate the competence of those invited to read the Scriptures and address the people. He also ran the financial affairs of the synagogue and was responsible for ensuring correct behavior at worship. *This position* was unpaid, and it was held by those who were greatly respected in the community. Such a person was aided by a paid assistant who took care of the many practical details of maintaining the synagogue and its services (the "attendant" of Luke 4:20).

We know then that Jairus was an important man who held a respected religious and governmental post. It is significant that at least some persons of high standing—as well as the disadvantaged and the oppressed—had a real faith in Jesus.

Parties to the miracle. The central figures are Jesus, Jairus, and Jairus's daughter. We are also given glimpses of some people gathered at Jairus's home.

Jesus. Jesus was responsive to the synagogue president's request to come and heal his dying daughter. But on the way, Christ stopped to deal with a woman who had an unstoppable menstrual flow (see page 201). Given the urgency of Jairus's request, it may seem strange that Jesus paused for so long. His delay is explained when he went to the home and brought the girl, who had died, back to life. By waiting for the worst to happen, Jesus brought even greater joy to Jairus and offered proof of his power.

Jairus. Although he was an important man, he did not hesitate to hurry to Jesus to plead for help for his dying daughter. Jairus clearly was a man with faith in Jesus, for he believed that if Jesus would come and lay hands on his little girl, she would live.

We can only guess at Jairus's agony when Jesus delayed to speak with the woman whose flow of blood had been healed. Likewise, we can only imagine his joy when Jesus later delivered his daughter to him, alive and restored.

Jairus's daughter. Luke noted that the girl was twelve years old. This was just before the marriageable age of 13. Her death just before the experience of becoming a wife and mother adds to the sense of tragedy that Luke conveys.

The people gathered at Jairus's house. These are described as "those who wept and wailed loudly" (Mark 5:40). The implication is that they were professional mourners—women hired to accompany a funeral procession and loudly bewail the loss. When Jesus announced that the little girl inside was not dead but sleeping, those making the commotion ridiculed him. Their attitude may reflect their preference for a day's pay over the life of the young girl. Selfish self-interest is sometimes stronger than concern for the suffering.

How the story unfolds. Jesus responded to the urgent request of Jairus to go with him to save his young daughter's life. As they pushed through the crowds, a desperate woman touched Jesus and was cured of a chronic flow of blood that had ruined her life. Jesus then stopped and talked with her!

By the time Christ was ready to move on, messengers reported the child's death. But Jesus told Jairus not to fear but "only believe, and she will be made well."

When they arrived, they discovered that professional mourners had already filled Jairus's house and were making a great commotion. Jesus was ridiculed when he told them the girl was not dead but "sleeping." Jesus then removed the mourners, went into a room with the body of the girl, and called her back to life. The parents were amazed when he opened the door and told them to get her something to eat.

"He fell down at Jesus' feet and begged Him" (Luke 8:41). No matter how important we may be, there are times when our need is so desperate that there is no room for pride. It was this kind of situation which Jairus faced that day. How wonderful that we can go to Jesus with our needs, as Jairus did.

"Your daughter is dead. Do not trouble the teacher" (8:49). The messengers who came from Jairus's house were wrong on two counts.

They assumed that death limited Jesus' power. Soon they would see Jairus's daughter alive and well again. Even death submits to the word of Jesus Christ.

They assumed that Jesus would not want to be bothered with Jairus's suffering. Even when God does not intervene to help, Christ does care for us and feels with us in our pain.

"Only believe, and she will be made well" (8:50). It would be easy to misunderstand this sentence. Jesus did not say, "Only believe *in order that* she may be made well." Jairus's belief was not a condition of the girl's healing. Jesus said, "Only believe *and* she will be made well."

Belief in Jesus would calm the father's fears and give him hope until Jesus actually made her well. Then the father would not need faith; he would possess what faith had led him to expect.

It was Jesus, and not Jairus's faith, that performed the miracle. Jesus' ability to exercise his power doesn't depend on human faith. Faith in Jesus will carry *us* through our dark times, until God acts to meet our needs. Then faith's expectation will be rewarded with the thing for which we had hoped.

"She is not dead, but sleeping" (8:52). This seems a strange saying, because the girl *was* dead. But the key to understanding these words is to realize what they and he meant by "dead."

To the parents and the mourners, "dead" meant gone—cut off from the realm of the living, forever lost to loved ones. To Jesus, biological death was as temporary as that peaceful unconsciousness into which we slip each night. Jesus knew there will be an awakening for the dead, just as there is an awakening each morning for the sleeping. Paul captured the glory of this truth in 1 Thessalonians 4:13, 14, where he encouraged believers not to

sorrow as others who have no hope. For if we believe that Jesus died and rose again, even so God will bring with him those who sleep in Jesus.

Our dead sleep now. But when Jesus returns, there will be a grand awakening!

The meaning of the miracle. This miracle reminds us that Jesus controls both death and life. As with Jairus's daughter, the death of our loved ones brings grief and fear. Yet this miracle account reminds us that while we wait for

the great reunion that will come when the dead in Christ are raised, we wait in faith. We will be "made well" in that glorious time.

JESUS HEALS TWO BLIND MEN
Matthew 9:27–31

Jesus healed two blind men who cried out to Him as "Son of David."

Background of the miracle. Blindess has been common in the Middle East since before biblical times. Yet the Old Testament records no such miracle of restoring sight as Jesus performed (see Matt. 4:23; 8:16–17; 9:35). Each of the Gospels reports several incidents of him restoring sight to the blind. Why such an emphasis on these events and on other healing miracles?

Isaiah 35:5, 6 associated such healings with the messianic age. Isaiah predicted for Israel that when God "comes to save you,"

> Then the eyes of the blind shall be
>   opened,
> And the ears of the deaf shall be
>   unstopped.
> Then the lame shall leap like a deer,
> And the tongue of the dumb sing.

The miracles that Jesus performed fulfilled this prophecy. They should have been recognized by the Jewish people and their teachers as proof of who Jesus was. We learn in this miracle story, however, that the first people to clearly see the significance of what Jesus did were two blind men!

Parties to the miracle. The miracle account, told in just three verses and recorded only in Matthew, mentions only Jesus and the two blind men.

Jesus. Jesus is given two titles in these verses: Son of David and Lord. Both are significant for understanding the implications of the event.

The two blind men. They are the first persons in Matthew's Gospel to address Jesus as "Son of David." This was a Messianic title, for the promised deliverer was to be a descendant of

David and thus one qualified to inherit Israel's throne.

How the story unfolds. Just after Jesus left Jairus's house (see p. 203), he heard two blind men calling to him as "Son of David," asking for mercy. Jesus took the blind men inside the house [where he was staying?] and questioned them about their faith. Each professed faith in him, addressing him as Lord. Christ then touched their eyes and restored their sight.

Although Jesus "sternly warned them" not to tell anyone, they "spread the news about him in all that country."

"Do you believe that I am able?" (Matthew 9:28). Why the emphasis on faith in this miracle account? There are several reasons.

Faith, not desperation. When people are desperate, they often cry out to God without any conviction that he can help—or even that he exists. Jesus' questioning revealed that the blind men came to him not out of desperation but in faith.

Focused, not general. Christ asked in pointed fashion, "Do you believe *that I am able to do this?*" The power of God is made available to us in Jesus. Our faith is not to be in some abstract being "out there," but in the person of Jesus Christ, God the Son incarnate, our Savior. Jesus' questioning revealed that the blind men truly trusted him and his ability to save.

Effective, not futile. Some interpreters make a serious error with these words. They assume that when Jesus said "according to your faith," he meant that if they had *enough* faith their sight would be restored. Not at all. The healing was according to the object of their faith. They were healed because their trust was in Jesus.

Faith in Jesus still opens the channel through which God's love and power will flow.

"Son of David . . . Lord" (Matthew 9:27, 28). Christ's questioning of the two blind men established that their faith was truly in him. It also established that they understood who he

was. Their cry "Son of David" is the first public acknowledgment recorded in Matthew that Jesus was the promised Messiah. During their questioning by Jesus, they also acknowledged Jesus as Lord.

The word *Lord* in the first century was sometimes used in addressing a superior as a sign of respect. But its use in this context is far more significant. Jesus was not only Israel's Messiah; he is history's sovereign Lord.

To have real faith in Jesus, we must recognize and acknowledge him for who he truly is.

Jesus "warned them sternly" (Matthew 9:30). The Greek word used here is *embrimaomai,* which occurs only five times in the New Testament (Mark 1:43; 14:55; John 11:33, 38). Always it is connected with deep emotion. Why the emotion here, and why the stern warning?

When this miracle took place, Jesus had been teaching and working miracles in Judea and Galilee for some time. Now, at last, the message of his miracles to Israel had been recognized by the two blind men. No wonder Jesus felt strong emotion at that moment. And no wonder Jesus questioned them so closely about their faith. Had they *really* understood? They had!

But Jesus knew that the rest of the people would *not* understand. Neither would they respond with a faith like that of these two men. It was best that this miracle, so briefly stated but so meaningful to Jesus, not be reported to the doubting crowds.

But the blind men, excited by their healing, couldn't keep quiet. They spread the news everywhere. They couldn't sense what the miracle healing had meant to Jesus. They only knew what it had meant to them.

How important it is to realize that the miracles God performs may be as significant a blessing to him as they are to us.

JESUS CASTS OUT A MUTE SPIRIT
Matthew 9:32–35

Jesus cast out an evil spirit that had blocked a man's ability to speak.

Background of the miracle. Matthew indicates this miracle took place as two blind men whose sight had been restored (see page 205) were leaving Jesus' house (Matt. 9:32). The two miracles are linked also by Matthew's intent to contrast the responses to Jesus by the blind men, the crowds, and the Pharisees. The two miracle accounts should thus be examined and taught together.

Parties to the miracle. The three brief verses that contain this account focus our attention on the interaction of Jesus, the mute man, the multitudes, and the Pharisees.

Jesus. Jesus had just been recognized by two blind men as Israel's Messiah and sovereign Lord. His miracles, performed in fulfillment of prophecy, offered proof of his identity (see "*Background of the miracle,*" above).

The mute man. The Greek word used of his disability is *kophos,* which generally has the meaning of "deaf mute." The text makes it clear that the cause of his malady was not organic, but oppression by an evil spirit.

The multitudes. Matthew emphasizes the astonishment of the crowds which witnessed this miracle and their awareness that "it was never seen like this in Israel" (9:33). No Old Testament prophet worked miracles like those which Jesus was performing.

The Pharisees. These influential men had a reputation for piety because of their strict observance of Mosaic Law. They had decided that Jesus' power must come from Satan, not God.

How the story unfolds. As the blind men whose sight Jesus had restored left, a mute man was brought to Jesus. Jesus cast out the evil spirit who had blocked the man's powers of speech, and the mute began to speak. The crowd was amazed, because in all of sacred history nothing like Jesus' miracles had been witnessed. The Pharisees, confirmed in their hostility toward Jesus, muttered and accused him of being part of a satanic conspiracy.

Three responses to the two miracles. This miracle must be examined with the healing of the two blind men which immediately preceded it. Matthew's point in linking the two was to demonstrate the differing responses to those who observed Jesus' performing miracles.

The two blind men. The two blind men realized that Jesus' miracles marked him as the Messiah, and they put their trust in him (Matt. 9:27, 28).

The crowd. The crowd acknowledged that "it was never seen like this in Israel." No healings such as these had been performed by Israel's prophets. But the phrase "seen like this" is significant. While such miracles had never been *seen,* they had been *predicted by Isaiah* (see p. 205)! And that prediction associated the miracles Jesus performed with the coming of the Messiah. In fact, the first two miracles mentioned In Isaiah 35:5 are:

> Then the eyes of the blind shall be
> opened,
> And the ears of the deaf shall be
> unstopped.

If we understand *kophos* to mean "deaf mute," these are the very miracles Matthew recorded in this passage!

The crowds, like the two blind men, had all the proof they needed that Jesus was the Messiah! But unlike the blind men, they simply could not "see."

The Pharisees. The judgment of the Pharisees is harsher and more revealing. These men who took such pride in their knowledge of the Law should have noticed immediately the relationship between the miracles Jesus performed and the messianic promises. Unlike the crowds, they were *willfully* blind. In ascribing Christ's miracles to Satan, they rejected the testimony of the Scriptures which they claimed to honor.

No wonder John reported Christ saying at another time, "You search the Scriptures, for in them you think you have eternal life; and these are they which testify of Me. But you are not willing to come to Me that you may have life" (John 5:39, 40).

The meaning of the miracles. These miracles have a unique function. Note that these two miracles are found only in Matthew's Gospel and that his Gospel was directed primarily to a Jewish audience.

In selecting these two miracles and focusing attention on the response of various groups to Jesus, Matthew presents a strong argument for Jesus' Messiahship. These miracles are linked in prophecy with the messianic age to be instituted by God.

But do people respond when Jesus offers his miracles as proof of his messiahship? A few recognized him and respond with faith (the two blind men). Most were confused and unable to grasp the meaning of what they had witnessed (the crowds). And the religious leaders, who knew most about the Scriptures and should have understood the significance of Jesus' wonders, were simply "not willing" to submit to him. They not only rejected him; they turned others against him by charging that he was part of a satanic conspiracy.

Jesus presents himself today as the wonder-working Savior, and we must also decide for or against placing faith in him.

JESUS FEEDS 5,000 PEOPLE *John 6:1–14; Matthew 14:13–21; Mark 6:30–44; Luke 9:10–17*

Jesus fed a large crowd which followed him into the wilderness, using only a few small loaves and fishes.

Background to the miracle. It was the responsibility of the head of each Jewish family at mealtime to look up to heaven while thanking God, and then to break and distribute bread for the meal. One of the most common of such mealtime prayers was, "Blessed art Thou, O Lord our God, King of the Universe, who brings forth bread from the earth."

In performing this miracle, Jesus assumed the role of head of the family as well as the role of God, bringing forth bread to meet the needs of his people.

The Gospel writers followed Jewish custom in counting only the men when reckoning the crowd. While the ideal woman of rabbinic lore stayed at home, it is clear from the Gospels and from various references in early rabbinic literature that women went to the market and worked in the fields with their husbands at harvest time. Some have estimated that the crowd Jesus fed, if the women and children were added, might have been fifteen or twenty thousand.

This is an especially significant miracle, for it is reported in all four of the Gospels.

Parties to the miracle. The significant figures in this miracle account are Jesus, the disciples, the thousands who had followed Jesus into a wilderness area, and a boy who shared his lunch.

Jesus. Jesus' revealed his deity by creating bread, as if in answer to the usual mealtime prayer.

Jesus' disciples. The disciples showed sensitivity to the needs of the crowd for food and shelter (Matt. 14:15). But their solution, to "send them away, so they can buy bread," was not acceptable to Jesus. The disciples were stunned when Jesus ordered, "You give them something to eat" (Mark 6:37).

The crowds. Great crowds had followed Jesus into a "deserted" (uninhabited) area. They had come hastily, without bringing food to eat on the way. Jesus saw them as sheep, wandering aimlessly, helpless without a shepherd.

The boy. The boy who provided the food Jesus multiplied is mentioned only by John (6:9). How strange that in many Sunday school lessons, he is made the focus of this story rather than Jesus.

How the story unfolds. Jesus had been surrounded and harried by crowds of people coming and going. He told his disciples it was time to rest, so they set out by boat to find a deserted place.

But other people recognized him as the boat passed. By the time the boat landed, a new multitude had gathered to greet him. Jesus couldn't escape, even for a moment. Rather than being irritated, Jesus was deeply moved; these ordinary people to him were like sheep without a shepherd. So he began to teach them.

When evening drew near, the disciples reminded Jesus that it was late, and they were in an uninhabited area. Jesus needed to send the people away soon, so they could "buy themselves bread." Jesus shocked the disciples by his reply: "*You* give them something to eat" (Mark 6:37).

Confused, the disciples objected. It would take at least eight month's wages to buy enough bread for such a crowd, even if that much bread were available. Jesus asked, "How many loaves do you have?"

The disciples reported they could come up with five loaves (each about the size of a modern dinner roll) and two small fish. Jesus told the disciples to have the crowd sit down in groups, as they would at mealtime. Christ then blessed the bread [i.e., said the prayer used before eating] and began to break the bread and fish into smaller pieces. The food was miraculously multiplied. After everyone had eaten, twelve flat wicker baskets of food were left over.

Jesus then sent the crowds away. While he went up into the mountains to pray, the disciples set out by boat to cross the sea.

Sheep not having a shepherd (Mark 6:34). Jesus' imagery has deep Old Testament roots. Moses prayed that God would provide a successor who "may lead them [Israel] out and bring them in, that the congregation of the Lord may not be like sheep which have no shepherd" (Num. 27:17). God's answer in that situation was to set apart Joshua—which is the Hebrew version of the name "Jesus."

Even more significant is the use of the image in Ezekiel 34. In that passage, the prophet condemned the false shepherds who mistreated God's flock and who led them astray. God promised,

"Indeed I Myself will search for My sheep and seek them out. As a shepherd seeks out his flock on the

Jesus blessed the bread and fish and gave it to the disciples to distribute.

day he is among his scattered sheep, so will I seek out My sheep and deliver them. . . . I will feed My flock, and I will make them lie down," says the Lord God. "I will seek what was lost and bring back what was driven away, bind up the broken and strengthen what was sick" (Ezek. 34:11–12, 15–16).

What happened that day by the Sea of Galilee identified Jesus with the Lord God of the Old Testament, whose concern was for the well-being of the flock. In Christ, God was seeking out and feeding Israel not only with bread but with truth as well.

"You give them something to eat" (Mark 6:37). Jesus didn't expect the disciples to perform a miracle. But the command, with its emphatic "you" in the Greek, is significant.

Jesus challenged the disciple's solution. The disciples had been concerned for the crowd. But their solution was to send them away so they could "buy themselves bread" (Mark 6:36). But Jesus did not come to send people away. He came to draw them to him. He came because the people could not "buy themselves" what they required to meet their deepest need. Only Jesus could meet that need, and he did so supremely on Calvary.

Jesus challenged the disciple's vision. Jesus was training his disciples so they would be able to meet the needs of the shepherdless. "*You* give them" was a challenge to help them catch a vision of the mission for which they were being prepared.

Jesus challenged the disciple's understanding. The answer to their confusion on how to fulfill Jesus' command was not to buy bread but to look to Jesus. Christ never asks us to do anything without providing the needed resources to complete the task.

The miracle that followed illustrates this principle. Jesus took what the disciples had and multiplied it. No matter how limited our resources, God's ability to multiply them is as unlimited as they were on that day in the wilderness.

Twelve baskets of fragments (Mark 6:43). The Gospel writers report that everyone in the crowd ate and were filled, after which they took up 12 baskets of fragments. Some have seen significance in the number 12. There were 12 tribes of Israel. Messiah's provision was so generous that even his scraps can supply the needs of Israel, as represented by the 12 surplus baskets.

"Take him by force to make him king" (John 6:15). John adds a detail not mentioned in the other Gospels. After the meal, the enthusiastic crowd decided that Jesus must be the prophet promised by Moses (Deut. 18:18). Why not then acclaim Jesus king?

Jesus later commented on their motive. "You seek me, not because you saw the signs, but because you ate of the loaves and were filled" (John 6:26). The people had not seen the meaning of the miraculous sign which identified Jesus as the Lord God, their Shepherd. All they knew was that he was someone who could feed them. Self-interest, not faith, lay at the root of their enthusiasm. No wonder they were ready to proclaim Jesus king.

How ironic are the phrases "take him by force" and "make him" king. Those who acclaim a person king will be willing to submit to his will. The crowd intended to make Jesus submit to their will, thus robbing him of his royal authority. Let's be careful not to do the same. When we come to God in Jesus' name, may our prayers be for that which is in his will. As true followers of Christ, we should not attempt to cajole him into doing our will.

Miracle and message (John 6:26–66). John's Gospel follows a pattern noted before (p. 186). He describes a miracle, then records a lengthy teaching of Jesus which is related to it. That lengthy teaching in John 6 has been called Jesus' "Sermon on the Bread of Life."

In this sermon, Jesus pointed out the selfish motives of the crowds who followed him. But Christ himself is the true bread, the source and sustainer of life. He is the true bread of heaven, who has been sent by the Father to give eternal life to everyone who believes in him. The ancestors of his hearers who had eaten manna in the wilderness were all dead, but those who would appropriate Christ—figuratively eating his flesh and drinking his blood—would live forever.

John notes that after this sermon "many of his disciples [used here in the sense of loose adherents] went back and walked with him no more" (John 6:66). They had eagerly received the bread that sustained physical life, but they rejected the Word that promised eternal life.

Some people today preach a false gospel, which promises material prosperity to those with enough faith. How eagerly the crowds in Jesus' day would have welcomed such a gospel. And how quickly we turn away from the true gospel as well. The authentic gospel promises us new life, but then it calls us to live this new life not for ourselves but for the Lord.

The meaning of the miracle. Commentators tend to follow many side trails in discussing the feeding of the 5,000, but we must not forget this miracle's central message. In each Gospel, this miracle is an acted-out parable. Jesus declared himself to be the Lord God, come to shepherd his people, as he had promised through the prophet Ezekiel.

JESUS WALKS ON WATER   *Matthew 14:22–33; Mark 6:45–52; John 6:15–21*

Jesus walked on a stormy sea and joined his disciples in their small boat.

Background of the miracle. After Jesus fed the 5,000, he "made" his disciples get in their boat and go on ahead of him (Matt. 14:22). The strong Greek verb in this passage is often translated "compelled."

What was the urgency?

- Jesus may have sent the disciples ahead to help diffuse the crowd that wanted to make him king (compare John 6:15).
- Jesus wanted to escape both the crowd and the disciples, to get some rest (Mark 6:31–32).

- Jesus definitely wanted to spend some time alone with his Father in prayer (Matt. 14:23).

The separation of Jesus from his disciples provided the occasion for this miracle.

When the disciples first saw Jesus approaching them on the lake, they mistook him for a ghost. Their fear reflected the common first-century belief that ghosts were hostile beings, the shades of malevolent men who had died, and who would harm human beings.

Parties to the miracle. Jesus is the central figure. The others involved are the twelve disciples, with the emphasis on Peter.

Jesus. After resting and praying Jesus was walking on the surface of the Sea of Galilee, apparently crossing it to join the disciples who had gone on ahead by boat. The miracle displayed Christ's control of the forces of nature.

The disciples. The disciples' initial reaction of fear was transformed to worship as the miracle impressed them with the fresh realization that Jesus was "the Son of God" (Matt. 14:33).

Peter. Peter is both a good example and a bad example in this miracle account. He alone had faith enough in Jesus to step out of the boat into the stormy sea. But once on the waters, his gaze was torn from Jesus and fixed on his surroundings. We are also asked to risk in response to Jesus' call. Peter's experience reminds us not to take our eyes off Jesus in difficult situations.

How the story unfolds. Jesus hurried his disciples into a boat and away from the crowds. It is likely that he told them to wait for him until a fixed time and if he had not arrived by then, they should set out to cross the lake. But the sea was stormy and the wind was in their face. By four o'clock in the morning, the disciples were only halfway across the lake.

When they noticed a figure walking on the water, the disciples were terrified, assum-

Jesus approached the disciples, walking on the water in the midst of a storm.

ing it must be a ghost. But Jesus called out and identified himself. Peter then asked the Lord to tell him to join him on the waters. Jesus did, and Peter stepped out into the stormy waters. He walked a few steps toward Jesus but was distracted by the raging winds and began to sink.

Jesus caught Peter's hand and lifted him up, calling him a "little-faith" person and asking, "Why did you doubt?" (Matt. 14:31). When Jesus and Peter got into the boat, the winds and the sea calmed down.

Amazed, the disciples worshiped Jesus. For the first time in Matthew's Gospel, they expressed the belief that Jesus was "the Son of God" (Matt. 14:33; see also Matt. 16:16; 26:63; 27:40, 43, 54).

"The fourth watch of the night" (Matt. 14:25). The Romans divided the night into four watches, the Hebrews into three. The Roman system was adopted by all the Gospel writers. Thus, Jesus approached the boat between 3:00 A.M and 6:00 A.M

"It is I" (14:27). The Greek phrase is *ego eimi*, and it may reflect the Old Testament name *Yahweh*, meaning "I AM." No wonder Jesus could encourage his disciples to "take courage" [rendered "be of good cheer" in our text], and "do not be afraid." Since God was with them, they had no reason to fear.

"Command me to come to You" (14:28). The incident with Peter offers an interesting commentary on Jesus' words of encouragement.

"Lord, if it is You" (14:28). The conditional here has the meaning, "*Since* it is You." Jesus had announced, *ego eimi* ("it is I"). Peter had confidence that Jesus truly was Lord.

"When Peter had come down out of the boat" (14:29). Jesus said, "Take courage." Peter showed his courage by stepping out boldly into the surging waters.

"He was afraid, and beginning to sink" (14:30). Jesus had said, "Do not be afraid." Out on the waves alone, Peter did fear. And he began to sink. Fear may overcome us also when we take our eyes off Jesus and concentrate on our circumstances.

"O you of little faith" (14:31). It is far better to be a "little faith" person than a "no faith" person. But best of all is to be a person of "great faith."

"Why did you doubt" (14:31)? At first, the answer seems obvious. Peter doubted because the circumstances were fraught with danger. But the question encouraged Peter and the disciples to look deeper. Jesus had announced "It is I." No matter how hazardous the circumstances may be, there was no reason to doubt when Jesus was present.

This is one of the most important messages of this miracle for us today. We can become so obsessed with difficulties and dangers that our doubts overwhelm us. Yet if Jesus, the Son of God, is with us, he is in control of every circumstance. We need to be as bold as

Peter in walking through our stormy waters, yet wiser than Peter by never forgetting Jesus' presence in our lives.

"They had not understood" (Mark 6:52).
Mark's account of this miracle displays a slightly different emphasis than Matthew's. Mark draws our attention to the disciples' hardened hearts. The phrase indicates an underlying attitude which accounts for their amazement at Jesus' ability to walk on water and at the immediate calming of the waters when Jesus entered the boat. They had just seen Jesus feed 5,000 people. They should have recognized his claim to be the Lord, come to offer himself as Shepherd to his people (see p. 208f.).

While this emphasis is different from Matthew's, the two accounts are actually in complete harmony. The private miracle performed on the Sea of Galilee taught the disciples what the feeding of the 5,000 had not—

that "truly, You are the Son of God" (Matt. 14:33).

The meaning of the miracle. With this miracle, we have evidence that the true identity of Jesus was beginning to dawn on his disciples. They would grasp the full meaning of that confession—"You are the Son of God" (Matt. 14:33)—only later, after the Cross and the Resurrection.

Looking back from that perspective today, we can see in this miracle more evidence that Jesus was who he claimed to be. We can see something of what it means to live in relationship with the Son of God.

The life of faith calls for a boldness like Peter's. He was willing to risk leaving the security of the boat to walk alone on the stormy lake. Faith also calls for a continual awareness that Jesus is with us. This will dispel our doubts, no matter how difficult our circumstances may be.

CHAPTER 11

JESUS: MIRACLES OF THE SON OF GOD

ASSURANCE OF THE RESURRECTION
Matthew—John

Miracles accompanied Jesus throughout His public ministry. Even as Jesus hung on Calvary's cross, wonders took place around Him.

The miracles of Jesus mark Christ as God's messenger. And Jesus' own words mark Him as the Son of God. As we read the accounts of the wonders this Man performed we are confronted with evidence that supports His claims about Himself.

But all Jesus' miracles, as wonderful as they were, pale before the grand miracle of the Resurrection (see pages [15–17]). In the words of the apostle Paul, by His resurrection from the dead Jesus was "declared to be the Son of God" (Romans 1:4).

JESUS HEALS A SYRO-PHOENICIAN GIRL   Matthew 15:21–28; Mark 7:24–30

Jesus first ignored and then responded to the plea of a Gentile woman who begged him to cast a demon from her daughter.

Background of the miracle. This miracle took place in the region once controlled by the cities of Tyre and Sidon, which lay on the Mediterranean coast about thirty and fifty miles, respectively, from Galilee. While Jesus often "withdrew" from the crowds to rest (Matt. 4:12; 12:15; 14:13) this is his only recorded retreat to Gentile territory. His search for solitude was thwarted, however, as "he could not be hidden" (Mark 7:24). He was apparently recognized by some people who had come from this region earlier to hear him (Mark 3:8; Luke 6:17).

The woman from this region who appealed to Jesus was called a "Greek" by Mark. He used the term as a synonym for "non-Jew." Matthew identified her as a Canaanite, one of the ancient pagan peoples who were Israel's traditional enemies. While the Bible reports healings by Jesus of non-Jews in Jewish territory, this is the only miracle he performed for a pagan in Gentile lands.

Parties to the miracle. The persons in this miracle story are Jesus, the Canaanite woman, and the disciples.

Jesus. Jesus left Jewish territory to escape the crowds so he could rest. But even here, he was recognized. The most striking feature of this account is Jesus' apparent coldness to and initial rejection of a desperate woman. It seems so out of character for Christ, normally so compassionate, to fail to respond to anyone who requested his help. Especially troubling to some interpreters is Jesus' comparison of the Jews to "children" and Gentiles to "dogs."

The Canaanite woman. Following Jesus in spite of his apparent indifference, the woman begged him to help her "severely demon-possessed" daughter (Matt. 15:22). When Jesus finally spoke to her, her reply showed her wisdom and faith.

The disciples. The disciples were puzzled observers. They were irritated when the woman trailed after them, constantly crying out for Jesus' help. They suggested that Jesus help her in order to get rid of her. This shows they misunderstood the critical issues involved.

How the story unfolds. Jesus' attempt to get some rest was frustrated when he was recognized even in gentile territory. One persistent woman annoyed the disciples by following Jesus around, crying out loudly for help. When they urged Jesus to heal her and get rid of her, Christ explained that he was "not sent except to the lost sheep of the house of Israel" (Matt. 15:24).

The woman fell at his feet and begged him to help. Jesus refused, saying it wasn't good to throw the children's bread to dogs. The analogy was clear: the Jews were the children; she and other Gentiles were dogs! The woman agreed, but pointed out that dogs do eat the crumbs that fall from the table as the children eat. Christ commended her faith and indicated her request had been granted. At that moment, her daughter was healed.

"Son of David" (Matthew 15:22). This title is reserved for Israel's Messiah, the promised King from David's line. In using this title, the Canaanite woman acknowledged Jesus as the Jewish Messiah. Later she worshiped him as "Lord" (Matt. 15:25), a term which emphasized Jesus' rule over humankind. Christ was

"Son of David" for Israel; "Lord" for all mankind.

"Send her away, for she cries out after us" (15:23). Jesus' reply (Matt. 15:23) made it clear that the disciples were urging Jesus to send her away with her request granted. But note their motive. The disciples were moved by annoyance, not compassion.

"Not sent except to the lost sheep of the house of Israel" (15:24). Jesus at an earlier time had sent his disciples on a preaching mission with the warning, "Do not go into the way of the Gentiles, and do not enter a city of the Samaritans. But go rather to the lost sheep of the house of Israel" (Matt. 10:5, 6). Christ was Israel's Messiah. His mission required him to concentrate his initial efforts on recalling straying Israel to relationship with God.

Mark, writing to the Gentiles, included a detail that Matthew left out. He quoted Jesus as saying to the woman, "Let the children be filled *first*" (7:27). God always intended that the gospel message have a universal impact. Yet it was only right that Jesus should first present himself to Israel as the fulfillment of the prophets' hopes and dreams.

"Throw it to the little dogs" (15:26). It is true that first-century Jews dismissed Gentiles as dogs. But Christ's analogy in this verse is not a condemnation of the Gentiles. He pictured a familiar household scene. When the family gathered for a meal, the parents didn't take food prepared for the children and put it on plates to feed puppies. Mom and dad may have a real affection for the puppies, but they don't give them the meal prepared for their children.

God had prepared the meal of miracles and wonders for Israel, the covenant family, who like lost sheep had strayed far from God. Miracles and wonders were not to be "thrown away" on Gentiles. Most of them would not be tuned in to spiritual matters.

"Crumbs" (15:27). The woman didn't argue or plead. In saying "Yes, Lord," she acknowledged the validity of Jesus' position. But she used Christ's own analogy. While it was true that the meal is prepared for the children, the puppies do get any crumbs that fall from the table. All she was asking for was one of those crumbs.

What a faith this Canaanite woman displayed. The miraculous healing she asked for would not be a problem for Jesus. She knew his power was so great that such a miracle would be a mere crumb from a table laden with goodness. And she was right.

"Great is your faith" (15:28). Jesus acknowledged and praised the faith in the woman's statement, then healed her daughter. While the woman had no right to a miracle healing—for these were intended as signs and witnesses to God's chosen people—her faith caused a crumb to fall into her life.

What a lesson for us. The healing we need—whether inner spiritual healing or physical restoration—is no great challenge for God. Our healing is only a crumb that falls from a table that groans under the weight of the wonders God has prepared. How can we fail to have faith in a God so great, whose miracle-working powers know no limits.

JESUS HEALS A DEAF AND DUMB MAN   *Mark 7:31–37*

Jesus healed a man who was deaf and dumb.

Background of the miracle. Mark places this miracle immediately after the healing of the Syro-Phenician woman's daughter (see p. 214). In her case, Jesus had emphasized the fact that his miracles and wonders were intended especially for Israel. This miracle, performed along the shore of the Sea of Galilee, emphasizes this fact as well. It is just the kind of miracle which the prophets said would mark the ministry of the Messiah (see Isa. 35:5). The healing miracles of Jesus unmistakably marked him as the promised Saviour-King.

Parties to the miracle. The parties mentioned in this miracle account are Jesus, the deaf and dumb man, and an undefined "they."

Jesus. Jesus was back in Jewish territory, where he responded without hesitation to those who sought healing.

The afflicted man. We are told nothing about this disabled individual.

"They." Unnamed persons play a significant role in this miracle account. "They" brought the deaf and dumb man to Jesus. "They" were cautioned by Jesus to tell no one about the miracle. And "they" were astonished by what Jesus did.

How the story unfolds. Jesus left the Gentile region where he had healed a Syro-Phenician woman's daughter. Back in familiar territory along the Sea of Galilee, he encountered a deaf and dumb man brought to him by some of the man's friends. He healed the man so he could both hear and speak. Jesus cautioned the witnesses to tell no one about the healing, but they spread the report everywhere. Everyone reacted with astonishment and approval.

"Departing from the region of Tyre and Sidon, he came . . . to the Sea of Galilee" (Mark 7:31). The geographical reference connects this miracle with the healing of the Syro-Phenician woman's daughter. We need to read the account of the two miracles together and interpret the second in view of Jesus' remarks to the woman.

"They begged Him to put His hand on him" (7:32). This may simply be Mark's way of describing a request that Jesus heal the man. Or it may imply that they expected Jesus to heal *their way.* When we come to the Lord with our requests, we do well if we come without any expectation of the precise way in which Jesus will meet our needs.

"He took him aside from the multitude" (7:33). This is one of only two times that Jesus took someone aside for private healing (compare Mark 8:23). At the same time, it fits Mark's emphasis on Christ's desire to have closer personal contact with those whom he healed. The special touching of ears and

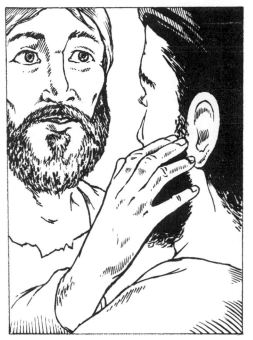

In healing a deaf-mute, Jesus touched his ears and tongue and said, "Be opened."

tongue may have been a response to the "conditions" implied in the request of those who brought the victim that Christ might "put his hand on him."

Christ will often touch those who are weak in faith in ways that strengthen the faith they have.

"Ephphatha." It was not Jesus' touch that healed. The healing took place "immediately" when Jesus pronounced, "Be opened." He who created the universe with a spoken word (Gen. 1:3, etc.) needed no more than a word to perform this miracle.

"They were astonished beyond measure" **(7:37).** Mark reports this as a delayed reaction from the crowd. Jesus had told the people crowded around to tell no one, but they proclaimed it "widely." Even after they had time to consider what had happened, they were overwhelmed. They understood *what* Jesus had done: "He makes both the deaf to hear and the mute to speak." Although they felt

positively about Jesus ("he has done all things well."), they did not catch the significance of the miracle.

Yet a Gentile woman had recognized Christ as the Son of David, Israel's Messiah (Matt 15:22). She had even agreed when he explained that his miracles were "bread" provided for God's "lost sheep," Israel (Matt. 15:27). They were more than acts of kindness, in spite of the compassion that moved Jesus for those whom he healed. Jesus' miracles were signs which identified him to Israel as the Messiah predicted by the Old Testament prophets.

A pagan woman had understood the meaning of Jesus' miracles, but his own people—for whose instruction the miracles were intended—were astonished. All they could say was, "Good job!"

JESUS FEEDS FOUR THOUSAND PEOPLE *Matthew 15:30–38; Mark 8:1–9*

Jesus miraculously provided food for another crowd, which had been with him for three days.

Background of the miracle. Some interpreters have assumed this account is not a separate miracle but a doublet—a repetition of the earlier story of the feeding of five thousand people (Matt. 14:21; Mark 6:44). There are similarities between these accounts:

- Both happened in the country.
- Both featured bread and fish.
- Both portrayed Jesus giving thanks and breaking bread.
- Both portrayed the disciples distributing the food.
- Both ended in a boat trip.

At the same time, there are significant differences which indicate the two feedings were separate events.

- The numbers fed differ: five thousand and four thousand.
- The locales differ: northeast and southeast shores of the Sea of Galilee.

- The seasons differ: green grass is emphasized in the story of the five thousand.
- The initial amounts of food differ.
- The number of baskets of food left over differ.
- Different baskets are specified: in the story of the five thousand they are shallow woven trays; in the story of the four thousand the baskets are giant, hamper-sized containers.
- The length of time the people were with Jesus differs.

The two accounts not only report different events; they intentionally parallel the works of two of the Old Testament's premier prophets, each of whom miraculously fed God's people twice (Moses—Ex. 16; Num. 11; Elisha—2 Kings 4:1–7, 38–44).

See pages 208–211 for a discussion of parallel elements in the two miracle accounts.

Parties to the miracle. The miracle report featured Jesus, his disciples, and a hungry crowd.

Jesus. Jesus expressed his concern for the crowds that had been with him for some time. He took what little food the disciples could find and multiplied it to feed about four thousand men.

The disciples. Although they had witnessed the earlier feeding of five thousand people, the disciples again expressed confusion about how this crowd could be fed. Again they said "Where could *we* get enough bread" (Matt. 15:33). We often forget what Jesus has done for us before, never thinking of turning to him for help when faced by a new need.

The crowd. "Great multitudes" followed Jesus into the wilderness to receive and witness his healing miracles (Matt. 15:30). According to how the Jews reckoned time, the "three days" the crowd was without food doesn't imply they hadn't eaten for 72 hours. An evening, the following day, and the next morning—as little as 30 hours—would be considered "three days."

The four thousand counted were the men only. If women and children are added, the crowd may have been as large as twelve thousand to fifteen thousand.

How the story unfolds. Jesus had been performing healing miracles for a great crowd. On the third day, Jesus expressed compassion and concern. If sent away without being fed, some people might "faint on the way" (Matt. 15:32). Jesus' disciples were frustrated. Where could they find enough food in such an isolated spot to feed such a great crowd?

Jesus sent them to find out how much food was available. Then he seated the crowd, gave thanks for the bread and fish, and had the disciples distribute them to the crowd. After everyone had eaten, the disciples filled seven large baskets with leftover food.

"How many loaves do you have?" (Matthew 15:34). In each account, Jesus took the little food his disciples had and multiplied it to supply thousands. If we give Jesus what we have, however small, he will use it to supply the deeper needs of many.

"Seven large baskets full" (15:37). The "large baskets" in this account were *spuridas,* large woven baskets about the size of a large laundry hamper. The apostle Paul was let down over the walls of Damascus in this kind of basket (Acts 9:25)!

These baskets were much larger than those used (*kophinoi*) after collecting leftovers following the feeding of the five thousand. What a reminder to the disciples, and to us, of the superabundance of Christ's ability to satisfy our needs.

JESUS HEALS A BLIND MAN   Mark 8:22–26

Jesus used an unusual method to heal a blind man.

Background of the miracle. Typically, Jesus' healings took place instantaneously, and they were implemented by a verbal command from him. This incident is distinctive in that the restoration of a blind man's sight was gradual, and the text doesn't mention a spoken command. It is also unusual in that Christ touched the blind man not once, but twice.

We can understand the reason for Christ touching some people whom he healed. Jesus touched a leper he restored out of compassion: he knew how much this man, isolated as he was from others, needed to feel a human touch (p. 181). Jesus also touched a deaf and dumb man whom he made well, possibly to increase his faith (see page 216). But there is no suggestion in Mark's account of the reason why Jesus took this man aside and twice touched his eyes to implement the healing.

Parties to the miracle. The text focuses on Jesus and the blind man, who was taken aside from the crowd for healing.

Jesus. Jesus responded to a request that he put his hands on a blind man (i.e., heal him).

The blind man. All we know about this blind man is that he had lost his sight as a youth or adult. When his sight began to return, he reported that "I see men like trees, walking" (Mark 8:24). He recognized the blurred, wavering images of trees, so he must have known what trees looked like before losing his sight.

How the story unfolds. In Bethsaida, a fishing village beside the Sea of Galilee, a blind man was brought to Jesus for healing. Christ took him aside, spat in his eyes, and laid hands on him. The man's sight was only partially restored, and he told Jesus what he could make out. Jesus then "put His hands on his eyes again." This time the man's sight was fully restored. Then Jesus sent the man away with orders not to tell anyone what had happened.

"Put His hands on his eyes again" (Mark 8:25). Commentators have wondered why Jesus abandoned his usual method of instantaneous healing by command. Some have seen a symbolic meaning: the spiritual sight of his disciples also grew gradually.

A better suggestion was made by John Calvin: "He did so most probably for the purpose of proving, in the case of this man, that he had full liberty as to his method of proceeding, and was not restricted to a fixed rule. . . . And so the grace of Christ, which had formerly been poured out suddenly on others, flowed by drops, as it were, on this man."

Calvin's comment is helpful. We often yearn for instantaneous grace; yet God's grace may be best measured out drop by drop, that we may savor it day by day. Both grace that is poured out and grace which is measured out drop by drop bring healing.

JESUS DELIVERS A DEMONIZED BOY
Mark 9:14–29; Matthew 17:14–21; Luke 9:37–43

A desperate father brought his demon-possessed son to Jesus after Christ's disciples were unable to exorcise the demon.

Background of the miracle. Mark gives the most complete account of this miracle and of the conversation of Jesus with the father and his disciples. There is one significant difference among the three reports of the event.

Matthew identified the son's malady as epilepsy. Both Mark and Luke identified it as demon possession. This is not a contradiction. Matthew spoke of the symptoms, while Mark and Luke identified the underlying "disease." The symptoms as reported in Mark were clearly like those of epilepsy: Mark reported that whenever the demon seized the boy "it throws him down; he foams at the mouth, gnashes his teeth, and becomes rigid" (9:18).

In many ancient cultures, all diseases were assumed to be caused by evil spirits. In Egypt two medical traditions developed: one in which diseases were treated medically, and the other in which illnesses were treated by incantations and invocation of the gods. In later Egypt these traditions merged and the magical approach became dominant.

The New Testament writers distinguished between illnesses which had natural causes and maladies caused by demons. Many of the afflicted are spoken of as cripples, blind, or deaf while others—often with the same problems—are identified as afflicted by demons.

The activity of the demons portrayed in the New Testament makes it clear that these spiritual beings are *hostile* to humankind. When demons dominate an individual, they don't use their powers to bring that person health and happiness. Persons who seek contact with the demonic under the naïve assumption that they will gain some sort of power or privilege are deceived indeed.

Parties to the miracle. This miracle account reports on Jesus' lengthy interaction with the father and his disciples. It also contains significant information about the demon who tormented the son.

Jesus. Jesus was again shown to have power over Satan's hosts. We also sense Christ's frustration with the father as well as his disciples. In spite of all that Jesus had done to demonstrate who he was, none seemed to understand or to respond with appropriate faith.

The father. The father came looking for Jesus. When he arrived, Christ was on the Mount of Transfiguration with three of his disciples (Mark 9:1–13). Since Jesus was not around, the father looked up some of his disciples and asked them to perform the healing.

Jesus' remark about a "faithless generation" (Mark 9:19) was made immediately after the father told of the disciples' inability to help (Mark 9:18). The implication is that Jesus was frustrated by the father's failure to realize that he was the source of the healing power which marked him as the Messiah. We can never substitute reliance on "faith healers" for faith in Christ, even though the healers may claim to be Jesus' representatives. We should bring our needs to Jesus.

The disciples. After the miracle healing, the disciples asked Jesus why they couldn't cast out the demon. This was a relevant question, since Matthew 10:1 reports that Jesus had earlier sent his disciples out to preach and had given them "power over unclean spirits." Yet the dis-

ciples were not able to help the son. Why? Jesus gave two reasons.

First, the disciples had "little faith" (Matt. 17:20, see footnote). Jesus immediately went on to explain that he didn't mean a "little *amount of* faith." If faith were to be measured by its size, the tiniest amount [a "mustard seed"-sized faith] could move mountains (Matt. 17:20). No, faith's effectiveness depends on its *object,* not its amount.

The disciples had assumed *they* could cast out the demon. After all, hadn't they done it before when Jesus sent them out by two (cf. Matt. 10:8)? The implication is that they had slipped into the error of relying on *their* authority rather than Jesus' authority in trying to cast out the demon.

Second, Jesus commented that "this kind [of demon] does not go out except by prayer and fasting" (Matt. 17:21; Mark 9:29). This reflects the teaching of Daniel 10 that Satan's angels, the demons of the Old and New Testament, are of different ranks and powers. The demon which had entered this man's son was no ordinary demon, but one of unusual rank. He had resisted every effort of the disciples to cast him out. "Prayer and fasting" represent the need for total dependence on the Lord's power.

In spite of the strength of this particular demon, it also recognized and reacted to Jesus (Mark 9:20). When Jesus rebuked [commanded] the evil spirit, it convulsed the child—then left him (Mark 9:28). Even the strongest demons cannot resist Jesus or believers who command them in Jesus' name. (For more on demon possession and exorcism, see *Every Good and Evil Angel in the Bible.*)

The demon. Mark's Gospel gives us much information about the demon. It was of unusually high rank and power (Mark 9:29). It had taken possession of the son when he was a child (Mark 9:21). It showed its intense hostility toward human beings by throwing the boy into fire and water, as if intent on destroying its host (Mark 9:22). This account of demon possession, along with Luke 8, provides vivid images of the evil intent of demons and clear descriptions of their major characteristics.

How the story unfolds. Jesus returned from the Mount of Transfiguration and found scribes and Pharisees debating a recent event with his disciples, while a crowd looked on. As Jesus approached, a man cried out, begging Jesus to look at his son. The son was demon-possessed, and the demon regularly threw the boy down, injuring him. The man told Jesus he had asked his disciples to heal the boy, but they couldn't.

Jesus expressed his frustration at this fresh evidence of unbelief, but he told the father to bring the son to him. When the demon saw Jesus, it threw the boy into a seizure. As the child writhed, Jesus asked how long this had been happening to him, learning he had been afflicted since childhood. The demon had often tried to kill his host!

"If you can do anything," the father pleaded, "have compassion on us and help us" (Mark 9:22).

Jesus told the father that all things are possible to the person who believes. The father, torn by hope and doubt, declared, "I believe, help my unbelief."

Jesus then rebuked the unclean spirit, commanding it to leave the child. The boy was racked with a last great convulsion, and then fell down as if dead. The demon was gone!

Later the disciples asked Jesus why they were unable to cast out the demon. Jesus replied that the reasons were complex. They lacked the necessary faith, and the demon was unusually powerful. After this, Jesus and his disciples moved on through Galilee.

"If You can do anything" **(9:22).** The father in this story stands in contrast with others who came to Jesus in the assurance that he could help. Even a Roman centurion had so much confidence in Jesus that he didn't even ask Jesus to visit his sick servant—only to speak the word. This father, however, came to Jesus not with confidence but with a last, desperate hope.

This demonstrates that whatever motivates a person to turn to Jesus, it is coming to Jesus that counts.

"Lord, I believe; help my unbelief" **(9:24).** The key word in this verse is "Lord." When our faith wavers, we are to reflect on who Jesus is, and remember that he is Lord.

"Lord" **(9:24).** This single word sums up the message of this miracle. Jesus is Lord. This truth was disputed by the religious leaders of Jesus' day. It was doubted by those who most needed his help. Even the disciples did not fully realize it. But Jesus demonstrated his authority by casting out the unusually powerful demon that had taken possession of the young victim. Jesus is Lord of all. Even a little faith, as long as it's centered on Jesus, can change our lives.

JESUS PRODUCES TAXES FROM A FISH'S MOUTH   *Matthew 17:24–27*

Jesus told Peter to catch a fish and take the temple tax from its mouth.

Background of the miracle. Exodus 30:13–16 specified that every Israelite male age 20 and older should pay a half-shekel into the temple treasury annually. This religious tax was used with other funds to support the temple ministry. The collection of this tax was the occasion for one of Jesus' most unusual miracles.

Parties to the miracle. The parties to the miracle were the collectors of the religious tax, Peter, and Jesus.

The tax collectors. The collectors of this tax were temple officials. Their behavior seems strange. Rather than asking *for* the tax, they asked Peter *if Jesus paid it.*

Peter. Peter hastily answered the tax collectors' question with a "Yes." Edersheim suggested that Peter sensed a trap in the officials' question, and said "Yes" in order to avoid the trouble that a different answer might have made for Jesus.

Jesus. Jesus' gentle questioning of Peter made it clear that Peter had spoken before he thought. Jesus resolved the issue by providing the tax money in an unusual way.

How the story unfolds. Peter was questioned by collectors of the temple tax. Did Jesus intend to pay it? Peter answered "Yes." When Jesus next saw Peter he asked, "From whom do the kings of the earth take customs or taxes, from their sons or from strangers?" Peter answered correctly, and Jesus summed up: "Then the sons are free."

Without explaining further, Jesus sent Peter to cast a line into the nearby waters. The fish Peter caught had in its mouth a coin that would pay both Peter's and Christ's annual temple tax.

"From whom do the kings of the earth take customs or taxes" (Matthew 17:25). In Christ's day Rome ruled the world, collecting taxes from all over the Mediterranean world. But taxes were not collected in Rome. Much of the foreign tax money was used to provide free grain and entertainment for the Romans. This was well known in Judea and Galilee, which groaned under taxes imposed not only by the Romans but also by the Herods.

Thus when Jesus asked Peter this question, Peter rightly answered that earthly rulers collected taxes from strangers.

"Then the sons are free" (17:26). Jesus' conclusion is significant. Because he was the Son of God, he was not obligated to pay the temple tax! Peter had given the wrong answer, whatever his motive had been.

There was, of course, another implication. If God required Israel to pay the temple tax, then the Jewish people could not be "sons." The common first-century assumption that physical descent from Abraham guaranteed a place in God's family was wrong! Faith in Jesus the Messiah, not physical descent from Abraham, makes a person a child of God.

"Lest we offend" (17:27). Jesus instructed Peter to pay the temple tax with money provided

miraculously. There was no need to make an issue of the symbolic meaning of the temple tax. The real issue then as now was Jesus himself, and nothing should be allowed to distract the people's attention from the question of who he was.

JESUS HEALS A MAN BORN BLIND
John 9

Jesus set off an intense controversy when he gave sight to a man who had been blind since birth.

Background of the miracle. John 8:12 records Jesus' affirmation to the Pharisees that "I am the light of the world. He who follows Me shall not walk in darkness, but have the light of life." The event reported in John 9 is an acted-out parable, demonstrating the truth of Jesus' statement and applying it both physically and spiritually.

Physically, Jesus gave sight to a man who was born blind. This was no restoration of lost sight. It was a creative act; bringing something into being that had not existed before. In the same way, God's creative act is involved when a person is given spiritual sight.

Spiritually, there's a difference between light and darkness, seeing and being blind. The man to whom Jesus gave sight gradually came to realize who Jesus was. This was indicated by his descriptions of the One who healed him. Note the sequence: the Healer was "a Man called Jesus" (John 9:11); "a prophet" (John 9:17); "from God" (John 9:33); and, "Lord" (John 9:38).

In contrast, the religious leaders who were finally forced to acknowledge that Christ had performed a notable miracle insisted that "this Man is a sinner" (John 9:24). The blind man saw, while the sighted men were blind to "the light of the world" (John 9:5).

Parties to the miracle. The entire chapter is devoted to this miracle and its effects. While Jesus performed the miracle and later spoke again with the man who had been healed, the man himself was the focus of the account. The chapter reports a series of intense conversations—between Jesus and his disciples, between the man and the Pharisees, between the parents and the Pharisees, and between the man Jesus. The chapter contains seven scenes:

1. The miracle—John 9:1–7
2. The man is questioned by neighbors—John 9:8–12
3. The man is cross-examined by Pharisees—John 9:13–17
4. The parents are cross-examined—John 9:18–23
5. The man is cross-examined again—John 9:24–34
6. Jesus seeks out the man—John 9:35–38
7. Significance of the miracle—John 9:39–41

How the story unfolds. One Sabbath as Jesus and his disciples passed by, they asked him about a man born blind. "Who sinned?" Jesus replied that sin was not the cause of his blindness. Acting as the "light of the world" (John 9:5), Jesus restored the blind man's sight.

The miracle set off a furor. Even the man's neighbors couldn't believe he was the same person. The man explained what happened and how Jesus gave him sight.

The neighbors brought the man to the Pharisees, who cross-examined him. The miracle caused a debate among these religious leaders. Some argued that a person who would "work" on the Sabbath couldn't possibly be from God. Others objected, "How can a . . . sinner do such signs?" When the man himself was asked, he replied, "He is a prophet."

The Jews [a term John used of the religious leaders] refused to believe the man was born blind until they questioned his parents. The parents insisted that this was their son, and that he had been blind since birth. But they were afraid to say any more, because they knew the leaders had agreed to expel from the synagogue anyone who declared that Jesus was the Christ.

Frustrated and angry, the Jews again called for the man whose sight had been restored. Under their hostile probing, the man asked, perhaps tongue in cheek, if "you also want to become his disciples." The "also" re-

vealed this man's commitment to his Healer. When the leaders reacted angrily, the man expressed amazement. "Since the world began," no one had opened the eyes of one born blind. "If this Man were not from God, He could do nothing" (John 9:33). This obvious conclusion was scornfully rejected by the religious leaders, and the man was ejected.

Jesus then found him and asked if he believed in the Son of God. As soon as the man learned that Jesus was the Son, he believed and worshiped. Christ then explained the significance of the miracle. He had come to differentiate between the blind and the sighted. His presence showed that those in Israel who claimed to have spiritual insight were actually blind, while those considered spiritually blind recognized Christ, and were given sight. The remark insulted the Pharisees, who challenged him: "Are we blind also?"

Christ's answer underlined the truth that a deliberate rejection of the One who is the light had condemned them to God's judgment.

Scene one: the miracle (John 9:1–7). Jesus restored the sight of a man born blind.

"Who sinned" (9:2). It was commonly believed by the Jews that serious disabilities were punishment for sin. The question of whether the man or his parents had sinned reflected a misunderstanding of Exodus 34:7. This verse stated that punishment of the guilty extended to the third and fourth generations. Sin corrupts our relationships so deeply that several generations of any family will be affected by serious sin.

"That the works of God should be revealed in him" (9:3). Tragedies give God an opportunity to reveal himself in unique ways. It was a tragedy that robbed Joni Erickson Tada of her ability to move. But through Joni, the Lord has encouraged thousands, and he continues to display his glory.

We cannot choose how God will glorify himself in us. But we can seek to glorify him whatever our situation.

"Spat on the ground and made clay" (9:6). Commentators have linked the mode of healing used by Jesus in this situation to the original creation of man from the earth. Irenaeus, an early church father, wrote "That which the artificer—the Word—had omitted to form in the womb he supplied in public, that the works of God might be manifested in him" (Adv. Haer. 15:2).

Scene two: the man was questioned by neighbors (9:8–12). The stunned neighbors could hardly believe the now-sighted man was the one who had sat and begged. The man explained what happened, giving credit to "a man called Jesus."

Scene three: the man was cross-examined by Pharisees (9:13–7). The neighbors brought the man to the Pharisees, who were confused and upset by the reported healing.

Pharisees. Members of this influential group were committed to keeping every detail of God's Law as interpreted by the rabbis.

"Does not keep the Sabbath" (9:16). By the Pharisee's definition, Jesus' healing of this blind man was "work," for he had "made clay" (John 9:6). The Pharisees' legalistic interpretation of Sabbath-keeping was more important to them than a stunning act of God. Let's be careful not to let our theology keep us from recognition of a true work of God.

"How can a . . . sinner do such signs?" (9:16). There were only two possible answers. Either Jesus was not a sinner or Jesus did not perform the miracle. The "Jews" [the religious leaders] chose not to believe in the miracle—until they questioned the parents and found they couldn't deny it. They were not willing to admit the only other reasonable possibility—that Jesus was not a sinner but a man of God.

Scene four: the parents were cross-examined by the Pharisees (9:18–23). The Pharisees were finally convinced that the man had been blind since birth. But the parents refused to say any more out of fear that they would be "put out of the synagogue" (John 9:22). A person put out of the synagogue would be cut off from assistance if he fell into poverty or dire need. A person with a business would not be able to trade with people in the community. Many who had been friends would no longer speak to the ostracized person. To confess Christ in the face of the threat of being "put out of the synagogue" took a courage that the parents lacked.

Scene five: the Pharisees cross-examined the man again (9:24–34). The Jews refused to consider that their interpretation of Sabbath Law might be wrong. Instead, they rejected a sign which, like so many others, had identified Jesus as God's spokesman. The key word in these verses is "know."

The Pharisees claimed to know based on rabbinical interpretations of the biblical command not to work on the Sabbath. They concluded:

- We know this man is a sinner (9:24).
- We know God spoke through Moses (9:29).
- We do not know where this man came from (9:29).

The man claimed to know based on the miracle and the obvious:

- I know that while I was blind, now I see (9:25).
- We know that God does not hear sinners (9:31).
- We know that God hears anyone who worships him and does his will (9:31).
- If this man were not from God, he could do nothing (9:33).

The once-blind man saw the issues clearly and held fast to his convictions in spite of pressure from the religious leaders. What moved the man was not fear of these powerful leaders but wonder at their claim not to know where Jesus was from. There was no question in his mind—Jesus was a man sent from God.

The leaders followed through on their threat and "cast out" the man. The implication is that he was put out of the synagogue, not just their presence (John 9:34). We suspect that the man cared little for their punishment. He could see! Nothing Christ's enemies could take away was a loss—compared with the wonderful gift Christ had given him.

Scene six: Jesus sought out the man (9:35–38). When Jesus found the man, he led him to the full commitment of faith. Christ identified himself as the Son of God, and the man immediately affirmed, "Lord, I believe! And he worshiped Him" (John 9:38).

How often a gracious work in our lives gently leads us to faith's full commitment.

Scene seven: the significance of the miracle (9:39–41). Christ's own comment brought the miracle's meaning into focus. Jesus himself is the pivot on which every person's eternal destiny turns.

Only those who admit they are lost and blind, then look to Christ for spiritual sight, will find the salvation he offers. Any who claim they can see—like the Pharisees—will remain blind to the gospel offer. And their sin will remain.

Deliberate rejection of Jesus, the light of the world, leaves a person in eternal darkness. How good it is to see the light, and come to know God in his Son.

JESUS HEALS A WOMAN BOUND BY SATAN   *Luke 13:10–17*

Jesus healed a woman with a chronic back problem on the Sabbath.

Background of the miracle. This is another Sabbath healing. Like other healings on this holy day, it offended the religious leaders. Their rules for what was proper on the Sabbath went far beyond the simple biblical proscription against work (Ex. 20:8–11).

The rabbis' rulings made allowance for a physician to attend a person with a life-threatening emergency on the Sabbath. But in their eyes, it was not lawful to help a person with a chronic illness. Such an illness could wait for treatment on some other day!

Jesus as God had created the Sabbath. He was not bound by their human regulations.

This particular healing also revealed the fatal flaw in rabbinic Judaism. Rules had become the ultimate reality, and the true message of God's Word had been missed.

Centuries before, the prophet Isaiah had predicted this misuse of Scripture and described its consequences. In chapter 28 of his book, the inspired prophet characterized the message of God's Word as "the rest with which you may cause the weary to rest," and as "the refreshing." Yet Israel refused to listen. And so to Israel the Word of God was to become

> Precept . . . upon precept, precept
>   upon precept,
> Line upon line, line upon line,
> Here a little, there a little (Isa.
>   28:10).

What was the result of this focus on the details of the divine Law to the exclusion of its meaning? The divine judgment was,

> That they might go and fall
>   backward, and be broken
> And snared and caught (Isa. 28:13).

By turning God's Word into lists of rules to keep, the grace of God had been overlooked. By piling up precept upon precept, Israel committed itself to a religion of works which so hardened the religious leaders that they would not acknowledge the Messiah. The irony is that his coming was intended to free God's people from everything that bound them.

Both the grace of God and the blindness of legalism are shown clearly in this Sabbath miracle.

Parties to the miracle. In relating this miracle, Luke draws our attention to Jesus, the infirm woman, and the reactions of the ruler of the synagogue and "all the multitude."

Jesus. Jesus initiated the healing, without being asked.

The woman. The woman was referred to as "a daughter of Abraham" (Luke 13:16). The reference was not to her physical descent from Abraham, although the people in the synagogue may have understood it this way. The reference was to her faith: she had a faith like Abraham's. He believed God and was declared righteous (Gen. 15:7).

The ruler of the synagogue. One of the responsibilities of the *archesynagogos* or ruler of the synagogue was to maintain order in the Sabbath services. This man was committed to the strict interpretations of the Law which characterized the Pharisees. His indignant reaction was typical of those described in Isaiah 28. He missed the refreshing intent of the law, transforming it into precepts which blinded him to God's grace.

The "multitude." This was Luke's term for the ordinary people, who saw what Jesus did and responded openly without the blindness of the religious leaders.

How the story unfolds. As Jesus was teaching, he saw a woman with a bent back. She had not been able to stand upright for 18 years. Je-

❖

"Woman, you are loosed from your infirmity."

sus called to her and announced that she was loosed from her infirmity. Then he touched her and she straightened up. This scandalized the ruler of the synagogue, who rebuked Jesus for healing on the Sabbath.

Christ called him a hypocrite, pointing out that even the legalistic Pharisees untied their animals on the Sabbath to give them a drink. How much more precious was the daughter of Abraham whom he had loosed, after she had been tied in knots by Satan all these years!

The response shamed Jesus' opponents, but the common people rejoiced over the wonderful things he was doing.

"He called her to Him" (Luke 13:12). This was no response to prayer or faith by the woman. Jesus initiated the encounter and acted to heal the woman. Christ showed compassion. His action showed the dramatic contrast between God's attitude toward the hurting and the attitude of the nation's religious leaders.

"Loosed from your infirmity" (13:12). The terms Luke used in describing this event were common among physicians of that time. He also provided a careful description of the stages of the healing. First the woman's cramped muscles were relaxed [loosed]. Then Jesus touched the woman to strengthen her spine so she could stand upright.

"Glorified God" (13:13). The woman was thrilled by what God had done. What a contrast with the indignant reaction of the ruler of the synagogue. Would the *archesynagogos* have been upset if *he* were the person healed? The capacity to rejoice with others who are blessed by God is one indication of God's work in our own lives.

"Hypocrite!" This word described Greek actors who held masks over their faces to represent the person whom they portrayed. It came to mean play-acting or inconsistency—pretending to be someone you are not or behaving differently in public than in private.

Jesus' charge was leveled at the inconsistent behavior of the Pharisees. Their rules allowed for the needs of farm animals on the Sabbath, while refusing to give consideration to the needs of people. And they claimed to represent God!

Christ's concern for a woman who had suffered for 18 years revealed the heart of God while exposing the grudging attitudes of the Pharisees. No wonder Jesus' adversaries were "put to shame" (Luke 13:17)!

"Loose his ox" (13:15). Note the play on words in the story. Jesus loosed the woman (Luke 13:12) and was criticized by a man who would never hesitate to loose a farm animal.

"Satan has bound" (13:16). This was not a case of demon possession but of demonic *oppression.* Satan was identified as the cause of this woman's physical disability, but Jesus did not indicate that he dominated her personality. The apostle Paul's "thorn in the flesh" was another example of this phenomenon (2 Cor. 12:7). (See *Every Good and Evil Angel in the Bible.*)

"All His adversaries were put to shame" (13:17). This phrase does not mean that Jesus' adversaries *felt* ashamed. "Put to shame" means that the emptiness of their claim to represent God was exposed for everyone to see.

This miracle of Jesus revealed clearly the heart of God. Other hearts were revealed that day as well: the woman's, the synagogue ruler's—and even the hearts of the onlookers, who praised God for Jesus' good works.

JESUS HEALS A MAN WITH DROPSY
Luke 14:1–6

While eating Sabbath dinner at a Pharisee's house Jesus healed a man with dropsy.

Background of the miracle. This is the fourth Sabbath miracle reported by Luke (6:6–11; 13:10–17). It reminds us that healing on the Sabbath was a major cause of conflict between Jesus and the Pharisees. See pages 186 and 225 for background.

Parties to the miracle. Luke focuses on the interaction between Jesus and a hostile group of "lawyers and Pharisees" who were observing Jesus closely. The parties to this miracle are:

Jesus. Jesus was dining at the home of a "ruler of the Pharisees." The phrase suggests that the man (an *archon,* ruler) was a member of the Sanhedrin and belonged to the Pharisee party.

Lawyers and Pharisees. A "lawyer" was a person versed in the written Law [Old Testament] and the oral Law [traditional interpretations]. The Pharisees were members of a small but influential group that argued for the strictest interpretation of written and oral Law.

The man with dropsy. Dropsy was an illness caused by a "serious abnormal accumulation of fluid in the body's tissues."

How the story unfolds. Jesus was eating at the home of a leading Pharisee, where he was being watched closely by the other guests. These guests were also members of the religious elite. A man with dropsy was also at the meal.

Jesus took the initiative and asked whether it was "lawful" to heal on the Sabbath. When no one was willing to risk an answer, Jesus healed the man with dropsy.

Jesus then asked which of them would not "immediately" help one of their farm animals which had fallen into a pit on the Sabbath. They couldn't answer! They couldn't rebut Christ's actions or his argument.

"A certain man who had dropsy" (Luke 14:2). Many commentators have suggested the man with the dropsy had been planted at this gathering by Jesus' enemies. There is good reason for this theory. In the first century, serious diseases were thought to be God's punishment for sin. The host was a "leading Pharisee," and his guests were members of the religious elite. These men normally would have been unwilling to sit down to a meal with any "sinner."

The man was seated directly "before him," so Jesus could hardly fail to notice him (Luke 14:2). Finally, when the man was healed, Jesus "let him go" (Luke 14:4).

How like the Pharisees to use others in an effort to trap or discredit Jesus.

"They kept silent" (Luke 14:4). No one was willing to risk answering Jesus' question about whether it was lawful to heal on the Sabbath.

"Which of you?" (14:5). After healing the man with dropsy, Jesus asked another question. Which of them wouldn't pull from a pit an animal which had fallen in on the Sabbath? Members of the Qumram sect held that an animal which fell into a pit should not be lifted out on the Sabbath. But the dominant view in Jesus' time was that an ox or donkey which had fallen into a pit could be helped out "immediately" (*Shabbat 128b*).

To this they "could not" reply. There was no answer they could give without condemning themselves.

The significance of the miracle. Jesus' miracles had several vital functions. On one level, they served to reveal God and demonstrate his compassion. On another level, they served as signs which marked Jesus as the promised Messiah. On yet another level, they exposed human hearts, showing some to be filled with faith and others to be hypocritical and far from the attitudes of the Lord. In this miracle report, God's compassionate heart and the hypocrisy of Jesus' antagonists are clearly revealed. The Pharisees would rush to save one of their valuable animals, but they cared nothing for a person in need.

The miracles of Jesus show not only who he was, but who we are apart from God's transforming grace.

JESUS RAISES LAZARUS   John 11

Jesus restored life to Lazarus three days after his death.

Background of the miracle. Jesus had already restored the life of a widow's son (Luke 7) and Jairus's daughter (Luke 8; Mark 5). Each of these restorations occurred immediately after the person had died.

The custom in first-century Judaism was to bury an individual on the day of his death. But the Jews were aware of the possibility of a coma, so they would check a tomb for three days after the burial to see if the victim had revived. After three days, all hope of awakening from a coma was gone, and the body would have begun to decay.

The raising of Lazarus was significant because it took place the full three days after he had died, plus one extra day (John 11:39)! There could be no doubt in anyone's mind that Christ had restored a person who was truly dead.

It is no wonder that this most spectacular of Jesus' miracles troubled the chief priests and Pharisees. After this, they were certain that "if we let him alone like this, everyone will believe in him, and the Romans will come and take away both our place and nation" (John 11:48). Thus the greatest proof of who Jesus was became the critical event that drove the Jewish hierarchy to seek Jesus' death (John 11:53).

There can be no vacillation for modern believers. We must accept Jesus for who he is, acknowledging him as Lord. If we fail to do this, we take sides with the rulers of first-century Israel and choose to force him out of our lives.

Parties to the miracle. The entire chapter is devoted to this miracle account and Jesus' interaction with the people involved. These include: Mary and Martha, the sisters of Lazarus; the disciples, and especially Thomas. John also reports the reaction of those who had come to comfort the sisters as well as the response of the Jewish leaders.

Jesus. Jesus is portrayed in this account as one who dearly loved Lazarus and his sisters. Yet he failed to respond to an urgent plea to come and heal his friend. The delay seems out of character. But when Jesus finally did arrive, Mary—perhaps with some hint of rebuke—declared, "If You had been here, my brother would not have died" (John 11:32).

Jesus called on the sisters to believe that he had power over death in the present as well as at history's end. Then Jesus called to Lazarus, who stumbled out of his tomb—still wrapped in the strips of linen that served as burial clothes.

The disciples. Jesus and his disciples were across the Jordan River in Perea when word of Lazarus's illness arrived (John 10:40). They had retreated in part because the hostility of the leaders had become so intense that Christ was in danger of being stoned (John 11:8).

After the messenger's arrival, Jesus stayed in Perea for two more days. Then he told his disciples, "Let us go to Judea again" (John 11:7). The disciples were afraid. They objected when Christ told them that "Lazarus is asleep," assuming that Jesus meant that Lazarus was resting after the crisis had passed. But Jesus meant that Lazarus was dead. He stated his intention to wake him. The disciples' fears were reflected by Thomas, who declared, "Let us also go, that we may die with Him" (John 11:16).

Thomas. This disciple is commonly known as "doubting" Thomas because of his refusal to believe in Christ's resurrection until he could touch the wounds in Jesus' hands and side. But here we see Thomas in a different light, as "loyal" Thomas.

Thomas was certain that danger awaited all of them in Judea. But he encouraged the disciples to stay with Christ. Thomas had no hope; he did not expect to die *for* Jesus, or to be able to turn the danger aside. The best Thomas and the others could expect was to die *with* Jesus. And this Thomas was ready to do. Nothing could separate loyal Thomas from his Lord.

We are blessed because God has said, "I will never leave you nor forsake you" (Heb. 13:5). Courageous Thomas reminds us that we are to be as committed to God as he is to us—whatever the danger, whatever the cost.

Martha. She and her sister Mary were close to Jesus. They often sheltered him in their Bethany home when he visited Jerusalem. Bethany, about twenty miles from Perea, was only two miles outside Jerusalem. Christ stayed at Bethany when Jerusalem was crowded with pilgrims during the annual festivals.

When Martha saw Jesus, she expressed faith in him: "if you had been here, my brother would not have died." But Martha went on to say that "even now" (11:28) she believed God would give Jesus whatever he asked.

This statement was one of great faith, but even Martha's faith couldn't grasp Jesus' meaning when he told her, "Your brother will rise again" (John 11:23). She assumed that Jesus was speaking of the final resurrection at history's end. Jesus then affirmed that he was the resurrection and the life. The eschatological hope was present in his person. God's plans and promises were fulfilled *in him.*

Martha, still unaware of what Jesus intended, confessed her belief that Jesus truly was the Christ, the Son of God.

How often Martha is remembered only for her attention to dinner preparations and her criticism of Mary, who chose instead to listen to Jesus' teachings (Luke 10:40, 41). Here we see Martha in a far more flattering light, as one whose faith in Jesus burned bright and true—and one whose faith was about to be rewarded!

Mary. Mary, the second sister, then came out to greet Jesus. Like Martha, she expressed her faith: "If You had been here, my brother would not have died." But unlike her sister, Mary sobbed as she spoke. Even if she shared her sister's hope, she must not have felt it in her moment of loss.

Lazarus. We know little about Lazarus. He is not mentioned elsewhere in the Bible, although we are told that Jesus had developed a deep affection for him. Even after Lazarus was raised, John's account mentions nothing of what Lazarus felt or said or did. But he was a silent and powerful witness to the power of Jesus.

There are many unknown people whose actual words have not been passed on to future generations, but whose restored lives serve as powerful witnesses to Jesus Christ. Many times a believer does not need to say anything: the difference Jesus makes in his or her life will shine through brightly. May our lives, renewed and transformed by Jesus, be the witness to our neighbors that Lazarus was to his.

The mourners. The mourners who had come to comfort Mary and Martha were stunned by Jesus' miracle. Many "believed in him" (John 11:45). But others rushed to report to the Pharisees what Jesus had done. By this time, the entire city of Jerusalem was aware of the attitude of the Pharisees toward Jesus. Those who hurried to them certainly didn't go with an intent to witness!

The chief priests and Pharisees. These men had to admit that "this man works many signs" (11:47). But they didn't intend to submit to him. Instead, their hostile attitude toward Jesus became even more fixed, and they determined to kill him—one way or another.

Caiaphas. As the Jewish high priest, Caiaphas served as president of the Sanhedrin. He summed up the fears of the religious leaders and passed judgment. Jesus must die.

In saying "it is expedient . . . that one man should die for the people" (11:50), Caiaphas was representing the leaders' concern. As the founder of a messianic movement, Jesus' teaching might stimulate a rebellion, bringing Roman armies against Judea. Some interpreters have argued that Caiaphas' reference to the Romans' taking away "both our place and nation" expressed fear for the temple ("our place"). It is far more likely he was referring to the privileges enjoyed by his own priestly class.

While Caiaphas had one thing in mind, his words were prophetic. Christ would die for the nation—not to keep the Roman armies away, but to defeat sin and Satan and make eternal life available to all.

How the story unfolds. Jesus and his disciples were about twenty miles from Bethany when a messenger arrived with word that Lazarus was sick. For two days Jesus did nothing. Then he told his disciples it was time to return to Judea, explaining that Lazarus was "asleep" (has died). The fearful disciples accompanied Jesus on the day-long walk back to Bethany.

Martha hurried out to meet Jesus, expressing her belief that if Jesus had been there her brother would not have died. Jesus announced that he was the resurrection and the life, leading her to confess her belief that he was the Christ, the Son of God.

Martha then brought out Mary, who also expressed her belief that if Jesus had been with them her brother would not have died. Mary was weeping, heartbroken; and as Jesus followed her to Lazarus's tomb, he also wept.

At the tomb, Jesus told the onlookers to roll away the stone that closed the burial place. Martha objected. Lazarus had been dead and buried for four days: there would be a stench. But Jesus reminded her of their earlier conversation, and the stone was rolled away.

Jesus then thanked the Father aloud for always hearing him. He offered this prayer for the sake of the bystanders, that they might believe God had sent him. Jesus then shouted, "Lazarus, come forth!" (John 11:43). And the dead man, restored to life, stumbled out into the light, still wrapped in his grave clothes and his face covered with a cloth.

On Jesus' command, the tight wrappings were removed, and many of the stunned onlookers believed in Jesus.

Other witnesses to the miracle hurried into Jerusalem to carry word to the religious leaders. These men gathered almost in despair. What could they do? Jesus was performing such amazing miracles that soon everyone would believe in him!

There was no thought in their minds that *they* should consider his claims. Jesus was too great a threat to their own position and to the *status quo!* They concluded that Jesus must die. From that day forward, they set about get-

Jesus called to Lazarus and he came out of the tomb, still in graveclothes.

❖

ting rid of this "Christ." John revealed in his Gospel that they even plotted to kill Lazarus, whose existence was a convincing witness to Jesus' power (John 12:10, 11).

Jesus, knowing their intent, withdrew with his disciples to a remote town (John 11:54), where he stayed quietly until the next Passover arrived (John 12:1).

"He whom you love is sick" (John 11:3). The sisters had no doubt of Jesus' love for their brother. How they must have anguished as the messenger hurried to Jesus. But before he could cover the 20 miles to tell Jesus, Lazarus died.

"For the glory of God" (11:4). Although Lazarus was dead when the messenger arrived, Christ said that the sickness would not *end in death.* The end would be life restored, and Christ glorified.

Our sicknesses too—even our last sickness—will not end in death. History is rushing even now toward God's intended end—resurrection and life eternal for Christ's own. For the glory of God!

"Jesus loved Martha and her sister and Lazarus" (11:5). It is often harder for those left behind to sense God's love for them than to be-

lieve that God loved the person who has died. John through his Gospel wanted us to know that Jesus does care, deeply, for the grieving.

"Our friend Lazarus sleeps" (11:11). The Bible appropriately speaks of death as sleep (1 Cor. 15:51; 1 Thess. 4:14). We can be confident as we lie down at the end of our earthly existence that we will awaken, and rise again.

"He groaned in the spirit and was troubled" (11:33). This—and the shortest verse in Scripture, "Jesus wept" (John 11:35)—reminds us that even as God permits our suffering, he feels with us.

Christ knew that he was about to bring Lazarus back to life. But he did not discount the pain of his dear friends. Instead, he entered into their pain, felt it deeply, and wept with them.

It is good for us to remember that God is committed to bringing good out of all the things that happen to us (Rom. 8:28). Yet it is important to remember that God takes our hand in the meantime and does not abandon us in our sorrow. He feels our pain. And he weeps with us as we grieve. And then, when the time is right, God will wipe away all tears from our eyes, welcoming us into the glory he intends for us and our loved ones to share (Rev. 21:4).

"I am the resurrection and the life" (11:25). There is no clearer statement in Scripture of the significance of Jesus for us individually. He is the resurrection and the life. His is the power; he is the source. Those who believe in him may die physically, but they will live eternally. This is his promise to us if we will trust in Jesus as the resurrection and the life.

This truth points us toward the ultimate significance of the miracle. Jesus' claim to be the resurrection and the life was proven by the restoration of Lazarus. Jesus' deeds always backed up his words.

Today we can contemplate this miracle, finding in it a foreshadowing of what lies ahead. One day Christ will return and shout to our dead, "Come forth." Then we will arise, and together with the believers alive in that day, rise up to meet the Lord in the air (1 Thess. 4:16, 17).

Truly Jesus is the resurrection and the life.

JESUS CLEANSES TEN LEPERS   *Luke 17:11–19*

Jesus healed ten lepers, but only one, a Samaritan, returned to give glory to God.

Background of the miracle. In the first century, the ancient Jewish hostility toward the Samaritans had been revived. The Samaritans were despised as offspring of pagan peoples brought into the territory of the old Northern Kingdom, Israel, by the Assyrians in the 720s B.C. The Samaritans claimed descent from the Jewish patriarchs, but this claim was angrily disputed by the Jews.

A little over 100 years before Jesus was born, John Hyrcanus had ruled in Judea and had destroyed the Samaritan temple on Mount Gerazim. In Christ's time, the Samaritans showed their hostility by refusing shelter to anyone traveling to Jerusalem (Mark 3:17). One of the most serious insults hurled at Jesus by the religious leaders was to call him a Samaritan (John 8:48).

Against this background, we understand Luke's observation that as Jesus was going to Jerusalem, he "passed through the midst" of Samaria and Galilee (Luke 17:11). The Greek word is *dia meson,* "along the border between" the two territories. Jesus apparently avoided the direct route to the Holy City from Galilee, which would have taken him through Samaria.

There, along the border of Samaria, ten lepers called out to Jesus and asked for mercy. At least one of these lepers was a Samaritan. In their misery Jew and Samaritan formed a bond that the healthy were unwilling to consider.

Parties to the miracle. The account identifies ten men who were lepers. Apparently most were Jews, as Jesus told them to show themselves to the priests. This action was prescribed for those who had been lepers but had become free of the disease. Only a priest could certify that a person had been healed. This assured the person could retake his or her place as a member of the community.

How the story unfolds. When Jesus entered an unnamed village, ten lepers—standing at an appropriate distance because of their uncleanness—cried out for mercy. Jesus told them to show themselves to the priests, and "as they went" (17:14) they were cleansed [healed]. One of the ten hurried back to thank Jesus and praise God when he realized he had been healed. And this man was a Samaritan. Jesus wondered aloud where the others were. Commending the foreigner's faith, Jesus sent the man on his way.

"As they went, they were cleansed" (Luke 17:14). The lepers trusted Jesus enough to set out to see the priests. They were cleansed "as they went."

Some believers hope God will give them "faith" so they can obey him. What a tragic misunderstanding. Faith is expressed in our obedience; as we obey God, he works in our lives.

"Were there not ten cleansed?" (17:17). Only one of those who realized he had been healed returned to thank Jesus, giving glory to God. Commentators have been sharply critical of the other nine. About the kindest thing said of them is that they were ungrateful. Others have wondered whether the nine were afraid Jesus might place demands on them if they returned. Still other interpreters have suggested that the nine, once healed, wanted nothing more to do with their benefactor.

The text doesn't explore the motives of the nine. Perhaps they were so eager to go home again that they didn't pause for even a moment. Whatever their motive, we are hardly in a position to condemn them. How often we have also taken our blessings for granted. Many of us are strangers to thanksgiving, just like these nine healed lepers.

"This foreigner" (17:18). The fact that the one who did return was a foreigner is significant. Jesus was drawing near the end of his earthly ministry. He had healed hundreds in Israel; yet his own people would soon join in the cries of "crucify him!" As history records, it was mostly foreigners who rejoiced in Israel's Christ and glorified him with their praise.

"Your faith has made you well" (17:19). The nine missed hearing Jesus' explanation of their healing. As the nine hurried to the priests, they may have assumed that it was their obedience that made them well. Perhaps they thought their willingness to undergo the ancient ritual examination was critical to their healing. Jesus had somehow made them well. But hadn't they played their role in their own healing?

The Samaritan knew better. It was Jesus himself who had brought about the cure. It was faith in Jesus which had channeled the power that flowed from our Lord. Faith in Jesus, demonstrated by doing as Jesus said, had made all the difference.

JESUS GIVES SIGHT TO BLIND
BARTIMAEUS   *Matthew 20:29–34; Mark 10:46–52; Luke 18:35–43*

While on the way to Jerusalem and the cross, Jesus stopped to heal a blind beggar.

Background of the miracle. There are two critical differences in the details given in the three gospel accounts of this miracle.

Mark indicates the miracle took place on the way out of Jericho, while Luke says the miracle occurred when Jesus was entering the city. But in the first century, there were two Jerichos: old Jericho, which was largely a ruin; and new Jericho, an attractive city built by Herod just to the south of the old town. Apparently the miracle took place on the border between the old and new cities, as Jesus was leaving one and entering the other.

Mark and Luke mention only one blind man, whom Mark identifies as Bartimaeus. Matthew indicates that Jesus healed two blind men. It is clear from the other details that the Gospel writers describe the same incident, so we can assume that Bartimaeus was the more prominent of the two. For a discussion of this type of supposed contradiction in the biblical text, see the discussion of the demoniac of Gadara, p. 198.

More significant than the supposed contradictions is the fact that this last of Jesus' healing miracles took place on his way to Jerusalem and the cross. In Matthew, this miracle concludes a major section dedicated to the theme of greatness.

Jesus' disciples had asked about greatness (Matt. 18:1). Jesus called a little child and taught, "Whoever humbles himself as this little child" is greatest in the kingdom of heaven (Matt. 18:4). After showing the disciples how to live together as God's little children (Matt. 18:5–35), Matthew records a series of incidents exposing the fallacy of seeking greatness through keeping the Law (Matt. 19:1–15), through humanitarian works (Matt. 19:16–29), and through relying on works rather than on God's grace (Matt. 20:1–19). Then, when two of the disciples sent their mother to ask Jesus for the most important posts in his coming kingdom, Jesus used the occasion to instruct them on true greatness.

The Gentiles thought of greatness as lording it over others. But, Jesus said, "Whoever desires to be first among you, let him be your slave—just as the Son of Man did not come to be served, but to serve, and to give His life a ransom for many" (Matt. 20:27, 28).

Immediately after this—while he was on his way to the cross and burdened with the awareness of his coming fate—Jesus paused in answer to the cry of the blind men and asked, "What do you want Me to do for you?" (Matt. 20:32).

How clearly this last healing miracle illustrated what Jesus had just taught his disciples. The truly great of God's kingdom set aside personal burdens and say to others "What do you want me to do for you?" Like Jesus, the great in God's kingdom give of themselves to meet other people's needs.

Parties to the miracle. The story in Matthew is told simply, with three major voices.

Jesus. In spite of his own heavy burden, Jesus stopped to meet the needs of two blind men.

The blind men. The blind men realized that someone special was passing by. When they learned it was Jesus, they cried out to him as "Son of David" and begged for mercy.

The crowd. The crowd tried to silence the blind men. Jesus was too important to be bothered by such as them! The crowd thus revealed a lack of concern for individuals which contrasted with the servant attitude exemplified by Jesus and to which he calls his followers.

How the story unfolds. Jesus was on his way to Jerusalem and the cross. Although the roads were filled with travelers heading to the holy city for Passover, an unusually large crowd was following him. When two blind men, one of whom was named Bartimaeus (Mark 10:46), realized that Jesus was near, they began to shout. Addressing Jesus by his messianic title as Son of David, they begged for mercy.

The crowd told them to be quiet, but they cried out even louder. Responding to their cries, Jesus stopped and called them to him. At that, the crowd's attitude changed, and they told the blind men to cheer up. Jesus was waiting for them (Mark 10:49)!

Jesus asked the blind men what they wanted, and they told him they wanted their sight. Christ, again moved by compassion, touched their eyes (Matt. 20:34) and told them to receive their sight (Luke 18:42), indicating that their faith had made them well.

"They told him" (Luke 18:36). Luke describes the blind man's curiosity as he heard a large crowd passing by. We can almost hear him asking, "What's happening? Who is it?"

"Have mercy ... Son of David" (Matt. 20:31). Each account agrees that the blind man/men addressed Jesus as the Son of David. This was a messianic title, reflecting the conclusion reached by Bartimaeus and his companion that this Jesus, of whom they had heard many stories, was indeed the Messiah. He had power to help, so they cried out to him.

"Bartimaeus, the son of Timaeus" (Mark 10:46). Mark frequently provides details not mentioned by the other Gospel writers. In this miracle account, Mark alone reports the crowd's change of attitude (10:49), revealing that when Bartimaeus realized that Jesus was waiting for him, he discarded his outer cloak to hurry to Jesus (10:50). It is likely that he had spread the cloak over his knees so passersby could drop in coins.

In view of Mark's typical attention to such detail, we should not be surprised that he gave the name of one of the two blind beggars.

"What do you want Me to do for you? (Matt. 20:32). This one sentence sums up the servant attitude which Jesus displayed. This is the attitude which he desires for all who would be truly great in his kingdom.

"What do you want Me to do for you?" (Mark 10: 51). There is no question that Jesus knew the need and the cure. Why then did he ask this question?

Some suggest he wanted to increase the blind man's faith. But it is more likely a reflection of a teaching on prayer found in James 4:2: "You do not have because you do not ask." Prayer is to be specific. We are to identify our needs and bring them to Jesus, asking him to meet these needs.

It may be helpful for us when we pray to raise the question Jesus asked. What do we want God to do for us? We must not tell him how to meet the need. But we must define our needs, and then bring them to him.

"Jesus had compassion" (Matt. 20:34). Caring about others is essential if we are to be servants. Jesus was not acting a part. Unlike some whose claims to "feel your pain" is mere posturing, Jesus was deeply moved by the suffering of those in need. Servanthood is not technique, but a heart response to others which reflects Jesus' deep concern.

They followed Him (20:34). This comment most likely means that the blind men literally followed Jesus up the steep fifteen-mile trail from Jericho to Jerusalem, where Passover was about to be celebrated.

"All the people, when they saw it, gave praise to God" (Luke 18:43). The road to Jerusalem led through Jericho. Thousands of Jewish families would have passed along it on their way to celebrate the religious festivals in the Holy City. Bartimaeus and his blind friend were probably fixtures in Jericho, known and recognized by many.

This verse shows that servanthood brings praise to God. The people praised God when they witnessed the miracle. On the other hand, Jesus' servanthood did not protect him from that hostility from others which ultimately brought him to the cross.

The meaning of the miracle. Jesus' last miracle of healing is significant in several ways. The miracle shows what blessings were available if only Israel, like the blind men, had acknowledged Jesus as the Son of David. It also illustrates Jesus' servant attitude and serves as an example for us.

Through this miracle, we are also reminded that the key to claiming the blessings that God is eager to pour out is faith in Jesus Christ and his ability to meet our every need.

JESUS CURSES A FIG TREE   *Matthew 21:17–22; Mark 11:12–14, 20–24*

Jesus cursed a fig tree whose leaves promised a fruit it had not produced.

Background of the miracle. Fig leaves appear about the same time as the fruit, or a little after. Thus the fact that this tree was in leaf should have indicated it was also bearing fruit, although it was not yet the season for figs (Mark 11:13). The tree's appearance promised something which it didn't deliver.

Most interpreters take this miracle as an acted-out parable. The fig tree represents Israel, which had the appearance of bearing fruit but which in fact was barren. Jesus cursed the tree not because of its failure to bear fruit but because its appearance was a lie. The tree's leaves advertised a fruitfulness that did not exist—just as Israel's outward honoring of God and his law advertised a relationship with the Lord which they didn't have.

When it was cursed by Jesus, the fig tree withered. Its appearance at last matched the reality of its fruitless state. How soon Israel would also wither. In A.D. 70, just a few short decades after this incident, the Romans destroyed Jerusalem. With its temple destroyed, the priesthood set aside, and its familiar worship patterns forever lost, the nation of Israel withered indeed.

While Matthew's arrangement of this account is topical, Mark provides a chronological account. Between the cursing of the fig tree and its withering, Jesus cleansed the temple—an event which showed the bareness of Israel's worship.

Parties to the miracle. The story mentions only Jesus, his disciples, and the fig tree.

Jesus. This is the only event in the Gospels in which Jesus used his power to destroy rather than to heal or restore. The withering of the fig tree reminds us that God is not only a God of grace but a God of judgment as well.

The disciples. The disciples were amazed when the tree that Jesus cursed withered away so quickly. Their question about how this was possible led to a brief teaching by Jesus on prayer.

The fig tree. The fig tree is an image of Israel, just like the vineyard of Isaiah 5:1–7 and the figs of Jeremiah 8:13 and 24:1–8. The "sin" of the fig tree was to make a show of fruitfulness when in fact it was barren, even as Israel's response to Jesus revealed the spiritual emptiness of God's people.

How the story unfolds. Jesus was on the way to Jerusalem the day after his triumphal entry when he saw a fig tree with leaves but no fruit. Jesus cursed the tree, declaring, "Let no one eat fruit from you ever again" (Mark 11:14).

In Jerusalem, Jesus entered the temple and drove out those who "bought and sold" in it. The temple was supposed to be "a house of prayer for all the nations," but God's people had made it a "den of thieves" (Mark 11:15–17). The scribes and chief priests wanted to kill Jesus, but they hesitated to act out of fear of the people.

The next morning when Jesus and his disciples were returning to the city, Peter pointed out the tree that Jesus had cursed the day before. It had withered away, "dried up from the roots" (Mark 11:20).

Jesus used the occasion to encourage his disciples to "have faith in God," and reminded them that with prayer, even the impossible could become a reality.

"Jesus went into the temple" *(Mark 11:15f).* The report of Christ's second cleansing of the temple (see John 2:13–17) is sandwiched between the two parts of the story of the fig tree. Jesus drove out the moneychangers and the merchants who were buying and selling in the temple court. The temple was supposed to be a house of prayer for all nations. But Israel's leaders had made it a "den of thieves."

After Jesus cursed a fig tree, it withered.

The temple area referred to in this account was the outer court, or "court of the Gentiles." The priests supervised the merchants who sold sacrificial animals here and exchanged foreign coins for "temple currency." These businessmen were permitted to charge a fee of about 4 percent of the value of any money exchanged. But the high priestly family which controlled the temple at this time was known for its greed. Jesus' characterization of the market as a "den of thieves" suggests that these limits had been exceeded.

Even more serious, however, was the corruption of a place which God intended to be set apart as a "house of prayer for all nations" (Isa. 56:7). Israel's fig tree had leaves; its temple erected to the glory of God was one of the wonders of the ancient world. But the traffic in the temple court revealed that the practices of her people were barren indeed.

"Whoever says to this mountain" *(Mark 11:22).* The disciples, shocked at the rapid withering of the fig tree, stimulated a brief teaching on prayer. In the first century, any great difficulty or impossible task was frequently referred to as a "mountain." Jesus was speaking metaphorically, reminding his disciples that God was able to do what human beings cannot. We are thus to rely on him and bring life's challenges to the Lord. We can have complete confidence that God will deal with the greatest of our difficulties, even though a way out may appear to be as impossible as commanding a mountain to move itself into the sea.

The meaning of the miracle. The cleansing of the temple and Jesus' comments on prayer should not distract our attention from the miracle itself. The barren fig tree, whose leaves promised a fruit which the tree did not produce, was judged by Christ. It would never deceive hungry travelers again.

In a similar way, Israel would also be judged. Its way of life would wither when the temple and its sacrifices were taken away. A different form of Judaism would take the place of its familiar pattern of life and worship. Root and branch, the old would soon be gone.

JESUS RESTORES MALCHUS'S EAR
Matthew 26:51–56; Mark 14:46,47; Luke 22:50, 51; John 18:10, 11

When Peter struck a member of the mob that had come to take Jesus, he cut off part of the ear of a man named Malchus. Jesus touched the ear and healed it.

Background of the miracle. Jesus' last miracle before his death was performed on the night of his capture and trial, just hours before his crucifixion. A mob led by Judas arrested him on the Mount of Olives in the garden of Gethsemane.

Only John, who was from a wealthy family which maintained a large house in Jerusalem, names Malchus. He was "the" servant of the high priest, an important official in his own right and clearly a person whom John knew. It is ironic that Jesus' last miracle of healing was performed for an enemy who had come with the mob to make sure Christ was arrested.

Parties to the miracle. The miracle is not the focus of the story, but it seems almost an aside. Judas led a mob to Gethsemane to take Jesus prisoner. Peter, named only in John's Gospel, resisted the arrest and struck out with his weapon, cutting off part of Malchus's ear. Jesus restored the ear, then told his disciples not to resist and left with the crowd as they went back to Jerusalem.

Jesus. Although he was being arrested, Jesus was clearly in command of the situation.

Peter. Frightened by the crowd, Peter drew a weapon and struck one of the mob that had come to take Jesus away.

Malchus. As an important official of the Jewish high priest, Malchus was probably in charge of the detail which had come to bring Jesus in for trial. He was accompanied by a mob carrying torches and weapons.

How the story unfolds. Jesus had finished a time of prayer and returned to his disciples when a mob led by Judas appeared. Judas pointed out Jesus. As the mob surged forward to seize him, Peter drew a weapon and struck at the group. He cut off part of the ear of the servant of the high priest, whom John identified as Malchus.

Jesus told Peter to put his sword back in its place. Jesus could have called legions of angels to defend him. But the Scriptures had to be fulfilled, so it was necessary that he be taken away.

"Drew his sword" (Matthew 26:51). The word for "sword" and "knife" are the same in Greek, so we can't be sure what kind of weapon Peter drew. It is clear that he attacked the crowd with it in an attempt to defend Jesus.

"Cut off his ear" (26:51). Mark uses the diminutive Greek word *otarion* for ear, suggesting that perhaps only the ear lobe was cut off. This would explain why Luke 22:51 indicates that Jesus healed the ear rather than reattaching it. In any case, this was a gracious miracle which he performed for an enemy.

"Put your sword in its place" (26:52). Luke 22:38 indicates the disciples had two swords, and 22:49 points out that other disciples were only awaiting Jesus' word to fight back. But Peter didn't wait for Jesus' command; he drew his weapon and struck! This was so like Peter.

Pacifists have argued for nonresistance from this passage, while their opponents have noted that Jesus told Peter to put his sword back, not throw it away. But this account of Jesus' capture is hardly one on which to base arguments over pacifism. Jesus himself said he could have called on legions of angels to fight for him, if this had been God's will.

Christ allowed himself to be taken so "the Scriptures be fulfilled, that it must happen thus" (Matt. 26:54).

The meaning of the miracle. This last miracle, taking place just before Jesus was arrested and sentenced to death, is a striking reminder. Christ was not *forced* to the cross. He was never overpowered by his opponents. He could have escaped the fate they intended for him at any time.

Jesus' last miracle was actually a warning to his accusers, who refused to believe his claims to be the Christ—in spite of the evidence of his signs and wonders. As Jesus warned them during his trial, "I say to you, hereafter you will see the Son of Man sitting at the right hand of the Power and coming on the clouds of heaven" (Matt. 26:64).

Those who refuse to accept healing at Jesus' hand will surely face his judgment.

WONDERS AT CALVARY

Jesus performed no miracle while on the cross, but his death was accompanied by wonders.

It is appropriate to note several wonders associated with the death of Jesus on the cross. These, like his miracles, were extraordinary events with a religious purpose caused by God.

The cross is one focus of fulfilled prophecy. It is a wonder indeed that hundreds of years before Jesus came to earth, his crucifixion was described in great detail.

Psalm 22 was acknowledged to be messianic long before Christ was born. It contains the following verses:

> "My God, My God, why have
>   You forsaken Me" (22:1).

> They shoot out the lip, they shake
>   the head, saying,
> "He trusted in the LORD, let Him
>   rescue Him;
> Let Him deliver Him, since He
>   delights in Him" (22:7, 8).

> They pierced My hands and My feet
>   (22:16).

> They divide My garments among
>   them,
> And for My clothing they cast lots
>   (22:18).

As we read the Gospels, we discover that each of these verses describes something that was said or something that happened at Calvary.

Isaiah 53 describes Jesus' death in the company of criminals (Isa. 53:9, 12), predicting that he would be buried in a rich man's tomb (Isa. 53:9). Psalm 34:20 predicts that none of Jesus' bones would be broken. This is a striking prediction, for the legs of the thieves with whom he died were broken to hasten their deaths (John 19:32, 33).

These and other prophecies fulfilled at Calvary on the day Jesus died are one of the wonders of God's Word. They remind us that the Cross was always a central element in God's plan and that the death of Jesus was decreed by the Father, not by human beings.

To find the meaning of the Cross, we must understand it not as a tragedy, but as the key to God's triumph over Satan, sin, and death.

The wonder of the torn veil. Matthew reports that at the moment of Jesus' death the veil of the temple was "torn in two from top to bottom" (Matt. 27:51). The same event is reported in Mark 15:38 and Luke 23:45.

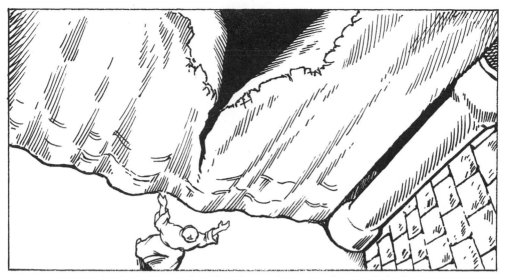

At the death of Jesus, the veil of the temple was torn from top to bottom.

The veil that hung between the Holy Place and the Holy of Holies in the temple was a thick, woven tapestry of multiple colored strands. No known force could rip it apart.

The veil was also spiritually significant. Only once a year could the high priest go behind this veil—and then he carried sacrificial blood to sprinkle on the cover of the sacred ark of the covenant as an atonement for Israel's sins.

The writer of the book of Hebrews reveals that the veil which separated the two inner rooms of the temple indicated that "the way into the Holiest of All was not yet made manifest" (Heb. 9:8). The veil cut off not only the people but even the priests from direct access to God. It was a symbol of the reality that no avenue of approach to God existed in Old Testament times.

But with the death of Christ, a radical change took place. He took our sins upon himself and opened the way to God through his sacrifice. And so the writer of Hebrews declares, "Let us therefore come boldly to the throne of grace, that we may obtain mercy and find grace to help in time of need" (Heb. 4:16).

The wonder of the torn veil symbolizes the end of one age and the beginning of another. In this new age, all believers can enter the holiest of all boldly and with confidence, knowing that God's throne is a throne of grace for all.

The wonder of the opened graves (Matt. 27:52, 53). Matthew alone reports this extraordinary event. He indicates that an earthquake struck the area at the moment of Jesus' death, opening a number of graves. Many of the saints were restored to life and seen in Jerusalem after Jesus' resurrection.

The implications of this wonder are clear. Jesus' death brought life to some who had been dead. What a symbol of victory over death, and of the resurrection life that Jesus offers to all who trust him as Savior.

EASTER MIRACLES—AND BEYOND

Each Gospel devotes much of its space to the story of Jesus' trial and crucifixion. Yet each Gospel account ends on a note of triumph. Jesus has been falsely accused and foully murdered. Yet death cannot hold Jesus. In an unmatched exercise of the power of God, Jesus is raised from the dead!

The account of events on and beyond the first Easter focus our attention on a number of

RESURRECTION APPEARANCES			
Who Sees Him	**Where**	**When**	**Reference**
Mary Magdalene, Mary the mother of James, and Salome	At the tomb	Early Sunday morning	Matt. 28:1–10; Mark 16:1–8; Luke 24:1–12; John 20:1–9
Mary Magdalene	At the tomb	Early Sunday morning	Mark 16:9–11; John 20:11–18
Peter	Jerusalem	Sunday	Luke 24:34; 1 Cor. 15:5
Two travelers	Road to Emmaus	Midday Sunday	Luke 24:13–32
Ten disciples	Upper room	Sunday evening	Mark 16:14; Luke 24:36–43; John 20:19–25
Eleven disciples	Upper room	One week later	John 20:26–29; 1 Cor. 15:5
Seven disciples	Fishing in Galilee	Dawn	John 21:1–23
Eleven disciples	Galilee	Much later	Matt. 28:16–20; Mark 16:15–18
500 followers	Probably Galilee	Later	1 Cor. 15:6
James the apostle	Unknown	Later	1 Cor. 15:7
Disciples, leading women, Jesus' brothers, and others	Mount of Olives	40 days after the resurrection	Luke 24:46–53; Acts 1:3–14
Saul of Tarsus	Road to Damascus	Midday, years later	Acts 9:1–9; 1 Cor. 15:8

wonders associated with the Resurrection, which is the greatest wonder of all. As we look first at the associated wonders and then at the Resurrection itself, we realize how utterly central the bodily resurrection of our Lord is to authentic Christian faith.

WONDERS ASSOCIATED WITH THE RESURRECTION

The tomb's stone seal was rolled away (Matt. 28:2; Mark 16:1–3; Luke 24:1–2). The tombs of wealthy first century Jews like Joseph of Arimathea, where Jesus' body was placed, were hewn into rock cliffs. Such tombs generally had several niches carved into the rock, where the bones of several generations of the family could be stored. These tombs were sealed by large stone "wheels," which would be rolled along a track cut into the rock to seal the tomb. When on the first Easter morning several women set out for Jesus' tomb to wrap His body in linen strips interwoven with sweet-smelling spices, they worried. How could they roll away the heavy stone that sealed the tomb?

When they arrived at the tomb, they discovered the tomb already opened! Matthew tells us that an earthquake had jolted the stone from its track, and an angel had moved it away from the tomb's opening!

The guard posted at the tomb was unconscious (Matt. 28:4). The Jewish leaders had asked Pilate, the Roman governor, to put a military guard at the tomb. They remembered that Jesus had promised a return to life, and while they did not believe Him, they thought His disciples might try to steal the body.

But the appearance of the angel and the earthquake shocked the military guard into unconsciousness. Later, when they awakened, some of the guard reported what had happened to the chief priests. These religious leaders who had conspired to see Jesus executed then bribed the soldiers with "a large sum of money" to say that the disciples stole Jesus' body while they were asleep.

The leaders must also have promised the soldiers protection, for the penalty for a Roman soldier who slept while on guard was death. And, of course, if the disciples had actually stolen Christ's body while the soldiers slept, the soldiers could hardly have been credible witnesses. How would they know *what* happened, if they were asleep? Like most political cover-ups, this attempt to confuse the population about Christ's resurrection was destined to fail.

Angels informed visitors to the tomb that Jesus had risen from the dead (Matthew 28:3; Luke 24:4–7; John 20:12–13). This is a third wonder associated with the Resurrection. One or more angels appeared to groups of women who came to the tomb, and testified to Jesus' resurrection. In each case the angels appeared in their natural, radiant state, rather than as ordinary persons. There could be no mistaking the supernatural character of these witnesses to the raising of Jesus.

The undisturbed graveclothes (John 20:2–10). When Peter and John heard that Jesus' tomb was empty they ran to see for themselves. Peter stooped and stepped into the tomb and was stunned by what he saw.

In biblical times bodies were loosely wrapped in strips of linen, and a cloth was placed over the head of the deceased. What Peter saw was the cloths in which Jesus had been wrapped, still in the shape of the body around which they had been done up! But there was no body inside! Jesus had somehow

Faithful women were the first to discover Jesus' empty tomb.

passed through the grave cloths, leaving them as an empty husk!

The apostle John tells us that when he saw this, he believed (John 20:8)!

Mary saw Jesus Himself (John 20:12–18). Even after Mary had seen the angels at the tomb, she wept uncontrollably. She was still convinced that "they" had taken Jesus away.

Then through her tears Mary saw a figure standing nearby. Supposing him to be the gardener she asked the figure where the body of Jesus had been placed. Jesus then spoke only one word to Mary: her name. Immediately Mary recognized His voice.

Jesus appeared unrecognized to two disciples on the Emmaus road (Luke 24:13–35). Another striking incident is reported in Luke. As two disciples return to their home in Emmaus from Jerusalem they are joined by an unknown man. The man questions them, and when they share their vanished hopes that Jesus might have been the Christ, the man leads them through the Old Testament prophets, showing from Scripture that it was foretold that the Christ would suffer as Jesus had!

On arriving home the two travelers invited the stranger to take a meal with them. As the stranger broke the bread and gave thanks for it, in the traditional Jewish table blessing, they suddenly realized that their companion was Jesus Himself, raised from the dead. Jesus then disappeared, and the two hurried back to Jerusalem to tell the disciples that Jesus was alive.

Jesus appeared in a locked room (Luke 24:36–43; Mark 16:14). The text tells us that Jesus came to His disciples and spoke with them personally shortly after the Resurrection. Luke adds a fascinating detail. The room where the disciples had gathered was a locked room, where the disciples were hiding for fear of the religious leaders who had manipulated Jesus' death.

The sudden appearance of Jesus in the room is one of the proofs that the resurrection body is not limited in the way our mortal bodies are limited. Jesus appeared and disappeared at will, most likely freely crossing the barrier between the material and spiritual universes which no mortal can cross.

Jesus' resurrection body bore the marks of crucifixion in its hands and side (John 20:24–31). The disciple Thomas had not been present the first time Jesus appeared to the gathered disciples. He would not believe the report of the others that Christ had shown Himself to them, alive. Thomas bluntly stated that he would not believe unless he touched Jesus' hands and side, and confirmed that the One who now lived was indeed the same One who had been crucified.

Yet when Jesus did appear, and invited Thomas to touch His wounds, Thomas found he did not need this confirmation after all. Thomas knew Jesus, and fell down before him, confessing "My Lord and my God."

These events, each closely linked to that first Easter morning, were wonders indeed. Yet they pale in comparison to the event with which they are associated: the literal, bodily resurrection of Jesus Christ.

THE SIGNIFICANCE OF THE RESURRECTION: *Romans 1:4; 1 Corinthians 15*

Some contemporary "theologians" have argued that it doesn't matter whether the resurrection of Jesus was literal and historical or not. They claim that a "spiritual" resurrection is all that is required. What mattered is not whether or not Jesus' body was raised and transformed. What mattered is that the disciples *believed* that Jesus was raised. What mattered is that they experienced Him in a different way than when He lived among them.

But the Bible makes it very clear that the resurrection of Jesus was a literal resurrection of the material body, and that the Resurrection took place in space and time as a true historical event. Romans 1:4 reminds us that by His resurrection Jesus was "declared to be the Son of God with power." The Resurrection is the capstone miracle, which confirms once and forever Jesus' claim to be God the Son and Son of God.

The apostle Paul provides a thorough discussion of the Resurrection in chapter 15 of his first letter to the Corinthians. Tracing that discussion we gain some insight into both the nature of Jesus' resurrection, and its significance to our faith.

Christ's death, burial, and resurrection are all historical events prophesied in the Old Testament (1 Corinthians 15:3–4). This is significant, as prophecy which has been fulfilled has invariably been fulfilled literally. We can conclude from this that the death of Jesus was a real death, and the resurrection of Jesus was a real, historical resurrection.

Christ was seen alive after His resurrection by many witnesses who knew Him, and who could not have been deceived (1 Corinthians 15:5–11). Paul not only mentions the Twelve, but also some 500 others, most of whom were alive when Paul wrote the Corinthian letter.

Christ's was raised as the first of many (1 Corinthians 15:12–20). Christian faith promises resurrection to all who believe in Jesus. If Christ was not raised, this critical promise is an empty one. On the other hand, because Jesus did experience a bodily resurrection, our own future resurrection is assured.

The Resurrection is a critical element in God's eternal plan to destroy death itself (1 Corinthians 15:21–28). Adam's sin introduced death. Biblically "death" is not only the cessation of biological life; it is also that corruption of human moral nature which separates human beings from God and brings them under divine judgment. In dying Jesus paid the penalty for our sins. In His resurrection Jesus provided eternal life for those who believe in Him. When God's plan reaches its culmination believers will be resurrected also, and the last taint of sin and death will be forever done away.

The dynamic power of Jesus' resurrection life will accomplish the resurrection transformation of believers, that once again God may be all in all.

While mortal and resurrection bodies are related, the resurrection body is of a different order (1 Corinthians 15:35–48). The great apostle struggles to find analogies that will help us understand resurrection. In a real sense, we will never understand the glorious prospect God holds up to us until the final resurrection comes. Yet Paul does suggest a series of contrasts which helps us sense something of the transformation that took place when Christ was raised, and that will take place when we are raised from the dead.

Corruption vs. incorruption (1 Cor. 15:42). The natural body is subject to dissolution. The resurrection body is not.

Dishonor vs. glory (1 Cor. 15:43). The contrast is explained in the verse. Our natural body is weak and subject to all sorts of disabilities. The resurrection body is infused with power.

Natural body vs. spiritual body (1 Cor. 15:44). This contrast points out that our mortal body is governed by principles implicit in the material universe. In contrast, the resurrection body operates on principles that are supernatural, i.e., "spiritual."

Earthly source vs. heavenly source (1 Cor. 15:47–49). The first man, Adam, was molded from the earth, and his material body was infused with life by God. But Christ's origin is heaven itself, as is the origin of the transformation that produced His resurrection body. In the same sense the essence and origin of our resurrection bodies will be heavenly. In the resurrection "we shall also bear the image of the heavenly Man."

The bodily resurrection of Jesus is most certainly one of the three Grand Miracles of our faith, as described on pages 15 through 17 of this book. The literal, bodily resurrection of Jesus also serves as a miraculous confirmation of our own destiny, and as such is foundational to authentic Christian faith.

JESUS CAUSES A GREAT CATCH OF FISH *John 21:1–14*

After his resurrection, Jesus appeared to his disciples by the Sea of Galilee and caused a great catch of fish.

Background of the miracle. This is the second miraculous catch of fish reported in the Gospels. The first was associated with the calling of the disciples as Jesus' followers (see p. 176). This extraordinary catch of fish is related to the recommissioning of Peter and Jesus' call to "follow Me."

Parties to the miracle. The parties to this miracle were the resurrected Jesus and his disciples, with the focus on Peter.

Jesus. This was the third time the disciples had seen Jesus following his resurrection. The other two took place in Jerusalem. This appearance was by the Sea of Galilee.

Peter. Back in Galilee, Peter took the lead and announced that he was going fishing (John 21:3). A man of action, Peter may have been unable to wait patiently for Jesus to come to them (see Matt. 28:7). Peter must have been uneasy as well. On the night before Jesus was crucified, Peter had denied the Lord three times.

Peter was so eager to see the Lord that he leaped into the water and swam to shore when Jesus appeared. Then he lingered behind to drag the full nets ashore and count the catch.

After a shared meal on the shore, Jesus spoke to Peter, asking three times about Peter's love for him. After each response, Peter was told to tend or feed Christ's sheep. Peter was thus recommissioned for the ministry to which all the disciples had been called.

But the spiritual significance of this miracle is not Christ's dialogue with his disciple. It is found in a miracle within the miracle.

How the story unfolds. The disciples had returned to Galilee. Peter announced he was going fishing, and the others went with him. Although they fished all night, they caught nothing.

Then as morning dawned, a person was seen on the shore. The figure called to them to cast their net on the right side of the boat. When the fishermen obeyed, they caught a school of large fish so heavy it could not be pulled into the boat.

At this point, John said to Peter, "It is the Lord!" (John 21:7). Peter grabbed his outer garment and leaped into the sea to swim to shore. The other disciples brought the boat into the shallows, dragging the heavy net. When they reached the shore, they saw that Jesus had a fire going, with bread and fish already laid on the fire.

Jesus instructed them to bring some of the fish they had just caught. The net was pulled on shore and the catch counted. They had caught 153 large fish. Christ called them to the meal, serving them the bread and fish he had prepared.

After this meal, the dialog with Peter occurred.

"They caught nothing" (John 21:3). The disciples were professional fishermen. But this night their best efforts were futile.

"Cast the net on the right side" (21:6). Some interpreters have suggested that Jesus could see from the shore the school of fish that the disciples could not. Given the conditions, and the fact that Christ himself was only an indistinct figure in the dawning light, this theory is as absurd as it is unnecessary.

Before his resurrection, Jesus had directed the path of fish in the seas (page 176). He was surely able to cause this school of fish to swim into the net of his disciples.

"A fire of coals there, and fish laid on it, and bread" (21:9). This is a miracle within the miracle. Jesus caused the disciples to catch fish. But before they brought their catch ashore, he was already preparing fish for them to eat—fish they had not caught, fish which Jesus obtained and prepared for his followers.

The significance of the miracle. The meaning of the miracle lies in three verses that speak of fish.

John 21:3 indicates the disciples caught no fish. Their best efforts were futile, even though they were expert fishermen.

John 21:6 reveals that by following Jesus' instructions they caught a "multitude of fish."

John 21:9 tells us that while the disciples were still out on the lake, Jesus was already preparing for them fish which they had not caught.

As the disciples set out on their mission to spread the gospel of the risen Christ, they left their old occupations. However skilled they were at these jobs, there was nothing more in them for persons called to guide Christ's church.

Jesus' instructions to the disciples to cast their nets in the path of a school of fish remind us that Christ is able to make us successful in any chosen pursuit, as long as we are obedient to him.

The meal Jesus served the disciples was a promise that they could rely on him to supply all their needs as they carried out their mission. This miracle within a miracle—Jesus' supply of fish which the disciples did not catch—was the most significant miracle of the two.

Both miracles speak to us today. We learn from one that our success depends on living by Christ's Word. And we learn from the other that we are free to obey him completely. We can rely on his ability to meet our every need.

CHAPTER 12

MIRACLES OF THE APOSTLES

PROVING CHRIST'S POWER

Acts

Jesus was gone.

He had been raised from the dead, but within a few days Jesus returned to heaven. With Jesus gone, would miracles cease?

The answer of the book of Acts is, "No!" Even from heaven Jesus continued to perform miracles through His followers. Miracles performed by the apostles provided proof of their claim that Jesus is Lord, and proof that the power of Jesus is unlimited still!

MIRACLE CLUSTERS IN SCRIPTURE

As noted earlier, Scripture records several periods during which clusters of miracles took place. Typically these periods were marked by establishing miracles, which served to underline some great new revelation.

Thus, the ten great miracle plagues in Egypt, associated with the name Yahweh, demonstrated that the Lord was God, and that he was faithful to the covenant promises given earlier to Abraham. These miracles also established Moses as God's representative, who would unveil the next stage in God's eternal plan.

In a similar way, the next cluster of miracles, performed by Elijah in the eighth century B.C., were establishing miracles. King Ahab had launched an intensive campaign to make Baal worship the official religion of Israel. God's historic and written revelation were under direct attack. The miracles performed by Elijah, and particularly the miracle on Mount Carmel, demonstrated conclusively that the Lord is God, turning the tide against the advocates of Baal.

Each of these two clusters of establishing miracles was followed by a series of supportive miracles. The supportive miracles showed the continuing presence of the Lord, further confirming the revelation authenticated by the establishing miracles.

During the Exodus a number of miracles served this purpose, and miracles continued on through the time of the conquest of Canaan. God had promised Abraham that his descendants would occupy Canaan. The ten plagues established the Lord as God, and the later miracles revealed his continuing presence with his covenant people.

In the eighth century the miracles of Elijah again established that the Lord alone is God. The supporting miracles of Elijah's successor, Elisha, revealed the continuing presence of the Lord with his people, who had returned to him.

THE MIRACLES OF JESUS AND THE APOSTLES

The miracles of Jesus clearly fit the pattern and purpose of earlier clusters of miracles. A new aspect of God's eternal plan was being unveiled. The miracles of Jesus were establishing miracles. They proved that Jesus was God's spokesman as well as the promised Messiah.

Earlier miracles had proven that the Lord is God. Christ's miracles, and especially the Resurrection, proved that Jesus was the Lord.

But Christ had died and been raised, and had returned to heaven. So the question might well be raised, How could the presence of the risen Jesus be proven by those who set out on the new path that Jesus had revealed? In the past, establishing miracles had been followed by supporting miracles. It was the same with Jesus' miracles. The early days of the Christian church were marked by wonders and miracles performed by the apostles. As supporting miracles, these demonstrated the presence of Jesus with his followers, authenticating the movement Jesus founded as a work of God.

SUPPORTING MIRACLES IN THE BOOK OF ACTS

The book of Acts includes reports of 14 distinct wonders or miracles and references to others. The distinct wonders and miracles are:

The miracles of Jesus proved He was God's spokesman and the Messiah.

GENERAL REFERENCES TO MIRACLES IN ACTS

Many passages in Acts reveal that miracles, wonders, and signs accompanied the ministry of the apostles and others as the Christian church was established in Jerusalem, spread through Judea and Samaria, and ultimately radiated out into the wider Roman world.

We can sense how common miracles and wonders were in these early days by looking at the verses which give general descriptions of miracles during this period.

Then fear came upon every soul [in Jerusalem], and many wonders and signs were done through the apostles (Acts 2:43).

After being ordered to stop preaching, the apostles prayed,

"Look on their threats, and grant to Your servants that with all boldness they may speak Your word, by stretching out Your hand to heal, and that signs and wonders may be done through the name of Your holy Servant Jesus" (Acts 4:29, 30).

And through the hands of the apostles many signs and wonders were done among the people (Acts 5:12).

They brought the sick out into the streets and laid them on beds and couches, that at least the shadow of Peter passing by might fall on some of them. Also a multitude gathered from the surrounding cities to Jerusalem, bringing sick people and those who were tormented by unclean spirits, and they were all healed (Acts 5:15, 16).

And Stephen, full of faith and power, did great wonders and signs among the people (Acts 6:8).

And the multitudes with one accord heeded the things spoken by Philip, hearing and seeing the miracles which he did. For unclean spirits, crying with a loud voice, came out of many who were possessed; and many who were paralyzed and lame were healed (Acts 8:6, 7).

Then Simon himself also believed; and when he was baptized he continued with Philip, and was amazed, seeing the miracles and signs which were done (Acts 8:13).

Therefore they stayed there a long time [in Iconium], speaking boldly in the Lord, who was bearing witness to the word of his grace, granting signs and wonders to be done by their hands (Acts 14:3).

Then all the multitude kept silent and listened to Barnabas and Paul declaring how many miracles and wonders God had worked through them among the Gentiles (Acts 15:12).

God worked unusual miracles by the hands of Paul, so that even handkerchiefs or aprons were brought from his body to the sick, and the diseases left them and the evil spirits went out of them (Acts 19:11).

These were indeed supportive miracles, performed in Jesus' name. They made it plain to all that God was with these followers who proclaimed that Jesus was the Son of God. The new revelation introduced and established by the miracle-working Christ was further confirmed by a great number of supportive miracles performed by his followers.

THE ASCENSION OF JESUS *Acts 1:9–11*

The Ascension was Jesus' return to heaven, mentioned three times by Luke in his Gospel and Acts: Luke 24:50–51; Acts 1:2; and Acts 1:9–11. As the disciples watched in wonder, two angels joined them, promising that Jesus would come back "in like manner as you saw him go into heaven."

Jesus was taken up and received into a cloud (Acts 1:9). The miraculous departure of Christ contrasts with the Old Testament's report of Elijah's departure. That Old Testament prophet was swept up into heaven by angels, carried away in a fiery chariot (2 Kings 2:11).

The description of Jesus' departure seems

almost casual. One moment the resurrected Christ was blessing his disciples outside Bethany (Luke 24:51). And the next, he was taken up into the air and received into a cloud.

However, this departure was less casual than the description suggests. When associated with the miraculous, clouds have a special significance.

We're reminded of Luke 9, which describes Jesus' transfiguration in front of some of his disciples. Luke indicated that a cloud "overshadowed them" and that a voice speaking from the cloud announced, "This is My Beloved Son, hear him!" (Luke 9:34, 35). The cloud also reminds us of Jesus' words about himself and his return, "in the clouds with great power and glory" (Mark 13:26).

In each case, the image of the cloud is rooted in the Old Testament era, where a bright cloud symbolized the glory of God, the *shekinah*, which once filled the tabernacle and later filled the temple built by Solomon.

❖

Jesus was taken up into heaven.

Thus, the apostles' last glimpse of Jesus was of him being enveloped in a cloud which spoke of the divine presence. Even the manner in which Jesus was taken up was a powerful affirmation of his divinity.

Jesus was carried up "into heaven." The Greek phrase *eis ton ouranon,* "into heaven," is used in Luke 24:51 and repeated in Acts 1:10 and three times in Acts 1:11. It is clear that locating the risen Jesus in heaven was of central importance to Luke in reporting this wonder.

The message of the two angels further emphasizes this point. The angels told the watchers that "this same Jesus, who was taken up from you into heaven, will so come in like manner as you saw him go into heaven" (Acts 1:11). The angels' words established two things: Jesus was now in heaven and Jesus would return to earth.

The continuing emphasis on Jesus' location "in heaven" is the most significant feature of this first wonder described in the book of Acts.

Why Jesus' presence in heaven was so significant. The importance of establishing this point is reflected in a prayer offered by the apostles after a confrontation with the leaders who had conspired to have Jesus executed. The disciples prayed that the Lord would stretch out his hand to heal, and that signs and wonders might be done through the name of Jesus (Acts 4:30). Because he was in heaven, Jesus could now answer his disciples' prayers and act through them to perform fresh wonders on the earth!

In fact, the New Testament mentions a number of the present ministries of Jesus Christ.

- Jesus in heaven is preparing a place for us (John 14:2, 3).
- Jesus, as the vine, is the source of that spiritual vitality which enables us to bear fruit as we stay close to him (John 15:4, 5).
- Jesus, as head of the church, guides and directs us (Eph. 2:20, 21).
- Jesus, as our High Priest, sympathizes with our weaknesses and provides mercy

and enabling grace when we come to his throne of grace (Heb. 4:15, 16).

- Jesus, as our High Priest, intercedes for us, guaranteeing our salvation (Heb. 7:25).
- Jesus, as our advocate, represents us when we sin, pledging his own blood as the basis for our salvation (1 John 2:1, 2).

These and other ministries which Jesus performs for believers today make his living presence in heaven vital for us. And the wonder of the Ascension focuses our attention on the fact that Jesus lives, and that in heaven today he ministers to us and our needs.

THE WONDERS OF PENTECOST
Acts 2

The disciples had assembled in Jerusalem to wait, as Jesus instructed them, for "the Holy Spirit to come upon you" and provide the spiritual power required for their mission (Acts 1:8). On the day of Pentecost, 50 days after Jesus' resurrection, the Spirit swept into the room where the apostles and other believers in Jesus had gathered.

The day of Pentecost (Acts 2:1). This day fell on the fiftieth day from the first Sunday after Passover, and thus fifty days after the resurrection of Jesus. It was the day on which the first produce of the wheat harvest was presented to God. The Jewish rabbis had concluded from Exodus 19:1 that Pentecost was also the day on which God had given Moses his Law.

How significant that the Holy Spirit who would write God's law on the hearts of those who trust in Jesus (2 Cor. 3:6–8) should come on the anniversary of the day when the Law was given in written form. A new era began that day.

Visible signs of the Spirit's coming (Acts 2:2–4). The coming of the Spirit was marked with visible wonders:

And suddenly there came a sound from heaven, as of a rushing mighty wind, and it filled the whole house where they were sitting. Then there appeared

to them divided tongues, as of fire, and one sat upon each of them. And they were all filled with the Holy Spirit and began to speak with other tongues, as the Spirit gave them utterance (Acts 2:2–4).

It was the combination of these three miraculous signs that marked the coming of the Spirit as a unique event in sacred history.

The "rushing mighty wind" (Acts 2:2). Wind is a symbol of God's Spirit in both the Old Testament and the New Testament. The Hebrew word *ruah* and the Greek word *pneuma* mean either wind or spirit, depending on the context.

The prophet Ezekiel had spoken of the wind as God's breath, blowing over the dry bones that represented Israel and filling them with new life (Ezek. 37:9–14). Jesus in speaking with Nicodemus had referred to the wind/spirit or meaning of *pneuma* to draw an analogy: "The wind blows where it wishes, and you hear the sound of it, but cannot tell where it comes from and where it goes. So is everyone who is born of the Spirit" (John 3:8).

John the Baptist had spoken of Jesus as One who "will baptize you with the Holy Spirit [wind] and fire" (Luke 3:16). There is little doubt that in describing the events of Pentecost, Luke saw in the rushing wind and tongues of fire the fulfillment of John the Baptist's prophecy.

Divided tongues, as of fire (2:3). Fire also has a long history as a symbol of the divine presence. The roots of this image are found in the appearance of the Lord to Moses in the burning bush (Ex. 2:2–5), in the cloudy-fiery pillar that led Israel through the wilderness, and in the fact that the Lord "descended upon [Mount Sinai] in fire." The tongue-like flames which burned over the head of each believer in the book of Acts was a clear, visible sign of the presence of God—this time the presence of the third person of the Trinity, the Holy Spirit.

They . . . began to speak with other tongues, as the Spirit gave them utterance (2:4). There is a clear

"Tongues, as of fire, sat upon each of them."

difference between the "other tongues" of Acts and the ecstatic utterances also called "tongues" in 1 Corinthians 12—14. In the 1 Corinthians passage, the tongues were unintelligible and the church needed an interpreter to understand what the speaker was saying (1 Cor. 12:10; 14:2, 5). In Acts, the wonder was that Jews from many foreign lands who had come to Jerusalem for the festival heard in their "own language in which we were born" (Acts 2:8, 11).

The lasting significance of the Spirit's coming. The Acts passage doesn't give a name to the Spirit's Pentecost activity. Acts does report that the disciples were "filled with" the Holy Spirit, an experience which was repeated on several occasions (Acts 4:8, 31). Later in Acts, however, the apostle Peter identified the initial experience and gave it a name.

Reporting the conversion of the first Gentile who became a Christian—a Roman centurion named Cornelius—Peter reported that "the Holy Spirit fell upon them, as upon us at the beginning. Then I remembered the Word of the Lord, how he said, 'John indeed baptized with water, but you shall be baptized with the Holy Spirit'" (Acts 11:15, 16). Peter's reference to "the beginning" in this context was clearly to the day

of Pentecost. And the ministry the Spirit exercised on that day was his baptizing work.

While believers in most Christian traditions speak of Pentecost in terms of the baptism of the Holy Spirit, Christians differ as to the meaning of that term. Yet this work of the Spirit was clearly defined in 1 Corinthians 12:13: "For by one Spirit we were all baptized into one body—whether Jews or Greeks, whether slaves or free—and have all been made to drink into one Spirit." The baptism of the Holy Spirit is thus that work of the Holy Spirit by which every believer is made a part of the body of Christ, linked forever to Jesus and through Jesus to every other believer in the Lord.

When the Spirit came on Pentecost, the church as the living body of Christ, a spiritual organism, was born (see 1 Cor. 10:16; 12:27; Eph. 4:12). After Pentecost, every believer has been joined to that spiritual body upon trust in the Lord.

The significance of the wonders that marked the Spirit's coming. While the three visible signs together served as the unique mark of the Spirit's coming, the focus of the text is clearly on the third sign—tongues.

As those from the western Roman world

Places represented on Pentecost.

and from the east heard the Christians speaking in their own tongues, "they were all amazed and perplexed, saying to one another, 'Whatever could this mean?'" (Acts 2:12). The question was answered by the apostle Peter, who stood up and preached history's first gospel message. Peter quoted the prophet Joel, announcing that what the visible signs meant was that the promised age of the Spirit had actually arrived!

Peter quoted,

"And it shall come to pass in the
    last days, says God,
That I will pour out of My Spirit
    on all flesh" (Acts 2:17).

Peter continued to quote the passage, which promised a display of wonders, and concluded his quote with these words:

And it shall come to pass
That whoever calls on the name
    of the Lord
Shall be saved (Acts 2:21).

While a number of the signs mentioned in Joel are associated with the judgments linked to Jesus' second coming, Peter's emphasis was clear. The wonders of Pentecost marked the *beginning* of the last stage of God's plan for humankind. That stage, which continues to our own day, is marked by the vitalizing work of God's Holy Spirit and the

promise of salvation to "whoever calls on the name of the Lord."

The wonders of the day of Pentecost established a link between the Old and New Testaments. They marked the initiation of an era predicted by the Old Testament prophets—a period in which each individual, Jew and Gentile alike, is faced with the necessity of making a personal decision about Jesus Christ.

THE HEALING OF A LAME MAN
Acts 3:1–26

Peter and John healed a man who had been a cripple from birth on their way to worship at the temple. The miracle amazed the other worshipers, who crowded around to listen as Peter seized the occasion to preach another evangelistic sermon.

Worship at the temple (Acts 3:1). The first Christians were observant Jews, who worshiped in the traditional ways and continued to practice their ancient religion. For many years Christians were simply known as practitioners of "the Way" (Acts 9:2). During this period Christianity was considered a sect of Judaism and not a separate religion. It was only as the gospel message spread in the gentile world that leaders like the apostle Paul had to struggle to define the lifestyle to which faith in Christ called believers.

So it was not surprising that the two apostles of Jesus were on their way to the temple "at the hour of prayer, the ninth hour" (Acts 3:1). Two principal daily services were held at the temple, one accompanying the morning and the other the evening sacrifice. It was the evening service the two intended to attend.

The lame man (3:2). The "lame man" was a cripple who had to be carried to the gate where he begged daily. The text emphasizes that he had been lame "from his mother's womb." This was no psychosomatic illness that could be "cured" by suggestion.

The lame man was probably familiar to those who had passed for years on their way to the temple. Many would have given him alms, which was considered a *mitzvah,* a meritorious act.

The fact that the lame man was well known as well as the serious nature of his disability contributed to the amazement of the people at his healing.

"In the name of Jesus Christ of Nazareth" (3:6). While passing by, Peter drew the attention of the cripple and announced that while he had no silver or gold, he would give what he had. In the name of Jesus, Peter told the man, "Rise up and walk."

The supportive miracles performed by the apostles were done in "the name of Jesus." That is, the apostles called on Christ to act and to demonstrate the power which he alone possessed.

There is a significant difference between the apostle's pronouncements of Jesus' name and the magical use of "names" in biblical times. For centuries magical formulas had included the supposed names of demons and deities, manipulating them to do the will of the sorcerer. This is the way some people interpret the healings in Acts. But an incident reported in Acts 19:13f makes it clear that this was not the case.

In Ephesus, Paul performed such stunning miracles in Jesus' name that a group of Jewish exorcists tried to cast out a demon using Christ's name. The demon then beat them and chased them from the house, saying "Jesus I know and Paul I know; but who are you?" (Acts 19:15).

There was no magic involved in Peter's miracle of healing. The power of Jesus flowed through his servant and performed the miracle. These were supporting miracles indeed, revealing Jesus' presence with the leaders of the movement founded in his name.

"Entered the temple with them, walking, leaping, and praising God" (3:8). The complete healing of the crippled man was advertised by his actions. He was quickly recognized. Luke emphasizes the reaction of those who knew him. They were "filled with wonder and amazement" and were "greatly amazed" (Acts 3:10, 11).

There is a story that Thomas Aquinas once visited Pope Innocent II in Rome. Pointing out his riches, the pope said, "See, Thomas, the church can no longer say 'silver and gold have I none.'" Aquinas agreed. "True, holy father. Neither can she say, 'Rise and walk.'" This miracle reminds us that no Christian congregation should be more concerned with its facilities than with seeing the transforming power of Jesus at work in people's lives.

"Men of Israel . . ." (3:12). Peter used the occasion to address the crowd. It was not by Peter's or John's own godliness that the man was made to walk. The power was that of Jesus: "And his name, through faith in his name, has made this man strong, whom you see and know. Yes, the faith which comes through him has given him this perfect soundness in the presence of you all" (Acts 3:16).

Peter was not saying that the lame man had faith. He was not even claiming credit for his own and John's faith. Rather, Peter was saying that the *Jesus who was the object of their faith* had performed the miracle.

Peter then explained who this Jesus was. He was the one whom they had crucified but who had been raised again by God. He was the one predicted by prophets, whom God in faithfulness sent first to bless Israel. To have faith "in his name" was to have faith in him as the Scriptures defined him.

We must also accept Jesus on his own terms, as he is defined in the Word of God— not as he has been redefined by those who would keep the name but rob the person of his glory by viewing him as a good man or a simple Jewish rabbi. Jesus was and is the Christ, the Son of God; and for this reason alone power resides in his name.

The significance of the miracle. This was not the first of the confirming miracles worked by Jesus' followers (compare Acts 2:43). It was, however, the *defining* supportive miracle. All the miracles and wonders of Acts were performed through faith in the name of Jesus Christ. Each miracle demonstrated to all who saw the continuing presence of one whose own miracles had established him as the Son of God.

THE DEATHS OF ANANIAS AND SAPPHIRA   *Acts 5:1–11*

A couple eager to gain a reputation in the new Christian community sold some property. They kept part of the money for themselves but claimed the amount they brought to the apostles was the entire proceeds of the sale.

"Why has Satan filled your heart" (Acts 5:3). When Ananias brought the money to Peter, God revealed their dishonesty. Peter rebuked Ananias for an act which was in essence a "lie to the Holy Spirit." Ananias immediately collapsed and died. It is clear that Peter had no direct role in the death of Ananias. Ananias was struck dead by God.

"About three hours later" (5:7). In harmony with Jewish custom, Ananias was taken out and buried. Three hours later his wife came in. When she was questioned, she repeated the lie told by her husband (Acts 5:8). At that moment the men who had buried her husband returned, and Peter announced that they would bury her too. "Immediately" she also fell and died, and was buried beside her husband.

What was the sin of Ananias and Sapphira? Their plan to deceive the apostles and the church was a "lie to the Holy Spirit" (Acts 5:3). As such, the lie served "to test the Spirit of the Lord."

We need to remember that the purpose of confirming miracles and wonders was to demonstrate the continuing presence of God with his people. The events of the day of Pentecost (Acts 2) and the healing of the lame man (Acts 3), along with many other miracles (Acts 2:43), had demonstrated the living presence of God with this company which was committed to Jesus. The "lie to the Holy Spirit" by Ananias and Sapphira was a denial of God's presence—an act which put God to the test.

The significance of the miraculous deaths. In the critical early days of the church, the challenge issued by Ananias and Sapphira could not go unanswered. God struck the pair dead, confirming the reality of the divine presence within the Christian community.

The impact of the miracle (5:11–13). This miracle had its intended effect within and outside the church. Acts indicates that "fear came upon all the church and upon all who heard these things" (v. 11). We should not understand this fear as terror but as a deep, abiding awe. The reality of God's presence was impressed on Jesus' followers, and thus their faith was strengthened.

The miracle had an unusual effect on "the rest" of the people of Jerusalem as well. Acts 5:13 reveals that "none of the rest dared join them, but the people esteemed them highly."

Sometimes people have "joined the church" for reasons other than trust in Jesus as God's Son and Savior. When Jesus was on earth, many followed him not because they understood or accepted his claims but because he healed their diseases and fed them when they were hungry. The shocking deaths of Ananias and Sapphira sent a powerful message to anyone who might link themselves with the Christian movement without a real faith in Christ: it was dangerous to be a "pretend" Christian!

So while the people of Jerusalem had a high regard for the apostles and the followers of Christ, the movement never became "popular." The next verse reveals that while more and more people were added to the church, it was only those who "believed in the Lord" (Acts 5:14, NIV).

THE APOSTLES ARE MIRACULOUSLY FREED FROM PRISON   *Acts 5:17–42*

The flurry of miracles performed by the apostles after the death of Ananias and Sapphira (Acts 5:15) and their vigorous preaching of Christ aroused the anger of the Sadducees, who imprisoned the apostles.

They "laid their hands on the apostles" (Acts 5:18). The Sadducees were the priestly party in Judaism. They controlled the Levites, who served as the temple police. It was the temple police who arrested the apostles and put them in jail, where they would be tried by the Sanhedrin the next day.

"An angel of the Lord opened the prison doors" (5:19). The opening of the prison doors was not a miracle done by the apostles—but a miracle performed for them by an angel. For a discussion of the incident, see *Every Good and Evil Angel in the Bible.*

Luke provided specific details of this happening, so the miraculous nature of the release is clear. Acts 5:23 recounts the report of the detail of guards sent the next morning to bring the apostles before the Sanhedrin. "Indeed we found the prison shut securely, and the guards standing outside before the doors; but when we opened them, we found no one inside."

Reports of miraculous releases from prison in first-century literature. Jeremias has commented on the widespread popularity of legends in the ancient world which recount the opening of prison doors. Jeremias wrote,

The threefold repetition of the motif of the miraculous opening of prison doors in Ac., its distribution between the apostles in Ac. 5:19; Peter in 12:6–11, and Paul in 16:2ff, and the agreement with ancient

An angel released the apostles from prison.

parallels in many details, e.g., liberation by night, the role of the guards, the falling off of chains, the bursting open of the doors, the shining of bright light, earthquake, all suggest that in form at least Lk. is following an established *topos* (*Jerusalem in the Time of Jesus,* p. 176).

While Luke wrote the most fluid Greek in the New Testament and was undoubtedly familiar with this literary convention, the content is always more important than the form. The important thing to remember is that the events Luke relates in Acts actually happened.

The apostles witnessed boldly (5:25). While the confused members of the Sanhedrin pondered this report, they were told that the apostles were now standing in the temple and teaching the people. The temple police then approached the apostles and politely asked them to appear before the Sanhedrin. The members of this supreme court of Judaism attempted to silence the apostles, who answered with boldness that they would obey God rather than men (Acts 5:29).

The court was restrained from killing the apostles by a Pharisee named Gamaliel, whose fame is known from rabbinic writings. Gamaliel pointed out that other messianic movements had died out. He suggested that they beat the apostles, command them not to speak in Jesus' name, and let them go. Hopefully this movement would also just go away.

The result was that "daily in the temple, and in every house, they did not cease teaching and preaching Jesus as the Christ" (Acts 5:42).

SAUL'S MIRACULOUS CONVERSION
Acts 9:1–20

A zealous young Pharisee named Saul saw a vision of Jesus while on the way to Damascus to seize Christians and return them to Jerusalem for trial.

WAS SAUL RIGHT TO PERSECUTE CHRISTIANS?

There is no doubt that Saul felt justified in persecuting Christians. In Old Testament times, God had commended Phinehas for slaying a sinning Israelite (Num. 25:6–15). In more recent history, the Maccabees had shown their zeal for God by rooting out apostasy (compare 1 Macc. 2:23–28; 42–48). The writer of one of the Dead Sea Scrolls saw zeal against apostates as a natural expression of one's commitment to God. He wrote, "The nearer I draw to you, the more I am filled with zeal against all who do wickedness and against all men of deceit" (IQH 14:13–15).

There is no doubt that Saul the Pharisee felt justified in persecuting Christians. He also saw it as his religious duty—until that day on the Damascus road when Jesus spoke to him, and the foundation was laid for the transformation of Saul into the apostle Paul.

The background of Saul's journey (Acts 9:1). Saul, who later became the apostle Paul, is pictured as *"still* breathing threats and murder against the disciples of the Lord."

Earlier Saul had taken part in the stoning of Stephen (Acts 7:58; 8:1). Following Stephen's death, nearly all the Christians were driven from Jerusalem (Acts 8:1). The "still" in 9:1 tells us that this crusade against Jesus' followers had not satisfied Saul. So Saul obtained letters from the high priest authorizing him to bind believers and return them to Jerusalem.

In the Roman Empire, ethnic groups were allowed to keep their own religions and their own systems of law. Letters from the High Priest as the head of the Sanhedrin, the supreme court of Judaism, would be recognized as authorizing the arrest of any Jew. Saul was on official business, and his business was the persecution of the church.

"Suddenly a light shone around him from heaven" (Acts 9:3). While on the road to Damascus, Saul was suddenly blinded by a bright light. He fell to the ground and heard a voice from heaven calling to him. The voice asked why Saul was persecuting the Lord. Saul, "trembling and astonished," could only ask, "Lord, what do you want me to do?"

When Saul arose, he was blind. His companions led him by the hand to Damascus, where he neither ate nor drank for three days.

"Ananias" (9:10). The vision on the road to Damascus was not the only miraculous element in Saul's conversion. God spoke in a vision to a believer named Ananias and sent him to Saul. Reassured by God that the hostile Saul was "a chosen vessel of Mine to bear My name before Gentiles" (Acts 9:15), Ananias went. When he reached Saul, Ananias laid hands on him and "immediately there fell from his eyes something like scales" (Acts 9:18). Saul got up and was baptized. After recovering his strength, Saul began to preach in the synagogues in Damascus that Jesus was the Christ, "the Son of God" (Acts 9:20).

The three accounts of Saul's conversion. Three accounts of Saul's conversion occur in Acts. They are found in Acts 9, 22, and 26. At first glance, the three accounts seem to conflict in important details. In Acts 9:3 and 22:6,

A bright light from heaven blinded Saul.

the light radiated around Saul only; in Acts 26:13, it shone around everyone. Acts 9:4 says that Saul heard the voice, and 9:7 adds that his companions heard it as well. But Acts 26:14 indicates that Saul alone heard the voice.

The solution to this apparent contradiction lies in the fact that the Greek noun *phone* means both "sound" and "intelligible speech." What happened is that all saw the light that enfolded Saul. While Saul distinctly heard Jesus speak, his companions heard sounds they could not understand.

What everyone understood, however, was that something miraculous had happened. There had been a *bat qol,* the "daughter of a voice," or a "voice from heaven,"—a phrase used in the first century to indicate that God himself had spoken.

How stunned Saul was when the voice from heaven—obviously that of God—asked why Saul was persecuting him! Saul certainly didn't think he had been persecuting God! When the speaker identified himself as Jesus, everything Saul had believed was swept away.

The miracle convinced Saul that those believers he had been persecuting were right. By the time Ananias appeared, Saul was ready to commit himself to Jesus.

The significance of the miracle. The miraculous conversion and the restoration of Saul's sight foreshadowed the significance of Paul in the spread of the gospel. It also demonstrated the continuing active presence of Jesus, whose own miracles had established him as the Son of God.

PETER PERFORMS MIRACLES AT LYDDA AND JOPPA *Acts 9:32–42*

The conversion of Saul was followed by a relaxation of the persecution of Christians. During this time, Peter traveled through Judea, Galilee, and Samaria. The book of Acts recounts two miracles which he performed.

The first miracle occurred in Lydda and the second in Joppa. These cities west of Palestine were populated by both Jews and Gentiles. The location suggests a further extension of the gospel message, laying a foundation for the conversion of the Roman centurion Cornelius. He would have heard of these nearby miraculous events.

"Jesus the Christ heals you" (Acts 9:34). The first miracle, which took place in Lydda, was the healing of a paralyzed man named Aeneas, who had been bedridden for eight years. Peter healed in the name of Jesus, and Aeneas "arose immediately."

"Tabitha, arise" (9:40). When a much-beloved woman in nearby Joppa died, the believers sent to Lydda for Peter. The woman's Hebrew name was Tabitha, while her Greek name was Dorcas. Both names mean "gazelle." She is described as a "disciple" (the only occurrence in the New Testament of the feminine form of the word) who "was full of good works and charitable deeds" (Acts 9:36). In response to the urgent request, Peter quickly traveled the ten miles to Joppa.

Peter prayed beside Tabitha's body, and then called on the dead woman to "arise." She opened her eyes and sat up. Peter led her out alive and presented her to the assembled widows and believers.

The significance of the miracles. These two miracles mimicked miracles performed by Jesus during his time on earth. They confirmed the continuing presence of Jesus with his followers, demonstrating that presence outside traditional Jewish territory.

These supportive miracles provided continuing proof of Jesus' power. As the restoration of Tabitha became known throughout Joppa, "many believed on the Lord" (Acts 9:42).

PETER'S DELIVERANCE FROM PRISON AND HEROD'S DEATH
Acts 12:1–25

Herod had executed the apostle James (Acts 12:2). The act pleased his Jewish subjects so much that he imprisoned Peter, intending to execute him after the Passover celebration. But the miraculous intervention of an angel in answer to the church's prayer freed Peter. This miracle was followed shortly afterward by a clear divine judgment against the king.

Who was the Herod of Acts 12? The Herod of Acts 12 was Herod Agrippa I, the grandson of Herod the Great of the Christmas story. Herod grew up in Rome as an intimate of the imperial family. Even so, he had to flee Rome at age 33 to escape his creditors. A few years later the emperor Caligula made him tetrarch of two northern Palestinian territories, with the right to be addressed as king. In A.D. 41, when Herod was 51, the emperor Claudius, a childhood friend, added Judea and Samaria to his territories, extending his rule over all the lands that had been ruled by his grandfather.

Herod Agrippa sought the support of his Jewish subjects. He played the part of an observant Jew, following every ritual rule. He moved the administrative seat of the province to Jerusalem from Caesarea and began to rebuild Jerusalem's northern wall. He was also able to prevent the emperor Caligula from erecting a statue of himself as a god in the Jerusalem temple.

It's not surprising that Herod saw suppression of Christians, a divisive element in Jerusalem, as a wise policy. When Herod executed the apostle James—who with his brother John was one of Jesus' earliest followers—the Jewish leaders were delighted.

To please them further, Herod seized Peter also. Herod was unable to have Peter brought to trial until after the Passover religious holidays. So Herod put Peter in a cell under heavy guard. Peter's execution would serve Herod's political purposes very well. Whether Peter had done anything to deserve death was immaterial.

Peter's prison (12:4, 5). Peter was imprisoned in the Fortress Antonia, just beyond the magnificent temple Herod the Great had spent 38 years and enormous sums to enhance. Important prisoners kept under guard were usually chained to one soldier. The political significance that Herod attached to Peter is seen in the fact that the apostle was "bound with two chains between two soldiers" (v. 5). In addition, guards were posted outside the locked cell door.

Herod's arrangements were futile. The Bible reports that "an angel of the Lord stood by him, and a light shone in the prison; and he struck Peter on the side."

Stories of angelic deliverance from prison were imbedded in the popular lore. Peter at first assumed he was dreaming. Peter saw the chains drop from his wrists. He could see the soldiers seated there, unmoving. He stooped to pick up the outer cloak he had used as a blanket as he slept on the stone floor. Peter even tied on his sandals, wrapping the leather thongs carefully around his leg.

Then Peter followed the angel. He passed the guards, still alert at their posts but totally unaware of Peter and his companion. He watched as the great iron gate that led out into the city swung open of its own accord. But it wasn't until they had walked some distance from the fortress and the angel had left that Peter realized this was no vision.

Peter's release was an answer to prayer (12:5). When Peter was imprisoned, many Christians gathered to pray. Even as Peter was being led from the prison, one group was praying in the home of Mary, the mother of John Mark. It was to this house that Peter walked that night.

In first-century Jerusalem, the wealthy lived in walled homes. Large gates were set in the outer wall. These were opened only on special occasions. Smaller doors were built into these large gates. It was on this smaller "door of the gate" that Peter knocked when he arrived at Mary's house.

That night a girl named Rhoda was serving as doorkeeper. It was her duty to respond to anyone who knocked. When she called out "Who?" the visitor responded, "It is I." The doorkeeper was expected to recognize the voice of a friend and would open the gate without actually seeing the person.

Rhoda recognized Peter's voice. But she was so happy that she neglected to open the door, running instead to tell the congregation inside the good news. The believers tried to calm her down, certain she must be wrong, but she kept on insisting.

The incident is encouraging for those who have the notion that our prayers are answered only if we have unshakable faith. The church was praying earnestly, but it was certain that Peter couldn't possibly be outside the door.

Peter's release from prison in answer to prayer was another miraculous confirmation of the presence of Christ with his people and also of Christ's power. Jesus even commanded angels to intercede for his own.

The miraculous death of Herod. The details and the timing of the subsequent death of Herod Agrippa I was portrayed as a miracle by Luke, and it was undoubtedly viewed this way in the early church.

Josephus, the first-century Jewish historian, gave an account of Herod Agrippa's death in his *Antiquities* (XIX, 343–50 [viii.2]). His account and Luke's narrative were clearly in-dependent, but they are similar in structure and many details. Both make it clear that Herod was struck down as the crowds praised him as a god.

This way of honoring rulers was common in the Hellenistic world. For instance, an entry in a child's exercise book read: "What is a god? That which is strong. What is a king? He who is equal to the divine" (quoted in A. D. Nock's *Conversion,* Oxford, 1933, 91). Sacrifices in honor of kings often slipped over the already blurred line to become sacrifices made *to* the king. One first-century inscription honored King Antiochus I of Commagene as "The Great King Antiochus, the God, the Righteous One, the Manifest Deity."

In Judaism, however, this practice was viewed as a form of blasphemy. When Herod accepted the divine honors offered him, according to Acts, "immediately an angel of the Lord struck him, because he did not give glory to God" (12:23).

Luke provided a medical explanation in his comment that Herod was "eaten by worms." The king was probably killed by intestinal round-worms, which grow to a length of ten to fourteen inches. Clusters of roundworms can obstruct the intestine, causing severe pain. The sufferer will vomit up worms, but in a case so advanced will die an excruciatingly painful death.

Josephus gave a graphic description of Herod's demise. He wrote that Herod was "overcome by more intense pain. . . . Exhausted after five straight days by the pain in abdomen, he departed this life in the fifty-fourth year of his life and the seventh of his reign."

These two events, the release of Peter and the death of Herod, were connected by the angelic agency and linked in Luke's history. They were undoubtedly linked in the minds of first-century Christians. A pagan king who pretended to live as a pious Jew had threatened the existence of the early church. The angel that protected Peter from execution was also God's agent in carrying out the divine sentence of death passed on the persecutor.

The conclusion was inescapable: Jesus lived, and his presence hovered over the church even as his miracle-working power protected believers and threatened the lives of the enemies of his people.

THE BLINDING OF ELYMAS
Acts 13:4–12

On their first missionary journey, Paul and Barnabas preached on the island of Cyprus. When a renegade Jewish sorcerer opposed them, Paul struck him with blindness.

Paul's history. The miraculous conversion of Saul of Tarsus is described in Acts 9 (see p. 255). After his converson, Saul became such a fiery evangelist in Damascus that the Jews plotted to kill him, and he barely escaped with his life (Acts 9:22–25). He returned to Jerusalem, where he again spoke out so boldly that his life was endangered (Acts 9:26–29). The believers brought him to Caesarea and saw him off on a ship to his home city of Tarsus (Acts 9:30).

During the next several years, Saul studied the Scriptures and was given a deeper understanding of the implications of Christ's coming, death, and resurrection. Barnabas, who had befriended Saul in Jerusalem, eventually brought Saul to Antioch to help lead the gentile church in that city (Acts 11:19–28).

Some time later the Holy Spirit led the church at Antioch to send Saul and Barnabas on a mission to spread the gospel to other parts of the Roman Empire. Their first stop was in Cyprus, where they traveled and preached throughout the island.

Cyprus (Acts 13:4). The island of Cyprus was named for its primary export, *cyprium,* or copper. It had been annexed by Rome in 57 B.C. When the missionaries preached there, it was classified as a senatorial province, administered by a *proconsul* (Acts 13:7).

The missionaries landed on the east coast and traveled across the island, preaching first in the Jewish synagogues. Traveling west, the missionaries reached Paphos, the seat of the provincial government. The proconsul, Sergius Paulus, summoned Paul and Barnabas to question them about their message.

The Sergius Paulus family was prominent in the first and second centuries. Various members of the family have been proposed as the Sergius Paulus of this story. The governor's summons of the missionaries was likely motivated by his sense of responsibility to investigate any unusual happenings in his realm. However, Luke's account suggests that the governor was open to the Word of God that Paul preached (Acts 13:7, 8).

Elymas the sorcerer (13:6–8). We are told several things about this sorcerer, whose name in Hebrew was Barjesus (Son of Jesus, i.e., "the Deliverer"). First we know he was a Jew, but a renegade Jew. No traditional Jew would violate the proscription against occult practices in Deuteronomy 18 and seek a reputation as a *magos,* a "magician" or "sorcerer." He is also called a false prophet, not in the sense of foretelling future events but claiming to channel divine revelation. The statement that he was "with" the proconsul indicates he had gained some influence with him.

Elymas apparently saw Sergius Paulus's interest in the gospel as a threat to his position, so he "withstood" the missionaries, "seeking to turn the proconsul away from the faith" (Acts 13:8).

Paul's response to Elymas (13:9–11). The apostle openly condemned Elymas as a "son of the devil." Elymas was no Barjesus (deliverer). He was a *huie diabolou* (deceiver, or son of the devil)! As such, he was an "enemy of all righteousness" who was intent on perverting the "straight ways of the Lord." That is, Elymas was intent on twisting the truth.

Having exposed Elymas for what he was, Paul pronounced judgment. "You shall be blind, not seeing the sun for a time" (Acts 13:11). Luke makes it clear that this pronouncement was not an impulsive one. Paul was "filled with the Holy Spirit" (Acts 13:9) when he acted, and "the hand of the Lord" caused the blindness (Acts 13:11).

Some commentators have seen echoes of Paul's own temporary blindness in this judgment. Although both Saul and Elymas opposed Christianity, there was a significant difference between them. Elymas was a renegade Jew who had knowingly violated Old Testament Law; Saul was a Pharisee zealous for God's glory. The fact that the blindness of Elymas was temporary is a striking indication of God's grace.

A judgment miracle. The miracles performed by Jesus were "positive" miracles, involving restoration to health and well-being. Demons were cast out, the disabled were healed, the dead were restored to life. Even nature miracles such as those on the Sea of Galilee stilled storms rather than created them.

In contrast, several of the supportive miracles and wonders that demonstrated Jesus' continuing presence with his people were miracles of divine judgment. Ananias and Sapphira were struck dead when they conspired to lie and thus test the Holy Spirit. Herod Antipas was struck dead by an angel. Now Elymas, who resisted the preaching of the gospel to Sergius Paulus, was struck with blindness.

It is appropriate that all of Jesus' miracles were worked on behalf of people. But it is also appropriate that in the apostolic age the Lord supported the preaching of the gospel with both miracles of healing and miracles of judgment.

The outcome of the miracle (13:11, 12). When Paul pronounced judgment, Elymas "immediately" was blinded, and "he went around seeking someone to lead him by the hand." This phrase is significant. Elymas had to search for someone to lead him, because all would draw back! Elymas had been cursed by God, and all who knew would fear association with him.

What a reversal of fortunes. Elymas instantly lost all influence with others. Those who had honored him now feared him, and no one would have anything to do with him.

Luke revealed that the miracle had an impact on the proconsul of the island as well. Sergius Paulus "believed, when he saw what had been done" (v. 12). It is uncertain whether "believed" is used in the sense of being con-

Elymas was blinded for opposing the gospel.

vinced that Paul was God's spokesman, or whether "believed" is used in the sense of having saving faith in Jesus. While the Sergius Paulus family is known from other documents, no evidence for or against a Christian branch of that family exists.

PAUL HEALS A CRIPPLE AT LYSTRA
Acts 14:8–20

In the Lycaonian city of Lystra, which had become a Roman colony in 6 B.C., Paul healed a cripple. The missionaries were hailed as gods, come down in the likeness of men.

A violent response to miracles and wonders (Acts 14:1–7). When Jesus performed his miracles, the people responded by giving glory to God. Many may not have accepted his messianic claims, but Christ's healings were met with approval and praise.

In Acts, as the gospel message spread into the Roman world, we see a different kind of response. Before going to Lystra, Paul and his missionary team had preached in Iconium.

Many people, both Jews and Greeks (i.e., non-Jews), believed. Luke tells us that the Lord bore witness to the message in Iconium by "granting signs and wonders" to be done by the apostles (14:3).

But most of the Jewish population resisted Paul and his message. The dispute spread so that the entire population of the city was divided. Finally, "a violent attempt" that involved the city officials, Jews, and Gentiles to "abuse and stone" the missionaries forced the missionaries out of Iconium.

The "signs and wonders" failed to create openness to the gospel. Just as the miracles of the Exodus had the effect of hardening the heart of Pharaoh (see page 68), these miracles of Paul seemed to polarize public opinion and intensify hostility to the gospel message.

The Healing in Lystra (14:8–10). After leaving Iconium, the missionary team moved on to Lystra. While preaching there, Paul noted that a disabled man was listening intently. Luke emphasizes the seriousness of the man's disability: he was "a cripple from his mother's womb, who had never walked" (Acts 14:10).

Luke also emphasizes another element in this healing. Paul perceived that "he had faith to be healed" (Acts 14:9). The observation is significant.

It implies divine revelation. "Faith" is not something that is observable. While the Bible does teach that faith will produce works, in this case the necessary time for faith's flowering was lacking. Paul was given insight by God to see into this hearer's heart.

It implies a spontaneous miracle. Paul had not planned to launch his ministry in Lystra with a miracle. But he perceived an awakened faith in his crippled hearer, so he responded spontaneously by commanding him to "stand up straight on your feet" (v. 10).

It implies a "family" miracle. When Paul perceived that the man had faith in Jesus, he called on him to stand. The man's faith was not the cause of the healing, although it was the cause of his response to Paul's command. What seems significant, however, is that this was a family miracle, performed to meet the need of a new brother in Christ. It was not a miracle intended to authenticate Paul as God's spokesman.

The majority of New Testament miracles were family miracles. They were performed for those who had confidence in Jesus and who showed that confidence. We need to remember that the faith spoken of in such incidents is *not* faith in healing, but faith in Jesus. How gracious he is to his own.

The people of Lystra mistook Paul and Barnabas for gods (Acts 14:11, 12). What is most impressive about Luke's account of this miracle is the excitement of the onlookers. They shouted that "the gods have come to us in the likeness of men" (v. 11). Immediately the priest of Zeus prepared a sacrifice to offer to the two startled missionaries.

The details in passages of the Bible often refute the claims of critics. Luke's report of the reaction of the people of Lystra and their identification of Barnabas as Zeus and Paul as Hermes (Apollo) is one of those details that rings especially true.

The people of the area worshiped these two pagan gods. An ancient legend recorded by the poet Ovid (43 B.C.—A.D. 17) about fifty years before the missionarys' visit told of how these two deities visited the hill country of Phrygia where Lystra was located. The two gods came disguised as mortals looking for a place to stay and were turned away from a thousand homes.

Finally they were welcomed to the simple straw cottage of an aged couple. The homes of the inhospitable thousand were destroyed by the gods, while the cottage of the two old people was transformed into a golden temple. They were ordained priest and priestess of the temple and transformed into ever-living trees.

With this background, we can understand why the citizens of Lystra were so eager to honor "gods" noted for rewarding—and punishing!

"They tore their clothes and ran in among the multitude" (Acts 14:14). The people of Lystra had apparently been speaking in their own language. When the sacrificial animals [*taurous,* bulls] were brought out, the apostles realized what had happened and ran in among the crowd to stop them.

It is clear from later events that Paul's words to this crowd about the emptiness of idolatry and the goodness of the true God fell on deaf ears. When Jews from Iconium and Antioch arrived, the crowds not only turned against the missionaries but even stoned Paul, dragging him outside the city and leaving him for dead!

The miracle of healing had failed to open a door for the gospel. As in Iconium earlier, the miracle had only caused confusion and heightened antagonism against Paul and Barnabas.

Paul revived (19:20). Some have interpreted Paul's revival after the stoning as a miracle. But the text does not say that Paul was dead. It states that the people of the city dragged him outside and left him for dead. When the rest of his party gathered around him, Paul revived and got up. The next day they left Lystra for the nearby town of Derbe.

The significance of the miracle. On one level, the report of this and other miracles by Paul parallel the miracles of Peter, who had also healed a man who had been lame from birth (Acts 3; see p. 251). While Paul had not been one of Jesus' original disciples, he was personally called and commissioned by Jesus. The parallel between the miracles of Peter and Paul confirm his role as an apostle of equal authority to Peter and the others.

This miracle, however, like those performed by Paul in Iconium, highlights an important reality. Like the miracles of Moses in Egypt, these miracles hardened resistance to God's Word rather than producing faith.

It seems unwise to argue, as some do, that we should expect miracles to be performed by missionaries in territories where

the gospel is being introduced. The apostle Paul reminds us that faith comes by hearing, and hearing by the Word of God (Rom. 10:13–15). While a miracle was performed for a cripple who had faith, that miracle did not lead to the mass conversion of the crowd who listened to Paul without faith.

CASTING OUT A DEMON IN PHILIPPI   *Acts 16:16–40*

In Philippi Paul cast a demon out of a slave girl who told fortunes. Her angry masters incited a riot, and Paul and Silas were beaten and imprisoned. An earthquake opened the prison doors, leading to the jailer's conversion.

Fortunetellers in the New Testament world (Acts 16:16). Awe of the occult and a superstitious reliance on oracles was common in the first-century Hellenistic world. People with epilepsy were considered touched by the gods, and words they muttered in an epileptic episode were viewed as divine utterances. Cult oracles, like the Oracle of Delphi, inhaled fumes to put them in a trance. Their troubled mutterings were interpreted by priests, who recast them as cryptic or ambiguous proverbs which permitted several interpretations.

In Philippi, however, the apostles met a slave girl whose utterances were stimulated by a demon who possessed her. This girl's utterances were not muttered phrases but plain speech: "These men are the servants of the Most High God, who proclaim to us the way of salvation" (v. 17).

It's not surprising that a fortuneteller with a supernatural source of information, and especially one who spoke plainly, should earn her masters a significant income.

Paul exorcised the fortuneteller's demon (16:17–18). Paul was annoyed by the fortuneteller's attention. For a few days he said nothing as she followed the missionaries around, screaming [*ekrazen*] her utterances. The demon-inspired words were not only tainted testimony; they received more attention than the gospel itself, as observers discussed her rather than Christ.

Finally, Paul commanded the spirit who possessed the girl to leave her.

The girl's owners incited the crowd against Paul and Silas (16:19–21). This first miracle freed the girl from the evil being who inhabited her. But it also stripped her of her powers, and this made her owners furious. Their hope of profit was gone; the girl was now useless to them. Their reaction was to strike out at Paul and Silas.

The angry owners of the slave girl aroused a mob by accusing Paul and Silas of being Jews who taught an illicit [unauthorized] religion. At this time, Jews made up about one-tenth of the population of the Roman Empire, and it was not illegal for Jews to seek converts. But a great deal of anti-Semitism existed in the first-century Roman Empire, in part because of the Jews' separatist ways and their religious beliefs. The girl's masters fanned the flames of this anti-Semitic sentiment by labeling Paul and Silas "these Jews," while appealing to their listeners' pride of "being Romans."

Paul and Silas were taken before the city magistrates and beaten (16:22, 23). The hostile mob dragged Paul and Silas before the city magistrates. Without questioning Paul and Silas, the magistrates tore off their clothes and ordered them flogged and imprisoned.

Paul and Silas imprisoned (16:23–24). The jailer rigidly followed the magistrates' order to keep the two men "securely." He not only put them in the *esotera*, the innermost cell in the prison, but he also placed their feet in stocks. These wooden instruments, anchored to the floor, were designed with several holes or notches, so the prisoner's legs could be forced apart and held in an unnatural position. Stocks were as much an instrument of torture as imprisonment, since it was impossible to avoid cramping. The fact that the apostles were immediately placed in stocks indicates that torture was intended.

BIBLE BACKGROUND:

ROMAN PRISONS

Prisons have been excavated in various first-century Roman cities. Many references in literature of this era also provide insight into prison conditions. Prisons were frequently overcrowded, and prisoners slept on the floor wrapped in their cloaks (compare Acts 12:8; 2 Tim. 4:13). Hot in the summer, freezing in winter, with little or no ventilation, prisons were breeding grounds for disease. The stone cells were dark, admitting little light from outside. This was especially true in the most secure cells, like the one where Paul and Silas were left that night. The Greek word commonly rendered "dungeon" is *tenebrae*, which means "darkness." The apostle's stay in prison in Philippi was probably in complete darkness.

The darkness associated with prisons was viewed in ancient literature as one of their primary torments. An item in the *Theodosian Code* of A.D. 320 contained this word on prison reform:

> When incarcerated he [the prisoner] must not suffer the darkness of an inner prison, but he must be kept in good health by the enjoyment of light, and when night doubles the necessity for his guard, he shall be taken back into the vestibules of the prisons and into healthful places. When day returns, at early sunrise, he shall forthwith be led into the common light of day that he may not perish from the torments of prison [Cod. Theod. 9.3.1 (=Cod. Just. 9.4.1 [353 AD].

This item in the code explains how the other prisoners could listen to the two Christians singing hymns and praising God. Rather than double the guard at night, the Philippian jailer jammed all the prisoners into the most secure "inner prison" (v. 24) along with the two missionaries. This also explains why, after the earthquake, the jailer rushed first to the innermost cell of the prison, and how Paul could assure the jailer that none of the prisoners had escaped.

Paul and Silas praised God in the prison (16:25). The reaction of Paul and Silas to imprisonment must have stunned their fellow prisoners. In spite of the pain of the untreated wounds and bruises received during the beatings, the two Christians spent the hours between sunset and midnight "praying and singing hymns to God."

By their actions, the two missionaries set a precedent that other believers in the Roman Empire were to follow. As the Christian message exploded across the empire, it began to threaten the social fabric. As the decades passed, both informal and official persecution of Christians developed. Many thousands were imprisoned, while others were martyred for their faith. The bright faith of these dedicated men and women is a reflection of that which led Paul and Silas to sing in the darkness.

As a later writer asked, "Well now, pagans, do you still believe that Christians, for whom awaits the joy of eternal light, feel the torments of prison or shrink from the dungeons of this world? . . . Dedicated as they are to God the Father, their brothers care for them by day, Christ by night as well." [Mart. Mar & James: 6.1, 3, 259 AD] The gloom of Roman dungeons was never able to extinguish the flame of faith—a faith that seemed to burn brighter in the darkness.

A miracle earthquake opened the prison doors (16:26–29). At midnight an earthquake hit. The foundations of the prison were shaken, the doors swung open, and everyone's chains were loosed.

The prison keeper rushed from his residence and saw the prison doors open. His suicide attempt reflects the fact that in the Roman Empire a jailer who let a prisoner escape was

Paul and Silas prayed and sang hymns in the Philippian jail.

to receive the penalty due the prisoner [see *Code of Justinian* 9.4.4] and that in Roman culture suicide was considered an honorable alternative. Suicide would prevent the forfeiting of all family assets in some cases, and a man who cared for his wife and children might kill himself to preserve their inheritance.

Before he could act, however, Paul shouted out, assuring the jailer that "we are all here" (v. 28). The jailer's reaction suggests that he had heard the missionary's message. He called for a light, carried it into the dark innermost cell, and fell trembling at Paul's feet.

The jailer and his household found Christ (16:30–34).

The earthquake, miraculous because of its timing rather than its occurrence in this geologically unstable area, did not win the release of the prisoners by itself. Rather, the earthquake was interpreted by the jailer as proof that these men were indeed "servants of the Most High God." The words of the fortuneteller had not moved this practical retired soldier. But the earthquake compelled conviction. Shaken in heart as well as body, the jailer asked, "Sirs, what must I do to be saved" (v. 30).

Paul's answer has often been misunderstood. "Believe on the Lord Jesus Christ, and you will be saved" is direct and clear. But then Paul added "you and your household." What did he mean?

In the Roman world, the "household," or family, was not defined primarily by kinship but by dependence and subordination. Aristotle's *Politica,* 1,2,1 showed the same notion in Greek culture. He pointed out, "The household in its perfect form consists of slaves and freedmen." The head of the Roman household was responsible for—and expected some degree of submission from—his wife and children, his slaves, former slaves, hired laborers and tenants, clients, and sometimes even business associates.

It is not at all unusual in ancient literature to find references to an individual's "house" or "household," with the added phrase "and his wife and children." In the five times in Acts that Luke mentions "houses" (10:2; 11:14;

16:15; 16:31; 18:8), it is clear that the references are to individuals of relatively high social status and that the term encompasses more than the individual's immediate kin.

What did Paul imply, then? First of all, Paul was saying that the salvation by faith in Jesus Christ which he offered the Philippian jailer was not just available to him. It was available to everyone in the jailer's household, whatever his or her social status. The gospel is for adult and child, for master and slave, for high and low.

But Paul implied more. In the Roman world, the father as head of the household was responsible for carrying out religious rituals and maintaining a pious household. It was assumed that the family would practice the religion of the *pater familias,* the father [head] of the family.

With a few brief words, Paul reassured the Philippian jailer that responding to the message of Christ did not threaten the established social order! The Philippian jailer could accept Christ and the salvation he offered, confident that the gospel was for his whole household, and that his role in the family was not threatened by the new faith.

Ultimately, of course, each member of the household would accept or reject the gospel for himself or herself. But the influence of the head of the household was such that most would follow his lead and make a true heart-commitment to the Lord. This is exactly what happened in Philippi, for the jailer "rejoiced, having believed in God with all his household" (v. 34).

This incident had begun with the miracle of casting out a demon and continued with the miracle of a quake that opened doors. It concluded with the miracle of salvation experienced by the Philippian jailer and his household—perhaps the greatest miracle of all.

PAUL RESTORES THE LIFE OF EUTYCHUS   *Acts 20:7–12*

One night as Paul was speaking, a sleepy young man fell from a window and was killed. Paul restored him to life.

Paul's journey (Acts 20:1–6). The apostle Paul had determined to go to Jerusalem in time for the feast of Pentecost. Although he was in a hurry, Paul used every spare moment to teach in churches along the way.

Teaching in Troas (20:7–9). Paul and his friends spent seven days in Troas. On the Sunday before taking ship, Paul spoke to the believers "until midnight." Luke describes the setting. Paul taught in an upstairs room, lit by torches. The heat they generated and the lateness of the hour caused a young man named Eutychus to doze, finally "sinking into a deep sleep."

Eutychus's death (20:9). The "window" where Eutychus was sleeping was probably a slitted opening in the wall. He tumbled from this perch and, according to Luke the physician, who was present, "was taken up dead."

Paul restored Eutychus (20:10). Paul went downstairs, "embraced" Eutychus, and announced that "his life is in him." Some have taken this as a diagnosis rather than a miraculous restoration. However, Luke does not say that Eutychus "appeared" dead, but that he was dead. Luke wanted us to understand that Paul, like Peter, restored life to a person who had died.

Miracles of resuscitation. This miracle performed by the apostle Paul completes the series of resuscitation miracles recorded in Scripture. Seen together, there is compelling balance.

Resuscitation Miracles in the Bible

1 Kings 17:21	Elijah	restored a widow's child
2 Kings 4:34–35	Elisha	restored a Shunamite's child
Mark 5:35–43	Jesus	restored Jairus's daughter
Luke 7:11–14	Jesus	restored a widow's son
John 11	Jesus	restored Lazarus
Acts 9:36–42	Peter	restored Dorcas
Acts 20:7–12	Paul	restored Eutychus

Thus, two Old Testament prophets raised the dead while two New Testament apostles raised

the dead. In each of these four instances, the individual who was restored had died recently, probably within a few hours. Jesus, appropriately, restored the dead three times. And the third restoration, that of Lazarus, took place after Lazarus had been dead four days.

There were also two similar miracles mentioned in passing. A dead man dumped into Elisha's grave was restored to life when his body touched that prophet's bones (2 Kings 13:20–22). And when Jesus died on the cross, an earthquake opened a number of graves and "many bodies of the saints who had fallen asleep were raised" (Matt. 27:52).

The pattern of these miracles demonstrates a striking symmetry. Elijah and Elisha stand parallel with Peter and Paul. But Jesus remains supreme, both in the number of such miracles and in the level of difficulty displayed in the raising of Lazarus.

Scripture wants us to remember that Christ truly is the source of life. He who was the lifegiver as Yahweh of the Old Testament era is also lifegiver as Lord of the New Testament. Jesus is both Yahweh and Lord.

PAUL'S HEALING OF PUBLIUS'S FATHER   Acts 28:7–10

The last miracles recorded in Acts are healing miracles. They were performed by Paul while he was shipwrecked on the island of Malta.

The situation. Paul had been arrested in Jerusalem. Because he was a Roman citizen, he was transported to Caesarea, the seaport city which served as the Roman administrative center for Jewish lands. He remained under house arrest at Caesarea for two years. Finally, Paul exercised his right to be tried in Rome and officially "appealed to Caesar." Paul was then sent under guard on the long sea journey to Rome.

Caught in a terrible storm, the ship was driven aimlessly for two weeks before running aground on the island of Malta. Paul, encouraged by an angel, had promised that if everyone stayed with the ship, no lives would be lost. It happened as he said, and all 276 persons on board got safely to land.

On shore, Paul was bitten by a deadly snake as he carried wood to the fire they had built to warm and dry the ship's company. The natives, who observed the poisonous creature hanging from Paul's hand, assumed he was a murderer whom "justice does not allow to live" (Acts 28:4). When Paul showed no effects from the bite, the people of the island decided he must be a god.

Paul's healing ministry (Acts 28:7–8). The survivors were sheltered by the "leading citizen" of the island, Publius. Inscriptions from Malta suggest that "leading citizen" was an official title. The father of the leading citizen was ill. Again Luke, the physician, provides a medical diagnosis. He suffered from "a fever and dysentery."

Paul prayed, laid hands on him, and healed him.

The reaction to the healing miracle (28:9, 10). The response of the islanders was twofold. First, all the diseased of the island came to Paul and were healed. Second, the islanders "honored" the missionaries, and "when we departed . . . provided such things as were necessary."

What is notable, however, is what was *not* recorded. Luke does not state or even suggest that any conversions resulted from the miracles! In fact, there is no mention of any conversions on Malta at all.

The significance of the miracle. This account of Paul's miracle-ministry again parallels that of Peter. Like Peter, Paul restored the life of a person who was dead. Like Peter—who gained such a reputation as a healer that he attracted crowds—Paul also won a reputation as a healer and crowds of sick and diseased persons came to him.

Paul, like Peter, was an apostle, authenticated by God through miracles.

Peter's miracles were performed in Jewish territory, demonstrating the continuing presence of Jesus with the early Jewish Christians. But Paul's miracles were performed in gentile lands. And these supportive miracles showed Jesus' world-wide power and presence.

THE MIRACLES OF ACTS *Summary and Review*

The book of Acts traced the history of the church from the ascension of Jesus through the next thirty years, up to the first imprisonment of Paul in Rome in approximately A.D. 62.

Luke built his history around the experiences of two leaders of the early Christian church—Peter and Paul. Peter, one of Jesus' original 12 disciples, preached the first gospel message to both Jews (Acts 2) and Gentiles (Acts 10). But most of Peter's ministry was to Jews in Jewish territory and in Jewish sections of cities of the Roman Empire.

Paul, on the other hand, was a reluctant convert, whose miraculous conversion transformed him into a committed missionary, dedicated to planting churches in Gentile lands. Paul's experience with Jesus commissioned him as an apostle, and he established churches in key cities in Roman Asia Minor and in Europe. Paul's letters to these churches stand, with the Gospels, as foundational Christian documents.

It is not surprising that Luke recorded miracles performed by both Peter and Paul. As we have noted, there is a pattern in the occurrence of the miracles recorded in Scripture.

First, they come in paired clusters. Second, they are associated with critical moments in the history of God's revelation of his purposes to humankind. Third, the first cluster in each pair (1) establishes a new body of truth, and (2) authenticates the person who introduces that body of truth as God's spokesman. Fourth, the second cluster in each pair demonstrates God's presence with those who accept and live by the new revelation.

The following chart compares these paired clusters, showing the function of the miracles in each period.

Exodus Miracles

Cluster One: The Plagues on Egypt

1. Yahweh is the God of Abraham, who keeps his covenant promises.
2. Moses is God's authentic messenger.

Cluster Two: Miracles in the Wilderness and Canaan

1. God is present to bless and judge his people when they live in accordance with Moses' Law.

Eighth-century Miracles

Cluster One: The Miracles of Elijah

1. Yahweh, not Baal, is the true God.
2. Elijah is God's authentic messenger.

Cluster Two: The Miracles of Elisha

1. God is present to bless a people who honor him as Lord.

First-century Miracles

Cluster One: The Miracles of Jesus

1. Jesus is the bringer of the promised new covenant which replaces Moses' Law.
2. Jesus is God's authentic messenger, the Messiah and Son of God.

Cluster Two: The Miracles of the Early Church

1. Jesus is present to bless those who accept him as Messiah and Lord.
2. Peter and Paul are God's authentic messengers, and their teachings are true.

When we think about how miracles touch the lives of believers today, we should begin with an understanding of the function of miracles in biblical times, as reflected in the chart above.

Miracles marked the introduction of a fresh revelation of God's purpose. And miracles authenticated as God's spokesmen the individuals whom God called to speak for him.

CHAPTER 13

MIRACLES PAST—
AND FUTURE!

SIGNS AND WONDERS
The Epistles; Revelation

Another age of miracles is coming!
The apostle Paul writes about it in 2 Thessalonians. The apostle John predicts it in Revelation. But these miracles are to be Satanic in origin. How can we tell the difference between real miracles and "lying wonders"? The New Testament epistles teach us many things about miracles. And Revelation provides a picture of future miracles.

REFERENCES TO MIRACLES AND WONDERS IN THE EPISTLES

The language of miracles occurs only eight times in the New Testament Epistles. Romans 15:19 refers to signs and wonders. The Greek word translated miracles (*dunamis*) occurs in 1 Corinthians 12:10, 28, 29 and in Galatians 3:5. "Miracles, signs and wonders" are used together in 2 Corinthians 12:2 and Hebrews 2:4. And 2 Thessalonians 2:9 speaks of "all power [*dunamei*, "miracles"], signs and lying wonders."

ROMANS 15:18, 19

I will not dare to speak of any of those things which Christ has not accomplished through me, in word and deed, to make the Gentiles obedient—in mighty signs and wonders, by the power of the Spirit of God, so that from Jerusalem and round about to Illyricum I have fully preached the Gospel of Christ.

The context in which this verse appears. Romans 15:14 marks a change of subject in the letter. The apostle Paul moved from instruction and exhortation to share more personal matters. He reminded the church in Rome that he was writing to them as an apostle called by God to minister to Gentiles. Paul went on to share the passion which had motivated him, a passion to preach the gospel "not where Christ was named," but in lands where no one has yet heard the good news (Rom. 15:20). He mentioned "mighty signs and wonders" as miracles which the Holy Spirit had performed through him as evidence of Christ's calling to his ministry.

The interpretation of the verses. Paul appealed to miracles as evidence of a very special "grace given to me by God" (Rom. 15:15). The miracles which he has performed are divine

Paul wrote letters to churches he had established, and some he had never visited.

proof of his position as a apostle of Jesus Christ.

1 CORINTHIANS 12:9, 10, 28–30

Gifts of healing by the same Spirit, to another the working of miracles (1 Cor. 12:9, 10).

And God has appointed these in the church: first apostles, second prophets, third teachers, after that miracles, then gifts of healings, helps, administrations, varieties of tongues. Are all apostles? Are all prophets? Are all teachers? Are all workers of miracles? Do all have gifts of healing? (1 Cor. 12:28–30).

The context in which these verses occur. In 1 Corinthians 12—14, Paul took up an issue which had troubled the church in Corinth. The Christians there had taken the more obviously supernatural workings of the Holy Spirit through believers as evidence that those with such gifts were more "spiritual" than others. In fact, the Corinthians had fastened on the gift of tongues (speaking in an unintelligible "spiritual" language) as the premier indicator of a believer's closeness to the Lord.

In order to correct this misunderstanding, Paul taught in 1 Corinthians 12 that every believer has at least one spiritual gift. He pointed out these gifts were the method by which the Holy Spirit ministered through people to build up other believers. The exercise of any gift was an expression of the Holy Spirit's working, and spiritual gifts were distributed by the Spirit as he willed (1 Cor. 12:7, 11). According to Paul, this meant the gift a person had was *not* an indicator of spirituality (i.e., one's closeness to the Lord, or harmony with his will).

Paul then went on in 1 Corinthians 13 to show that the true indicator of spirituality is love, not the gift a person may possess.

Finally, in 1 Corinthians 14 Paul returned to the question of tongues. He pointed out that if gifts were to be ranked, this should be done on the basis of the contribution the gift makes to the edification of the body. On this basis, prophecy or teaching would be near the top of the list. Tongues would rank near the bottom because they are unintelligible and thus not edifying to others.

References to miracles and healings in the passage. The subject of this extended section of 1 Corinthians is not miracles or miraculous gifts. This makes their mention in the passage even more striking. Paul clearly assumed miracles and healings were not unusual events in Corinth. It seems the Corinthians had been experiencing both miracles and healings. Apparently, these were commonly recognized ways in which the Holy Spirit had been at work in this Christian community.

At the same time, it is perhaps significant that this is the only passage in Scripture in which both miracles and healings are spoken of in this way. In two other passages in which spiritual gifts are listed—Romans 12 and Ephesians 4—no reference to tongues, miracles, or healing occurs.

The almost casual references to miracles and healing as spiritual gifts in this passage, but not in other passages on gifts, raises an important question. Just what can we assume from the biblical evidence? And what can we *not* conclude?

Miracles and healings are valid spiritual gifts. It is clear from 1 Corinthians 12 that in Corinth at least the Holy Spirit did gift believers with the ability to perform miracles and to heal. As the Holy Spirit is free in his sovereignty to distribute gifts "as he wills" (1 Cor. 12:11), we have no basis for saying that the Holy Spirit cannot or will not distribute the same gifts in our own day—or any other time.

Miracles and healing gifts are referred to only in 1 Corinthians. This raises several questions. Why aren't these gifts mentioned in parallel passages on spiritual gifts? Why aren't healings mentioned in *any* other New Testament epistle as elements in Christian experience?

One possibility is that these gifts functioned in Corinth, but they did not operate in the other New Testament churches. This is certainly a possibility. There may have been

———————— ❖ ————————

Jesus' miracles continued with His apostles.

unique factors which called for these gifts in Corinth but not, say, in the church at Ephesus. But we have no idea of what these factors might have been. And we have no reason to suppose that conditions in one city of the Roman Empire were radically different from the situation in another city.

In short, we simply don't know why these gifts are mentioned only in reference to Corinth. It's impossible to say why miracles and healings seem to have been performed by some Corinthian believers, and why no mention of miraculous healing is found in any other epistle.

Were miracles and healings for the first century only? First Corinthians 13:8, in speaking of the value of love, declares, "Whether there are prophecies, they will fail; whether there are tongues, they will cease; whether there is knowledge, it will vanish away." Some have argued from the reference to tongues "ceasing" that this gift operated only during the decades during which the church was founded.

Even though 1 Corinthians 13:8 says nothing about miracles or healings, those who hold this position argue that "tongues" represents all the supernatural gifts of 1 Corinthians 12 which were visible. Their conviction is that these supernatural gifts operated only in the period before the canon of Scripture was complete. With the writing of the last book of the New Testament, the need for the miraculous ended.

This is an interpretation which assumes more from the biblical text than is obvious. It is always a problem to build an important doctrine on a single verse of Scripture, especially when only indirect evidence and supposition support the interpretation.

A more serious objection to this position is that it tends to rule out the *possibility* of miracles, healings, or tongues in our day. In essence, it puts God in a box, declaring that the Holy Spirit cannot work today through believers in a method which he used in the first century. Any affirmation which places limits on God's freedom to act is suspect.

We really cannot limit the possibility of miracles, healings, and tongues to the first century or to the Corinthian community.

Miracles, healings, and tongues are a possibility in any age, including our own time. It is important to remember that agreeing such happenings are a possibility today is not the same as saying that miracles and healings are commonplace. Neither should we declare on the basis of the limited evidence we have that they happen infrequently. All we can affirm from the 1 Corinthians passage is that God can and does perform miracles, and that the Holy Spirit can enable believers as agents to perform miracles and to heal. Whether he chooses to do so in any given situation is entirely up to God.

2 CORINTHIANS 12:12

Truly the signs of an apostle were accomplished among you with all perseverance, in signs and wonders and mighty deeds [*miracles*].

The context in which this verse appears. Paul's second letter to the Corinthians contains an extended defense of his ministry. Paul's apostolic authority had been challenged in Corinth by persons representing themselves as leaders of the Jerusalem church and carrying letters of commendation to establish their "authority." In this most revealing of Paul's letters, the apostle shared freely the principles on which his new covenant ministry had been based.

Evidence of apostolic calling and authority (2 Corinthians 12:12). In these verses, Paul called his ministry "in signs and wonders and mighty deeds [*miracles*]" the "signs of an apostle." These were proof that "in nothing was I behind the most eminent apostles" (2 Cor. 12:11).

It is somewhat surprising that Paul called these wonder-working abilities "signs of an apostle." After all, Paul had spoken in 1 Corinthians 12 of such powers as gifts of the Holy Spirit, implying that ordinary believers might possess them. Yet it is clear from the book of Acts that the ministries of both Peter and Paul were often marked by miracles, especially healing miracles. This may indeed be the difference. The apostle worked many such miracles, and thus was authenticated as God's spokesman. The number, frequency, and function of gift-miracles may have been significantly less.

Conclusions. All we can conclude from this passage is that the ministry of Jesus' 12 apostles and Paul were marked by the performance of miracles and wonders. We have no information on how common non-apostolic miracles were in the New Testament era.

GALATIANS 3:5

Therefore he who supplies the Spirit to you and works miracles among you, does he do it by the works of the law, or by the hearing of faith?

The context in which this verse appears. In the book of Galatians, Paul wrote to a congregation which had been led astray concerning the role of faith and works. Paul's careful argument in the book demonstrated that salvation is by faith alone, and that the Law given by Moses had no role in establishing personal relationship with God.

Paul also argued that the believer relates to God by being responsive to the Holy Spirit, not by keeping the Law. The Galatians received the Holy Spirit by faith and not by "the works of the law" (Gal. 3:2). Why then would they imagine that progress in the Christian life comes by making an effort to keep God's law rather than by walking in the Spirit (Gal. 5:25) and letting the Spirit produce in us his own unique fruit (Gal. 5:22, 23)?

The reference to miracles in Galatians 3:5. Here, as in 1 Corinthians 12, the passage in which miracles are mentioned is not *about* miracles. Paul referred to miracles, *as though the Galatians were familiar with them.* In fact, the text spoke of working "miracles among you" as though miracles were even commonplace occurrences.

Clearly in the experience of at least two New Testament Gentile churches, miracles seem to have been more or less expected.

While we cannot generalize from this to conclude that miracles were commonplace in all the New Testament churches, this text—along with similar comments in 1 Corinthians 12—is certainly suggestive. Yet we cannot generalize from the experience of the churches in Acts and the Epistles by declaring that miracles *ought* to be found in churches of our day.

HEBREWS 2:4

God also bearing witness both with signs and wonders, with various miracles, and gifts of the Holy Spirit, according to his own will.

The context in which this verse appears. The book of Hebrews was written to demonstrate to Jewish believers the superiority of the new covenant initiated by Jesus to the old covenant introduced by Moses. In Hebrews 1, the author carefully established the superiority of Jesus to angels. The reason for this was that the Jews believed angels had been mediators of the Law given on Mount Sinai.

In chapter 2 of Hebrews, the writer drew an initial conclusion. If the "word spoken through angels" was binding, and every transgression was punished, how much more dangerous it was to neglect the great salvation first spoken by the Lord himself (Heb. 2:3).

Miracles confirmed the message spoken by Jesus. Hebrews 2:4 points out that the words spoken by Jesus were confirmed by God himself. The miracles, signs, and wonders Jesus performed were God's witness to him and to the truths he revealed.

This reference views miracles as authenticating signs, which confirmed the One who performed them as God's spokesman, and which served as the divine stamp of approval on what Jesus said and did. This reference refers back to the ministry of Jesus on earth. It is not relevant to the questions of modern miracles or to questions about the role of miracles in first-century Christianity.

2 THESSALONIANS 2:9

The coming of the lawless one is according to the working of Satan, with all power [*dunamis,* "miracle"], signs and lying wonders.

The context in which this verse appears. In his second letter to the Thessalonians, Paul corrected certain misunderstandings about the future. Some believers in the church had assumed that Jesus' second coming had already taken place. Paul described what would happen when Jesus did return—openly and accompanied by mighty angels—to punish and judge the unbelieving world (1 Thess. 1:7–10).

In chapter two, Paul pointed out that this day could not possibly have happened yet because certain events must precede Jesus' return. In particular, a "lawless one" [the Antichrist] would be revealed. There would be no mistaking his appearance because it would be marked by a new age of miracles! But this time, the extraordinary events would be caused by Satan rather than God! In judgment, God will send a "strong delusion" (2 Thess. 2:11) on those who have rejected Christ. They will be convinced by the "lying wonders" of Satan and follow the Antichrist in the great rebellion against God which precedes Jesus' return.

The implications of 2 Thessalonians 2:4. In previous chapters of this book, we have noted that clusters of miracles are associated with the introduction of significant new revelations from God. Groups of miracles have clustered around the Exodus story and the 40-year ministry of Moses in the 1400s B.C. They have clustered around the ministries of Elijah and Elisha in the 700s B.C. And they have clustered around the ministry of Jesus and the founding of the church.

What Paul suggests in 2 Thessalonians is that a fourth cluster of miracles lies ahead. But this cluster of miracles will involve "lying wonders" performed by Satan to deceive mankind into following the Antichrist in open rebellion against the Lord.

Implications of Paul's teaching in 2 Thessalonians. The first implication is that God is not the only one who can cause extraordinary events. Satan also seems to have the power to perform what we call miracles. Throughout biblical history, God has been the one who performed signs and wonders, but we must be open to the likelihood that "lying" wonders have been part of pagan religious experience.

We must also be aware that no miracle *in and of itself* is necessarily God's work. We need something more than miracles—or perhaps other than miracles—to show that a person or teaching is approved by God.

This is an issue that we will take up in the next chapter on miracles in the book of Revelation. For now, it is enough to note that we must be careful not to take miracles or wonders alone as sufficient authentication of anyone who claims to be God's spokesperson.

SITUATIONS WHICH MIGHT HAVE BEEN RESOLVED BY MIRACLES BUT WERE NOT

Our review of references to miracles and wonders in the Epistles has established several things.

First, miracles and signs and wonders did authenticate the ministry of Jesus (Heb. 2:4) and serve as authenticating signs for those with apostolic authority (2 Cor. 12:12).

Second, healing and miracles are also identified as spiritual gifts which God the Holy Spirit distributes. These clearly functioned in the Corinthian church, even though neither healing nor miracles is found on other New Testament lists of spiritual gifts.

Third, in letters to both the Corinthians and the Galatians the apostle Paul referred to miracles in such a way that it is clear they were familiar if not common occurrences in these congregations. But these miracles (*dunamis,* works of power) clearly did not have the same function as the numerous miracles which authenticated Jesus and then Peter and Paul as God's spokesmen.

Fourth, a new thought is introduced in 2 Thessalonians 2:4. Extraordinary events may be "lying wonders" caused by Satan rather than God. The experience of a miracle in and of itself is not sufficient proof that God's hand is involved—or that a person credited with performing miracles is God's servant.

But we have not yet established whether we should expect miracles in our day. The evidence from references to miracles in the Epistles is inconclusive on this point. So we need to look for additional evidence and ask other questions. One of the most important questions we can ask is, Did believers *expect* miracles when they had problems?

BELIEVERS AND THEIR SICKNESSES

Believers and their illnesses. Several passages speak of sickness among New Testament Christians. How did the writers of the Epistles deal with sickness? Four passages are particularly helpful in answering this question.

Paul's thorn in the flesh (2 Corinthians 12). Paul was troubled by a "thorn in the flesh." Most commentators believe this was a chronic illness of some kind, and many take it to refer to an eye disease. Paul tells us that his problem was a "messenger of Satan to buffet me" (2 Cor. 12:7).

Paul relates that he pleaded with the Lord three times, asking for healing (2 Cor. 12:8). But God told Paul "no," reminding the Apostle that God's strength is expressed through human weakness. Paul then stopped praying for the "thorn" to depart, and chose to praise God for his infirmity.

The life-threatening illness of Epaphroditus (Philippians 2:25–27). Epaphroditus, a close friend of Paul's, had come to visit the apostle, bringing an offering from the church at Philippi. While he was with the apostle, Ephaproditus became sick "almost unto death." This "brother, fellow worker, and fellow soldier" of Paul's did recover, which Paul credited to the mercy of God (Phil. 2:27).

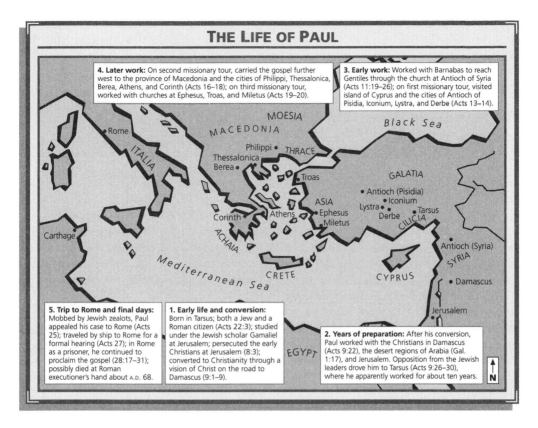

THE LIFE OF PAUL

4. Later work: On second missionary tour, carried the gospel further west to the province of Macedonia and the cities of Philippi, Thessalonica, Berea, Athens, and Corinth (Acts 16–18); on third missionary tour, worked with churches at Ephesus, Troas, and Miletus (Acts 19–20).

3. Early work: Worked with Barnabas to reach Gentiles through the church at Antioch of Syria (Acts 11:19–26); on first missionary tour, visited island of Cyprus and the cities of Antioch of Pisidia, Iconium, Lystra, and Derbe (Acts 13–14).

5. Trip to Rome and final days: Mobbed by Jewish zealots, Paul appealed his case to Rome (Acts 25); traveled by ship to Rome for a formal hearing (Acts 27); in Rome as a prisoner, he continued to proclaim the gospel (28:17–31); possibly died at Roman executioner's hand about A.D. 68.

1. Early life and conversion: Born in Tarsus; both a Jew and a Roman citizen (Acts 22:3); studied under the Jewish scholar Gamaliel at Jerusalem; persecuted the early Christians at Jerusalem (8:3); converted to Christianity through a vision of Christ on the road to Damascus (9:1–9).

2. Years of preparation: After his conversion, Paul worked with the Christians in Damascus (Acts 9:22), the desert regions of Arabia (Gal. 1:17), and Jerusalem. Opposition from the Jewish leaders drove him to Tarsus (Acts 9:26–30), where he apparently worked for about ten years.

Timothy's chronic stomach trouble (1 Timothy 5:23). In his first letter to Timothy, Paul gave his younger protégé advice on many matters. One of the most mundane pieces of advice was about Timothy's chronic stomach trouble, a common complaint in the first-century world where the water supply was often tainted. Paul's advice was, "No longer drink only water, but use a little wine for your stomach's sake and your frequent infirmities." That is, mix some wine in the water you drink to purify it.

James' advice concerning the sick (James 5:14–15). In his epistle, James, the brother of Jesus, said, "Is anyone among you sick? Let him call for the elders of the church, and let them pray over him, anointing him with oil in the name of the Lord. And the prayer of faith will save the sick, and the Lord will raise him up. And if he has committed sins, he will be forgiven." One interpreter commented on these verses:

This passage linking prayer, sickness, church elders, anointing with oil, and confession of sins has fascinated Christians throughout the ages.

Several things are clear from the text. (1) Prayer is needed when sickness comes. (2) One role of the elders of a church is to pray for the sick. (3) Prayer is primary, an active verb, and anointing with oil is secondary, expressed as a participle. (4) Oil was the most common ingredient in ancient medical treatments, and the verb describing its use (*aleipho*) means to "smear on" rather than the sacramental "to anoint" (*chrio*). Thus the passage teaches applications of both prayer and normal medical treatments. (5) "Confession" is important if sin should happen to be the cause of the sickness, and thus the sickness is disciplinary. (6) Since confession and prayer are associated with good health, it is important for Christians to be sensitive to sin, confess their sins to each other, and pray for each other (The *Bible Reader's Companion*, Chariot/Victor, 875).

Conclusions. It is clear from this brief survey that the normal approach in the first century when a Christian became sick was to come to

God in prayer and ask the Lord for healing. At the same time, the believers utilized the normal medical treatments available at the time. This is essentially the way most Christians today deal with sickness.

What is significant is that Paul did not perform a miraculous healing of either Epaphroditus or Timothy. Neither James nor Paul advised calling someone with the gift of healing or miracles when a brother fell sick. Instead, both advised prayer and medical treatment.

It seems from these facts that—in spite of the references to miracles in 1 Corinthians 12 and Galatians 3—it was neither typical nor "normal" to expect miracles or healings when Christians fell ill.

It is undoubtedly true, however, that the early Christians looked to and relied on the Lord to provide healing when sickness struck. But the healing they looked to God for was apparently what we would call "natural" healing—a normal recovery.

CHRISTIANS AND THEIR TRIALS

One of the things we realize if we read the New Testament carefully is that the early Christians didn't have an easy life. Their faith in Christ carried them through their sufferings. Most of them didn't expect deliverance through instant miracles.

Paul's account of his own sufferings (2 Corinthians 11:23–28. Earlier we looked at the Acts 16 description of Paul's miraculous release from prison in Philippi. It would be easy to assume that whenever the apostle was in difficulty, God simply performed a miracle and got his servant out of the uncomfortable situation. But Paul's own description of his life as a missionary quickly dispels any such impression:

Are they ministers of Christ?—I speak as a fool—I am more: in labors more abundant, in stripes [i.e., beatings] above measures, in prisons more frequently, in deaths often. From the Jews five times I received forty stripes minus one. Three times I was beaten with rods; once I was stoned; three times I

was shipwrecked; a night and a day I have been in the deep, in journeys often, in perils of waters, in perils of robbers, in perils of my own countrymen, in perils of the Gentiles, in perils in the city, in perils in the wilderness, in perils in the sea, in perils among false brethren; in weariness and toil, in sleeplessness often, in hunger and thirst, in fastings often, in cold and nakedness (2 Cor. 11:23–27).

Surely Paul was subject to intense pressures and danger. And just as surely, Paul did not expect or experience miracles to deliver him from these problems.

Peter's advice in view of coming persecutions (1 Peter). Peter's first epistle shows a great sensitivity to believers who are "grieved by various trials" (1 Peter 1:6). Nowhere in this letter did Peter offer any hope of miraculous interventions. Rather Peter told believers to commit themselves to a godly lifestyle and remember that Christ "suffered for us, leaving us an example, that you should follow his steps" (1 Peter 2:21). Peter even spoke of situations in which Christians do what is right, but suffer anyway (1 Peter 3:14f). In fact, Peter quite bluntly says,

Beloved, do not think it strange concerning the fiery trial which is to try you, as though some strange thing happened to you; but rejoice to the extent that you partake of Christ's sufferings, that when his glory is revealed, you may also be glad with exceeding joy (1 Peter 4:12, 13).

It should be clear from Paul's experience and from these words of the apostle Peter that Christians were not promised daily miracles. In fact, even when they faced extreme difficulty, the early Christians did not expect nor were they encouraged to expect miraculous deliverance.

Passages like these could be multiplied. But it is clear from this brief survey that miraculous deliverance from difficulties was not the norm in the early church. Whatever we may think of contemporary miracles, Scripture does not support the idea that we should expect them as commonplace. Rather, we are to trust the Lord, expecting him to provide the strength to live godly lives in and through our trials.

A miraculous earthquake freed Paul and Silas from the Philippian prison.

AUTHENTICATION OF GOD'S SPOKESMEN IN THE EPISTLES

We've seen that one function of the miraculous in Scripture was to mark individuals as authentic spokesmen for God. This was true in Old Testament times, and it was true of Jesus, Peter, and Paul as well.

AUTHENTICATION OF GOD'S SPOKESMEN IN OLD TESTAMENT TIMES

The Old Testament provided four tests by which a person who claimed to speak for God could be authenticated. Deuteronomy 18 taught that God's true prophets would be an Israelite (Deut. 18:18), who would speak in Yahweh's name (Deut. 18:19). In addition, whatever a true prophet spoke in the name of the Lord would "happen or come to pass" (Deut. 18:22). If a prophet's predictions did not come true, he could be ignored. He did not speak for the Lord.

The fourth test, in Deuteronomy 13:1–2, makes it clear that even the miraculous was not a sufficient test. What the prophet says must also be in harmony with God's revealed word.

If there arises among you a prophet or a dreamer of dreams, and he gives you a sign or a wonder, and the sign or the wonder comes to pass, of which he spoke to you, saying, 'Let us go after other gods—which you have not known—and let us serve them,' you shall not listen to the words of that prophet (Deut. 13:1–3).

This fourth test is important because it highlights the possibility that a fulfilled prediction, a sign, or a wonder might not come from God.

AUTHENTICATION OF GOD'S SPOKESMEN IN THE NEW TESTAMENT EPISTLES

There are several passages in Scripture which state principles for distinguishing God's authentic spokesmen from false teachers. Not one of these passages mentions miracles, signs, or wonders as valid authenticating signs.

A theological test. The apostle John in his first letter gives Christians a theological test. In chapter four John warned Christians to "test the spirits, whether they are of God; because many false prophets have gone out into the world" (1 John 4:1). John affirmed, "Every spirit that does not confess that Jesus Christ has come in the flesh is not of God" but is of the Antichrist (1 John 4:3). Belief in Jesus as God the Son incarnate is a theological test which Christians are always to apply to those who claim to be God's messengers and ministers.

This same emphasis is seen in 2 Peter 2:11, where false teachers are described as those who deny the Lord who bought them.

A lifestyle test. Both Jude and Peter described the personalities of false prophets and false teachers. They were bold and arrogant (2 Peter 2:10; Jude 16), they despised authority (2 Peter 2:10; Jude 3), they followed the corrupt desires of the sinful nature (2 Peter 2:10; Jude 4, 19), and they loved money and wealth (2 Peter 2:15; Jude 12).

These lifestyle descriptions contrast sharply with the lifestyle appropriate for Christian leaders, as given by the apostle Paul in 1 Timothy 3:1–9 and Titus 1:5–9.

A discernment test. In addition to these tests which help to identify false prophets and teachers, the early church was to rely on Spirit-led discernment to test specific teachings. In 1 Corinthians 14, Paul turned to the topic of orderly worship in a church meeting where all were welcome to participate. After establishing rules for the exercise of the gift of tongues, Paul said, "Let two or three prophets speak, and let the others judge" (1 Cor. 14:29). The word *judge* means to distinguish, to discern, to evaluate, and thus to judge. The "others" mentioned here were the elders of the church who had the responsibility of guarding the congregation.

This function was especially important in the early church, as the New Testament canon had not been completed. This meant there was no written revelation against which to measure the teachings of those who claimed to speak for the Lord.

Conclusions. It is significant that while the New Testament Epistles showed a deep concern for distinguishing true and false prophets and teachers, not one passage even suggested a miracle test like that for Old Testament prophets. Instead, the Epistles provided theological, lifestyle, and discernment tests to be used by the early Christians.

It seems clear that miracles and wonders simply were not considered to be authenticating tests which could be applied in local church settings. While "signs and wonders and mighty deeds [*miracles*]" were understood to be "the signs of an apostle" (2 Cor. 12:12), they were not expected of the itinerant teachers and evangelists who traveled from church to church across the Roman Empire.

MIRACLES AND WONDERS IN THE EPISTLES: A SUMMARY

Our review of references to miracles in the Epistles has led to several conclusions.

First, miracles and signs and wonders did authenticate both the ministry of Jesus (Heb. 2:4) and did serve as signs authenticating those with apostolic authority (2 Cor. 12:12).

Second, healings and miracles were identified as spiritual gifts which God the Holy Spirit distributed. These clearly functioned in the Corinthian church, even though neither healings nor miracles are found on other New Testament lists of spiritual gifts.

Third, in his letters to the Corinthians and the Galatians the apostle Paul's references to miracles implied that in both congregations these were familiar if not commonplace experiences. Yet such miracles (*dunamis,* works of power) did not have the same function as the numerous miracles which authenticated Jesus—and then Peter and Paul—as God's spokesmen.

When we raised the question of how the Epistles described dealing with sickness, we found a surprising fact. When the apostle Paul or his close friends became sick, Paul did not perform a healing miracle, or call for a person with the gift of healing. Paul simply prayed and, like the apostle James, recommended medical treatment.

In the same vein, the apostle Paul in 2 Corinthians 11 recounted his many trials. In none of them did the apostle expect or rely on miraculous deliverance. Similarly, 1 Peter's guidance on how Christians were to meet persecution and suffering made no mention of calling for or expecting miraculous divine intervention.

We find a similar pattern if we examine how the early church distinguished between true and false prophets and teachers. While the Epistles provided doctrinal and lifestyle tests, and expected Christians to exercise Spirit-led discernment, there is no evidence at all that miracles or wonders were means by which authentic messengers of God could be distinguished.

When we take all the evidence of the Epistles together, we are forced to conclude that miracles were not common in the apostolic age, nor were they normative for vital Christian churches.

While God can and does perform miracles, Christians apparently are not to *expect* miracles when faced with sickness or troubles. Instead, we are to meet life's trials with faith in Christ, finding in him the strength to endure and to overcome.

INTERPRETING THE BOOK OF REVELATION

Church history records a variety of ways in which the book of Revelation has been understood by Christians.

Revelation as a book of prophecy. The early church fathers saw Revelation as a book of prophecy. They linked its teachings with those of the Old Testament prophets and with Jesus' statements about the future, as recorded in Matthew 24 and Luke 13. During these early centuries Revelation was understood to describe future events which would surely take place on earth.

For instance, Justin Martyr drew from Revelation when he wrote, "I and as many are orthodox Christians, do acknowledge that there shall be a resurrection of the body, and a residence of a thousand years in Jerusalem, adorned and enlarged, as the prophets Ezekiel, Isaiah, and others so unanimously attest" (*Ante-Nicene Fathers,* Vol. I, 239).

Irenaeus, another church father who was also a famous missionary, gave this picture of the future as held by the early church. Again, this vision of the future incorporates information found in Revelation with the vision of the Old Testament prophets:

When the Antichrist shall have devastated all things in the world, he will reign for three years and six months, and sit in the temple at Jerusalem; and then shall the Lord come from heaven in clouds, in the glory of the Father, sending this man, and those who follow him, into the lake of fire (*Ante-Nicene Fathers,* Vol. I, 560).

The understanding of Revelation as prophecy destined to be literally fulfilled was maintained through the first four hundred years of church history.

Revelation as an allegory. About A.D. 390, a leader of the African church, Tyconius, allegorized Revelation. He assumed that the visions recorded in Revelation referred symbolically to hidden spiritual truths. The allegorical view of Revelation dominated until about A.D. 1200.

Revelation as a chronological document. Joachim of Fiore divided history into three ages—of the Father, Son, and Holy Spirit. Joachim divided Revelation according to this scheme. The Reformers adopted this chronological approach, and identified the Antichrist of chapter 13 and the harlot of Revelation 17—18 with the papacy and Rome. Catholic scholars were quick to respond and argue that the Antichrist was an individual who would appear at some future time. Yet neither Catholics nor Protestants attempted to relate the book of Revelation to the Old Testament prophets, as had the early church fathers.

Modern approaches to interpreting Revelation. In modern times, two views of Revelation predominate. Some hold the view of the early church, considering Revelation a prophetic description of things to come. Others continue to take revelation primarily as an allegory, filled with symbolism but powerfully conveying the truth that God is sovereign and that he will triumph at history's end.

MIRACLES IN THE BOOK OF REVELATION

Whatever approach we take to interpreting Revelation, we must be struck by two things about references to wonders and miracles in this fascinating book.

The first is that when the language of miracles is used, it describes extraordinary events produced not by God but by Satan or demonic powers. The second is that this book is filled with descriptions of extraordinary acts of judgment executed by angels at God's direction.

"LYING WONDERS"

Lying wonders were predicted by the apostle Paul. In writing to the Thessalonians, Paul presented a decisive argument to prove that Christ's second coming had not yet occurred. Paul wrote in his second letter to this church that "that Day will not come unless the falling away comes first, and the man of sin [the Antichrist] is revealed, the son of perdition, who opposes and exalts himself above all that is called God or that is worshiped, so that he sits as God in the temple of God, showing himself that he is God" (2 Thess. 2:3, 4). In making this statement, the apostle linked his teaching to Old Testament prophecies by Daniel (see Dan. 11:31; 12:11) and to Christ's own description of the future (Matt. 24:15f).

Paul then went on to state that "the coming of the lawless one [again, the Antichrist] is according to the working of Satan, with all power, signs and lying wonders" (2 Thess. 2:9). The appearance of this great enemy of God, a person who is energized by Satan himself, will initiate history's fourth great age of miracles.

We've seen that at pivotal points in history, fresh revelations by God of himself and his plans have been marked by clusters of miracles. What Paul is saying is that when a fourth age of miracles dawns, they will be worked by Satan and not God! They will be wonders. But they will be lying wonders, for God will not be their source. And the person they seem to authenticate will be Satan's man and not the Lord's.

These lying wonders are further described in the book of Revelation. When we scan Revelation for the language of miracles, we find the biblical words for miracles, signs, and wonders occur in the following verses.

Revelation 13:13, 14. "He performs great signs, so that he even makes fire come down from heaven on the earth in the sight of men. And he deceives those who dwell on the earth by those signs which he was granted to do in the sight of the beast."

The context of these verses. Revelation 13 introduces "the beast," an individual who is named the Antichrist only in 1 John 2:18 and 4:3. This individual is given political power and authority by "the dragon," another name for Satan (Rev. 20:2). The first beast, or Antichrist, is supported by "another beast." This second individual, identified as the "false prophet" in Revelation 16:13 and 19:20, is the one who performs the "great signs" described in this passage.

The purpose of the false prophet's signs. The miracles performed by the false prophet are in support of the Antichrist. These miracles help to convince humanity to worship both "the dragon who gave authority to the beast" and the Antichrist (Rev. 13:4, 15). They also help to consolidate his political power (Rev. 13:15–18).

There is no doubt, as reflected in the quotes from Justin Martyr and Irenaeus above, that this passage reflects the early church's understanding of Revelation 13.

Revelation 16:13, 14. "And I saw three unclean spirits like frogs coming out of the mouth of the dragon, out of the mouth of the beast, and out of the mouth of the false prophet. For they are spirits of demons, performing signs, which go out to the kings of the earth and of the whole world, to gather them to the battle of that great day of God Almighty."

The context of these verses. John's next mention of lying wonders is of demons "performing signs." Here as throughout the Old and New Testaments, "signs" are miracles which serve to authenticate a messenger and/or his message.

Again, the language of the verse has deep roots in the Old Testament. The phrase "that great day of God" is a constant theme of the Old Testament prophets. One interpreter notes that

this phrase, along with its shorter version, "that day," occurs often in the OT prophets. It always identifies a critical period of time during which God personally intervenes in history, directly or indirectly, to accomplish a specific purpose which fulfills his announced plan for the ages. Most often the events of "that day" take place at history's end, as in Isaiah 7:18–25 (The *Bible Readers' Companion,* Chariot/Victor, 413).

For instance, there are 45 references to the "day of the Lord" or "that day" in Isaiah. In each case, it refers to a time of judgment as history reaches a climax (see Isa. 13:9–13; 24:1–23; 32:1–20; 63:1–6).

The purpose of these demon-produced signs. It is clear from the text that the purpose of the signs mentioned in Revelation 16:13, 14 is to guarantee the allegiance of the nations of earth for a final great struggle against God. Reading a few verses further, we see that the place where the final battle is to occur is named Armageddon (Rev. 16:16).

Revelation 19:20. "Then the beast was captured, and with him the false prophet who worked signs in his presence, by which he deceived those who received the mark of the beast and those who worshiped his image. These two were cast alive into the lake of fire burning with brimstone."

The context of the verse. Earlier uses of the language of miracles in Revelation is associated with the appearance of two individuals called "beasts" and identified as the Antichrist and a false prophet. These two are portrayed as agents of Satan, who gives the false prophet the power to do "lying wonders." These lying wonders are miracles which mimic the works of God but are actually works of Satan.

This cluster of miracles produced by Satan's henchmen is used to consolidate the political power of the Antichrist and to deceive humanity into worshiping him as a god. The miracles are also used to guarantee the allegiance of earth's nations to Satan as history's terminal battle, Armageddon, approaches.

The outcome of the battle. Chapter 19 of Revelation describes Christ's conquest of Satan and his armies. The victory is decisive and total, and Jesus is established as King of kings and Lord of lords (Rev. 19:16). The Antichrist and the false prophet are cast into a "lake of fire," a place which we know as "hell."

The miracles which will accredit those who will lead humanity into history's climactic rebellion against the one true God will be lying wonders indeed.

DIVINE JUDGMENTS

The most striking feature of Revelation is its vivid descriptions of divine judgment poured out on earth. If we understand miracles as extraordinary events caused by God with a religious purpose, the great judgments described in Revelation are certainly miracles.

Before we look at several of these miracles, we need to understand something important about the language of this powerful but difficult-to-understand book of the Bible.

THE APOCALYPTIC LANGUAGE OF THE BOOK OF REVELATION

The *American Heritage Encyclopedic Dictionary* defines *apocalyptic* as "of or pertaining to a prophetic disclosure or revelation" and "portending violent disaster or ultimate doom." It is common these days to assume that all such language is symbolic or metaphorical. However, while there clearly are symbolic elements, the critical problem in understanding the apocalyptic literature of the Bible is lack of vocabulary.

An image of divine judgment (Revelation 8:7–10).

The apocalyptic visions of Revelation begin with Revelation 4. John introduces them by telling us that an angel called him up into heaven, where the angel would "show you things which must take place after this" (Rev. 4:1). Thus, John tells us that what he describes is to take place in the future, and that he sees the future from the viewpoint of heaven, not earth. From that viewpoint, John not only can observe events on earth but he can also see their heavenly cause.

In chapter 8 of Revelation, John describes seven angels being given seven trumpets. As each trumpet is sounded, another judgment strikes the earth and its population. From the vantage point of those on earth, only the effect will be experienced. John, in heaven, sees both the cause and the effect.

In Revelation 8:7–10, John describes the effect caused by the sounding of the first three trumpets:

The first angel sounded: And hail and fire followed, mingled with blood, and they were thrown to the earth. And a third of the trees were burned up, and all green grass was burned up. Then the second angel sounded: And something like a great mountain burning with fire was thrown into the sea, and a third of the sea became blood. And a third of the living creatures in the sea died, and a third of the ships were destroyed. Then the third angel sounded: And a great star fell from heaven, burning like a torch, and it fell on a third of the rivers and on the springs of water.

It is clear from this sample that we can't really tell just what John is describing. Is the "great star" a massive meteorite? What could "something like a mountain burning with fire" possibly be? And what does John mean by hail and fire mixed with blood?

It is easy to dismiss this language, or to consider it strictly metaphor, just because we can't imagine what John is talking about. No wonder many interpreters assume this language can't be taken literally.

A contemporary example.

Before we consider whether the language of Revelation is "literal," we need to try an experiment. We need to imagine ourselves among the first colonists to land in America. We disembark from our tiny ship and set out to carve a home in the wilderness. We build log shelters, struggle to clear land on which to grow crops, and huddle together in winter around flickering fires.

Now let's suppose that suddenly we were transported hundreds of years into the future. There we are shown three scenes of the twentieth century. We are shown a television program depicting Americans landing on the moon. We are shown a Los Angeles freeway, with cars zipping by. And we are shown the Dallas–Fort Worth airport, with jets landing and taking off.

Now let's suppose that we awaken. Stunned and awed by what we've seen, we try to share these realities with our fellow colonists. What would we say? What words would we have to use to enable them to visualize what we have seen? Remember, we can only use the vocabulary of our own time. And we can only compare the things we are trying to describe with things that are familiar to us and our companions.

I suspect that—given these limitations—what we said or wrote would sound very much like John's description in Revelation of the events which he witnessed. Our report of what we had seen would sound, well, apocalyptic. Or at the very least, we would be accused of using symbolic language and metaphor. Nevertheless, what we described would be real to us. And in this sense, our depiction would be "literal."

The issue in understanding apocalyptic language is not whether it can be taken "literally," if by literally we mean that the writer is describing as actual events what he has observed. The problem is that the vocabulary available to describe what one sees in apocalyptic literature is so limited by the writer's time and place that we cannot tell what is being described.

If John had been a twentieth-century man, would he have called the burning star that falls from heaven a meteorite? Or would hail and fire mingled with blood have become the eruption of a string of volcanos? We simply do not know.

What we do know is that whatever events John is describing, they represent extraordinary events caused by God. And we know that in Revelation these events have a clear and distinct religious purpose. They are elements of God's judgment on a sinful humanity which has rejected the gospel of grace, and which prefers Satan's ways to those of the Lord.

THE OUTCOMES OF THE DIVINE MIRACLE: JUDGMENTS DESCRIBED IN REVELATION

The miracle-judgments do not produce faith (Revelation 6:15–17). We've noted earlier in this book that miracles tend to confirm faith in believers, but at the same time they tend not to produce faith in unbelievers. As miracle judgment followed miracle judgment in the time of Moses, Pharaoh's heart became more and more hard. In spite of the wonderful miracles Jesus performed, which identified him as the Messiah, Israel rejected and crucified him rather than extended a welcome.

It should be no surprise, then, that the miracle judgments of Revelation also fail to produce faith in those who experience them. In a telling passage, John describes the reaction of individuals who recognize the divine origin of the judgments. Rather than turn to God for forgiveness, they "hid themselves in the caves and in the rocks of the mountains, and said to the mountains and rocks, 'Fall on us and hide us from the face of him who sits on the throne and from the wrath of the Lamb!' " (Rev. 6:15, 16).

In another passage John writes, "But the rest of mankind, who were not killed by these plagues, did not repent of the works of their hands, that they should not worship demons, and idols of gold, silver, brass, stone and wood, which can neither see nor hear nor walk. And they did not repent of their murders or their sorceries or their sexual immorality or their thefts" (Rev. 9:20, 21).

The judgment miracles of Revelation are just this—judgment miracles. They are not intended to call human beings to God, but to punish those who have refused to heed his call in Christ, and who have remained committed to a lifestyle of sin.

The miracle judgments are preparation for history's end (Revelation 20—22). The book of Revelation ends with Christ triumphant, the sinful dead judged, and a new heaven and earth created by the Lord. The sin which plagued the first creation has been dealt with at last. Those who trusted Christ are now the joyful inhabitants of a new and perfect universe. Those who turned their backs on God and refused to respond to his gospel have been dismissed to the lake of fire.

The grand drama is over, and justice and love have been vindicated. As the contemporary worship songs affirm, "Our God rules."

IMPLICATIONS OF THE LYING WONDERS AND DIVINE JUDGMENTS

As we have explored what the Bible says about miracles, we've noted a consistent pattern. Miracles come in paired clusters. As new revelation is introduced or old revelation reaffirmed, there is first of all a cluster of establishing miracles. These authenticate a divine messenger and validate his message. The establishing miracles are followed by a cluster of supportive miracles, which demonstrate the presence of God with those who have responded to the new revelation. This pattern can be seen in each of the three historic ages of miracles in the fourteenth century B.C., the eighth century B.C., and the time of Christ and the apostles.

But the pattern is broken in the Bible's fourth age of miracles, which lies in the future.

The first cluster of miracles of that time are indeed establishing miracles. But they are lying wonders, energized by Satan, intended to establish the Antichrist as the world's political and religious ruler.

What happens then is a cluster of judgment miracles caused by God. Rather than support the claims of the Antichrist established by the first cluster of miracles, these judgment miracles demolish those claims, even as they demolish the pretensions of the Antichrist and the false prophet.

In the battle of miracles, God is shown to be supreme. This is Revelation's great and final contribution to Scripture's teaching on miracles.

MIRACLES TODAY

GOD WORKING IN AND THROUGH US

MIRACLE: An extraordinary event caused by God for a religious purpose.

If this defines a biblical miracle, are such miracles for today? The author suggests, probably not. But he believes that God does perform compassionate miracles today—and anonymous miracles as well. There is no doubt that God can perform such miracles today. And there is good reason to believe that He does!

BIBLICAL MIRACLES: NOT FOR TODAY

We must say this hesitantly. It's always presumptuous for a mere human being to announce what God will and will not do. God is Sovereign, and free to act in any way he chooses and at any time.

With this caveat, let me explain what I mean by saying biblical miracles are not for today. As we have seen, biblical miracles occur in history in paired clusters. These clusters of miracles were intended to introduce or reaffirm significant truths revealed by God.

The first cluster of miracles in each pair are *authenticating* miracles, which validate the new revelation. They also clearly identify the individual who coveys the new revelation as God's spokesman. This first cluster of miracles is followed by another cluster of miracles

which are *supportive* miracles. These miracles demonstrate the living presence of God with those who welcome and follow the path marked out by the new revelation.

Historically, the agents of the authenticating and the supportive miracles have differed. Moses was God's agent for the authenticating miracles of the Exodus and many of the supportive miracles; Joshua was the agent of additional supportive miracles. Elijah was God's agent for authenticating miracles in the 700s B.C.; Elisha was God's agent for the supportive miracles. Jesus was God's agent for the authenticating miracles of the first century; Peter and Paul were his primary agents for the supportive miracles.

We should not expect this kind of miracle cluster in our day. The New Testament has completed God's revelation of his plans and purposes, and no new revelation is to be expected. In fact, the apostle Paul in 2 Thessalonians and John in Revelation make it clear that the next cluster of miracles to occur will be "lying wonders," worked by Satan to validate a false revelation. Rather than being followed by supportive miracles, the "lying wonders" will be followed by a series of devastating judgment-miracles poured out on an unrepentant humanity by God.

It is for this reason, and with this understanding of the role and function of miracles in Scripture, that we conclude that biblical miracles are not for today.

GOD DOES PERFORM MIRACLES FOR BELIEVERS TODAY

Although what we have called "biblical miracles" are not for today, we must also conclude that God really does perform miracles for believers today.

Christ's miracles revealed God's compassionate nature. One of the most beautiful truths expressed by the miracles performed by Jesus is that they were expressions of God's compassionate nature. It is true that the miracles Christ performed were exactly the kinds of miracles that the Old Testament prophets associated with the Messiah and the messianic age. Thus Jesus' miracles served to authenticate his claim to be Israel's promised deliverer. Yet the kinds of miracles predicted and performed were by their nature compassionate.

Isaiah wrote of the messianic age when God would come to save his people:

> Then the eyes of the blind shall
>   be opened,
> And the ears of the deaf shall be
>   unstopped.
> Then the lame shall leap like a
>   deer,
> And the tongue of the dumb sing
>   (Isa. 35:5, 6).

How easy it would have been for God to choose other kinds of miracles as authenticating signs. He could have made mountains leap, or blinded his enemies. Instead, God chose miracles of compassion to mark his Messiah, demonstrating the loving compassion of One who cares deeply about human beings.

The Gospel writers recorded on 14 separate occasions that Jesus had compassion on the persons for whom he performed miracles. The miracles of Jesus stand as a permanent monument to the compassion and love of God.

Modern Christians report miracles of compassion performed by God. Paul Prather was a skeptic about miracles. In his book, he told of an experience that began to change his outlook:

My father was a Southern Baptist preacher as well as a school teacher and, for several years, an administrator at a Baptist college. My mom, a housewife, was an equally staunch Baptist. In those days some Southern Baptists, including my parents, held the theological view that the age of miracles had ended in the first century with the death of the original apostles. They looked askance at other Christians who acted as if God was very much in the miracle business today, such as the ragged Pentecostals who met in a small, white frame building on the poorer end of one town where we lived.

Our understanding of miracles changed in 1976, while I was a ne'er-do-well student at the University of Kentucky. By the time cancer was discovered, it had invaded my father's entire body: his head, a kidney, his bones. First, doctors operated on a tumor on his skull. They opened him up and stitched him shut after removing only enough tissue for a biopsy. Surgery wouldn't do the job, they'd known as they saw the tumor. Dad's neurosurgeon told me a few minutes afterward that the cancer had spread so far that they could draw marrow from any bone in his body and it would be malignant.

And then something happened that I still find hard to grasp. One day I visited my father in his hospital room. He told me that God had spoken to him as he was praying. The Lord had told him he was going to be healed. I can't remember exactly what I thought, except that I was puzzled and sad. My father didn't normally claim to have received divine revelations regarding faith healings, or anything else (*Modern-Day Miracles,* 1996, pp. 8, 9).

Prather went on to tell how the cancer vanished before his father had received a single medication. A kidney tumor which had been clearly visible on X-rays disappeared. Bone marrow tests returned negative. His team of doctors sent their findings to another hospital, assuming they had missed something or that his dad had never had cancer. The doctors at the other hospital agreed with the original diagnosis. Prather's father had had cancer. Then he didn't. Twenty years later, Prather wrote in his book,

God still performs healing miracles, but believers can't claim them as their right.

Say what you want, but my father told me what was going to take place before it happened: God had said he intended to heal Dad. Then, apparently, God did just that. I bear witness that I saw what I believe to have been a miracle (p. 9).

Others bear witness to similar happenings. Extraordinary things, for which there seems to be no explanation but God, do occur. Doctors may speak of "spontaneous remission." But many who experience such things call them miracles and give God and prayer the credit.

Certainly this experience and many others like it are in complete harmony with what we know of the power and compassion of our God.

But what about those who are not healed or delivered? One of the troubling things about what we might call "miracles of compassion" is that not everyone who is sick or in need experiences a miracle. In our survey of the New Testament Epistles, we saw that even men of faith such as Paul and James did not expect or claim miracles as their right. Instead, they advised prayer and normal medical treatment.

Some would say that whether a person is granted a miracle depends on his or her faith. If we believe strongly enough, God will supply the miracle. Aside from the fact that texts used to support this position are misinterpreted, this teaching makes God dependent on us rather than us dependent on God. Ultimately, this position pictures a God who is captive to human beings—who must behave in a certain way if we have enough faith, pray believing, purge ourselves of sins, or meet some other condition.

The fact is that God is sovereign, and his freedom to act is not dependent on anything that any human being does. The reason why God seems to provide miracles for some and not for others is a mystery to us, hidden in his inscrutable will.

How are we to respond to this mystery? We have an example in the three Hebrews who faced Nebuchadnezzar's fiery furnace with quiet faith. Like them, we are to appeal to the Lord, and then say with confidence, "Our God whom we serve is able to deliver us from the burning fiery furnace, and he will deliver us from your hand, O king. But if not, let it be known to you, O king, that we do not serve your gods, nor will we worship the gold image which you have set up" (Dan. 3:17, 18).

Our God is able to deliver.

But if not . . . we will continue to trust only him.

In God's hands. The June 29, 1996, edition of the *St. Petersburg Times* carried a story on parents whom the writer described as having "a faith that has no limits." The article told the poignant story of Fred and Lu Langstone, whose 18-year-old son suffered a massive heart attack and was in a coma. The article reported:

"We are just struggling parents who trust their God in hard times," said Fred Langston. "This is the darkest valley I could ever walk."

"I would have never thought I could have lived through this," said Lu Langston. "I have watched and read about others and wept and sobbed. But I know where my strength comes from."

This was after the family got jolted at 7:30 Wednesday when a neurologist at University General Hospital in Semanole told them their son, Leighton, suffered from a brain hernia. With a swelling, there was no penetration of blood to the brain.

No one has ever survived a similar condition.

"From the standpoint of one doctor," said Fred Langston, "it means there is absolutely no hope. This would be a first and won't happen unless God does something on a par with the parting of the Red Sea."

The family asked for a second opinion and called in another neurologist Wednesday night. The neurologist confirmed the findings of the other specialist. It is possible they might take Langston off life support today. He still will have a tube that feeds him food and water and keeps his throat clear.

Leighton Langston, 18, a high school soccer star, suffered a massive heart attack Friday and has been in a coma ever since. Tuesday evening, he turned his head toward his dad's voice but showed no such signs Wednesday.

"A lot of people think what we are is all about religion," said Fred Langston. "If it were just about religion, we would not have made it through Friday night. This is about the knowledge of God and an ongoing relationship with him that is sustaining."

The 75 to 100 young people who have spilled into the hospital's halls are witness to this.

"People will say how they [the Langstons] need to get a little reality," said Cameran Brenner. "They just don't understand what they say all leads back to God. They really make you want to believe. When you drive down the street, you start crying.

Then you realize, 'Why should I cry when they are so strong.'

"I'm Jewish," said Doug Bird, "but I went to their prayer service [at Pasadena Presbyterian Church in St. Petersburg], and it is something I have never seen before in my life. So many people coming together, singing and praising Jesus.

"You would cry, even if you were a complete stranger."

Tuesday night, the third of such gatherings in the chapel drew 300 for a 9:30 service. It wasn't until 6:45 that someone suggested it.

The scene was repeated Wednesday, even though the service didn't begin until after 10 P.M.

"This thing just wipes you out," said Fred Langston, "but you keep drawing on the resources of a loving Lord and he'll get you through."

Fred and Lu Langston were not granted a miracle. Leighton died. And why one is saved by a miracle and another is not is something that we simply cannot explain. All we can do is remember that our God is a God of love and compassion. And trust that what he chooses to do is best, for reasons we may never know.

Does God perform miracles of compassion in our day? May he perform miracles for other reasons of his own? Of course God does, and he can.

But when we ask whether we are to *expect* miracles, or whether we have any basis on which to claim miracles as our right, the answer must be "No." Our relationship with God is no guarantee of miraculous intervention. But as Fred and Lu Langston discovered, "the knowledge of God and an ongoing relationship with him . . . is sustaining" indeed.

ANONYMOUS MIRACLES

One of the great convictions that Christians have shared across the ages is that God is sovereign. God is at work in history and in our individual lives.

Recently I ran across a saying penned by an unknown writer: *Circumstances are God's way of doing miracles anonymously.* What the author wants us to contemplate is that God is always at work in the circumstances of our lives. When we suffer a serious illness and respond to medical treatment, God is no less involved than when our healing cannot be "explained" by doctors. God works through the natural as well as the supernatural to show his grace to us.

Recently my wife was pondering the unusual events that led up to our meeting and subsequent marriage. She made a list of all the unusual things that had happened in her life that had brought her to the place where our paths crossed. These included moves from one part of the country to another, two personal tragedies, the wise advice of a Christian counselor, and a number of other experiences. She realized again that if any of the things she listed had not happened as they did, she would either never have met me or she would not have been attracted to the qualities she had come late to value.

To Sue, this series of events which many would dismiss as "coincidences" were no less a cause of wonder and amazement than if we had both been guided by an audible voice to a meeting place, and told by that voice that God intended us to marry. The path that brought us together seemed to her to bear the mark of the miraculous. And rightly so.

For us, and for you as well, God has often performed his miracles anonymously. He has worked through circumstances in which only the eye of faith can see his hand.

And it is with the eye of faith that we are to look not only at Scripture, but at our daily lives as well. In the Word of God, we meet the author of history's grand miracles. He is the Creator, at whose Word the universe sprang into being. In Jesus, God the Son became incarnate, entering our world to live among us as a human being and die for mankind's sins. In the grand miracle of the Resurrection, Jesus was displayed to all as the Son of God with power—history's living and coming Lord.

When we know him and appreciate his power and love, doubt disappears. The miracles of Scripture and the anonymous miracles which fill our lives become occasions of wonder, awe, and praise.

And we affirm, together, that our God truly is a miracle-working God.

EXPOSITORY INDEX

An expository index organizes information by topic and guides the reader to Bible verses and book pages which are critical to understanding the subject. It does not list every verse referred to in the book, but seeks to identify key verses. It does not list every mention of a topic in the book, but directs the reader to pages where a topic is discussed in some depth. Thus an expository index helps the reader avoid the frustration of looking up verses in the Bible or the book, only to discover that they contribute in only a small way to one's understanding of the subject.

This expository index organizes references to miracles and wonders by topic. Topics and sub-topics are identified in the left-hand column. Key Bible verses and passages are listed in the center column under "Scriptures." The far right column identifies pages in this book where the topic is covered.

In most instances, several of the key verses in the "Scriptures" column will be discussed on the book pages referred to. Very often additional verses will be referred to on the pages where the topic is covered. Our goal is to help you keep in focus the critical Bible verses and passages. Similarly, the book pages referred to are only those which make a significant contribution to understanding a topic, not every page on which a topic may be mentioned.

Please note that material under sub-topics is sometimes organized chronologically by the sequence of appearance in Scripture, and sometimes alphabetically, depending upon which organization will be most helpful in understanding and locating information.

TOPIC	SCRIPTURES	PAGE(S)
ABSENCE OF MIRACLES, IMPLICATIONS		
For the sick	2 Cor. 13; Phil. 2:25–27; 1 Tim. 5:23; James 5:14–15	274–276
For those undergoing trials	2 Cor. 11:23–28; 1 Pet. 1:6; 2:21; 4:12, 13	276
ATTACKS ON MIRACLES		17–19
Early Jewish		17
Early pagan		17–18
Spinoza		17–18
Hume		18–19
Paulus		19
Bultmann		19
Contemporary		19–20
AUTHENTICATING ROLE	Deut. 13:1, 2; 18:18–22	157–158, 277–278

SCRIPTURE INDEX

(Bible references are in boldface type, followed by the pages on which they appear in this book.)

THE "EVERYTHING IN THE BIBLE" REFERENCE SERIES

Every Covenant and Promise in the Bible. From the Old Testament covenants God made with Noah, Abraham, Moses, and David through the promises that still apply to our lives, this volume helps you develop a new appreciation for God's dependability and the power God's promises can afford to believers today. (Available)

Every Good and Evil Angel in the Bible. The Bible leaves no question about the reality of angels, even though humankind has not always been clear on their nature and function. This volume takes a thorough look at every mention of angels in the Bible—both those working for God and those working against Him. It also looks at the place of angels in the lives of contemporary believers. (Available)

Every Miracle and Wonder in the Bible. A God who created all that is certainly is capable of working miracles. Beginning with the miracle of Creation, this volume reviews God's wondrous works in dealing with His people. Major emphasis is given to the special evidences of God's activity in the Exodus, the ministries of Elijah and Elisha, and the ministry of Jesus. (Available)

Every Prayer and Petition in the Bible. The Bible is filled with evidences of prayers offered to God—some intensely private and others joyously public. Individuals are seen coming to Him with their requests and their complaints, their confessions and their praises. Three chapters look at the powerful prayers in the Psalms. Four chapters focus on Jesus' teachings about and practice of prayer. (Available)

Every Woman in the Bible (Available Spring 1999)

Coming soon

Every Man in the Bible

Every Name and Title of God in the Bible

Other titles are being planned.

OTHER BOOKS BY EDMUND PHELPS

Rewarding Work: How to Restore Participation and Self-Support to Free Enterprise

Enterprise and Inclusion in Italy

Seven Schools of Macroeconomic Thought: The Arne Ryde Memorial Lectures

Structural Slumps:
The Modern Equilibrium Theory of Unemployment, Interest, and Assets

Political Economy: An Introductory Text

Studies in Macroeconomic Theory (2 volumes)

Economic Justice (editor)

Inflation Policy and Unemployment Theory

Microeconomic Foundations of Employment and Inflation Theory (with others)

Fiscal Neutrality toward Economic Growth

MASS FLOURISHING

MASS FLOURISHING

How Grassroots Innovation
Created Jobs, Challenge, and Change

EDMUND PHELPS

The 2006 Nobel Laureate in Economics

PRINCETON UNIVERSITY PRESS

Princeton and Oxford

Published by Princeton University Press, 41 William Street, Princeton, New Jersey 08540
In the United Kingdom: Princeton University Press, 6 Oxford Street, Woodstock, Oxfordshire OX20 1TW
press.princeton.edu

Jacket design by David Drummond, Salamander Hill Design

ISBN 978-0-691-15898-3
Library of Congress Control Number: 2013936720

British Library Cataloging-in-Publication Data is available

This book has been composed in Calluna with Filosofia and DIN display by
Princeton Editorial Associates Inc., Scottsdale, Arizona.

Printed on acid-free paper. ∞
Printed in the United States of America
1 3 5 7 9 10 8 6 4 2

CONTENTS

PREFACE

When I first saw Los Angeles I realized that no one had ever painted what it looked like.

DAVID HOCKNEY

WHAT HAPPENED IN THE 19TH CENTURY that caused people in some countries to have—for the first time in human history—unbounded growth of their wages, expansion of employment in the market economy, and widespread satisfaction with their work? And what happened to cause many of these nations—by now, all of them, or so it would appear—to lose all that in the 20th century? This book aims to understand how this rare prosperity was gained and how it was lost.

I set out in this book a new perspective on what the prosperity of nations is. Flourishing is the heart of prospering—engagement, meeting challenges, self-expression, and personal growth. Receiving income may lead to flourishing but is not itself a form of flourishing. A person's flourishing comes from the experience of the new: new situations, new problems, new insights, and new ideas to develop and share. Similarly, prosperity on a national scale—mass flourishing—comes from broad involvement of people in the processes of innovation: the conception, development, and spread of new methods and products—indigenous innovation down to the grassroots. This dynamism may be narrowed or weakened by institutions arising from imperfect understanding or competing objectives. But institutions alone cannot create it. Broad dynamism must be fueled by the right values and not too diluted by other values.

The recognition by a people that their prosperity depends on the breadth and depth of their innovative activity is of huge importance. Nations unaware of how their prosperity is generated may take steps that cost them much of their dynamism. America, judging by available evidence, does not produce now the rate of innovation and high job satisfaction it did up to the 1970s. And participants have a right not to see their prospects of prospering—of self-realization, as John Rawls termed it—squandered. In the past century, governments sought to move the unemployed into jobs so they could prosper again. Now there is a larger task: to reverse losses of prosperity among the employed. That will require legislative and regulatory initiatives having nothing to do with boosting either "demand" or "supply." It will require initiatives based on an understanding of the mechanisms and mindsets on which high innovation depends. Yet surely governments can do it. Some began clearing paths for innovation two centuries ago. These thoughts were on my mind when I conceived this book. I believed the sole problem was the terrible unawareness.

Eventually I began to sense another kind of problem: a resistance to modern values and modern life. The values that supported high prosperity ran up against other values that impeded and devalued flourishing. Prosperity has paid a heavy toll. Questions are being asked about the sort of life it would be best to have and thus the sort of society and economy to have. There are calls in America for traditionalist goals long familiar in Europe, like greater social protection, social harmony, and public initiatives in the national interest. These were the values that have led much of Europe to viewing the state in traditional, medieval terms—through the "lens of corporatism." There are calls too for more attention to community and family values. There is little awareness of how valuable modern life, with its flourishing, was. There is no longer in America or in Europe a sense of what mass flourishing was like. Nations with brilliant societies a century back, say, France in the Roaring Twenties, or even a half-century ago, say, America in the early sixties, have no living memory of wide flourishing. Increasingly, the processes of a nation's innovation—the topsy-turvy of creation, the frenzy of development, and painful closings when the new things fail to take hold—are seen as a pain that upstart materialist societies were willing to endure to increase their national income and national power, but that we are unwilling to endure any longer. The processes are not seen as the stuff of flourishing—the change, challenge, and lifelong quest for originality, discovery, and making a difference.

This book is my response to these developments: It is an appreciation of the flourishing that was the humanistic treasure of the modern era. It is also a plea to restore what has been lost and not to reject out of hand the modern values that inspired the broad prosperity of modern societies.

I first set out a narrative of prosperity in the West—where and how it was won and how to varying degrees it has been lost in one nation after another. After all, much of our understanding of the present comes from trying to put together some pieces of our past. But I also study cross-country evidence of the present day.

At the core of the narrative is the prosperity that broke out in the 19th century, firing imaginations and transforming working lives. Widescale flourishing from engaging, challenging work came to Britain and America, later to Germany and France. The step-by-step emancipation of women there and, in America, the eventual abolition of slavery, widened the flourishing. The making of new methods and products that was part of this flourishing was also the major part of the economic growth that coincided with it. Then, in the 20th century, flourishing ultimately narrowed, and growth slipped away.

In this narrative, the historic run of prosperity—from as early as the 1820s (in Britain) to as late as the 1960s (in America)—was a product of pervasive indigenous innovation: the adoption of new methods or goods stemming from homegrown ideas originating in the national economy itself. Somehow the economies of these pioneering nations developed dynamism—the appetite and capacity for indigenous innovation. I call them *modern* economies. Other economies gained by following the modern ones in their slipstream. This is not the classic account by Arthur Spiethoff and Joseph Schumpeter of entrepreneurs jumping to make the "obvious" innovations suggested by discoveries of "scientists and navigators." The modern economies were not the old mercantile economies, but something new under the sun.

Understanding the modern economies must start with a modern notion: original ideas born of creativity and grounded on the uniqueness of each person's private knowledge, information, and imagination. The modern economies were driven by the new ideas of the whole roster of business people, mostly unsung: idea men, entrepreneurs, financiers, marketers, and pioneering end-users. The creativity and attendant uncertainty was seen through a glass darkly in the 1920s and 1930s by those early moderns, Frank Knight, John Maynard Keynes, and Friedrich Hayek.

Much of the book is occupied with the human experience in the innovation process and the flourishing it brings. The human benefits of innovation are a basic product of a well-functioning modern economy—the mental stimulus, the problems to solve, the arrival of a new insight, and the rest. I have sought to convey an impression of the rich experience of working and living in such an economy. As I considered this vast canvas, I was excited to realize that no one had ever depicted what a modern economy felt like.

My account of the phenomenon of dynamism recognizes that myriad economic freedoms are a key element—freedoms that we have our Western democracy to thank for. So are various enabling institutions, which arose in answer to business needs. Yet the rise of economic modernity required more than the existence and enforcement of legal rights and more than various commercial and financial institutions. My account of dynamism does not deny that science has been advancing but does not link prosperity to science. In my account, attitudes and beliefs were the wellspring of the dynamism of the modern economies. It is mainly a culture protecting and inspiring individuality, imagination, understanding, and self-expression that drives a nation's indigenous innovation.

Where a country's economy becomes predominantly modern, I argue, it goes from just producing known, specified goods or services to dreaming up and working with ideas about other things to try to produce—goods or services not known to be producible and perhaps never before conceived. And where an economy is pulled back from the modern—denied its institutions and norms or blocked by curbs or inhibited by opponents—the flow of ideas through it narrows. Whichever direction the economy is pulled, toward the modern or the traditional, the texture of working life is profoundly changed.

Thus the history of the West set out here is driven by a central struggle. That struggle is not between capitalism and socialism—private ownership in Europe rose to the American level decades ago. Nor is it the tension between Catholicism and Protestantism. The central struggle is between modern and traditional, or conservative, values. A cultural evolution from Renaissance humanism to the Enlightenment to existentialist philosophies amassed a new set of values—modern values like expressing creativity and exploring for its own sake, and personal growth for one's own sake. And these values inspired the rise of modern societies in Britain and America. In the 18th century they fostered modern democracy, of course, and in the 19th century they gave birth to modern economies. These were the first economies of dynamism. This cultural evolution brought modern societies to continental Europe too—societies modern enough for democracy. But the social disruptions brought about by the emergent modern economies in those nations were a threat to traditions. And traditional values—putting community and state over the individual and protection against falling behind over going ahead—were so powerful that, in general, few modern economies made much headway there. Where they made or threatened to make deep inroads, they were forcibly taken over by the state (in the interwar years) or hobbled by restrictions (in postwar years).

Many authors allude to a long struggle to free themselves from received wisdom, and I had to escape from a forest of unrecognizable descriptions and inapplicable theories to be able to talk about the modern economy, its creation, and its value. There was the classic formulation by Schumpeter—innovations are sparked only by exogenous discoveries—and the neo-Schumpeterian corollary that innovation could be increased only by boosting scientific research. These two views assumed as a foregone conclusion that a modern society could do without a modern economy. (No wonder Schumpeter thought socialism was coming.) There was Adam Smith's concept that people's "well-being" derived from consumption and leisure alone, and thus their whole business life was for these ends, not for the experience itself. There was the neoclassical welfarism of Keynes, in which failures and fluctuations are the main modern ills to be combated, since the challenges and ventures responsible for them have no human value. This was followed by the neo-neoclassical view, dominant in business schools today, that business is about risk assessment and cost control—not ambiguity, uncertainty, exploration, and strategic vision. There was the Panglossian view that a nation's institutions are not a concern, since social evolution produces the most needed institutions and every nation has the culture that is best for it. If this book gets at all close to the truth, all these ideas of bygone times were false and harmful.

The book devotes many pages to admiring descriptions of the experience that the modern economy offers participants. It was, after all, the marvel of the modern era. But that tribute invites the question of how this modern life, which the modern economies made possible, compares with other ways of life. In the next-to-last chapter I argue that the flourishing that is the quintessential product of the modern economy resonates with the ancient concept of the good life, a concept on which many variations have been written. The good life requires the intellectual growth that comes from actively engaging the world and the moral growth that comes from creating and exploring in the face of great uncertainty. The modern life that modern economies introduced perfectly exemplifies the concept of the good life. That is a step in the direction of justifying a well-functioning modern economy. It can serve the good life.

Yet a justification of such an economy must address objections. An economy structured to offer prospects of the good life, even to all participants, could not be considered a just economy if it caused injustices in the process or provided the good life in a way deemed unfair. The less advantaged and indeed all participants suffer—from workers who lose their jobs to entrepreneurs whose companies are ruined and families whose wealth takes a huge hit—when a modern economy's new direction turns out to be ill judged or very close to being a racket, like the housing boom rigged up in the previous decade. Governments fail to govern the distribution of the benefits of a modern economy—the primary one being the good life—in a way that is as favorable to the less advantaged as it could be. (But that may be the fault of the government more than of the modern economy.)

The last chapter sketches a conception of an economy that is modern but also just in going as far as feasible to provide prospects for the good life to the participants whose talent or background renders them less advantaged than the others. I note that a well-functioning economy of the modern kind can be governed in accordance with familiar notions of economic justice, such as focus on the least advantaged. If all are keen on the good life, they will be willing to take the risks of large swings to have that life. I also add that a justly-functioning modern economy is to be preferred to a justly-functioning traditional economy—an economy based on traditional values—under a wide variety of conditions. But what if some participants have traditional values? In an introductory exploration one has to stop at some point. But this much is clear: Those in a nation who want to have economies of their own, based on their traditionalist values, ought to be free to set them up. Yet those who aspire to the good life have the right to be free to work in a modern economy—not to be confined to a traditionalist economy, bereft of change, challenge, originality, and discovery.

It may seem paradoxical that a nation would countenance or even strive to make more effective a kind of economy in which the future is unknown and unknowable, an economy prone to huge failures, swings, and abuses in which people may feel "adrift," or even "terrified." Yet the satisfaction of having a new insight, the thrill of meeting a challenge, the sense of making your own way, and the gratification of having grown in the process—in short, the good life—require exactly that.

MASS FLOURISHING

Advent of the Modern Economies

It is true that modernity was conceived in the 1780s. . . . [But] the years 1815–30 [are] those during which the matrix of the modern world was largely formed.

PAUL JOHNSON, *The Birth of the Modern*

O VER MOST OF HUMAN EXISTENCE, the actors in a society's economy seldom did anything that expanded what may be called their economic knowledge—knowledge of how to produce and what to produce. Even in the early economies of Western Europe, departures from past practice that might have led to new knowledge and thus to new practice, or innovation, were uncommon. Ancient Greece and Rome made some innovations—the water mill and bronze casting, for example. Yet it is the dearth of innovation in the "ancient economy," especially over the eight centuries after Aristotle, that is striking. The Renaissance made pivotal discoveries in science and art and brought riches to royalty. Yet the resulting gains in economic knowledge were too meager to elevate the productivity and living standards of ordinary people, as the historian of everyday life, Fernand Braudel, observed. Familiarity and routine were the rule in these economies.

Was that because the actors in these economies did not desire to depart from past practice? Not exactly. Humans, it has been found, were exercising imagination and displaying creativity as long as a thousand generations ago.[1] Participants in the early economies, we can safely assume, did not lack the desire to create—they invented and tested some things for their own use. But they lacked a capacity to develop and provide new methods and products for society: early economies had not acquired institutions and attitudes that would enable and encourage attempts at innovation.

---

1. Researchers at the University of Tübingen recently unearthed some flutes fashioned from bones by the cave dwellers that colonized Europe 35,000 years ago. Nicholas Conard and colleagues reported the find in 2009 in the science magazine *Nature*.

The highest achievement of these early economies was the spread of commerce within each country and the spread of foreign trade with other countries. The commerce of 14th-century Hamburg and 15th-century Venice—two prominent city-states—stretched along Hanseatic trade routes, the Silk Road, and ocean lanes to increasingly far-flung cities and ports. With the establishment of the New World colonies in the 16th century, commerce spread within nation-states and foreign trade increased. By the 18th century, most notably in Britain and Scotland, most people were producing goods for the "market" rather than for their families or towns. More and more countries exported and imported at significant levels in distant markets. Business still involved producing, but it was also about distribution and trade.

This was capitalism, of course—to use a term that did not exist in those times. More precisely, it was *mercantile capitalism:* someone with wealth might become a merchant, investing in wagons or boats to transport goods to places where prices were higher. From about 1550 to 1800 or so, this system was the motor of what the Scots called a "commercial society." In Scotland and England, at any rate, many admired this society unreservedly, while others felt it lacked "heroic spirit."[2] In the mercantile age, though, these societies were certainly not lacking in aggressiveness. Merchants were pitted against one another in the struggle for supplies or market share, while nations raced to establish colonies. Military conflict was rampant. Perhaps with little to challenge people's minds and to tempt big leaps in their business, the heroic spirit sought outlets in military ventures.

In the mercantile age, to be sure, business life exhibited a good deal less of the familiarity and routine that had been so pronounced in the middle ages. Finding and penetrating new markets—and being found and penetrated—must have provided bits of new economic knowledge from time to time. No doubt expansion of commerce often turned up a new opportunity for domestic producers, or a new opportunity for foreign competitors—thus new knowledge about what to produce. Such gains could be public knowledge, falling into the laps of people "in the business," or could be hard-won and remain private knowledge. Less often, perhaps, the stimulus to switch to producing a good

---

2. Adam Smith in his *Lectures on Jurisprudence,* given in Glasgow in 1762–1763, saw "disadvantages" of the "commercial spirit." "[T]he minds of men," he wrote, "are contracted . . . education is despised or at least neglected, and heroic spirit is almost utterly extinguished." (See Smith, 1978, vol. 5, p. 541.) In his 1776 classic *The Wealth of Nations* he says that "in barbarous societies . . . the varied occupations of every man oblige every man to exert his capacity. . . . [Thus] invention is kept alive" (p. 51). Adam Ferguson in his 1767 *Essay on the History of Civil Society* quoted admiringly the American Indian chief who said, "I am a warrior, not a merchant."

not produced before might lead to advances in how to produce. By how much, though, did economic knowledge increase in the mercantile age?

Economic Knowledge in the Mercantile Era

Some scraps of early data from England's economy are revelatory. Increased knowledge of what to produce can be supposed, other things unchanged, to pull up productivity—to pull up output in relation to labor input. So if this know-how in the hands of the economy's participants, whether it was private knowledge or public knowledge, grew appreciably over the mercantile era, this would be manifested by *increased* output in relation to labor input between the era's start around 1500 and its end around 1800. If we see little or no such improvement in the relationship, that would be reason to doubt that there was important growth of production know-how during the mercantile era. What, then, does the evidence show?

Output per worker in England did not increase at all between 1500 and 1800, according to the estimates by Angus Maddison in his 2006 volume *The World Economy*, a trusted source. However, population, and thus labor force, increased enormously over that span—recovering from losses from the bubonic plague, or Black Death, of the 1300s. Conceivably that pulled down output per worker, through "diminishing returns," enough to mask an upward pull on output per worker exerted by increasing knowledge, if there was any. However, decadal estimates by Gregory Clark show that output per worker was as high in the 1330s and 1340s, when population had not yet fallen much below its pre-plague peak, as it was in the 1640s, when population was nearly back to that previous peak. Some rare micro data suggest that output per farm worker was no higher even in the 1790s than in the early 1300s. Another study comes up with a one-third increase over that span.[3] It is safe to conclude that available farming techniques did not improve

3. A study of grain output in England's Ramsey Estates found that average rates of output per man-day between 1293 and 1347 "either surpassed or met the literature's best estimates for English workers until 1800." See Karakacili, "English Agrarian Labour Productivity Rates" (2004, p. 24).

A broader study reports no reductions in the labor required for threshing, reaping, and mowing. Yet its findings on overall productivity suggest that over a 4½-century span knowledge of how best to use farm workers did increase somewhat. Workers produced 58 bushels of grain per 300 man-days in the early 1300s and 79 bushels in the 1770s. But this is a meager gain over so long a period. See Clark's 2005 working paper, "The Long March of History," figure 3 and table 6. Clark's figure 8 shows a single upward shift from the 1640s to the 1730s in the output-per-labor relationship—by about 20 bushels.

much over almost five centuries. (Yet measuring output per worker, product by product, misses the continual gains in aggregate output per worker from shifts of labor to production where prices or productivities are higher. In this respect, wages are more informative.)

Real wages per worker—the average wage in terms of a basket of consumer goods—reflects, among other things, knowledge of how to produce and what to produce. Start-up projects to develop new methods or products would create jobs and that would pull up wages sooner or later. New methods also tend to exert an upward pull. Did the mercantile economies see a strong lift in real wages, which would be consistent with important increases in economic knowledge? In English farming, real wages, like output per head, were falling during the first half of the mercantile age, 1500 to 1650, owing to population regrowth after the plague. Wages rose from 1650 to 1730, though about half of that gain was lost by 1800. The net result was that wages in 1800 were lower than in 1500. However, wages in 1800 *were* higher than in 1300—about one-third higher. But is that gain large enough to confirm increased economic knowledge through English innovations in products and methods? First, real wages were greatly increased by declining prices of imported consumer goods and the "arrival of new goods such as sugar, pepper, raisins, tea, coffee and tobacco," as Clark in his 2007 book records (p. 42). So the one-third gain in real wages is not a sign of English innovation so much as evidence of discoveries by navigators and colonizers. Second, 1300 marked the end of a century of wage decline. Real wages in 1800, as Clark's table 4 shows, were lower than in 1200! It is safe to "split the difference," agreeing that England saw little progress in wages from the middle ages through the Enlightenment.[4]

We must conclude that the mercantile economies brought strikingly few advances in economic knowledge even in their heyday from 1500 to 1800. As population increased dramatically in the 18th century and still more over most of the 19th, with population levels setting record highs every year, it might be supposed that the fixity of land must have slowed the rise of productivity that growth of economic knowledge would otherwise have brought. But as Britain's population grew rapidly, its economy devoted itself more and more to manufacturing, trade, and other services, which were activities

---

4. It is true that wages (and output per worker) in 1200 may have been pushed a little above the 1300 level by an abundance of land that was never matched again—a time when a Robin Hood could enjoy an entire forest. But land could hardly have been appreciably scarce in 1300 either. In neither period was labor pressed against the land. So there is no compelling reason to rule out 1200, with its good wages, as the base year from which to make comparisons.

requiring less land than farming did. For this reason, population growth mattered less and less for growth of wages and output per worker. The belief that rising population prevented or severely limited productivity and wages, thus thwarting and masking a rise of economic knowledge, is not persuasive. Something else was limiting growth of wages and output per head.

The remarkable similarity of economic development across the mercantile world is also a clue to what was driving them—and what was not. We now know that in the mercantile era 11 countries (or regions that become countries) were in the same club with respect to output per capita and wages per worker: Austria, Britain, Belgium, Denmark, France, Germany, Holland, Italy, Norway, Sweden, and Switzerland. (Even in the 1200s and early 1300s, England was not the backwater next to the European continent that it was thought to be.) By 1800, America had joined the club. We could say that these nations and others marched to the same drummer, though in a ragged way: each had its own fluctuations around roughly the *same trend path*—with Italy in the lead position in 1500 and Holland by 1600 (until the early 1800s). That fact suggests that their modest upward trend was the product of mercantile forces—global and felt about equally, at least within the club—not nation-specific forces.[5]

Anyone living in those times might have forecast that, once commercialization had spread as far as it could go, the national economies would settle into the routine of old, albeit in a more globalized way. As it turned out, however, the mercantile era would not be the last stage of economic development—not for these developed parts of the world, at any rate. In several of the commercial societies, the economy, while still engaging in commerce and trade, would soon take on a new character. Something happened that was strange for its time, something that would change everything.

Signs of Exploding Economic Knowledge

The indicators that were surprisingly trendless from 1500 (by some measures even from 1200) to 1800 took an astonishing turn within just a few decades. From the 1820s to the 1870s, Britain, America, France, and Germany broke out of the pack one by one. The trajectory of these countries' two indicators—output per head and the average real wage—was a phenomenal development in the history of the world.

---

5. The standard source is the rough estimates, drawn from a range of data, by Maddison, *The World Economy* (tables 1b and 8c).

Output per head in Britain, according to present-day measurements, began a sustained climb in 1815 with the end of the Napoleonic Wars and never turned back. It grew spectacularly from the 1830s through the 1860s. Output per head in America is now viewed as having gone into a sustained climb around 1820.[6] In France and Belgium, it began a bumpy ascent in the 1830s, with Germany and Prussia following in the 1850s. These extraordinary climbs are indelibly associated with the first scholar to dig them up, the American economic historian Walt W. Rostow. He dubbed them *take-offs*—take-offs into sustained economic growth.[7]

The average real wage generally followed suit. In Britain the daily wage in the crafts for which we have data began a sustained rise in 1820 or so—not long after the time that output per worker took off. In America, wages took off in the late 1830s. The countries that saw, one by one, an explosion of their productivity saw an explosion of their real wages. (Chapter 2 will quantify the ascents.) The wage take-offs were discovered in the 1930s by Jürgen Kuczynski, a German economic historian of Polish birth. An extreme Marxist, he saw in the transformed economies only "deterioration of labor conditions" and "increasing misery." Yet his own data, even after his adjustments, reveal wages to be taking off strongly by the middle of the 19th century in all of the countries he studied: America, Britain, France, and Germany.[8]

The countries pulled one another along. With the quickening of the four lead countries' growth in both output per head and wages, every other

6. An attempted climb in 1800 ended in a crash. Despite years of fast growth until 1807, all of that growth and more was soon lost and was not regained until 1818. In contrast, the years from the mid-1830s to the mid-1840s showed a slowdown but no loss of previous gains. See the 1967 paper by Paul David, "The Growth of Real Product in the United States before 1840."

7. The chief work is Rostow's 1953 *The Process of Economic Growth*. See also his 1960 *The Stages of Economic Growth*. His discussion, involving "linkages," of the causes of the take-offs was difficult and did not win over the profession. (That explanation of the take-offs does not resemble or appear to anticipate the one given here.) After a stint in the government in the 1960s he was not invited back to Harvard. Yet he deserved more recognition than he got, if only for calling attention to the take-offs.

8. Kuczynski's early research is in his *Labour Conditions in Western Europe* (1937) and *A Short History of Labour Conditions* (1942–1945, vols. I–IV). In a life suitable for a film noir, he was not afraid of controversy. He made several novel adjustments to the raw wage data he had compiled, which succeeding investigators could not replicate. Yet, even his real wage for Britain "net" of lost time in unemployment goes from 57 in the "trade cycle" 1849–1858 to 99 in the cycle 1895–1903 (vol. I, part 1, p. 67). The estimates cited above, however, are drawn from present-day sources: the 1995 international tables by Jeffrey Williamson et al. and tables by Broadus Mitchell, Paul Bairoch, Gregory Clark, and Diedrich Saalfeld. (Kuczynski's calculations portrayed the nations he studied as starting off highly unequal and finishing the century with roughly equal wage levels, thanks to technology "transfer" and migration of workers. Calculations by Williamson show less convergence, even some divergence among the four nations.)

member in the pack was able to grow faster simply by continuing to trade with the leaders and by stepping up trade to capitalize on emerging differences—in short, by swimming in their slipstream, like fishes behind a whale.

The pioneering observations of the take-offs, made by our two Galileos of modern economic history, Kuczynski and Rostow, crystallized the extraordinary journey that the West embarked upon in the 19th century. What, historians and economists asked, were the origins of these unprecedented phenomena? Economists turned to traditional economic thought.

Many traditional economists supposed that the answer lay in the sharply increasing stock of *capital*—plant and equipment—in farms and factories during the 19th century. But capital formation could not plausibly explain—even in part—the ascent of output per capita in the United States from the mid-19th century into the 20th. In fact, the rise of capital and land in use accounted for only one-seventh of this rise.[9] The growth of capital in the 18th century may have been sufficient to explain the somewhat meager and fitful growth of productivity in that period. But the growth of capital in the 19th century, though hastened, could not have powered the ascent of productivity and wages. Owing to diminishing returns, sustained growth of capital cannot singlehandedly yield sustained growth of output per worker and the average real wage.

Sensing that difficulty, some other traditional economists suggested that the answer lay in *economies of scale*. As labor multiplied and capital kept up, they suggested, output per worker (and per unit of capital) increased.[10] But the near-tripling of productivity between 1820 and 1913 in America and Britain is far too large an increase to attribute to economies of scale resulting from the expansion of labor and capital. And if such an expansion worked wonders in that period, why did a similar expansion from the 1640s to the 1790s have no comparable effect—or, in fact, any effect? Moreover, if economies of scale raised productivity and wages so significantly, why did they

9. The span analyzed, 1869–1878 to 1944–1953, had the earliest start date possible with the U.S. data available to researchers at the time. Today, one could make rough calculations from as early as 1840 without much change in the results. See Abramovitz, "Resource and Output Trends in the United States since 1870" (1956).

Historical research on Britain concluded that although the lion's share of 18th-century growth there was due to growth of capital rather than of knowledge, in the 19th-century growth it *was not*. See Crafts, "British Economic Growth, 1700–1831" (1983, p. 196). McCloskey's remark, quoted below, appears in this paper.

10. This thesis was advanced in 1969 by an important economic theorist of yesteryear, John Hicks, in one of his lesser works, *A Theory of Economic History*. The theoretical work on how integrated markets work out these scale economies was initiated by Paul Krugman in his 1992 book *Geography and Trade*.

not provide the same effect in Italy and Spain? Those countries' excess populations fled to the Americas, North and South, in search of better economic opportunities. Furthermore, achieving new economies of scale must have been harder over the 20th century in the take-off economies. The increases in labor and the resulting increases in capital that could feed new economies of scale subsided. Yet output per worker and wages kept right on growing over most of the 20th century—right up to the early 1970s. (Productivity rose at a blistering rate between 1925 and 1950, even during the Great Depression of the 1930s, then again from 1950 to 1975.)

Other traditional economists supposed that the answer lay in ongoing expansions of commerce within countries and expansions of trade among countries over much of the century—the shifts of people out of self-sufficiency and the creation of new canals and railroads connecting markets. Of course, the broader horizons added to the knowledge in economies— the take-off economies and the others—of what to produce and even how to produce. But we have been here before. If *all* the commercialization and trade from medieval Venice and Bruges to 18th-century Glasgow and London was not sufficient to lift output per worker and wages, we can hardly believe that the last expansions of commerce and trade in the 19th century increased productivity and wages so spectacularly. Moreover, even if commerce and trade were important to one or another take-off economy, they could not power the boundless growth of output and wages that appeared to be unfolding. Trade as an engine of growth runs out of fuel once globalization is total.

Almost nothing in the social world is absolutely certain. But it would appear that only increasing economic knowledge—knowledge of how to produce and knowledge about what to produce—could have enabled the steep climb in national productivity and real wages in the take-off countries. As Deirdre McCloskey put it, "ingenuity rather than abstinence governed." And, we might add, ingenuity rather than trade.

With time, the modernist emphasis on increasing knowledge—and the presumption that there is always more knowledge to come—triumphed over traditional emphases on capital, scale, commerce, and trade. But where did that knowledge come from? Whose "ingenuity" was it?

Finding the Wellspring of Economic Knowledge

Most historians coping after Rostow with the phenomenon of take-offs had no philosophical qualms about accepting the possibility that the mind can produce new ideas and that new knowledge may result. Further, if much of the future knowledge of consequence for society was not inevitable, or determinate, the future of society was not determinate. And what is indeterminate is unforeseeable, as Karl Popper wrote in his 1957 book against "historicism"— the view that the future grows determinably out of the historical situation.

However, even these historians, though not wedded to historical determinism, based their view of economies—19th-century economies and the take-off economies included—on an 18th-century conception handed down by Smith, Malthus, and David Ricardo. In that classical conception, a "market economy" was always in equilibrium. And, in equilibrium, this economy incorporates all of the world's knowledge potentially useful to its working: if the world discovers a new piece of knowledge, these market economies act at once to make use of it. In this view, there is no room for discovery within a nation's economy—no room for what we may call *indigenous innovation*, or home-grown advances in economic knowledge—since, in this view, the economy is already as knowledgeable as it can be. A nation has to look outside its economy—to the state (the legislature or the crown) or privately endowed nonprofit institutions, at home or abroad—for whatever ideas or findings might bring it new economic knowledge. It follows on this view that the onset in the 19th century of unremitting growth in productivity and wages reflected some new external force rather than a new force in the economy itself.

This view of economic history was explicit in the works of the last generation of the German Historical School of Economics. They regarded all material advances in a country as driven by the force of science: the discoveries of "scientists and navigators" external to the national economies. Without these godlike figures, there would be no material progress or anything else to exclaim over. The dazzling Austrian economist Joseph Schumpeter, not yet 30, added just one new wrinkle to the school's model: the need for an entrepreneur to develop the new method or good made possible by the new scientific knowledge.[11] In what became a hugely influential work published first in

---

11. The school grew famous and influential in Europe and America for its underlying theme that institutions are of central importance for economic performance—a theme going back to Wilhelm Roscher and even Marx. In the early 1900s the leader of this school, the German Arthur Spiethoff, and his Swedish successor, Gustav Cassel, were upstaged by the last member, Joseph Schumpeter. (Other notables were Werner Sombart, Max Weber, and Karl Polanyí.) Yet Spiethoff was important. The great British economist John Maynard Keynes traveled to Munich in 1932 for the *Festschrift* celebration marking Spiethoff's retirement—an occasion organized by Schumpeter.

Austria in 1911, he set out the dogma of the school, which may be fairly para-phrased as follows:

> What is knowable at present in the economy is already known. So no orig-inality is possible within the economy. It is discoveries outside the econ-omy that make possible the development of any new method or good. Though the opening of such a possibility is soon "in the air," its reali-zation, or implementation, requires an entrepreneur willing and capa-ble enough to undertake the demanding project: to raise the capital, organize the needed start-up company, and develop the newly possible product—"to get the job done." Though the project is onerous, the likeli-hood of the new product's commercial success—the likelihood of an "innovation"—is as knowable as the prospects faced by established prod-ucts. There is no chance of misjudgment, provided there is due diligence. An expert entrepreneur's decision to accept a project and a veteran bank-er's decision to back it are correct ex ante, even uncanny, though ex post bad luck may bring a loss and good luck an abnormal profit.[12]

Thus Schumpeter proposed a way to think about innovation while barely departing from classical economics. The two pied pipers, Schumpeter with his scientism and Marx with his historical determinism, profoundly mis-led historians and the general public. Economics remained mostly classical throughout the 20th century.

Difficulties with this mode of thinking quickly appeared. Historians relying on the German theory realized that by the time of the take-offs, the great navigators had nearly run out of navigable routes to discover. Histori-ans depended on "scientists" to link the take-offs to the step-up in the pace of scientific discovery over the period of the Scientific Revolution from 1620 to 1800, which includes the Enlightenment (defined as the years from 1675 to 1800 or so). Some scientific successes of that period remain legendary: Francis Bacon's 1620 *Novo Organum,* setting out a new logic to replace Aris-totle's *Organon* [*Logic*]; William Harvey's brilliant analysis of the "motion of the blood" in 1628; Anton Leeuwenhoek's work on microorganisms done in

---

12. These propositions express the main themes in Schumpeter's 1934 *The Theory of Economic Development* and the 1912 German edition from which it was drawn, *Theorie der wirtschaft-lichen Entwicklung.* Thus it serves as a window onto Schumpeter's theoretical perspective in the 1900s—a decade or two before the "moderns" of the interwar years, notably Friedrich Hayek. Influenced by Hayek's work, Schumpeter came around in his 1942 *Capitalism, Social-ism and Democracy* to believing that companies in the business sector, not just scientists in royal courts and universities, could be creative in conceiving successful innovations. In his mind, though, they needed industrial labs employing scientists to do it.

1675; Isaac Newton's 1687 mechanics; Pierre Simon Laplace's mathematics work around 1785; and Eugenio Espejo's 1795 work on pathogens. Is it plausible, though, that the findings and subsequent research of a handful of scientists in London and Oxford, and a few other sites, were the forces that propelled the explosive take-offs into sustained growth?

There are ample reasons to be skeptical of this thesis. It boggles the mind to think that the scientific discoveries during and after the Enlightenment had applications so comprehensive and profound as to triple the take-off nations' productivities and real wages in less than a century—and in *most* industries, not just a few—when all the world's past discoveries could do almost nothing to raise productivity. For one thing, the new scientific findings were just additions to a vast storehouse already there. Newton himself insisted that he and all scientists were "standing on the shoulders of giants." For another, the new findings may have had scant applicability to the economy's production; the scientists' discoveries enabled new products and methods only accidentally. Furthermore, most innovating—obviously in entertainment industries, fashion, and tourism—is remote from science. Where it is not, innovation often goes first: the steam engine preceded thermodynamics. The historian Joel Mokyr found that in cases in which entrepreneurs could have used some scientific understanding, the innovators typically ventured ahead of science, using their hunches and experimenting accordingly.

Schumpeter's scientism goes on to credit science with the rise of economic knowledge right through the 19th century. But this is equally problematic when tested against another kind of evidence. Any important new piece of scientific knowledge is accessible in scholarly publications at little or no cost—it is for this reason that it is called a public good. Scientific knowledge, therefore, tends to be roughly equalized across countries. So if we were to accept advances in scientific knowledge as the major explanation of the huge increases in economic knowledge in the take-off nations, it would then be very hard to explain the mounting disparities (starting from rough equality in 1820) in economic knowledge over the 19th century—the Great Divergence, as it has been dubbed. It would be necessary to string together a half dozen ad hoc explanations to account for Britain's early, unsustainable lead, followed by America's durable lead, Belgium's and France's advances, and Germany's progress late in the game. It would be necessary to explain from the perspective of scientism how America left France in its dust, then blew past Belgium and finally overtook Britain, when America was the country least schooled in science and, being exceptionally far geographically from the others, had least access to scientific discoveries. It would be an even greater challenge to explain how the Netherlands and Italy remained at the starting gate, despite their sophistication in science. (Schumpeterian historians might hypothesize that those two nations fell short in entrepreneurial spirit and financial expertise. But Schumpeter himself could not have expressed such doubts after building his theory on the zeal of entrepreneurs and the knowledgeability of financiers.)

We must conclude that advances in science could not have been the driving force behind the explosion of economic knowledge in the 19th century.

Some historians give the credit to the inventions of the applied scientists emerging during the Enlightenment—the most famous being the headline inventions of the so-called First Industrial Revolution. In Britain, examples include Richard Arkwright's 1762 water-powered spinning frame; the 1764 multispool spinning machine credited to the humble Lancashire weaver James Hargreaves; the improved steam engine designed by the firm of Boulton & Watt in 1769; the method for producing wrought iron from pig iron developed by the iron mill of Cort & Jellicoe in the 1780s; and the steam-powered locomotive invented in 1814 by George Stephenson. In America, John Fitch's 1778 steamboat comes to mind. There is no reason for these historians to focus on headline innovations, however. The advances too tiny to be recorded may well have added up to an amount of innovation—measured by the gain in output or wages—far larger than the total innovation prompted by the standout inventions. We may assume that the historians of the Industrial Revolution recounted the headline inventions only to make vivid the restless inventiveness that began to spread in Britain starting in the 1760s. But can we really interpret these inventions as drivers of advances in scientific knowledge—advances scored on the ground, rather than in the ivory tower? And were they drivers of the explosions of economic knowledge in the 19th century?

A point against this thesis is the fact that nearly all the inventors, even the headliners, were not trained scientists, nor were they even particularly well educated. Watt was the exception, not the rule. Arkwright was a wigmaker turned industrialist, not a scientist or engineer. Hargreaves, a Lancashire weaver, was of humble background—too humble to have invented the spinning machine. The great Stephenson was virtually illiterate. Paul Johnson observes that the vast majority of inventors were born poor and could afford little education. It was enough to be creative and smart:

> The Industrial Revolution, which first developed in the 1780s when
> Stephenson was a little boy, is often presented as a time of horror for
> working men. In fact it was the age, above all, in history of matchless

opportunities for penniless men with powerful brains and imaginations, and it is astonishing how quickly they came to the fore.[13]

This characterization of the headline inventors undoubtedly also applied to inventors of the myriad advances in methods that, being tiny, went unsung. So if the historians pointing to the famed inventions thought that their inventors were vessels bearing new scientific knowledge to the fertile field of 19th-century economies, they were sadly mistaken. Furthermore, this scientism does not explain why the explosion of inventions began early in the 19th century, and not before or after, and why the explosion occurred in some high-income nations and not others.

Some might think to say that gifted inventors, even if untrained, were adding to scientific knowledge when their tinkering led to an invention. But these inventors did not create *scientific* knowledge any more than bartenders inventing new drinks create chemical knowledge: they lacked the training to do so. An addition to scientific knowledge occurred if and when trained theorists managed to understand why the invention worked. (It took a musicologist to see how Bach's cantatas "worked.") If an invention at the proof-of-concept stage went on to be developed and adopted, thus becoming an innovation, it did create *economic* knowledge. (Failure also added knowledge of a sort—the economic knowledge of what apparently does not work.)

To regard inventions as the driver of economic knowledge is misleading by suggesting that they are exogenous forces acting on the economy. (Even an accidental discovery happens and has impact only if the discoverer is in the right place at the right time.) The inventions made famous by the major innovations they led to were not prime causes—not thunderbolts from outside the economic system. They were born out of perceptions of business needs or an inspired sense of what businesses and consumers would like to have—all drawn from the innovators' experience and guesswork in the business world. James Watt may have been a pure engineer at heart but his partner, Matthew Boulton, demanded a steam engine that would be widely useful. Invention and the curiosity and ingenuity behind it were nothing new, after all. What

13. Johnson, *The Birth of the Modern* (p. 188). Few would want to question the judgments made by this polymath in any of his several fields. Yet it is highly eccentric to conceive of the First Industrial Revolution as starting in the 1780s rather than the 1760s and unusual to conceive of it as stretching to the 1820s. (Some of the most important inventions and succeeding innovations of the Second Industrial Revolution, starting with the Bessemer process and the Siemens-Martin open hearth processes, were significantly science-based. But even here scientific advances were not generally the drivers of the inventions and certainly do not account for the greater part of aggregate innovation.)

was new, and tied up with the deeper causes, were the changes that inspired, encouraged, and enabled people to invent on a mass scale.

The headline innovations rarely move the mountain that is the economy. The brilliant innovations of Britain's 18th-century textile industry led to great gains in output per worker but, the textile industry being a small part of the economy, could not cause more than a very modest increase in output per worker in Britain's economy as a whole (so modest that output per worker barely increased, if at all, from 1750 to 1800). In the same vein, the economic historian Robert Fogel shook up his fellow historians with his thesis that American economic development would have proceeded as well without the railroads. The fruits of the Industrial Revolution are all one-off— one-time events rather than manifestations of a system or a process. They do not explain either the spectacular take-off in Britain or later take-offs. As Mokyr wrote, "[t]he Industrial Revolution itself, in the classical sense, did not suffice to generate sustained economic growth."[14]

We must conclude that neither the stirring voyages of discovery nor the splendid discoveries in science and the headline inventions that followed could be the cause of the steep and sustained climbs of productivity and wages in the 19th century in the take-off economies of Western Europe and North America. Rather, the explosions of economic knowledge in the 19th century must be the effect of the emergence of an entirely new kind of economy: a system for the generation of endogenous innovation decade after decade as long as the system continues to function. Only the structuring of these economies for the exercise of indigenous creativity and pathways from there to innovation—for what has come to be called "indigenous innovation"—could have put these nations on steep paths of sustained growth. If there was a fundamental "invention" here, it was the fashioning of economies that drew on the creativity and intuition that lay inside them to attempt innovation. These were the world's first modern economies. Their economic dynamism made them the marvel of the modern era.

14. He adds:
> It is easy to imagine the economies of the West settling into the techniques [of producing throstles, wrought iron, coke-smelting, and stationary steam engines] that had emerged between 1750 and 1800 without taking them much further. Such a development would have paralleled the wave of inventions of the 15th century, with the printing press, the three-masted ship and iron-casting settling into dominant designs and the process of improvement slowing down to a trickle subsequently.

See Mokyr's 2007 Max Weber Lecture, "The Industrial Revolution and Modern Economic Growth," p. 3.

We do not have to infer from data on productivity growth the presence (or absence) of dynamism—as physics inferred the existence of dark matter and dark energy. The revolution in the societies possessing take-off economies went far beyond the unprecedented phenomenon of sustained—and apparently sustainable—growth. As pioneering entrepreneurs multiplied, ultimately overshadowing merchants, and as more and more people were tinkering with methods and products or dreaming up new ones, the experience of work changed radically for increasing numbers of participants. From retail trade to textiles to Tin Pan Alley, masses of people in society were active in conceiving, creating, evaluating, and trying out the new and learning from the experience.

In this way, the modern economies brought to a society something of the "heroic spirit" that Smith hoped to see, such as standing out from the crowd and rising to a challenge. These economies also brought to ordinary people of varying talents a kind of flourishing—the experience of engagement, personal growth, and fulfillment. Even people with few and modest talents—barely enough talent to get a job—were given the experience of using their minds: to seize an opportunity, solve a problem, and think of a new way or a new thing. In short, dynamism's spark created modern life.

These modern economies, present and past—their rewards and costs, the preconditions for their rise, how some of them were unseated, their justification, and now, the weakening among the remaining ones—these are the subject of this book.

PART ONE

THE EXPERIENCE
OF THE MODERN ECONOMY

He was . . . a prey to homesickness for his own kind, for his own epoch,
for European man and his glorious history of desire and dreams.

WILLA CATHER, *Death Comes for the Archbishop*

CHAPTER ONE

How the Modern Economies Got Their Dynamism

The secret of brilliant productivity will always be discovering new problems and intuiting new theorems, which open the way to new results and connections. Without the creation of new viewpoints, without positing new aims, mathematics would soon exhaust itself in the rigor of logical proofs and begin to stagnate, as it would run out of content. In a way, mathematics has been best served by those who distinguished themselves more by intuitions than by rigorous proofs.

FELIX KLEIN, *Lectures on Mathematics in the 19th Century*

PART ONE SEES THE FIRST MODERN ECONOMIES as lying at the core of the modern societies that arose in the West early in the 19th century. Their unprecedented dynamism was mirrored by dynamism in other realms of society as well. The narrative describes how these economies changed not only living and working standards but also the very character of life: dynamism manifests itself in manifold ways. The narrative goes on to examine how and why these history-making economies came about.

A modern economy, as that term is used here, means not a present-day economy but rather an economy with a considerable degree of dynamism—that is, the will and the capacity and aspiration to innovate. One may ask, then, what makes a modern economy modern, just as one may ask what makes modern music modern. If a national economy is a complex of economic institutions and a fabric of economic attitudes—an economic culture—what structure of these elements equipped and fueled the modern economies for dynamism? To begin, it is necessary to be clear about the concept of dynamism and its relation to growth, with which it is often confused.

An innovation, to repeat, is a new method or new product that becomes a *new practice* somewhere in the world.[1] The new practice may arise in just one nation, before it spreads, or in a community that cuts across nations. Any such innovation involves both the *origination* of the new thing—its conception and its development—and the *pioneering adoption*. Thus innovations depend on a *system*. Innovative people and companies are just the beginning. To have good prospects for innovation, a society requires people with the expertise and experience to judge well whether to attempt development of a new thing; whether a proposed project is worth financing; and whether, when a new product or method is developed, it is worth trying.

Until recent decades, the innovation system was supposed to be the national economy. To innovate, a nation had to do its own development as well as its own adoption. But in a global economy, in which national economies are open to outside developments, the development could take place in one country and the adoption in another. If an innovation, joint or singlehanded, is then adopted by another country, that adoption is not regarded as an innovation—not from a global perspective. Yet selecting foreign products that would have good prospects of acceptance at home might require as much insight as selecting among new conceptions to develop. The distinction between innovation and imitation is basic, but the line between may be fuzzy.

We must also understand the concept of an economy's dynamism. It is a compound of the deep-set forces and facilities behind innovation: the drive to change things, the talent for it, and the receptivity to new things, as well as the enabling institutions. Thus dynamism, as it is used here, is the willingness and capacity to innovate, leaving aside current conditions and obstacles. This contrasts with what is usually called vibrancy: an alertness to opportunities, a readiness to act, and the zeal to "get it done" (as Schumpeter puts it). Dynamism determines the normal volume of innovation. Other determinants, such as market conditions, may alter the results. And there can be a drought of new ideas or a gush of them, just as a composer may have a dry or fertile spell. So the pace of actual innovation may exhibit marked swings without any change in dynamism—in the normal tendency to innovate. Post-war Europe saw a

---

1. This usage is not universal but is increasingly common. An example is Denning and Dunham, *The Innovator's Way* (2010). To economists, ever since Schumpeter's 1912 work, an innovation has meant a new practice, not just a new development. (For him, development and adoption went hand in hand, both being a sure thing.) Scientists tend to call the invention of a new method or product an innovation whether or not buyers are found for it.

sprinkling of innovation in the 1960s —the bikini, the Nouvelle Vague, and the Beatles, for example. By 1980, though, with wealth having recovered to its old level relative to income, innovation had fallen back. It became apparent that the dynamism of Europe had not recovered, even partially, to its healthy level in the interwar years, although that became clear only with mounting evidence.

One way to measure this dynamism is to gauge the aforementioned forces and facilities—the inputs producing dynamism. Another approach is to gauge the size of its estimated output: the average annual volume of innovation in recent years—the growth of total GDP not attributable to the growth of capital and labor—after allowance for unusual market conditions and after deducting the "false innovations" copied from other countries. The decadal average income earned by those in the innovation process, if we could observe it, would be a crude measure of that "output." Or we could size up many strands of circumstantial evidence: new firm formation, employee turnover, turnover in the 20 largest companies, turnover of retail stores, and the mean life of a product's universal product code.

The economic growth rate of a country is *not* a useful measure of dynamism. In a global economy driven by one or more economies of high dynamism, an economy with low or even no dynamism may regularly enjoy much the same growth rate as that of the highflying moderns—the same growth rate of productivity, real wages, and other economic indicators. It grows that fast partly by trading with the highflyers but mainly by being vibrant enough to imitate the adoptions of original products in modern economies. Italy provides a nice example: from 1890 to 1913, output per manhour there grew at the same rate as in America—it remained 43 percent lower, neither gaining nor losing ground in the *league tables* (the rankings of countries by the relative levels of their productivity (e.g., output per hour worked) and real wages), but no economic historian would suggest that Italy's economy had much dynamism at all, let alone the American level.

An economy with low dynamism might for a time show a faster growth rate than a modern economy does with its high dynamism. A transient elevation of the growth rate could result from any of a number of structural shifts in the economy, such as an increase in vibrancy or an increase in dynamism from low to not-as-low. While the economy is moving up to a higher place in the league tables—a partial "catch-up" to the modern economies—it will be growing at the normal, global, rate plus a transient, which fades away as the destination nears. But even a growth rate that is the world's highest should not suggest that the economy has just acquired high dynamism, let alone the highest. Sweden provides a good example. It held the world cup for the championship growth rate of productivity from 1890 to 1913. It started a raft of new companies, several of which endured and became famous. But it did not appear to acquire the high dynamism of America or, say, Germany. In ensuing decades its growth rate dropped below that of America and not one new firm has entered the top 10 on the stock exchange after 1922 even to this day. Japan's high growth from 1950 to 1990 is another example. Many observers inferred high dynamism, but this streak of growth reflected not the advent of state-of-the-art modernity throughout Japan—no such transformation occurred—but rather the chance to import or imitate practices pioneered for decades by the modern economies. The world-record growth in China since 1978 is the latest example: while the world sees world-class dynamism, the Chinese discuss how to *acquire* the dynamism for indigenous innovation, without which they will be hard pressed to continue their fast growth.

So a nation's "dynamism" is not a new word for a nation's productivity growth. Its own dynamism is not necessary for its growth if the rest of the world has dynamism—vibrancy is enough; and it is not sufficient if the nation is so small that its dynamism cannot go far. Dynamism over an appreciable part of the world leads to global growth, barring bad luck. The modern economies, with their high dynamism, are the engines of the growth of the global economy—today, as in the 19th century.

So, although the growth rate of productivity in an economy—say, output per manhour—over a month or even a year is no indicator of its own dynamism, we might think that the *level* of its productivity relative to the levels abroad would be an indicator. It is true, with few exceptions, if any, that the economies with productivity levels at or very close to the top level owe that position to a high level of dynamism. Yet a low position of a country's productivity level may reflect low dynamism *or* low vibrancy or both. So the relative level of productivity is not an altogether safe indicator of an economy's dynamism.

To gauge more deeply an economy's dynamism, we have to look under the hood to see what there is in the structure of an economy that might strongly nourish or inhibit dynamism.

Inner Workings of the Historical Modern Economies

Schumpeter's near-classical theory, with its concept of punctuated equilibrium, blocked all thoughts of a modern economy—an economy generating economic knowledge through its own talent and insight into the business of innovating. The dominance of this theory has had consequences: to this day, policymakers and commentators do not distinguish between modern economies, less modern ones, and nonmodern ones. They see all national economies, even exemplars of modernity, as essentially machines for producing products and doing so more or less efficiently at that—though some have natural handicaps or costly policies.

But if we just look, we can see the distinctive stuff that modern economies are made of: It is *ideas.* The visible "goods and services" of the national income statistics are mostly embodiments of past ideas. The modern economy is primarily engaged in activity aimed at innovation. These activities are stages in a process:

- conception of new products or methods
- preparation of proposals to develop some of them
- selection of some development proposals for financing
- development of the chosen products or methods
- marketing of the new products or methods
- evaluation and possible tryout by end-users
- significant adoption of some new products and methods
- revision of new products after tryout or early adoption

In an economy of substantial size, there are gains in expertise from a Smithian division of labor, and innovational activity is no exception: some participants work full-time in a team conceiving and designing a new products, some work in a financial company picking new companies to fund, some work with a start-up entrepreneur developing a new product, some are employees specializing in evaluating new methods, others specialize in marketing, and so forth. No less important, in an economy of dynamism, some portion of most participants' time is spent looking at current practice with the expectation that a new idea will occur for a better way to do things or a better thing to produce. This patchwork of activity is the *ideas sector.* In an economy high in dynamism, the idea-driven activity might amount to a tenth of total manhours worked. However, the work of investing in new ideas and new practices—though it may crowd out work in some familiar lines of investment activity—may spark a boundless amount of investment activity aimed at producing facilities to make the new products. The result is a strongly positive effect on employment. (Innovative activity in particular and investment activity in general are far more labor intensive, hence less capital intensive, than the production of consumer goods: food production, for example, uses much capital, such as wire fences, and much energy; energy production also uses much capital, such as derricks, dams, and windmills.)[2]

How do these modern economies *work*—those of the 19th and the 20th century too? We may begin at an almost physiological level, rather like Henry Gray's *Anatomy* (1862). We see in these modern economies multiple lines of innovative activity. These are parallel efforts, which represent the competition of ideas. In an economy of appreciable size, new commercial ideas are hatched every day, mostly inside enterprises. Development of such ideas will generally require enterprises with the right expertise. Among the projects with an eager entrepreneur, not all will find financial backing. Capital flows only to those projects judged by an entrepreneur and a financial backer to have good prospects of development and marketing. Among the projects carried forward, not all will manage to embody the idea in a product that would be cheap enough to be marketable. Among the new products brought to the market, sales or orders will come in only for those judged by end-users—managers or consumers—to be worth the risk of a pioneering adoption. Only a small proportion will show signs of wide enough adoption to continue production or to warrant stepping up production to break-even or profitable levels. This *selection mechanism* may leave one idea standing where there were thousands to begin with. (A study by McKinsey estimated that, from 10,000 business ideas, 1,000 firms are founded, 100 receive venture capital, 20 go on to raise capital in an initial public offering of shares, and 2 become market leaders.)

We can picture the corresponding competition going on in a socialist economy: the "enterprises" are state-owned, and the backing comes from a state development bank. We can also picture the corresponding competition in a corporatist economy: the enterprises, though under private ownership, are state-controlled, and their finances are allocated by state-controlled banks. However, the modern economies of the storied past possessed neither one of these structures. The modern economies of the past two centuries—primarily those of Britain, America, Germany, and France—were, and to varying degrees still are, specimens of *modern* capitalism.

In these real-life modern economies—and in any modern-capitalist economy—decisions to provide capital for the first steps toward innovation are made predominantly by investors, financiers, and share buyers drawing

---

2. The Austrian-born Fritz Machlup did some early work on measuring the importance of the industries aimed at producing new economic knowledge. The estimate above is not a precise calculation but is not just an impression either.

on their own private wealth or by managers of financial companies under private ownership. The collected investments and loans of these "capitalists," some of them with very small wealth, determine which directions, among those presented, the economy will embark on. Decisions to take the initiative of planning and seeking finance for development of a new idea are made predominantly by producers—managers by trade—starting a private venture or acting within established private enterprises. To distinguish producers of such undertakings from producers of established products, the former are called *entrepreneurs*. Typically, the entrepreneurs also bring some capital to the new undertaking. Both a project's entrepreneur and its investors stand to gain whatever pecuniary returns the project might bring and suffer the loss should the returns be negative. Of course, these returns are not determined in isolation: such projects compete against others, driving down the private returns and driving up rents to land and wages to labor. The pecuniary return is not unimportant to an investor with a large stake or to an entrepreneur—their livelihoods and standard of living may be at stake. An entrepreneur may need the prospect of winnings to obtain the moral support of family members.

The prospect of profit, which entrepreneurs and investors share after paying creditors, is not the only prospective return factored into the decision to start a new undertaking. Both entrepreneurs and large-stake investors favor projects that excite their imagination and enlist their energies. They may also want to play a part in the development of the community or the nation.[3] (Some entrepreneurs and financiers create enterprises primarily for the satisfaction of producing a social benefit—on top of whatever pecuniary return may be expected. These "social entrepreneurs" may coexist alongside the classic entrepreneurs, whether or not they are financed by the state. To the extent that this parallel system has dynamism, it helps make modern economies modern.)

It is unfortunate that most discussions, except for trivial distinctions like that between ships and factories, do not distinguish modern capitalism from

---

3. Do entrepreneurs generally receive large nonpecuniary returns? Schumpeter was skeptical. He writes poignantly of the successful entrepreneur who finds that admittance to polite society will not be one of the rewards. He also thought that the average realized pecuniary return of entrepreneurs was below normal: they were too sanguine or paid a steep price to have some fun. Now there appears to be a consensus that, even in the unromantic 20th century, modern entrepreneurs as a group find big nonpecuniary rewards—"the time of their lives," as some put it; but perhaps at some cost to their cash flow. None of this matters for how the modern economy *works,* however.

mercantile capitalism (also known as early capitalism or commercial society). Modern capitalism built on early capitalism, of course. The latter solidified property rights; won acceptance of interest, profit, and wealth-building; and taught the social value of individual responsibility. Mercantile capitalism also gave birth (in Venice and Augsburg) to banks that lent to or entered into business. But modern capitalism is as different from mercantile capitalism as innovators are different from merchants. The mercantile economy was about the distribution of products to consumers. (To exaggerate slightly, men and women scooped up nature's crops and took the excess supplies to market to exchange them for excess supplies of other crops.) Modern capitalism introduced innovation into capitalism. Entrepreneurs soon put merchants in the shade. As new practices welled up, many guilds founded in medieval times could not enforce standards. The state could not issue charters fast enough to meet the exploding demand.

Even more unfortunate, economies around the world that repress competition by limiting entry to the well-connected and do nothing else that might encourage or facilitate innovation are being seen as examples of capitalism by those suffering hardships in those economies as well as those who run the economies. (The American economy is seen as an "exceptional" case of capitalism.) In northern Africa, a tightly connected ring of politicians, elites, and the armed forces keep the business sector for themselves: outsiders are not licensed to enter industries in competition with incumbent enterprises. These economies are said to be "capitalist" on the thought that "capital" is in charge—the wealth of the oligarchy of the ruling families. But a hallmark of capitalism is that the capitalists are independent, uncoordinated, and competing with one another: no monarchy or oligarchy is in charge. And a hallmark of modern capitalism is that it permits and invites outsiders with a new idea to seek capital from capitalists willing to place a bet on the proposed project. These oligarchic economies are more accurately viewed as a kind of *corporatism,* a system in which the business sector is under some kind of political control.

This chapter began by asking what structure "equipped and fueled" the modern economies for dynamism. The discussion so far has cast some light on how the modern economies are equipped to select among new ideas for development and adoption. But what fuels the creation of new ideas?

The very concept of new economic ideas has been foreign to the rising numbers under the spell of scientism, which came to rule academia in the 20th century—not to mention historicism, which ruled out any new ideas! As noted in the Introduction, the German Historical School supposed that only scientists have new ideas, which, after testing, often add to scientific knowledge. That theory never worked well: from the time of Columbus to Isaac Newton's era there was little innovation and between the steam engine and electric power there was no epochal scientific advance. But the failure of a theory is not enough to stop it. Schumpeter, some 30 years after his first book, reaffirmed that only scientists can have ideas, allowing that they could have their ideas in the great industrial labs, such as DuPont.[4] The popular theory today is neo-German: gifted conceivers of new technology "platforms," such as Tim Berners-Lee, creator of the World Wide Web; Jack Kilby and Robert Noyce, the builders of the microchip; and Charles Babbage, inventor of the computer, are thought to provide the underlying advances that make possible successive waves of applications. This scientism easily persuaded the public. No one had to ask where scientists and engineers "get their ideas," since everyone knew they got their ideas from their observations in the lab and the findings reported in research journals. The investigators and experimenters are immersed in their science and engineering fields—though no more than entrepreneurs and financiers are immersed in their fields.

But the advent of the modern economy brought a metamorphosis: a modern economy turns people who are close to the *economy*, where they are apt to be struck by new commercial ideas, into the investigators and experimenters who manage the innovation process from development and, in many cases, adoption as well. (In a role reversal, scientists and engineers are called in to assist on technical matters.) In fact, it turns all sorts of people into "idea-men," financiers into thinkers, producers into marketers, and end-users into pioneers. The driving force of the modern economy in the past two centuries is this economic system—a system built of an economic culture as well as economic institutions. This system, rather than the brilliant *personaggi* of the popular theory, generates the modern economy's dynamism.

The modern economy, then, is a vast *imaginarium*—a space for imagining new products and methods, imagining how they might be made, imagining

4. See his 1942 monograph *Capitalism, Socialism and Democracy*. The brilliant 1912 book with which Schumpeter made his name portrayed his subject as an infallible machine, one that had no creativity but could promptly and faultlessly seize every opportunity for profitable investment soon after it arose. The 1942 book with which he closed his career went further in concluding that corporate managements could promptly and faultlessly seize opportunities for technological advances. That led to the question, if corporate managements could do it, why not state agencies and socialist enterprises? That may have deepened Schumpeter's feeling at the end of his career that the Western world was on an inexorable "march into socialism."

how they might be used. Its innovation process draws on human resources not utilized by a premodern economy. In Schumpeter's theory, premodern development draws on the capacities of premodern entrepreneurs to organize the projects made possible by outside discoveries—he spoke of human resources like hustle and the determination to "get the job done." As modern theorists have said, *modern* entrepreneurs are business owners or managers who, in the face of not very much real knowledge, micro or macro, demonstrate "a capacity for making successful decisions when no obviously correct model or decision rule is available"—nor can be—as a 1990 essay by Mark Casson put it. This capacity, which relies on financiers as well as entrepreneurs, is recognized to require the resources called *judgment,* or acumen—judgment about the unknown likelihood of things—and *wisdom*—the sense that there are forces not even conceived of, called the unknown unknowns. This judgment involves imagining in an effort to foresee the consequences of alternative actions. This entrepreneurial capacity is *modern entrepreneurship.* But it is not by itself a source of radical change or even novelty. It is not the same as *innovatorship.*

The indigenous innovation process of the imaginarium draws on a different set of human resources. A basic resource is the *imaginativeness,* or *creativity*, to conceive of things not conceived already that a firm could try to develop and market. There cannot be much departure from present knowledge if no one can imagine the existence of another way or another goal, or if no one can imagine the chance of beneficial outcomes. Imaginativeness is fundamental to successful change, as David Hume saw in his profound work so fundamental to the modern era.[5] The innovative capacity also requires *insight*—insight into a new direction that might turn out to meet desires or needs that could not have been known before. That insight is often called strategic vision—an intuition we cannot explain and a sense of whether other enterprises will be adopting the same strategy. Steve Jobs owed his huge success to his creativity and deep insights. Curiosity to explore and the courage to do something different must also be mentioned.

Yet no imaginarium will be present in economies where people are not motivated and encouraged to innovate or are not in a position to innovate.

---

5. Hume's great themes—the necessity of imagination for discovery or change, the importance and legitimacy of sentiment or "passions" in human decisions, and the danger of depending on past patterns to hold up in the future, all in his 1748 masterpiece *An Enquiry Concerning Human Understanding*—can be seen as prefiguring the modernity to come, in which imagination would run wild, the growth of knowledge would be rampant, and the future would be barely recognizable.

The fuel on which this system operates is a mixture of pecuniary and nonpecuniary motives. Pecuniary rewards make a difference: The prospects of significant money are apt to be helpful in persuading one's family to support the effort one may have to put in. So few participants in the economy will be available to conceive and develop a commercial idea if not legally free to monetize it—to sell it to an entrepreneur for a share of the resulting profit or, in the case of patentable concepts, to collect the royalties under the patent or sell the patent to others. Entrepreneurs and investors will not develop an idea if they are not legally free to start a firm, break into an industry, sell their shares in the firm later (nowadays in an initial public offering), and close down the company in the event that buyers do not turn up. Entrepreneurs have to know that potential end-users are free to abandon a current method or product in order to cast their lot with a new method or product. Without the incentive of such pecuniary protections and inducements, most entrepreneurs will draw back from undertaking such ventures, no matter the nonpecuniary rewards.

Some nonpecuniary motives, or drives, are also important—perhaps critical—for the functioning of the modern economy. To function, the modern economy feeds off a motivating economic culture as well as pecuniary incentives. High dynamism in a society requires people who grew up with attitudes and beliefs that attract them to opportunities that they expect will excite them with their novelty, intrigue them with their mysteries, challenge them with new hurdles, and inspire them with new vistas. It requires people in business brought up to *use* their imaginativeness and insightfulness to achieve a new direction; entrepreneurs driven by their desire to make their mark; people in venture investing willing to act on a hunch ("I like the cut of her jib"); and many end-users—consumers or producers—with the willingness to *pioneer* the adoption of a new product or method whose expected value is not knowable beforehand. This requires drives such as aspiration, curiosity, and self-expression. High dynamism in the system requires high dynamism in all its parts.[6]

6. Various observers have written on the subject. In Somerset Maugham's 1929 story, "The Man Who Made His Mark," a man fresh out of a job, noticing that the neighborhood has no tobacconist, has the drive to restart his life by opening a tobacco shop there. End-users, too, must share in the dynamism of Maugham's tobacconist. What became known as the Nelson-Phelps model of the adoption of an innovation, published in 1966, was an early attempt to highlight end-users in the innovation process, such as farmers risking adoption of new seeds and fertilizers. The focus there was on the importance of end-users' education. Amar Bhidé in his 2008 book focused on the need for "venturesome" end-users.

Innovating also draws on people's observations and personal knowledge. New business ideas come only to those who have been observing at close hand some area of a business, learning things about how it works and giving some thought to the possible size of the market for a new sort of product in that area or to the prospect for a better method of production; plausible business ideas rarely come to those remote from any business. People situated in some area of the business sector will gain knowledge and see opportunities that they would not otherwise have been aware of—or have known existed.

Hitting upon an idea for better use for retail space or a better route for delivering packages is not exactly what we mean by innovation. Yet, it may be argued, the detailed business knowledge that inspires new ideas for business investment also inspires ideas that may lead to business innovation. (Similarly, the attitudes that help stir the formation of new investment ideas also stir ideas for innovation.)

So there is an obvious answer to the question of where business people's ideas for innovation come from: they come from the business sector. Business people draw on their personal observation and private knowledge, in combination with the shared pool of public knowledge (such as economics), in coming up with conceptualizations that lead to a new method or product that might "work"—much as a scientist, immersed in his or her own experimental data, specialized expertise, and general scientific knowledge, arrives at a new formulation or hypothesis to be tested, which might add to scientific knowledge. Business people and scientists alike draw on private knowledge, based on individual observation, as well as on the public knowledge of the community to which the individual belongs. (Yet scientists will undoubtedly go on believing that business people get their ideas from outside business, just as most people say that composers get their ideas outside music. Giving the lie to this common illusion, Robert Craft reported an exchange between reporters and Igor Stravinsky: "Maestro, can you tell us where you get your ideas?" "At the piano," Stravinsky shot back.)

Friedrich Hayek, the Austrian-born economist who loomed large in the Austrian school, was the first economist to view economies from this perspective. His seminal works from 1933 to 1945 see producers and buyers in the complex economies around him as having valuable practical knowledge about how best to produce and what best to produce. Typically, such knowledge, being local, contextual, and kaleidoscopic, cannot be easily acquired by or communicated to others: it remains private knowledge. (Even if all of it were all costlessly accessible—open to the public—it is too enormous to be comprehended, let alone assimilated.) Therefore such knowledge is, and remains, dispersed over the economy's participants, each industry having much knowledge unique to the industry and each participant some further knowledge unique to that individual or to a very few. This leads to two propositions: First, an economy of complexity gains critically from markets, in which individuals and companies can exchange goods and services with one another, so that the specialization of practical knowledge can continue—so one does not need to be a jack-of-all-trades with only the thinnest knowledge of any. When new knowledge is obtained in an industry, this is "communicated" to society through the market mechanism: a drop in price, or the like. Second, such an economy, if unimpeded, is an organism ever-acquiring gains in economic knowledge of what and how to produce (while also deaccessing old knowledge once it is of no further use). The right prices are "discovered" in the process. Every company or participant is like a forward observer, or scout ant, responding alertly with adjustments in the level or direction of production to observations and analyses of any local development. If the output of some product is increased, the reduced price on the market will signal the society that it now costs less than before.[7] This was Hayek's *knowledge economy.*

Yet this work of Hayek is not about innovations. It does not envisage indigenous innovations, which develop from ideas sparked by the creativity of participants in the economy. In a much-cited 1945 paper, he makes it explicit that he is discussing *adaptations*—"adaptations," he calls them, to "changing circumstances." These adaptations do draw on some of the human resources of modern entrepreneurship mentioned earlier: judgment, and wisdom, and the drive to make their mark.

There is an air of predictability about adaptations, unlike innovations. They do not involve an intuitive leap but are repercussions that would take place sooner or later, barring some other change that erased the need for the adaptation. And they will not go on long if "circumstances" should stop "changing." They are not disruptive: they bring closure to a disruption rather than causing

---

7. This work begins with Hayek's 1937 presidential address to the London Economic Club, "Economics and Knowledge," and ends with his much-cited 1945 paper "The Use of Knowledge in Society," which has the notion of "changing circumstances." These and other papers collected in his *Individualism and Economic Order* (1948) were conceived in the period from the 1920s until almost the 1950s, when socialism and corporatism were hotly debated by many European economists. The present chapter, though, is focused on how Hayek's views contributed to the understanding of modern capitalism. Chapter 5 takes up the debate over socialism and Chapter 6 the modern economy's struggle with corporatism.

new disruptions. In contrast, innovations (from *nova*, Latin for new) are not determinate from current knowledge, thus are not foreseeable. Being new, they could not have been known before. Yet many business people have the mistaken notion that innovation means going out to find out what their customers want. The fallacy that innovations are foreseen is criticized by Walter Vincenti:

> The "technical imperative" of the retractable landing gear is . . . after-the-fact. Designers at the time, by their own testimony, did not foresee it. . . . Innovators see where they want to go and by what means they propose to get there. What they cannot do, if their idea is novel, is *foresee* with certainty whether it will work in the sense of meeting all the relevant requirements.[8]

Being unforeseen, an innovation may be disruptive, creating a new jigsaw puzzle in which to fit the pieces—to which to adapt. Innovations are the happenings to which "adaptations" adapt. (A big adaptation that comes far sooner than supposed could be disruptive.) An innovation may be ephemeral, yet most innovations tomorrow stand on the shoulders of today's innovations. Cumulatively they drive the economy's "practice" on a path to ports-of-call that would otherwise have gone unseen. Thus innovations pass a more demanding test than adaptations do.

Innovations, while requiring the intellectual faculties of imaginativeness and insight to envision a new objective, may also require the boldness to venture into unknown territory and thus to go in a different direction from one's peers and mentors. This causes us to see innovators as heroes—putting creation ahead of their comforts and braving failure and losses. However, there is no reason to think that innovators love risk. The Minnesota innovators Harold and Owen Bradley said that an innovation springs from conceiving a new *model* of the business or of the world in some respect. So it may be that innovators, whether the founders of companies or gifted CEOs or the pioneer end-users, are driven by an inner need to demonstrate to themselves or to others the superiority of their understanding.

Henry Ford's quest for the mass-produced car is a paradigm case of innovation. In the 2011 lecture "Eureka," Harold Evans told the story:

> Many Americans believe Henry Ford invented the car. Of course, he was preceded in Europe and by others in America and even in his home town of Detroit. He said: "I invented nothing. I simply assembled into a car the discoveries of other men." In fact, he did do something startlingly new.

8. Vincenti, "The Retractable Airplane Landing Gear" (1994, pp. 21–22).

Not so much in originating the automatic production line; an assembly
line that multiplied milling productivity fivefold was devised by Oliver
Evans in 1795 . . . Henry Ford's genius lay in an idea—the egalitarian idea
that everyone should have a car.

Although some people did not view Ford as highly innovative, like Ford
himself, his breakthrough was a farsighted vision of a new way of life,
which he proved realizable. Another instructive story is America's glorious
cross-country railroad. Evans's 2004 book *They Made America* discusses it:

Theodore Judah, of Sacramento, had the boldness to entrepreneur and
engineer America's first transcontinental railway. His wife Anna wrote
that "it . . . show[ed] what was in the man . . . to grasp the gigantic and the
daring." Detractors said that the idea had been around for years and it was
"just a matter of time" till the railway was built.

As Evans remarks, Judah's engineering feat was felt by some to be too foreseeable to be classed as an innovation. Yet it was only the *attempt* at construction that was "just a matter of time." *Success* was in doubt. Many engineers
thought that such a direct railway to northern California was not feasible. So
the successful construction was by no means foreseeable. Judah had a stunning intuition and proved he was right.

Some innovations are accidental. Thomas Edison absent-mindedly created a filament out of some tarred lampblack in his hand, and Alexander
Fleming made penicillin by mistakenly leaving a Petri dish uncovered. In
the economy, too, there are countless examples of an undreamed innovation. There is always some "Side B" or low-budget sleeper that becomes an
unimagined hit. Pixar was created to develop a new computing practice, but
when a technician showed some visitors he could use the technique to make
animated cartoons, their excitement turned the company into an animation
studio. These accidental innovations were so novel that the conceivers did
not even dream of the new product.

And virtually all innovations have an accidental or random element.
Success in developing the new product and gaining adoption for commercial production is in part a matter of chance. The iconic TV interviewer Larry
King commented more than once that his most famous guests all told him
that their enormous success depended on a stroke of good luck. Yet the success or failure in attempted innovation is not like a lucky or unlucky flip of
a known coin. Innovators travel on a voyage into the unknown, one with
some known unknowns and some unknown unknowns; so they have no
way of knowing whether—even with every lucky break—their creativity and

intuition will deliver the innovation they hoped for. Hayek, coming finally to innovation in 1961, was dismayed that the American economist John Kenneth Galbraith supposed that companies knew what the prospects were for their new products. For Hayek, a company can no more *know* the probability of this profit or that loss on a new auto design than a writer of a novel can know what his or her chances are of making the bestseller list.

Oddly enough, economists left it to Hayek to tie up the rudimentary theory he missed starting—though he may have inspired it. In 1968 he sees economies—evidently referring to what is called here the modern economy—producing "growth in knowledge" through the operation of a method he dubs a *discovery procedure.* The term refers to the process of determining whether the imagined product or method can be developed and, if developed, determining whether it will be adopted. Through internal trials and market tests, a modern economy adds to its knowledge of what can be produced and what methods work, and to its knowledge of what is *not* accepted and what does *not* work.[9] It might be added that the advance of business knowledge may very well be boundless, since, unlike scientific knowledge, it is not limited by the physical world. It is the scientists who should be worried that their discoveries are coming to an end.

Another source of growth in this knowledge, though this one has limits, comes from correction: the fact that much of current knowledge is incorrect both at the micro level of particular products and the macro level of the whole economy.[10] Conditions and structural relationships are apt to be changing in not-yet-perceived ways. (Northrop, using a wind tunnel, found the added drag from a fixed landing gear instead of a retractable one was negligible; they did not realize the added drag was serious on the much faster planes.) In addition, observations of the economy are not outcomes of a controlled experiment; the data themselves are constantly changing as knowledge (and misunderstanding) change in the economy. So there is room in economies for insight into the mistakes of others.

The modern economy takes on "the problem of discovering—or inventing—possibilities and making good use of them," as Brian Loasby wrote.

---

9. Hayek's 1961 piece is "The Non Sequitur of the 'Dependence Effect'" (reprinted in 1962). The later paper mentioned is the 1968 "Competition as a Discovery Procedure" (published in English in 1978). A 1946 paper contains the first hint of this new chapter in Hayek's thought.

10. The notion of "changing beliefs" figures in Hayek's *The Counter-Revolution of Science* (1952). To really understand a social phenomenon, he writes, one needs to know "what the people dealing with it think" (p. 156).

The more an economy devotes itself to this activity, the more modern it is. An economy can have the vibrancy to formulate, the diligence to evaluate, and the zeal to exploit new commercial opportunities opened by external discoveries, which was as much as Schumpeter could see and thought possible. Yet the same economy or another economy may possess the creativity to conceive its own new commercial ideas in response to conditions or developments within it and have the vision (or intuition) to point that creativity in plausible directions. Creativity and vision are resources; they exist in all human economies. Yet historically some countries were unable or unwilling to deploy them and others drew back after earlier use. A modern economy unleashes creativity and vision yet manages with some success to harness it to the expertise of entrepreneurs, the judgment of financiers, and the gumption of end-users.[11]

The basics of the modern economy—how it functions as an innovation system—have been set out. Participants have new commercial ideas, which grow out of their deep engagement and long observation in their respective industries and professions. The process of development of new methods and products involves a variety of financial entities—angel investors, super-angel funds, venture capitalists, merchant banks, commercial banks, and hedge funds; it involves various sorts of producers—start-up companies, large corporations and their spin-offs; and a range of marketing activity—marketing strategy, advertising, and the rest. On the end-user side, there are company managers making pioneering assessments of novel methods and consumers deciding what new products to try out. Both are learning how to use the new methods and products they have adopted. By the mid-19th century, building blocks for a modern economy were in place in Britain and America, later in Germany and France:

> There was a swarm of entrepreneurs enjoying rights to hold property
> and do business, rights against the state, and the protections of contract
> law. These entrepreneurs, in companies or proprietorships they founded,
> were heavily engaged in tinkering with new methods and dreaming up
> new products. Banks seldom lent or invested in entrepreneurs without
> a track record. Family and friends often acted as "angel investors" to get

---

11. It is not controversial to say that the economies that have stood out for their extensive and effective use of creativity and judgment are those making heavy use of a relatively well-functioning "free enterprise," or "capitalist" system—whatever the social and political systems they operate with. They have been the great historical examples of modern economies—leaving aside the issue of whether they are the sole examples. Yet well-functioning capitalism could perhaps be superseded by some new form of the modern economy.

the entrepreneur's project started. Many new businesses had to plow back earnings if they were to expand. In England there were country banks supplying entrepreneurs with short-term credit and trusted attorneys accepting deposits from clients and lending long-term to entrepreneurs. And sometimes individuals became partners in a venture or put up the fee to buy patent protection. A few banks virtually went into business, as the Fuggers had done in south Germany centuries before—some advising and investing in whole industries. In America, country banks tended to be more entrepreneurial. New England businesses not uncommonly went into banking, even selling bank stock to finance their business ventures. Other banks lent to family and friends. (Not many of these proto-venture capitalists could take equity stakes, as today's venture firms do, until entrepreneurs created joint-stock companies that could issue shares.)[12]

The modern economy, seen as a vast, unceasing project to conceive, develop, and test ideas about what would work and what people would like, has had profound consequences for work and society. Its predecessor, the mercantile economy, offered little work and what there was offered a wage and little else. It may have been a relief from domesticity, yet it was tedious. In modern economies, work is nearly universal: economic inclusion is far wider than in mercantile times. This work is central to people's experience, particularly their mental life, and shapes their development. Thus the modern economy institutes a way of life. The fierce struggles over economic systems, which came to a head in the 20th century, were all about the human experiences that came with the modern economy and the loss of what had gone before.

A Social System

Most innovative ideas envision adoption by others, not just by the conceiver or entrepreneur. And a multiplicity of entrepreneurial projects is going on at any one time. Most of the fuel for the modern system—and the worst complications—derives from its operating in a society, not on a one-person island. The multiplicity of the actors, each acting independently, adds enormously to uncertainty in the economists' sense. Frank Knight, an influential

---

12. After nearly two centuries in which most knowledge of how the system worked was lost, a new literature has sprouted up, much of it spearheaded by Cambridge University Press. Chapter 4 on the historical origins of the modern economy conveys some of that. In the above paragraph, the pieces of the financial puzzle were put together by the late Jonathan Krueger, a student of mine at Columbia in 2010.

American economist, contrasted the known risk when a known coin is flipped, such as one known to be fair, with the unknown risk when an unknown coin is flipped, which he called *uncertainty*. He saw that business was rife with this Knightian uncertainty. He seemed to appreciate that this uncertainty is a hallmark of the modern economy.[13]

Uncertainty about the end results of an entrepreneur's project for a new product is in part the *micro* uncertainty about whether end-users will like the new product enough to buy it. The entrepreneur lives in fear that end-users will like it but will like some other entrepreneur's new product more. (Crusoe had only to fear that he himself might not like his new product.) Furthermore, the results of other entrepreneurs' ventures will affect the results of the entrepreneur's own venture. (The micro uncertainty about whether those other products being readied will be liked raises uncertainty about whether output and income in the economy will hold up. And that creates a *macro* uncertainty about whether end-users of a new product will be able to afford to buy it.) Thus, as John Maynard Keynes was first to see, the uncoordinated nature of the modern economy's entrepreneurial projects spawns a future unfolding in ways and magnitudes that are very indeterminate. The future, after any considerable length of time, becomes largely unknowable. About the future, Keynes wrote, "we simply do not know." In the space of a generation, an economy can take a shape that would have been unimaginable for the previous generation.[14]

For both Keynes and Hayek it was bedrock that new ideas are drivers of economic history—contrary to the stark determinism of, say, Thomas Hobbes or Karl Marx—because they understood that new ideas are unforeseeable (if they were foreseeable, they would not be new) and, being unforeseeable, have an independent influence on history. Yet the unknowability of the future makes

13. Knight's radical book, *Risk, Uncertainty and Profit,* was published in Boston in 1921, delayed for several years by World War I. (Another brilliant though less influential book on uncertainty, Keynes's *A Treatise on Probability* (1921), suffered the same delay.) An idiosyncratic thinker, Knight was fascinated with the proposition that if there were no uncertainty, there would be no genuine profit earned by businesses, only a normal return that could be thought of as required to pay the competitive level of interest to creditors.

14. See Keynes's *General Theory* (1936), with its allusion to Plato's "animal spirits." (Hayek's 1968 paper on the discovery procedure could have made similar points but it steered clear of them.) Ideas were never far from Keynes's mind, it seems. His greatest line was, "the world is ruled by ideas and little else." It was stated in his discussion of the hold that prevailing policy ideas have over nations. But Keynes's own career demonstrated that new policy ideas sometimes break in. Similarly, the ideas in business and finance, both old and new, dominate the directions and the swings in the business world.

all the more uncertain the consequences of developing today's ideas. Hence, any plausible projection of economic development in a modern economy is out of reach, just as Darwin's theory of evolution cannot predict evolution's course. Still, we learn some truths by studying processes for "growth in knowledge" and innovation: Failed ideas are not always valueless, since they may indicate where not to try any further. Successful ideas—the innovations—may inspire further innovations in an endless virtuous cycle. Originality is a renewable energy, driving the future in unknowable ways, creating new unknowns and new mistakes, thus new scope for originality. We will do well to study the fertile soil that high economic dynamism requires.

The modern system thrives on diversity within the society. How willing and able to innovate a society is—its propensity to innovate or, for short, its economic dynamism—obviously depends not only on the variety of situations, backgrounds, and personalities among potential conceivers of new ideas. (The entries into the music business of Jews in the 1920s and blacks in the 1960s are familiar examples.) A country's dynamism also depends on the pluralism of views among financiers. The more opportunity that an idea has to be evaluated by someone who can appreciate it, the less likely it is for a good idea to be passed up for funding. (To let the king pick all the creative projects for financing would be a recipe for making a monochromatic country.) Dynamism depends, among many other things, on the variety of entrepreneurs from whom to pick the one most in tune or most prepared to embody the new idea in a workable method or product. Clearly the pluralism among end-users is also important. If they were all identical, finding an innovation they would all like would be like precision bombing.

If all this diversity is important, we have an answer to a question avoided earlier: Historically, the system of creativity and vision described above—thus, growth in knowledge and innovation—exploded in the private sector, not the public sector. Could a comparable system for growth in knowledge and innovation function inside the public sector? Not if diversity among financiers, managers, and consumers is quite important.[15]

The success of this system depends also on the degree of interactivity within it. A project to dream up a new product typically begins with the formation of a creative team. A project to develop a newly conceived product for

15. Whether the presence of a really large public sector, marked by massive state purchases of goods and services for defense, the environment, and so forth that add up to half the GDP greatly impairs the economy's creativity and judgment, thus seriously reducing innovation and growth in knowledge, is another question. It is best deferred to the last two parts of this book.

commercial production or marketing typically begins with the formation of a company staffed by a number of people. Anyone with experience operating in a group understands that, generally speaking, groups are capable of producing a set of insights far beyond what the members would have been able to do working in isolation. The belief of some social critics that one can have a good career working at home neglects the value of being pinged by the ideas and questions of others—especially those we learn to admire and trust. And the belief that a company can place large numbers of its employees in solitary locations, such as their homes, without any cost to its innovation overlooks the importance of serendipitous interactions at the watercooler and luncheon meetings.

Interactions also enhance individual powers. When the principal horn player of Amsterdam's Concertgebouw Orchestra was complimented on the high level he had reached, he replied that he never could have done it without interactions with the rest of the orchestra. A team—a well-functioning one, at any rate—achieves not just the productivity from combining their complementary talents, as a classical economist would say, but also, in management theorists' terminology, the "superproductivity" that comes as every member of the group acquires a heightening of his or her talent, thanks to their mutual questioning and resulting gains in insight, and their urging one another on, a point emphasized by the management philosopher Esa Saarinen.

There is also interactivity over distance and time. The ideas of a society combine and multiply. A person's fertility in producing new ideas is hugely increased by exposure to recent ideas generated by the economy in which the person functions and, these days, the global economy. If isolated, the person might have a run of failed ideas at some point and be unable to generate any more. In *Robinson Crusoe* the economist-novelist Daniel Defoe shows us how pitifully few ideas Crusoe has without a society from which to take inspiration. The contention that to maximize its prosperity, a country like Argentina must remain agrarian rather than become urban, in view of its natural advantage in producing sheep, overlooks the fact that rural life is not conducive to the intellectual stimulation and wide-ranging interchange that contributes so critically to creativity.[16] Thus wide participation and the huge

16. In a 1940s debate, the Argentine economist Raúl Prebisch advocated taxes on agricultural output and import duties on manufactures. He was opposed by the Chicago economist Jacob Viner, a classical advocate of free trade and laissez-faire. Both Prebisch and Viner were too classical to articulate the gain in innovativeness that could be expected from urbanization. In their shared perspective, there was no such thing as creativity, engagement, and personal growth in a modern economy—there were only resources, technologies, and tastes, and the consumption and leisure they enabled.

agglomeration in cities of people in diverse pursuits serve to amplify the creativity of the system.

This chapter has viewed the anatomy and functioning of modern economies—the historical ones of the 19th and 20th centuries. In its first decades, participants had little sense that elements for a new system were in place and were quickly developing. But with the growing awareness of the modern system in which they were operating, there was a gathering sense that the new system was opening up fantastic possibilities. The next two chapters tell the little-known story of the gains in productivity and living standards the system brought—the material benefits—and the gains in the character of work and the meaning of life itself.

CHAPTER TWO

Material Effects of the Modern Economies

Babylon had her hanging gardens, Egypt her pyramids, Athens her acropolis, Rome her Coliseum, so Brooklyn has her bridge.

Banner at the 1883 opening of the Brooklyn Bridge

THOUGH WE IDENTIFY THE KIND OF ECONOMY a nation has by its structure, as in the previous chapter, its real meaning is in its consequences. The sustained growth of productivity that the arrival of the modern economy brought to several nations as early as the 19th century was a momentous consequence. Karl Marx, though he opposed the developing system he saw around him, did not think that this sustained growth was unimportant. In 1848, even before the modern economies were running at top speed, Marx, with productivity partly in mind, noted the "progressiveness" of the modern economies before his eyes.[1] As noted in Chapter 1 this productivity growth was of global significance, since the new methods and products could be adapted and used by other economies, even many very far from modern. It may very well be that some countries saw their early modern economies become less modern in the 20th century—France, it is fair to say, appears to have lost much of its dynamism some time after World War II. (A few economies, such as Germany's, verged on the *un*modern or *anti*modern in the 1930s.) Yet some other countries have seen their economies become more modern—Canada and South

---

1. Marx and Engels, *The Communist Manifesto.* It was in this pamphlet that Marx and Engels called the capitalism around them "progressive." But it is important to be clear that mercantile capitalism and the primitive capitalism before that were not "progressive"—not perceptibly from one generation to another, at any rate. The term capitalism has since come to mean any system but socialism—the economies of the Philippines, Argentina, the Arab states, and every country in Europe and Eurasia—no matter that nearly all of them have plainly been far from "progressive." To repeat, the present book terms *modern* any economy that is chronically, indigenously innovative, like the several that transformed Europe and North America in the 19th century, some of which are still somewhat modern.

Korea are clear examples. All in all, then, the modern economy lives on: several economies are making widespread efforts to innovate and are succeeding at it, under most market conditions at any rate.

The aim here is to get a sense of the force and effect of the dynamism of a well-functioning modern economy. A Martian landing on the earth would have little idea what to attribute to what. But the miracle-like arrivals of the modern economy, which were timed when not much else was arriving, make it plausible to attribute the differences between 19th- and 18th-century life to the birth of the modern. Examination of the magnitudes of those things attributable to the advent of the modern is the nearest thing we have to a laboratory experiment. We have to remember here that finally achieving high *levels* is not good enough if the levels are not growing. (People in the movie business used to say that "you are only as good as your last picture.") And *growth* is no compensation for being at abysmal levels.

Fundamentally we are interested in the consequences of the modern economy for human life, or more accurately, the life people live in society—in short, for social life. The data on output per worker and the average wage per worker are dry as dust: they do not adequately suggest life in the modern economies—what the (proceeds of) the output and the real wage came to buy in the space of a few decades and what the rewards were of the experiences that achieved that output and wage. We want a sense of how modern economies transformed work and therefore life—ideally a vivid and sweeping survey of the range of benefits and costs for the participants in the modern economies.

This chapter and the next argue that the modern economies and the modernity that brought them had deep consequences, most of them good. The present chapter takes up some of the modern economies' tangible effects—the "material pleasures and cares." The next chapter devotes plenty of space to the sweeping effects on intangibles—the intangibles that people live for.

A Cornucopia of Material Benefits

The climb of output per worker—so-called labor productivity or productivity, for short—brought about by the modern economies was sustained and remains so. In qualitative terms, the nations with modern economies (and with varying lags, those of other nations that are plugged into the global economy) went from a stationary state to explosive, boundless growth. Had the growth rate of productivity been only one-half of one percent per year or less, though, that growth might not have been widely noticed. At that rate, it would take a nation 144 years for its output per worker to double. The modern economies brought not only boundless growth: they also brought fast growth.

How high output per worker climbed over the so-called long century (ending in 1913 on the eve of World War I) is breathtaking. By 1870, total domestic output per capita in Western Europe as a whole had risen 63 percent above its 1820 level. By 1913, there was a further rise of 76 percent over the 1870 level. In Britain, the first rise was 87 percent and the second 65 percent. In the United States, the first rise was 95 percent and the second 117 percent. (Such climbs may not make much impression on today's readers after the even more spectacular growth in China between 1980 and 2010. But China had the opportunity to acquire and adopt a vast amount of production knowledge from overseas, while there was no third area from which Europe or America could have done that.)

The cumulative increase from the time of take-off to 1913—almost a tripling in Britain and a quadrupling in America—provided a standard of living for ordinary people that in the 18th century would not have been thought possible. The change in living standards had transformative effects, some of which are mentioned below. There was also an indirect effect: With an economy's aggregate output and hence income growing without bound, households' wealth will not regain its former size relative to income. People, who were not saving much at all in the old stationary state, began to save more and tried to earn more (to save still more) than they did in the 18th century so that their wealth would not fall further behind the pace—the pace of income growth. On this view, we should expect to find that participation rates in the modern economy are much higher than they were in the mercantile economy. Unfortunately, the data do not exist to test that expectation.

But wages, not productivity, are the single most important indicator of the material benefits available to those people coming into the economy without appreciable inherited wealth or the prospect of it. Adequate wages were—and still are—a gateway to important benefits. In the 19th century especially, though less so now, the *wage* that a person could earn was the main determinant of the primary goods that ordinary wage earners could afford—basic material goods, such as shelter and health care, and nonmaterial goods for which virtually everyone has a deep need, such as holding a job that is not dangerous or deadening, having a family, or having access to community life.

An increase in productivity is not a guarantee of increased wages, just as increased wages may occur without an increase in productivity. As noted in the Introduction, Fernand Braudel, the foremost French historian of the postwar period, found that even though the great explorers and colonists of the 16th century brought back cargoes of silver to their rulers, these revenues did not lift wages.[2] Although the wage per worker and output per worker are connected (someone once said that in economics everything depends on everything else in at least two ways), special factors can alter the channel from productivity to wages. But never mind. Modern economies raised the wages of working people, which stores of silver did not.

As the Introduction's discussion of wages implied, the advent of modern economies broke the gloomy pattern that Braudel had observed. (It was in the 16th century, as noted earlier, and in the 18th century, from 1750 to 1810, not modern times—the age of the modern economies—that wages were falling—in Britain, at any rate, for which we have data.) In Britain, daily wages per worker expressed in real terms, or purchasing power, in the crafts for which we have data started a sustained rise in 1820 or so—around the time that output per worker took off. (In America such early data are virtually nonexistent.) In Belgium, wages started such a rise around 1850. In France, wages took off soon after, playing tag with Britain's until 1914. In German cities, wages had been on a roller-coaster and went downhill again from the early 1820s through the 1840s, thus helping to set off the 1848 uprisings; a sustained rise began in 1860 or, according to another source, in 1870. So the real wages of building labor, factory workers, and farm workers in the modern economies took off with the take-off of productivity.

The question arising here is whether wages showed the same impressive ascent that output per worker did. Perhaps wages lagged behind productivity, as labor suffered a reduced share of the growing product. In fact, the nominal daily wage of an "average urban unqualified male" expressed in the local money did not just keep up with the money value of output per capita: It gained ground. From 1830, Britain's wage-productivity ratio, after losing a bit of ground until 1848 (that bad year again), more than caught up in the 1860s, fell off again in the 1870s, and finally surged ahead in the 1890s and was still further ahead by 1913. In France, the ratio followed a similar pattern.

---

2. Braudel, in his 1972 volume on the Mediterranean world, writes that the rulers exchanged their silver for spices and silks from the Far East rather than for the products made by European labor.

In Germany, the ratio, after remaining firm from 1870 to 1885, was some-what weaker in the 1890s but ended at a high water mark in the 1910s, until the war came. And these data overlook that workers were not buying units of the gross domestic product with their pay; to an important extent, they were buying imported consumer goods at prices that were collapsing as sup-plies were increasing and transport costs were decreasing. One British study concludes that "after prolonged stagnation, real wages . . . nearly doubled between 1820 and 1850."[3] The thought that, in the modern economics, wages lost ground to nonwage income cannot be supported. What happened to the wages of the less advantaged, or underprivileged, in these economies could be different, however.

In the public mind, the new system that the 19th century ushered in was an economy from hell for the less-fortunate workers who had to work in fac-tories, mines, and menial jobs. Some believe that social conditions scarcely improved until a century later, when socialist ideas changed Europe and the New Deal changed America. Literary works may have given that impres-sion. Often the dates are wrong, though. Victor Hugo's *Les Misérables* was focused on tensions arising in the years 1815 to 1832 from the Louis Philippe monarchy, not on the downside of the modern economy that reached France some decades later. Yet there are impressive works from the mid-19th century too. It is Dickens's microscope on London poverty in his 1839 novel *Oliver Twist* and Honoré Daumier's graphic depictions of the struggles of Parisian workers, which ran until 1870, that give us the impression that when produc-tivity took off, the great mass of working-age people were harmed by reduced wages—or, at best, remained for a long time just as miserable, unengaged, and unfulfilled as they had been before. That proposition needs to be tested.

One test of that proposition is to see whether so-called working class wages—blue collar wages for manual and other physical labor—were stagnant (or even falling) while the modern economies were taking hold and becoming more effective. So, it has to be asked, *were* wages for blue collar work in fact

3. Lindert and Williamson, "Living Standards" (1983, p. 11). Results on wages as a ratio to pro-ductivity are from Bairoch, "Wages as an Indicator of Gross National Product" (1989). If these are not grossly inaccurate data, one wonders how another scholar could have reached a rather different conclusion: "[T]he rise in living standards in [1815–1850] was almost undetectable; it is but one of many minor fluctuations in the course of seven centuries. The gains from 1815 to 1850 were a cycle—and a minor one at that—not a trend" (Allen, "The Great Diver-gence in European Wages and Prices," 2001, p. 433). The explanation is that only two of Allen's dozen cities, namely London and Paris, are located in the emerging modern economies of that period. Both London and Paris showed sharp wage increases.

stagnant or falling? The popular impression is that the least-skilled workers did see their wages fall over the 19th century as a result of mechanization—or fall relative to the wages of skilled labor, at any rate.

This is another misimpression, however. According to the British study mentioned previously, the average wage per worker outstripped the wage of blue collar workers by about 20 percent between 1815 and 1850. But much of that was a result of lagging wages of manual labor in agriculture, and hard times in agriculture cannot easily be blamed on the modern sector. British estimates from another source show that the average wage of all skilled workers in the nonagricultural sector climbed only a little more over that period than the average wage of unskilled workers—by 7 percent.[4] Clark's 2005 data on the wage per day of craftsmen and the wage of "helpers" in Britain's building trade show that helpers began to lose ground to the craftsmen in the 1810s—this after no trend up or down since the 1740s—but the data show that the tide turned in mid-century; helpers regained their former position by the 1890s and went on to gain more ground in the next decade. That was the impression in those times too. Prime Minister Gladstone, seeing the gushing tax revenues pouring into the government from all sorts of wage earners, commented in the House of Commons:

> I should look with some degree of pain, and with much apprehension, upon this extraordinary growth if it were my belief that it is confined to the class of person who may be described as in easy circumstances. . . . But . . . it is a matter of profound and inestimable consolation to reflect that while the rich have become richer, the poor have become less poor . . . [I]f we look to the average condition of the British labourer, whether peasant or miner or operative or artisan, we know from varied and incontrovertible evidence that during the last twenty years such an addition has been made to his means of subsistence as we may almost pronounce to be without example in the history of any country and of any age.[5]

In Britain, then, the modern economy did not aggravate wage inequality—not systematically and never in any permanent way. Marx, obfuscating the data, never did acknowledge the facts to which Gladstone called attention.

The belief that labor in general suffered in the 19th century relative to capital fares no better than the other misimpressions. Recently available data

4. Jackson, "The Structure of Pay in Nineteenth-Century Britain."
5. Hansard (1863, pp. 244–245).

show the daily wage per employed worker as a ratio to the national output per capita. In Britain, the ratio went up, not down—from 191 around 1830 to 230 around 1910. In France, the ratio went up from 202 around 1850 to 213 around 1910. In Germany, the ratio went from 199 in the early 1870s to 208 in the early 1910s.[6] A stylized portrait was drawn in 1887 by Robert Giffen, a journalist and chief statistician of the British government, using individual income data collected with the start of British income tax in 1843. These data show that aggregate income of the "rich" doubled over the next 40 years, but so did their number; the aggregate income of manual laborers more than doubled, and their number increased relatively little.

> The rich have become more numerous but not richer individually; the 'poor' . . . are, individually, twice as well off on the average as they were fifty years ago. The poor have thus had almost all the benefit of the great material advance of the last fifty years.[7]

The favorable movement of real wages, notwithstanding a lengthy low in the relative wage for unskilled work over several decades in the 19th century, can be supposed to have two benefits that are generally considered to be of social value. One benefit is that an increased general level of wages is liberating: it enables persons confined to the lower reaches of the available wages—unskilled workers, in the usual terminology—to move from work they previously could not afford to reject to work that is more desirable. A person working in the "domestic economy" as a homemaker or as paid help in other people's homes could afford to move to a job that is not so isolating; someone working in the underground sector could afford to take a job in the legitimate economy with its greater respectability and lesser dependency; someone could afford to leave a job in the business economy for one with initiatives, responsibilities, and interactions that make it more rewarding. Thus higher wages also result in what may be called *economic inclusion.* More people end up participating and contributing to society's central project and thus finding the rewards that could only come from such involvement. To describe and confirm the value of economic inclusion requires a discussion like that in the next chapter, so it cannot be elaborated just yet.

6. See the 1989 paper by Bairoch, "Wages as an Indicator of Gross National Product." The curious units in which this ratio is measured may be disregarded.
7. "The Material Progress of Great Britain." Giffen was immortalized in Alfred Marshall's textbook *Principles* (1938) for the "Giffen good"—a good that people buy more of the higher its price is. However, scholars have been unable to find this concept explicitly formulated anywhere in Giffen's works.

The increase in wages has the further social benefit that it reduces poverty and pauperism. Observations by two distinguished economists of their day confirm that a noteworthy decline of poverty took place in all the modern economies emerging in the 19th century—those for which we have data, at any rate. Speaking of the trends in England and Scotland, Giffen noted in 1887 the steady decrease in the number of paupers (individuals relieved of debts)—in the teeth of the fastest population growth on record—from 4.2 percent in the first half of the 1870s to 2.8 percent in 1888. To quote Giffen again, in Ireland, to which the modern economy came only later, "there has been an increase of pauperism, accompanied by a decline of population." Writing in the 1890s about America, David Wells in a couple of pages on "pauperism" notes that the "number of poor as a proportion of the whole population have been generally decreasing; and this, notwithstanding the very great obstacles in the way of . . . checking pauperism, in a country like the United States, which annually receives such armies of poor from European countries."[8] Another way to weigh the claim that the modern economy hurts the masses is to examine the somewhat surprising evidence on infectious disease, nutrition, and the resulting mortality. The story, like the above stories, is not one of linear progress. It shows societies flowering in the 19th century after the trials of Job in the 18th. Strikingly, smallpox deaths, which are mainly found among young children, rose over the 17th century up to the heyday of the commercial economy in the mid-18th century, when two-thirds of all children died before their fifth birthday. The cause of the smallpox epidemic could not have been the functioning of the modern economy, since it was hardly functional then. The cause was the rise of international commerce!—"the importation of more virulent strains with the growth of world trade." Then smallpox deaths began to recede. By the second quarter of the 19th century, child mortality had fallen by two-thirds. This appears to be more the result of the modern economy dating from the 1810s than from the first stage of the industrial revolution in the 1770s, which, as noted above, was largely confined to a single industry in a short time span.[9] As the modern

8. From Wells's 1899 book, p. 344. A polymath of his time, Wells, after his college years at Amherst, studied science with the naturalist Louis Agassiz in Boston, invented textile machinery, and was prominent in American policymaking even before his bestseller. He appears to have known only the material side of the economy and saw material progress as solely the application of science.

9. See the 2007 paper by Razzell and Spence, "The History of Infant, Child and Adult Mortality," p. 286. Data there show a faster proportionate decline of burials per child from 1790–1810 to the modern interval 1810–1829 than from 1770–1789 to 1790–1810.

economies gained force over the 19th century, the decline of smallpox intensified. Wells reports that "for 1795–1800 the average annual number of smallpox deaths in London was 10,180; but for 1875–1880 it was only 1,408."[10]

Infectious diseases affecting adults more than children also fell sharply in the 19th century. Wells writes that "plague and leprosy have practically disappeared [from Britain and America]. Typhus fever, once the scourge of London, is said to have now entirely disappeared from that city." As a result, mortality rates were steeply declining. "In London, the death rate, which had averaged 24.4 per 1000 in the 1860s was down to 18.5 by 1888. In Vienna, the death rate had been 41 and fell to 21. In European countries, the decrease ranged from one-third to one-quarter. In the whole United States it was between 17 and 18 in 1880."[11]

Was all this a credit to science? That does not appear to be expert opinion. Referring to the reductions in the gamut of infectious diseases in London—smallpox, "fevers" (typhus and typhoid fever), and "convulsions" (diarrhea and gastrointestinal diseases)—Razzell and Spence point to the public health and hygienic measures made affordable by higher incomes:

> Most of these were dirt diseases. [The fall of mortality] occurred equally amongst the wealthy and the non-wealthy population. . . . It is possible that a transformation of the environment had an impact on a number of diseases. . . . The replacement of woolen underwear by linen and cotton garments . . . and more effective washing—involving the boiling of clothing—were probably responsible for the progressive elimination of typhus as well as lice.[12]

Wells points to the better diet that came with higher incomes:

> Now, while improved sanitary knowledge and regulations have contributed to these results, they have been mainly due to the increase in the abundance and cheapness of food products, which are in turn almost wholly attributable to improvements in the methods of production and distribution. . . . The American is apparently gaining in size and weight, which could not have happened had there been anything like a retrogression toward poverty on the part of the masses.[13]

10. Wells, p. 349.
11. Wells, p. 347.
12. Razzell and Spence, pp. 287, 288.
13. Wells, pp. 347, 349. He calculates that a good diet required a small fraction of the daily wage of manual workers and marvels at the decade-long explosion in imports of tropical fruits and fresh fish from the north Pacific.

In these ways, the modern economy helped to reduce disease and mortality. The improvements in productivity made by the economy on a daily basis provided the wherewithal for families and communities to combat disease through private measures and public health measures. Improvements in hospital practice, such as the use of antiseptics, helped to reduce many infectious diseases. Moreover, modern hospitals are a part of the modern economy. The insights and learning occurring in hospitals and their diffusion throughout the healthcare industry were a notable part of the explosion of knowledge produced by the modern economies.

With the development of the modern economies and the productivity gains that traveled to various other nations, the world embarked on a virtuous circle. With lower mortality came a larger population of young people, thus more persons around who might invent, develop, and test new concepts, and thus another round of increased wages and lower mortality.

Not a Rose Garden

Readers surprised at the very good news on wages in the modern societies may be expecting that the record of the fledgling modern economies on employment and unemployment will provide a corrective. In 2009 a British journalist, Maev Kennedy, reacting to the century of British newspapers just put online by the British Library, suggested that "anyone overwhelmed by today's political scandals, wars, financial disasters, soaring unemployment and drunken feral children can take refuge in the 19th century—its wars, financial disasters, political scandals, soaring unemployment and drunken feral children." But it was the commercial economy of the 18th century, in creating the first large cities, that marked the birth of the phenomenon of mass unemployment. It marked the start of the migration of people from subsistence farming with only the occasional paid work, or "wage labor"—a life in which no one was unemployed—to urban life in which lacking a paid job meant having few alternative ways to earn one's bread and the roof over one's head. People had to self-insure against unemployment by saving enough for a rainy day, if they could. If they couldn't, there were the mutual aid societies (the *Verein*) to which craftsmen might go for help; and many could fall back on family or friends. State-run unemployment insurance programs came to the rescue in France in 1905 and Britain in 1911.

The rise of modern economies in the 19th century multiplied the number of cities, thus multiplying the number of people unemployed. By expanding

the part of the country that was urban, with its unemployment, and thus contracting the part that was rural, which had only underemployment, it inescapably increased the national unemployment. That was not unambiguously bad. For urban dwellers, there was the risk of being unemployed. There was also the chance of finding some of the benefits that drew people to agglomerate into cities. Many people fled farming for city life because it was a trade-off worth making.

We lack the data to tell whether the modern economy drove the average unemployment rate in existing cities above the average of a century earlier. However, the available data show increasing labor force participation rates over the 19th century (among women) and unemployment rates that were not larger than the rates in the present age, say, since 1975. A recent study of France found that "a change in direction, first discernible in the 1850s, occurred from the 1860s onward: there was a marked acceleration in the growth of [the number] *working* [despite] a sharp check in the increase in the working-age *population*."[14] The advent of the modern economy in France appears to have pulled increased numbers of working-age people into nonfarm employment, there being no known force in the farm sector giving them a push. As for Britain, the classic work by A. W. Phillips on unemployment in relation to inflation presented data going back to 1861. These data show no evidence of any upward trend in unemployment in the next several decades as the modern economic system spread wider and its power to create new knowledge, and thus change, increased. Moreover the path of the unemployment rate in the early period of the series (say, from 1861 to 1910) does not appear to be elevated by comparison to the period from 1971 to 2010, a span over which Britain has not been a front-runner in knowledge or invention relative to its peers. The lesson is that rapid growth of knowledge, thus productivity and wages, managed through one or more channels to hold down unemployment, which latter-day Britain, with a less inventive economy in a less creative society, has found it difficult to do. Myriad subsidies and state agencies succeeded in moderating unemployment among low-wage participants but not in turning back the tide.

Why, then, has a poor reputation shadowed the modern economies—those emerging in the 19th century and later manifestations? They were stuck with William Blake's image of the "dark Satanic mills" he saw dotting the landscape in 1804—a decade before the invasion of factories came. The drudgery and deprivation of rural work was mainly replaced by the tedium,

14. Caron, *An Economic History of Modern France* (1979, table 1.7, p. 19).

grime, and noise characterizing many or most factories. Charlie Chaplin's image of the assembly line in his 1937 film *Modern Times* looked more mindless than oppressive. In any case, the factory was not unique to the modern economies of the 19th century and the first half or so of the 20th century. Similar or worse factories appeared in some of the least-modern economies ever seen: in the Russia of Lenin and Stalin and the China of Deng Xiaoping, for example. Furthermore, the rise of factories is not an inherent accompaniment of a modern economy at any stage. The next country to make a break for modernity may very well skip factories and go straight to offices and interactive webcasting.

There may be another explanation. For us, even now in the twenty-first century, we can still be appalled by the filthiness and suffocating pollution in the fast-growing cities of the modern economies arising in the 19th century. But we forget to appreciate what it meant for people to escape from the wages of medieval times to incomes two or three times the medieval level, as most people in Britain, America, France, and the German lands came to enjoy in the 19th century. Income is such an abstract, lifeless thing. Yet higher income cuts the incidence of poverty.

To countries where it came and even, to some degree, to countries where it did not come, the modern economy brought immense material benefits: In raising wage rates, it provided increased numbers the dignity of self-support, it liberated them to get out into society, and it opened up city life as an alternative to rural ways. In raising incomes, it improved living standards in very basic ways, reducing risks of early death through disease, so that one might live to enjoy the new living standards. A new middle class arose that could dine out, go to the stadium or the theater, and introduce their children to the arts. (In America, it was said, there seemed to be a piano in every parlor.)

It might seem that, now, this "sustained growth" is no longer important. Higher income *is* less important to people today than it was when consumption and health conditions were so desperately low—as evidenced by the major shortening of the work day and work week between the 1860s and the 1960s. It is a central theme of this book that, for an ever-increasing number of people in the modern economies, continued growth of their wage rates and salaries is not among the most important things in their lives. Research a decade ago on "happiness," however, has stimulated a different thesis. It has concluded from household survey data that, after a point, persons higher up the income ladder did not report higher levels of "happiness"—a Buddhist-like state where no more consumption or leisure is wanted. And

this is concluded even though higher responsibility and greater scope generally come with higher income. (Subsequent researchers have argued from similar data that this conclusion is not accurate.) Whatever the truth of that thesis, we have always known that "money cannot buy happiness." Happiness is not yoked to income. Earning a high income is a means to satisfactions not classified as "happiness"; otherwise, people would not seek the increased income that does not bring an increase in their reported happiness. A shortfall of one's income is an impediment to key goals: to personal development and a gratifying life. It is a great achievement of modern economies that, over their long history, fewer and fewer participants were lacking the income to pursue their nonmaterial goals.

Of course, had the modern economy not arisen in the West, leaving only the mercantile economy of the baroque era, wage rates and incomes might have grown as a result of some of the scientific advances exogenous to economies that would have occurred—whatever those might have been. But wages and incomes would not have grown nearly as fast. If exogenous science had been the main driver of 19th-century growth in the select Western economies that saw rapid growth, those scientific advances would have caused a rising tide lifting all boats, including the boats of the Dutch and the Italians, who were relatively productive and sophisticated when the 19th century started. The fact is that, although nearly all the Western countries started in the same place around 1820, the material achievements of some countries went far beyond those of the others—namely the modern economies' towering achievements.

To conclude: This chapter has not only quantified the rapid growth brought to several countries by the advent of the modern economy. It has also found evidence that, in the countries in which it took root, the modern economy, through its ceaseless creation of new economic knowledge, changed radically the material conditions of life. The modern economies performed this feat by doing what they were well structured to attempt and to succeed at: by mass innovating.[15] The massive effort to innovate evidently

---

15. Referring to the "hundred years' peace" from 1815 to 1914, Karl Polanyí, brother of the brilliant Michael Polanyí, suggested that the paucity of wars, civil and foreign, had much to do with the cumulative rise of capital and productivity in that period. See his *The Great Transformation* (1944). This was odd on the level of facts alone, since America had its Civil War, Britain had the Crimean War and the Boer War, and France and Germany had their wars. The achievement of modernity is therefore all the more remarkable. From the perspective he took, he was unable to see that the challenges and the engagement brought by innovation must have had much to do with the long stretches of peace. His book is in major ways 180 degrees to the present book.

permeated nations from the bottom up. As befits the grassroots character of this innovation, some benefits, such as income, went equiproportionately to the less advantaged; some other benefits, such as health and longevity, went mostly to the less advantaged. As a recent American history of this development put it, it was an economic "revolution" and was "in many ways the best thing ever to befall the ordinary people of America."[16]

Material change is not the only feat of the modern economy, though. The immaterial, or intangible, world of experience, aspiration, spirit, and imagination was, for more and more people, no less radically changed. That is the subject of the next chapter.

16. See H. W. Brands's 2010 book, *American Colossus,* p. 606.

CHAPTER THREE

The Experience of Modern Life

Europe was transformed by the new experience of metropolitan life between 1860 and 1930. Expressionism was a visionary expression of what it feels like to be adrift, exhilarated, in a fast-paced, incomprehensible world.

JACKIE WULLSCHLAGER, *Financial Times*

Young America . . . has a great passion—a perfect rage—for the new.

ABRAHAM LINCOLN, "Second Lecture on Discoveries and Inventions"

WITH THE MODERN ECONOMIES CAME something radically new—modern life. The results in consumption, leisure, and longevity pointed to in the previous chapter were very large, a few of them large enough to make a difference for what people were able to do. With a longer life in prospect, people might be willing to prepare for careers requiring a larger investment. However, these material gains, although they changed the standard of living (and of working), did not change radically the way of life—did not change the "way we were." Of those material gains, perhaps the one that comes closest was the decline in child mortality. It must have reduced the heartache and fear in having children. But did it change fundamentally the experience of having a child and raising a child?

The radical significance of the modern economy in those cities or nations where it emerged lies in its nonmaterial results. It transformed the work and career of a large and increasing number of participants. Thus it was life-changing: the new experience of work in the modern economy and, with it, the new experience of city life changed the *character* of living, not simply the standard of living. Of course, the full effect took time to build up, and it reached some jobs later than others or never. So it would not be surprising if early observers took less notice of this effect than did later observers, who could hardly miss the new tenor of the times.

To be sure, some of the great economists of the modern age came to recognize that the work experience was central to the lives of the working population. Alfred Marshall, the leading British economist in the quarter-century from 1890, emphasized that those employed in modern business find that the majority of the problems they have to solve arise in the course of their *work* in the economy:

> [T]he business by which a person earns his livelihood generally fills his thoughts during by far the greater part of those hours in which his mind is at its best. During them his character is being formed by . . . his work . . . and by his relations to his associates in work.[1]

Very likely, there is some British understatement here, and Marshall welcomes the mental stimulation and mental exercise being offered in the jobs he sees around him. A few decades later, the Swedish economist Gunnar Myrdal makes a stronger point in his always explicit way:

> [I]t is a stock phrase . . . in economics [that] consumption is the sole end of production. . . . In other words: Man works in order to live. But there are many who live in order to work. . . . [M]ost people who are reasonably well off derive *more* satisfaction as producers than as consumers. . . . [M]any would define the social ideal as a state in which as many people as can live in this way.[2]

Marshall and Myrdal were departing from orthodox economics in recognizing that, for growing numbers of people, business life—figuring out how better to produce and pondering what might be better to produce—engaged the mind.

Marshall and Myrdal's observation is striking in a couple of ways. To have so emphasized the mental side of work, they must have understood that this aspect had been uncommon. People—most people, at any rate—do not derive comparable stimulus and challenge from a lifetime of child care or other

1. Marshall, famous for the eight editions of his *Principles*, made this remark in his more popular 1892 textbook *Elements of Economics*, p. 2. Born in 1842, he rose to great heights at Cambridge University, becoming the most accomplished and prolific economist of his time. His students, Keynes, Arthur Cecil Pigou, and Dennis H. Robertson, were to become the great Cambridge economists of the next generation. Marshall, having grown up in the urbanized section of London called Clapham, had the advantage, almost unique among Oxbridge dons, of seeing and sensing what work was like in the second half of the 19th century.

2. Myrdal, *The Political Element in the Development of Economic Theory* (1953, p. 136), translated from the 1932 German edition.

domestic activities. (Had they found the world packed with mental stimulation and challenge at every turn, finding the same in the workplace too would have been nothing to write home about.) They must also have understood it was something new under the sun. They tacitly assume that work in bygone times was not widely engaging, except maybe for the king's work to keep power. It is the mental stimulation and intellectual challenge of work in the modern economy that is rich with satisfactions, not the agrarian work of traditional economies. Marshall and Myrdal implicitly understood that intellectual involvement was going on in workplaces, but they left unspecified what the stimulants and challenges were.

Another World: Work and Career Transformed

The distinctive experiences of the modern economy come from its distinctive activity of creating, developing, marketing, and testing new ideas. In many occupations, though not all, the experience of work is transformed from the sameness, or *stasis*, typical in the traditional economies to the change, challenge, and originality found in the modern economy. With a little observation and more than a little interpretation we can identify some of the modern experiences, or categories of experiences—though some may escape us. Perhaps not all of these experiences could be called rewards (see below). And even the clear rewards are not sufficient for a well-functioning modern economy to be found just, though they may be necessary for a just economy (see Chapters 7 and 8). But first, the experiences.

With modernity came continual change, which contrasted sharply with the sameness and tedium of work in the traditional economies. Ceaseless change arriving from outside a company brought mental stimulation to the participants. When a new product comes along, a user or potential user of it may be stimulated to ask whether there could be some gain from using it in some way that is overlooked. A producer may be stimulated to ask whether there could be a way to improve or change its functioning. A traditional economy may well have some existing products that could have new uses or could be improved upon—and thus some unexploited possibilities remaining—so there may be some stimulation to be found even in traditional settings. However, the stimulation that comes from the stream of new products is far more powerful.

Another experience brought by the modern economy is the process of solving the new problems arising from efforts to create change from the inside. Although artisans and farmers were gradually surmounting age-old hurdles in ancient and medieval times, they had evidently run out of hurdles or solutions over the 16th, 17th, and 18th centuries. Several Schumpeterian discoveries had occurred earlier, and some more were to occur from time to time. Yet a country can count neither on the force and frequency of such discoveries, nor on being the country best placed to develop a new opportunity. Only a country's modern economy is capable of creating for its working-age people the endless succession of new problems required to keep their work challenging. Philosophers refer to the resulting "expansion of talents" as *self-realization* or *self-actualization*—the full realization of one's potential. Managements use the term *employee engagement* to indicate both that their workforce is stimulated by novel developments and absorbed by the problems presented to them. Marshall and Myrdal can be interpreted as having in mind these qualities of modern work.

Relatedly, there is the social experience of *interchange* with workplace colleagues in the course of their work. No doubt, interactions, as well as problems and problem solving, are present at home too, where a parent interacts with the children and other parents. But the modern workplace is constantly offering new interchanges rather than a recycling of old ones, which no doubt makes a considerable difference.[3] Interchange outside the workplace also develops in a modern economy. Companies that competed with each other, not just those buying from each other or from the same pool of labor or of capital, found it convenient to merge or collude. An employee gained in a variety of ways from taking part in shop talk after work. A company with better access to the industry's rumor mill would have a better idea what not to produce.

In another category are the experiences of directing or taking part in an innovative kind of initiative. For the entrepreneur or team leader and for others on the team too, such projects offer opportunities to inject one's own creativity and judgment into decisions—for *self-expression* or *self-affirmation*. For many people this activity is apt to result in a greater sense of accomplishment than mere problem-solving does. In the traditional economies of the

---

3. The value to people of both problem solving and teamwork in solving problems are themes inseparable from the pragmatist school of American philosophers—Charles Peirce, William James, John Dewey, and Josiah Royce—especially Dewey. (Later members were Stanford's Richard Rorty and Harvard's Amartya Sen.) Somewhere in Dewey's vast work is the image of a team of shipbuilders solving the problems of making a battleship. Dewey, an anticommunist yet a critic of U.S. capitalism, shared the socialist vision of enterprises in which the manager or at any rate the foreman is replaced with workers' meetings and consensus. Dewey supposed their decisions would be as good as the boss's.

mercantile age and earlier, work was largely routine, and, aside from the occasional fire to put out, the opportunity and the need to exercise initiative were only occasional.

Another category of work experiences is the most distinctively modern. In the modern economy, careers almost force participants on a winding voyage of *exploration*—a leap into the void. Some of the unimagined experiences people have and the challenges they meet in these careers may be the most valuable episodes in their careers—and are certainly the most distinctively modern benefits of the modern economy. In earlier economies, expeditions of discovery were exceptional: Marco Polo's journey to China and Leif Ericson's expeditions to Vineland, for instance. In the commercial economy of mercantile capitalism there was, here or there, a leap into the unknown that was a privilege reserved for a handful of people. In the modern economy, however, these modern rewards of *self-discovery* are endemic.

Some end results of work and career are also among the nonmaterial rewards of modern work. The modern economy makes it possible for participants to rack up *achievements*, achievements that are very visible. The gratification from such success is a not unimportant benefit of the modern economy. Such satisfactions were out of reach of all but a tiny minority in traditional economies, including the mercantile economies of the commercial age, since not much out of the ordinary was achieved—other than swapping goods at greater and greater distances. Yet some household surveys do not find that people look for jobs offering the prospect of achievement. They seek personal experiences and inner growth, so we must be careful not to overemphasize this aspect.

There is also the experience of *freedom*. For a classical economist, it would be double counting to count the material blessings of the modern economy opened up by its enabling institutions and encouraging culture, and then to add the blessings of the freedoms that enable people to produce these material benefits. But in any real-life modern economy—not a theoretical model in which everything in the present and the future is known—the actors may sense or entertain opportunities and dangers about which there is little or no public knowledge. Individuals' *freedoms to act* (or not to act) on their unique knowledge, judgment, and intuition may be indispensable to people's sense of self-sufficiency and thus self-worth. In this view, the freedom to take charge of one's own heading and make one's own mistakes is a primary good itself, one of huge importance.

The concept of *attainment* appears in some discussions of the rewards from work in modern times. Some material attainments, such as the wealth amassed by a person, do not belong in the set of end results from participation in the modern economy. Wealth is primarily a means to various benefits, most obviously to the material benefits noted in the previous chapter and also to various work experiences as well. (Households may save now to be able to afford to take a job later offering experiences at some cost in terms of lower pay.) Nonmaterial attainments, such as honors and influence accumulated, are also problematic. They suffer from being positional goods—they are precious only to the extent that some others do not have them. (It has been said that the happiness of the Nobel Prize winners is outweighed by the unhappiness it causes the runners-up.) Nevertheless, it is unreasonable to believe that a society has no appreciation for the attainments of its people— that it gains only to the extent that the pursuit of these attainments helps motivate risks and sacrifices that serve to generate some of the other nonmaterial benefits identified above.

How does it feel to be alive in a country with a modern economy? How in particular did it feel to participate in the modern economies that arose in the 19th century and in those that stayed modern in the 20th? Answers to the question require some imagination on our part. Evidence of the significance that the experience of work and career may provide does not stare us in the face. Yet pieces of evidence exist here and there, some of them directly observable and even measurable, others highly circumstantial and speculative. The importance of this experience is the focus here. And if it is important, there is some presumption that people have found it valuable.

On the significance of interchange, a feature of modern work, there is direct demographic evidence. In the mercantile economies it was the exceptional industry that became concentrated in one town or region. When keeping up with new ideas was not an imperative, most industries spread out over the land. When, during the 19th century, keeping up with new ideas became crucial for decisions, the landscape was transformed. People went where the ideas were, and there was much agglomeration. Companies in an industry herded together—French textile makers in Lyon, English metalworkers in Birmingham, and Italian clothes makers in Naples. Later, in the 20th century, there were the German film makers in Berlin, American car makers in Detroit, and so forth. Rural areas depopulated, and cities sprang up. Germany, in spite of little increase in population, went from 4 towns that qualified as cities in 1800 to about 50 by 1900. By 1920, Americans went from living predominantly in rural areas to living predominantly in cities. For the first time in history people could conveniently interact with one another for business, professional, or other reasons. And people took advantage of their new situation. There was an explosion during the 19th century (and a detectable rise earlier) in both Britain and France in the number of taverns and cafes where people might talk. What Marxians saw as overcrowding leading to urban misery was, from this perspective, in the interest of both labor and capital—up to a point, at any rate. (No company broke from the city with its workforce delighted to follow—not until some internet companies headed for the hills in recent decades.)

On another modern experience, the pleasure of encountering the new, particularly new problems and the satisfaction of solving them, there is direct clinical evidence of the craving for mental stimulation and problem solving among primates. Zookeepers have talked about their findings:

> Once animals at the Bronx Zoo spent their days in idleness and boredom, pacing their small cages, eating meals handed to them on a platter. That made for listless animals. As the study of wildlife and animal behavior grew, it became apparent that boredom undermined animals' health. . . . Nowadays, the animals stave off boredom. Since the mid-'90s, New York's zoos have expanded their definition of care to include the animal's mental state. . . . Basically, the purpose is to prevent boredom. But scientists have higher goals, Dr. Diana Reiss, senior scientist at the New York Aquarium, said. "We're asking: How can we give animals . . . the chance to make their own choices? To deal with challenges? To solve problems and use their brains? To teach them to learn for themselves?" . . . The zookeepers are experimenting with ways of reproducing the tasks, puzzles, . . . in the wild. These include using various toys, hiding food. . . . "Novelty is very important," commented Dr. Richard Lattis, senior vice president of Wildlife Conservation Society, which runs the city's five zoos and its aquarium. The problem is "we have to keep inventing new things. The animals get tired of the same old toys."[4]

Though the same experiments have not been performed on humans, we can be pretty sure that there is at least as much craving for more mental stimulation and problem solving among humans. Prison reforms decades ago suggested that when inmates were allowed to play chess or other games and to study books, the inmates were healthier, emotionally and physically. Some nations have experimented with a drastic curtailment of work. In continental

4. Stewart, "Recall of the Wild: Fighting Boredom, Zoos Play to the Inmates' Instincts" (2002, p. B1).

Europe, where half the men are retired by age 55 and women are retired even sooner than the men—no more change, challenge, or originality for them!—a physician reported that the mortality rate of his patients spiked up in the months after they retired.

There is also statistical evidence. In the 2002 General Social Survey, nine in ten of the American adults who worked more than 10 hours per week in 2002 reported they were "very satisfied" or "somewhat satisfied" with their jobs. Job satisfaction is less among those taking less enriching work, of course. Yet even among those who categorized themselves as working class, 87 percent reported they were "satisfied." It is still a logical possibility that people simply love to exert and to tire themselves, while there are no mental and intellectual rewards. But that case appears to be far-fetched. Had the surveyees responded that they were dissatisfied with their jobs, it would be problematic to argue that the mental and intellectual side of work was highly valued though outweighed by the pain of the hard work. However, the fact that people *do* report considerable satisfaction from their jobs in spite of any fatigue, stress, nuisance costs, and interpersonal tensions, is quite impressive. (This refutes Robert Reich, the former Secretary of Labor, who in a radio show with the present author in October 2006 erupted with "Americans *hate* their jobs.")

Perhaps these first observations make it reasonably clear that the advent of the modern economy was a godsend to people, delivering rewards known only to a fortunate few in earlier times—employee engagement, intellectual gratification and the joy of the occasional discovery. It might be worthwhile, then, to look at the advent of the modern through another lens.

Modern Experience Mirrored in Arts and Letters

Is there other evidence of the profound change that the modern economy brought to working life, thus to life itself? There is the literature and the arts in the age of the modern economy. We expect literature to illuminate aspects of life in our time that we may not have been very conscious of. "Yes," we say in response to the more resonant works, "that's how it feels." And the mere fact that some are writing novels and some are composing symphonies may be a sign that people are in an excited state and are trying to express and understand the new system that has transformed life, as Vargas Llosa has remarked. So it is reasonable to check the greatest fiction to see whether there are some hints there of how life changed with the emergence of the modern economies. Of course, few writers reflected in concrete terms on the experiences of work and career in their time. But what is there may be suggestive.

There have always been writers who write about adventure, even when there was little of it to be seen in the world. The leading countries of the Baroque era, with their mercantile economies and state-sponsored explorers, did not offer writers an experience of change, challenge, and originality to write about. In Spain, Miguel Cervantes's 1605 novel *Don Quixote* was, from a literary point of view, a satire on the romances that some popular writers attempted to sell to the public. But from another viewpoint its theme is the deprivations of a life without challenge and creativity. Quixote, stuck on the Spanish desert, could have no experience of modern work and career. With his "squire," Sancho Panza, the don is driven to invent chivalrous challenges and causes. When, bedridden, he announces that their adventures are over, Sancho bursts into tears, for he needed the fantasies too. In Britain, Daniel Defoe, equipped better by his imagination than his background in economics, was interested in innovation, but, to write about it, he had to set his 1719 novel *Robinson Crusoe* on an island far from sea lanes on which Crusoe, a shipwrecked seaman, was to be trapped for 28 years. There Crusoe does what he could not have done in largely premodern Britain. He lives a life of innovation, at first to survive, then because he could. He starts by working for months to build a boat, only to find it is too heavy to get to the water. (In Defoe's 1721 novel *Moll Flanders,* the adventuress steals a horse, then, not knowing what to do with it, gives it back.) Defoe has been called the poet of mistakes, difficulties, and setbacks.

When modern economies do sprout up, there are few writers conveying much sense of it. Yet three towering novels stand out as suggesting that something of epic importance has been occurring. The earliest of these is the 1818 work *Frankenstein; or, The Modern Prometheus* by Mary Shelley (born Mary Wollstonecraft Godwin). For Romantic poets and artists in Britain, the heroic figure of Prometheus symbolized the capacity for free will, creativity, and destruction. *Frankenstein* became the most influential version.[5]

---

5. The original tragedy *Prometheus Bound*, by the ancient Greek Aeschylus, told of the captivity of Prometheus and his eventual release by the omnipotent Zeus (Jupiter). In the 1820 dramatic poem *Prometheus Unbound* by Percy Bysshe Shelley, Prometheus frees himself by withdrawing a curse he had put on Jupiter, which causes Jupiter to lose his power and leave the world to a benign anarchy. Mary, living with Percy and Lord Byron, started her horror novel in Switzerland in the summer of 1818 and described Percy's drama in a letter that September. It is fair to say that her Prometheus story was, in part, a reaction against the "rational-humanism," as Muriel Spark terms it, of her atheist father, William Godwin, and that of her Christian lover and husband to be, Percy. In his younger years, Percy was called Viktor.

The author could not foresee the modern economy, let alone warn against it, but as the modern economy grew powerful, readers continued to be drawn to the novel, no doubt seeing parallels between the monster created by Dr. Viktor Frankenstein and the innovative companies created by entrepreneurs. When in James Whale's 1931 film version Dr. Frankenstein, seeing the monster move, cries "It's alive!" he could have as well been exclaiming over the nascent modern economy in Britain or America. A company is generally inclined to be kind to customers and employers just as the monster was usually kind. And companies are feared, just as the monster was feared. But was the novel an indictment of Prometheanism? Against the modern economy? The poet Percy Shelley, worried that his wife's novel would be seen as a warning against these developments, opposed any such interpretation in the preface he wrote for the book. Yet he had little reason to worry. The book does not attack innovation. It laments Frankenstein's inability and that of the townsfolk to accept the monster. And it asserts that science cannot duplicate the creative powers of human minds.

Another novel of the Romantic period that is a marker of the modern economy is the 1847 novel *Wuthering Heights* by Emily Brontë. The backdrop of the tragic love story is the tension between the rural life that imprisons Cathy and the irresistible force that pulls Heathcliff to the big city where important careers are made.[6] By the middle of the 19th century the dynamism of London had seized the imagination of the young generation, though some would have to remain behind. In the classic film version, as Heathcliff leaves Wuthering Heights, Cathy expresses the excitement—hers or perhaps her sense of his—in a single line: "Go, Heathcliff. Run away. Bring me back the world!"[7]

Charles Dickens had views on the world of work that were more complex than is widely appreciated. His power as a writer was such that he could arouse public sympathy for destitute orphans and unskilled workers oppressed by the mindlessness of the most routine factory labor—as he did in his 1837 novel *Oliver Twist* and in his 1854 novel *Hard Times.* Dickens's own harsh introduction to London when he was a boy of 12 gave him deep

6. Heathcliff, who was of Gypsy origins, may also have sensed that London, where business acumen counted, would offer chances of skirting the traditional prejudices of the rural areas. Mid-century London must have been a locus for economic inclusion as well as economic dynamism.

7. This is the 1939 version—Hollywood's golden year—produced by Samuel Goldwyn and directed by William Wyler with screenplay by Ben Hecht and Charles MacArthur. Merle Oberon and Lawrence Olivier played the lead roles.

insights into the burdensomeness of unskilled work. But he became sensitive to a growing range of problems in English society.

> Even *Hard Times* is not concerned with the sorts of workers' suffering detailed by Mrs Trollope. . . . The novel's satirical focus is less industrial . . . more involved with those forces that would oppress individual and imaginative life. Stephen Blackpool's problems result not from industrialization . . . but from (in the first instance) the incapacity of the System, embodied in Parliament and the Establishment, to respond to the difficulties of his marriage; and (in the second instance) by his refusal to submerge his individuality in another dehumanizing system, Slackbridge's trade union.[8]

Dickens's views on industrialization changed too. By the 1850s he was delighted with the rise of new work opportunities across Britain while retaining a nostalgia for traditional life and an unsurpassed sympathy for the less fortunate. In his extraordinary night walks through the city he was fascinated by the vitality and variety he encountered—the "restlessness of a great city and the way in which it tumbles and tosses before it can get to sleep." In the 1836 work *Sketches by Boz* he describes the slow awakening of the city: shopkeepers, law clerks, office workers, and a new set of people entering by 11 o'clock: "The streets are thronged with a vast concourse of people, gay and shabby, rich and poor, idle and industrious, and we come to the heat, bustle and activity of NOON." After a second look at Birmingham factories he writes, "I have seen in [your] factories and workshops such . . . great consideration for the work people . . . I have seen the results in the demeanour of your working people, excellently balanced by a nice instinct, as free from servility on the one hand as from self-conceit on the other."[9] Nor was he as naïve as the solution George Orwell ascribed to him—to "give everyone turkeys." For example, Dickens warned factory operatives that a manipulative labor union organizer would use them to secure personal benefits or political ends that would not be beneficial to them.

Dickens came to see careers as a means, if not *the* means, to personal growth. His 1850 novel *David Copperfield* celebrates the development of David from childhood to maturity, contrasting it to the strategy of David's nemesis, the unctuous climber Uriah Heep:

8. Schlicke, *The Oxford Reader's Companion to Dickens* (1999, p. 294).

9. The first quote is from "Night Walks" in *The Uncommercial Traveller*, the second is from "The Streets—Morning," in *Sketches by Boz*, and the third is from a speech delivered in Birmingham on January 6th of 1853 and reprinted in *Speeches, Letters and Sayings*. These quotations also appear in Andrews, *Dickens on England and the English*, pp. 98, 84, and 69, respectively.

Heep's egocentricity prevents him from seeing work as a means of genuine liberation and self-affirmation. It is . . . David whose life assumes meaning because he finds the work that gives him both purpose and identity. The self-actualization that comes to David through his vocation as a writer constitutes Dickens's own endorsement of the worth of work. . . . [T]he oppressive situations Dickens opposed in so many of his novels were perversions of the work ethic. . . . [Dickens], the most striking nineteenth-century model for success through enterprising work, shared the basic assumptions that work is, in general, good and that workers are to be respected for their individuality and intrinsic worth.[10]

In Dickens's work, David is just one of many characters who take control of their lives. The richness and courage he saw in ordinary people is striking. So Dickens proves no less of a vitalist than Shakespeare or Cervantes.

A comparison of the writing of the mid-century novelist Charlotte Brontë, born in 1816, with that of the 18th-centuryish Jane Austen, born in 1764, may offer insight into the transformation of life in 19th-century England. Brontë's 1847 novel *Jane Eyre* can be read as the "story of a woman who succeeds in 'getting on.'" She strikes out courageously and independently and forges her own career, first as governess, then as an independent schoolmistress with her own business. . . . By the book's end, she has 'got on' very far, struggling against poverty and adversity for most of her early life, enjoying immediately none of the benefits of birth or patronage."[11] In contrast, in Austen's work, women's experiences are in the domestic economy, and her heroines look more toward marriage for their economic achievements. For them, money, which they legally had no right to in Austen's time, was basically an opportunity to raise their standard of living and social class: In *Sense and Sensibility* (1811), the Dashwood women, Elinor and Marianne, argue over the annual budget that will be required. Although many people in the present day and many contemporaries too, such as Samuel Coleridge in Britain and Thorstein Veblen in America, lamented the materialism in the mid- and

---

10. Bradshaw and Ozment, *The Voices of Toil* (2000, p. 199). Thus it would be wrong to view Dickens as writing about 18th-century or 17th-century capitalism as much as 19th-century modern capitalism.

11. Rick Rylance in *The Cambridge Companion to the Brontës* (2002, pp. 157–158) discusses the phrase "getting on" in the Victorian Britain of the 1840s. It meant making a success of one's life and was applied to a whole emerging class of "economically dynamic and socially mobile entrepreneurs." Interestingly, he comments that the literature seemed to disapprove of the changes in character that developed during the economic revolution though not objecting to the economic system itself.

late 19th century, evidence suggests that it was the 18th century in which the game of making money was an obsession. William Blake, the feminist writer Mary Wollstonecraft, and Thomas Carlyle were all contemporary critics of that materialism. In Austen's time, around the turn of the century, even a landowner of social rank has an intense interest in increasing the profits from land. But in her last novel, *Mansfield Park* (1814), making money begins to hold an intellectual fascination. Henry Crawford says that "the most interesting thing in the world [is] how to make money—how to turn a good income into a better [one]" (p. 226).

In the other countries where a modern economy had sprung up there are also literary works reflecting on the new business life, of course. In France, Balzac wrote approvingly for an entire volume on the phenomenon of the French cafes in the 19th century, and Émile Zola wrote about the changes taking place in Paris. In Germany, Johann Wolfgang von Goethe, the pioneering novelist of personal development, wrote with an eye on the new but his heart still in the old about the economic modernity arising along the Rhine in the 1820s. Thomas Mann's novel *Buddenbrooks*, first published in 1901, tells of four generations of a family, starting with the generation that made its fortune in business. The book charts the vitality that is lost as each generation moves farther from the world of business.

One would guess that America must have seen an outpouring of literature on the new economic life, since that life spread so far and so profoundly through the population. Americans were swept up in the movement to build new things, settle in new places, find adventure, test themselves, improve themselves, and get ahead. But for just that reason there were not many people who preferred writing about the new life to taking part in it. There was not much demand either. Had America been supplying as many new titles as Europe did, few of them would have found buyers willing to take time out to read them. Yet the novels by Herman Melville, the greatest master in 19th-century American fiction, hum with the undertones of the rising business world.

Two of Melville's major novels speak of confidence, trust, and uncertainty. In *The Confidence-Man*, his 1857 novel set aboard the ship *Fidele*, business is all about whether to entrust money to an entrepreneur or potential partner. As a friend of Melville's said, "[i]t is a good thing . . . and speaks well for human nature that it *can be swindled.*" Melville's grand success in 1851, *Moby-Dick*, devotes pages to describing the processes of whaling, suggesting the excitement and indicating the hazards, which we understand are not at all quantifiable. The "whaling lines" in which the seamen may become caught, perhaps fatally, serve as a metaphor for the developments in which the actors in the economy may become disastrously entangled.[12] Although business life—the good and the bad—and the profusion of occupations made big impressions on Dickens, it took an American observer with a poetic voice to capture the fascination and suspense of the new life.

Washington Irving's *The Sketch Book of Geoffrey Crayon, Gent.*, well received in England and America in 1820, featured stories dealing with profound changes to cities. In "The Legend of Sleepy Hollow," some 25 miles up the Hudson River from New York City, Irving depicts a town isolated from the sweeping economic changes of America: Sleepy Hollow is where "population, manners, and customs remain fixed, while the great torrent of migration and improvement, which is making incessant changes in other parts of this restless country, sweeps by them unobserved." A relatively learned man— Ichabod Crane—comes to work and teach in this town of "listless repose" only to be eventually shunned by its superstitious and stubborn inhabitants. Irving subtly hints at his critical view of those who may have "understood nothing of the labor of headwork." Engagement in work is harshly contrasted with idleness, which Irving associates with lost opportunity and isolation from change.

The emergence of the modern economy drove change not just in literature but in painting as well. Until the 19th century, painting was generally static and picturesque, not only the bucolic canvases of Claude Lorrain or Thomas Gainsborough and the portraits of domesticity by Joshua Reynolds or Diego Velasquez but even in what Willard Spiegelman (somewhat unfortunately) terms "action painting":

> [A]ction painting—whether dealing with mythic, religious or historical events, and even if violent in content—often lacked real energy. In France, the gorgeous colors and symmetries of Poussin in the 17th century, the chiseled nobility of David in the late 18th century and the shellacked beauty of Ingres at the start of the 19th all gave way to the explosion of Romanticism.[13]

---

12. I am indebted to Richard Robb for general discussion. In a course at Columbia University, he has used the "whaling lines" metaphor to make vivid the hazards of making decisions in conditions of radical uncertainty characteristic of the modern economy. Regarding *The Confidence-Man*, the friend of Melville's quoted above was Evert Duyckinck, who commented in 1850 in the periodical *Literary World* on newspaper reports of people being taken in by confidence men.

13. Spiegelman, "Revolutionary Romanticism: *The Raft of the Medusa*" (2009, p. W14). The

In France this Romantic movement started in the 1820s with Théodore Géricault's tempestuous painting *The Raft of the Medusa,* in which, as Spiegelman writes, the wind-blown and sea-tossed survivors, sighting the rescue ship, express a range of emotions, "from eagerness and exultation to incredulity [and] hysteria." The huge canvases by Eugène Delacroix soon follow. On his 1834 painting *Arabic Fantasy,* E. H. Gombrich comments that "there is no clarity of outline here, no pose and restraint . . . , [no] patriotic or edifying subject. All the painter wants is to make us partake in an intensely exciting moment, and to share his joy in the movement and romance of the sea."[14] In Britain, J.M.W. Turner, in such epochal paintings as the 1801 *Dutch Boats in a Gale,* the 1842 *Steamship in Snowstorm,* and the 1844 *Rail, Steam and Speed,* evoked almost palpably the dangers and excitements of modern business ventures:

> Turner is an artist of anxiety, of restless turbulent motion, of a world that on the surface might look like the old, immemorial pre-industrial planet painted by the masters he sought to rival, but in reality is being shaken from its moorings by war, industry and revolution.
>
> This Romanticism . . . sweeps you away like a cork on a tidal wave. . . . [W]hile [the 17th-century painter] Van de Velde's sea piece *A Rising Gale* . . . paints a picture of the wild sea, [*Dutch Boats*] makes that model seem as quaint as a toy windmill. . . . Turner captures the motion and menace of the waves as paint—his paint is the sea, not a picture of it. He gives objects and energy physical reality . . . while Van de Velde seems just to be creating a virtual nature on a computer screen.
>
> Turner's painting makes you doubt the solidity of the ground beneath your feet. His earth is not a pre-Copernican platform but an orb spinning in space. . . . Turner, as his champion John Ruskin claimed, is the very definition of a "modern painter."[15]

The sea and trains became symbols of the kind of economy that had emerged

---

titular "Medusa" was a frigate that ran aground in Mauritania, leaving 150 clinging to a raft. This canvas by Théodore Géricault bids to be the earliest action painting of 19th-century Romanticism.

14. Gombrich, *The Story of Art,* p. 382. Gombrich embraces the 19th-century "revolution" in painting, though, noting the "two possibilities in Constable and Turner," he declares that "those who followed Constable's path and tried to explore the visible world rather than to conjure up poetic moods achieved something of more lasting importance." Of course, any self-respecting art scholar wants art to be a subject in itself, not just a branch of social studies. However, it remains true that the spirit of some great painters' works does reflect the spirit of the society in which they worked.

15. Jones, "Other Artists Paint Pictures, Turner Brings Them to Life" (2009).

in the century—powerful, dangerous, and too unpredictable to control, yet also fascinating and thrilling.

This Romantic movement in art, as is widely said, rejected the ordered equilibrium of 18th-century neoclassicism as mechanical and impersonal. The Romantics turned to the directness of personal experience and to individual imagination and aspiration. The parallel with the transformation of the economy is quite clear. The 18th-century economies, in which the timepaths of production, investment, and work might have been supposed to be largely determinate and thus largely knowable—apart from occasional exogenous shocks, such as the plague and finding the New World—gave way to modern economies in which what can be produced is constantly being uncovered by innovations and in which decisions on what to produce and invest in reflect the imagination of entrepreneurs. But the parallel goes only so far. Did these paintings up to the 1850s signal high engagement and deep gratification from work in the emerging modern economies? Did they reflect moments of happiness from landing the desired job or proving the worth of the new commercial idea? Apparently not. But they do represent the thrill of the opportunities and dangers of the new era.

Expressionism sought to capture other aspects of economic life not successfully represented previously. Vincent van Gogh, the forerunner of the Expressionists and another nominee as the founder of modern art, brought high emotion to subjects from everyday life in his incandescent work painted in Arles, such as *Sower with Setting Sun, The Painter on the Road to Tarascon,* and *Café Terrace on the Place du Forum,* all in 1888. In the last, the outdoor cafe in summer is as glowing as the night sky, and we want to be there chatting, drinking, and eating with friends. In his voluminous letters to his brother, van Gogh showed he understood something about the modern economies. As a daring innovator himself, he understood the need of people to create and to leave a mark by innovating. As a professional, he also understood that innovation cannot go far in the absence of possibilities of observing, and learning and taking inspiration from the innovative activities of others:

> Man is not placed on this earth to be happy; nor is he placed here merely to be honest. He is here to accomplish great things through society.[16]

The Expressionists, following up on the breakthroughs of van Gogh, were fascinated by the fast-expanding urban life. Before them, there were paintings such as Kruger's *Parade in the Opernplatz 1822,* in which a traditional subject, with its royal figures, is transformed into an image of a "modern crowd"

16. Van Gogh, *The Letters* (2009, p. 57).

composed of ordinary citizens and celebrities.[17] The Expressionist Ernst Ludwig Kirchner with his half-dozen paintings titled *Berlin Street Scene* between 1913 and 1915 struck a new note in conveying the vitality, glamour, and rush of the new city life at the end of the century. Later, however, Oskar Kokoschka and George Grosz were extraordinarily dark about the modern life around them, having survived the horrors of World War 1 and the upheavals in the 1920s. A sunnier side was presented in the Mediterranean region with the Futurist painters of Italy, who caught the quickened pace of Italian life. An early example, the 1910 work by Giacomo Balla *Dynamism of a Dog on a Leash* must be mentioned. Later, Gino Severini celebrated in 1915's *Red Cross Train Passing a Village* the breathtaking speed and sleek design of the modern trains coming into being in Italy. (In contrast, the painters who took the road of Constable—Paul Cézanne and the great Cubists—were more interested in space and perspective than in life in business and the city.)

There is little expression in the visual arts of a key dimension of living that the modern economies introduced. Business life used to be full of derring-do—of going "down to the boats and into the sea," as the Vikings did. With the modern economy, life was full of cerebration—of "I'm going up to the attic to think." In painting and sculpture there are some acknowledgments of the new mental life, however. A portrait painted around 1900 by a Philadelphia artist depicts a businessman apparently deep in thought. *The Thinker,* about the most well-known work in all of sculpture, was produced in 1889 by Auguste Rodin, progenitor of modern sculpture and widely appreciated for representing ordinary men and women. Maybe *The Thinker* was the mythic Prometheus, yet "promethean" has long been a term used to characterize the modern economies; no one made such a sculpture until the modern economies and, with them, modern sculpture came along.

We do not find in literature or the visual arts much appreciation for the interior satisfactions and gratifications that surely arose and spread first in the 19th century. In *Field Notes from Elsewhere,* his meditation getting to the bottom of life, the philosopher Mark C. Taylor asks in his next-to-last chapter, "why is it so hard to write about happiness?" He suggests that writers tend not to write when they are happy and when the happiness passes, as it always does, they deal with their unhappiness by writing about it. Maybe doing so helps them to work their way out of their unhappiness. Another reason may be that, although moments of joy, glee, or ecstasy may be possible to

17. Foster-Hahn et al., *Spirit of an Age* (2001).

represent if put in a particular context, unremarkable everyday satisfactions and gratifications from being engaged in projects—alone or in teams—do not lend themselves to representation by words or paint.

In contrast, it appears that music has proved better able to resonate with those interior feelings, with the internal dimensions of much of our experience. Music appears to have captured the experience of meeting problems and resonated with the obstacles and exaltation of creating. Perhaps this is because a piece of music may be a hundred stanzas and thousands of bars, while a painting is a single frame. So their capabilities are different.

No doubt, the product delivered by music is not a mere depiction of others' creativity, innovation, the ensuing struggle, defeat and triumph. The music is its own thing; with exceptions, it does not represent anything in the social world. What the composer expresses is the composer's own feelings about the composer's own effort to create and, with luck, to cause a musical innovation. And if perchance the audience "resonates" with the task and the struggle expressed, the composition becomes a commercial success.

Europe and America in the 19th century were alive with the sound of music, increasingly so over the century. Music was no longer a sort of treasure reserved for European bishops and princes. So-called serious music came to be embraced by the middle class from the business world, and so-called popular music could be accessed by the working class as well. The audience for music was strong in America. In 1842 Vienna's Musikverein was founded to support the Vienna Philharmonic Orchestra while in the same year the Philharmonic Society of New York was founded to create a high-level orchestra there. Yet in the 19th century the great producers of music, serious and popular, were all European. In the next century, though, America took the lead in popular songwriting and, by the 1930s, pulled its weight even in the music of the concert hall.

Something important must have been going on in music that struck a chord with the life of the times. It is clear now what it was. Composers in the Baroque and classical periods of the 17th and 18th centuries routinely drew on the stock of preexisting folk tunes for material and were formulaic in developing their themes—as routine and formulaic as the mercantile economies of that era. Working in this style, a composer of Joseph Haydn's musicality could produce more than 100 symphonies. The subsequent eras were all about tearing down these rules. A poll years ago asked musicologists to name the three most innovative composers of all time. The winners were Ludwig van Beethoven, Richard Wagner, and Igor Stravinsky. (There would surely have been no consensus on the fourth.) They all broke rules in musical composition between 1800 and 1910 in company with the rise of the modern economies and the high business innovation that resulted.

Beethoven, most loudly with his 1804 Symphony No. 3 (*Eroica*), introduced a way of innovating by leaving it to some extent undetermined how the symphony will develop—much as the path of the modern economies was to an extent undetermined owing to the possibilities of innovation that were left open to entrepreneurs and financiers. Beethoven can break into a new theme unpredictably—for example, the last movement of the Symphony No. 2, with its frenzied strings, seems chaotic, and Symphony No. 9 breaks rules to express disorder—just as an entrepreneur might unpredictably start the development of a new product. Of course, Beethoven was not inspired by vast commercial innovation: the modern economies were just beginning to be developed enough to be able to carry out successful attempts at business innovation. What seems likely is that Beethoven rocketed to success over ensuing decades because the experience of hearing his symphonies struck a chord among people who were experiencing innovation—their own and, mostly, those of others—in their own business lives. It was the educated bourgeoisie who hoisted Beethoven up on their shoulders. They celebrated him; he was not celebrating them.

The next generation of composers raised the celebration of the hero to a fever pitch. Robert Schumann's overture *Manfred* caught the spirit of Shelley's poem and the propulsiveness of his piano quartet in E-flat major—played at breakneck speed—brilliantly expressed the rush of his times. Franz Liszt broke new ground with *Les preludes* (*d'apres Lamartine*), an orchestral work not structured along classical lines, which he dubbed a "symphonic poem." The title is thought to refer to an ode by the poet Alphonse de Lamartine and an epigraph in the published score evokes that poem:

> What else is our life but a series of preludes? . . . [W]hat is the fate where the first delights of happiness are not interrupted by some storm, the mortal blast of which dissipates its fine illusions, . . . where the soul . . . on issuing from one of these tempests, does not endeavour to rest in recollection in the calm serenity of life in the fields? Nevertheless man hardly gives himself up for long to the enjoyment of the beneficent stillness which at first he has shared in Nature's bosom. . . . [W]hen "the trumpet sounds the alarm" he hastens to the dangerous post, whatever the war may be, which calls him to its ranks, in order at last to recover in the combat full consciousness of himself and entire possession of his energy.

(The electrifying trumpet call lets the audience know when "recovery" has come.)

Richard Strauss's symphonic poem *Ein Heldenleben* [*A Hero's Life*] is inspired by the ups and downs in the early years of a career—his own. His last opera, *Capriccio,* has a business setting: the theatrical business. With the character of the theater director La Roche, Strauss draws a convincing warts-and-all picture of a vain but great man. Yet, in that opera and some others, Strauss is primarily interested in dramatizing the heroine's quest for self-knowledge. Women as well as men must go into the world to find out who they are. By Strauss's time, modern economies had wrought a cultural and psychological revolution and were beginning to break down even age-old gender barriers.

Nineteenth-century opera reflected the new aspirations of people for liberation and self-expression. Richard Wagner and Giuseppe Verdi, both born in 1813, reflected the tensions and emotions raised by the modern social life developing around them. In Wagner, heroines are at the center and it is passion, such as love, that gives life meaning—nowhere more so than in his four-opera cycle *The Ring of the Niebelung,* which premiered in 1869. He does not assert that there are no passions in business or that meeting challenges, experimenting, and exploring in the business world cannot give life meaning. But the *Ring* cycle is also about the meaninglessness and possible downfall that await those who indulge in a single-minded, unbridled pursuit of material wealth or arbitrary power. The sought-after golden ring is cursed. The cycle also expresses foreboding as the old order of throne and altar is brought down by the arrival of industrial nations and the end of the Holy Roman Empire. When Wotan, ruler of the world, steals the ring from Alberich, who had himself stolen it, he undermines all the old treaties and obligations—it is everyone for himself. Yet Wagner is not a pessimist. The downfall of the gods in the *Ring*'s last opera represents, according to Wagner himself, the beginning of the modern world, where human beings will be freer than before to shape their destinies. And befitting an artist of his talent and daring, Wagner was not a social conservative. He may have been a socialist on some ethereal level but he was no corporatist: his only comedy, *Die Meistersinger,* pays affectionate tribute to the traditions of the medieval guild, yet he comes down on the side of the individual and openness to the new.

Later operas in Italy, notably Verdi's *La Traviata* and the *verismo* works of Giacomo Puccini and Pietro Mascagni that followed, dramatize the modern theme of emancipation from oppression and repression. In the 20th century, the jazzy compositions of Maurice Ravel, Darius Milhaud, and Jacques Ibert celebrate the freedom and sheer fun of modern life in France in those times. The rise of jazz in New Orleans and Chicago in the 1920s was an expression of individuality and an imaginative spirit.

Evolving in tandem with modern music, modern ballet offers a respite from opera's heroism and revenge. Marius Petipa, the French dancer who, after stints in America and Europe, ended up in St. Petersburg, created the modern ballet of ecstatic leaps and twirls in collaboration with Peter Ilyich Tchaikovsky. *Swan Lake,* in its original 1877 version, centers on the conflict between the upright and dutiful Odette, turned into a Swan Queen, and the glamorous woman of the world Odile, a would-be seductress of the Prince, in love with Odette. The ballet can surely be seen as an allegory of the moral tensions in modern life, where there are new hazards in commitment—though a virtuous path can offer rewards too, and virtue is its own reward. Yet ballet certainly had further to go in modern directions, and another Russian, George Balanchine, took it there as he wended his way from St. Petersburg to Paris to London to New York. His revolutionary works, from *Apollo* in 1928 ("I learned I too could simplify") and *Prodigal Son* in 1929, to *Agon* in 1957, and *Stravinsky Violin Concerto* in 1972, depicted elements of modern life—journeys without destinations, the strangeness of it, and its exhilarating moments. Russia's economy was far from modern then—it still is. Yet, soaking up the spirit of the West's modern cities from an early age, Stravinsky and Balanchine became modern giants.

One wonders whether the decline of modern art and music during the 1960s—when Ezra Pound's "Make It New!" was replaced by the endless loops of Philip Glass and the irony of Pop Art—and the decline of economic dynamism that was already visible across Europe and beginning to set in across America both signaled a loss of commitment to the ideals of exploration and innovation.

Summing Up

The modern economies that broke out in much of the Western world had deep consequences for the temper of the times. The birth of the modern in the arts and letters is undoubtedly connected with the spirit of the modern economy in the countries where it sprang up and maintained its force. Yet the connections are two-way. The earliest expressions of the modern, very clearly in music and philosophy, appear to anticipate and perhaps to kindle the spirit without which modern economies would have been impossible;

these precocious breakthroughs in the arts and philosophy are harbingers of the modern economies to come. Nevertheless, the extraordinary waves of artistic innovation in the 19th century and the first half of the 20th are reflections and commentary on the new dimensions of life wrought by the modern economy. In general, the arts, normally critical of society and frequently dark, were positive about the modern life and celebrated the new dimensions of living. (The last two chapters take up the ultimate question of how we might reasonably weigh the positive effects of economic modernity against the costs.)

Readers by now will have gotten a sense of the ports of call ahead and where the ship is bound. Chapter 4, which closes out Part One on the rise of the modern, tackles the question of the evolving institutions, economic and political, and the economic culture that may have given birth to the modern economies hatched in the 19th century. Part Two takes up the 20th-century battles and controversies over the modern economy, some of which led to modifications of the modern system—for better or for worse.

CHAPTER FOUR

How Modern Economies Formed

The Bolsheviks understood that culture [has] a strong influence on people. . . . [They] knew the game was up when the sons
of the Communists themselves wanted to become capitalists and
entrepreneurs.

JOSEPH JANICEK, "Czechs' Velvet Revolution," *New York Times*

T HE EMERGENCE BY THE MID-19TH CENTURY of a pervasively modern
economy in much of the West altered human experience by enlisting
creativity, inviting experimentation, and fostering innovation. It thereby
earned its place as a watershed development in world history. One would
think, then, that historians would have taken up the big questions of its
origin: What was required for economic modernity and how were the
requirements met? What was present here and not there? Present then and
not before?

General historians did not address the questions. What they wrote under
"the rise of the West" are chronicles of the rise of the state and democracy.
Their drama opens with Gutenberg's printing press in 1444, the expansion-
ism of Europe's monarchs in the 1500s, Luther's "95 Theses" of 1517 challenging Rome, and the gradual recognition of the Magna Carta in the 1600s. This
was heady stuff. Yet the era's economies are mainly noted for little but the
growth of long-distance trade from 1350 to 1750.

A few historians, sociologists, and others did write of the rise of several
economies in the West, often under the heading of "the rise of capitalism." In
Jared Diamond's ecological work, abundant crops and animals and the towns
they could support enabled greater specialization of labor in Eurasia than was
possible in sub-Saharan Africa, Australia, and the Americas. That is why Eurasia became richer than the rest. But this thesis does not explain the rise of
innovation and why it arose in Britain, Belgium, France, and Germany but

not in Holland, Portugal, Ireland, Greece, and Spain. Economic institutions and culture are the suspects.[1]

The sociologist Max Weber pointed to a particular cultural shift, believing it was the key to where capitalism flowered. He argued that Calvinism and Lutheranism gave birth to an economic culture of thrift and hard work, which is why capitalism succeeded in the Protestant nations of northern Europe. Though Weber's treatise was well received by the public, critics have noted that some non-Protestant nations, such as Italy, have private saving and net wealth levels that dwarf those of Germany and workweeks that are longer than Germany's as well. What is most telling, however, is that Weber's vocabulary has no room for experimentation, exploration, daring, and unknowability—the hallmarks of indigenous innovation. His thesis may help explain high levels in the aggregate of all investment-type activities reached in several countries. Yet high saving is not necessary for high innovation. (A nation can finance innovative activity by increasing saving or by diverting a part of the unchanged flow of saving to innovation from projects that are relatively uninnovative—houses and conventional business investments. Or it could draw on foreign saving.) And clearly high saving is not sufficient for innovation.[2]

A few scholars did come to grips with Walt Rostow's 19th-century "take-offs into sustained growth." Alexis de Tocqueville, the French political thinker who made penetrating observations on Americans in 1837, thought that the richness of the country's natural resources was the reason Americans were

1. Diamond's book, *Guns, Germs and Steel* (1997), did suggest in passing that European nations became more innovative because, being small, they were forced to innovate or lose population to one another, while the vastness of Asian empires impeded exit. France and Germany were the biggest on the Continent and yet the most innovative.

2. Weber's treatise, known to the English-speaking world in the translation by Talcott Parsons, *The Protestant Ethic and the Spirit of Capitalism,* was first published in German in the 1904/1905 volume of *Archiv für Sozialwissenschaft und Sozialpolitik* (under the title *Die protestantische Ethik und der Geist des Kapitalismus*). It must have been read by every sociologist ever since and by Schumpeter, who is wrongly credited with coining "the entrepreneurial spirit." Yet this treatise was not the high point of Weber's social thought. His big book, 1922's *Wirtschaft und Gesellschaft,* translated in 1978 as *Economy and Society,* offers first drafts on several basic problems in the social sciences: the state, companies, bureaucracy, rationality, legitimacy, and more—topics that went on to enliven social sciences over the century. His most profound insight is his theme that (to paraphrase) an extraterrestrial watching from afar a terrestrial economy would not make sense of what people were doing—unless it was a traditional economy executing the same rhythm every year. (The puzzle would be like the cryptic action in Alfred Hitchcock's *Vertigo* or Michelangelo Antonioni's *Blowup.*) A meaningful analysis requires enough information about the subjects' intents and beliefs to put one's self figuratively in the economy. This is a difficulty physics does not face.

such energetic entrepreneurs. But innovation flowered as much in Britain in the early 1800s as in America. And several countries rich in resources, such as Argentina, became famous for failing to develop any economic dynamism—it was even suspected that natural resources were (or could be) a "curse." Arnold Toynbee, the British historian, took the position opposite to de Tocqueville's. He contended that the British were the first to embrace innovation because, being so poor in climate and natural resources, they had the most to gain if their ship came in. Nothing ventured, nothing gained.[3] But if natural wealth were the drag that Toynbee thought it was, the Americans would have been much less entrepreneurial and less innovative generally, which seems counter to the evidence. Toynbee's idea—*per aspera ad astra*—has some merit: rich kids tend to be short on the focus and hustle necessary for big success. But the exceptions in this case are notable.

The general problem in these four histories is that they never get down to brass tacks. They observe that in some nations more than others labor demand was high (Diamond, de Tocqueville) or supply was high (Weber, Toynbee); then, in a series of leaps, they conclude that high levels of work, saving, wealth, and willingness to take large risks resulted. But even if, where labor increased, great wealth and risk-taking resulted, it does not follow that processes of *innovation* started up. The idea that economic dynamism sprouted from natural and accidental causes implies that countries had no need to devise a set of economic institutions or possess an economic culture favorable to commercial innovation—it implies that the system was already there waiting. Though most if not all peoples, it appears, found self-expression in acting creatively and embracing novelty as far back as prehistoric times, it would be bizarre to exclude the possibility that some countries were more advantaged—politically or culturally—in identifying and building institutions that would enable and facilitate innovation and in fostering attitudes toward experimentation, exploration, and imagination that would inspire

3. De Tocqueville's book, *Democracy in America*, first published in 1835 in France, though it had many observations on economic life, was primarily about America's political life. Toynbee's life work, the 12-volume tome *A Study of History*, published between 1934 and 1961, has the theme that after the rise of wealth out of nothing, accumulation goes on until there is a great fall. His model of decline has a place alongside Gibbon's *Decline and Fall of the Roman Empire*, published in volumes from 1776 to 1789, and Spengler's 1926 prophecy, *The Decline of the West*. In Toynbee's model the difficulty is why Britain should have overexpanded its investments and imperial reach to unsustainable levels. Britain did recoup the huge losses suffered during World War II but never came close to regaining its previous levels of overseas capital and empire. An analogous paradox in every financial crisis is why banks impale themselves on an excess of short-term debt.

and encourage people. A case in point is the Afghan region, now synonymous with backwardness, yet a thousand years ago a place of shining cities and scientific discoveries undreamt of in the rest of the world. This region, to which nature had dealt a good hand, could never develop economic institutions or elements of an economic culture that would open the way to economic modernity—to flourishing business careers and high human fulfillment among all or most of the populace.[4]

If we are to reach an appreciable understanding of the causal forces, conditions, and mechanisms giving birth to a modern sector, pushing out the feudal sector and stealing the show from the mercantile sector, we will have to conceive of the forces and conditions capable of driving the economy's innovative process. We of course recognize that the story we tell can never be error-free, let alone complete. Just as the actors in a modern economy can have only imperfect knowledge of the effects that actions taken in the present are going to have in the future—too much is new and too many actors may be taking novel steps at the same time—theorists of the modern economy can have only imperfect understanding of how, if at all, the beliefs, institutions, and cultures built up over the past enable and encourage the creativity and innovation of the present. In the nations in which modern economies arrived, there were too many developments over previous decades or centuries for us to be able to identify with confidence a set of crucial elixirs. Like canny financiers, we must use judgment and imagination. The competition of ideas has left standing more than one story, or "myth," of the creation of the modern.

These stories are important, of course. Any story a nation tells about its modernization or the lack of it reveals that nation's understanding of the attributes to which it owes its modernization or failure at modernization. Such a story and its retelling are aimed at conveying a conception of things the nation has been right to do and things it was right not to do. Some, if not all, of these stories may therefore be of considerable influence. No doubt the late economist Paul Samuelson had that influence in mind when he said, reflecting on his own story-telling, "I don't care who writes a nation's laws . . . if I can write its economics textbooks." Of course, truth matters, not just influence (which Samuelson never lost sight of). A truer narrative would be a more valuable one—provided it is not so much harder to grasp than the next-truest. Better understanding would help a nation find (or re-find) its

4. See Starr, "Rediscovering Central Asia."

way to a modern economy or to avoid jeopardizing the modern economy it has. Any attempt at a truer narrative will do well to draw on core ideas in the stories already told. Yet the centerpiece of our narrative must be the emergence of the innovation that made some economies modern and even great.

Economic Institutions: Freedom, Property, and Finance

A part of the story of the rise of chronically innovative economies, nascent or mature, is about the creation and evolution of various economic institutions, called in some contexts framework conditions. Some set of economic institutions is necessary to protect and facilitate the activities and arrangements needed for innovation. Not every one of these institutions may be essential by itself—taken alone. Yet, generally speaking, each one makes the economy more able or more disposed to innovate.

It is a commonplace that the range of individual freedoms established relatively early in the West were dear to those who won them. Adam Smith writes of the importance of "dignity" and John Rawls of "self-respect." It is also a commonplace that the emergence of various economic freedoms, such as the freedom to exchange one's goods or services for the goods or services of others, enabled people to realize opportunities for mutual gain. In addition, since many contracts to exchange one thing for another could be violated, people need to see the state protecting economic freedoms by enforcing contracts in order to have the confidence to enter into them. Thus freedoms—to barter or receive income, for example—help weed out economic *inefficiencies*, as Adam Smith saw. But a study of the rise of dynamic economies has to consider the role of individual freedoms in gaining economic *dynamism.*

Economic freedoms were of key importance in enabling processes of innovation. Here, the basic point is that two heads are better than one. We should expect innovation in a nation's economy to be less widespread if large segments of society cannot gain inclusion or, if they could join, would be denied a legal right to share in the fruits of their work. Historians of personal liberty—self-ownership—find that, among traditional societies, those in the East gave a father ownership of his daughters, so they could be worked or sold, while those in the West gave husbands ownership of whatever their wives brought in. In both East and West, blacks could be sold into slavery. In the 19th century, however, the modern societies finally abolished slavery. Somewhat later, they established the legal right of married women to own property. It has been theorized that the evolving nature of work in an innovative economy made it advantageous to society that women have self-ownership, so they would be motivated to adapt and improvise as they see best.[5] Similarly, innovation in a nation's economy will tend to be more widespread if potential providers of inventive ideas are free to open new companies in existing industries. Such free entry permits entrepreneurs to develop and launch new products for testing in the marketplace or to introduce new methods for producing existing products. Also, innovation is more widespread when established firms are freer to offer new products or conduct their businesses in new ways. Thus the rise of such freedoms was to have unanticipated benefits going far beyond exchange—benefits that would ultimately take human development to a new plane.

It is also clear that people are better able and more apt to be involved in departures that may lead to innovation when they have been left free to venture from their homes, regions, and even countries to soak up information on old and new products and new lifestyles. As Weber would have said, people cannot remotely understand the structure and workings of an economy or even a small industry in it—an economy or industry in which future innovations will occur—unless they have considerable experience in it. For innovation to take place, consumers and enterprises, in making decisions as potential end-users, have to be free to adopt a novel product, to judge whether it best meets a need, and to learn how to use it.

The statement that freedoms are good, notably for the expression of creativity and the achievement of innovation, does not imply that freedoms are good in every case—the overstatement for which the libertarian Ayn Rand became famous. Not all freedoms are good for dynamism. A regulation curbing some producers' freedom may allow a consumer to risk trying a new product without having to fear electrocution, poisoning, or the like. A bankruptcy law restraining creditors from seizing what is owed them may allow an entrepreneur to risk attempting an innovative product without having to fear the loss of everything he or she owns (though such laws may dampen the credit made available). On the other hand, some regulations block innovations rather than pave the way for them. (While the libertarians are always contending that virtually all regulation is bad, statists suggest that there is

---

5. Furthermore, parents would see it in their interest to bring up daughters to haul in a good income in business. See the 2002 paper by Geddes and Lueck, "Gains from Self-Ownership and the Expansion of Women's Rights," and the 2011 survey in Edlund, "Big Ideas."

hardly any innovative product that ought not to be submitted for regulatory approval before trial in the market, lest it cause some pioneering users harm.) As the modern economies developed, a welter of regulations by local, regional, and central governments erected barriers to new products and facilities to produce them, thus quite possibly doing more harm than good. In the United States, airport construction has hit a wall not because travelers prefer congestion and delays to the added tax on their air tickets that would be entailed but because every community says NIMBY—"not in my backyard." It is thought that, better than banning some projects, it would be better to require the builder to compensate the community sufficiently to win approval. But that too would have a chilling effect on many innovative projects.

There are good reasons to believe that two more freedoms—the legal right to accumulate the income earned from a new successful product, such as a hit song or movie, and the legal right to invest it in private property, mainly capital—have been of historic importance in boosting dynamism. (We may leave aside for now how much wealth would be enough—whether, for ample dynamism, it might be sufficient for people to be permitted to own an abundance of personal effects, such as clothes and other household durables, a car, a boat, an apartment in the city, and a house in the country.) Here, we are going well beyond the proposition that the legal right to receive money in return is a rudimentary step toward making innovation gainful on a large scale. The proposition at issue is whether it was and is important that people be free to hold wealth in the form of owning firms (proprietorships or partnerships) and, going a step further, owning companies in the form of shareowning—companies privately held and those whose shares are publicly traded. The argument that such freedom is generally helpful to innovation and that some form of company ownership is possibly essential does not hold any surprises at this point. If we want creative ideas springing up from the grassroots and private entrepreneurs and private financiers judging which ones look to be worth gambling on, we will not want to limit the pool of idea-men, financiers, and entrepreneurs to those who would do it for just the usual stipend that the state pays everyone, or for just a chance at earning the annual wage income that workers receive with little or no risk. A nation would not get the right selection of people that way, and those selected would have little incentive to make decisions with the prospect of profit—rather than fun or fame. And there does not appear to be any obvious way of paying the conceiver of an idea, the developer, and the financier except by an arrangement that pays shares to these central actors. There has to be a social device that rewards those doing innovative work according to the fruits of their visions, insights, and judgments—the innovation achieved—not the hours put in. (It is left to the next chapter to take up the socialist argument that society does well to leave most or much of the economy's investment in capital—including economic knowledge—to the state.)

If we agree on the importance of these economic freedoms for innovation, are we then on our way to a freedom-based narrative of the birth of economic dynamism in the 19th century? To be sure, in prehistoric times, when families lived in small groups, a great many family decisions now regularly made with utter freedom must have been submitted to the group for approval. The day-to-day interdependencies could not have allowed much scope for individual initiative. The challenge to a narrative of the eventual flowering of innovation that bases itself on freedom, though, is that most of these valuable freedoms did not arise in Britain or anywhere else until a short gestation period before the modern economy was born—1815 or so. Indeed, recorded history shows that property rights go back more than 3,000 years before the explosion of innovation. In ancient Babylonia, the Code of King Hammurabi, proclaimed around 1760 BC, set out a body of law that assumed individual ownership of property and protected owners against theft, fraud, and violation of contract. Jewish law was established about the same time and came to form the basis for common law, including property rights. In ancient Rome, the civil law was codified and made accessible to citizens, whose property rights were defined and protected against confiscation by the government. The law also supported contractual agreements, and it defined private corporations and their ability to acquire property. These principles were applied throughout the vast Roman Empire.

These ancient freedoms of private ownership did not make it to the 19th century without a setback in the Dark Ages:

> [W]hen the Roman Empire faltered and failed, largely owing to corruptness at its higher levels of government, [t]he weakening of Roman authority diminished the force of Roman law. . . . Distant commercial dealings became more risky and, as a result, the settings for transactions became more localized and compact. . . . Private ownership gave way to collective ownership. Land and other resources, in larger measure than before, became the property of local abbeys, feudal villages and [family-run] peasant farms . . . [which] strove for and secured a large measure

of self-sufficiency. Mutual obligation and collective control of resources substituted for private ownership. . . . The church and feudal institutions were run as cooperatives . . . the peasant farm by the family.[6]

Yet private ownership never disappeared. The cities maintained extensive private ownership of resources. And as the long-distance trade of cities gradually recovered in importance, property law grew in importance. Elements of Roman law survived in the common law that arose in Britain and in the civil law that developed on the European continent. Many principles of Roman law were imported directly into French civil law with the Napoleonic Code of 1804. So, although the economic freedoms involving private ownership began to emerge, albeit fitfully, in ancient times, the gradual spread and codification of these freedoms was ongoing, even in the most modern societies in the West, well into the 19th century. After the middle ages, "[t]he march from status to contract and from collective to private ownership resumed," as Demsetz put it. And, as noted above, the extension of ownership rights to the enslaved and to women occurred only in the middle of that century.

It has to be interjected that a kind of property associated with innovation began to come under legal protections on the eve of the 19th century. Patents, copyrights, and trademarks developed, aimed (with varying success) at protecting *intellectual property.* Laying the groundwork for this shift, Britain in 1623 became the first country to issue patents in a significant volume, granting protection from infringement of "projects of new invention" upon payment of a stiff fee. The Patent Act in the United States offered much cheaper protection, with the result that patent applications soared. (Britain modified its system during the 19th century to make patents as affordable as in America but never reached a comparable volume.) The French patent system was created during the Revolution in 1791. In view of these dates, it might seem plausible that patents were the key—the open sesame—to innovation in the 19th century. Economics gives less support to that notion than may be supposed. In fact, a great deal of intellectual

---

6. Demsetz, "Toward a Theory of Property Rights II" (p. 668; the following quote is also to be found on that page). Harold Demsetz, writing in the shadow of the groundbreaking organization theorist Ronald Coase, sees the latter's work in the middle third of the past century as on the "consequences"—benefits, to be more precise—"of an existing private-ownership system" and sees his own work in the last third of the century as on the causes of private ownership—"why it came into existence."

property stays with the proprietor without benefit of any legal protection whatsoever. Much of a company's chronic improvements in the goods it sells and its methods of making them may simply pass under the radar of competitors, actual or potential. As Hayekian economists would say, much detailed knowledge stays with those "on the spot," who are immersed in it enough to understand it. Even if a company's new method of producing could easily be copied by a rival company, the latter would fear that constructing similar equipment to compete might only wipe out all profit or so much of the profit that it could not cover its cost, so it may not undertake the investment. In films, much of the profits are earned in the first couple of weeks, the rest within the year, so an imitation may succeed but not at the cost of the pioneer. Even when a new book or play is off to a good start, it is rare that another publishing house or theatrical company could imitate or improve on it well enough to overcome the advantages of the pioneering work—its reputation and fame or buzz. Where an innovator is sure it could set its price low enough to keep potential predators at bay and still make a profit, the loss resulting from the appropriability of its innovation might not be large enough to deter it from attempting the innovation.

These gains notwithstanding, demands on the state to provide protection of property rights and other services had the consequence of creating state powers with no counterpart in the middle ages and the mercantile era. And the monarchies and feudal baronies that protected commoners from one another did not protect them against state power. However, in England, Scotland, and colonial America there was a backlash against that power, as commoners began to insist on "rights against the king" as well as rights with respect to one another.

The concept of rights against the king found its first public expression in the Magna Carta Libertatum issued by King John of England in 1215, confirmed in 1297, and repeated in a 1354 statute. Kings were to rule in accordance with law and custom—a concept that sowed the seeds of constitutional government. Yet the great principles were flouted. (They did not stop William II from taxing the politically weak and economically poor farmers, which the outraged Robin Hood sought to redress.) The statute was put into practice only after a struggle in the 1600s between the kings of the House of Stuart and Parliament, culminating in the Glorious Revolution of 1688 and the Bill of Rights in 1689. The latter finally abolished such royal prerogatives as suspending laws, levying taxes without Parliament, and interfering with the courts. The "law of the land" was equated to "due process of law," and due process meant that no one may be deprived of liberty or property without proper adjudication.[7]

This constitutional development has been viewed as having put Britain and later other countries under the rule of law. The protection of businesses as well as households from confiscation by the crown and from new edicts to benefit favorites at the expense of others could have signaled to entrepreneurs and investors that Britain and similar countries had been made safe for enterprise in general and innovation in particular. The contracts clause in the U.S. Constitution of 1787 is seen as in the spirit of the rule of law, applied equally to the powerful and the weak. It became a bulwark against government actions taken in the interests of the politically powerful and at the expense of the politically weak.

But there have been doubts that the activation of the new rights in 1689 could have made the difference between day and night. The sentiment that "law should govern" and authorities should be "the servants of the laws" had been familiar in Aristotle's time in ancient Greece and in Jewish law before that. That it took nearly a century and a half after 1689 for innovation to explode suggests that instituting the constitution was not enough to cause a sharp break in the path of history and, by itself, to open the way to intensive innovation. And the very fuzziness of some elements in the "rule of law" concept—Is every change in tax law unjust? When is a tax a taking from political opponents?—suggests that protections of freedoms from the authorities must be taken with a grain of salt.

Though these freedoms were unquestionably necessary for the transformation from mercantile economies to modern ones, the fact that the explosion of innovation did not take place in the late 1600s or in the 1700s makes it hard to believe that that these freedoms, even taken together, were sufficient for the birth of the modern. We have still not found a spark that could be

---

7. Chapter 39 of the original Magna Carta states:
   No Freeman shall be taken, or imprisoned, or be disseised [dispossessed] of his Freehold, or Liberties, or free Customs, or be outlawed, or exiled, or any otherwise destroyed, nor will we pass upon him, nor condemn him, but by lawful Judgment of his Peers, or by the Law of the Land. We will sell to no man, we will not deny or defer to any man either Justice or Right.
   Sir Edward Coke, Chief Justice in the early 1600s, wrote in a series of opinions that in "the ancient constitution," which the Magna Carta enshrined, law must be based on courts alone, judges must be independent, and neither King nor Church could enter houses without warrants, raise taxes without legislation, and make arrests not according to the law. In the commentary on the Magna Carta in his 1797 *Second Institute* Coke equates the "law of the land" with "due process of law." Due process became the foundation of the common law.

confidently said to have ignited the fire of innovation—the equivalent of Mrs. O'Leary's cow, thought to have triggered the Chicago Fire. Yet we can search for *later* institutions that would plausibly explain the formation of chronically innovative economies, particularly those arising in the second quarter of the 19th century.

In fact there are other economic institutions that began emerging closer to the birth of the modern. Some key institutions had roots in mercantile times or even in ancient times but reached a mature stage only in the mid-1800s. The development of the company is one example. The oldest and still most common form of business organization is the sole proprietorship, which is run by an individual or often by a family. The proprietorship is not expensive to form or maintain, and there are not the moral hazards that owners face in later organizations. For larger operations, the preferred business form was the partnership. Partnerships could conduct businesses having capital requirements out of reach of the typical proprietorship, and they had the advantage that they combined the talents and personal knowledge of persons with managerial and investor backgrounds. From ancient Rome onward, a company was accorded various legal rights. It could, for example, conduct business in its own name. Early in the 19th century, partnerships were surely producing more output than businesses of any other form in Britain and America (with proprietorships, that is, family firms, surely second). And not all partnerships were small. Some grew large by becoming "holding companies" with central headquarters run by some highly senior partner and several subsidiary branches run by other partners. In America, the "investment banks" of the late 19th century were partnerships. Partners risked all their wealth.

The difficulty with many a partnership is that it puts a partner on the horns of a dilemma. If partners had latitude to act alone, a partner could be held liable for the actions, unscrupulous or ill-judged, of another partner. If instead partners were put on a short leash, they would face the nuisance of negotiating an agreement with one another and the risk that in the end no agreement would result. With such a downside, it would not be surprising that partners would not be inclined to take on the complex challenges and uncertainties of venturing on a highly innovative project. Furthermore, expanding a partnership could multiply the hazards hanging over the partners. For these reasons, liability fears must have severely limited the size and scope of most partnerships well into the 19th century—and thus were a drag on undertaking innovative projects when other conditions were making innovation a possibility.

A newer form of business organization eventually developed into a powerful vehicle for risk taking and, at least in that respect, for innovation. This was the joint-stock company—the business corporation, in modern terms. It issued ownership shares and, normally, limited a shareowner's losses to what had been paid to acquire the shares. Owners thus had limited liability. That could be a boon to entrepreneurs, and governments granted it only to companies they chartered. In the 16th and 17th centuries British and Dutch governments chartered several joint-stock companies to carry out public-private projects for trade, exploration, and colonization: the East India Company, Hudson's Bay Company, and the notorious Mississippi Company and South Sea Company. At the zenith of mercantilism about half of Britain's export revenues were produced by chartered companies. In the 18th century Britain began chartering companies in industry, notably in insurance, canals, and hard drink, creating near-monopolies in which owners and the state benefited. But these monopolies were not innovative. The joint-stock company proved unattractive to investors, who were wary of buying shares after the South Sea abuses and later scandals. So the cost of capital may have been too high to permit joint-stock companies to finance a novel expansion or a radical change. And most industrialists—including Boulton & Watt and Eli Wedgwood no less—saw drawbacks in a charter. A charter was costly, the process cumbersome, the profits of a joint-stock company would be taxable on top of applicable income taxes, regulations came with the charter, and the charter could be modified at will. In America, state charters continued to be restricted to "public works"—canals, colleges, and charities.

But radical changes in the joint-stock form came to America and Britain on the eve of the modern economy or hard on its heels. The contract clause of the U.S. Constitution, ratified in 1788, prohibited any state law retroactively impairing contract rights, yet charters did not obviously qualify as "contracts." In 1819, however, dealing with a suit by the Corporation of Dartmouth College, the Supreme Court ruled that all corporations have rights, including the right not to have their charter rewritten by new state laws. The 1830s saw restrictions loosened on business incorporation in one state after another: the Massachusetts legislature dropped its practice of limiting charters to public works, and Connecticut permitted companies to incorporate without a legislative act. In Britain, the Parliament, wearying of chartering a rash of railway lines, passed the Joint Stock Companies Act of 1844, allowing companies to incorporate simply by registering—though without the boon of limited liability, which was under debate. The Joint Stock Companies Act of 1856 granted these corporations limited liability. France followed in 1863, and Germany did much the same in 1870.[8]

A new creature was loose in the Western world—too late to claim paternity for the modern economy born in the 1820s or so, but not too late to contribute mightily to the great innovations in the age of industry—from the 1840s or 1850s to the 1910s or 1930s or 1960s. Adam Smith had criticized the joint-stock company for its poorly designed incentives. He was right about insufficient attention to costs and a weakness for short-term gains. But Smith, with his classical lens, missed the point. A corporation, acting for its hard core of one or a few big-stakes owners, could venture far into the unknown, employ a wide assortment of talent, and absorb a long spell of losses. It thus had some prospect of achieving significant innovations, owing to its ability to find shareowners who, able to diversify, would accept the risk and who, able to hold the stock for years or to sell it to others who could do so, would value profits far in the future. The benefit to investors and to society from the resulting innovations may well transcend the petty objections to corporate waste and managerial problems.

John Stuart Mill may have been saying the same thing when he observed that limited liability reduced an important deterrent to setting up a new business—a particularly daunting deterrent for poor people.[9] This was a splendid point, especially in Mill's time, when limited liability was granted only for 20 or 30 years. (It is a question whether it has a place in companies of an advanced age. The late Peter Martin, a business economist at the *Financial Times,* once suggested that companies be wound up after 20 years.)

---

8. *The Company,* an enjoyable book by Mickelthwait and Wooldridge, surveys the development of the company from ancient to modern times. Among the classics it draws on are Chandler's *Strategy and Structure* and, on Britain and Germany, *Scale and Scope;* DuBois's *The English Business Company after the Bubble Act;* Rosenberg and Birdzell's *How the West Grew Rich;* and Kindleberger's *A Financial History of Western Europe.* An account of the Chinese company is Kirby, "China Unincorporated."

9. Mill's 1851 "The Law of Partnership," reprinted in *Essays on Economics and Society Part II:*
 The liberty of entering into partnerships of limited liability, similar to the *commandite* partnerships of France and other countries, appears to me an important element in the general freedom of commercial transactions, and in many cases a valuable aid to *undertakings* of general usefulness.
 No one, I think, can consistently condemn these partnerships without being prepared to maintain that it is desirable that no one should carry on business with borrowed capital; in other words, that the profits of business should be wholly monopolized by those who have had time to accumulate, or the good fortune to inherit capital: a proposition, in the present state of commerce and industry, evidently absurd.

One of the last of the new institutions to fall into place was bankruptcy. In America, there was widespread imprisonment of persons unable to discharge their debts until 1833, when federal imprisonment was abolished. There are many reasons to celebrate this human advance, but one of them was that people did not have to fear that if they started a business they might land in prison through bad luck or a mistake. Defaults went on of course—they even increased. In an 1836 lithograph depicting Liberty Street in the heart of New York's financial district, four of the nine firms shown were bankrupt within the next five years.[10] The Bankruptcy Acts of 1841, 1867, and 1898 further eased the penalties of default by permitting voluntary bankruptcy and a workout of the debts in federal bankruptcy courts. In Britain, punishments evolved from deportation and death to prison in Victorian times, though debtor's prison was not pleasant. (References to it are recurrent in Dickens, whose father did time at London's Marshalsea Prison.) With the 1856 law, business owners registered for limited liability were saved from the prospect. Then the 1869 Debtors Act abolished imprisonment for debt by allowing proprietorships, partnerships, and all people to file for bankruptcy. This almost surely was good for innovation.

Finally, among economic institutions, there is the rise of financial institutions importantly oriented (whether or not totally dedicated) toward financing business investment projects or financing the early development of new businesses. Credit institutions, along with so very many other institutions, can be found as far back as the inventive Babylonians. Wealthy landowners and temples lent to proprietorships and partnerships for purposes of production or trade, with farmland, houses, slaves, concubines, wives, and children put up as security. In medieval times, some families created banks to which they devoted their careers—most famously the Fuggers in southern Germany and the Medicis of Florence. They were known for their loans to kings and princes in Europe. In the 18th century, there were the Baring family in London and the Rothschild family, whose five sons spread out to Frankfurt, London, Paris, Vienna, and Naples. The former was known for its loans to governments, such as for the Louisiana Purchase, the latter for its loans to Britain for its war with Napoleon. All of them engaged also in merchant banking. Yet it is hard to see in

---

10. See Balleisen, *Navigating Failure*. The author notes the financial panics of 1837 and 1839. Informed estimates, he adds, suggest "among proprietors engaged in market exchange, at least one in three and as many as one in two succumbed to an insupportable load of debt" (p. 3). The casualties in his case studies included many who went on to great success, such as Arthur Tappan (of Tappan Zee bridge), James Watson Webb, and Silas Stilwell. Mark Twain was another.

these merchant banks any new development that could be seen as paving the way for an age of innovation.

Early 19th-century banks in America hold some basic lessons. These banks have been generally viewed as a source of instability and thus a drag on entrepreneurship and economic development, a failure at achieving the "mobility" of capital extolled by neoclassical economic theory, and not the success in driving economic development that the "universal bank" developed in Europe has been seen as. The U.S. system had two kinds of banks. One was the commercial banks, chartered by state governments to accept deposits, issue notes, and finance production and commerce. The other was the private banks, which could neither issue notes nor accept deposits and depended on their own capital. Both sorts of banks thrived. (The latter banks attracted much foreign capital and developed into investment banks, lending to businesses to finance investment projects.) So complex and subtle a system does not lend itself to a quick judgment. Recent thought and scholarship, however, argues that these banks were well suited to serve regional entrepreneurship and development—not perfect, of course, but helping more than hindering. In sticking mostly to the region they knew, they were in the forefront of responses to shifting opportunities. And they practiced the rule of knowing their customers and monitoring their borrowers:

> For economic development to have proceeded, manufacturing enterprises needed to arise and grow. . . . For that growth to occur in a timely manner, manufacturers needed access to external finance, notably bank credit. . . . Bankers—typically being merchants themselves—tended to lend to enterprises and entrepreneurs with whom they were familiar, namely other merchants.[11]

In this revisionist view, the absence of universal banks from the American and British contexts was not an impediment, whatever benefits France and Germany may have derived from them.

---

11. Bodenhorn, *A History of Banking in Antebellum America*, p. 24. The author's thesis as it appears on page 12 is that
> a decentralized, federal, Madisonian polity encouraged experimentation and the adaptation of institutions to local needs or preferences. Nowhere were the results more evident than in banking policy. With the exception of the First and Second Banks of the United States, antebellum banks were creatures of the states themselves, reflecting the desires, even the whims, of local residents. . . . The decentralized nature of the polity allowed for a regional flexibility with the result that banks "grew more and more different over time, like the beaks of Darwin's finches."

Political Institutions: Representative Democracy

Political institutions arguably played a significant role in the creation of the modern economy. One of these was representative democracy, which arose rather close to the emergence of economic modernity. The development of modern democracy alongside that of the modern economy is suggestive, to say the least.

In most countries, seats in the national parliaments continued to be held right through the mercantile era by noblemen and landowning aristocrats. With any sense of economic justice centuries away, their lawmaking was mainly animated by narrow self-interest. Yet, in the 18th century, the idea of a representative democracy—a more representative democracy, at any rate—captured popular imagination in both America and Europe, in large part in response to the growing demand of the urban working class and business people for equal representation. America's Declaration of Independence in 1776 proclaimed the right of the people to self-government, free of all kings and aristocracies, although this vision was fully realized only with the abolition of slavery some 90 years later. The French Revolution of 1789 was the rallying cry in Europe for the creation of democracy. The Polish-Lithuanian Constitution of 1791 called for political equality between townsfolk and nobility. Some historians say that the court at Versailles diverted landowners from thinking about better practice, with the consequence that innovation came to France only when the state got out of the way.

This democracy has posed some downside risks for the economy, to be sure. It was more short-termist than hereditary monarchies were inclined to be. It permitted a tyranny of the majority, which constitutions put some limits on. It also put people into government who were so short of money in relation to many of the governed that they were more susceptible to bribery than the aristocratic legislators were. Yet it may very well have been, on balance, rather good for innovation.

The right of the people to govern themselves has long been thought to have had benefits for economic performance in general. And there are reasons to believe it created beneficial conditions for the rise of economic dynamism. For instance, a representative democracy may establish economic institutions and policies that an autocrat would refuse or repress. A democracy would push the public sector to support the interests of the lower and middle classes, thus to protect and nourish individual initiatives, such as serving business activity and encouraging public education. Innovation, which derives so much from inspiration, exploration, and experimentation at the grassroots, could be expected to benefit from this feature of democracy. In contrast, an autocracy would be expected to use the public sector for projects that serve autocratic interests, such as national power or aura. (The other side of the coin is that a democracy may lead to legislative logrolling in the service of a welter of special interest groups that cover all or virtually all the society. The result may be a public sector so swollen that it does more harm to innovation than good. That was unlikely in the 19th century, though, when governments were still so small, except in France.)

Representative democracy may naturally support institutions and a culture for a modern economy that an autocracy would be less apt to do. Where governments have legislated and thus legitimized institutions protecting economic functioning in spite of the uncertainty, change, reversals of fortune, profits and losses, and the rest, the would-be entrepreneur and innovator can be more confident that their company will not be subjected to extortionate holdups by agencies of the government or social partners, to postcontractual threats by creditors or employees, and to mobs allowed to plunder shops and factories without police protection. The argument is that when an institution has been established by a large society of diverse-thinking voters, the probability that the net sum of the changes of mind will be large enough to cause repeal of a previous law is smaller than the probability that an autocratic ruler would have such a change of mind. (This follows from the proposition known in statistical theory as the law of large numbers.)

This thesis bears on the question whether the rule of law can be robust enough to be relied on. As everyone agrees, autocratic rulers heed the rule of law only when it suits them; even a constitution like the Magna Carta does not make it certain that the law will not be circumvented by one device or another. Democratic parliaments can also change laws, though, or circumvent them with added laws. The argument above suggests that the legislature of a large and diverse democracy has difficulty contravening or circumventing an existing law, unlike an autocrat. The "rule of the people" lends credibility to the rule of law.

Another aspect of democracy may also have contributed to innovation. De Tocqueville in his travels through America in 1835 speculated that self-government helped to breed self-reliance and self-expression in business. The fund of experience Americans acquired in governing themselves, from taking part in town meetings to serving as public officials, was constantly useful to them in negotiating contracts, working with employees, and making the contacts needed in setting up a new business. By the same logic, the experience Americans had supporting themselves in the economy provided them with the skills—the self-confidence, easy sociability, and so on—they would need in governing themselves. In the Tocquevillian model, voluntary associations were the "great free school" in America, and they were not much found in Europe.

One more feature of democracy may have been important for the emergence of the modern economy. Representative democracy is a system in which, compared to autocracy, a great many voices are heard and heeded—if only politicians cater to them in hopes of getting their vote. The autocrat is apt to be unaware of many of the needs, particularly new needs. Thus a representative democracy was likely to have been more responsive to the needs for new institutions during the decades of its embryonic modernity.

If it is granted that the governmental mechanisms of a democracy operate in favor of innovation, there remains a historical question: Did the mechanics of representative democracy commence operation in the right places at the right times to have been the *trigger* for the explosion of economic dynamism in each nation to which it came? Did Britain, America, Belgium, France, and Germany develop their modern economies *after* their representative democracies? *Before?* Britain's venerable Houses of Parliament came to represent new wealth and new cities with the revolution of 1688. The Reform Act of 1832 extended the vote in contests for the House of Commons to men without reference to property qualifications and redistributed seats to urban areas. In America, the House of Representatives and Senate created by the U.S. Constitution in 1788 were radically more representative than England's two chambers: voting was open to all men having property qualifications— between a third and a half of the male adult population, citizen or not. (The franchise was soon broadened by steps: to men without property in 1812, to nonwhites in 1870, and to women in 1920.) It appears, though, that both democracy and dynamism were slow to arrive in France. The French Revolution was followed not by democracy but by Napoleon until 1815, the monarchical Restoration until the Revolution of 1830, and the rule of Louis-Philippe until 1848. Democracy in the form of elections with universal male suffrage came with the Revolution of 1848. Likewise, though a modicum of innovation and a resulting degree of prosperity came to France after Napoleon and grew stronger in the reign of Louis-Philippe, it was in only the second half of the century that France, with its productivity take-off, demonstrated relatively high innovation. Belgium is less clear-cut. A long wait for democracy is also found in Belgium, which was ruled by France until Napoleon's fall in

1815 and by the Dutch until 1830, when the Belgian Revolution established a parliamentary democracy. Innovation appears to have gotten ahead of democracy but did even better under democracy than under foreign rule: even before 1830 Belgium saw entrepreneurial advances in mining and steel-making in the French-speaking Wallonia that gave it a jump over any region in France. In contrast, innovation continued in Belgium after 1830, including notably the creation of the rubber industry, and the country was a world leader in industrialization until 1914. Germany is the exception. It saw little democracy except at local levels throughout the 19th century, while its innovation grew powerful over the last half of that century. That fact leaves open the possibility that Germany would have done far better with democracy, and that most countries were so structured that they did need democracy to support innovation. In any case, the reasonable inference is not that modern democracy caused the modern economy or vice-versa, but that both sprang from the same matrix of values and beliefs—the same culture.

Economic Culture: Differences and Changes

What is a modern economy? From the perspective described above, its distinction is the rewards it offers, pecuniary and experiential, for conception, embodiment, and pioneering of new commercial ideas—thus encouraging the use of resources for attempts at innovation. From the perspective of the present chapter, any society's economy operates on the society's institutions and its cultures. Such a culture is the attitudes and beliefs in the social heritage—though not all members inherit exactly the same culture and a culture does not include the nation's economic policy or any moral philosophy. So we may think of an economy as consisting of its economic institutions and its *economic culture* or cultures. An economic culture is the attitudes and beliefs about business and economic matters. For an economy of one kind or another to work there has to be a supporting culture. But not all behavior is "culture," and much behavior may be effect rather than cause.

Before historians, mostly in the 20th century, sought explanation of the take-offs and prosperity of the modern economies that sprouted in the 19th century, some of the best minds of the 18th century pondered explanations of the rise of notable commercial economies in the 16th and 17th centuries. In Adam Smith's explanation of the rise of commerce in Britain, the end of intrusive and confiscatory government allowed the rise of "truck and barter"—the constant search for better prices. In making people feel it was safe to hold wealth, it allowed thrift to arise. And, in causing wealth to accumulate, trade could be conducted on an ever-larger scale. Thus materialism flowered in the commercial era. Yet Smith saw the desire for material goods as universal and constant through time, not as something unique to the commercial era or to Britain—hence not a prime mover. "The principle which prompts [us] to save," he wrote in *The Wealth of Nations,* "is the desire of bettering our condition, a desire which . . . comes with us from the womb and never leaves us till we go into the grave" (p. 324). (Marx, of course, agreed that the "fetish" of commodities and wealth was not a cause of the commercial economy; he said it was an effect.) The mercantile economies exhibited some other distinctive behavior as well. There was honesty, respect for the laws, keeping promises, trading favors, and all the other commercial virtues known as trustworthiness. Yet David Hume and Adam Smith did not see this bourgeois respectability as behind the mercantile economy either. Hume in his 1740 *Treatise of Human Nature* argues (in a way that would seem conventional to present-day economists) that these commercial practices evolved from merchants' self-interest, including their interest in their reputations. Smith's 1763 *Lectures on Jursiprudence* views a merchant's interest in his commercial reputation as resting on the profit at stake, not his pride in it, and his 1776 classic *Wealth of Nations* views the commercial virtues as effects of the commercial economy, not as preconditions for it.

Our focus is on the emergence of modern economies, not mercantile economies. The essential point to be made is that even if increased effort, thrift, and wealth were the consequences of a cultural shift toward industry, frugality, and bourgeois respectability, as Weber argued, it is hard to see how such a cultural shift could spark the unprecedented feats of the modern economies of the 19th century, since long work weeks, high saving rates, and respecting law and agreements all appear to have been present in the 17th and early 18th centuries, as Smith and Hume imply. (If the work week and saving rate rose to greater heights in nations where a modern economy arrived, there are good reasons to view that as motivated by the fast economic growth and high investment demand that came with the dynamism of the modern economies.) At best, it can be argued that bourgeois respectability was necessary to or supportive of the development of the modern economies just as they were supportive of the commercial economies before them.

There were genuine cultural shifts that can be seen as causes of the emergence of the modern economies, however. It is evident that the Western world came to acquire—much more in some nations than others—an *ethos,* or spirit, that, as the elements of it came together, ultimately provided the impetus for the dynamism that is the essence of the modern economies. This ethos that built up was part of *humanism* (though humanism was broader than this ethos). In countries, regions, and cities where these strands reached a critical mass, they sparked the creation of a modern economy. (It does not matter that the earliest of the elements of the new outlook, or culture, emerged some centuries earlier, as long as other crucial elements were more recent.) This ethos may aptly be called *modernism.*

The meaning of "modern" in the present context is familiar: a modern woman, a modern city, modern life, modern as untraditional, modern as novel, and modern as disruptive or subversive. The modern society creates change within it, and the new ideas of those participating in the modern economy are the main sources of that change. The first modern societies begin in 1815, as argued in Paul Johnson's *Birth of the Modern.* Modern thought, however, begins around 1500, as documented in Jacques Barzun's vast survey of what he calls the "modern era," *From Dawn to Decadence.* Some ideas we reasonably think of as modernist existed in ancient times but were not widespread or they were driven out in the middle ages.

Modern values—attitudes and beliefs—continue to the present day to be prevalent—to significantly differing degrees—in the nations of the West. Modernist values include norms like thinking and working for yourself and self-expression. These values also include attitudes toward others: readiness to accept change caused or desired by others; eagerness to work with others; the desire to test one's self against others, thus to compete; and the willingness to take the initiative, thus to go first. (These cultural elements were not integral to the production, trade, and accumulation in the commercial economies.[12] As noted earlier, complaints were made from Smith to the young Marx that the commercial economies did not enlist these elements of their culture.) Other modernist attitudes are the desire to create, explore, and experiment, the welcoming of hurdles to surmount, the desire to be intellectually engaged, and the desire to have responsibility and to give orders. Behind these desires is a need to exercise one's own judgment, to act on one's

12. Neo-Schumpeterians might protest, arguing that when an external discovery occurs, some entrepreneur does have to take the initiative of undertaking the commercial application of the new possibility if it is to be realized. The general public with some economic background has been led to believe that this is what the entrepreneurial spirit is all about. But Schumpeter himself theorized, especially in his more formal analyses, that it would become clear among the entrepreneurs in the city or town which entrepreneur was best suited to undertake the "obvious" development. None was required to exercise any initiative.

own insights, and to summon up one's own imagination. This spirit does not involve a love of risk—hence enjoying a bet on the toss of a fair coin. It is a spirit that views the prospect of unanticipated consequences that may come with voyaging into the unknown as a valued part of experience and not a drawback. Self-discovery and personal development are major vitalist values.[13]

Modernist beliefs include some distinctive ideas of what is right: the rightness of having to compete with others for positions of higher responsibility, the rightness of greater pay for greater productivity or greater responsibility, the rightness of orders from those in responsible positions and the rightness of holding them accountable, the right of people to offer new ideas, and the right of people to offer new ways of doing things and to offer new things to do. All this stands in contrast to traditionalism with its notions of service, obligation, family, and social harmony.

The first signs of this new spirit appear in the Renaissance. In the middle ages, notions that engaging the world could hold deep rewards (and not just for kings), that not everything is already known and mankind's imagination might uncover more knowledge were undreamt of. The humanist Giovanni Pico della Mirandola (1463–1494), who was in the center of the movement, argued, using the religious constructs he had grown up with, that if human beings were created by God in his image, they must share in some degree God's capacity for creativity. In his funeral oration for Michelangelo, Pico calls man "the sculptor who must chisel out his own form from the material nature has endowed him." Thus Pico depicted an "individualism" in which men and women have to carve out their own development.[14] The influential humanist Desiderius Erasmus (1466–1536) wrote of "the expansion of [a person's] horizon that results from the hope of immortality, the quickening of

---

13. The value people commonly find in identifying and connecting with others is dubbed "altruism" in Nagel, *The Possibility of Altruism*. The value found in self-discovery and personal growth was dubbed "vitalism" by Jacques Barzun, a towering historian of Western thought at Columbia University. A sizeable discussion appears in his 1962 essay "From the Nineteenth Century to the Twentieth." (By the time he wrote his great 800-page tome *From Dawn to Decadence* in 2001, his many other interests squeezed "vitalism and volunteerism" into a few paragraphs.) Vitalism is also prominent in the writings of the eminent literary critic Harold Bloom, such as 1961's *The Visionary Company* and 1994's *The Western Canon*. The vitalism here is not to be confused with the 18th-century metaphysical craze of that name—the idea that there exists a "spark of life," like a shock of electricity, that brings a creature or organism to life. Luigi Galvini gave electrical shocks to dead frogs in an effort to bring them back to vitality. (The muscles did contract, but they did not get their jump back.)

14. Cassirer, "Giovanni Pico della Mirandola" (p. 333).

new aspirations, the suggestion of endless possibilities," which he attributed to the "spirit of Christianity."[15] The demand by Martin Luther (1483–1546) that members of the Roman church be accorded the "Christian liberty" to read and interpret the bible for themselves was a landmark in the emancipation of people from unproductive or dysfunctional government.

The Age of Discovery was another formative epoch. A profound vitalist spirit swept from Italy through France and Spain and on to Britain in barely 70 years. (Whether vitalism was a response to the heroism of the great navigators or their explorations, another expression of the new vitalism hardly matters.) Born in 1500, Benvenuto Cellini, the great sculptor and subject of the Berlioz opera of the same name, bared himself in his *Autobiography* as a questing, no-holds-barred artist-entrepreneur, the very embodiment of the liberated individualist bent on achievement and success. Born in 1509, John Calvin lauds careers as extending God's work. Born in 1533, Michel de Montaigne, in his collection *Essais,* chronicles an inner life—his own—and the personal growth that he calls "becoming." Born in 1547, Miguel Cervantes in his *Don Quixote* tells of the don and Sancho Panza, stuck in a place without challenges and going so far as to hallucinate them to find the vitality of a fulfilling life. Born in 1564, William Shakespeare in *Hamlet* and *King Lear* portrays the interior struggle and courage of his larger-than-life protagonists.

The wave of investigations between 1550 and 1700, called the Scientific Revolution, was another landmark. It demonstrated that observation and reason could be deployed to discover many of the workings of the natural world, such as William Harvey's model of the circulatory flow of the blood. The lesson to be drawn was that with study and thought it might be possible to figure out how something worked or could be made to work.

The 18th-century Enlightenment represented another step. Looking at the wealth accumulated by venture-merchants in the commercial economy, these philosophers and political economists saw entrepreneurial effort as having individual merit and social value. In France there was a total embrace of the entrepreneur. Nicolas de Condorcet elevates the productivity of business entrepreneurs over the political rent-seekers vying for political favor. Jean-Baptiste Say extols entrepreneurs for constantly reinventing the economy in their quest for higher yields. Voltaire, especially in his 1759 work *Candide,* championed a life of individual initiative and economic independence over conformity with convention and joining with others—*Il faut*

15. Dods, *Erasmus and Other Essays* (p. 300).

cultiver notre jardin.[16] In America, Jefferson likewise advocated an economy filled with participants in "pursuit of happiness" through smallish proprietorships engaging in grassroots entrepreneurial endeavors. Such thinking led to the corollary that such individual enterprise on a wide scale could change the world. This "progress" did not mean that the world would become perfect nor that there would not be missteps, only that societies might whittle away some of their imperfections and advance some of their capabilities. In these respects, humanism and its vitalist subdivision became part of the West's core beliefs.

The Enlightenment also brought the first glimmer of understanding of how creativity comes about. Hume, the first modern philosopher, had the insight that imagination was the key to advances in all kinds of knowledge. In his 1748 *An Enquiry Concerning Human Understanding* he explains that new knowledge does not spring from sheer observations of the world and existing ideas. Our knowledge is never a completely closed system, so originality may break into it. New knowledge starts from imagining how parts of the system not yet studied might work. (Such imaginings may be sparked by new data, but they do not require new data.) It was left for Hayek to point out that nothing will be imagined without considerable familiarity with those observations and ideas.

Something else very important came from the Enlightenment. Few expressed it at all, and no one expressed it more deftly (or succinctly) than Thomas Jefferson. With his imperishable phrase "life, liberty, and the pursuit of happiness" he put two propositions into the minds of contemporary Americans. One is the notion that every person has the moral right to seek his or her fulfillment. This was an idea that had not been widely articulated. It ran contrary to the tradition of the preceding era, which held that lives should be devoted to others—to family, church, and country. (To be sure, there is pleasure in giving, but Jefferson is surely talking about a journey of human development. He saw America as already "flowing with all the necessaries and comforts of life," so he must have meant "pursuits" on a higher plane.) The other notion, later set out by Søren Kierkegaard and by Friedrich Nietzsche, is the existential idea: a real life can come only through one's own endeavors. We may or may not find this "happiness," but we need to pursue it. These two propositions epitomize what we often call modernism. They are inimical to the ideas of traditionalism, which made the individual subservient to the group.

16. See Rothschild, *Economic Sentiments* (p. 33).

No one today can doubt that these revolutionary ideas changed what it was like to be alive. Following the Enlightenment, some European societies were excited and anxious over the Faustian possibility of profound advances in knowledge. Business people—farm and nonfarm—could see themselves as possessing creativity, and their political representatives could advocate the establishment of an economy engaged in exercising creativity and insight in their business. Vitalism became the spark of the modern economies—the elixir of their dynamism. The 19th century saw in the participants in a modern economy a rush of confidence in the power of discovery that they were testing and in the rewards. For the first time in human history there were heady anticipations of new methods, new products, and resulting advances in income. In Britain a growing part of the population was drawn into the new, mainly urban, enterprises, in which people spoke of "getting on." In America they were also getting on. When de Tocqueville journeyed through America in 1831–1832, he noted the self-confidence and the determination. The "American frontier," the borderline of settlements out west, could have been a symbol for the frontier of business methods and products.

Yet de Tocqueville *did* doubt that a new vitalism had come to America—or, if it had, that it was not the same as in France:

> Among ideas that occupy me, two bulk large, the first that this population is one of the happiest in the world, the second that it owes its immense prosperity less to its characteristic virtues, and even less to a form of government intrinsically superior to all the others, than to its peculiar conditions. . . . Everyone works, and the vein is still so rich that all who work it succeed rapidly in gaining the wherewithal to achieve contentment. . . . Restlessness seems to abet the prosperity. Wealth is the common lure. . . . Unless I'm sadly mistaken, man is not different or better on one side of the Atlantic than on the other. He is just differently placed.[17]

Now, nearly two centuries later, de Tocqueville's position looks 180 degrees to the truth. To have laid some of the bustle and drive in the American economy to "peculiar conditions," mainly the opportunities to develop virgin land, made sense in the first half of the 19th century. However, America virtually ran out of virgin land by the century's end, and yet the drive to experiment, explore, and create did not completely stop in the entire 20th century. Had Americans' place as "happiest" hung on an Eden, they would have lost that place by 1920, by which time America was urban.

17. De Tocqueville, "Letters from America" (pp. 375–376).

De Tocqueville was also wrongheaded to suppose that economic culture tends to be the same—in the Western world at any rate. Today we have evidence that de Tocqueville did not have. Present-day evidence on attitudes and beliefs shows beyond any doubt that people *are* "different" across oceans and across nations. Survey data in *World Values Surveys* display not only differences in attitudes and beliefs from one individual to another but also differences in mean attitudes and beliefs from one nation to another— differences in the national averages. (Many of the differences can be shown to be systematic, not simply random or the persisting after-effect of a temporary disturbance.) It is hard to see how it could have been otherwise in de Tocqueville's time. If the 19th century, when vitalism was riding high, was different from the 15th century and even the 18th, it would have been unlikely that all nations' average attitudes and beliefs moved in lockstep. Some countries must have been faster to embrace the new values of the Renaissance and Enlightenment than other countries were.

Finally, de Tocqueville seems wrong again when he suggested that some of the "characteristic values" in America (whether or not these values were also the values held in France) contributed "less" than other influences did, such as institutions, to America's greater drive in the 1830s—greater than Europe's and greater than before. Judging by recent studies of contemporary data in the attitudinal surveys, elements of the economic culture do matter for economic performance: for productivity, labor force unemployment rates, and also for reported job satisfaction and reported happiness. Differences in these respects across nations contribute quite a lot to differences in performance, even among nations as alike as the advanced economies of the West, as Chapter 8 shows.[18]

Of the many attitudes toward job and career reported in the household surveys, several can be interpreted as reflecting some aspect of vitalism—the acceptance of new ideas, the importance of work, the desire to have some freedom on the job and some initiative, the willingness to follow, the acceptance of competition, and the desire for achievement. It is noteworthy that about half of these attitudes have significant power in the explanation of inter-country differences in some economic performance indicators. There are so many of them, though, that only the fittest or the luckiest can significantly explain the differences in all the performance indicators. In response, the two recent studies place the various attitudes found in the attitudinal

---

18. Phelps, "Economic Culture and Economic Performance" (2011); Phelps and Zoega, "Entrepreneurship, Culture and Openness" (2009); Bojilov and Phelps, "Job Satisfaction" (2012).

surveys into a smallish number of affinity groups. Vitalism is the most powerful group in explaining differences across countries in the indicators of economic performance, generally speaking. The next most powerful group can be interpreted as measuring consumerism, or materialism. A traditional group, the one interpretable as a measure of social trust, is also important, as is the group interpretable as measuring self-reliance.

The remaining question is whether differences in economic institutions matter for economic performance to a comparable extent. The two more recent studies suggest that most of a nation's economic institutions, laying aside for the moment its political institutions, do not improve our explanation of how countries rank in economic performance. In accounting for how nations rank, it seems we can get along with cultural data alone, because the economic institutions are merely expressions of the economic culture. A qualification: it appears that one exception is the degree to which institutions offer the "economic freedom" to invest, innovate, compete, and enter.[19]

We have come a long way in a short space, so a summing up may be welcome to reinforce the main points so far: Seeking and acquiring wealth was, in contrast to vitalism, *not* an element of culture that came along at about the right time to launch the modern economy. What one could say was that in the dark ages of feudal times, wealth was regarded as filthy ("filthy lucre"). Wealth seeking and pleasure from the pursuit of or the prospect of acquiring more wealth became acceptable in time for the commercial economy and helped encourage merchants to expand their markets and take on bigger risks. But for the modern economies to emerge, a new sense of the possibilities of life beyond wealth accumulation was required and thus the construction of the required economic and political institutions.

Missing Piece: Population and Cities

This chapter has told the story of how some nations possessed the culture and acquired the institutions that would be important for indigenous innovation. Compelling reasons were found to regard the spread in these nations

19. The supremacy of economic culture is found in Bojilov and Phelps, "Job Satisfaction" (2012). Nevertheless, it is unlikely that no institution makes a difference for economic performance once the economic culture is taken fully into account. A composite element, labeled economic freedom, composed of some data on economic institutions as well as economic culture, was found to have some explanatory power in Phelps and Zoega, "Entrepreneurship, Culture and Openness" (2009).

of key economic freedoms, the rise there of vitalism, and the development of democracy as milestones on the way to modern economies. It is plausible that modernity would not have gone so far without the *acceptance* of the corporation—the joint-stock companies with their controversial limited liability; and, more broadly, without myriad institutional arrangements and policies offering people wider economic scope.

Yet something is missing. Why was it that, next to innovation in the 19th century, especially after the first quarter with its wars, innovation was so paltry throughout the 18th? The answer may be that something may have grown to multiply or amplify the faint impulses of innovation—to potentiate the democracy and the vitalism that were already present at relatively high levels by the last quarter of the century. But what might that something be? Economic historians appear not to have identified it. Why did innovation come earlier to Britain, America, and possibly Belgium than to France and Germany? We do not have to share de Tocqueville's impression that culture is everywhere the same to wonder whether differing intensities of the above forces argued to be central—the corporation, democracy, vitalism, and economic freedom—can wholly or largely explain why France and Germany got their dynamism later than the others.

The missing piece, which is obvious once one hits on it, is population density—the number of working-age persons in the country, excluding remote areas. Not many innovations in a country can be encouraged by its culture and promoted by its institutions if there are few minds. (Why, then, are Icelanders, with their small numbers, not backward and therefore poor? The reason is their proficiency in English and Scandinavian languages virtually integrate them into the economies of America and Europe.) Having more persons, all energized by vitalism and encouraged by democratic limits on arbitrary powers, surely increases the total number of new ideas being generated, even if it leaves unchanged the number per generator. Further, if the resulting new products and methods generally lead not to private use by the developers but to adoptions over the country—to diffusion—the end result is an increase in the number of innovations: the new products developed by companies themselves and those developed by other companies, which grew in number with the increased population. Thus, the more people there are in a rather integrated country to inspire, develop, market, and try out new ideas, the greater is its prospective rate of indigenous innovations per capita—provided the necessary institutions and culture are in place. (Why, then, was China, despite a population far greater than that of Britain or America, not generating many innovations in the 19th century? Or earlier? There was a phenomenal abundance of entrepreneurs in China's cities in the 18th century, the Irish economist Richard Cantillon reported in his 1755 study. The reason is China was seriously lacking in the economic institutions or the economic culture or both needed for innovation, indigenous or exogenous. It is far less lacking in the 21st century.) If the economy of the West experiences more innovations per capita now than 100 years ago, it is mainly because there are many more people engaged in innovation in that economy; it does not follow that every (or any) subpopulation of a given size generated more new products and methods.[20]

The benefits of increased population come not only from more creations, most of them available for adoption by others. If new ideas and new products based on them are striking a country, they are likely to spread faster through the economy the more dense the population is—just as heat travels faster when there are more molecules and a disease is apt to spread faster (and farther) through the world the greater the population size. Ideas are communicated very much like diseases. More people, more relays. Also: more people, bigger market. The Beatles could play 1,000 nights in Hamburg, that city being big enough, but not in Liverpool.

A sufficiently large population leads also to a city, simply as a result of various advantages of crowding together—of agglomeration. A still larger population leads to a second city. If land cannot expand proportionally, cities grow larger as well as more numerous as the population increases. It is now understood that cities have some special benefits that go beyond the benefits of more minds or more density over a large space. The urban economist Jane Jacobs, confronting the bulldozers of New York's titan planner Robert Moses, came up with a central insight:

> [P]eople gathered in concentrations of city size and density can be considered a positive good . . . and their presence celebrated.
>
> [B]ig cities are natural generators of diversity and prolific incubators of new enterprises and ideas of all kinds. Moreover, big cities are the natural economic homes of immense numbers and ranges of small enterprises. . . . Dependent on a huge variety of other enterprises, they can add further to

20. The first lines of argument began turning up in the 1960s after social commentators had begun to warn that the increase in world population then being projected would cause a general worsening of living standards. One was an 1960 paper by Simon Kuznets, "Population Change and Aggregate Output." The other paper, written in 1968 independently of the first, was Phelps, "Population Increase." The germinal idea is that there is a sort of production function relating the flow of new ideas to the stock of minds. The latter work led to a series of books by Julian Simon.

that diversity. This last is a most important point to remember. City diversity itself permits and stimulates more diversity. . . . Without cities, [these small enterprises] would not exist. The diversity . . . that is generated by cities rests on the fact that in cities so many people are so close together, and among them contain so many different tastes, skills, needs, supplies, and bees in their bonnet.[21]

Samuel Johnson's remark "he who is tired of London is tired of life" evokes the creativity that can be expected only in a city. But Jacobs goes further with her point that only a city can be expected to breed new diversity and originality, thus possibly innovation.

What do the data on historical population changes have to say? Do they support the above thoughts about the effect of population increase on the creation and communication of new ideas? Do they thus help answer the question of why Britain, Belgium, and America could produce so little gross national innovation, so to speak, as late as the last quarter of the 18th century in comparison with the heated innovation they were to produce in the middle decades of the 19th? Data on population size are so spare that we have just three benchmark years to go by. From 1700 to 1820 and on to 1870, population in the Western world (i.e., Western Europe and the "Western offshoots") increased from 83 million to 144 million and on to 208 million. (Growth was far slower between 1600 and 1700.) Britain was helped by a major increase in its population—from 8½ to 21 million and on to 31½ million. America came to have the largest population in the West—rising from 1 million to 10 million and on to 40 million. Belgium's population more than doubled—going from 2 to 3½ million and on to 5 million. Germany's did the same after a slower start—going from 15 to 25 million and on to 39 million. France's population less than doubled—from 21½ to 31 million and on to 38½ million.

---

21. Jacobs, *The Death and Life of Great American Cities.* Jacobs's book was just a salvo in her battle against Moses. She also took to the streets—and ultimately won. See the PBS documentary *The American Experience: New York—The Planning Debate in New York, 1955–1975.* In a later work, which is more of a textbook, Jacobs tries another exposition of her insight:

> [I]nnovations were exported from the cities to the countryside, transplanted to the countryside or imitated in the countryside. . . . This is so not because farmers and other rural people are less creative than city dwellers. The difference lies in the contrasting natures of rural and city economies, for it is in cities that new goods and services are first created.
>
> Cities are places where adding new work to older work proceeds vigorously. . . . [Since] cities have more different kinds of divisions of labor than villages, towns and farms do[,] cities contain more kinds of work to which new work can be added than other settlements.

Jacobs, *The Economy of Cities* (pp. 8–9, 50).

Equally impressive is the emergence of cities in the 19th century. Take cities with a population more than 100,000, which were big in their day. The benchmarks are 1800 or thereabout and the period 1846–1851. In this span, Britain went from one to nine such cities. America went from none to six, Belgium from none to two. Prussia went from one to two, and France from three to five.[22]

In societies, the past is not fully determinable. It seems a good bet, though, that even if judgments should sometime shift to the belief that all the attitudes and institutions fueling innovation in the 19th century were present in the 18th after all, contrary to the above sections of this chapter, there were simply not enough minds hatching new ideas to cause innovation to take off until Western populations had reached a critical mass.[23]

Final Comments on Part One

Karl Marx and Max Weber both wrote texts for a *History of the World Part II*. As they saw the Western world after 1600 or so, the wealth accumulation of venture-merchants emerging outside the feudal system of the manor created capitalists, who established standalone factories hiring wage labor in the growing populations of the towns. The manorial lords soon began siphoning for sale to the towns some of the agricultural produce that had been distributed to the serfs. The enclosure movement was another historical force pushing labor from farmlands to towns. This is a story about industrialization, but not much of a causal account. With or without a feudal system dotting the countryside, there would have been towns, cities, stores, and factories springing up along with the massive increase in population that began early in the 18th century.

The story told by Marx and Weber about the *effects* of industrialization is not much better. Their *History* saw this industrialization as the first stage in

---

22. The population data are in Maddison, *The World Economy*. The city data are from Weber, *The Growth of Cities in the Nineteenth Century*.

23. It is worth noting as an aside that demographic influences lead to related points. The steep rise of population in barely more than a century operated in the direction of raising the returns, current and prospective, on capital by lowering wages. At the same time, the opening up to commercial use of new lands and natural resources in the New World, though bringing a mass relocation of labor from Europe to the Americas, was in many ways no different from discovery of new lands and resources in Europe: it too operated to raise the prospective returns on capital. These increases in prospective returns must account for some of the increase in investment activity in the Western world in the 19th century and, through similar mechanisms, some of the increase in innovation activity too. (And the increase in wages brought by the new lands may have brought an increased willingness to sacrifice some income for greater adventure and standing in the community, which could induce an increased interest in engaging in innovative activity.)

a kind of modernization, about which they were ambivalent. Marx claimed there was a tendency for wages to fall, notwithstanding increases in efficiency and in the capital stock. But this claim, once an article of faith in labor movements, had to be quietly retired with the findings that wages had not fallen over the 18th century, had risen strongly over the 19th, and continued rising in the 20th. (Marx himself came to recognize in his and Engels' 1848 *Communist Manifesto* that the modern capitalism he witnessed was "progressive.")

Both Marx and Weber went on to assert that 19th-century modernization brought a dreary rationalization and impersonal bureaucratization to economic life. But it was preposterous to insinuate that the traditional economy of feudal manors provided workers with much "liberating activity." It has never been the prevailing opinion of people who experienced both rural and urban life and labor that rural is better than urban. Migration to the city has been a fixture of demographic history for many centuries.

Present-day versions of their *History* end with the hope that the "knowledge economy," especially the service sector, will bring long-awaited opportunities for work and career that satisfy the "realization of talents." This postindustrial modernization will spread the human development that industrialization never delivered.[24]

The first four chapters of this book take a radically different perspective and tell a different narrative. The modern economies emerging in the 19th century were a stunning success in both nonmaterial and material dimensions: intellectual engagement and personal development as well as sustained economic growth and an inbuilt tendency toward inclusion. This depended on the rise of a new force: economic dynamism. And what sparked this dynamism was a new economic culture. Its necessary nutrients were representative democracy and a cultural revolution originating in Renaissance humanism, Baroque vitalism, and Enlightenment modernism. Representative democracy ensured property rights but also stimulated self-reliance and social engagement. Altruism, vitalism, and modernism caused people to reach out to the world and find meaning through innovative activity. The resulting culture and the economic institutions it led to provided people with the urge and the capabilities to innovate. Adequate numbers of people was the last of the necessary, but not sufficient, conditions.

The series of modern economies, starting with Britain and America, seems to stop arbitrarily—with Germany as the last of the modernizers. Why not

---

24. For example, Inglehart and Welzel, *Modernization, Cultural Change, and Democracy* (2005, p. 1).

Sweden and the rest of Scandinavia? Japan? Italy and Spain? No doubt, indigenous innovation did develop in some industries in those nations. The difficulty is that the economies there were so late in showing what could have been signs of widespread dynamism that those signs could have been in large part the result of those economies' catching up with the new products from the pioneers. The evidence is ambiguous. Similarly there is a continuing debate over how much is indigenous innovation instead of catch-up by imitation and adaption in the economies of Hong Kong, South Korea, Singapore, Taiwan, South Korea, and now China and India. These economies have developed some visible enclaves of innovation, but it is hard to know how extensive and intensive innovation is in these economies—or in any economy for that matter.

Obviously the new kinds of economies, at least the new ones of the 19th century, involved capitalism. Yet these modern economies were a far cry from the mercantile economies, which achieved important expansions of trade and accumulations of wealth though precious little lift to productivity, wages, job satisfaction, and the human spirit—and perhaps little gain in employment too. Of course, all the modern economies emerging in the 19th century represented improvements in the capitalist system of the 16th and 17th centuries—for example, financial institutions became better at selecting and facilitating projects aimed at innovation. Yet these modern economies belonged to modern societies, which made more radical contributions: These societies possessed political institutions and an economic culture that would galvanize their capitalist economies. The result was *modern capitalism*. The world's first modern economies—the first to possess dynamism—were an amalgam of capitalism and the modern.

Although the modern capitalist economies were the first example of a modern economy, it did not follow that they would be the last. In the 20th century the West became a debating platform for discussions of whether a country might build a modern economy—one possessing dynamism, thus given to innovation—that is *not* a *capitalist* economy. The Europeans, who created capitalism, debated whether there might be one or more other systems on which a modern economy could be built—an economy of comparable dynamism. They debated whether economic modernity could be justified in spite of the costs it might be shown to have. And they debated whether economic modernity was even desirable. The question of the justification of capitalism and of modernity itself turned Europe not only into a debating platform but also, at times and places, into a battleground.

PART TWO

AGAINST THE MODERN ECONOMY

Socialism and Corporatism

How much must perish so that something new may arise!

JACOB BURCKHARDT

CHAPTER FIVE

The Lure of Socialism

I am convinced there is only one way to eliminate [the] grave ills [of capitalism], namely through the establishment of a socialist economy. . . . A planned economy, which adjusts production to the needs of the community, would distribute the work . . . and guarantee a livelihood to every man, woman and child.

ALBERT EINSTEIN, *Why Socialism?*

Communism is socialism plus electrification.

V. I. LENIN

You don't understand something until you can build it.

Paraphrase of J. CRAIG VENTER's variation on RICHARD FEYNMAN

THE ECONOMIC INSTITUTIONS AND THE SOCIAL NORMS, or economic culture, on which the world's first modern economies operated were not chosen by the people—by their democratic assemblies or judicial bodies. Legislatures and courts occasionally had to decide for or against this or that piece of the system, but there was never a public choice between one system and another.

Britain and America were the nearest to exceptions. By 1800, so many people had left the traditional economy for a commercial and cosmopolitan life and so many of them were engaged and rewarded in what they were doing that both capitalist institutions and norms—its private property and profit seeking—and the modern economy—its freedom, inquisitive and adventurous spirit, and indeterminacy—had wide support. In America's Constitution and Britain's judicial rulings, capitalism and modernity were implicit. There was hardly an alternative. Few wanted a return to feudalism.

But in the high period of the modern economy, from the mid-19th century well into the 20th, people participating in a quite modern economy were having a highly varied experience with it—much more varied than the experience with the mercantile economy. Even if there were few who did less well than they would have done in mercantile times, it was how well they were doing relative to what they supposed would be *possible* that mattered to them. One who had good luck or advantages could disregard whatever inefficiencies or biases in the system had made the outcome less brilliant than it might have been. But one with bad luck or a disadvantage could be right to blame some of the outcome on the system, pointing to this or that supposed "flaw" while leaving it to scholars to decide whether it was a real flaw and, if so, whether it caused real net harm. The discontent must have been far worse among Russian serfs and eastern European peasants, who worked in conditions untouched by the modern economy. Workers' discontent about inequalities of income and wealth, about unemployment and economic instability, were at the origins of the socialism that emerged in Europe in this period.

Modern Discontents

The evidence does not support popular beliefs of the time that modernization drove down the wages (relative to the median wage in the economy) of the working class—Marx's proletariat—effectively shearing them from the mainstream of society. Neither is there evidence that middle-income earners dwindled as many were pushed into the "proletariat." In fact, from the dawning of the modern economies to the eve of World War 1 in 1913, the working class shrank and the bourgeoisie grew. Nor did wage inequality appear to increase within the set of working class jobs. The term had not been coined yet. Nor is there evidence that labor's share had contracted. (These points were made in Chapter 2.) Yet the modern economy did have a revolutionary effect on the pattern of incomes and wealth levels.

Modern economies opened up opportunities for individuals to make large-stake bets—betting their whole minds and bodies over months, even years—for highly uncertain prospects of reward: from a very large gain to the loss of the whole bet. As a result, enormous differences in economic results could occur—and there is no law that present winnings will sooner or later be offset by future losses. One person might suffer lengthy unemployment, while another not obviously different person might be working overtime. A person might have been led to an industry in decline, while another was led to an industry that was booming. A person's pay might double in a few decades, while another's might quadruple. It is not surprising that those left in the dust by others should take a jaundiced view of the system. Observations by contemporaries and piecemeal historical records all give evidence of an enormous rise in the inequality of income and wealth, though there are not the comprehensive records needed to construct the statistical data we take for granted now. Appreciable numbers of moguls and magnates in the business sector and speculators in the financial markets acquired staggering wealth, some displayed garishly, some tastefully, some hidden from view—especially in the gilded age. Capturing a share of the income from this wealth, if not the wealth itself, through taxation was to become an item high on many socialist agendas. But it was not at the top of the discontents with the modern economy. Great riches were nothing new. It was the democratization of opportunities to get rich that was new. People could take the presence of old wealth among a handful of aristocrats, the origins of which had become shrouded in the mists of time. They could not swallow so easily the "new rich" sprouting up in unexpected places.

Uppermost among the discontents with the modern economy was the precariousness of jobs and wages—the ever-present possibility of the loss of one's job or a major decline of wages in one's line of work. Episodes of high unemployment in the economy as a whole (aggregate unemployment) and sometimes in particular industries were endemic to the modern economy in this period. There had been sharp speculative bubbles and crashes in the era of mercantile capitalism, of course: the bursting of the Dutch tulip mania in 1637 and the bursting in 1720 of both the South Sea bubble in Britain and the Mississippi bubble in France, though these events were not broad enough to drive total employment either high or low. The wars of the period caused booms, often followed by recessions. In 1815, at the cusp of the modern, the end of the Napoleonic Wars sent many countries (but not France) into recession and Britain into a long slump. Though the 19th century was generally peaceful, downswings came with greater frequency and amplitude with the rise of the modern economies: there were the financial panics of 1792 (Wall Street's first crisis), 1796–1797 in Britain and America, 1819 in America, 1825 in Europe except France, 1837 in America, 1846 in all of Europe and, in America, 1857, 1873, and 1893—in addition to minor recessions. Since business was far more tightly tied to the financial sector in the modern economies, employment was far more affected by these financial panics than by earlier ones. Evidence of the time indicates that jobs were on the whole a great deal more precarious than they were in the previous century. (Some of the precariousness in the first half of the century was the result of the financial fragility of companies, especially small firms, and this lessened by degrees over later decades.)[1]

Yet as finance loomed ever larger in the modern economy, the macroeconomic fallout of speculative excess and reckless financing grew capable of producing important slumps. In the mid-1840s railroad overbuilding led all Europe into a slump, which triggered the 1848 revolutions that swept over the Continent. Deeper slumps followed—the renamed Long Depression of 1873–1879 (first called the "Great Depression"), when U.S. unemployment exceeded 10 percent for years, and the more severe Depression of 1893–1898, when U.S. unemployment exceeded 12 percent for four straight years. Observers at the time must have wondered why, if these breakdowns were part of the "performance characteristics" of the modern economy, countries should want to continue with such a system. And countries with a less-than-modern economy must have wondered why they should aspire to one.

Not only was industrial life treating people very differently, the people in the cities also represented an ever-increasing variety of backgrounds. Large numbers of Chinese, then Irish, and later Jews from eastern Europe and Italians from the *Mezzogiorno* came streaming into London, New York, and San Francisco. Although the evidence is not quantifiable, it appears that, compared to the yeoman farmers and tradesmen and business owners in 1800 or even 1850, the new populations were more accustomed to communitarian ways—to habits of sharing, equalitarian notions of fairness, and an alienation from capitalist owners, who may have been indistinguishable to the newcomers from the inherited and entrenched owners of property and businesses found in the old country. Many or most of the older populations would have rejected the idea of belonging to a trade union, or crafts union, while many or most in the new populations would have thought it was wrong not to belong.

Talk of socialism arose in these times. The burgeoning diversity of experience and background that gave a boost to commercial innovation—discussed

1. Job security in America looks to have improved with the Galbraithian era—the early 1950s to the early 1970s—when Americans were safely employed in big entrenched companies enjoying stable growth and Europeans were steadily engaged in the process of "catching up." It is a question, though, whether jobs were also more secure in the 30-year era from the mid-1970s to the mid-2000s—though that span includes the 20-year Great Moderation dating from the mid-1980s. This era saw the U.S. slump of 1973–1983, the continental European slump of 1978–1988, the global 1987 stock market crash, the 1990 U.S. savings-and-loan crisis, the slump Japan entered in 1990, the East Asian economic crisis in 1997, the collapse of Long Term Capital Management, and the correction of the U.S. tech stocks in 2000–2001. The "Great Moderation" was an egregious misnomer.

in Chapter 1—must have been an impetus to thinking up new elements in the institutions and norms of society. Henri de Saint-Simon was an early socialist.[2] He criticized the economic system that had arisen around him as unscientific and irrational, thus wasteful of resources, and was the first to say that the system was not advantageous to the working poor. The *Communist Manifesto* by Marx and Engels, first published in January 1848 on the eve of the uprisings, was a strong condemnation of the waves of unemployment and its seemingly upward trend in Europe.

The uprisings of 1848 brought expressions of discontent with wages, employment, and working conditions to a new peak, though many of those rebellions were no more than a democratic opposition to the aristocracies, such as the February Revolution in Paris overthrowing the constitutional monarchy of Louis-Philippe and the March Revolution in Berlin and some German states demanding German national unity and a national parliament. Marx was to complain that the workers had no clear objectives or program, so it was not surprising that the workers gained nothing. It was only in the next decades that an extensive socialist agenda was proposed and debated.

The Idea of Socialism

The very idea of socialism was fraught with difficulties. Defining the set of ends that socialism would serve was never completely resolved. Some purposes of socialism in the minds of one might run counter to some purposes in the mind of another.

> Socialism's appeal, when it had one, was to say, at one and the same
> time, that its mission was to transcend capitalism while improving
> it; that everyone was equal but that the proletariat was the leading
> class; that money was the root of all evil but the workers needed more
> of it; that capitalism was doomed but the capitalists' profits were as high
> as ever; that religion was the opium of the people but that Jesus was the
> first socialist; that the family was a bourgeois conspiracy but it needed

2. An early statement of his criticisms is his *Lettres d'un habitant de Genève à ses contemporains* (1803). The "anarchy" of the modern economies was a major theme of Friedrich Engels in Germany and Thomas Carlyle in England. Saint-Simon went on to propose that business people and scientists direct the state and society's use of resources. His last book, *Nouveau Christianisme* (1825), states that the resources ought to be directed for the purpose of improving the conditions of the poorest class. He is believed to have coined the term *socialisme*, first used by Pierre Leroux in an 1834 essay "De l'individualisme et du socialism," that is, "On Individualism and Socialism." (Leroux, an economist and philosopher, was skeptical of both.)

defending from untrammeled industrialization; that individualism was to be deplored but that capitalist alienation reduced people to undifferentiated atoms; that there was more to politics than voting every few years while demanding universal suffrage; that consumerism beguiles the workers but they should all have a color television, a car and go on holidays abroad.[3]

Thus "socialism" was a fuzzy concept, and a variety of conceptions were advocated—Christian socialism, Marxian socialism (called communism), state socialism, market socialism, guild socialism, and Fabian (or evolutionary) socialism.

Declared socialists on the Continent began efforts around 1860 to reach agreement on a core set of values or rights—mostly in meetings of worker associations, intellectual periodicals, and conferences of Germany's Social Democratic Party. Socialist countries were to be guided by a socialist ethic that was an alternative to the spirit of modernity and the capitalist ethic that motivated individuals working in a modern capitalist economy.

In this ethic, access to employment was a right, not only because a job was a worker's livelihood—even in socialism nonparticipants judged of sound mind and body could not claim the wage paid to participants—but also because of its necessity for a person's sense of self-respect. Joblessness was to be combated.

Another part of this ethic had to do with the conditions and opportunities provided to the worker in society's enterprises, private (if any) and public. The right to a job meant the right to a job offering dignity. The abuse of power by the employer was not acceptable, so that dismissal without a hearing or without compensation was not to be permitted. To his credit, Marx brought up the normal need of human beings for a mental life, about which he felt deeply:

[Adam] Smith has no inkling whatever that this overcoming of obstacles [in work] is in itself a liberating activity . . . hence as self-realization, objectification of the subject, hence real freedom, whose action is, precisely, labor.[4]

---

3. Sassoon, "All Shout Together."

4. Marx, translated from *Grundrisse der Kritik der politischen Ökonomie* (1858, p. 611). Some would say that Smith was better than that. He deplored repetitive tasks, by which he meant unchallenging tasks. (Flying jet planes on the milk routes is repetitive but sometimes severely challenging. "It's hours of sheer boredom," as someone said, but "punctuated by moments of sheer terror.") It could be that Marx's hostility sprang from his anxiety that Smith had thought of the point and others before he did. It could also be that Marx felt impelled to diminish Smith by portraying him as a rightwing zealot.

Similar expressions were to be heard from a range of social thinkers, not all of whom thought of themselves as socialist.

Another socialist value was that wealth and power must not be so disparate in society that some participants are denied the ability to realize their potential. Under socialism, large accumulations of wealth would not be allowed and, upon instituting equal opportunity, "to each according to his contribution" would rule in wage setting.[5] If all auto workers are necessary and interchangeable in producing a car, their wages would be equal; and a farmer would be construed as contributing as much as an auto worker. (Under communism, as *The Communist Manifesto* conceived it, "the free development of each is the condition for the free development of all.")

The socialist ethic saw private business as unattractive—as "money grubbing"—whether it made a profit or a loss. In the capitalist ethic, personal growth is, in part at any rate, a climb up the greasy pole to obtain better terms for oneself in one's career—better pay, higher fees. In the socialist ethic, personal growth comes from the love of one's work and mastering one's craft or profession.

The socialist ethic also condemned amassing and holding great wealth. The aim was to cultivate a "new person" (*Neuer Mensch*) who will be guided by instincts to serve others rather than by the shallow values of an "acquisitive society." In his 1860s cycle of four operas telling the story of the cursed ring of the Niebelungs, Wagner, a passionate socialist, dramatizes movingly the moral that when we choose wealth and power over love, we condemn ourselves to our own destruction. Audiences, especially if they know that Wagner was a dedicated socialist, reasonably interpret the Ring cycle as contrasting the greed of capitalism with the idyll of socialism. (Yet entrepreneurs and investors touched by Wagner's music drama apparently go right back to taking satisfaction from their lives as entrepreneurs and investors.)

Still another socialist value was attached to allocating resources by the principle of where they are most needed rather than by the profit motives of capitalism. Centralized coordination was deemed superior to decentralized

---

5. See Marx's 1875 *Critique of the Gotha Program*. The Gotha Program was a draft statement of socialist goals prepared for the founding conference in May 1875 of Germany's new Socialist Democratic Party in the town of Gotha. In a letter to friends, Marx vented his anger at the program's conception of a socialist state as merely subsidizing "producers associations," and he stated his ideas on the rewards to work in a socialist economy. Marx's *Manifesto, Grundrisse,* and Gotha letter are his basic short works.

competition and individual initiative. "Production for use rather than profit" is shorthand for this principle.

But a functioning economy has to have means to its ends, means in the form of economic institutions and economic culture. These are the norms, rules, institutions, and laws by which it enlists participants; opens them to know-how and experience; inspires them to exercise creativity; and, as neo-classical economics says, allocates land, labor, and capital over enterprises and industries and sets rules for the distribution of income or goods. How, in these terms, did a socialist economy work?

The socialists, though far from united in their ends, instinctively came together on what the means would be—figuring that they could thrash out later the main ends to which the means would be put. A key instrument, both at the communal level and at the national level, would be some mechanism for centralized control over the main directions of investment activity. There would be neither capitalists nor private entrepreneurs to veto investment projects. Another instrument would be the wage paid to workers—miners, nurses, musicians, and so forth. The state would supplement this wage with a "social dividend"—what would be profits under capitalism. The production method and the assignments of workers to jobs in an enterprise would be decided cooperatively with an eye to the workers' satisfactions as well as their productivity; a worker would be motivated by how stimulating the job was, not how long the worker would expect to be in the unemployment pool in the event he or she were fired in favor of a better worker. Finally, the allocation of labor and capital across enterprises and industries would be decided politically, by the workers' representatives, rather than by seeking the lowest cost, highest price, and greatest valuation—the market mechanism.

The various factions within socialism differed in matters of scope. The thoroughgoing, classical socialists, including Marxian socialists, sought centralized control of the capital available and the prices chargeable in all enterprises, large and small, and all industries, from farming to film making. More moderate socialists sought state control only over the "commanding heights" of the economy, including heavy industry. Proponents of *market socialism* wanted state-owned companies, as well as those under private ownership, free to buy and sell their products and intermediate goods in open markets (though prohibitive company taxation was always an option). Britain's Fabian socialists advocated starting small and feeling their way to the right scope over the economy. They wanted some "reforms" of capitalism; for communists, capitalism could not be reformed, only overthrown.

Could a Viable Socialism Be *Built*?

The classic debates of the 1920s and 1930s, the interwar years, were not about what anyone today would suppose they were about, namely the desirability of the socialist values. These new debates were on the feasibility of designing economies that would have the properties sought by socialists. Could the socialists succeed on their own terms? For a pragmatist, the question may have looked entirely empirical: let's wait to see how the socialist experiments turn out. But in the 1920s there was only the experiment starting in Russia and the chance that another one or two might start in Germany or France. So evidence was going to have less weight—and theory, such as it was, more weight—than it would have in an agronomy experiment conducted on several different plots of land. If the socialist economy on Russian soil succeeded in all respects or failed in all respects year after year, that would be no guarantee that the same results would follow experiments in other countries, or even that Russia's results would continue.

Enter Ludwig von Mises, a Viennese economic theorist of fiery temperament who founded the Austrian school of economics with his former student, Friedrich Hayek. Mises, so near to the revolution in Russia and socialist measures in Germany, could be said to have been an eyewitness of the creation of socialism. He immersed himself in the debate from 1920 to the early 1930s.[6] As Mises saw it, trying out socialism was an experiment without a theory. "[I]n the cloud-cuckoo land of their fancy," he wrote, "roast pigeons will in some way fly into the mouths of the comrades, but they omit to show how this miracle is to take place." He went on to argue that a socialist economy is not viable—not just uninnovative but ultimately impossible (*unmöglich*).

Mises's objections to socialism were based on the idea that in the modern economies around him the actors were restlessly trying out departures from normal practice in hope of obtaining higher prices for what they sell or lower prices for what they buy; in that way, new methods were tested and economic gains discovered. While socialists, including Marx, supposed that industrial workers, peasants, and craftsmen would somehow engage in the experiments necessary to achieve high efficiency, Mises argued that a socialist economy, in which nobody really owns anything—even one's own labor—would

---

6. Mises's first publication (in German) was the 1920 landmark, "Die Wirtschaftsrechnung im sozialistischen Gemeinwesen," translated in Mises, "Economic Calculation in the Socialist Commonwealth," where the quote that follows above can be found on page 88 and the next extract on 110. His big work, published two years later, was *Die Gemeinwirtschaft*, translated in Mises, *Socialism* (1936).

not present the incentives and the information needed for the deviations, or experiments, by individuals that ultimately make market prices and wages reflect the costs of products and the value of labor in each use:

> [I]n a socialist state . . . rational conduct might still be possible, but in general it would be impossible to speak of rational [i.e., efficient] production any more. There would be no means of determining what is rational, . . . hence . . . production could never be directed by economic considerations. For a time the remembrance of the experiences gained in a competitive economy . . . may provide a check to the complete collapse of the art of economy . . . [though] . . . the older methods . . . would meanwhile have become irrational, as no longer comporting with the new conditions. . . . [I]n place of the "anarchic" economy, recourse will be had to the senseless output of an absurd apparatus. The wheels will turn, but to no effect. . . . The administration [in a socialist state] may know exactly what goods are urgently needed. But in so doing it has only found what is, in fact, but one of the two necessary prerequisites for economic calculation. . . . It must dispense with the other—the valuation of the means of production. . . . Thus in the socialist commonwealth, every economic change becomes an undertaking whose success can be neither appraised in advance nor retrospectively.

Mises gives as an example the question of whether a new railroad should be built. A market economy, he says, enables an estimate of what the savings in transport costs would be. Mises concedes that the socialist state might have a decent estimate. But if the values of labor, energy, iron, and so forth required for the project's construction are not available in a common unit—in money—it is impossible to calculate whether the savings would cover the cost of the railroad. (In the jargon of economics, a socialist economy does not reveal to the "administration" each input's *opportunity cost*, or *shadow price*, which is equal to the value of its use in production elsewhere; in contrast, a market economy presents to entrepreneurs observable prices, which Mises views as adequate approximations of opportunity costs.)

Mises could have supplied a simpler example. Under a socialist economy in which equality of wages is regimented, no worker would ever try to see whether being more diligent or industrious than the others would be rewarded. Said worker would not receive an increased wage in return, since all wages are equal. And the worker would not save his or her job that way, since their jobs are very secure anyway. No worker has an incentive to exercise greater care and put greater energy into his or her work *no matter how valuable to society.* The system never allows the market to "discover" the correct general level of effort—and the correct general level of wages that corresponds to it—even when everyone is alike and has the same preferences, since no market process of trial moves takes place.[7] The conclusion is that private ownership of the fruits of one's own labor permits and encourages experimentation, without which the pattern of wages and prices in the economy could continue without a tendency toward correction.

The analysis by Mises may have been abstract to most of his readers. History, however, would provide graphic illustrations of Mises's points. The failure of Soviet personnel policy to reward workers taking greater care and to promote workers showing greater talent must have led to a sense of futility, and this helplessness must have been behind the massive alcoholism that plagued Soviet life in its last decades. This was a waste of the natural inclination of people to pitch in, to do a good job, and to try to make something of themselves. An appalling decline in the work ethic resulted, with severe effects on efficiency. There is a story of a foreigner living in Moscow in the 1980s who decided to gather field data by following a large truck as it left a brick-making factory. According to the observer, as the truck bumped along the streets and highways, about as many bricks fell out of the truck as it unloaded on its stops. If workers had had individual earning power and the freedom to make investments that would increase that power, their efforts and wages and self-respect would all have ended up being at far higher levels. For these insights, Mises is regarded as the originator of *property rights theory.*

A second argument by Mises turned on the "profit motive." He hammered away, primarily in *Socialism*, at the theme that enterprises operating as arms of a bureaucracy would not even attempt to operate with efficiency, in contrast to enterprises driven by the profit motive:

> The motive force of the whole process which gives rise to market prices
> for the factors of production is the ceaseless search on the part of capital-
> ists and entrepreneurs to maximize their profits. . . . Without these private

7. The socialist theoreticians could reply that there remains in the socialist system a healthy incentive to perform well: failing to perform up to prevailing standards would likely cost a worker his or her promotion to jobs with greater scope for taking on responsibility. Thus there has to be some inequality, though not wage inequality. But the force of that counterargument would depend on how much more rewarding the jobs higher on the ladder were. Mises could have retorted that if the socialist plan envisioned an essentially stationary economy, in which only the occasional natural disaster interrupted the general tranquility, it is not obvious that there would be any nonpecuniary rewards from moving up the ladder that would be enough to motivate the workforce. And an economy that does not revolve around innovation would not need deep ranks of managerial personnel to begin with.

owners the market loses the mainspring that sets it in motion and keeps it in operation. (pp. 137–138)

Socialist managers would be lacking in this motive. They would have relatively little incentive to seize opportunities for increased profit regardless of inconvenience or political cost: If the profit increased, the central government would not know to what to attribute this increase, so the manager might not get the credit, and if the profit decreased, it might raise suspicions that the manager was less competent than others. A manager or worker who knows there is no way to protect his or her idea from being claimed by others is not apt to think of a new idea. When nevertheless an enterprise does have a new idea, there is apt to be no good way by which that enterprise can signal its belief in the benefit of the idea. Furthermore, the incentives of socialist managers would be mostly undesirable. They would always do the bureaucratic thing of "following the rules" and attending to appearances. They could compete for promotion up the ladder, but that incentive would lead them to avoid any risk of failure. For these insights, Mises could be seen as the originator of *public choice theory*—the decisionmaking of self-dealing individuals in a bureaucracy, such as a state agency.

Mises's warning led to one of the most famous exchanges in the annals of economics. Oskar Lange, a brilliant theorist rising into prominence in the West in the 1930s before returning to his homeland, communist Poland, challenged Mises's contention that a thoroughly socialist economy must ultimately lead to collapse.[8] Lange argued that a nation wanting a socialist economy without the failings warned of by Mises had open to it a way to put the right prices on labor, iron, railroad track, and all the fruits of production. It could use the same markets made use of by capitalist economies. Enterprises would, in general, be state-owned, as before. These socialist enterprises would supply each of their products to the market, where other socialist enterprises and households might convey their demands. Some of these markets might be auction markets, as in capitalism, while others would not be, just as in capitalism. Thus, the market would determine prices. Wages could be determined similarly, as enterprises communicated terms and individuals offered their services. Competition would ensure equal pay for indistinguishable labor working the standard workweek. (When some enterprises offered a high wage for greater effort, the other enterprises would have to offer the

8. The original article appeared in Lange, "On the Economic Theory of Socialism," *Review of Economic Studies*, October 1936 and February 1937. It is reproduced in Lange, "On the Economic Theory of Socialism" (1938).

same. There could be two or more tiers of workers, differentiated according to their category of effort.) Confident of his triumph, Lange joked that every socialist town in Europe will put up an ironic monument to Mises for having provoked insights showing that socialism was not "impossible" after all. In fact, *market socialism* was tried in Poland and Hungary in the 1980s.

But most of those studying Lange's argument tended to conclude that market socialism would not really work either. It might be an improvement over the more regimented system adopted by the Soviet Union but not an escape from the limits that a thoroughgoing socialism would impose. Mises's profit-motive argument suggests that socialist enterprises will not be driven to supply the socially desirable amount of output in response to any given market price; so where that undersupply is relatively acute, prices will be driven to relatively high levels. Mises scored again in noting that it is one thing to expect the government to motivate socialist managers to "play" at being profit-maximizing producers—some might do a fair job of it. It is another thing to expect the government to delegate to the managers the responsibility for *investment decisions*. No managers would declare it was their duty to let their enterprises shrink in the interest of the economy's "efficiency." The socialists themselves, far from being grateful for the idea of competitive socialism, were all against it—because they wanted to take over the power heretofore residing in the marketplace and/or because for them the whole point of socialism was to direct the reshaping of the economy—to plan.

The young Hayek, turning his attention to the controversy over socialism, cast a new light on the debate over "socialist calculation."[9] The arguments of Hayek are knowledge-based, while those of Mises were incentive-based. Hayek starts with his idea that the know-how in any complex economy—complex either because it is very modern or highly diversified—is necessarily dispersed over the participants in the business sector. Yet, as he says, any individual or agency desiring to "plan"—from scratch—such an economy's allocation of resources over industries would need all this know-how to set up the most suitable methods of production. Diverting everyone with know-how to advise in planning would be prohibitively costly. Even if all the possessors of know-how could be put in one stadium, the mass of detail would swamp any attempt by the planner to use it all. The planner would not be able to put it all together. Therefore, central planning cannot work satisfactorily.

9. Hayek, "Socialist Calculation" (1935, pp. 201–243), reprinted in Hayek, *Individualism and Economic Order* (1948).

Hayek was fond of a shorter route to the same conclusion. A modern economy, with its institutions and culture and with its production methods and the capital goods it uses, could not have been *built* by one individual or one company or any one body of any kind—the thing is too complex. So a government could not have built one either. Nor build it now.

A socialist state might succeed well enough at first by copying some similar economy abroad, making what socialist changes it could. But inefficiency in resource allocation would grow as the economy took its own path— as product demands rose here and fell there and as older people retired and younger ones entered the workforce. In Hayek's view of the modern capitalist economy, increases in relative prices and wages in some industries or lines of work indicate to participants elsewhere that they might do well to gather know-how in those industries or lines of work. In the socialist economy, people have little incentive to choose an industry or occupation on that basis, and they may be faced with bureaucratic obstacles to moving to the industry or occupation of their choice. An industry in a socialist economy might finally lose the key to how to produce because of its failure to provide individuals with motives to maintain or acquire the needed know-how.

Another Hayekian argument is that a good business decision may often require the input of practitioners whose know-how, born of long experience, offers them insights with which to appraise the difficulty of carrying out some investment project or the difficulty of developing a product that the enterprise had not produced before. This problem appears in a free-enterprise economy as well. How to produce a new thing and how costly it will be are questions to which the answers are not known beforehand. If the state were to decide whether to take an initiative in some industry, the full opportunity costs of the project to all other industries in the economy could not really be known to anyone in the government. Even the experts on the ground would have to make educated guesses. From this Hayekian viewpoint, the private entrepreneur deciding whether to build a new rail line (in consultation with engineers, financiers, and so forth) will usually come to a far better sense of the costs of acquiring the new line, having been in the business for years, than would the administration of a socialist economy, no matter how transparent the prices of things. Here is Hayek in his classic 1935 paper on socialist calculation:

> In a centrally planned society the selection of the most appropriate among the known technical methods will be possible only if all that knowledge can be used in the calculations of the central authority. . . . It is hardly

necessary to emphasize that this is an absurd idea even in so far as that knowledge is concerned which can properly be said to "exist" at any moment of time. But much of the knowledge that is actually utilized is by no means "in existence" in this ready-made form. Most of it consists in a technique of *thought* which enables the individual engineer to find *new* solutions rapidly as soon as he is confronted with new constellations of circumstances.[10]

Over the years, more and more in the general public came to be persuaded by the arguments of Mises and Hayek against the socialist economy—though some needed to see the malfunctions and mounting stagnation of the Soviet economy in the 1980s to feel sure. But what persuaded them was not so much the argument that limitations in a socialist economy would saddle it with growing inefficiencies—an economist's argument. It was the idea, which people read between the lines or simply supposed was a part of the broad critique, that if a relatively well-functioning modern economy went socialist, it would become *less innovative*. It would be saddled with increasingly obsolete products and production methods. People cared more about economic growth, it seems, than they did about dry-as-dust efficiency.

In fact, the socialist economies were fatally lacking in dynamism. The innovatorship of the former state managers was tested when massive privatization began in eastern Europe after the collapse of the Soviet Union. These managers, fearing they would lose their post to a rival or see their enterprise close if they *did not* succeed in innovating, made frenzied efforts to create and market new products. Yet they met with almost total failure. They were willing entrepreneurs, when their backs were to the wall at any rate, but they were not *able* at entrepreneurship. The Darwinian process in the communist economies had not selected managers for that talent, so those managers who had that trait were few and far between.[11]

Mises *seemed* set to make the innovation argument. He implied that those in control of a socialist enterprise, doubting they would win much of the credit for an innovation and fearing they would have much to lose from failure, will be far less willing to attempt an innovation than private owners of such an enterprise would, since the latter can expect to pocket any winning

---

10. Hayek, "Socialist Calculation" (p. 210). The italics have been added.

11. The construction of the survey of managers and the statistical findings are described in Frydman et al., "When Does Privatization Work?" (Mises could have said in defense that his argument about prices being increasingly wrong in a socialist economy clearly implied that innovative effort in that economy would go increasingly awry.)

and, thanks to limited liability, escape much of the loss. Mises also understood that the "ceaseless search" for profit has also the function of tending to weed out the wrong people from various jobs and to put in new people to be tested. Lacking the profit motive, a well-functioning socialist economy—far more than a well-functioning modern economy would—would let into managerial positions people whose talents did not lie in either the conception or the development of ideas for novel commercial products. But Mises did not make the point explicit.

Hayek's conception of the modern economy may have seemed to lead to the innovation argument. In his bottom-up, grassroots theory, the modern market economy, in the process of creating new products, whether goods or methods, draws on the freedom of individuals in that system to exercise their originality and thrives on the individuality of their situation and their know-how. Hayek opened the door to a model of indigenous innovation—innovation indigenous to a country's economy—based on the new and diverse ideas that strike individuals in the economy. In contrast, the socialist economy does not confer on individuals any right to apply for financial support for an innovative project. At best, an individual would be free to suggest an innovative idea to the manager of the socialist enterprise, and a manager would be free to apply to the national bank for a loan to develop such an innovative idea into a new product. From Hayek's perspective, a socialist economy could not realize its potential for innovation, since diverse entrepreneurs are not free to compete with one another for market share through new products and methods, diverse financiers are not free to bet on their private judgments in deciding which new ideas to back, and diverse creative types are not free to compete with one another for an entrepreneur to help develop their new ideas.

The loss of innovation would be particularly clear and pronounced in the case of a knowledge economy. Government takeover of enterprises in which the talents and services of most participants are idiosyncratic, such as architectural firms, soccer teams, comedy clubs, oil drillers, gourmet restaurants, ballet companies, and wine growers, would be unworkable for the Hayekian reasons that the government would have little or no knowledge of the business and of which ones to invest in. Moreover, worker management would typically vote no to moving, to newcomers, and to innovation. Those who had dreamed up new ideas would lack the clear channels they had used before. (In modern economies there are companies called ESOPs in which employees are the shareowners, but they are seldom as successful as their owner-managed competitors.) A socialist state with a knowledge economy would thus be particularly hard-pressed to acquire dynamism.

Why, then, did Mises and Hayek not make these innovation arguments? For one thing, Mises and even Hayek, writing as late as the mid-1930s, were still Schumpeterian in their thinking about innovation. Had they warned of a dearth of indigenous innovation in a nation choosing a socialist economy, acute readers would have commented that a socialist economy is as free as a modern capitalist economy to *import* the magnificent new technological advances wrought by scientists and inventors around the world. The concept of the modern economy—creative and successful at indigenous innovation— had not surfaced in their 1920s and 1930s papers or even in Hayek's famous 1944 tract.[12] For another thing, to argue that the nations like czarist Russia that had gone socialist could realize high dynamism if they just returned to private ownership would have been seen as absurd. (It was nations like America, Germany, Hungary, and France that would lose their dynamism if they switched to socialism—as those that tried soon found out.)

Over the decades most economists, including many on the left, came to declare the Austrian team the winner of the debate. The Austrian school persuaded the economics profession that a socialist economy would cause a decisive deterioration of efficiency. The Austrian side did not have to claim that the modern capitalist economy was free of its own inefficiencies—the misdirections and the waste brought by financial panics hardly needed to be acknowledged. They had only to argue that such an economy, once socialized, would suffer a sickening slide into greater and greater inefficiency.

The Austrians lost another battle, though. They seemed to believe that *every country* that threw out its capitalist economy in favor of a socialist

---

12. In his *The Road to Serfdom* (1944) the terms innovation, creativity, originality, invention, growth, advance, and progress do not appear in the index. Hayek scholars might agree that the first flicker of recognition that—as was virtually pointed to in his own work!—indigenous creativity could occur within a nation's economy, not just its scientific establishment, may have come when Hayek was sent a lecture by Oskar Morgenstern in 1937. Hayek had supposed in influential work in 1927 that the economy has a tendency to home in on some equilibrium path, though errors could cause disequilibrium for some time. Morgenstern's lecture argued that to suppose that was to assume that the actors in the economy possessed perfect foresight, which they could not do in a world of endogenous innovation (nor, for that matter, in scientific research outside economies). Certainly Hayek saw the problem. His recognition of the uncertainty within an economy caused by innovators (and more generally the pluralism of views among participants) became explicit in the 1960s. Hayek's 1961 paper "The Non-Sequitur of the 'Dependence Effect'" teased J. K. Galbraith for supposing that would-be innovators bringing out new products know they would succeed or know the probability of any given level of sales.

economy would soon be worse off owing to growing inefficiencies. But it was one thing to argue that there would be, generally speaking, a decisive loss of efficiency from socializing in its entirety an economy of great complexity and sophistication, which had required a long evolution of institutions and culture to achieve—a modern economy or merely a knowledge economy. It was quite another thing to suggest that *every* economy, no matter how ineffective, would be still worse off by going socialist. And it was yet another to argue that *any* amount of socialism, no matter how moderate and how aimed, would spell worse inefficiency than would otherwise have been experienced. The socialist movement could live! And it did.

Socialism managed to take power in economies that were not advanced and were not rapidly becoming advanced through modernization. It was no use to tell the Russians that their socialism would not be as efficient as well-functioning capitalist economies were, since the Russians had no experience with such an economy. And it would not have been persuasive to tell them that their socialism would not be as innovative as an economy of high dynamism, since they had no experience with that either. In fact, Soviet Russia had an extraordinary run of *Schumpeterian* innovation from the 1920s to the 1960s as electrification and other advances were quickly introduced. No one yearned for the return of the czar.

Socialism also managed to take over limited sectors in some economies— the less-advanced economies, to be sure, but also in some economies that were relatively advanced. The notion grew that socialist ownership and control would work well in the "commanding heights" of the economy—energy, telecommunications, railways, ports, and any heavy industry. The unexpected revival of this thinking in China was confirmed in an address by Prime Minister Wen Jiabao in Beijing in March 2010. "The socialist system's advantages enable us to make decisions efficiently, organize effectively and concentrate resources to accomplish large undertakings."[13]

The socialist discussion, especially in the more advanced economies, shifted from the workability of a socialist economy to the workability of state ownership and control in one or more sectors. It also shifted toward the regulation and taxation of the private sector. The Austrians' perspectives were applicable to this discussion, of course. The power of Hayek's perspective can hardly be overestimated. There was a Hayekian moment in the past decade when Western governments took measures to encourage the

13. As reported on the *International Herald Tribune*'s website, www.iht.com, March 5, 2010.

use of biofuels instead of the conventional fossil fuels, coal and oil, by induc-
ing farmers to switch land from raising the usual crops to producing soy-
beans, which could be used for making soy biodiesel. The reallocation of land
caused a catastrophic rise in the price of various staple foods and thus led to
hundreds of thousands of deaths by starvation. It was also a cause of the further deforestation of the Amazon basin. On top of all that, the soy biodiesel
produced was later found to have virtually no advantage over conventional
fuels in terms of overall greenhouse gas emissions.[14] There was great irony
in the failure of "planning," since the socialists in particular and government
planners in general were always asserting that socialism, by virtue of being
rational, would look to the long term in contrast to the short-termism of capitalism. But it was precisely capitalism, with its huge step forward in introducing shareowning, that solved the problem that the principal owner would
not be expecting to live forever. It was the single proprietorship and, earlier,
the feudal barony that were apt to suffer the problem of no heirs.

In particular, even an incremental move toward social ownership raises
the question of why the government should nationalize to undertake projects that veterans of private industry presumably rejected. Mises's point that
a socialist government does not face the right prices does not apply if the part
of the economy under social ownership and control is too small to change
the configuration of prices in the economy. But in the Hayekian perspective,
the lack of the needed know-how in the socialist government may cause it
to proceed in the wrong direction or to fail when it is moving in the right
direction.

Yet the Austrians overgeneralized, supposing that their theory applies
in every case and must always trump other considerations. It can happen
that business people, not having worked much in government, do not know
everything known by the state. Possibly the state has knowledge about some
industries that would make state ownership and control better on balance
than private ownership. On the issue of nationalization of any particular
kind of production, then, the Hayekian bias in favor of private ownership
may be outweighed. However, Hayek was certainly correct to see the dangers
of totalitarian control of the economy—by the state or by anyone. He was
not the extremist he was taken to be. He never proposed a zero-level of state
activity in production. In his famous wartime tract, *The Road to Serfdom*, he

14. Ammous and Phelps, "Climate Change, the Knowledge Problem and the Good Life"
(2009). See also Volpi, "Soya Is Not the Solution to Climate Change" (2006).

proposed a range of roles for the state, including research to increase longevity.[15] Hayek was not an ideologue.

Socialism's Strange Side

It is clear now, from the distance of time, that something was very odd about the socialism debate of the interwar decades. The Austrians made the strange assumption that the goal of the socialists was economic efficiency. But the socialists were not plotting revolutionary changes in the structure of the Western economies for the sake of bringing economic waste under better control. Output per head in Western Europe had quadrupled between 1820 and 1920. So even the most earnest socialists could have afforded to let go whatever loss of output resulted from the occasional panic and the unemployment that accompanied the modern economy.

Most socialists, in fact, held aloft their goals of stability, equality, dignity, and contentment. They had no wish to smash the individual. But to the extent the individual is encouraged to excel in the social sphere, it is through his alignment with the state. The values expressed in this set of goals represented a fundamental shift from the core values of the Western world—some from as far back as ancient Greece. Absent from the socialist terms was the vocabulary of the humanist tradition—terms like exploration, creation, and exhilaration.

---

15. In a 1933 paper, "The Trend of Economic Thinking," Hayek wrote that laissez-faire is not "the ultimate and only conclusion." (p. 134). In *The Road to Serfdom* he speculated that "nothing has done so much harm to the liberal cause as the wooden insistence of some [libertarians] on certain rules of thumb, above all the principle of laissez-faire" (p. 13). That tract brought a range of reactions. A mild one was from Keynes, who in a letter expressed great admiration for the book, then said he differed with it at only one point. He favored a radically different list of activities for the state to do—an agenda as odd from present-day perspectives as from Hayek's. The fury of some of the reactions is incomprehensible to scholars in the present age. On its sixtieth anniversary in 1994, *The Road to Serfdom* won high praise from Amartya Sen, writing in the *Financial Times*. It remains true that Hayek was alarmed as few others were by the loss of individual freedom he expected to result from British economist William Beveridge's plan for a massive system of social insurance and other interventions.

Incidentally, many imagine that *Road* was a broadside against Soviet socialism based on Hayek's previous theoretical work. In fact, it was Hayek's answer to those in Britain who claimed there was no reason to fight a war with Nazi Germany. It was a warning against the state-sponsored corporatism in Germany more than against communism in the Soviet Union, though Hayek often alluded to the latter. Maybe Hayek saw corporatism in Beveridge's extreme welfare state. During the war, Hitler's economists got hold of a draft of the Beveridge blueprints after it was air-dropped over Nazi-occupied Europe. The Nazis apparently exclaimed, "This is what we need here in Germany!" See "Commission on Social Justice: Beveridge's Appeal for an Attack on Five Giant Evils" in *The UK Independent*, October 25, 1994.

The socialist goals were pursued with fanatical zeal. The socialist experiments, dating from Lenin's to Castro's, made a fetish of enforcing rigid equalities, controlling population in the name of "full employment," and forbidding virtually all individual initiatives in the economy. These economies became faceless, suffocating, boring—not just grossly inefficient.

So it was odd that, at first, Mises and Hayek did not criticize these goals. They gave the impression that efficiency was decisive in the choice of an economic system. It seemed they would have been willing to accept socialism—the limitation on wealth, bars against opening a business, workers voting on the conduct of businesses, and so forth—if they could be persuaded that no loss of total output, or economic efficiency, would result. Economists effectively voted to award victory in the debate to the Austrians on the narrow grounds on which the Austrians made their arguments. Had there been, following the debate, a consensus that, all things considered, the socialist economy's avoidance of unemployment and swings in employment would increase output more than new inefficiencies would decrease it, Mises and Hayek would have lost their debate.

Later, in *The Road to Serfdom,* Hayek conveyed his sense of tragedy over the loss of *freedom* suffered in Italy and Germany since the 1930s with the rise of authoritarianism. There could be no longer any doubt about his feeling for humanity. If Sen's reading is right, freedom in Hayek's thinking is a means to other goals. Yet *The Road to Serfdom* did not indicate what goals would be infringed on by a loss of economic freedom at the hands of the authoritarians other than efficiency—except to warn that output, or efficiency, would be diminished if the freedom of businesses is crimped by the authoritarian leaders. (Most of the book is concerned with the importance of political freedom.)

With hindsight we can see that missing in the discussion of socialism was a debate between socialist values and Western humanist values. It has come to be clear that neither the proponents of the modern economy nor its opponents—the advocates of socialism and those of corporatism—could formulate a justification of the system they favored until they could show that it served compelling social values.

The Fear of Socialism

For many of those who feared the coming of socialism, the problem was not that socialism might fail but that it could succeed well enough by its own lights to go on and on. One could not be sure that a robust majority would always be there to stop socialism in one's own country—in Italy, say, where the capitalist economy paled next to those in America, Britain, and Germany. By 1919, little more than a year after the Bolshevik revolution, several countries—Italy, Germany, and America too—were in the grip of the Red Scare.

In Germany and France, an incremental socialism was making some headway. Germany's Social Democratic Party (known as the SPD), which sought a socialist economy, headed the coalition that gained control of the parliament in 1919. The socialists won the establishment of factory councils (*Betriebsrat*) in which workers would have a say in various company matters. An arbitration mechanism was set up for labor disputes. Private capital retained ownership but lost some control. The work day was shortened not to 10 or 9 hours but to 8 hours. Social reforms that ought to have been discussed in the society at large and, if chosen, paid for by taxpayers because they wanted the reforms, were squeezed out of the business sector. The West was started in the direction of regulations, mandates, and fees that were to take a toll on investment and innovation.

As the 1920s dawned on the West, there was a great sense of foreboding about the economic future. A revolution had started, and no one could know whether it was going to spread.

CHAPTER SIX

The Third Way:
Corporatism Right and Left

Corporatism is not an internal reform to satisfy the selfish interests of each of us. . . . [I]t represents the end of civic and economic individualism, the coming of a new social and economic regime, and the revelation of an organized nation made up of mutually supporting bodies.

GEORGES VALOIS, "La Coordination des forces nationales"

WHEREVER THE MODERN ECONOMY ARRIVED, with its institutions and culture, there were preexisting social customs and social values going back centuries. Over the latter half of the 19th century, extensive modernization in parts of continental Europe, including France and Germany, rode roughshod over traditional ways of life. Though socialists went on with their critique of capitalism—the modern capitalist economies not excepted—other social critics arose to deplore other things about the modern economy. By the mid-1920s, these critics had formulated the standard 20th-century indictment of the modern economy. While the unemployment and wages that socialists complained of in capitalism could have been addressed and eventually were, the new indictment struck at the heart and brain of the modern economy.

Corporatism's Indictment of the Modern Economy

The modern economy, as argued earlier, was driven by the altruistic individualism of Renaissance humanism, the vitalism of the Baroque, and the modernism of the Enlightenment. That last current, in adding to (as well as building on) the earlier currents, made the critical mass that fueled the modern economy. At modernism's core was the idea that individuals ought to be free to pursue their own happiness, with some regulations for their own benefit. In arts and letters, the author of a work should be emancipated from service to extrinsic moral and political ideals. Art for art's sake, as Oscar Wilde and E. M. Forster proclaimed. In business, the entrepreneur should—on the same grounds—be freed from service to society. Business for business's sake.[1]

In social life, a "modern woman" felt free to depart from tradition or even break taboos. Ordinary people went from being dependents on mutual protection to adventurers out in the world in quest of career challenges and whatever other chances might lie ahead. Men and women might become heroic figures on a small or large scale, far more so than in the mercantile age that Smith saw as unheroic. In some countries, important political leaders and activists were early champions of such a society, voicing little or no support for the state's pursuing social goals other than the goal of individual prosperity and individual development for all. In *Common Sense*, first published as a pamphlet early in 1776, Thomas Paine's argument for American independence from Britain was built on the proposition that it would boost Americans' prosperity; if Paine recognized another social value, it was not evident. Jefferson, in the second draft of the Declaration of Independence in July 1775, wrote that the institutions of America "opened . . . to the unfortunate & to the enterprising of every country . . . the acquisition & free possession of property," thus suggesting that self-support, a career, and some wealth were markers on the road they took in pursuit of happiness and the reason they came to America. In a 1925 speech after his election, President Calvin Coolidge saw Americans as still on the course that Paine and Jefferson evidently supposed they were on and left little doubt that his government would be oriented accordingly. "After all," he said, "the chief business of the American people is business. They are profoundly concerned with buying, selling, investing and prospering." Even more strikingly, Lincoln's second lecture speaks of Americans' "rage for the new."

Also at the core of modernism was the idea that everyone who enjoys the legal rights of a modern society and pays little for them has obligations of responsibility: to respect the laws and people's rights, so as not to cheat others; and obligations of independence: to bear the consequences of one's mistakes so as not to be a burden on others. Responsibility implies that persons, alliances, and even the state may not violate property rights of persons or companies; extort payments from them; induce the state to block competitors from

1. See Sidorsky's "Modernism and the Emancipation of Literature from Morality" and his "The Uses of the Philosophy of G. E. Moore in the Works of E. M. Forster."

introducing new products; or solicit subsidies, grants, and indemnities from the state. (The modern state may make investments to open up new innovation and enterprise, as the Louisiana Purchase did, and may take actions to prevent external forces from crippling innovation and enterprise—if these are not judged to cost too much. And the state may act to combat what is seen to be economic injustice in the rewards from cooperation. But it is *not* a function of the modern state to block development of innovative products or block new investments to protect competing producers from the new competition or to indemnify them if it is too late to protect them. In a modern society, even a just state is not in the business of comprehensive insurance.)

This modernism that impelled the emergence of modern economies was nothing less than a cultural revolution, and the modern economies it was injecting were a cultural shock, especially in continental Europe. In the last half of the 19th century, whole operas dramatized the costs of modern self-finding and self-expression in societies still heavily traditional: Mascagni's 1890 *Cavalleria Rusticana*, Wagner's 1868 *Die Meistersinger,* and Verdi's 1853 *La Traviata.* ("A subject for our age," Verdi wrote to a friend. To obtain a theater he changed the setting to "Paris and environs, 1700.") Modernism and modernity stimulated counter-currents in those Continental countries where a modern beachhead was substantial but traditions remained strong. The most important counter-current began in late 19th-century Germany—one eventually culminating in an economic system that came to be called *corporatism.* But why was it bound to elicit a backlash? In a classic treatise on the healthiness of traditional life, which became a fount of corporatist ideas for decades, the Prussian sociologist Ferdinand Tönnies points to the trader who, armed with the "contracts" created by Roman law, makes offers that put others out of business. For Tönnies, this trader is the force destroying the traditional community, not the "division of labor" brought by factories, which Marx had emphasized.[2] Much of the corporatist critique of modernity consisted of unfavorable comparisons of city life with community life. More

2. Tönnies witnessed this disruption as a youth in rural Schleswig. He further distanced himself from Marx in arguing that specialization had existed in communities for centuries and had actually strengthened them. Neither was he a fascist. He joined the Socialist Party in 1932 just to spite the Nazis. Tönnies's magnum opus, in German, was first published under the title *Gemeinschaft und Gesellschaft* in Leipzig in 1887, when he was still young. Though *Gesellschaft* often refers to a business, so one might think the title meant "Community and Business," Tönnies used *Gesellschaft* to mean modern civilization, business included. Editions in 1912 and 1920 gained wider attention. A new 2001 translation into English is *Community and Civil Society.*

generally, a large part of the corporatist critique of modernity protested features and properties of the modern economy that broke with traditions.

A corporatist critique of the modern economy developed over the next several decades. One of the corporatist criticisms of the modern economy was that it had no leadership, thus no course, its heading being the net resultant of millions of individuals pulling in myriad directions. In the medieval past, corporatists supposed, attempts to innovate were directed by the economy's communal authority, with results generally along the lines of what the community had hoped. When such communal goals came to be largely crowded out by the unannounced, largely unobserved, and often inscrutable initiatives of a welter of individuals and companies in the business sector, the economy could be said to have been left *rudderless*, which gave rise, understandably enough, to a sense of disorder. And that sense, no doubt, lay behind some of the unease felt across Western Europe in the last years of the 19th century and the early decades of the 20th. The desire for direction (for *dirigisme*, as the French said) was a major strand of corporatist thought.

Many corporatists saw the *uncoordination* in capitalism as another source of disorder. They sought a system of concerted action. At the micro level, a company's owners could act on a proposal only if "stakeholders," such as employees, agreed (codetermination or *mit Spreche*). At the macro level, legislative action needed the consent of the main players, capital and labor (*Concertazione*). Later they spoke of the "social partners."

Conservative corporatists sought not just order but the *old* order. As they saw it, the modern culture with its yen for change was eroding the economic order in traditional communities, where members had a sense that they were working toward the shared goals of their traditional culture. They bewailed the lack of *solidarity*. For Freud, the conflict between modern and traditional was, ultimately, "the struggle between the claim of the individual and the cultural claims of the group."[3] The yearning for the traditional culture is evidenced not just in the writings of corporatist theorists but also in artistic works of a splinter group of classicists who broke away from modernism in the 1920s. A return to the harmony and perfectionism of the classical

---

3. Freud, *Civilization and Its Discontents* (p. 50). He wanted aggressions to be constructive, lest another war broke out. The title of the 1930 German original, *Das Unbehagen in der Kultur*, raised the problem of translating *Unbehagen*. (Freud suggested "discomforts." His 1930 translator Joan Riviere proposed "discontents.") What Freud meant by *Kultur* was the entire acquisition of knowledge, practice, attitudes, and even "tools." Today, tools and even technology are usually kept out of "culture" but included in "civilization."

order was evoked in sculptures such as Aristide Maillol's *Ile-de-France*, paintings such as those from Picasso's period of classical portraits, and film, notably Leni Riefenstahl's documentary film *Olympia*.[4]

Many social critics, most of them in continental Europe, saw failings that had to do with the *materialism* of the societies around them. They charged that the quality of life in society had been debased by what they saw as a spread of money-grubbing. They complained of the economic disparities between those who scurried to make the most of their material advantages and those who lacked them. They also complained of the outbreaks of violence between owners and workers, neither of whom seemed to have limits on the means they would use to achieve material gains. These were the themes of the Roman Catholic Church and the articles of what came to be called Catholic corporatism. For the mitigation of this misery the 1891 papal encyclical of Leo XIII titled *Rerum Novarum* called upon those who hire labor to pay a wage adequate for raising a family. Today this would be called exercising social responsibility. (One wonders why the Church's economists did not look for a way that would not destroy jobs; the public could have paid a tax to finance subsidies for hiring factory workers.) *Rerum* also threw its support behind the establishment of labor unions to negotiate improved conditions. The 1931 papal encyclical of Pius XI, *Quadragesimo Anno,* gave its approval to the corporatist invention of vocational groups and to producer associations. Neither of these encyclicals attacked private property but rather appealed to private owners for a kinder face. By this time, both the Church and many, if not most, intellectuals had turned away from the socialist contention that state ownership would serve any good purpose. Freud wrote in *Civilization and Its Discontents* (p. 60) that "[i]n abolishing private property we deprive the human love of aggression of one of its instruments," such as amassing more wealth than our neighbors, no doubt, "but we have in no way altered the differences in power and influence which are misused by aggressiveness, nor have we altered anything in its nature." The stark inequalities that were fast developing in the Soviet Union bore out this prophecy.

Much animosity toward the modern economy, though, expressed not a desire for order, whatever the new order might be, or even nostalgia for the

---

4. The classic study is the 1925 essay by Franz Roh, reprinted in 1995. Many examples of the period are reproduced in Silver, *Chaos and Classicism.* Silver's earlier book *Esprit de Corps* covers some of this ground.

old order, whatever order that was, so much as the fear and anger of various social classes whose social status and very survival were threatened. The modern economy was dissolving the social hierarchy and the distribution of power. In the societies of medieval Europe, the classes were imbedded in a system of mutual protection: peasants could appeal to authorities, such as the lord of the manor, for protection when the actions of another raised their costs or reduced their revenues. Competition among manufacturers might be forestalled by limiting production to the manufacturer granted a royal charter. Merchants formed merchant guilds, which served to control the sale of staples such as food and cloth, thus exercising a degree of monopoly power. Artisans and craftsmen formed the craft guilds, which sought to regulate standards for, thus entry into, their line of work. There was a sense that the terms demanded by the various producer groups were sanctioned by an unwritten social compact, whether or not the terms were exactly the "just price" conceived by some theologians.

In contrast, modern capitalism did not offer a social contract—it could not and be true to the values for which it stood. Thus the various groups of producers, merchants, artisans, and the rest experienced a newfound *powerlessness*, though some of them were on the rise, so they were not materially suffering. In some countries, the manufacturers in the new infant industries tended to be protected by an import tariff, but few manufacturers, if any, faced the reliable and stable demand that manufacturers enjoyed in the traditional economies, owing to the economy's evolution and advance over time. And few manufacturers enjoyed monopoly power for very long. As a consequence, individual producers and producer groups had no power to set their terms outside a narrow range—they went from price setters to price takers— and they lost some of their power to set standards and maintain prestige. The sense of powerlessness in trades, industries, and professions could have been for many people a gnawing frustration to be set against the satisfactions that they found in their work. If they loved the business they were in and the work they did, that was all the more reason to suffer from their inability to set their own terms in hopes of maintaining their social position. The corporatism of 1920s Europe held out the promise of some defense against the relentless innovation of the modern economy and against the desertion of consumers—defense that they later dubbed "social protection." Farmers could go on producing, even if not all of their produce could be sold in the marketplace. Movie makers could be subsidized even if their former audiences now preferred not to watch them. This broad "social protection," as it became known, was one of the last strands of corporatism to fall into place.

In continental Europe all these intellectual strands and the political forces championing them came into a confluence during the 1920s: the elites in a city like Munich or Rome, many of them nationalists who felt the need for a return to unity and purpose in society; the intellectuals who felt the need for economic order; the peasants, artisans, and other interest groups losing ground to modernization, who wanted protection; the scientists who wanted state support for research and artists who wanted it for the arts; and, not least, the Christian corporatists, who advocated restoration of traditional communities and vocations through curbs on mobile capital and the "trader spirit" in profit-driven businesses.[5] True, the socialists had already decried the scramble for social status, money, and power, most dramatically the socialist-sympathizer Wagner with his opera cycle, *Ring of the Niebelung*. To pick up votes, the corporatists took up that socialist theme and other parts of the socialist agenda, such as some sort of codetermination, without saddling themselves with the socialist baggage of social ownership and without making a fetish of wage equality and full employment.

All these factions hoped for some way of curbing or overriding the various tendencies and impulses of the modern economy with its modernist culture. The result was the corporatist economy. Its core function was to keep the private sector under public control. To what ends? The corporatists' main aims were state-led investment, industrial peace and solidarity, and social responsibility. There was much thinking about economic growth too. Economies on the fringe of modernity were growing so slowly as to leave a widening gap between their productivity and that in America and Germany. Italy and Spain were being passed by others in the league table of productivity.

---

5. There was an ethnic dimension to the politics of protection. The competition from which the Christian Social Party sought to protect the Catholic lower class came from predominantly Jewish businesses. The German nationalist parties wanted government to use its power to protect people of their ethnic background against competition from Slavs and especially from Jews. The socialists were no different. The Social Democratic Party boasted that it, not the corporatist group, was the true opponent of the "Jewish big capitalists," "Jewish exploiters," and "rich Jews." It went out of its way to characterize its targets as Jewish where the targets were disproportionately Jewish. Anti-Semitism was endemic in Europe during this period. See Muller, *The Mind and the Market* (p. 353). It is fair to ask whether the advancing entrepreneurs were opposed because they were Jewish or the advancing Jews were opposed because they were entrepreneurs. The answer would appear to be the former, since Europe had long exhibited a bias against Jews. It was more than that, however. The problem that the corporatists later called the "Jewish question" was not the Jewish identity of so many in Germany but rather that many successful Jews were mostly in the "liberalism" camp, which was integral to the birth of economic modernity, rather than in the corporatist camp. The first solution was to take over their businesses, the "final solution" was the Holocaust.

Some corporatists, Benito Mussolini included, laid Italy's problem to the cautious performance of the small family businesses that dotted Italy. Others, corporatist or socialist, laid the problem to the degree of monopoly and cartelization among the big businesses. The corporatist theoreticians supposed that, with the concerted effort of all society, and in particular its community of scientists, a country could drive scientific advances at a faster pace. And the state might act to steer scientists toward projects that would yield, with the involvement of engineering and other specialities, advances in useful technology—thus possibilities for better methods of production and new kinds of goods. This was the doctrine dubbed *techno-nationalism* by Richard Nelson. It is one manifestation of the more general belief called *scientism*— the belief that scientists, equipped with the tools of their science, more effectively advance the flowering of new products and methods than do the diffuse and poorly directed initiatives taken in a free enterprise economy. (It was under Mussolini in 1923, then prime minister, that Italy founded its national science foundation, the Consiglio Nazionale delle Ricerche, a full 27 years before America's National Science Foundation.)

The corporatist system also aimed to enlist artists. The preservation and promotion of the culture of the nation was a natural outgrowth of the elevation of the society over the individual. And the belief grew up, which could be called *culturalism,* that artistic advances could drive a country's economic progress, just as scientism held that scientific advances could be such a driver. Article 9 in Italy's constitution charges the government with responsibility for maintaining and promulgating the nation's cultural heritage. (This culturalism persists today: When the Milan opera house La Scala saw its budget cut back by the government in 2011, some opera fanatics called the move unconstitutional. Only increases are constitutional, not decreases.)

All this control had to mean putting the private-enterprise economy under political control—not back under propped-up lords of the manor, of course, but under some sort of political governance. If the main direction or directions of the economy were to be determined politically, the corporatists supposed, there would be progress along the lines they ardently wanted. By what means was this control to be achieved? The economy was to be organized into groups of companies and workers, large and small. The impression was that workers and indeed all groups, from taxi drivers to pharmacists, suffered from competition—from others and each other. Some socialist thinkers had argued that workers' wages were depressed by the power of capital to "divide and conquer." A company's workers had to expect to lose some jobs to workers in competing companies or industries to the extent that a wage increase would push their company to raise its price relative to others' prices. If represented by a very broad labor union, best of all a nationwide one, the workers would find themselves with the monopoly power of their dreams. In the thinking of this unionism, it was not imagined that the increase in wages would or could bring a decrease in jobs. Oddly, corporatist thinkers thought that grouping producers into a few large cartels would solve the problem—that, with the formation of cartels, the balance of power between labor and capital would be restored, and jobs would not be lost as a result of either the unions or the cartels. It seems to have escaped notice that enabling an increase in mark-ups by companies constituted a contraction of supply on top of the contraction of supply caused by enabling an upward push on wages. The last argument of the corporatists, however, was that, with labor and capital talking together in their "chamber," a new economy of unity and purpose would arise that would put an end to lockouts and threats of mass dismissals on the part of employers and to shirking, work stoppages, and general strikes on the part of employees. This new industrial peace would improve the efficiency of business operations and thus might end up expanding rather than contracting employment while raising wages and profits too.[6]

Whatever the merit of the corporatists' beliefs, aims, and means, the attraction they held for Europeans would be hard to overestimate. Corporatist doctrine was soon put into practice over a vast swath of Europe and the rest of the world.

Early 20th-Century Corporatism

Italy can be said to be the first country to build an economy along the lines of corporatist thought. Benito Mussolini, born in 1883 (like Schumpeter and Keynes) to a poor family in the province of Forli, became the most forceful champion of a corporatist economy in Italy and eventually its chief operating officer. A school teacher briefly, he became a political journalist, editing the Marxist weekly *Avanti!* Deciding that private ownership of enterprises

---

6. Some scholars define "corporatism" in terms of its structure rather than its aims. In a 1974 paper, "Still the Century of Corporatism?" Philippe Schmitter writes that corporatism could be defined as "a system of interest representation in which the constituent units are organized into a limited number of singular, compulsory, noncompetitive, hierarchically ordered and functionally differentiable categories, created, recognized, or licensed by the state and granted a deliberate monopoly" (p. 97).

could better serve high economic performance than either worker ownership or worker control, he broke with the socialists as World War 1 approached and founded the daily paper *Il Popolo d'Italia,* which would be his organ. Italy, after its costly combat against Austria in World War 1 with no rewards to show for it, needed a leader to give them hope for greater importance in the world. A forceful speaker and a shrewd tactician, Mussolini was well suited to take on the role. He was able to enlist to his side most of the corporatists and many of his old socialist allies, becoming the leader of the Fascist Party. Rapidly gaining popular support, he was elected a deputy in the Parliament in 1920, organized the March on Rome in early 1922, and was named prime minister by King Vittorio Emanuele III soon after. In 1925, Mussolini reduced the powers of the parliament, becoming dictator. There was no constitution in Italy, nor elsewhere in Europe at the time, hence no judicial review to put a check on such moves.[7]

In these years, Mussolini's program had been critical of Italy's capitalism. The Fascist Manifesto of 1919 demanded a heavy capital levy, workers' participation in company management, and a minimum-wage law. There was much emphasis on productivity. When the Mussolini government formed, it quickly aimed for a revival of economic growth. Yet the policies that were attempted led to another lurch in his thinking.

The Mussolini government saw Britain and America as having shown the way to a 100 years of growth in the form of 19th-century liberalism. Mussolini moved to repeal much of the socialist legislation of the previous decade: to end the state ownership of the insurance business in 1923 and the telephone network in 1925. Also in 1925, he disempowered the trade unions that had been empowered by the socialists and moved to exempt inward foreign investment from taxation and to make trade agreements. In moves reminiscent of the travails of present-day capitalism in some countries, the government bailed out the banks in 1926 following speculative attacks on the currency. In the end, Italy's experiment with cosmopolitan mercantile capitalism failed to generate appreciable economic growth and failed to protect the population from a sharp recession. Mussolini concluded that laissez-faire, or (classical) liberalism, was a weak reed on which to depend for rapid economic growth.

By then Mussolini's thinking had graduated to a conception of the corporatist economy. What Mussolini was seeking was more than a pickup of the

---

7. Sardinia's Statuto Albertino, which King Charles Albert's son had imported to all of Italy on his ascension to the throne, did not create review.

growth rate. It was a radical modernization of the Italian economy through a fundamental recast of Italian institutions, values, and beliefs. Mussolini took pains to register his dislike of "super-capitalism," with its mass production of homogeneous consumer goods, and his dislike of socialist cartel or monopoly capitalism, with its loss of the innovative spark and increased bureaucratization. His discontentments with capitalism were no doubt real enough, though he was not a philosopher of corporatism—that role fell to Giovanni Gentile, who would later ghostwrite *The Doctrine of Fascism* for him in 1932. Though no corporatist philosopher, Mussolini was nonetheless a builder of a corporatist economy. And the system he built could hardly have differed more from modern capitalism.

The architecture of his corporatist economy is laid out in his own publications.[8] The molecules of the institutional framework are entities called "corporations" (*corporazioni*). In the industrial classification there were finally 22 categories, for example, cereal, textiles, steel, hotels, arts, and credit. Each such *corporazione* was required by the Sindical Laws of 1926 (the "Rocco Laws") to have one employers association (*Associazione*) and one labor union (*Sindicato*):

> The class struggle in the Marxist sense between workers grouped on one side and masters grouped on the other is replaced by debates on matters concerning various categories of producers. Disputes . . . may arise between various categories of workers or between various categories of masters, or even between masters and workers, but they are viewed as one of the inevitable forms of human restlessness, indeed of human life. . . .
>
> The *corporazione* was conceived as an organ where managers and workers might come in touch with one another and establish cooperation. The *corporazione* took definite shape through the Act of February 1934 as an organ for collaboration.[9]

This was a big change from the socialist period before the war. By the early 1910s Italy had a spate of trade unions, some legally recognized by the socialist government only recently. In 1910, a broad employer association, the Italian Confederation of Industry, was founded to work with the unions and to

---

8. His main speeches in the early 1930s and a sort of handbook of the structure of the corporatist economy were published in the original Italian in Mussolini, *Quattro Discorsi sullo Stato Corporativo* (1935), and in English translation the same year under the title *Four Speeches on the Corporate State*. ("Corporatist" or "corporative" would have avoided a seeming reference to corporations in the English sense.)

9. Mussolini, *Four Speeches on the Corporate State* (pp. 81–82).

serve as a lobbying organization. But conflict arose after the war with the militancy of the working class. The unions led the "factory councils" movement in 1919–1921 for the sharing of company management between capital and labor; the Confederation, relaunched as Confindustria, worked to save owner control. The Fascist regime then acted to marginalize these unions by creating Fascist unions. Historians date the emergence of corporatism in Italy to October 1925, when Confindustria and the new unions concluded a pact at Palazzo Vidoni recognizing each other as the only legitimate representative of capital and labor.[10]

Mussolini's corporatism was not exactly the restoration of the control of private owners, however. Article 43 of the Decree of July 1926 declared that "the *corporazione* is not a civil person but an *organ of the state*." Article 44 adds that "corporative organs are endowed with powers to conciliate disputes that may arise between the affiliated organizations."[11] The Labor Charter of April 1927, while reaffirming rights to private "ownership," asserted the state's right to intervene even in companies' hiring of workers. So the Italian government was free to reject agreements between employers and employees until it got the agreement it wanted and free even to dictate company employment. Mussolini spoke of this power to intervene in his January 1934 speech, explaining that it would be invoked only when the decisions of Italy's patriotic owners and employees suffered from some miscalculation or coordination failure:

> Corporate economy introduces order in the field of economy. . . . In what way should this order be put into practice? Through self-discipline of the various categories concerned. *It is only when various categories fail to come to an agreement, or to establish the proper balance, that the State may intervene, although the State always has the undisputed power to do so, because it represents the other aspect of the phenomenon, which is consumption.*[12]

In this passage, Mussolini was being naïve or cynical, though. Italian corporatism with its *corporazioni* created or aggravated problems that it then called upon the government to solve. Corporatist theoreticians, by perverting capitalist industries into employer "associations" that were larger and had more pricing power than the capitalist cartels, and "syndicates" that were larger and in some cases more powerful than the traditional craft unions, increased the

---

10. James, *Europe Reborn* (p. 99).
11. *Four Speeches on the Corporate State* (p. 83).
12. *Four Speeches on the Corporate State* (p. 33).

monopoly power of many bodies and coalitions to the point where it would require pervasive and invasive government action to curb. Yet it would be quite a leap to conclude from this bit of analysis alone that corporatist economies were bound to perform worse on the whole than the modern economies or, at any rate, worse than the relatively well-performing among them.

This tripartite system began operating in piecemeal fashion by 1926, and the scaled-up system was operational by 1935. The system was something new in the firmament, and references to it—admiring or envious—were made by Winston Churchill, George Bernard Shaw, and John Maynard Keynes. It hardly needs saying that, in the second half of the decade, Mussolini, done with his economic designs, moved on to pursue his imperial designs on Ethiopia and the Adriatic, and then tainted his government forever by turning the force of the state against homosexuals, Gypsies, and Jews. Yet in the first half of the decade, Italy's construction of a functioning corporatist economy fascinated much of the world and surely played a part in emboldening some other countries to proceed along corporatist lines.

Germany, for one, had already been incubating its own corporatist philosophies before the full realization of Italy's example. In fact, the development of corporatism there started sooner than in Italy. Even before Leo XIII pontificated for social responsibility, Germany had had its early corporatist critics of capitalism: Ferdinand Tönnies, with his thesis in 1887 that communities and guilds were being destroyed, and Émile Durkeim, who argued that capitalism raised conflicts without rules. In the 1920s, German politics gradually gave voice to the elements of corporatist thought that Italy did—the revulsion against individualism, the rejection of laissez-faire economic policy, and disdain for the petit bourgeoisie. Yet some other strains of thought were more salient, and socialism was more embedded in Germany than in Italy, so the rise of an Italian-style corporatist economy was more complicated and took longer.

Adolf Hitler played a pivotal role in much the same way as Mussolini did. A former art student born in Austria and working in Munich for the German military in 1919, Hitler was sent to spy on the leftwing German Workers Party, an upstart rival of the venerable Social Democratic Party, and found that its ideas—German nationalism and anti-Semitism—were like his own. A stirring orator, he gained mounting leverage in the German Workers Party, recruited some of the military to it, and in 1920 proposed it be renamed the National Socialist German Workers Party, known as the NSDAP, and later nicknamed the Nazi Party to underline the nationalism and to retain votes that still lay in socialism.

A theme of the Nazi Party in the 1920s and later was their desire to see a return of the economy to high performance (*Leistung*), much as Mussolini's party harped on *productività*. In 1920 the party's first program, known as the "25 Points," was as anti-capitalist as the Italian manifesto of 1919. It demanded the abolition of unearned income, the nationalization of trusts, land reform, and the nourishment of a "healthy middle class." And it vented an opposition to self-interest verging on hatred:

> The activities of the individual must not clash with the interests of the whole . . . but must be for the general good. . . . We demand ruthless war upon all those whose activities are injurious to the common interest . . . usurers, . . . other profiteers . . . the Jewish materialist spirit. . . . The Party is convinced that our nation can achieve permanent health from within only on the principle: the common interest before self-interest.[13]

The Nazis gained a plurality in the Reichstag, and Hitler was named chancellor in 1933, a win paved by Germany's 1929 Depression, or "slump," and the Nazi's portrait of the Weimar government as weak on the issue of German reparations (even though it had twice negotiated them down and little had been paid). The National Socialists set out to construct a corporatist system of the tripartite type—capital, labor, and government—in 1933. The 1934 Act for the Organization of National Labor established a number of industrial groups, each with "followers" under a hierarchy of "leaders." In 1935, labor unions were regulated and called on to find noncommercial incentives to raise productivity. Cartels were spread over nearly the entire economy, and joining them was made compulsory. The National Economic Chamber was formed atop all these associations, with power to issue laws and decrees. The system was such that the state could intervene as widely or as little as it wished.

For a time, the government attempted to direct a large part of the economy: conscripting labor to work as desired, telling companies what to produce and how much, and imposing price and wage controls. But by 1937, the government drew back: the Chamber was directed not to engage in any more price and market regulation, and the cartels resumed setting prices and wages. The focus of the Nazi government swung to foreign policy, and companies were largely free to compete for customers in the marketplace and to compete for government contracts. Yet the limitless power of the state ensured that no company would dare go far against the government's

---

13. Quoted in Heinz Lubasz, *Fascism: Three Major Regimes* (p. 78).

manifest desires. Companies might also become arms of the state, vying for government contracts and subsidies. Hayek thought, as he said in his 1944 *Road to Serfdom*, that the German business people were deluded in believing they retained the autonomy from the state they had enjoyed when Germany's economy was relatively modern.

Germany, like Italy, had possessed elements of corporatism long before the interwar years. Mercantile guilds, craft guilds, and guilds of professionals, which were relatively important in German lands as far back as the 1100s, sought to control prices and standards of manufactures and also to exert influence on the provincial—or national, if there was one—ruler and legislature. But the waves of competition brought by capitalism had weakened them, and Napoleon had banned them throughout his empire, so their influence was at least diminished in the modern economies of the 19th century. Germany reached a turning point when in 1871 Otto von Bismarck completed the unification of the German states under Kaiser Wilhelm's Prussia, the states having lost their unification under the Austrian Empire in 1866. The historian Ulrich Nocken dates German corporatism from 1871, while Werner Abelshauser puts 1879 as "the birth-point of the modern system of corporatist interest mediation."[14] Germany's emerging modern economy went corporatist to some extent. Employer associations, called "chambers" of commerce and of industry, arose, which served to lobby, set wage norms, and agree on prices. Industrial unions, mostly small, arose too, though they were weak (especially from the enactment of anti-socialist laws in 1879 until their repeal in 1890) compared to the German unions in World War I and post-World War II. The employer confederations and to a small degree the unions were players in the "wheeling and dealing" with the government that characterized the Wilhelmine economy. Bismarck, the Reich's chancellor from 1871 to 1890, failed in his efforts to set up a National Economic Council that could both veto and propose legislation in the parliament (Reichstag) like the Prussian Economic Council he set up to curb the Prussian Diet. But though he had to share power over economic matters with the Reichstag (unlike Hitler), the Iron Chancellor exerted great influence and later wielded his power to pave the way for financing the iron and steel industry in the 1880s and 1890s. Thus, the German Empire could be said to have developed a version of what historians have variously called a voluntary or consensual corporatism

14. See Nocken, "Corporatism and Pluralism in Modern German History"; Abelshauser, "The First Post-Liberal Nation" (p. 287).

in the late 19th century, in contrast to the mandatory and generally comprehensive corporatism of the 1930s. Germany's voluntary corporatism went on to embrace labor unions in the early Weimar years from 1919 to 1924, when the employer associations, caving in to the stronger labor unions of the war years, agreed to sit down with them as equals at the bargaining table.

Interwar corporatism's popular appeal is evident in the mass rallies and wide support it inspired, as well as in the direct reports of contemporary observers and the indirect responses of artists to the era's shifting mood. There was in many quarters a sense of a new path with new discoveries along the way. The impetus, all or most of it, behind the corporatist project is easily seen. It was the public's mounting rejection of both capitalism and socialism. Corporatism was the *third way* (*la terza via*). It was "neither right nor left," in the telling phrase of the historian Zeev Sternhell—neither the old right nor the old left, at any rate. (One could say—getting ahead of the story—that, well into the postwar period, a new corporatism was to become the medium of both a new right and a new left.) Thus corporatism could capture both the interest groups that felt ill-used by capitalism as well as the interest groups that feared socialism. The former grasped at corporatism as an escape from all the ills that modernism and the modern economy brought or threatened to bring: the perils from market competition, the instability of jobs, and the rudderlessness of industry. The latter saw corporatism as an alternative to the arbitrariness and dreariness of a socialist economy: the loss of their savings and the loss of their fun—the bars to building companies, and the difficulties of building careers. Corporatist politicians could argue that the corporatist structure would resolve the capitalist conflict between workers and owners and dissolve the socialist conflict between the proletariat and the rest by reengineering men and women to pursue the common good—the state would take care of their vestigial needs for pedestrian private goods. That the politicians could not first build a prototype corporatist economy for the populace to test under laboratory conditions against their actual capitalist economy gave them an excuse to scrap much of the capitalist structure and put in its place the new corporatist economy. Ridding the country of the capitalist economy was their primary objective; fine tuning the corporatist economy for best results was secondary. That the world economy was in crisis in 1929, with the Great Depression looming ahead, made it all the easier to portray the existing capitalist economies as systems to be jettisoned as quickly as possible. Finally, the politicians could boast that they were taking action, which the legislatures, in a stalemate between those who would remake their capitalism and those who would step up their socialism, were unable to do. The politicians, once in power, could be seen as *doing* something—not simply standing idly by with the sole justification that they were not making things worse. In a string of countries with elements of corporatism, the populace was thrilled at the prospect of a new start.

Corporatism did not stop at Italy and Germany. With the 1936 coup, General Francisco Franco ended the socialism of the Spanish Republic, although corporatist thought in Spain never became as pervasive and the corporatist superstructure never as vast as in Italy. Portugal's Antonio Salazar, a professor of economic sciences at Coimbra and an admirer of the author Charles Maurras and Leo XIII, drew on corporatist ideas in his presidency between 1932 and 1968. (The experiment was of great interest in France.) Austria was next in 1934 when Engelbert Dolfuss, on becoming chancellor, adopted some of the corporatist doctrine of Monsignor Ignaz Seipel. Corporatism came to Ireland in 1937, where it was championed by anti-capitalist parties such as Sinn Féin and supported by the Church.

What of France? Early in the century the salons of Paris were full of militant intellectuals with visions of a fusion of socialism that would end individualism and democracy—Maurice Barres, Georges Sorel, and Charles Maurras among them. Yet France did not adopt in the interwar years the Italo-German corporatist apparatus introduced by Mussolini and Hitler. But when German soldiers marched into Paris in 1940, the Vichy regime they installed in the summer of 1941 quickly established a system of economic planning in the corporatist spirit. Less than half a decade later, Vichy was out, but General Charles de Gaulle's 1944–1946 government introduced the *plan indicatif* in 1946, and the Fourth Republic of 1946–1958 adopted Five-Year Plans, taking a leaf from the Four-Year Plans in 1930s Italy and Germany. In this way the government tried to point French industry in the directions in which they wanted it to go.

In South America, elements of corporatism came to Brazil during the regime of Getúlio Vargas, especially the dictatorship of 1937–1945. The labor law was taken verbatim from Italy's law, cartels were set up to control key products, and the government sought to steer industrialization. (Yet the mild-mannered Vargas, like Salazar, suppressed the Fascist and Nazi parties. He was also the undoing of Plínio Salgado's radical Catholic party Acao

Integralista Brasileira.[15]) Corporatism of another color came to Argentina in the first presidency of Juan Perón, 1943–1955. Industrial labor unions became the backbone of the Peronist party in its sweeping interventions in industry and agriculture.

In Asia, Japan's large vertical monopolies, called *zaibatsu,* typically controlled by a single extended family, became so prominent after World War I (even though they emerged in the Meiji period in the last decades of the 19th century) that they were necessarily in close contact with the central government. A corporatist arrangement resulted, as the imperial government did not keep them at arm's length or break them up. Korea fell into a corporatist structure with the end of Japan's rule in 1945, when the government awarded Japanese plants and other favors to a handful of Korean businesses in return for kickbacks.

As for the Anglo-Saxon countries, it would be an immense distortion to say that they too installed in the interwar years a corporatist system like that introduced by Italy and Germany. During the 1920s and 1930s, labor unions grew in power and size in America and Britain while they were being hobbled in Italy and Germany. The Americans continued the opposition begun by the Progressives while the Continent was busily creating cartels. The question is whether the American and British economies possessed a corporatist character more or less equivalent to that in Italy and Germany. America saw widespread governmental intervention in the economy after its horrendous slide from 1929 until 1933 into the Depression. Franklin Roosevelt was swept into the presidency, taking office in 1933, and a spate of New Deal legislation soon followed. In 1933 the National Recovery Act established the National Recovery Administration (NRA) to organize a team of leaders in each industry to set codes for prices and wages aimed at arresting their downward spiral, which Roosevelt believed had greatly amplified the downswing of employment. Joining was not compulsory, but reserving a Blue Eagle seal of approval to every company that complied with the code must have exerted social pressure on companies. (TV viewers can still see the seal in the first frame of the Marx Brothers movie *Duck Soup.*) Many commentators, including some

15. Salgado and his *Integralistas* wanted to abolish self-interest and put in its place pity, charity, and sympathy. Vargas needed them for a crackdown on the communists and the success of his 1937 coup establishing a single-party state, the Estado Novo. Once in power, however, he had no more use for them. The *Integralistas,* in a midnight attack on the presidential palace, attempted a takeover, called the Pajama Putsch. The army arrived barely in time to put down the assault, and the *Integralistas* were finished.

widely considered to be thoughtful, viewed the NRA as a worrisome step toward the "collectivism" of a corporatist economy:

> The vital essence of the whole conception was that each codified industry would enjoy an approximate monopoly of the American market, and that its monopoly profits would enable it to pay high wages. But in order to protect the monopoly, competitors had to be excluded. Thus, in the more "advanced" codes, barriers were raised against new enterprises and new processes, and the whole establishment was then protected . . . by the power to lay an absolute embargo against any imports.[16]

To most observers, though, the New Deal interventionism did not match that on the corporatist Continent, where intervention was unbridled—where no legislation was required, legislatures were disempowered and no court had powers of judicial review. As it turned out, the NRA was ruled unconstitutional in a unanimous decision by the Supreme Court in *Schechter v. United States* in 1935. Roosevelt soon after enlarged the Court, making it more to his liking. The NRA was not resurrected, however, and the Court's reputation seemed to improve, not to decline.

With the New Deal, social thought in America—if not always social action—radically distanced itself from 19th-century liberal thought. A statement by the NRA's head, Donald Richberg, is arresting:

> There is no . . . return to the gold-plated anarchy that masqueraded as "rugged individualism." Unless industry is sufficiently socialized by its private owners and managers so that great essential industries are operated under public obligation appropriate to the public interest in them, the advance of political control over private industry is inevitable.[17]

Yet the bark was more fearsome than the bite. A range of unfamiliar initiatives, some verging on the radical, were taken by the government in the Depression years, which created new classes of jobs. For instance, the Civilian Conservation Corps employed photographers and documentarists to record the look and sound of rural America before it became nearly extinct. The Works Projects Administration undertook major construction initiatives at a time when the federal government had previously lent money for the railroads and state governments had built canals, but the massive federal dams, such as Hoover Dam, were not a familiar sight. These novel initiatives resembled some of

---

16. Walter Lippmann, *The Good Society* (p. 139). Lippmann, whose newspaper columns made him a household name, was immortalized (along with Schopenhauer) in the burlesque number "Zip" in Rodgers and Hart's *Pal Joey*. Hart clearly drew on his courses at Columbia.
17. Quoted in Schlesinger, *The Coming of the New Deal* (p. 115).

those undertaken in Germany. Yet these new frontiers could be regarded by the public as temporary measures rather than a shift from the capitalist culture to the corporatist culture. "Things have to change," Prince Don Fabrizio Salina says in Visconti's *The Leopard*, "so that they can stay the same."

The New Deal also wrought a range of changes supposed to be permanent. In response to the abuses and failures to disclose conflicts of interest in the banking industry and the securities business, as uncovered by the Pecora Commission, Congress enacted the Glass-Steagall Banking Act of 1933 to separate commercial from investment banking; the Securities Act of 1933 on filing false information in stock offerings; and the Securities Exchange Act of 1934, which created the Securities and Exchange Commission to regulate the stock exchanges. The National Labor Relations Board was created in 1935 to prevent and remedy "unfair labor practices by private sector employers and unions." Yet these measures too were hardly daggers at the heart of modern capitalism. The protections they provided potential investors and potential employees brought a considerable renewal of confidence in markets.

A big step in the corporatist direction was the establishment of rights of employees to organize or to join an already organized labor union in the National Labor Relations Act of 1935, the Wagner Act. Congress argued that "unequal bargaining power" between employees and employers leads to "economic instability" and that the refusal of companies to negotiate leads to strikes, both of which impede the flow of commerce. This was new: previous governments did not boost organized labor; they only broke up organized business—cartels and sprawling monopolies. The progressive movement, led by Theodore Roosevelt in the 1910s, was aimed at busting the monopolies. So was Woodrow Wilson. ("I am for big business, and I am against the trusts.") After the Teapot Dome scandal of 1923, a case of bribery of federal officials, the government tried harder to keep businesses at arm's length and not to award them increased legal protections. Relations between business and Washington were distant in the 1930s.

These changes and others did not make Americans feel there had been an abandonment of what they held to be the traditional social values of the country. One may view Franklin Roosevelt as having made accommodations to corporatism that served to preserve modern capitalism from wholesale replacement by corporatism. It is arguable that corporatism began to make deep inroads that threatened to kill modern capitalism only long after Roosevelt was gone.

What was the performance of the newly corporatist economies of continental Europe, particularly Italy and Germany, compared with the economies that remained in the category of modern capitalism, such as America and Britain? Italy's corporatist economy was operational only by the late 1920s, Hitler's by 1933, and World War II was breaking out by the end of the 1930s. So the time span offers few "natural experiments" from which to learn. One of these "experiments" was the onset of severe slump—Britain's in 1926 and the others' in 1929. Both Hitler and Roosevelt came to power in early 1933.

It is widely believed that Hitler wielded corporatist tools so as to pull Germany out of its slump in short order, while Roosevelt, burdened by the laissez-faire thinking in most of the country, was compelled to look on while the slump lengthened into a depression that would go on for the next eight years.[18] But the national output numbers in Germany and America tell a quite different story:

> By [1936] German GDP in real terms had recovered to roughly the same
> level it had stood at in [1929]. This was no doubt a rapid recovery. But
> it was not superior to the recovery achieved [over the same span] in the
> United States under a very different policy mix. Nor, in terms of the rate
> of growth, was it superior to the rebound from the Weimar Republic's
> first severe recession over the winter of 1926–27, when the twelve-month
> growth rate was higher than at any time during the Third Reich. It is pos-
> sible therefore to imagine a similarly rapid recovery taking place even
> under a very different policy regime. In this strict counterfactual sense,
> Nazi economic policy cannot claim to have "caused" the German eco-
> nomic recovery.[19]

Moreover, had Roosevelt and his predecessor, Herbert Hoover, expanded the building of capital facilities, that would not have made the economy fundamentally corporatist (or closer to being fundamentally corporatist) and it might have made the American economy recover faster—faster than the Germany economy recovered. ("Might have" because a government action intended to boost aggregate employment does not work with the classical certainty of a lever and fulcrum lifting a heavy weight.) A look at all four of

18. One historian of the period writes, "Three years after [Hitler's] accession to power the German economy was booming. Unemployment was reduced so drastically that labour short-ages became a problem." See Nicholls, "Hitler's Success and Weimar's Failure" (p. 156).

19. Adam Tooze, *The Wages of Destruction* (2007, p. 65). Tooze referred to 1928 and 1935 rather than the bracketed dates 1929 and 1936, but both versions are true, and it is the recovery from 1929, not 1928, in which we are interested.

the large economies recovering from a deep slump—Britain's in 1926 and the others' in 1929—shows that national output in all of them gradually began recovering within a half-dozen years or so.[20]

More striking, productivity—as measured by national output per man-hour or more sophisticated measures—leapt ahead in America at a record-breaking speed from 1930 to 1941, a speed even faster than in the previous decade, while productivity growth in Italy and Germany was far slower than America's in the 1930s and gained only moderately in the 1930s over the 1920s rate. According to one explanation, America achieved a surge of innovation over the 1920s, much of which involved the development of many new products and processes sparked by electrification. But the innovation had not completely diffused through much of the economy by the decade's end. As a result, the ground was laid for further diffusion of the new products and processes in the 1930s. This latter diffusion caused an immense number of workers to lose their jobs—a situation made worse by the over-valuation of the dollar and the resistance of overseas nations to increased American exports.

The growing disparity in productivity was at first no more than a thorn in Hitler's side. In his "table talk," he complained that German automakers in the 1930s had barely reduced the number of workers required to produce one car while Ford Motor Company had reduced the labor requirement to a small fraction of its former level. As historians later noted, this extraordinary productivity in America made it possible to produce the many thousands of tanks, trucks, and fighter planes that ultimately defeated Germany in World War II—not so much the bombing of cities. The surge of productivity that threatened America's modern capitalism for awhile in the 1930s eventually saved that modern capitalism from the threat of takeover by corporatist thought.[21]

The defeat of the Axis powers in World War II toppled the national governments and prepared a return of the old democratic political systems in Italy and Germany as well as in the nations they had occupied. In 1947, Italy produced its first constitution, which made provision for judicial review of policies carried out by the executive branch and laws enacted by the

---

20. To a varying degree, employment rose slower than output did, owing in part to productivity growth.

21. Hitler likely had in mind the years 1935–1941 when U.S. output rose at a torrid pace, punctuated by the 1937–1938 recession, while Germany hit a soft patch after the door was closed to trade in 1938. Hayek may have had that in mind when he wrote in *Road* that German producers would suffer from corporatism.

parliament. Germany followed in 1949 with a constitution that was closer in spirit to the Weimar constitution's goals of social democracy than to Bismarck's imperial constitution of 1871.

Some political parties of the radical right survived, and new ones emerged after the war. They echoed several fascist themes: "fears of decadence and decline, assertion of national and cultural identity, a threat by unassimilable foreigners to national identity, and the need for greater authority to deal with these problems."[22] But to gain enough votes to be represented significantly or at all, most of these parties had to espouse programs of the moderate right and to drape themselves in the obscure term "postfascist," whatever that meant. And not even the far right parties attacked democracy and the rule of law.

These gains on the *political* side presented Germany and Italy with an opportunity to reexamine the character and effectiveness of the national economies that had developed over the interwar years. Did these reappraisals lead European nations to retrench in their corporatism, in its institutions, policies, and thinking? Or did the subsequent decades see a growth of corporatism on the whole? What precepts of corporatism have been sloughed off and what new ones, if any, have been added?

Evolution of Corporatism after the War

In the popular mind, the influence of corporatist ideas waned after the war because the strength with which these ideas were held has since diminished. And the strength with which these ideas were held has diminished because the social tensions wrought by the interwar catastrophes—the wreckage caused by the Great War, the Great Inflation, and the Great Depression— have passed. It is also suggested that popular democracy is now so strong that people can obtain the protection at the ballot box that they once needed unions, lobbies, and a strong state to obtain. But social democracy and a corporatist economy are not contradictory ideas, so it is not obvious that they could not coexist. A small number of serious economists in Europe argued in the 1960s or 1970s that their countries did not understand the continuing damage they suffered from a failure to keep enterprise relatively free— Herbert Giersch in Germany, Raymond Barre in France, and in Italy, Luigi Einaudi and Paolo Sylos-Labini. Yet there was little systematic research into corporatism in the second half of the 20th century.

22. Robert Paxton, *The Anatomy of Fascism* (p. 186).

Did Germany and Italy in the decades after World War II show evidence by any of the measures suggested here of shedding their corporatism and developing further modern institutions, policies, and cultures? Or evidence of keeping or renewing or even intensifying their corporatism? And what about Britain and France? And America? These questions have received little study.

The Western European continent in general and Germany in particular made in the early years after the war a number of economic reforms in the direction of laissez-faire, or neo-liberalism—quite a change from interwar corporatist policy. Continental economies became vastly more open to foreign trade (first, bilateral trade, or barter, then multilateral trade). Later they opened themselves to capital outflows, thus denying their governments the power to imprison private capital within their borders. And finally they permitted financial companies and businesses to compete across borders and move headquarters. (Much of the organization of all this took place at the European Economic Commission, established when West Germany, France, Italy, and the Benelux countries founded the European Union.)

In Germany, a sharp turn in policy was prophesied with the announced Economic Reform of 1948 under Economics Minister Ludwig Erhard. It declared that neo-liberal principles opposite to those of the corporatist model were to be embodied in the "social market economy" of the Federal Republic created in 1949. In his 1957 book *Wohlstand für Alle,* titled *Prosperity through Competition* in the English translation, Erhard credits the near-doubling of West Germany's national product between 1949 and 1956 to the rebirth of competition in the economy and the restoration of confidence that inflation would not rob lenders of their gains. Erhard believed that the nation gained by rejecting the corporatist tendency to dispense with individual incentives and rejecting also the socialist tendency to think of the distribution of wealth more than of the level to which productivity might bring it.

Erhard's analysis suggests, cleverly or unconsciously, that when in 1949 German output regained its last fully-peacetime level of 1936, there was no more damaged capital left to restore, so all of the subsequent doubling of output is to be attributed to increased competition and greater confidence than existed in the Hitler years—and the new investments and productivity gains that resulted. Never mind the obvious omission that in fact there may have been capital structures, such as rail lines and factories, still needing repairs, so that huge output gains were a certainty for more years to come—increased competition or not. The more important omission deluded all of Europe into believing they had stumbled onto a road taking them to Rostow's "sustained growth" forever. It was not understood that productivity on the Continent was shooting up in large part because companies could cheaply boost productivity and profits by identifying, adapting, and adopting the new goods and methods of production that had been developed and embraced in America and to a lesser extent Britain and a handful of other non-Continental nations in the 1920s and 1930s but which had not been adopted on the Continent owing to its upheavals and the lurch under corporatism toward closed economies. For this brilliant "catch-up" growth, neo-liberal competition and confidence were not sufficient: there had to be bountiful low-hanging fruit across the Atlantic for the taking.[23]

Was corporatism put back in place after the bricks and railway ties were restored? After 1949? If, at this point, we were playing statisticians seeking to measure the degree of corporatism's return, we would need a checklist of measures, yearly or decadal, of the force of corporatism, such as its effects on policies. These measures include state interventions in *production*: the volume of regulation (statutes and rulings), bureaucratic "red tape" (permits, etc.), limits on entry in industries and professions, "industrial policy," and tax collection. (Socialism, it may be noted, cares more about how things are made than what things are made.) Another set of measures capture the diversion or control of *income*: subsidized social insurance, "coordination" of wage determination by industries and unions, the depression of share prices viewed as evidence of the state's overriding of shareowners' property rights, and the prevalence of zombie companies impeded from selling or scrapping. High employment in the public sector is another measure, since intervention in the private sector requires personnel to conduct it. There are quantifiable measures of the strength of *values*—desires and beliefs—allied with or opposed to corporatist thought. (Several of these measures of corporatism's force are used to test the claims made on behalf of corporatism in the next two chapters.)

We are playing historians in this chapter, though, so we focus on significant events: the high points—or low points. Two developments suggest that

---

23. The German results do not prove that competition is necessary either. Spain provides an intriguing case. Though notorious for an economic system and economic policies that were considered disadvantageous by a range of economic opinion, Spain nevertheless posted phenomenally rapid growth both in real domestic product per person employed and in real hourly earning in manufacturing consistently over the period 1960 to 1980—much faster than the German growth.

corporatism did not have to wait very long for its comeback. Amid a crisis precipitated by the "Korea boom" in Germany, Abelshauser writes, "influential sections of German industry [began] reformation of [the] state corporatist system of the interwar period" (ibid., p. 308). The cooperation between various employer associations that reemerged in the early 1950s reminded one scholar of the "well-proven German tradition . . . which survived the end of the Nazi economy and the . . . Reform of 1948 virtually unbroken."[24]

The other development was the shift of power between capital and labor within the corporatist framework. From one perspective, corporatism results in a merger of government with the business sector, so that much of business activity is decided through negotiation with the government rather than through the market, though much of that activity is nevertheless influenced by the market. But that leaves open how much of a connection to the government organized labor would have. By the end of the 1960s Europe had greatly increased the voice of labor—making the "tripartism" of the classic corporatist doctrine into a reality replacing the earlier "bipartism."

One aspect of labor's new power was its seats on the supervisory board of directors of the large companies. This was not considered of any great moment in Germany, where the socialist hostility to big business had never completely died out. It went further, however, in the 1990s, when the labor unions managed to get a seat on the investment committee. This time, Germans blanched. There were fears that this change might block profitable investments or block efforts of companies to make reforms in order to survive—and some jobs to survive with them. But the economists need not have worried. It was disclosed in 2005 that Volkswagen, the German auto maker, had been paying bribes to union officials for over a decade.

The Economics Ministry in 1967 made tripartism explicit, undertaking a program of Concerted Action that brought labor, capital, and the government to the bargaining table. Although this formal tripartism lasted only 10 years, *informal* trilateralism has continued with the cooperation of "liberal" corporatists on both the union and the employer side. In these same years Italy was developing its own trilateral structures. It was at this time that the term *Tavola di concertazione* came into use in Italy to refer to the practice of formal consultation among labor, capital, and government. But was this postwar trilateralism on the Continent all "sound and fury," or did it have influence?

---

24. H. Adamsen, quoted in the useful survey by Berghahn, "Corporatism in Germany in Historical Perspective" (p. 117).

Trilateralism has had its good moments. The Wassenaar Agreement, reached in 1982 by organized labor and employer organizations amidst the European slump of that time, inaugurated a new era of wage moderation and appeared to create some jobs in the Netherlands. But it is not clear that either result has been lasting. The Organisation for Economic Co-operation and Development (OECD) tabulates national data for the member countries. Those data show that, two decades later, in 2004, the Dutch unemployment rate was in the middle of those for the OECD nations—between the British and the American rates—and hours worked per employee near the bottom. Thus a permanent influence on the labor market is not discernible with the naked eye. On the other hand, under the coaxing of Chancellor Gerhard Schröder of the Social Democratic Party, Germany negotiated a series of measures in 2003, called Agenda 2010, to cut wage costs and increase the "flexibility" of the nation's labor market. The reduction of labor costs in the business sector has lasted the decade and is credited with much of the German export boom of recent years. Yet, today, the labor market statistics in Germany are not seen as outstanding. The German unemployment rate in recent years has been typical of European rates if the high rates in crisis-torn Italy and Spain are set aside, and hours worked per employee is only a little higher than in Holland and Norway. (Unemployment may nevertheless be lower than it otherwise would be.) However, the influence of corporatism, embodied formally or informally, could reach far beyond wage setting, as the discussion above has tried to make clear.

It might be guessed that the graduation to tripartism and, more broadly, the idea that nothing important may be done without the "social partners" on board, were harbingers of a new springtime for corporatism in Germany and Italy—and perhaps in much or all of continental Europe too. What, then, do some of the corporatist statistics proposed in the previous pages show? There are data on the rise of the public sector in several countries over the course of the postwar decades. And there are census data from interwar Germany. The public sector in Germany employed 9 percent of all employees in 1933, and the number rose to 12 percent in 1938, owing to an increase in the armed forces. In 1960, this statistic stood at 8 percent. But it grew to virtually 15 percent in 1980–1981 (OECD 1983, table 2.13). It may be significant that the size of the public sector grew to be even larger than in the peacetime years of the 1930s corporatist economy. Another striking corporatist statistic is the rise of total government outlays—for consumption-type goods and services and for purchases of capital (plant, equipment, etc.)—over the same span from 32½ percent of the gross domestic product (GDP) to 49 percent in 1981 (OECD 1983, table 6.5). Italy's public sector employment statistic went from 9 percent to the German level of 15 percent; and the total government outlays statistic went from 30 percent to 51 percent.[25] The German figures were very nearly peaks. In 2006, before the onset of the huge downswing, Germany's public sector employment statistic was at 12 percent, and its total government outlays stood at 45½ percent. In Italy, the size of the government by either measure reached new peaks in the early 1990s. By 2006, though, the public sector employment statistic was again around 15 percent, and the government outlays statistic was back at 49 percent. In the Western world, at any rate, these measures indicate unprecedented levels of government involvement and lend weight to the hypothesis that corporatism on the Continent, far from fading, actually grew more influential. We are curious, though, whether these countries grew to be more corporatist than some comparator countries.

France's corporatism dates back in some respects to the time of Jean-Baptiste Colbert, finance minister of Louis XIV. Yet in the present era, judged by how they score on various measures of corporatism, France is not easily distinguished from Italy (and some other European nations). France's public sector employment also grew—from a jumping-off point of 13 percent—and reached 16 percent in 1981, and an astonishing 22 percent in 2006. France's total government outlay statistic also started higher, reaching Italy's 49 percent level in 1980 and going ahead to 52½ percent in 2006.

How do these three countries compare by another measure of corporatism, bureaucratic "red tape"? In this respect, France tied Italy in exceeding all the others according to a 1999 survey. Germany had less red tape but markedly more than Britain and the United States.[26]

French and Italian labor relations continue to look conflictual to foreign observers, while the unions complain that they do not have the power that the public imagines. A spate of "boss-napping" broke out in France during

25. Over that same span, Germany's government *consumption*-type expenditure, that is, purchases of good and services, rose from about 13½ percent of GDP to about 20½ percent. And social security outlays (benefits under old-age, sickness, and family allowance programs, plus social assistance) rose from 12½ percent to 17 percent (OECD 1983, tables 6.2 and 6.3). Italy's employment statistic started higher, at 9 percent, and its government expenditure statistic started lower, at 10 percent, but both statistics ended precisely at Germany's levels in 1981.

26. The red tape estimates were published in *The Economist,* July 1999. The scores were United Kingdom, 0.5; United States, 1.3; Netherlands, 1.4; Sweden, 1.8; Spain, 1.8; Germany, 2.1; Belgium, 2.6; France, 2.7; and Italy, 2.7.

2008–2009, and general strikes in France and to a lesser degree Italy—the awesome "manifestations"—sometimes paralyze the economy. Certainly in its outspoken rhetoric there was no country in Europe more hostile than France to "market society" and more alienated from business life.

Looking back at the history of these three countries since the war, the most influential development in corporatism appears to be the rise of labor unions to positions of political power verging on equality with business interests. Labor power did not substitute for company, or "corporate," power. (In product markets, it effectively added to the total amount of monopoly.) The concept gained strength that workers and investors could exert myriad and profound influence on the behavior and direction of the economy—generally to protect their vested interests—by mobilizing labor unions, companies, and business federations to exert influence through nonmarket channels. A huge increase in the activity of the public sector and a thicket of regulations has resulted. The question at this point is the extent to which and the ways by which this new system and accompanying culture, in narrowing the possibilities of change, of innovation, has choked off the possibility of the deeper rewards of business life in return for stability and the status quo.

In Britain, the experience with corporatism was comparable to that of France until a turnaround in the early 1980s. The share of total jobs located in the public sector by 1960—at about 15 percent—was already the highest in Europe and skyrocketed to the extraordinary level of about 23 percent by 1981. Britain's total government outlays statistic was at the Italian and German level in 1960 and rose to a level, 47 percent, just below the level in those two countries. But by 2005 it had fallen to 45 percent, well below Italy's 48 percent and still under Germany's 47 percent. What happened in the 1980s is becoming better known in recent years. The debate about the economy that polarized Britain for a decade was not over its "socialism." There cannot have been any other advanced economy with as small a share of enterprise output produced by state-owned enterprises (SOEs), which hardly budged from 1.3 percent from the early postwar years to the present. The debate was over corporatism, a debate that began in 1979 when Margaret Thatcher became prime minister.

> It is hard to recall now what a shock Mrs Thatcher's election in 1979 brought to employers as well as to trade unions. Her bracing dose of free markets and deregulation [led to] the most tumultuous period in Britain's postwar history. . . .

The Confederation of British Industry was marginalized by the Thatcher government and many of its members reacted with horror as high interest rates and a strong pound deepened the early 1980s recession and drove many manufacturing businesses to the wall. But as the economic medicine and tough trade union laws began to work, attitudes softened. Sir James Cleminson, who got on well with Mrs Thatcher, did much to dispel the CBI's reputation as a bunch of "moaning Minnies" always seeking government help. "Business is now recognizing that four-fifths of the things it wants done it can do for itself; it is saying that all we can expect government to do is clear the path," he said in 1985. That attitude largely survives today.[27]

After this period, Britain slowly turned the corner in the corporatist standings, leaving France in top place followed by Italy. Among countries in the G7, Britain was estimated in 1999 to have by far the lowest amount of red tape impeding business.

Last, we come to the corporatist influence in America. By 1960, despite the postwar cutbacks in the standing army, public sector *employment* as a share of the labor force was already higher than Britain's at that time—thus the highest in the G7. By 1980 the American level continued to exceed that in Germany, Italy, and France, though passed by Britain. In contrast, America's total government *outlays* as a share of GDP, which was in the middle of the pack, at 27.5 percent, in 1960, was the lowest in the group by 1980, standing at 35.5 percent. And, measured by red tape in 1999, the United States was well below the levels in Italy, Germany, and France.

The corporatist influence in the decade past must be judged to have increased. The Federal Register of Regulations has continued to rise steeply. Some of the new regulations, such as the Sarbanes-Oxley law, which holds chief executives legally responsible for the way in which the accounting of their corporations is presented, could be argued to have reduced the willingness of corporations to embark on novel projects shrouded in uncertainty.

The state's intrusion into resource allocation was most remarkable in the individual income tax code. The so-called Reagan tax cut legislation of 1981 abolished myriad tax "loopholes," thus bringing in billions of dollars of additional revenue, in return for cuts in the structure of tax rates—the marginal

---

27. Groom, "War Hero Who Became Captain of British Industry" (p. 7). The second sentence is from Groom, "Gloom and Boom" (p. 16). "Jimmy" Cleminson was an industrialist and later president of CBI from 1984 to 1986. Incidentally, fame came to him as a parachute captain at the battle of Arnhem. His exploits are a part of Richard Attenborough's 1977 film *A Bridge Too Far.*

tax rates in the tax brackets from lowest to highest. But loopholes and even rulings individualized to benefit particular persons or companies have mushroomed. The U.S. tax code runs to 16,000 pages. In contrast, the French have a tax code with only 1,900 pages.

A no less stunning development in America is the spectacular rise of litigation and the consequent fear of lawsuits. While Americans may not have as many unions to protect and defend them as they did in the 1930s, they now have access to rich legal resources and a vast court system with which to protect and defend themselves from being set back by others in the to-and-fro of society's pursuit of change and advance. The fear of being sued has noticeable consequences for individual initiative and judgment, and thus on efforts at innovation:

> [W]e have created a society paralyzed by legal fear. Doctors are paranoid.
> . . . Principals [are] paralyzed. Teachers don't even have authority to maintain order in the classroom. With no one in charge, the safe course is to avoid any possible risk. . . . A huge monument to the unknown plaintiff looms high above America, casting a dark shadow across our daily choices.[28]

It would be hard to argue, therefore, that corporatist influences in the American economy abated after World War II. It is easier to make the case that corporatist influences have intensified.

The conclusion to which this evidence points is that, generally speaking, corporatism gained or at least consolidated its influence in Europe over the decades, taken as a whole, since World War II. The drift in America may not be obvious to some, but there is evidence it has grown there too. Britain is an exception in having registered a decline of corporatism after a long rise until 1980. The major evolution in corporatism over the postwar decades was surely the rise of the labor unions to positions of power comparable to or at times exceeding that of business interests in some countries.

The concept that the market was never to be presumed right, that the voices of capital, labor, the professions, and other key groups could exert their influence through nonmarket channels such as lobbies, was a profound change. The big question not resolved in the 1930s was whether corporatism, in narrowing the market, removed or impaired the dynamism required for the pursuit of indigenous innovation.

---

28. The classic indictment is Howard, *The Death of Common Sense*. The quotation is from Howard's *The Collapse of the Common Good* (2001).

The New Corporatism

As seen above, the classic corporatism of the interwar years can be said to have survived to a degree in several countries in the past half-century. Although corporatism sooner or later allowed organized labor to become a social partner on a par with organized business in most economies, it was still *classic corporatism*: Classic corporatism widens government powers (relative to that under 18th-century liberalism) in order to forge a *state-led* economy. This corporatism, it will be recalled, refers to a set of aims: *directedness* rather than disorder, *solidarity* rather than individualism, and *social responsibility* rather than anti-social behavior. After the war this basic corporatism added to the agenda *codetermination* instead of owner-control and *stakeholderism* instead of companies maximizing the income to be divided between owners and workers. These ideas radically widened what the state may grant to interest groups—and where it may take the economy—in the name of the national interest. Now, time has added new dimensions to corporatism.

A new kind of corporatism has developed in recent decades. What we may call the *new corporatism* either reverses the flow of power or provides a two-way flow. The state is less a guide choosing the heading than a pilot paid by the passengers to take them where they ask. Some of the power has shifted to large-wealth owners and holders of powerful positions in business. (Even if all of them were mere atoms, the government might heed what the bond market and other markets have to say.) The state may retain some of the scope found in classic corporatism, though. It still takes it upon itself to act when society or a large part of it is in difficulty or faces the prospect of it.

The new corporatism also goes beyond the groups of classical corporatism—the groups that may bargain collectively and the groups yoked together in "concerted action"—by embracing the idea of a social compact: every person in a society is a signatory to an implicit contract with the others—its terms understood by all—and, according to this contract, no person may be harmed by others without receiving compensation.[29] This populist corporatism had vast consequences. Where in the past a group of lawyers,

---

29. Something like this emerged in economics during the 1970s when it became fashionable to suppose that the entire workforce of the country was in a lifetime implicit contract with existing employers. In every community the employers were seen as providing insurance to their employees in the event of poor business prospects warranting layoffs, and banks in the community provided employers insurance when conditions warranted some rationing of credit. This new wave of theorizing made it seem as though the feudal economy, with its lifetime employment and "relational banking" was the economic optimum after all, not laissez-faire with all its rigors—its cold showers and thin gruel.

pharmacists, or garment workers might have been granted the status of a *corporazione* with which to exert monopoly power, now all sorts of groups can demand a voice, request powers to protect themselves, or seek to be protected by the state. This new element of corporatism goes beyond the classic demand for state control that improves the conditions of society—national growth through state direction and industrial peace through "concertation" and co-determination—to the demand that the course of development at no time set back some while propelling the rest. The new thinking sees the state as undertaking to protect everyone from everyone else—or as close to it as is practicable. Social protection for all is the motto of the new corporatism.

A panoply of new roles has been given to the state. The state may compensate those hit domestically by a range of developments, from foreign competition to storm damage. Government grants of unlimited scope may be made to regions and cities, even if their latent function (in Robert Merton's term) is to dispense patronage in return for support, political or financial. Lobbyists are welcome to submit requests for legislation, regulations, and interpretative rulings, especially if they come with bribes. Regulations of industries are instituted, aimed at shielding companies or workforces from competition. Bans spare influential communities from new airports, landfills, and the rest. Shakedowns of companies by communities, nonprofits, or governments extract donations or other accommodations. Class action suits add to the diversion of income from earners to those receiving compensation or indemnification. (Other features of the new corporatism are mentioned in Chapter 10.) The result was not necessarily an extremely large government, but it was in important ways unlimited government.

The new corporatist economy, then, is pervaded by fears of holdups by the government, by stakeholders, by organized labor, and by an ocean of persons and companies ready to litigate. It is a familiar point that in economies where labor and capital are protected from having to compete, thus frozen indefinitely in companies producing the same old products, investment activity is generally meager. It is also familiar that the powers in a corporatist society to threaten existing companies can weigh heavily on the prospects for profit at affected companies and thus on their share prices, and thus depress the economy's investment activity and employment levels.[30] It needs to be

---

30. That high share prices usually lead to high investment activity and thus high employment—they induce the investment or they reflect impulses to invest inside the companies—is shown in Phelps, "Behind This Structural Boom" (1999).

added that if would-be innovators fear to embark on novel undertakings for fear of a feeding frenzy of pressure groups demanding a cut of any potential resultant innovation and profit, it becomes impossible for ordinary people to thrive and flourish. Indeed, the whole economy may gradually become obsolete and fall into a mounting depression.

Corporatism's Dark Side

The next two chapters undertake some economic research to test the central claims made on behalf of corporatist economies. But some of the false claims of corporatism can be detected with no economics at all, only a little common knowledge.

The corporatist system was idealized as having dispensed with individualism and competition, which were demonized as ugly and inhuman. But the system merely transplanted individualism from the market to the state, where individuals would elbow their way to increased power. The system would end competition among producers for the many buyers in the markets. But it replaced that with the insidious competition of producers and professionals for a share of government contracts and a place in government-sponsored enterprises—for a single, all-powerful buyer. The system was idealized as having put an end to the conflict between capital and labor, but in the end the postwar systems simply conferred large monopoly power to unions as well as large employers, thus licensing both of them to contract output. The system was portrayed as restoring the balance between materialism and high culture, but the system then undermined most of the great literature and art because they were individualistic. The system was extolled as scientific in contrast to the chaos of the modern system it replaced. But the system would replace uncertainty about what the myriad would-be innovators were up to with uncertainty about the outcome of the *state's* attempts at innovation. That might create more uncertainty than before. The corporatists demonized the power that the modern economy conferred on the industrial mogul or financial speculator who became rich, portraying their new system as a servant of society as a whole. But their system concentrated far greater power in the hands of *political* moguls and their financial backers.

It is understandable that, under early capitalism, market forces caused participants to feel they are like sheep being driven by snows, floods, and the rest. (The saving grace of the market in this respect is that it drove people to do voluntarily what needed to be done for a better allocation of resources.) The times of mercantile capitalism may not have been very happy for that reason. But with the advent of *modern* societies, participants in the economy were able for the first time on a mass scale to conceive and look for new ways of producing and new products to produce, thus to make new careers. Individual opportunity meant opportunities for mental stimulation, engaging work, and rewarding lives of challenge and personal development. Corporatism suppressed this individual opportunity, forcing participants to gain permissions to enter an industry and possibly to curry favor to enter an industry or win business. Thus it was an oppressive system. The idea of corporatism inspired systems of varying totalitarianism (to use Mussolini's own term) that turned most participants back into sheep.

CHAPTER SEVEN

Weighing the Rivals on Their Terms

The hen is the wisest of all the animal creation because she never cackles until after the egg has been laid.

ABRAHAM LINCOLN

H OW WELL HAVE THE CHALLENGERS to modern capitalism—corporatism and socialism—done? As the above narrative suggests, Bismarck's Germany, which had elements of corporatism, did well, though whether much of that success was owed to corporatism would be hard to say. The corporatist economies of Mussolini and Hitler rebounded from national crises no better than the American and British economies did. But what about the new corporatism or the new socialism of the mid-1960s to the present? We are now poised to study their consequences and influences over the past half century.

This chapter will explore whether the neo-corporatist and neo-socialist economies have performed as claimed. In the chapters that follow, this book will go on to argue in favor of a criterion for judging the performance of an economy that is radically different from corporatist and socialist thought. But first it ought to show how socialist economies failed to achieve socialist goals, and how corporatist economies failed to deliver corporatist benefits.

Socialism—Claims and Evidence

Socialism means many things but at its core is social ownership of a range of enterprises: economies with wider state ownership are generally seen as more socialist than those with markedly narrower state ownership. In the most basic sort of socialism, state-owned enterprises (SOEs in the jargon) are largely confined to health care, education, and some insurance industries, while highly socialist economies extend state ownership more widely.

So we would like data with which to test the socialist belief that state ownership boosts economic performance. Fortunately, evidence on the scale of state enterprise started to be available two decades ago. Estimates of the share of total domestic output (GDP) produced by SOEs were published in a 1995 study by the World Bank, *Bureaucrats in Business*. Among the advanced economies—our focus here—the percentage share of GDP in 1986–1991 produced by the SOEs was 10.0 percent in France, 7.1 percent in Germany, 5.6 percent in Italy, 4.0 percent in Spain, 3.0 percent in the United Kingdom—down from 5.9 percent pre-Thatcher—and 1.0 percent in America. (The data exist for two smaller countries, Austria (13.9 percent) and Portugal (14.2 percent).) A wider coverage of countries was provided by Branko Milanović in a 1989 book *Liberalization and Entrepreneurship*, and some further countries were added by using the SOEs' share of total *employment*, rather than output. In these calculations, covering 1978–1983, France is again at the top, now followed closely by Italy and Austria; next Sweden and Finland; then Germany and the United Kingdom (before Thatcher shrank state ownership in the next decade); next Norway and Canada; then Australia and Denmark; and lastly Spain, Holland, and America. See Table 7.1 for the full data.

Most proponents of a relatively socialist organization of economies—the so-called advanced ones, whether or not the low- or middle-income ones—stress the *availability* and *steadiness* of work they believe it provides. As for the availability of work, they see the socialist enterprise as more willing to hire and retain marginal workers at risk of chronic joblessness than capitalist enterprises are; also more willing to retain workers in the face of downswings, thus shaving off troughs in the employment cycle. Yet these two points, even if valid, are not conclusive, since new enterprise formation in modern capitalism may generate as many new jobs as are lost by established enterprises during slumps.

Belief that the more socialist economies were superior at job creation gained credence in the shining period from the mid-1950s to the mid-1970s. Using the "standardized" unemployment rates calculated by the OECD, we see that the American rate had an average level of 4.4 percent from 1960 to 1973. The rates in the European countries widely considered relatively socialist were at a spectacularly low level in that period: 0.8 percent in Germany, 1.3 percent in Norway, 1.8 percent in France, and 1.9 percent in Sweden. (The European Economic Community as a whole had an average unemployment level of 2.6 percent in that period.) But that impression was dispelled in subsequent decades. By the mid-1980s unemployment rates were markedly higher in the entire West. Europe had largely run out of the remaining new products and processes it could "transfer" from the rest of the world, so labor supply and business investment both retracted. America suffered a milder retraction

TABLE 7.1 Importance of Public Corporations and
State Sector in Some OECD Countries

Country*	In terms of output (%)	In terms of employment (%)
High share (above 15%)		
France (1982)	16.5	14.6
Moderate share (10–15%)		
Austria (1978–1979)	14.5	13.0
Italy (1982)	14.0	15.0
France (1979)	13.0	10.3
New Zealand (1987)	12.0	n.a.
France (1973)	11.7	9.3
Turkey (1985)	11.2	20.0
United Kingdom (1978)	11.1	8.2
West Germany (1982)	10.7	7.8
United Kingdom (1983)	10.7	7.0
West Germany (1977)	10.3	7.9
United Kingdom (1972)	10.2	7.8
Sweden	n.a.	10.5
Finland	n.a.	10.0
Low share (5–10%)		
Portugal (1976)	9.7	n.a.
Australia (1978–1979)	9.4	4.0
Denmark (1974)	6.3	5.0
Greece (1979)	6.1	n.a.
Norway	n.a.	6.0
Canada	n.a.	5.0
Negligible share (below 5%)		
Spain (1979)	4.1	n.a.
Netherlands (1971–1973)	3.6	8.0
United States (1983)	1.3	1.8

Source: Milanović, *Liberalization and Entrepreneurship* (1989).
Notes: Excludes government services proper (i.e., includes only state-owned enterprises in commercial activities). n.a., not available.
*Ordered according to share in output (when available).

from a different cause—a sharp drop of innovation from a high level. (Chapters 9 and 10 tell that story.) By 1995, the lowest unemployment rates among the larger countries were 5.6 percent in America, 6.5 in Holland, 7.0 in the United Kingdom (in 1997), and 8.2 in Germany. The *highest* joblessness was in Spain (22 percent), Italy (11.7), and France (10.3). Here too, the more socialist economies *cannot* be said to have demonstrated a widespread tendency to lower unemployment. And they may very well tend to have higher unemployment but act to contain that tendency through aggressive interventions. Most of the relatively socialist economies—Germany, Finland, France, and Sweden—have huge state programs aimed at reducing unemployment, thus masking to a degree their tendency to high unemployment. In contrast, most of the least socialist countries—namely, the United States, the United Kingdom, Canada, Australia, and Norway—make such interventionist expenditures least often. (See OECD, *Employment Outlook*, 2005.)

Socialism has traditionally stood for high participation in the labor force, not just low unemployment among those participating. Yet labor force participation rates, expressed in percentage of the working-age population, do not show a connection between socialism and participation. In 1995, as estimated in the OECD *Economic Outlook* for June 2000, the participation rates among the "major countries" were 76.9 percent in the United States, 75.8 in Canada, 75.3 in the United Kingdom, 71.2 in Germany, 66.7 in France, and 57.4 in Italy. (Denmark at 80.2 percent and Holland at 77.7 are two other countries low in state ownership and high in participation.) Hence, relatively socialist economies *cannot* be said to show a tendency toward high labor force participation. It appears pretty safe to infer just the opposite. (There are just two anomalies: Austria had a high 76.5 percent participation despite a high state ownership. Spain, which Milanović did not cover, had an abysmally low participation rate of 61.5 percent despite its dislike of state ownership.)

The disappointing performance in both unemployment and participation is a striking failing of European socialism in view of the oft-expressed dedication of most socialists to economic inclusion—the absorption of working-age people into the mainstream economy at terms allowing them the normal sorts of participation in society. Some socialist leaders have complained that they are up against the obstacles posed by "multiculturalism," though the continental European nations ranking high in socialism are not unique in facing cultural, ethnic, and racial diversity—there is surely more diversity in America. The source of this failing may be that the horror of business that fueled the socialist movement also fuels low labor force participation. It may also be that participation is apt to be low—and unemployment high— among countries in which the workplace is very bureaucratic—in which post office jobs at post office wages typify existing work. In such countries, large numbers of working-age people prefer to be occupied at home or in what is known as the informal sector, or underground economy. Rainer Werner Fassbinder's movie *The Marriage of Maria Braun* immortalized a period when German women entered the economy in the last years of World War II and even after, but German socialism could not stop them from going back as soon as they could afford it to *kinder, küche, kirche* (children, kitchen, church).

Another possible explanation for the disappointing performance in unemployment and participation of some economies is that the households in those countries exhibit high levels of household saving in relation to household disposable income. Among the large economies in the OECD in the early 2000s, the standout savers were Belgium, France, Italy, and Spain (*Economic Outlook* 2011); and the ones ranking the lowest in labor force participation were Italy, France, Belgium, and Spain. The lowest savers were the United States, Canada, and the United Kingdom; and highest in participation were Canada, Germany, the United Kingdom, and the United States. The most direct causal link is from high saving to high wealth to high demand for leisure, and late entry and early retirement from the labor force. (Wealth data are available only for the G7 nations.) An indirect link runs from wealth to the wherewithal for a welfare state that weakens incentives to work by offering so many things free of charge. (Mario Draghi, president of the European Central Bank, quotes the late Rudi Dornbusch as saying, "the Europeans are so rich they can afford to pay everybody for not working.")

Socialists' other claim of superiority on the employment front is that work is less precarious in a socialist economy. They could argue that work is steadier because there is less job change owing to less innovation. Most socialists, however, would prefer not to premise their argument for the superiority of socialism on an assumed lid it wisely puts on innovation. (It is imaginable that socialist economies innovate as much but do it better, setting higher hurdles for innovative projects at enterprises while compensating by undertaking projects of a longer term. But most observers of the more socialist economies see weak dynamism.) What admirers of a socialist economy argue is that, by its nature, it has key tools to moderate cyclical swings in employment that a capitalist economy lacks.

America in the 1930s gave the impression that it was lacking in just these kinds of tools. When its economy went into the steep downswing that was followed by the Great Depression, the government's monetary weapons were pinned down supporting the price of gold until the gold standard's demise in 1933. In any case, those weapons would not have been sufficient against structural forces moving labor away from building houses or farms and into making cars and other consumer durables. (The lesson was learned: In the 2008–2009 downswing, the world's monetary authorities did not sell their gold stocks to block a rise of gold prices.) The government had little fiscal weaponry with which to combat the unemployment arising. With no thought of taking over private industry, President Hoover, an engineer by training, resorted to massive construction projects to tame rivers and create dams for hydroelectric power. But some strain of conservatism held back the government from dotting the whole country with dikes and dams. The employment problem was finally thrown back on the modern capitalism on which the economy was built. In contrast, the central government of a socialist economy, when faced with a downswing, can compel SOEs to maintain or boost their investment expenditures—as if money were no object. This was the case with China in the aforementioned global recession, when it induced local governments to turn on the spigot of funds for increased local construction projects.

Yet the experience of recent decades does not bear out belief in the greater resistance of socialist economies to swings. The relatively socialist economies of continental Western Europe suffered an immense swing in employment (and other measures of economic activity) from the late 1970s to 1985—truly a Second Great Depression.[1] Yet the Europeans did not reach far into their arsenal of fiscal weapons, while the United States, faced with a similar downswing, however weaker or stronger it may have been, deployed fiscal weapons unknown in Hoover's time—higher investment tax credits and lower corporate profits tax rates—and fashioned some new ones—revenue-neutral cuts in marginal tax rates and increases in the earned income tax credit. (The monetary weapons at Paul Volcker's Federal Reserve were aimed at putting out the fires of inflation.) In the global downswing of 2008–2009, the more socialist economies were again more restrained in combating the slump. And it would be hard to decide which area suffered the wider downswing: the euro zone, which holds many of the more socialist economies, or the United States.

---

1. The earliest treatment of this episode is the 1988 monograph by Jean-Paul Fitoussi and Edmund Phelps, *The Slump in Europe.*

If there is a dimension in which the relatively socialist economies are still widely thought to have surpassed the others, it is in the measures taken to reduce *income inequality* and in the apparent effects of such inequality. While classical socialism meant full employment and less unequal wages, latter-day socialism has meant less unequal income. Some relatively socialist countries, namely France, Finland, and Sweden, as well as some not apparently socialist countries, namely Germany, Denmark, and Holland, have achieved reductions in inequality—say, between the bottom 30 percent and the top 30 percent—by instituting services free of user charges for all, thereby narrowing the inequalities in consumption levels.[2] Yet the relative narrowness of wage inequality in these countries has been the result not of redistribution by the state through spending and taxes, but the result of relatively low inequality to begin with: pre-tax incomes differ far less than in the Anglo-Saxon countries, for example. The Scandinavian nations are very homogeneous. Much of the remaining part of the explanation may be that there is less opportunity to innovate, thus to strike it rich. Various moral philosophers, from Immanuel Kant to John Rawls, opposed measures that would reduce inequality at a cost to everyone. But these qualifications miss the crucial point.

A deep decline of economic inclusion, particularly among less-qualified workers, swept over the Western economies in the 1980s—socialist, corporatist, and capitalist alike. Germany, France, Italy, and Sweden reacted strongly. In the first two, the *relative wage* of the *least-educated men* actually increased between the late 1970s and the mid-1990s; in the latter two, the relative wage slipped 1 or 2 percent. Holland, at the other extreme, apparently did not do enough, allowing the relative wage to fall 10.5 percent. In the United Kingdom and the United States the relative wage fell by 8 percent and 6 percent, respectively. It is striking, however, that the countries that pushed up the relative wage in the face of a strong headwind paid a stiff price—a far greater rise of unemployment among less-educated individuals over the 1980s than in the other advanced economies. The countries that settled for resisting most of the relative wage decline, Italy and Sweden and to some extent the United States, paid a much lower price. Holland suffered the smallest increase in the unemployment rate by far. What evidently happened is that France, led by a socialist party, and Germany, which refers to its "social market," used blunt instruments, such as statutes or labor union actions, to

---

2. The 2011 book by Vito Tanzi, *Government versus Markets*, provides expert discussion and helpful data.

force companies to pay higher wages to the poorly educated; Italy and Sweden, both relatively socialist-minded, used similar methods to resist a significant decline of the relative wage. These crude measures had the side effect of reducing the numbers of the least-educated that companies could afford to employ. The "catch" in the socialist progress on the wage front was a forced retreat on the employment front.[3]

Proponents of socialism widely think of the more socialist economy as more scientific, owing to the better organization of state enterprises and enterprises generally. It is also thought to have an education system that is better at supplying the middle and lower strata of society with the human capital they will need in the economy. If these claims are valid, we should expect the more socialist economies to exhibit higher levels of productivity—output per unit labor and output per basket of labor and capital, called total factor productivity (or multifactor productivity). In fact, some of the more socialist countries in Europe have been rocked by international studies evaluating their educational institutions far more poorly than imagined. But never mind. We may as well let the productivity data speak. What may be the first statistical study of the effects of socialism used cross-national data to estimate the relationship between the growth of output per worker and the share of national output produced by state enterprises.[4] A negative association was found. In short, a high SOE per unit of GDP hampers the rise of GDP. (That does not mean that even the best corporatist economies may never catch up to the leaders. It means that if they do catch up, it will take longer.)

There could be more here than meets the eye. It could be that high state ownership and low growth are both effects of a third influence—a heedlessness toward property rights or an outright antagonism toward private property with resulting fears of expropriation for any wealthy private investor

3. Phelps, "The Importance of Inclusion and the Power of Job Subsidies to Increase It" (2000/2, p. 86). See also figure 1 in that report. The article adds that "in the first half of the 1990s France and Germany again compressed low-end pay and again saw the steep rise in unemployment of low-skilled labor (see Figure 2)." The paper set out the case for an approach to raising low-end wages that is more employment friendly, namely a system of low-wage subsidies to be paid to employers for their ongoing employment of low-wage persons. In presenting this paper at the OECD Secretariat in Paris, I was going into the eye of the storm. Participants applauded the proposal except the U.S. delegation, which saw the proposal as endangering the Earned Income Tax Credit, which was designed primarily to encourage low-income mothers to earn some of their own support.

4. No statistical analysis was done, surprisingly, until the paper by Darius Palia and Edmund Phelps presented at the 1996 Villa Mondragone conference of Rome's Tor Vergata University. The conference volume, Paganetto and Phelps, *Finance, Research, Education and Growth*, came out in 2005.

brave enough to venture his or her capital. In such a country, SOE is better than no enterprise. That does not really alter the implications of the findings. Where a country opposes private ownership of enterprises—where it is socialist minded—it suffers poor economic performance.

Corporatism—Claims and Evidence

Classic corporatism, such as Mussolini's, sought to restructure the capitalist economy so as to speed economic growth—growth of productivity and of various national capabilities—far beyond the puny capacity of Continental capitalism. This meant more initiative in the public sector and more direction of the private sector—thus "ownership without control" for the owners. The quest for greater national growth and national power was to be subject to considerations of solidarity and, in particular, "social protection." That meant "concertation" of the state with the "social partners," and, more broadly, subsidies for regions or industries. In an equivalent view of classic corporatism, the state is free to take whatever measures it chooses in the name of solidarity and protection, constrained only by the need to take steps aimed at restoring growth when growth has slowed too much and too long.

This system, in which, in principle, the state may intervene at its own discretion without any restraints, poses serious moral hazards; and insofar as politicians fall into these hazards, their misconduct becomes part of the workings of the system. A constitutional democracy might be able and willing to curb such intervention but may fail to do so. Even in a democracy, self-interested legislators are apt at times to use their votes, and agency heads their powers to award projects, to win the support of interest groups that can keep them in office. In this political process, "growth" may take a back seat or be altogether neglected—even if it continues to be paid lip service. And, with the politicians focused primarily on their own political support, "social protection" is not really the rule either. Politicians may also be so venal as to dispense patronage to regions, companies, and labor unions in exchange for money under the table—kickbacks. (In 1990s Italy, bribery became so rampant that Italians saw themselves living in *Tangentopoli*—Bribesvilles.)

The hazards of a corporatist system do not stop there. If only *insiders* are well-enough connected to become clients of the politicians, the system may operate to protect insiders *against outsiders*. The clients and cronies of the state have no need for contracts paid with scarce taxpayer money if their enterprises can be awarded monopoly power. The gain of the insiders is the loss of the outsiders, who may be unable to start a business, break into an industry, or have a rewarding career—whether or not "protected" with subsidies for medical care, food, and heat. This is the burden of extreme corporatism: the deprivations of some, few or many—deprivations of basic goods like careers—who are not morally compensated by the spoils of the advantaged, few or many.

To rate how well the more corporatist economies perform their mission we need criteria and evidence with which to judge which countries are relatively corporatist and, preferably, to judge the degree of corporatism. It makes sense to begin looking under a lamppost where there is plenty of light. The directiveness of the state in the economy is widely seen as measured by the sheer size of the government, but not every such measure is helpful. Though a highly corporatist economy would need armies of bureaucrats to direct it, a swollen public sector is not a safe measure of corporatism. In 1960, the United States had, among G7 nations, the highest share of total employment working in the government—15.7 percent. It may have been the most corporatist in capabilities, with all its soldiers and schoolteachers at the ready. But few, if any, would believe it was the most corporatist in spirit. And, in fact, the other countries were fast pulling up their capabilities. By 1980, the United Kingdom and Canada exceeded—and France, Germany, and Italy were near—America's 16.7 percent. Evidently, government employment levels do not differentiate the advanced economies. (See OECD, *Historical Statistics 1960–81*.)

A better measure of the state's reach is government purchases of all kinds (not just labor) plus subsidies encouraging certain things and transfer payments awarded to certain people. Government purchases and subsidies are a standard measure of the extent to which the government guides the use of resources in the economy; transfer payments may in some cases be part of a social bargain to pursue corporatist goals. On this broad measure, the high-income economies had come to differ enormously by 1995. At one end, Sweden stood at 65.2 percent of GDP (55.0 percent in 2005), France at 54.4 (53.3), Italy at 52.5 (48.1), Belgium at 52.3 (52.1), and Holland at 51.5 (44.8). At the other end, America stood at 37.1 percent (36.3 in 2005), Britain at 43.9 percent (44.1), and Spain at 44.4 (38.4). In the middle were Germany at 48.3 percent of GDP (46.8) and Canada at 47.3 (38.0).[5] Among

5. Tanzi, *Government versus Markets.*

the smaller countries, Finland was at 61.5 percent of GDP (50.1), Denmark at 59.3 (52.6), and Switzerland at 34.6 (35.0). But before we declare Sweden the most corporatist nation (and Belgium third-most) we had better widen our investigation.

Among the larger high-income economies, France, Spain, and Italy rank worst in legal barriers to entry in industries; Spain and Italy in barriers to entrepreneurship; Italy, France, and Spain in economy-wide product market regulation; Spain and France in competition law and its enforcement; and Holland, Spain, Sweden, and Germany are seen as the most excessive in their employment protection legislation (EPL). On the whole, Italy, France, and Spain rank worst on these counts, while Britain, America, and Canada rank best—with Sweden, Holland, and Germany in the middle. Among the smaller high-income nations, Switzerland generally ranks in the middle, Ireland ranks high, and Denmark even higher. A broad measure of business interference, derived from OECD data, which *The Economist* in July 1999 dubbed an index of "red tape," differs a little: it puts Italy and France at 2.7, Belgium at 2.6, next come Germany at 2.1 and both Spain and Sweden at 1.8; Britain is best at 0.5, next America at 1.3, and Holland at 1.4. (Canada and Austria were omitted.) All these results are informative, although they are better at detecting levers of control and an obstructiveness that might be economy-wide than at gauging selective meddling and directing.[6]

While the above indicators describe the arms of a corporatist economy, another dimension of corporatist economies is the extent to which wage setting uses a trilateral mechanism connecting the state with labor unions and business confederations. This institution is still at the heart of Italian corporatism—both the rhetoric of Mussolini and the reality after the war. Indexes of "union and employer coordination" constructed by Stephen Nickell show only trace amounts in the United States and Canada, with very little in the United Kingdom (though the CBI still exists). We find the highest levels of coordination in Sweden, Austria, and Germany; next are France,

6. For these data see OECD, *Going for Growth: 2007,* a project led by Jean-Philippe Cotis. It might be suspected that these indexes of hindrances to innovation and to the conduct of business generally purport to measure the unmeasurable. However, the indexes are compounded out of concrete and measurable things, such as the number of days it takes to obtain a license to build a warehouse, which ranges from about 80 days in the United States and Canada to about 170 days in France and Germany and 284 days in Italy. It might also be wondered whether these differences among economies matter at all. However, a nation's investment in information and communications technologies (ICT) exhibits a rather tight relationship to its product market regulation index. Nations' unemployment rates have been shown to have some relationship to their EPL indexes.

Italy, Belgium, and Holland; tied for the lowest levels are the United States, the United Kingdom, and Canada.[7]

Another dimension of corporatism is the hazardous and uneven *playing field* on which private property has to operate. Some markers here are the amount of corruption in the public sector, the risk of expropriation borne by private enterprises, and the risk of government repudiation of contracts. How nations rank in these respects may help us rank nations according to their corporatism. Of course, corporatism does not have a monopoly on these bad traits, but that is not a decisive objection to their use as signs of corporatism. However, measurements of these qualities are generally proprietary information. What is available is an average of these three indicators and two other indicators (namely, law and order and quality of the bureaucracy), which are in turn averaged with an indicator of openness to foreign trade. The advanced economies rank in descending order as follows: Switzerland, the United States, Canada, Germany, Iceland, Denmark, Norway, France, Belgium, Austria, Britain, Japan, Australia, Italy, Spain, Portugal, Ireland, Korea, and New Zealand.[8] Taken at face value, this ranking suggests that, among the nations under examination here, Spain, Italy, Britain, Belgium, and France are relatively corporatist.

The evidence on the differing degrees of corporatism in the advanced economies cannot be entirely satisfying until we have evidence on the scope of *statism* in the advanced economies. We need data on the degree to which the state goes around the capitalist institutions and the competition of the marketplace to exert its influence on industries and the companies—enabling or privileging some activities or players and not others. To that end, we could use data on the extent of lobbying and government contracts. We could use data on informal pressures exerted by the state on businesses—such as offers or denials of positions in the government. (France is thought to be a revolving door of executives who shuttle between jobs in the private and public sector.) We could use data on the presence or absence of a constitution that allows the government only "limited" roles in the economy. Some countries lack constitutions that, with judicial review by the highest court, would restrain the government from playing a directive role in the business sector, while some other countries have constitutions prohibiting the government from

7. The data can be found in Layard and Nickell, *Handbook of Labor Economics.*
8. This last ordering, dubbed the Index of Social Infrastructure, can be pulled off figure II in Hall and Jones, "Why Do Some Countries Produce So Much More Output per Worker Than Others?"

interfering with the direction of the business sector.[9] A readily available statistic that may well reflect the privileging of some companies over their competitors is capital's relative share of the income generated in the business sector. (When a company is anointed a national champion in its industry, it can raise its price; its competitors, seeing it has become easier to compete, will up their prices.) Capital's share in national income may also be a clue. In 1995–1996, among large economies, Italy and France ranked highest, with a capital share of 42 percent and 41 percent, respectively. Germany and Belgium were in the middle at 37 percent. In the bottom group were the United States at 34 percent and Britain and Canada at 32 percent.[10] (Among smaller economies, Austria was highest at 41 percent, Spain and Holland were at 40. Switzerland and Sweden were low at 31 and 33 percent, respectively [1996–1997].)

These data all show that in almost no part of the world is the government a silent partner in the business sector. They also suggest that the degree of involvement by the state varies a great deal from one country to another, even among those countries commonly thought to have the same economic organization. The totality of the above evidence suggests that the economies of Italy and France have relatively high degrees of corporatism, America and Canada the lowest, with Britain and Germany between these two poles. Corporatism is also rather high in Spain, Holland, Belgium, and Ireland while rather low in Switzerland, Denmark, and Norway. Sweden, so oft-discussed, is a mixed case: interventionist yet pro-business.

Sensing now which countries had relatively corporatist economies in recent decades, we are ready to answer the main question of this chapter: what was the outcome of the corporatist project in which these countries were engaged between the war's end in the mid-1940s and the last years of the 20th century? Painting with a very broad brush, one could say that in that half-century productivity levels came close to converging. But how close is "close," and what happened after near convergence?

Consider first output per (employed) worker. According to OECD calculations, the GDP per employee of Italy, Ireland, and Belgium came near the U.S. level in 1996. (Italy weighed in at 62,500 dollars, while the United States was at 67,500.) In a lower group was France along with Norway, Canada, and Holland. Below them were Germany alongside Austria, Sweden, and Denmark.

9. Early political philosophy touching on the scope of government is the subject of Andrzej Rapaczynski's 1987 volume, *Nature and Politics*.

10. See *OECD Economic Outlook,* Annex table 24, Capital income shares in the business sector, p. 214.

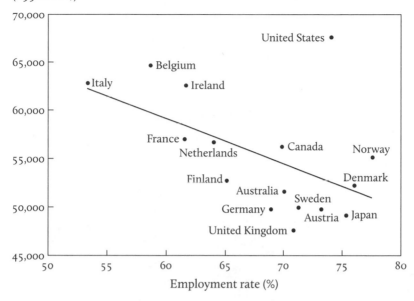

Real GDP per employee
(1996 PPP $)

FIGURE 7.1 Real GDP per employee and the employment rate (employment per working-age person). GDP, gross domestic product; PPP, purchasing power parity. (Source: OECD.)

See Figure 7.1. These results do not appear to be a success for the corporatist experiment: after 50 years, only three of the high corporatists beat Canada and not one beat the United States. And there is more that must be said.

The GDP per hour worked has also been calculated by the OECD. See Figure 7.2. By 1996, the U.S. level was reached in Italy, Ireland, and France—more or less. Germany and Canada reached somewhat lower levels, while the United Kingdom and Sweden occupy a still lower notch. But there is less there than meets the eye. For several reasons, these observations have little significance. For one thing, Europe is a continent of many nations, so it should not surprise us that there are a couple of "outliers," such as Holland and Norway, that have higher levels of output per manhour than the United States. If we looked at America's 50 states, we would also see outstanding levels in California and Massachusetts. For another thing, the employed are a rather narrow section of the working-age population in the many corporatist economies with an employment problem. For example, Italy's 1996 GDP per hour, at almost 39 dollars, is so high next to America's, at only 36 dollars, because Italy's economy fills

Labor productivity
(output per person-hour, 1996 PPP $)

FIGURE 7.2 Labor productivity (real GDP per hours worked) and employment rate (employment per working-age person). (Source: OECD.)

only jobs that are rather productive and it fills them with its most productive workers—low-wage employment is not permitted. Had Italy employed 75 percent of the working-age population, as America, Norway, and Denmark did, its GDP per hour would have been 32 dollars—a great deal less than Norway's 40, Denmark's 34, and America's 36. Differing levels of labor-force participation in Europe and America spoiled productivity comparisons from the mid-1970s to the mid-1990s. Finally, data on total output per total number of hours worked in less-corporatist America, Canada, and Britain are further biased downward by the fact that people there tend to work longer hours, which drives down their output per hour, while the reverse is true in corporatist Italy, France, and Spain, where people tend to work far fewer hours per year.[11]

11. Another point: Whatever the Continental and Anglo-Saxon productivity levels, measured by output per hour of labor, Continental productivity levels would be *decreased* relative to Anglo-Saxon levels if they were all measured by output per basket of labor and capital—the measure called *multifactor productivity* (or total factor productivity)—because Continental economies *raise* their output per labor ratios by investing more capital with which labor can work than Anglo-Saxon economies do. For this extra output, it may be argued, the Continentals must suffer the reduction in consumption levels required to meet the interest payments on the extra capital.

On this evidence, then, it *cannot* be said that the corporatist economies delivered on their claim to be superior in productivity to the remaining modern economies—those in America, Canada, and Britain. Quite the contrary: taking account of the considerations just noted, America's relatively modern economy retained its edge in productivity. And two other relatively modern economies, those of Canada and Britain, gained ground in the past two decades.

A stronger argument can be made using Figure 7.2, where the shortest distance of a country from the sloping line can serve as a makeshift measure of how well it performs in *both* employment, which is the socialist focus, and productivity, which is the corporatist. Among the large economies, the relatively corporatist ones—France, Italy, and Germany (not to mention the smaller Austria and Sweden)—*all* lie some distance *southwest* of the sloping line, while the relatively modern ones, including America, lie some distance *northeast* of the sloping line. Canada, though it is in the southwest, is not as far away as Sweden, Finland, and Australia, which have all come under suspicion of possessing significant corporatism in their economies.

Furthermore, the seeming catch-up of Italy and Germany by 1995 proved ephemeral. From 1995 to 2005, their participation rates recovered, with the predictable result that the added jobs offered diminished productivity. (A Cambridge don of yesteryear, Dennis Robertson, perhaps hoping to make his lecture on the law of diminishing returns more vivid, imagined that the 10th man in a construction crew, though they had no shovel left for him, could go to get the beer.) Over the same period, America saw workers of low productivity or whose jobs offered low productivity leave the labor force, with the result that U.S. output per employee clambered from its former (rising) track onto a higher track. Thus American output per manhour (and per employee) distanced itself further from the Italian and German levels.

This chapter has been focusing on dimensions of economic performance—all highly materialist—to which corporatism and socialism have been dedicated. We could look at other dimensions without straying from the materialist ones. The notable emigration of young people from France over the past two decades could be indicative. That evidence may, to some extent, reflect failures by the Continent's corporatism to deliver economies gleaming with productivity and brimming with jobs. (The fact that the high tide of unemployment since the 2007–2008 international financial crisis has damped that migration is not evidence that the corporatist economies have improved or that the less corporatist ones have worsened. It is too risky to quit in search of greener pastures.) The drawback is that the emigration phenomenon does not identify which deficiencies of corporatism and socialism are at work—only that they have deficiencies. The deficiency may be nonmaterial, such as oppressive companies or a repressive economic culture.

Wage inequality or, more aptly, unjust wage inequality is another dimension of performance on which corporatism might be judged. In view of the data discussed earlier on wage inequality, it is accurate to say that the relatively corporatist nations—Italy and France, and to a lesser degree Spain, Holland, Belgium, and Ireland—have less wage inequality than the exemplars of the modern economy: Canada, America, and Britain.[12] But, as stressed before, this may mean only that Canadians, Americans, and Britons are rolling the dice with greater frequency than the Continentals do. Yet their considerable ethnic and racial diversity may also have some array of effects on unjust wage inequality. However that may be, this chapter has set out to examine whether corporatism achieved its goals, and uprooting wage inequality was never a part of the corporatist manifesto. (Some corporatist countries, for example, have been notorious for leaving substantial minorities unintegrated.) If, as corporatism holds, the accomplishments and initiatives of the nation are what matters—and not personal freedom or individual aspiration and rewards—then the very idea of economic justice ceases to have any possible meaning. And, in fact, among the larger of the relatively corporatist countries, neither Italy nor Spain nor Germany did much to address wage inequality with training programs or employment subsidies. (On the European continent, only Holland and France put appreciable resources into pulling up wages at the low end of the labor market.) The countries that have long developed sophisticated machinery for raising the rewards to low-wage work are Britain and America, neither among the relatively corporatist nations, with their program of wage supplements for the working poor.

A Paucity of Innovation

It is apparent by direct observation that in the past three decades, up to the 2007–2008 crisis, the growth of the Big 4 on the European continent—France,

---

12. These OECD data are shown in Phelps, "The Importance of Inclusion" (2000/2); see figure 3a, "Trends in Wage Rate Dispersion, 1997." The gauge here is the 50-10 ratio, that is, the ratio of the mean of the wage rates of workers one-tenth of the way up the population of employed persons, thus at the 10th percentile, to the mean wage rate at the 50th percentile. It is also known as the D1/D5 ratio.

Germany, Italy, and Spain—continued to be driven by advances *external* to their economies, mainly (but not exclusively) advances made in the United States. Thus, the *degree* of these economies' catch-up with the American economy was not powered by a great rebirth of the indigenous innovation that was visible in continental Europe from about the 1870s to the 1930s. The corporatist economies must have come close to catching up with the American economy mainly by imitation. If growth relied on outside forces, by the way, the same is true of employment. A total cessation of American innovation would have sent the Continent into a long slump.

But what did the corporatism in some continental European countries *do* to inhibit or fail to promote innovation? One can imagine that the welter of bars put up by the relatively corporatist economies, such as barriers to entry and the OECD's barriers to entrepreneurship, would hinder or block various advances in productivity. However, it would be satisfying to see evidence that this barrier or that deficiency operated to dampen or fail to spur *indigenous innovation.*

A piece of the mechanism has been detected. A country's stock markets offer a clue to the dynamism of its economy. The current inventory of promising yet unexploited commercial ideas is a key kind of capital in the business sector of an innovating economy. The prospective size of this inventory in the near- or medium-term future, following the arrival of additional ideas, is a major determinant of the value of businesses in an enterprise economy: the larger this prospective inventory is, the greater the value of these business enterprises, and the greater, we may suppose, will be the capital market's estimation of that value. That might be the only value of start-up companies in their first day of life, but not of companies in general. The other component of the value of enterprises is the equipment and plant owned by them—the physical capital. Hence the "market capitalization" of a nation's enterprises, which is the value of the shares outstanding plus the bonds outstanding, taken as a *ratio* to the acquisition cost of the physical capital, is an indicator of how good the prospects for unexploited ideas are in relation to the physical capital stock. The same ratio, which came to be known as *Tobin's Q,* was used by James Tobin, who saw it as an index of speculative fever or fear, to predict the ups and downs of a nation's investment activity. For our purposes, taking the nation's annual business output as a crude proxy for the physical capital, we construct the ratio of "market cap" to the size of business output and reinterpret that ratio as an indicator of how significant the prospective new ideas are in relation to the

Market capitalization
(% GDP in logarithms)

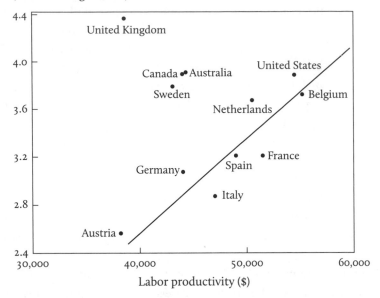

FIGURE 7.3 Market capitalization and labor productivity: business output per employed worker. Market capitalization variable measures the value of shares in the corporate sector in 1988. Labor productivity is calculated as business output per employed worker in U.S. dollars. The employment rate is the ratio of total employment to working-age population. (Sources: Morgan Stanley International; OECD.)

size of the economy or its business sector. Theoretically, this is a very natural indicator of an economy's dynamism. In Figure 7.3, this hypothesis receives considerable support. We see that the market-cap-to-output ratio in a country is a surprisingly good predictor of its labor productivity some years ahead.

This wonderful ratio is an even better predictor of *national employment* a few years ahead, as Figure 7.4 shows.[13] Remarkably, the size of the market-cap-to-output ratio in 1990 would have permitted one to forecast rather accurately the countries that rode the wave of the internet revolution arising in the second half of the 1990s. While it is intuitive that a relatively high rate of idea formation, in leading very probably to a high rate

13. See Phelps, "Reflections on Parts III and IV" (2003, figures 3 and 4).

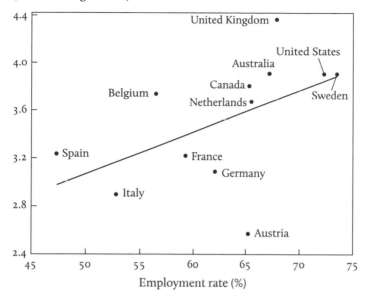

Market capitalization
(% GDP in logarithms)

FIGURE 7.4 Market capitalization and employment rate: employment as a share of the working-age population. The market capitalization variable measures the value of shares in the corporate sector in 1988. Labor productivity is calculated as business output per employed worker in U.S. dollars. The employment rate is the ratio of total employment to working-age population. (Sources: Morgan Stanley International; OECD.)

of innovation, tends to result in high productivity, a reader might wonder whether the path from high innovation to high employment is on safe ground. Might innovation destroy more jobs than it creates? It might at any given place and time. It may be that the phenomenal economic advances occurring in the 1930s hindered the climb out of the Great Depression more than they helped. But in the most common (and most studied) case, two positive effects are working. First, innovation in the form of new consumer goods or in the production of existing consumer goods, which tend to be capital intensive, by lowering their prices, lifts up the real value that firms making capital goods place on having added labor, just as it raises the value of the enterprises that make them; and that sparks new hiring. Second, when productivity is streaking ahead, pulling wages in its train, workers' wealth feels smaller to them—it is smaller relative to their improved wages—so they are

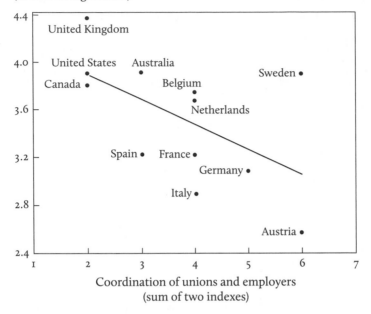

Market capitalization
(% GDP in logarithms)

FIGURE 7.5 Coordination and market capitalization. Market capitalization is the value of shares in the corporate sector in 1988. The coordination variable is calculated as the sum of Nickell's indexes of union and employer coordination for the years 1989–1994. (Sources: Morgan Stanley International; Layard and Nickell, *Handbook of Labor Economics* (1999).)

more willing to work, to move, and to take a chance on a different career. An innovation must be very labor-saving to overturn these effects.[14]

Now we ask whether some of the corporatist elements discussed above impact unfavorably on our market-cap-to-output ratio. One such element is the twin institutions so emblematic of corporatist economies—wage setting by labor unions and employer confederations. Figure 7.5 shows that an increase

14. It is often commented that employment will be falling if output is growing slower than productivity: the growth rate of productivity is the "stall speed" of the economy. That may suggest that a decline in productivity growth would have the silver lining of reversing the fall of employment. But little is known about the short-run effect of that on the direction of employment. It is known that there is no long-run, sustained link going from the productivity growth rate to the growth rate of employment; the latter is a matter of demographics. There are long-run connections between the *level* of employment and the productivity growth rate, as pointed out above. (Moreover, a drop in the productivity growth rate certainly would reduce the long-run growth rate of output.)

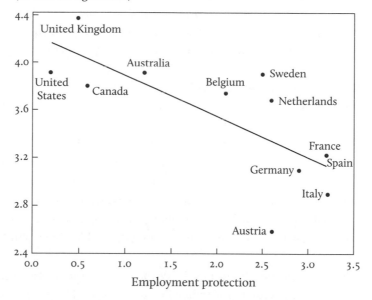

Market capitalization
(% GDP in logarithms)

FIGURE 7.6 Employment protection and market capitalization. Market capitalization is the value of shares in the corporate sector in 1988. Employment protection is the number of months of salary that goes in mandatory redundancy payments. (Source: Morgan Stanley International.)

in coordination between unions and employers is associated with a decrease in the market-cap-to-output ratio. Another element of the relatively corporatist economies is the extremism of their EPL. The benefits and harms from EPL have been much studied yet with very little consensus resulting. Figure 7.6, however, is rather persuasive in indicating that, though the beneficiaries of protection may have appreciated it, there is an ill effect on the market-cap ratio, which, as just argued, reflects a decrease in the actual and prospective stock of innovative ideas. There are other elements of corporatism that line up rather nicely with low market capitalization, of course. But there would be little utility in proliferating additional correlations. It is time to sum up.

To the question, how did corporatist elements prevent countries from reaching American levels of productivity and employment, the answer in *this* chapter is that some of the corporatist elements slowed the inflow of new commercial ideas and that constriction of the inflow was a drag on the advance of productivity, which in turn imparted a drag on hiring, thus causing relatively low levels of employment as well. Thus, the relatively corporatist economies failed to deliver because they lacked something needed to enable, stimulate, and spur experimenting, exploring, and trying things out. Therefore their economies were missing the ingredients required for operating at the productivity frontier and thus for having high mean levels of employment.

Postscript: There is a puzzle outstanding. How did the Big 3 of continental Europe—France, Germany, and Italy—come as close as they did to catching up with the American economy in terms of productivity and in terms of employment (in Germany and Italy) if, as has been observed here and elsewhere, they suffered such a paucity of endogenous, indigenous innovation? One would think that if the growth of the Continent's productivity was founded on its being behind the leader from whom all innovations flow, its growth would stop if somehow it caught up, just as greyhounds in a race would stop running if they were no longer behind the rabbit. (Greyhounds do not run for the fun of it.)

That is what happened. In the mid-1970s the American economy stopped running like a rabbit. Output growth had fluctuated around 4 percent annually from the mid-1950s to the mid-1970s—of which 3 percent was productivity growth and 1 percent employment growth. Then the Great Productivity Slowdown came in the mid-1970s. From 1975 to 2005, output grew at rates around 3 percent per year—relatively fast in the 1990s and relatively slow in the 2000s. With its growth engine having lost power, America was a sitting duck for catch-up by the rest of the world. A tendency to convergence arises as the leaders slow.

With America no longer producing the greater part of the world's innovation, which it had done in the 1920s and 1930s, then again from the mid-1950s to the mid-1970s, Europe, devoid of indigenous innovation, had little choice but to slow likewise. Further, once operating at reduced speeds, Europe became more vulnerable. It felt the rise of competition from the nations emerging into the global economy far more keenly than it would have in its "30 Glorious Years"—the 26 years stretching from 1955 to 1980. Also, upon resorting to fiscal deficits to make up for slow growth, Europe became increasingly tangled up in public debt.

By the late 2000s the entire West saw its economic growth reduced to slow motion and its employment levels depressed as the boom, stimulated by massive tax cuts, new entitlements, and new subsidies, fizzled out, as it had to do.

CHAPTER EIGHT

The Satisfaction of Nations

[The] big thing that's missing is a technocratic understanding of the facts, where things are working and where they're not working.

BILL GATES, quoted in the *New York Times*

T HE PREVIOUS CHAPTER, weighing the rivals on their own materialist terms, sought the effects of corporatism (and socialism) on the material economy—mainly on employment and productivity. Yet there is a *nonmaterial* dimension in a modern economy, as in modern life in general. Much of what is most valued about participating in a relatively modern economy is the challenge and experience it usually offers, and the intuitions and ideas it excites, rather than the material goods and services produced. As emphasized from the start, the modern economy is a vast imaginarium, a virtual laboratory in which to dream up and try out ideas. The modern revolution in arts and letters mirrored the new experience sought and widely found in modern working life. Household surveys have provided evidence for the nonmaterial rewards of work in the more modern economies, and their respondents often say that they look for kinds of compensation beyond the material reward of the paycheck.

The question here is whether, as this book has been arguing, the relatively modern-capitalist economies are *more* rewarding in nonmaterial terms than the relatively corporatist or socialist economies. To approach that directly would require neatly decomposing each country—"this one 1 part modern capitalism, 3 parts corporatism," "that one 2 parts modern capitalism, 1 part socialism," and so forth. That would be highly subjective. Our approach will necessarily be indirect. Some features found in economies are thought to be most pronounced or more common in corporatist (or socialist) economies, other features most pronounced in modern-capitalist economies. We will investigate some signature features of corporatist, socialist, and modern-capitalist economies to see whether they are conducive or inimical to nonmaterial rewards—features such as corporatism's high "employment protection," extensive welfarism, short regulation work week, and collective bargaining; socialism's gigantic public sectors; the bureaucratic "red tape" found in both of the latter systems; and capitalism's individual freedoms. Not knowing exactly how to measure the degree of, say, modern capitalism in each country, we use data measuring the size of the "modern" organs— the organs understood to function in the generation of dynamism and thus inclusion—to see how they correlate with nonmaterial rewards.

Yet, as important as institutions and policies may be, we must recognize that every economy is a *culture* or mix of cultures, not just policies, laws, and institutions. The *economic* culture of a nation consists of prevailing attitudes, norms, and assumptions about business, work, and other aspects of the economy. These cultural forces may affect the generation of nonmaterial rewards indirectly through their influence on the evolution of institutions and policies, but also very directly through their impact on participants' motives and expectations. An economy may owe its vibrancy—its readiness to apply newly discovered technologies and adopt newly proven products— to one or more components of its economic culture; an economy may owe its dynamism—its success at using the creativity of people to achieve indigenous innovation—to some other components in its cultural repertoire. A *political* culture may also suit a nation for innovation under some conditions, at any rate. To the extent that cultural differences are important, inter-country differences in nonmaterial rewards are to be explained not by crude labels—modern capitalism, corporatism, and socialism—and not only by the size and settings of a few institutions or policies, each characteristic of one kind of system or another, but also by measurements of some elements in the culture, each thought to be a key force in modern capitalism or corporatism or socialism.

In the economics that has been standard from David Ricardo and John Stuart Mill to the present day, the concept of a culture does not come up, as if there were just one culture in Western civilization—despite the dissents of Thorstein Veblen and Max Weber. Outside standard economics, however, anthropologists recognized that not all societies' cultures are alike and the differences matter. Claude Lévi-Strauss argued that every society's culture deserved respect, having arisen to meet its own special needs, and Ruth Benedict maintained that some societies had cultures that were not the best for them. The psychiatrist Erich Fromm said that some cultures were extremely bad, arguing that fascism took over where the culture did not value individual freedom.

In the past decade, though, culture has been making its way into economics. It is increasingly hypothesized that culture is the glue or "missing link" that loosely ties a country's economic performance in the present to that in even the distant past. "The apple does not fall far from the tree," good tree or bad.[1] Many observers have remarked at how effortlessly some countries, after being down and out, climbed back to a high place in the league tables: most European countries climbed back more or less to the position they had before their interwar traumas.[2] However, there can be no doubt that new experience and new ideas can change a country's culture. Nazi opposition in the 1930s to women working had a long-lasting effect, but over the past decade Germany's female participation rate has rebounded. Margaret Thatcher's campaign in the 1980s to sweep away British companies' aversion to competition has left a mark in the view of most observers, but there are now calls in Britain to return to "industrial policy." Historians of China are suggesting that China's economic reformation in 1978 under Deng Xiaoping succeeded thanks to a deeply seated culture that could be traced back to 1500. The West's modern era brought new thinking and, to varying degrees, new ways of behaving, as this book has argued at several places.

Disparities in Job Satisfaction

It is widely assumed that the "economically advanced" countries do not differ significantly in their *nonmaterial* rewards. Since they are about equally productive, the reasoning is, they must produce things the same way, and so the *work experience* must be the same too. (Standard economics supposes that the robotized economies of their theoretical models have no culture.) But that is a profound and serious misconception.

In fact, there are striking differences in job satisfaction within the West. That became clear with the publication of a wave of survey data gathered in

1. This theory sees the culture as a slow-moving causal force that may ultimately trigger an abrupt change of institutions—as shifting tectonic plates finally provoke an earthquake. See Roland, "Understanding Institutional Change" (2004). (There the culture is another institution—the slow-moving one. This book breaks out culture from institutions.) The hypothesis here allows new ideas to drive institutions and possibly culture too. Things would change even if culture never did.

2. A Spanish economist, chatting with me at a 1993 meeting in London, observed that in the early 1920s Spain's GDP per person put it in 8th place in the league tables, Western division— trailing America, Germany, France, Belgium, Holland, Britain, and Italy. After all that Spain had been through since then, from the Spanish civil war to Franco's reign and the post-Franco decades, Spain was again in 8th place.

Mean job satisfaction

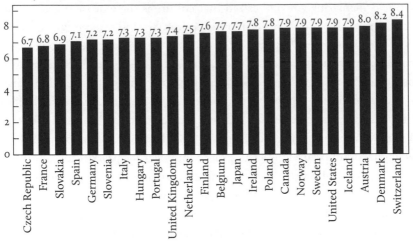

FIGURE 8.1 Mean job satisfaction, 1990–1991. (Source: World Values Surveys.)

1991–1993 for World Values Surveys (WVS)—a mine of data on individuals' satisfactions as well as "values," that is, attitudes, norms, and beliefs. The bar chart in Figure 8.1 gives graphic evidence of differing levels of mean job satisfaction among Western countries.

Understandably, doubts are raised. Is job satisfaction another term for wages or wealth? Empirically, ranking high in national wealth and wages is not a predictor of a high rank in job satisfaction. David Blanchflower and Andrew Oswald comment that job satisfaction was very high in one of the poorest countries in their 1990s sample, Ireland, and low in Mediterranean nations. It may be wondered whether the disparities in job satisfaction are merely transitory differences. Happily, the 1999–2000 job satisfaction data gathered by WVS in its subsequent survey, which unaccountably omitted the United States, do not rank the countries much differently from the first survey, as Figure 8.2 shows.

It is sometimes asked why it is useful to study *job* satisfaction. Why not go directly to the overall measure called *life satisfaction*? The answer is that we come to understand better what determines life satisfaction by studying job satisfaction on the way. It would be neglectful to study life satisfaction without studying the components: satisfaction with jobs, with family, and with economic situation ("financial satisfaction"). When we can study the sort of

Mean job satisfaction

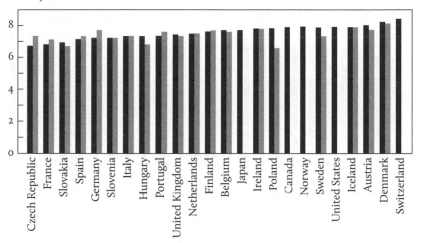

FIGURE 8.2 Mean job satisfaction, 1990–1991 (black) and 1999–2000 (gray). (Source: World Values Surveys.)

satisfaction that is specific to jobs and the effects that economic institutions and cultures have on it, we should prefer to start there for the sake of clarity.

One issue is urgent, however. Conventional opinion holds that if a society's economy is geared to create jobs that offer significant challenge and reward, it pays a steep price in the form of reduced *family satisfaction:* harried couples and neglected kids. That traditionalist perspective views it as an open question whether a modern economy makes a net positive contribution to *life* satisfaction. Observation is all on the side of the modernist perspective, however. Children clearly benefit from parents engaged in their jobs and having interesting things to talk about at the dinner table. So while intensive involvement in work and career detracts from the time available for the family, it has benefits for the value of the family time that remains. In a survey a decade ago, kids expressly said that they wanted their parents not to sacrifice more of their careers for the sake of children but rather to solve their problems and get on with their lives.[3] The WVS adds its support for the modernist view. Its data show that the countries lowest in job satisfaction are *lowest*

3. One authority setting out the family tensions thesis is Anne Marie Slaughter. Lucy Kellaway, with evident relish, set out in the *Financial Times* the counter-thesis.

Mean job satisfaction (black),
Mean life satisfaction (white)

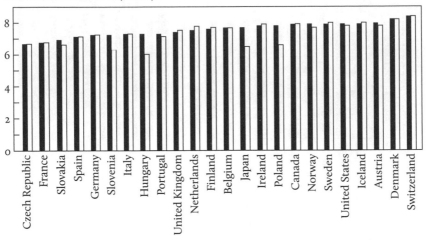

FIGURE 8.3 Mean job satisfaction, 1990–1991 (black) and mean life satisfaction, 1990–1991 (white). (Source: World Values Surveys.)

in family satisfaction, and the ones highest in job satisfaction rank—such as Denmark, Canada, America, and Ireland—are *high* in family satisfaction. All of this telegraphs the punch line in Figure 8.3: *life* satisfaction is positively correlated with job satisfaction and strongly so. Case closed.[4]

The waves of data on reported job satisfaction that have washed up in recent decades have led to misuses and misinterpretation. Some observers, pointing to Sweden's high score in job satisfaction, take this to be evidence that the Swedish economic system—a unique mixture of capitalism and welfarism with little dynamism—is the "best system." Others, pointing out that Denmark scored even higher, conclude that the Danish system—with its Flexicurity or some other attraction—is the best. That way of using the data is absurd. It is a schoolboy error in Statistics 101 to draw inferences from "outliers" rather than from the data as a whole. "Well, yes," one might say, "but it is fair to conclude that the United States does not have one of the best systems!" That too is a methodological error. A country's finishing on

---

4. The tight relationship between job satisfaction and life satisfaction, also known as total satisfaction, is shown in Bojilov and Phelps, "Job Satisfaction" (2012). In a paper given at a conference some five years earlier, Phelps and Zoega, "Entrepreneurship, Culture and Openness," the authors treat life and job satisfaction as interchangeable.

top in some test may be the effect of some purely *temporary* boost either from an extraneous force or from an unsustainable improvement of its system. When the best tennis player is put up against many contenders, one of them may win the tournament, but we know enough not to infer the winner is the best player. If there are many contenders, the best player may have only a small chance of being the winner. In fact, after all the hoopla over Denmark, the 2002 *International Social Survey Programme* delivered a sharp downgrade to Denmark's job satisfaction. The second wave of WVS data, from 2000 to 2002, shows a similar drop in Sweden.[5]

A common misinterpretation is to suppose that reported job satisfaction mainly reflects the job's pay, not the nonpecuniary satisfactions that household surveys were intended to measure. First, if wages among the countries in the West differ little, we cannot attribute differences in reported job satisfaction to differences in wages. Second, if pay were the main source of reported job satisfaction, one would wonder why the United Kingdom, with very low wages relative to their wealth, reports a pretty decent level of job satisfaction and why Germany, with its fairly high wages relative to wealth, reports a middling level of job satisfaction—like Italy and Austria. Third, what slender association there is between high reported job satisfaction and high income is significantly explained by the tendency of high-income job holders to have attitudes and beliefs conducive to high nonpecuniary satisfactions.

The plausibility of the reported job satisfaction levels receives a big boost from the reported satisfactions from work of particular kinds—pride in one's work and the importance to one of one's job. See Table 8.1. The rankings of countries by these two reported satisfactions, Pride and Importance, are very similar to their ranking by reported job satisfaction. Among the G7, one of the top countries in mean job satisfaction, the United States, scored highest in both Pride and Importance. (It scored above Sweden and tied Denmark in these respects.) The country at the bottom in mean job satisfaction, France, was at the bottom in Pride and Importance. (Perhaps the importance that the Scandinavians place on their jobs, the pride they take in them, and even their job satisfaction owe more to the Lutheran attitude of seriousness and

5. A quite different problem is that, when we ask whether some causal force raises or lowers performance of economies on the whole, the effect in each small country—Finland, Sweden, Luxemburg, Denmark, and Iceland—receives the same weight given to the effect in the entire United States. It might be better to start with a sample in which California, Oregon, Massachusetts, Illinois, and other U.S. states receive the same weight as each of the European countries.

TABLE 8.1 Indicators of Mean Nonmaterial Reward in the G10 + 2

Country	Mean job satisfaction	Pride in your job	Importance to you of your job	Net migration* (%)	Immigrants per 100 persons (%)	Participation rates of males 55–64 (%)	Participation rates of females 55–64 (%)
Canada	7.89	2.70	0.15	2.6	19.5	58.31	36.22
France	6.76	1.74	0.04	1.0	10.6	36.08	27.12
Germany	6.98	1.79	0.11	4.6	12.9	53.92	31.06
Italy	7.26	2.03	0.08	1.4	05.2	46.50	14.07
Japan	7.66	2.20	n.a.	-0.1	01.6	84.83	48.54
United Kingdom	7.42	2.80	0.07	0.4	09.7	62.46	40.76
United States	7.84	2.87	0.17	2.8	13.0	65.99	49.23
Spain	7.02	2.31	0.05	0.0	10.7	55.39	19.78
Holland	7.48	2.16	0.07	1.8	10.6	42.26	18.60
Sweden	7.93	2.63	0.11	2.0	12.3	70.92	63.91
Austria	8.03	2.03	0.18	1.5	14.0	44.71	19.07
Switzerland	8.40	n.a.	n.a.	3.9	22.3	82.56	46.77

Sources: Data are from Inglehart et al., *Human Beliefs and Values* (1997); Stock of Immigrants per Person (2005); United Nations Development Program, *Human Development Report on Mobility* (2009).

Notes: Job satisfaction responses are numbers between 1 and 10 (c033 in the World Values Surveys codes). Responses to "Do you take pride in your job?" (c031) are between 1 and 3. Responses to "Is your job the most important thing in your life?" (c046) are between 0 and 1. The table shows the mean of the responses. These data are from the wave of surveys taken during 1990–1993. n.a., not available.

*Net migration is for 1981–1990 as a percentage of the 1981 population.

the Calvinist significance of work than to a humanist delight in challenge and testing one's ingenuity and one's vision.) So it appears likely that the scores on job satisfaction *are* based on respondents' consideration of various non-pecuniary, or nonmaterial, rewards from work.

A contrarian interpretation argues that a country's low score on reported job satisfaction may be more about how demanding the respondents are than how unstimulating their jobs are. They may suffer low job satisfaction because, as in Italy and France, they are spoiled by their wealth. But America and Canada did not lack for wealth, especially in 2001, coming after the dot.com boom, and they have continued to rank high in job satisfaction. And Figure 8.2 reminds us that when Ireland went from poor to rich in a decade, it remained near the top in job satisfaction. Furthermore, if high levels of reported high job satisfaction are not genuine, one would be left with no explanation of why foreign populations flock to the countries with the highest reported levels—namely, Canada, the United States, and Sweden plus Germany. (Immigration into Germany may be laid in part to its proximity to the outflows of people from Eastern Europe.)

Institutional Causes of the Disparities

Comparative studies in recent decades of various dimensions of economic performance in the economies of Western continental Europe have implicitly assumed that the basic economic system in these nations—a corporatist system that lets big business, big labor, and big government (plus any smaller special interests that can win influence) have a veto over market outcomes— were about as effective as the modern-capitalist system in meeting a variety of goals. What the authors argued was that the European countries tripped up by injecting one or more impediments and hindrances in the market, apparently on the belief that their cost was negligible or modest enough to be worth paying. Some economists hypothesized that EPL helped explain the relatively low economic performance found in several of the 18–22 advanced economies of the West.[6] Some others hypothesized that the high unemployment

6. Lazear, Elmeskov, and Nickell are among the leading investigators into the matter. An interesting paper by Bentolila and Bertola, "Firing Costs and Labour Demand," built a hypothetical model of the representative firm in which theoretically the adverse impact of EPL on the rate of hiring is more than offset by the negative effect on the rate of firing, which pointed to the conclusion that, on balance, EPL reduces unemployment. That analysis, however, overlooked a "systems effect"—that the insiders, entrenched by the job protection, drive employers to raise wages and thus trim jobs throughout the economy.

insurance benefits financed by a payroll tax that are pronounced in some of these countries led to their inferior performance.[7] Other studies suggested that the combination of big unions and big industrial confederations bargaining over wages (and many other things) is significantly damaging.[8] The rate of the value-added tax and the average tax rate on labor income were also suspect—either as a measure of after-tax wage reduction or a measure of the scale of the social insurance benefits that the "social charges" on wages were paying for.[9] Also suspected were the short work week or work year,[10] so beloved on the Continent, and the protectionist interferences with imports.[11] A clever hypothesis was that the drag on the Continental countries was not the corporatism of their economies but the Roman law they stayed with in preference to the Common Law in the Anglo-Saxon countries.[12] The trouble is there is no end to such hypotheses, and many of the supportive findings would likely be spurious—correlations that are just happenstance, not causal. Our interest is in differences in economic dynamism between corporatist and modern-capitalist economies and any resulting effects on job satisfaction, which EPL, unemployment insurance benefits, and value-added tax might have little to do with in the larger scheme of things.

It is a theme of this book that the Continental countries in adopting EPL and the rest were not starting with a system as good as (or better than) the relatively modern-capitalist economies. Differences in the deep institutional structure as well as deep differences in economic culture between the relatively corporatist and the modern-capitalist economies are mainly responsible for the disparity in their dynamism and thus in their job satisfaction: corporatist economies underperform in job satisfaction mainly because they fail to develop fully modern-capitalist institutions and a modern culture that meet the requirements for high economic dynamism. That contrasts sharply

7. Jackman et al. (1991); Phelps and Zoega (2004).

8. See for example the 2001 paper by Nickell, and the 2004 paper by Phelps and Zoega titled "The Search for Routes to Better Economic Performance in Continental Europe: The European Labour Markets." Lars Calmfors argues that the ill-effect of this bargaining, organized in the corporatist way, disappears if a single union represents all the economy's workers, for in that case the union will see any wage increase as costing more jobs than it would if it knew the industry could raise its price relative to other industries so as to pass along the cost increase.

9. Phelps and Zoega (2004).

10. Phelps, "Economic Culture and Economic Performance."

11. Phelps and Zoega, "Entrepreneurship, Culture and Openness" (2009). After discussing job satisfaction as well as life satisfaction, the study focused on life satisfaction.

12. Balas et al. "The Divergence of Legal Procedures."

with the view, implicit in most economic investigations, that some countries, which happen to be corporatist, in injecting EPL, unemployment insurance benefits, high value-added tax, and the rest, threw a monkey wrench into the works of their otherwise perfectly fine economic systems. This latter view, pronounced by academic economists from Chicago to MIT, is a tenet of neo-liberalism, which holds that a country has only to prohibit governments and market actors alike from overturning competitive, or free-market, prices and wages, to have successful economic performance. It is conceivable and maybe plausible that the elimination and avoidance of interferences with competition would be sufficient for satisfactory performance, as a line of economists descending from Adam Smith maintained with qualifications, in an age when performance—even the best-possible performance—was only a matter of productivity and jobs. But in the modern era, those neo-liberal institutions are insufficient. Ever since the modern era finally began planting the ideas that blossomed into the first modern economies—economies with a demonstrated aptitude and capacity for indigenous innovation—a country cannot have *high* economic performance without high economic dynamism. And it cannot have much dynamism without institutions and an economic culture that potentiate conceivers of new commercial ideas, facilitate entrepreneurs to develop these new ideas, allow employees to contract to work long and hard, and protect against fraud financiers willing to invest in or lend to enterprises and consumers (or other end-users) willing to try products found in the market. Many of the institutions performing those functions—a virtual infrastructure of legal rights and procedures—arose in the formation of commercial capitalism over the 17th and 18th centuries, but they helped to support innovation as well.

In this thesis, the *modern* capitalism arriving here and there in the 19th century boasted new institutions aimed expressly at potentiating or facilitating innovation, such as a well-designed system for patents and copyrights, and some other institutions aimed at encouraging participants to bear the heightened uncertainty that attends ventures into the unknown, such as limited liability, protection of creditors and owners in the event a company fails, and protection of the manager against shareowner suits. Similarly, some elements of modern economies' economic culture originated in earlier eras, such as the notion of the good life originating in ancient Greece, while modern morals germinated only at the dawning of Barzun's "modern era." That is the theory. Does it to a degree explain differences in job satisfaction? Differences in dynamism?

A wide-ranging study in 2012 by Gylfi Zoega and the present author explores the parts played by *capitalist institutions* in determining mean job satisfaction in the OECD countries studied.[13] Note first of all that countries differ in the strength and breadth of several categories of institutions. Some legal institutions of the capitalist type appear to be strongly developed in Ireland, Canada, Britain, and America and weakly developed in the others. For example, the Fraser Institute since the mid-1990s has been ranking a large number of countries by their score in a category labeled Legal Structure and Security of Property Rights. (A country's score is the value of an index, or average, of the numerical measures of its institutions under that category.) In 1995, Ireland and Canada ranked 8th and 11th, respectively, and the United Kingdom and the United States were 14th and 15th. On the low side were Belgium in 24th place, France 25th, Spain 26th, and Italy 108th. The highest-ranking nations tended to be northern: Finland 1st, Norway 2nd, Germany 5th, and Holland 6th.[14] But property rights are just one institution that may help account for differences in job satisfaction.

Three categories of financial institutions are at the core of capitalism. One is represented by the capital access index, which is compiled by the Milken Institute from its measures of the "breadth, depth, and vitality of capital markets." Another is the number of companies choosing to list their shares for public trading on an organized stock exchange, expressed as a percentage of the number of firms in the economy. The third is the market value of the shares traded on the exchange, called stock market capitalization, expressed as a percentage of the GDP. The worth of these institutions for innovation might be questioned in view of the problems with so-called corporate governance in recent years. (The next chapter sets out some serious defects of the present-day system.) However, even a highly *imperfect* institution, if it helps both new and established firms to obtain capital through an initial public offering or a flotation of additional stock, may well be superior

---

13. Phelps and Zoega, "Job Satisfaction: The Effect of Modern-Capitalist and Corporatist Institutions."

14. These data are in Gwartney et al., *Economic Freedom of the World* (country data tables). Another Fraser category bearing on innovation is Freedom to Trade Internationally. (Clearly it is a boost to dynamism if aspiring innovators can expect adoption overseas, not just at home.) Here, Ireland ranked 4th, Britain 10th, America 18th, and Canada 31st, while Spain ranked 19th, Italy 24th, and France 32nd. Here, though, Belgium ranked 5th and Germany 9th. (The Nordics do not stand out here.) So the Continentals do not score badly at all in the institutions affecting foreign trade. But America is large enough to trade mostly with itself, so it suffers less from its failings in the free trade department than would a small country.

to a system without public capital markets. New companies, being small at first, have some key advantages in developing radical new ideas; while ever-small companies, generally family owned, that are able to hang on by reinvesting their profits or by borrowing and then seeking bankruptcy protection are holding on to resources that could have been used in innovative enterprises. So what do the data show? The statistical study in the aforementioned working paper by Phelps and Zoega finds that underdevelopment (or atrophy) in these two time-honored capitalist institutions—access to capital and public stock exchanges—help explain deficiencies in job satisfaction. A society benefits from a Jeffersonian freedom to *start* small companies, but it also benefits from institutions enabling them to *grow* to larger ones.

Are differences in the spread or well-functioning of *modern* institutions, such as those at the birth of *modern* capitalism, not also significant in accounting for differences in job satisfaction? Yes, of course, though the measurement of many of those institutions—the measure of a well-designed patent law, for example—is somewhat challenging. Since generally speaking, radically new ideas are best developed in new firms, the dismantling of feudal and mercantile barriers to the entry of new firms and the formation of new industries, which America accomplished when it gained independence from the tight rein of King George III, is one of the key institutional steps for the functioning of modern capitalism. In concept, then, institutions that remove red tape, if we had measures of such institutions, would help to explain high job satisfaction in modern-capitalist economies. But the granularity and idiosyncratic nature of many institutions in this area make it hard to represent them with numerical measures. So a couple of telling anecdotes might not be out of place: the founder of eBay, the Frenchman Pierre Omidyar, told an audience at Aix-en-Provence in 2005 that he would not have been able to found eBay in France, but he did not articulate why; perhaps he could not easily do it. Another prominent entrepreneur told Britain's Prime Minister David Cameron recently that he could not have started his business there owing to Britain's lack of some key institutions.

An institution that is basic to the operation of modern capitalism is company law: bankruptcy protection of companies from creditors, protection of companies from self-dealing by managers, protection of companies from employees who do not perform, limits on what companies may ask employees to do, and so forth—a concept articulated to a degree by Heritage under the rubric of business freedom. Under the proto-capitalism of pre-modern times, a landowner might contract labor to harvest the crop.

Under modern capitalism, companies and individuals come together, each party investing time or money in the relationship, without being able to foresee the tasks, some of them emergencies, which may arise in the future. It is impossible for an employee and employer to write a contract that would take account of all possible contingencies. Law is needed to set limits on the resolution of conflicts when the contract does not cover the state that the company is in. Without such legal support, an entrepreneur or an investor might hesitate to embark on the creation of an untried product if it would be problematic to hire or fire as necessitated by unforeseeable developments, or to replace an ineffective manager with a better one. Creation does not always cause destruction, but destruction-prevention makes it harder to obtain resources for creation.

Finally, the *economic policy* in a country is an institution that may significantly induce or thwart entrepreneurship aimed at innovation. Relying on scant data and an overly specific theory, Conservatives leap to the conclusion that every element of economic policy providing a role for the government has a cost exceeding the benefit—with few exceptions. But while there may have been a presumption that this or that intervention by the state in the activities of the business sector—more corn or less cloth—would be harmful in the pastoral economies of mercantile capitalism, there is no presumption that, say, more money for education or less money for education would disturb innovation from its optimum equilibrium—or disturb innovation at all. We do not know whether this or that concrete governmental activity would be constructive or detrimental for the dynamism of the economy and thus for job satisfaction. Yet research on such a question is often possible and may turn up results that force rethinking. For example, the evidence of the working paper cited above does not corroborate the supposition that subsidies to low-income workers, such as America's Earned Income Tax Credits, intended to draw the disadvantaged into employment and greater self-support reduce job satisfaction. It could be that integrating marginalized people into the business world has served to enlist the creativity of a whole section of society whose talents would not otherwise have had an outlet.

The welfare state offers another example. The same working paper by Phelps and Zoega finds that countries with high levels of state spending for social insurance, that is, medical care, and retirement benefits, let alone education, do not tend to have depressed levels of job satisfaction, though that finding may be driven by the data from some very peculiar nations, such as

Norway, with its oil, and Austria, with its waltzes.[15] Jean-Baptiste Say, the great French economist of the late 18th and early 19th century, identified a problem with big government in his 1803 treatise *Traité d'économie politique.* To paraphrase Say:

> Where the government's purchases are spread thick over the whole economy, the thoughts of entrepreneurs, which would have been occupied with a better method or a better product that caused incomes to grow, inevitably turn to how to exercise influence in order to beat out competitors for the government's new contract. So a high level of government consumption costs an economy some of its dynamism and thus, in turn, some job satisfaction.

In contrast, the working paper does not find that all that corporatist intervention for the "protection" of employees and industries *raises* job satisfaction either. The corporatist belief that core elements of human fulfillment would be lifted by making people more secure appears to be an illusion.

Regulatory institutions appear to be a significant depressant on job satisfaction, particularly credit market regulations (such as interest rate controls) and goods market regulations. The institutions of collective bargaining and regulations on hiring and firing are also estimated to depress mean job satisfaction. *Some* corporatist institutions, such as a willingness to run large export surpluses to finance interest and dividend payments to foreign creditors and investors, may have helped these nations attract foreign investment and transfer foreign technologies and foreign capital. However, if the evidence does not mislead, corporatist institutions nevertheless led to reduced job satisfaction.

Cultural Causes of the Disparities

An economy, it will be recalled, consists of an economic culture as well as a set of institutions; and that is especially true of a modern economy. (Schumpeter says in his 1942 book *Capitalism, Socialism and Democracy* that a capitalist economy is essentially a culture, but he meant that it develops habits and standards.) The hypothesis here is that a basic element of the culture, namely

---

15. It is interesting and not hugely surprising that there is no such baleful effect of government investment expenditure. Perhaps capital projects, from the federal highways to NASA and NIH, raise the job satisfaction of the engineers, technicians, and scientists engaged in them—just as innovation and investment in the private sector lift the satisfaction of the people participating in them.

prevailing attitudes and beliefs, has consequences for one's efforts at work and for the effectiveness with which one can collaborate with others; in both ways, one's job satisfaction is affected. These attitudes and beliefs are often called values. (The economic culture also includes attitudes such as those developed in companies, so that we often speak of the company culture at outstanding firms like Google.)

What values spark economies capable of offering high satisfaction with economic life? We will draw on the data gathered on attitudes, norms, and beliefs by anthropologists, ethnologists, and sociologists to see whether inter-country differences in the prevalence or intensity of these cultural values help account for inter-country differences in job satisfaction. (The analysis leaves aside the question of whether the influence of values held by employees, managers, and customers on satisfaction are indirect, in that they lead to a change of institutions, or direct, in that no change in institutions results unless the institutions adjust accordingly.)

The mention of economic culture brings immediately to the mind of many social scientists the characteristic called *trust*. It would seem that, very generally, a society works better if people are brought up to be law-abiding and respectful. The idea burst forth around 1970 with *The Gift Relationship* by the sociologist Richard Titmuss and, slightly later, *The Possibility of Altruism* by the philosopher Thomas Nagel. The issues were aired in a conference and ensuing volume organized by the present author.[16] But trust is left aside in the argument at hand for two reasons. One is that it might seem rather confusing to mix altruism with culture for the same reason that we keep morality separate from ethics. (Morality is about what ought to be done universally for the common good—such as, be altruistic—and ethics is about what an individual person is wise to do for her own good.)

16. Phelps, *Altruism, Morality and Economic Theory* (1975). At a 1974 meeting of the Law and Economics Seminar at the University of Chicago I set out the reasoning behind the belief of those at the conference that a dose of altruism contributes to an economy's efficiency. (I had not begun to think about economic dynamism at that time.) George Stigler, the lion of the seminar, demanded an example. I replied that people will be more willing to pay their full income tax if they are glad to make a small contribution to the work of the government or if they feel that other income earners will be paying their full tax too. Gary Becker, then a flaming neoclassical, said, "We'll give you that one but can you give us one more?" I suggested that people would be afraid to venture out into the street or use a car if they were not confident that others want to obey the traffic laws in order not to do harm. Professor Stigler rejected that, arguing that people observe the traffic laws only to avoid their own inconvenience. Warming to his theme, he said, "People don't want to have to stop to peel off the flesh on the windshield."

The recent literature on the effects of economic culture appears to have put altruism aside. The more powerful reason trust is omitted here is that there is no clear presumption that economic dynamism would be helped (or would be hindered) by more altruism, and, even if there were, there is no strong presumption that altruism is the preserve of modern-capitalist nations and not corporatist ones (or vice versa). So altruism is best left aside in this study.

The French businessman Philippe Bourguignon, whose working life has been divided about evenly between America and Europe, has portrayed the two regions as having quite distinct cultures.[17] In his analysis, the differences originate in the very different upbringings of children. French mothers, he observed, watch their children closely in the playground; they are attentive and warn them to be careful. American mothers, on the other hand, pay little attention and do not teach caution. As a result, Americans grow up taking failures in stride and moving on, so they are relatively undaunted by high rates of failure.

Another observer found a deep divide between the vocabulary of values on which business life is viewed in continental Western Europe and the normative concepts deployed in America, Canada, Britain, and Ireland. Investigative reporting by the journalist Stefan Theil found that France and Germany view private enterprise and market outcomes through radically different ethical lenses:

> The three-volume history book used in French high schools, *Histoire du XXe*
> *siècle*, . . . describes capitalism at various points in the text as "brutal" and
> "savage." "Start-ups," it tells its students, are "audacious enterprises" with
> "ill-defined prospects." German high schools . . . teach a similar narrative
> with the focus on instilling the corporatist and collectivist traditions. Nearly
> all teach through the lens of workplace conflict between . . . capital and
> labor, employer and employee, boss and worker. . . . Bosses and company
> owners show up in caricatures and illustrations as idle, cigar-smoking pluto-
> crats, sometimes linked to child labor, Internet fraud, cell-phone addiction,
> alcoholism and undeserved layoffs. One might expect Europeans to view

17. Bourguignon, "Deux éducations, deux cultures." The notion of "two cultures" will remind many readers of a famous lecture *Two Cultures* by C. P. Snow, who as a novelist and a scientist deplored that artists are ignorant of science and its remarkable culture. He could have added in the spirit of Bourguignon that the culture of scientists, like the culture of innovators, accepts failure: it is an integral part of the game. A game in which there was a certainty of success would be incredibly boring. It is true, though, that the scientific research and the entrepreneurial development we do tends to express who we are, so it hurts to fail.

the world through a slightly left-of-center, social-democratic lens. The surprise is the intensity and depth of the bias being taught in Europe's schools.[18] Theil's investigation suggests that the lenses through which people look at their world are quite different from country to country—more different than the worlds being viewed are. It also suggests that such differences result from some marked differences in the values that people have or in the way they rank some shared values, such as safety and security, invoked by Bourguignon.

The WVS, which this book has drawn on previously, produce large sets of survey data on values around the world. These surveys show that the prevalence of almost every value—precept or attitude or worldview—differs considerably from country to country. Statistical analysis of the individual responses to questions about values shows that little of the inter-country differences can be ascribed to the chance variations that result from the random sampling of individuals possessing a degree of uniqueness; the inter-differences far exceed what might be forecast from the observed differences. As could be expected, some values in these surveys are markedly stronger in the relatively modern-capitalist economies than in the corporatist economies, some other values markedly stronger in the corporatist countries.

It is a central proposition of this book's thesis that several values play a part in a country's generation of high economic performance—a proposition that, up to now, has been a hypothesis in search of confirmation. Some of these values affect the capacity and desire to conceive novel ideas, to develop these ideas into new products, and to try out the new products. Other values may affect economic conditions that support or damage the commercial prospects for innovation. In these ways, many values in the West—whether associated with modern capitalism or with corporatism—can be presumed to affect job satisfaction. They could affect job satisfaction through their *direct* effects on the stimuli and challenges of the workplace or through *indirect* effects by opening possibilities for new institutions that served to make the economy more challenging and rewarding. The moment has come to confront this hypothesis with the available survey data.

A research program at Columbia's Center on Capitalism and Society has been testing the influence on economic performance—ultimately, the effect on job satisfaction—of the West's culture of problem-solving, curiosity, experiment, exploration, and novelty and change. The first results were announced in a paper given at the 2006 conference in Venice on what ails

18. Theil, "Europe's Philosophy of Failure."

the Continental economies.[19] The paper injected the values of the economic culture into the discourse. It selected nine workplace attitudes from WVS to study their possible effects on economic performance. Several of these values were significantly associated with high economic performance in one or more dimensions. How the survey respondents in a country valued the "interestingness of a job" (c020 in the WVS classification) was significantly related to how well the country scored in several dimensions of economic performance. The acceptance of new ideas (e046) was also a good predictor of performance. The desire to have some initiative (c016) was also a good sign. A low willingness to follow (c061)—to take orders, which is conspicuous in some European nations—exacts a significant toll on a country's economic performance. A readiness to accept change (e047) and a willingness to accept competition (e039) are quite helpful. A desire to achieve (c018) matters little: it is the experience—the life—that people want, not some object.

It appears that the hypothesized influence of the various cultural elements is borne out rather generally. It appears also that the WVS values that are so successful are modern-capitalist values; they are values in which the countries suspected of being corporatist—France, Italy, Holland, Belgium, and so forth—are lacking relative to the usual comparators—America, Canada, and Britain—and small seafaring nations, such as Denmark, Ireland, and Iceland. But the paper did not test for effects on the performance indicator that is the focus of the present chapter: job satisfaction. It would be feasible to return to those data to check that the attitudes found to affect significantly the time-honored measures of economic performance—labor force participation, relative productivity, and unemployment—also significantly affect job satisfaction. There is no doubt about the results, though. And a more structured approach is more interesting.

The history told in this book suggests another way to test the importance of economic culture for job satisfaction (and, more widely, for economic satisfaction in general). The history speaks of the modern ethic—a desire for self-expression through the exercise of imagination and creativity—and the modern morality—the right of individuals to pursue this search unchained from traditionalism: obligations to family, community, country, and religion. The history of the world, Part Two, is all about this seesaw battle between modernism and

---

19. Phelps, "Economic Culture and Economic Performance," given at the Center's 2006 conference and republished in the 2011 volume *Perspectives on Performance of the Continental Economies.*

traditionalism—the great, endless struggle in the West from the early 1800s to the present. Where modernism gained the upper hand, traditionalism losing ground, a modern economy developed and society flowered, as in Britain and America. Although France, with its fraternity and equality, differed somewhat, as did Germany, where traditionalism (and socialism) remained a force, these nations also fashioned relatively modern economies. But with the revivals of traditionalism over much of Europe in the 1900s, national economies there drew back from the modern end of the spectrum.

If that is a fair history, we should expect to find a more impressive flowering and very likely a wider one, thus a higher level of mean job satisfaction, in a society where the cultural values of modernism are strong. And although elements of traditionalism might have their uses, we should not be surprised if job satisfaction is also higher where the values of traditionalism are weak.

A 2012 working paper by Raicho Bojilov and the present author tests whether modernist values in a country contribute to mean job satisfaction. It measures in each nation under study the attachment to some values found in the WVS that are a sign of a modernist culture or a lack of it.[20] The measures were calculated from the responses to the following yes-or-no questions: Do you think that it is fair to pay more to the more productive workers? (c059). Do you think that the management of firms should be under the control of their owners? (c060). Do you agree that competition is good? (e039). It also asks questions that call for a response on a scale from 1 to 10: Should one be cautious about major changes in life? (e045). Are you worried about new ideas? Do you believe ideas that have stood the test of time are generally better or may new ideas be worth developing and testing? (e046). Do you worry about difficulties that change may present or do you welcome whatever possibilities something new may present? (e047). By quantifying the responses in a country to these questions, we calculate the mean strength of that value in the country. By taking an average of these six quantitative measures, we obtain an index of modernism.

An index of traditionalism is constructed in a somewhat similar way. Survey questions were selected that would presumably pick up a strong concern for obligations to family and community, a concern strong enough that economic developments that would draw children away from the family or the community would not be well received. Some traditional values are captured by four of the WVS questions: Do you feel that service to others is important in life? (a007). Do you think that children should have respect and love for

20. Bojilov and Phelps, "Job Satisfaction: The Effects of Two Economic Cultures" (2012).

Mean job satisfaction

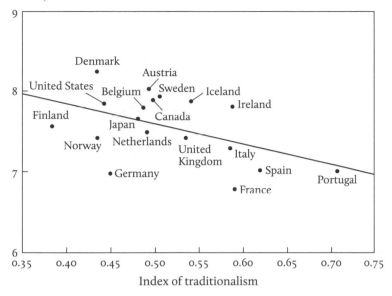

FIGURE 8.4 Traditionalism and job satisfaction, 1991.

their parents? (a025). Do you think that parents have responsibilities to their children? (a026). Do you agree that unselfishness is an important quality for your children to have? (a041). It is not being suggested here that it's a terrific aid to innovation to have economic actors who are monsters toward their parents or neighbors, only that innovation could be suffocated by a fixation on family and community to the exclusion of the individual.

What are the results? It might be thought that the traditional values are a precious glue holding society together and thus indirectly raising job satisfaction and other rewards from participation in the economy. It might also be thought that a little bit of modernism goes a long way; that important amounts of modernism weaken coordination, causing angst and a loss of the deep job satisfaction known to craftsmen in olden times. Continental politicians pay tribute to these cherished beliefs in every speech. The findings from the study, however, strongly suggest that neither one of these prejudices is true.

The results are shown in graphic terms in Figures 8.4 and 8.5, which draw on the indexes of modernism and traditionalism tabulated in Table 8.2. In the first of these figures, traditionalism appears to be an impediment to high job satisfaction. There are three countries, Finland, Denmark, and America,

Mean job satisfaction

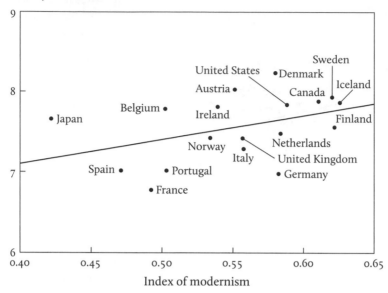

FIGURE 8.5 Modernism and job satisfaction, 1991.

that score conspicuously low in traditionalism and quite high in mean job satisfaction—countries often cited for their high dynamism too. And there are three countries, Portugal, Spain, and France, that score conspicuously high in traditionalism and very low in mean job satisfaction. Furthermore, the (negative) statistical correlation in the sample as a whole is highly significant. Sweden, Canada, Ireland, and Denmark have higher satisfaction than their modest or low traditionalism explains, but they have something that most of the others do not—as the next figure shows.

Figure 8.5 shows that modernism gives a strong boost to the level of job satisfaction. The countries scoring high on modernism scored high on job satisfaction. The nations with the most modern cultures—Iceland, Finland, Sweden, Canada, and America—did very well in job satisfaction. (In 2001, though, Sweden's job satisfaction fell considerably.)

The two figures together show that Italy's mediocre satisfaction is well explained by its high traditionalism, which its above-average modernism could not offset. France's low satisfaction is explained by the above-average traditionalism and below-average modernism. Germany's depressed workers and Austria's delighted ones are a puzzle. Evidently, values are not everything.

TABLE 8.2 Indexes of Modernism and Traditionalism

Country/region	Index of modernism	Index of traditionalism
Austria	0.55	0.49
Belgium	0.50	0.49
Canada	0.61	0.50
Denmark	0.58	0.44
Finland	0.62	0.38
France	0.49	0.59
Germany	0.58	0.45
Iceland	0.63	0.54
Ireland	0.54	0.59
Italy	0.56	0.58
Japan	0.42	0.48
Netherlands	0.58	0.49
Norway	0.53	0.44
Portugal	0.50	0.71
Spain	0.47	0.62
Sweden	0.62	0.51
United Kingdom	0.56	0.54
United States	0.59	0.44
Average	0.58	0.51

It may be surprising that so many countries ranked higher in modernism than America did in the last available measurement—the country that most embodied it in the 19th century and much of the 20th. Could something have happened over time? Significant changes in a country's culture are rare in 10 years' time, as we saw in Figure 8.2, but not so rare in the space of several decades. Whether the American economy has suffered a loss of dynamism in recent decades and whether, behind that, is a decline of modernism or a rise of traditionalism are questions for the next chapter.

PART THREE

DECAY AND REFOUNDING

How Some Dynamism Has Been Lost and
Why It Is Right to Try to Regain It

It is only in the shadows when some fresh wave, truly original, truly creative, breaks upon the shore, that there will be a rediscovery of the West.

JACQUES BARZUN

CHAPTER NINE

Markers of Post-1960s Decline

I called Silberman collect one morning . . . crazed on acid. . . . So what came up was this "Death of the American Dream" thing, and I thought, well, the best way to do that is to take a look at politics.

HUNTER S. THOMPSON, *Songs of the Doomed*

THE AMERICAN ECONOMY IS NOW QUITE DIFFERENT from the modern economy that was so scintillating over most of the 19th and 20th centuries. The central dimensions of performance—job satisfaction, unemployment, and relative productivity—make this very clear. Data show deterioration setting in on all three fronts as early as the mid-1970s, with only a temporary uptick in job satisfaction in the last giddy years of the internet boom. A similar deterioration came sooner or later to the rest of the West: to Germany in the 1980s and to both Italy and France in the late 1990s. These nations, so lacking in indigenous innovation, could not prosper any longer on the back of the American economy when it was similarly lacking.

The secular deterioration of the American economy was at first a mystery. The torrent of women and young people entering the labor force from the late 1960s to the late 1980s caused some rise of unemployment and somewhat reduced wages, but the effects of such demographic shocks on productivity growth were surely transient. That the deterioration has been lasting suggests that the economy was undergoing a shift of its tectonic plates—a systemic, qualitative change.

Early Data on Diminished Performance

Although evidence of a serious slowdown of productivity in the American economy became unmistakable by the early 1970s, it had actually begun several years earlier, only to be masked by booming employment. In the fall of 1962, John F. Kennedy campaigned for the presidency with the slogan "Get

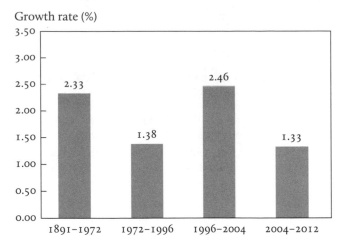

Growth rate (%)

FIGURE 9.1 Average growth rates of U.S. labor productivity over selected intervals, 1891–2012. (Source: Robert J. Gordon.)

America Moving Again." Ironically, present-day data show that a discernible slowdown of productivity began around 1964 and gained force—off and on—until the mid-1970s. Productivity growth remained very slow until 1993, and after recovering nicely during the build-out of the internet, fell back to the snail's pace set in the 1970s.

The anatomy of the productivity slowdown helps us understand it. There are two types of productivity. The more familiar is the relation between output and hours worked, called labor productivity. The growth rate of labor productivity is charted in Figure 9.1.[1] For a great many decades, the growth rate of labor productivity averaged 2.33 percent per year until 1972. Since then it has averaged 1.57 percent. For a time, it could have been supposed that the rapid growth of hours worked from the early 1970s to the early 1980s had brought diminishing returns to labor. However, the underlying slowdown was marked by an even greater reduction of the growth rate of output *per unit of capital*, which could hardly be laid to larger labor inputs. We may as well cut to an amalgamated measure of the two: the growth rate of so-called total factor productivity or multifactor productivity, as previously defined in

1. The calculations in Figure 9.1, based on standard data from the U.S. Commerce Department, and the very effective organization of the chart were set out by Robert J. Gordon. Figure 9.1 is Figure 4 in Gordon, "Is U.S. Economic Growth Over?" (p. 13). He kindly provided to me for use here the further calculations, based on the same data set, shown in Figure 9.2.

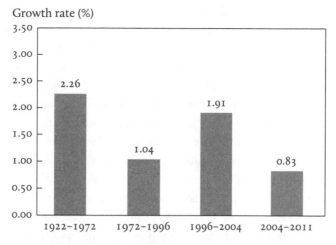

Growth rate (%)

FIGURE 9.2 Average growth rate of multifactor productivity over selected intervals, 1922–2011. (Source: Robert J. Gordon.)

Chapter 7: roughly output per basket of capital and labor inputs. The growth rate of productivity is charted in Figure 9.2. The data show the growth rate of total factor productivity to have run around 2.26 percent before 1972 and then around 1.17 percent after 1972. The slowdown of total factor productivity is more severe. As Figures 9.1 and 9.2 suggest, the slowdown was put in doubt by the productivity speedup during the years of the build-out of the internet, but since then the growth rate has been even worse than before the internet years.

By 1973, when the fall of the growth rates was already pronounced (and on its way to becoming even more so), a towering rise of the unemployment rate began—from lows of 3.4 percent over much of 1968 and 1969 to a high-water mark of 9.0 reached in May 1975. The rate averaged 6.6 percent in 1972–1981 after two decades when the average was 4.6 and the non-war years from 1900 to 1929 when it was 4.95. The urban unrest in this period was extraordinary. Sharp rises in oil prices in 1973 and 1979 added fuel to the fire, but they proved transitory (in inflation-adjusted terms). In the next three decades the unemployment rate averaged 6.3 percent: 7.0 in 1982–1991, 5.4 in 1992–2001, and 6.5 in 2002–2011. The increases in unemployment in European nations during this era were comparable. Throughout the West, heightened joblessness was as emblematic of the era as slower growth of productivity.

Are the fall in growth and the rise of unemployment cause and effect? Two decades of observing a variety of economies, some still quite modern and some no longer modern if they ever were, suggest a systematic connection from the slowdown to the joblessness. Starting from levels *below* the American level, the unemployment rate in the United Kingdom climbed above the American level in the early 1980s; the rate in France climbed further above the American level later in the 1980s; and the rate in Germany climbed further still by the mid-1990s, as *The OECD Jobs Study* (OECD 1994) records. Correspondingly, the decline in the growth rate of productivity was greater in the United Kingdom than in America, still greater in France, and greatest in Germany. So slower growth was systematically followed by increased unemployment, a fact uncovered in a 1997 paper by Hoon and the present author.[2] (It was so clear in the minds of journalists that they began to use "growth" as a *synonym* for high employment. It took the "jobless recovery" of 2010–2011 to break the habit.) It is noteworthy that the growth connection was very tight despite the fact that the slower growth in Europe had origins different from those in the United States. Still, the 1930s saw blistering productivity growth in America alongside a depression of employment—the Great Depression. (And economists remind us that high innovation is liable to create some frictional unemployment.) But that mass unemployment cannot plausibly be laid to rapid productivity growth; other monetary and nonmonetary forces pushed up unemployment. Unemployment might have been worse without that productivity growth—without men laying electric cable across the land.

Three mechanisms connect employment to the rate of innovation. One of these is direct. A firm raises prices and lowers employment if it expects a reduced threat of new products or new methods to come from new or old competitors.

The second mechanism connects a firm's employment to its own innovation prospects. If it expects its productivity to be growing at a reduced rate, it will place a reduced value on each additional employee it hires. (The fall in the growth rate is like a rise in the interest rate.) That will lead the firm to cut back its hiring.

The third mechanism works through wages and wealth. The simplest setting is an economy in which output is produced by labor without any physical capital; its capital is the investment companies have made in transforming new recruits into production-ready employees, as in the Hoon and

2. A simple analysis measured a nation's slowdown by the decrease of the growth rate from 1950–1970 to 1970–1990. See Hoon and Phelps, "Growth, Wealth and the Natural Rate" (1997).

Phelps paper. Here an increase in the productivity of labor would raise labor demand—that is, it would raise the wage that employers are willing to pay a given work force—and that, taken alone, would pull up employment and the going market wage. What if, after a long period without any change, the technology is suddenly *improving*, so that output per man is suddenly on a rising trend? The *wage* will then likewise start rising, and employment will be pulled up at least for a while. But how far? What matters for employment is the wage relative to *wealth*—the value of households' shareholdings. As levels of productivity and hence income go higher, saving per year will be correspondingly higher, so wealth will be rising. And the increase in household wealth will contract labor supply: it raises the wage required by workers so that it pulls employment down and pushes the wage up. Yet wealth is *not* going to grow large enough to bring employment back down as long as wealth has not caught up with the wage. And if productivity and the wage go on increasing steadily, wealth will never catch up to wage. (There is a phase, then, in which wealth, while rising, will be falling relative to the wage; that phase ends when the wage-wealth ratio is so elevated that wealth, though reduced as a ratio to the wage, is at last growing at the same rate as the wage.)[3]

Hence, a *decline* in productivity *growth* in the American economy and in some others can be seen as having two *deleterious* effects on employment and unemployment. First, when the pace of productivity growth slowed, saving did not drop, so wealth did not slow at first: as a result, the *ratio* of wage to wealth, which had reached a postwar high of .38 by 1968, fell over the 1970s to .32 in 1980 and to .29 by 1990. Disgruntled with their wages, many demanded higher wages—else they would retire or look elsewhere. (The corresponding swelling

---

3. This argument is along the lines of Hoon and Phelps, "Growth, Wealth and the Natural Rate." Households will be enjoying rising profits alongside the rising wage, but that does not alter the conclusion: saving does not jump, so wealth falls behind the wage. The implications are clouded if households extrapolate the observed income growth into the future: Then consumption would jump, saving would drop, and the drag on wealth adds to the rise of the wage-wealth ratio. Yet the sense of future riches—of increased "expected wealth"—operates, considered by itself, to boost "expected wealth" and thereby to encourage increased consumption and decreased work. However, the analysis in the text could still carry the day.

Once the argument is broadened to economies using physical capital for production as well as labor, real complications arise. Declining labor requirements and declining capital requirements have different results. Falling labor requirements in producing capital goods would exert a downward push on the relative price of the capital goods, which would reduce the wage that these industries would be able to pay but also reduce the wage that households would require. Falling capital requirements in producing consumer goods would raise relative prices received in capital goods industries, thus boosting the real wage in the latter labor-intensive industries while also raising wealth.

of the wealth-to-wage ratio boosted consumption relative to income as well as wage demands: consumption rose from about 62 percent as a percentage of domestic output in 1970 to about 69 percent in 2001.) See Figures 10.2a,b. Second, as the lowered expectations for growth of profitability lowered valuations of business assets—employees and customers included—share prices turned down sharply in 1968; as poor results reinforced the lowered expectations, shares did not level off until 1974. Reduced employment resulted. Workers in consumer goods industries, finding themselves devalued as a business investment by employers, would have had to accept a much reduced real wage to salvage their jobs, and many of these workers would not have accepted lower real wages, since their real wealth had largely held up or had not so dramatically fallen. Similarly, workers in capital goods industries, finding that the market value of their output was depressed, would have had to accept a steep real wage cut if they were to hold on to their jobs. Yet some degree of gradual recovery is normal as wealth falls, though a full recovery of wages and employment from a such structural shift cannot be expected.[4] Share prices ultimately regained their 1968 level in 1992. But the opportunities of the labor required to produce additions to the capital stock had improved by 1992—thus the opportunity cost of labor in producing capital goods was greater by then—and 1992 workers had much greater wealth than they had in 1968, so many had to be paid more to stay on.

Does all this imply the paradox that saving is bad? No. Acts of saving are necessary to finance investing and projects aimed at innovation. Current stocks of capital and hard-won knowledge are proud monuments to people's savings. Yet this wealth makes additional investing and innovating harder by reducing people's need to save and work in the future. Normally, productivity

---

4. In some conventional representations of the economy, all products are produced with the same method or recipe, capital goods and consumer goods alike. A fall in the valuations put on capital goods—plant and equipment—in some use does not cause *total employment* or the real wage to be depressed in the *long run*: The idled quantities of capital and labor finally regain their use and regain their rental and wages in parts of the sector where relative prices did not dip. But in fact consumer goods production is, generally speaking, relatively capital intensive, unlike capital goods, not to mention the capital firms have invested in employees. In *two-sector* economies, for example, the relative, or real, prices might fall over a great range of the capital goods sector, owing to a slowdown of the productivity in the consumer goods sector or a slowdown (or possibly a speedup) of the productivity of labor in the capital goods sector. Then workers in the capital goods sector will face the problem that most of the consumer goods producing sector is relatively capital intensive, much of it dramatically so—as Hitchcock impressively illustrated in *North by Northwest,* where on the vast cornfield there is no labor in sight, only the Cary Grant character looking out of place. So labor can find work only at a wage so reduced that some workers with high wealth levels may not accept it. In Phelps, *Structural Slumps* (1994), this model, the customer market model, and the trained-employee model offer escapes from the conventional model.

growth brought by saving helps an economy to "grow out" of the wealth that saving brings. But when innovation is nil or weak, saving brings less and less productivity growth, so the economy cannot go on growing out of the wealth that saving has brought.[5] The cause of the slump and the accompanying malaise, then, was the sustained and still prevailing slowdown of total factor productivity—known also as multi-factor productivity. And this slowdown can only be laid to a contraction of indigenous innovation, since grassroots innovation—not scientific advance—was the main source of innovation in America from the 1830s to the 1960s.

A concomitant effect of the decline of innovation was a reversal of the gains in *inclusion* that innovation had brought. When prosperity comes to a region, it is the marginal workers and the marginal properties that see the largest gains—even going from a zero level to a positive level. Likewise, depression visits the worst damage in percentage terms on the marginalized in society—not the advantaged or the wealthy. This development was to become an increasing part of the discussion in subsequent years.

In summary, investment activity of all kinds—investing in new machines, new employees, and the like—and the innovation that underpins investment provide the force essential for high employment as well as growth of labor productivity. The waning of innovation was largely behind the increased joblessness and downward pressure on wages that have been endemic to the post-1972 period.

Policy reactions and other feedback. The policy reactions to the decline of growth and the rise of unemployment—and the subsequent failure of

---

5. The question of which did the worst damage, the slowdown of labor productivity or the rare fall of capital productivity, would be difficult to answer. Some observers have made that discussion all the more difficult in claiming that there was a speed-up of innovation in new information and communication technologies (ICT), which *raised* labor productivity in making transistors, semiconductor chips, and other capital goods used in making consumer goods; and this productivity increase pulled up real wages and thus employment. Of course, no employment boom is apparent in the aggregate data. Yet such a spurt of labor's physical productivity in producing capital may very well have occurred. However, a speed-up in the productivity of labor in making capital goods, if it occurred, might *not* have been a force in the direction of raising "total output" and real wages at all: productivity advances in the production of semiconductor chips and other capital goods could have driven down the prices of the capital goods produced by enough to be a force for lower real wages and employment. So productivity gains in capital goods industries may have contributed to the *reduction* of real wages and increase in unemployment (relative to trend)! But aggregate technical progress almost stopped between 1968 and 1978, so it would be odd to blame such progress for the slumping economy. (A related paper that explores some of these insights in its beginning pages is Hoon and Phelps, "Effects of Technological Improvement in the ICT-Producing Sector on Business Activity.")

those policies—are a major part of ensuing events. It was apparent by the 1980s that productivity growth was still slow, with no hint of when, if at all, fast growth would resume. Businessmen stopped banking on the fast productivity growth of previous times. (An employee today would not be a super-employee in the future.) Economists and politicians understood that to engineer a sustained lift of total factor productivity growth by as much as it had fallen would require moving mountains, but no one knew which ones to move. However, they could consider steps that would offer prospects of symptomatic relief: medicine for swollen unemployment and for the disproportionate privations among the less advantaged.

In 1981, Ronald Reagan, just elected president and keen on the prescriptions of supply-side economics, wanted cuts in income tax rates across the board, believing they would boost employment by raising people's incentives to join the labor force and to work hard in hope of better pay. He also proposed tax credits to business for their investment outlays. (More investment in plants and equipment, while not raising total factor productivity, would increase growth of output per unit of labor.) In those times, fiscal responsibility in the Congress was not as elastic as it had become by the 2000s. Kennedy's tax cut bill had been enacted by the grieving Congress after his assassination. Rather similarly, Reagan won passage of the tax cut bill after he was shot in an assassination attempt. (Tax loopholes were closed with the hope of bringing in nearly as much revenue as the rate cuts would lose—thus achieving so-called tax neutrality.) With the Reagan cuts, the unemployment rate rose some more, peaking at 10.4 percent in 1982, before falling to 5.4 at the end of 1989.

In 1989, George H. W. Bush, just elected and suspicious of supply-side economics—he once called it "voodoo economics"—wanted to address the lingering fiscal deficits. When in 1990 Democrats refused to agree to expenditure cuts, the Congress voted and Bush signed into law a 1990s bill increasing tax rates. The unemployment rate began rising in mid-year, reaching 7.5 in 1992, then shrank to 6.1 in 1994. When in 1993 Bill Clinton took office, thinking changed: his advisers argued that budgetary *surpluses* would create more jobs within a few years than they would destroy in the meantime. In any case, the second half of the 1990s saw the internet revolution and the dot.com boom. Then, in 2001, with joblessness heading up again, the newly elected George W. Bush, subscribing to the supply-side model, pushed through income tax cuts in 2002, then the invasion of Iraq and the expansions of entitlements in 2003, and finally measures to heat up the housing boom. Yet the boom did not last, and unemployment grew higher than before. (That massive numbers of baby boomers were absorbed into the economy—upping the employment-population ratio from 58 percent to 60 in the 1970s, 60 to 63 in the 1980s, and almost 64 in the 1990s—is evidence of effective labor market institutions.)[6]

Evidently, even in those years of initially low public debt, Keynesian stimulants to consumer demand and supply-sider fillips to the supply of labor could not push back the tide of slow growth and enlarged unemployment. This is not to say that every effort was futile, only that the action taken could bring temporary relief but little lasting benefit—and less benefit over cost, if any.

Fallout: Inclusion, Inequality, Job Satisfaction

A setback of another kind started toward the end of the 1970s and grew until the early 1990s: a decline of economic inclusion. This "inclusion" generally refers to the relative unemployment rates and the relative wages among the disadvantaged. A rule of thumb has long been that the unemployment rate of disadvantaged groups is nearly twice that of the rest. A setback in relative unemployment rates was not evident over this period. However, there was a widening gap between the lower reaches of the labor force and the middle strata of the labor force in terms of *wages*—the magnitude of which is captured by the 10-50 ratio: the size of the wage earned by workers found 10 percent of the way up the distribution as a ratio to the wage of workers found 50 percent of the way up (better known as the median wage). The decline in the position of low-wage *men* was particularly deep. In the 1940s, the position of low earners relative to median wage earners improved strikingly—men included. Yet this era of improved wages for workers at the low end of the spectrum sputtered out in the last quarter of the 20th century. Low-wage men in fulltime jobs fell farther behind the median earners by 9 percent in the 1970s and by another 10 percent in the 1980s. They lost ground at about the same rate in the early 1990s and stabilized in 1995. As a result, the relative wage of low-wage men by the mid-1990s was about 20 percent below its 1975 level.

---

6. These fiscal experiments have inspired a basic proposition in public finance: when an income tax cut increases the after-tax wage, which makes work more attractive in the normal case, saving goes up (not just consumption); so wealth rises faster until it catches up to the after-tax wage, after which work no longer looks more attractive. Leaving aside the effect of whatever uses the government would have put the lost revenue to, across-the-board tax cuts have no long-lasting effect on unemployment—only a lasting effect on the fiscal deficit. See Hoon and Phelps, "Payroll Taxes and VAT in a Labor-Turnover Model of the 'Natural Rate.'"

Since the wage gap was rising markedly by the late 1970s, a few scant years after the slowdown took hold, it is natural to suspect that the productivity slowdown was behind the widening of the gap. The links from the former to the latter are still rather speculative, though not improbable. Much has been made in this book of the point that innovative activity itself, quite apart from its stimulating higher valuations of capital goods and thus driving productivity, wages, and employment onto a steeper path, generates jobs *directly,* since product development, marketing, and evaluation are apt to be quite labor intensive. But the phenomenon for discussion here is the decline in the wage going to low-wage workers relative to the median wage. The answer *could* be that the emergence of high-tech systems—ICT systems—raised the skill requirements for most business innovating. Steve Jobs had to acquire an understanding of these technologies to be able to judge well whether some new product would be feasible. The new high-tech systems also required more highly skilled workers for their operation. In short, rapid innovation has been the problem. But the data on the productivity slowdown suggest that, in the economy as a whole, the rate of innovation sagged from the mid-1960s onward and recovered only partially in the sub-period 1996–2007. Imagine the misery if innovating had kept to its rapid pace! A more realistic hypothesis is that companies innovating or adopting innovations are constantly driving down the costs of what they make, and when the innovation stops, their prices stop falling—at a cost to disadvantaged workers and most of the working class.[7]

The U.S. government made efforts, starting in the 1970s, to roll back or contain this increase in inequality. Prophetically, Rawls's *Theory of Justice* opened the decade. He argued for a conception of economic justice that would require the state to intervene with subsidies or other tools to raise the lowest wage rates as high as it could raise them. A few years later, Wilbur Mills in the House of Representatives led the way to passage of the Earned

7. Another possibility is that productivity slowed down in the consumer goods industries, which slowed the *decline* of consumer goods prices relative to capital goods prices, while productivity in the capital goods industries actually increased, which slowed the *rise* (or caused a fall) of *capital goods* prices relative to consumer goods prices. Both developments would lower the path of prices—relative to the past trend—for the goods that low-wage labor had the greater stake in, namely, capital goods. Similarly, it is shown in a recent paper that a technical improvement in the ICT-producing industry, in lowering the real price of ICT equipment, reduces the "demand wage" employers will pay, thus lowering employment as well as the real wage. See Hoon and Phelps, "Effects of Technological Improvement in the ICT-Producing Sector on Business Activity."

Income Tax Credit (EITC) in 1975. Those with low wage earnings for the year could take a credit against future taxes owed. Seven hundred dollars might turn into a thousand. This measure was just in time, as the wages earned by the bottom tenth slipped in the late 1970s and continued to do so until the early 1990s. The 1985 Reagan Tax Act amended the EITC, making it more biased toward working families with dependent children than it was at the outset, and therefore it became more of a child raising subsidy than a work subsidy. In any case, the annual expenditure never approached even 1 percent of GDP.

The efforts to address inequality were mainly directed not at raising earnings and thus stirring people to help themselves by continuing to work—Smith's "self-help." They were directed at providing economic support of low-income persons *whether or not* they were employed. The modest flow of income from the EITC was a drop in the bucket next to the sums a low-income person was provided in food stamps, Medicaid, low-income housing projects, aid to mothers of dependent children, disability benefits, and many smaller programs, all of which added up to a massive flow of income compared to the wage they could earn. OECD data record that "social transfers" in the United States grew from 7.26 percent of the GDP in 1960 to 10.21 in 1970. But in the 1970s these transfers grew to 15.03 percent, thus almost matching the United Kingdom, then grew to 21.36 percent in the 1980s, far outstripping the United Kingdom. As the slowdown remained, so did the trend in social benefits. Data from the U.S. Census Bureau record that the percentage of the population living in a household receiving some government benefits climbed in a virtually straight line from 29 percent in 1983 to 48 percent in 2011. Hence the income from not working skyrocketed as low-end pay for work stagnated:

> The entire bottom decile earned only $15 billion in 1990, which is about $1,200 per person. (This compares with economy-wide earnings per member of the labor force that year of about $25,000. . . .) How could 12 million workers have survived on so little? In large part the answer lies in the scale of welfare payments, particularly [but not only] those for which active and potential workers are eligible. . . . Total public spending for Medicaid, food stamps, housing benefits, and supplementary security income, all of benefit to the employed, came to about $150 billion that year. Thus the income received under current entitlement programs dwarfs the wage income of those in the bottom decile. We have here a measure of their dependency:

they earn only a small fraction of the total income (cash and in-kind income) they receive. But removing the support of the welfare system would not make them independent. . . . [T]hey would still be dependent, their dependency shifting to relatives and charities.[8]

Thus work was seriously devalued. No wonder fewer low-wage people found it convenient to work in a fulltime job or any job.

Another response of the policymakers in recent decades was the near-abolition of taxation in the lowest 40 percent—essentially the lower half of the population. Those who did choose to work, mostly people farther up the wage ladder, were taxed at rates that are lower than almost any other country in the Western world: very nominal tax rates on income, no tax on the ownership of residential property, no federal value-added tax, and so on. By running a huge budgetary deficit on the lower half, the government had very nearly scaled after-tax wages, wealth, and consumption back to the size they would have had in the absence of the decline in their relative wages. Yet this policy did nothing to restore the lower half's integration in society and their sense of self-support through the earnings from their contribution. The country's lower half went from running their careers but having no share in running or monetarily supporting the government to having no careers but a say in the running of government without sharing in the cost of it.

But all these efforts of the state to redress the damage where it could be seen and treated to a degree were superficial. The economy had fundamentally changed. Furthermore, even if the tax credits, the social expenditures, and the tax cuts had been enduringly effective in reducing unemployment and inequality back to their initial levels, there would have been a problem. If the economy was weighed down by diminished innovation, the satisfactions of economic life would likely have been depressed too. The policy measures were not of a nature to treat the effects of the slowdown on the *texture* and *experience* of economic life.

The losses in job satisfaction and the issue of job security. Job satisfaction did in fact suffer a significant decline in the new era of slowdown. In theory, with new products and methods coming up much less rapidly after the early 1970s, especially new methods and products that were the fruit of indigenous grassroots imagination, we would expect that work in the business sector

---

8. Phelps, *Rewarding Work* (1997, p. 23). The book discusses how the devaluation of work might be reversed.

soon became much less rewarding than previously; so data on the trend of job satisfaction provide a test of the thesis of important economic deterioration. It should not be surprising that, among all the many questions about job satisfaction asked by the several household survey organizations, *some* of the responses show no downward trend after the early 1970s. But overwhelmingly, the surveys found a marked decline. Surveys by Gallup and Ipsos-Reid asked, "Do you enjoy your work so much that you have a hard time putting it aside?" The percentage that said "yes" was 51 in 1955, 33 in 1988, and 23 in 2001. Roper asked, "Is work the most important thing and the purpose of leisure to recharge batteries . . . or is it leisure?" The percentage saying "work" was 48 in 1975, 46 in 1985, 37 in 1995, and 34 in 2000. Finally, Gallup asks whether you are "satisfied or dissatisfied with your job/the work you do." The percentage saying "satisfied" averaged 86 around 1966, was 77 in 1973, 70 in 1984, 73 in 1995, and 70 in 2001.[9]

The analysis of job satisfaction data from General Social Surveys by David Blanchflower and Andrew Oswald, pioneering economists in investigating job satisfaction data, likewise confirms "a small but systematic" downward trend across the period. Blanchflower and Oswald point out that this is a startling result precisely because physical working conditions steadily improved over the decades in question. The trends are not very different between men and women.[10]

One might wonder whether the downward trend in job satisfaction reflects only some ill effects on morale or on the worker-employer match resulting from the shift to higher unemployment rates following the great slowdown. After all, the unemployment rate shot up to 10.8 percent in November and December 1982—the worst months in the campaign to slay the dragon of inflation. However, the decline is barely less steep when we

9. See the valuable compilation of several survey results in AEI Public Opinion Studies, *The State of the American Worker 2009: Attitudes about Work in America,* updated August 21, 2009. http://www.aei.org/publicopinion17. Of the half-dozen surveys, two recorded no decline of job satisfaction between the early 1970s and the early 1990s. The National Opinion Research Center asked whether "work gives a feeling of accomplishment." The percentage saying "yes" showed *no trend* between the mid-1970s and the early 1990s, then a drop-off in the 2000s. Asked by Harris Interactive "how satisfied are you with your job—very satisfied, somewhat satisfied . . .," the percentage saying "very satisfied" was 59 in 1974 and the *same* in 1984 (after dipping to 45 in 1978). The later percentages were lower: 46 in 1994 and 49 in 2002.

10. Blanchflower and Oswald, "Well-Being, Insecurity and the Decline of American Job Satisfaction." The authors comment that the last finding "might be viewed as unexpected because of a presumption that gender discrimination has dropped over the last few decades."

Job satisfaction
(% very satisfied)

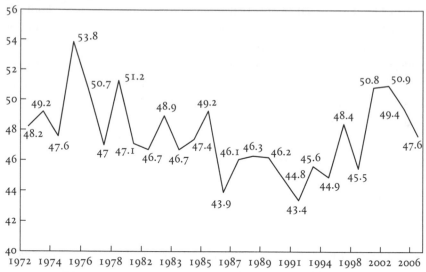

FIGURE 9.3 Job satisfaction in the United States, 1972–2006. (Source: David Blanchflower and Andrew Oswald.)

restrict our attention to the (increasingly rare) years when the unemployment rate was as low as that in the early 1970s.[11]

Declining job satisfaction was not confined to America. Although internally generated innovation in Western Europe, which had been a large source of job satisfaction there, had paused in the 1940s and finally died in the late 1950s, the flow of designs for new products and blueprints for new methods coming into Europe from overseas, largely from America, had been filling the gap with little let-up from the late 1950s to the late 1970s, thus providing jobholders with a modicum of job satisfaction in those years. But America's slowdown in the 1970s and the Continent's running low on overseas ideas in the 1980s sharply reduced opportunities for job satisfaction in Continental workplaces—just as

11. Of those over age 30, asked by General Social Surveys, "How satisfied are you with the work you do?," the percentage replying "very satisfied" was 54 in 1972 (when the yearly unemployment rate was 5.6 percent), 51 in 1988 (the year when the unemployment rate recovered to 5.5 percent), and 47 in 1996 (a year with a 5.4 percent unemployment rate—the new normal of that era). Blanchflower and Oswald, "Well-Being, Insecurity and the Decline of American Job Satisfaction" (table 1B). This development is presented in Figure 9.3.

it reduced available jobs. So we should be prepared to find that Europe experienced a moderate decline in job satisfaction in the 1980s—a lesser decline since it had less to lose. In fact, drawing on the earliest and smallest wave of data collected by WVS in 1980, we see that Britain suffered a serious decrease of job satisfaction from 1980 to 1991 and an equal decrease from 1991 to 2001. Italy suffered a decrease from 1980 to 1991, and Germany a smaller one. Ultimately, Europe's own productivity had to slow down. Italy went into a sharp productivity slowdown around 1997 and France in 1998. (France enjoyed an upswing of job satisfaction between 1991 and 2001 but a decline in the 2000s.) Germany has had recurrent periods of slow growth since 1984.

Many suppose the loss in reported job satisfaction reflects a loss of job security. Those who only think of security would suppose that. So do some who take a broader view: Several experts in household surveying suggest that job security is a part of job satisfaction. Their thinking seems to be that if you draw immense satisfaction from "the work you do" and something makes you fear you will lose it, you will say you are dissatisfied with your *job*! (But wouldn't it then be more accurate to say that your *economy* is dissatisfying?) At least one survey directs respondents to include their feeling of job security in their reported job satisfaction by presenting it to them as one of three or four components of what the survey defines as job satisfaction. Do we see a statistical correlation between job satisfaction and job security? One can be seen if enough underbrush is cleared away. But that statistical relationship may not be causal, running from security to satisfaction. Low job satisfaction and low job security may be a feature of economies with large numbers of *low-level* jobs. Job security is not sufficient for job satisfaction: Hungarians report great job security but miserable job satisfaction. In any case, the historical data of the era of diminished performance do not show significant downward trends in job insecurity—in the perception of precariousness. Gallup reports that the percentage of U.S. jobholders "completely satisfied" with the "job security aspect of your job" went from 45 percent in 1989, the first year of the survey, to 55 in 2002 and again in 2006. (These data, drawn from the AEI compilation of job satisfaction data, do not go back further.) The General Social Survey reports that the percentage who felt it "not at all likely" or "not too likely" they would lose their jobs or be laid off in the next 12 months fell insignificantly: from 91 percent in 1977–1978 (the earliest data available) only to 89.5 in both 1990–1991 and 1994–1996. The percentage who felt it was "very easy" or "somewhat easy" to find another job with the same remuneration went from 59 percent in 1977–1978 *up* to 60 percent in 1990–1991, then down to 57 percent in 1994–1996.[12] It appears that the lost dynamism caused little insecurity.

In fact, there was little basis for supposing that the loss of dynamism would cause increased insecurity. With productivity growing more slowly, one would suppose that Schumpeterian "job destruction" *fell* along with "job creation." And the evidence confirms the prediction. In 1989, 8 percent of jobs were measured as destroyed, while the percentage destroyed fell to the 7s in 1992–2000 and to the 6s in 2002–2007.[13] This may seem improbable, but it is not. Job insecurity *is* heightened in recessions. But the two long stretches in the 1990s and the 2000s each came *after* a recession. In recoveries and even in flat times, jobs are not particularly prey to destruction—even if the previous recession has left employment depressed—since the storm and its destruction have passed: the loss of dynamism and the wave of dismissals, while not reversed, are over for the foreseeable future.

A new development in the era of diminished performance was the onset in the 1990s of a *structural shift* from manufacturing to services and to finance. Employment in heavy industry—in durable goods manufacturing—started and finished the decade at 11.5 million persons. The number employed in *nondurable* goods manufacturing, though, fell from around 7.2 million to 6.7 million by 2000. Since manufacturing is worker intensive, especially intensive in workers without a college education, the shift of expenditure to the other sectors did not create enough new labor demand to absorb the loss of old labor demand. A full recovery of employment would have required a much greater level of total output. The insufficiency of the output rise for a full recovery of employment came to be known as a "jobless recovery." The decline of manufacturing steepened in the next decade—the 2000s—as a result, in part, at any rate, of increased imports from China. For awhile, however, the boom in construction soon took up the slack and more. (Resources for a rise in domestic investment—in construction expenditure—were made available by a shift from buying domestic products to products imported from China, with no change in domestic saving. When the latter decreased and the boom increased, all that

12. Blanchflower and Oswald, "Well-Being, Insecurity and the Decline of American Job Satisfaction" (1999, table A1, *a* and *b*). It is only the most secure who felt a noticeable loss of security. The percentage who felt it "not at all likely" they would lose their jobs or be laid off in the next 12 months went from 68.5 percent in 1977–1978 to 64.5 percent in 1990–1991 and on to 62 in 1994–1996.

13. These data were reported in *Business Dynamics Statistics,* a product of the U.S. Census Bureau that measures business openings and closings, startups, job creation, and job destruction by firm size, age, industrial sector, and state.

was necessary were counterbalancing increases in the import surplus—fewer exports or still more imports from China.)

Last, but not least, in the era of reduced performance is the greater *fluctuation* of employment. The tendency toward elevated unemployment has been noted, but job separations and the resulting dislocation are another dimension of economic performance. The era produced five downswings in little more than three decades: the recession of 1975 (when the monthly unemployment rate brushed 9.0 percent), 1982 (when the rate hit 10.8), 1992 (when the rate hit 7.8), 2002–2003 (when the rate hit 6.3), and the Great Recession of 2008–2009 (when the rate touched 10.1). It is fair to infer that the post-1972 economy became more recession prone. A familiar explanation draws an analogy to the bicyclist who is more likely to go off course when forced to go at a slow speed. While a slowdown of innovation is apt to be the cause of a slowdown of productivity and hiring, a recent paper makes the point that companies are apt to draw back from an innovative venture when, on top of the possibility that the new product may fail because it is rejected in favor of other products, there is the strong possibility that the demand will be critically weak because of another recession.[14]

The violent slide of 2008–2009 is in a special category not because it is the deepest of these, which it is not, but because it became the prelude to the protracted slump from which the economy is emerging only haltingly. (In contrast, the 1933–1937 recovery from the Great Depression set a speed record for rate of recovery. But deep troughs often reflect overshooting, not fundamentals, and thus are followed by a period of high-speed recovery.) Yet *all* the recoveries from the aforementioned recession were unusually protracted. The bicycle explanation argues that a rapidly growing economy is more robust to recessions, just as a bicyclist going at high speed is quicker to get back on track. In the 1949 recession, at a time when the American economy was gaining back the rapid growth of old, the unemployment rate, after peaking at 7.9 percent (up from 3.7 a year earlier), was back to 4.2 in just a year. In the 1975 recession, after peaking at 9.0 percent (up from 5.1 a year earlier), the unemployment rate took 3 years to fall back to 6.0. It is fair to infer that in the post-1972 era America's recoveries from downswings were much more protracted than they were in the

14. Aghion and Kharroubi, "Stabilization Policies and Economic Growth" (2013). If it is expected the economy is heading down, the cost of innovation is still high, but the future benefit, if the effort achieves an innovation, will be reduced. Symmetrically, if the economy is thought to be on the uptick, the cost of innovating is still low and the benefit contingent on success will be high.

golden years 1950–1972. Even in the high-growth period 1920–1941, the American economy was not *highly* recession prone or *chronically* in great flux: it suffered its steep downswing following the speculative excesses of the late 1920s, a downswing exacerbated by policy errors.

The set of actions that caused the 2008–2009 collapse to be so powerful are widely known: government actions aimed mainly at widening home ownership, unsophisticated efforts to make a profit on the naïve speculation that housing prices could only go higher (long enough to sell), fraudulent practices of mortgage originators, big banks greatly leveraging their capital by borrowing huge sums with which to bundle mortgages into packages to be sold to banks overseas—"originate and distribute"—and other practices.[15]

Yet the 1975 and 2008–2009 downswings and many of the other stresses of the era we are examining show the influence of many households stretching thin their income by drastic cuts in saving, the national economy stretching its national wealth by borrowing heavily from overseas, and, not least, the government stretching thin its revenues by borrowing heavily and deploying one ingenious measure after another to pump up investment, output, and employment in ways that would prove unsustainable and thus disappoint expectations. Through it all there has been a dogged denial of the era of slowdown and thus refusal to make a sober reckoning of the domestic consumption that the future would make possible. The result was a sick society, an electorate to whom political leaders did not dare to speak the truth. This state of affairs need not have followed the Great Slowdown. One could not have predicted that the slowdown would send society into a manic mode leading inevitably to speculative excess. (It could have sent the society into a mode of depression and paralysis.) In any case, it is important that we understand why the slowdown took place and what best we can do to end it.

---

15. The epilogue is a vehicle to take up the degradation of the financial sector that developed in the past decade and the new policies needed from the perspective of this book. The body of the book focuses on the questions raised by a well-functioning modern-capitalist economy— questions about stability, economic inclusion, and especially unemployment, and kinds of inequality; the questions raised by diminished economic dynamism, which even an economic system free of malfunctions can suffer; and the question of whether modern capitalism is politically sustainable and morally justifiable.

CHAPTER TEN

Understanding the Post-1960s Decline

> [Life] used to be about trying to do something. Now it's about trying
> to be someone.
>
> MARGARET THATCHER, quoted in *The Iron Lady*

I N ONE OF THE STORIES TOLD ABOUT THE AMERICAN DECLINE, the postwar
decades had been a golden age: The federal government supplied social security to working people—old age and disability insurance—while state governments supplied unemployment compensation. Regulations provided safety
for workers and consumers and protected people's savings from bank failure
and their investments from fraud. Big, diversified corporations provided de
facto tenure for employees, giving them more reason to remain loyal. Unions
fought against layoffs and for seniority rights. In addition to widespread economic security, unemployment was low and stable, and growth was fine.

Then, in this narrative, the golden age passed. Businesses shed the mantle of paternalism that was their redeeming feature and became models of
efficient managerial capitalism: putting shareowners ahead of employees,
corporations were Machiavellian in their efforts to push up share prices.
Underperforming managements became targets for corporate raids and
private equity buyouts; jobs were axed so that other jobs might live. Governments, caught up in the new spirit, cut tax rates to enhance corporate
incentives and, if government revenue was squeezed, they cut back programs.
Unions decamped from the private sector. As a result, unemployment rose,
workers felt insecure, firms felt uncertain, and investors saw nothing attractive to invest in.

The moral of this story—security lost, efficiency gained—is that America
would do well to return to the postwar corporatism. Some who accept the
narrative differ about the moral, saying that the paraphernalia of protection
arising in the "golden age" were sustainable only as long as the wind was at
America's back.

On the left, there is a persistent suggestion that . . . the midcentury model could have been sustained, that the private equity "vultures" could have been held at bay, and that what worked for the United States when Europe was in ruins and half the world was Marxist-Leninist could have worked in the age of globalization as well.[1]

However, most economists would say that even if that corporatist-communitarian model had been propped up, it would not have staved off wage stagnation brought on by external and internal forces, such as global competition, domestic demographics, and rising social charges on employment—not to mention slower innovation.

There are basic faults with this populist narrative. For one thing, the postwar era was not exactly a golden age. Its growth rate was a far cry from that in the interwar years, and both its unemployment and its participation rates were not outstanding next to the 1920s and earlier. The anomie of the 1950s workplace became the subject of David Riesman's *The Lonely Crowd*. For another, though globalization caused collateral damage, any standard analysis would see important benefits amid the costs: The expansion of the market to global proportions—increasingly perceived in the 1980s and 1990s—could only have stimulated American innovation; and the low interest rates at which China would lend might have been a stimulus to innovation too—or would have been had U.S. economic policy not redirected the stimulus to residential investment by speculators and sub-prime borrowers. Lastly, although the drive to increase profits through increased efficiency cost some jobs and cost unions some of their power, trimming jobs served to save the remaining ones, and the new freedom from unions can only have helped open up new jobs. There are no good grounds for believing that the corporatist spirit in postwar American business assured dynamism or created jobs; and no good grounds for believing that the neo-conservative swing to putting business first and restoring owner control cost the business sector its dynamism or job growth.

In another story of the decline, a longer and different golden age had started decades earlier and lasted into the 1960s. Free enterprise received strong support from both the public and government. Regulations were few and manageable. Most tax rates were still comparatively low in America. College attendance was the highest in the world. The medical and education industries saw new private colleges and new private hospitals enter,

---

1. Ross Douthat, "The Benefits of Bain Capitalism," *New York Times,* January 15, 2012.

expecting to be profitable. Even big corporations like DuPont and IBM were innovative. As prejudices waned, ethnic minorities broke into the professions and business. Growth was good and, the 1930s aside, unemployment low. It was the age of enterprise.

In this story too, the golden age passed away. Mushrooming regulation increasingly narrowed investment opportunities. Dysfunctional public schools and family environments deprived companies of people equipped for recent technologies. (People who can staff the phones are hard to find, it is said, and companies pay for BAs to run errands.) Taxes on savings and investments became comparatively stiff. Even small firms generally felt compelled to obtain limited liability. Only 65 percent of business income is left after corporate taxes and just 55 percent after the tax rate of 15 percent on dividends and capital gains. Growth slowed and unemployment rose.

The moral drawn by conservatives is that America would do well to return to textbook capitalism: The economy needs fewer and simpler regulations and sharply lower corporate rates to restore employment and growth. Some observers friendly to capitalism question whether America's social setting would make that any longer possible:

> Most of the Republican candidates talk as if all that is needed is . . .
> lighter regulation and lower taxes. . . . But [those steps] won't, on their
> own, help the . . . 40 percent born out of wedlock and [lacking] commu-
> nity support—get the skills they need to compete. . . . To ensure there is
> skilled labor . . . Obama would have to champion different policies.[2]

An economist would comment, however, that even if social institutions and "community support" had sustained the necessary skills, it is doubtful that market forces exerting a drag on wages—notably forces choking off innovation—would have been overcome.

The basic fault in the moral drawn is that although low taxes and stiff competition may be necessary conditions for very low unemployment and high efficiency,[3] those precepts of sound economic management are not sufficient conditions for the high dynamism that low unemployment and high job satisfaction require. The argument has appeared before in this book: Rolling back the government expenditures and the taxes on wage income and employer wage bills to pay for them would raise private saving and ultimately

---

2. David Brooks, "Free-Market Socialism," *New York Times,* January 24, 2012, p. A19.

3. Some observers say that the experience of Sweden and Norway proves that they are *not* necessary conditions.

private wealth, so paychecks would no longer look elevated. On this count, employment would no longer be higher than where it would have been without the reforms.

In a third story, a detachment from the ethos of business and individual responsibility in the postwar decades has been breeding a dysfunctional culture among disadvantaged communities and families, fueling social problems and threatening society's ability to support free enterprise or to sustain itself. The moral here is neither left nor right. In my 1997 book, *Rewarding Work,* I argued for a system of graduated subsidies to corporations to employ low-wage workers. This would immediately build inclusion by increasing employment and paychecks. Now many argue for improving education, upbringing, and community support in ways aimed at significantly reducing those disadvantaged in the next generation. It is clear that subsidies to improve the terms offered to less-fortunate workers and investments to improve their preparation could not be enough to restore their rates of employment and participation to the pre-decline levels of the 1960s. The reason is that returning to the self-support, education, upbringing, and social norms of old would not greatly lift the economy's overall dynamism and thus restore low general unemployment rates and fast growth of productivity and wages.

This book's narrative of the modern economy differs from these popular stories. The narrative points to a *deterioration* in the *core functioning* of the (surviving) modern economies that must have caused a significant loss of economic dynamism and, with it, a loss of economic inclusion. It does not fault the decrease of human capital (years of schooling, etc.) faced by companies nor the modest rise of taxes. It sees evidence to suggest that the handful of modern-capitalist economies *have been weakened by flaws in their institutional-cultural operating system and further weakened by political reactions.*

The moral of this narrative is not a call for more spending and regulation by the state or more libertarianism or even more intervention in education and business hiring, however welcome some measures of this sort might be. It is a call to rehabilitate *modern capitalism* by clearing away blocks to its dynamism both in society's values and in its institutions.

Sources of the Decline

What flaws account for the apparent weakening of the dynamism of America's modern-capitalist economy—its desire and capabilities for indigenous innovation? The progressive era was rife with criticisms of American capitalism, many valid enough to act on—the emergence of monopolies, for example. But the objections were on grounds of static resource allocation: monopoly power was used to constrict output to raise price relative to costs and thus create a monopoly profit. The so-called "natural" monopolies, where maximum economic efficiency is achieved by single-firm production, were turned into public utilities subject to price controls. Progressives also leveled criticism at the crude libertarian dogma that no wage ought to be subsidized and no interest income ought to be taxed. But the flaws we seek to detect in the history of our current situation are those impairing the capacity for innovation, which is the object of this book's study.

Structural Faults in Large Firms, Mutual Funds, and Banks

Worldly students of American business and finance found acute faults as early as the 1930s. Some of these faults have spread, and certain ways of organizing companies, once beneficial from the standpoint of efficient production, must now be reexamined from the standpoint of innovation.

The prominent business historian Alfred Chandler used the buoyant term *managerial revolution* to characterize the rise of a "professional management" able to bring "multiple product lines" under the control of a "hierarchy" of middle and top managers.

> By the middle of the twentieth century these enterprises employed hundreds and even thousands of middle and top managers who supervised the work of dozens and often hundreds of operating units employing tens and often hundreds of thousands of workers. . . . Rarely in the history of the world has an institution grown to be so important and so pervasive in so short a period of time.[4]

The new management methods were credited with finding "least-cost" methods of production—achieving economic efficiency. And the new methods were themselves significant innovations that changed managerial practice across the world. Moreover, the vast scale of these new big businesses made it possible to self-finance radically novel projects that smaller companies could not have funded. Yet other impediments to innovation arose: In a company of traditional size, even the lowest-paid employee, if he had an idea for doing

---

4. Chandler, *The Visible Hand* (pp. 3–4). Dupont impressed Schumpeter in the 1940s, though not enough to cause him to believe that capitalism had much time left. General Motors was Chandler's greatest fascination.

something new or different, could expect a chance to get the ear of someone well up the ladder, if not at the top. So employees of the company were alert to new ideas crossing their minds and were, for that reason, more likely to have new ideas. There is no such prospect in giant companies larded with managerial hierarchies.

One might wonder why owners would not intervene to limit company size and improve communication. Large companies, even those spectacularly successful in breaking into, or even creating, an industry, are vulnerable to the same self-dealing that befalls most large bureaucracies—even if the chief executive is also the largest owner and chairman of the board. That is what reportedly happened at Microsoft.

> Early in my tenure, our group of very clever graphics experts invented a way to display text on screen called ClearType. . . . Although we built it to help sell e-books, it gave Microsoft a huge potential advantage for every device with a screen. But it also annoyed other Microsoft groups that felt threatened by our success. Engineers in the Windows group falsely claimed it made the display go haywire when certain colors were used. Then the head of Office products said it gave him headaches. The vice president for pocket devices was blunter: he'd support ClearType and use it but only if I transferred the program and the programmers to his control. As a result, even though it received much public praise, internal promotion and patents, a decade passed before a fully operational version of ClearType finally made it into Windows.
>
> Internal competition is common at great companies. It can be wisely encouraged to force ideas to compete. The problem comes when the competition is uncontrolled and destructive. At Microsoft, it has created a dysfunctional corporate culture in which the big established groups are allowed to prey upon emerging teams, belittle their efforts, compete unfairly against them for resources, and over time hector them out of existence. . . . It's an open question whether Microsoft has much of a future.[5]

These problems arise even when the chief executive has the extra power that comes with also being the chairman of the board or even the founder of the company—as Bill Gates was during the ClearType controversy. Founders often lack the talent and the time to run a complex organization.

5. Dick Brass, "Microsoft's Creative Destruction" (p. A27). Mr. Brass was a vice president at Microsoft from 1997 to 2004.

At Facebook the visionary founder, Mark Zuckerberg, was canny enough to hire a chief operating officer, Sheryl Sandberg. Nevertheless, difficulties mount as an organization becomes complex and depends on decentralization of self-interested middle managers. These various problems have not been enough to stop innovation, but they have reduced it.

While large companies can be mismanaged by even the most motivated leader, they are apt to fare worse in the hands of a manager who is not a founder and not a controlling shareowner—in short, a professional manager, or hired gun. It came to be argued, not long after they appeared, that corporate governance of large companies run by professional managers was deeply flawed: the critique by Adolf Berle and Gardiner Means in their 1932 book *The Modern Corporation and Private Property* is the classic account. The device of share owning brilliantly enabled companies to reward present stockholders with immediate capital gains from undertaking projects expected to pay off only when many stockholders have since died—a masterstroke promising a long-termism that socialism could not match. Yet the manager of a large corporation is presented with an incentive—whether or not he or she acts on it—to sell the shareowners out: to pursue projects offering prospects of short-term gains—gains within his prospective tenure at the helm—to the disadvantage of projects with superior prospects over the long term. To deter such practices, directors on the board setting the manager's compensation have understood that they might reward the manager with a bonus when the stock goes up and, in some cases, even a negative "bonus" when the stock goes down. But managers, especially those with dependents, would then need a larger fixed salary to cushion negative bonuses; and that would present the manager with an undesirable incentive to avoid all projects that could put her job at risk, namely, long-term projects of high cost. Long-termism remains difficult to encourage. The governance problem is sometimes solved by aggressive shareowners with a large stake, although it can be aggravated by institutional shareholders whose interest is just as short term as that of the managers.

The short-termism at large corporations has been exacerbated in recent years by the rise of mutual funds—a theme of Louis Lowenstein and his son Roger Lowenstein's work. Hedge fund profits depend heavily on investors who remain with the fund rather than move about. Thus the fund is extremely averse to any appreciable risk that the stock of any company in which it holds shares might suffer a substantial drop in price. This leads to harsh pressure from mutual funds to announce the company's earnings "target" for the next quarter and to be intent on hitting it. As a result, the manager of a company with shares traded on a public exchange will spend much of his time setting and aiming at quarterly earnings targets rather than formulating strategies for long-term investment and innovation.

Mutual funds create the further flaw that their capacity for vast diversification reduces the incentive of wealth owners to use their specialized Hayekian knowledge of particular companies, industries, and technologies in favor of simply turning over their wealth for management by one or more funds. Scientific portfolio diversification, which seemed a wonderful gain in economic welfare to the fundamentally neoclassical economist Paul Samuelson, was actually a huge step backward for modern capitalism, as Amar Bhidé pointed out in "The Hidden Costs of Stock Market Liquidity" in 1993. What is most significant in the present context is that companies may see little rise or fall in their share price despite local knowledge about their shifting opportunities, owing to the determination of mutual funds to maintain the relative weight they give to each category of company. Thus investing and innovating for the future is delayed. Moreover, people who leave their investments to professionals will have less incentive to acquire local or specialized knowledge.

Most seriously, multiple flaws in the modern economy arose inside the large investment banks. Imperfections in many financial markets were whittled away, and assets became highly liquid. Large investment banks came to devote much of their borrowing capacity—and divert much of the expertise in the financial sector—to speculation on currencies and government bonds rather than to evaluating companies and industries and judging the merits of new directions. Furthermore, these banks greatly stepped up the amounts they had at risk. To do that, the banks, which had always been partnerships, wherein the partners had most of their fortunes at stake, changed into corporations listed on public exchanges where the shareowners had little control. If things went wrong, the shareowners suffered the losses, while the manager, no longer a partner, was free from personal liability for any investment decisions, no matter how egregious. (In one respect, it is not *casino* banking, since a casino takes virtually *no* risk. But, ironically, it *is* banking that pretends it can depend on the law of large numbers to manage its risk scientifically and precisely.)

Speculation by banks also puts the economy at risk of wider asset-price swings and bigger crashes. Banks love to borrow short term when the rates are low and lend long when, as usual, long rates have not fallen as far; it looks like easy money. But while the odds may continue to be rather favorable, it is uncomfortably close to a game of "gambler's ruin." If an unexpected revival of short rates occurs, pushing up rates on long bonds, their prices fall—just as the prices of houses fell after the long speculative boom in housing—and the banks incur huge losses on their borrowings. Most nations with capitalist economies have long failed to require that investment banks must borrow long to lend long—so that the banks have a chance of recovering before the bonds come due. Another social effect of this unbridled financial speculation is to push nations toward capital controls and other populist restrictions that harm innovation by making it easier for marginal incumbents already possessing capital to hang on, while making it harder for start-ups to raise capital and be confident they can get through their project before the next crisis strikes. (None of this means there ought to be a blanket prohibition against all speculation by persons, businesses, or even banks.)

In many respects, America's commercial banks—banks where households and companies keep their bank deposits—were reined in by the Glass-Steagall Act of 1933, after the crash of 1929 caused a fifth of all commercial banks to fail. Ferdinand Pecora, a former prosecutor, gave evidence to Congress that the banks had played a role in the speculative excess. The new law prohibited commercial banks from engaging in the underwriting business of handling new issues of securities, in the brokerage business of buying and selling stocks and bonds for customers, and in trading them on its own account. In 1999, though, the law was repealed. In the next several years these banks, like Citibank and JPMorgan Chase, built or acquired investment banks, leveraging their capital through massive short-term borrowing.

A severe flaw in the banking industry and a similar one in the airline industry arose from what came to be called ruinous competition—until the very concept fell out of use. An airline plunges into more routes and a bank goes on a lending spree on the calculation that overhead costs can be spread over more routes or more assets, so that profits are increased. But as all airlines do it, they ruin one another's chances of any profit. The loan frenzy of originate-and-distribute in 2005 and 2006 was based on the calculation that losses might be in store if additional assets were not acquired. What was not taken into account was that the competitors were simultaneously making the same calculation, with the result that the industry overexpanded. Consequently, the recurrent crises in these industries have cost the industry jobs and profits and have been costly for the rest of the economy as well.

The banking industry betrayed the very concept of a modern economy by betting on enormous piles of assets without exercising the vision and judgment essential to the well functioning of the modern economy.

The "Money Culture," Self-Importance, Doing, and Thinking

In an interview with RTL radio shortly before she died, Danielle Mitterrand, whose husband, François Mitterrand, was president of France in the 1980s, railed against French economic culture. "Everybody knows that the foundation of the system today is money. Money is the guru, money decides everything." In this statement is the thinly veiled suggestion not simply that there is a stronger orientation toward money than there was in past times but that capitalism operates on money while the corporatism of Mitterrand or Pétain or Colbert did not. But such systems of rent seeking or patronage are as much about money as the systems of capitalism are—pre-modern and modern. In modern capitalism, unlike corporatism, the economy is largely driven by people who, while attending to the bottom line, want to make a difference—to contribute to society or build monuments to themselves or connect with exciting ventures—not just make money.

Even in America, money lures all too many in both public life and private life. It is impressive how intent the top 1 percent of income earners are on keeping their taxes down and—if the discussion in the press is accurate—how keen the bottom 99 percent are on putting the nation's hands on top incomes. The question here, in our search for sources of reduced dynamism, is whether money "decides things" *more* than it did in the 1960s or the 1920s. A renowned philosopher, John Dewey, was a thoughtful observer of the role of money in 1920s America. (Thinking that almost all those engaged in a company play no imaginative, intellectual, or emotional part in its activities—only the manager does—he sought employee cooperatives to nurture a "new individualism." Yet he was important for having put the imaginative, the intellectual, and the emotional into public discussion. Process is important: Desired ends may not justify the means.) In 1929 Dewey wrote:

> [W]e are living in a money culture. . . . Worth is measured by ability to
> hold one's own or to get ahead in a competitive pecuniary race. . . . [T]he
> chief ambition of parents in the [working] class [is] that their children
> should climb into the business (and professional) class. . . . [T]he personal

habits most prized [are] clear-sighted vision of personal advantage and resolute ambition to secure it at any human cost.[6]

Dewey went on to suggest how the new "money culture" could have come about:

Industry and business conducted for money profit are nothing new . . . they come to us from a long past. But the invention of the machine has given them a power and scope they never had in the past from which they derive. . . . [W]e depend on a novel combination of the machine and money, and the result is the pecuniary culture characteristic of our civilization. . . . There is a perversion of the whole idea of individualism to conform to the practices of a pecuniary culture.

Dewey's argument can be taken in other directions. Just as the size of markets, measured by revenue, heightened the desire to make a top salary by driving up the salaries of those in top positions, so the Reagan cuts of the high-end tax rates faced by top managers, bankers, and investors fueled a craze for money in the 1990s—a craze refueled by the Bush tax cuts in the 2000s.[7] On the Deweyan view, the "pecuniary culture" must have received another boost around the world—from Shanghai to Munich to Silicon Valley—with the globalization of the 1970s and 1980s and the information and communications revolution of the 1990s. The sight of companies going global and people making billions naturally excited the imagination of many more firms and people. The big gains won in the stock market in the 1960s, the fortunes made in corporate raids by private equity firms in the 1980s, and the speculative fever of the dot.com years of the 1990s suggested the possibility of endless and enormous gains.

The question in this chapter is not whether "greed is good." What the good *is* belongs to the next chapter. The question here is whether the heightened aspirations for money or wealth help account for the economic decline that was clearly underway in America by the early 1970s: the slower growth, higher unemployment, and lower job satisfaction, as well as for the massive fiscal stimuli, dereliction of regulators, and the speculative manias. The answer is yes. Wealth seeking competes with innovation seeking, so many turned away

6. Dewey, "The House Divided against Itself," republished in Dewey, *Individualism Old and New*. This extract appears on p. 6 of that volume; the following extract appears on p. 9.

7. These tax cuts may have been unintended consequences of technical papers by Phelps in 1973 and Efraim Sadka in 1976 arguing that if the marginal tax rate in the highest bracket is a positive number, the rates cannot be tax-efficient: cutting rates at the top could coax income earners to step up their income and so pay a larger tax while doing so taxes unchanged incomes at the old rates.

from innovating. Also, investors and managers became more interested in the quick buck. The financial sector thus leveraged its equity to make huge bets in the areas it had long known—home lending and trading in government securities and foreign currencies—and to step into areas about which there was no empirical knowledge—asset-backed securities and credit default swaps. Business expansion and business investment were squeezed. Given the monetary rewards, more and more able and talented young people chose to go into the financial sector, rather than into the business sector. Significant amounts of capital, too, were redirected from the business sector to the financial sector. Since this development was global, not all financing could come from foreign saving: some domestic business investment was necessarily displaced.

The nearly obsessive focus on money no doubt lies behind the much-commented rise in the litigiousness of American society. Those who envy the talent of others know that little can be done about it, but people who envy the wealth of others can seize opportunities—or manufacture them, if necessary—to sue other people. The lawsuit culture undoubtedly costs an innovative economy some of its dynamism. People devoting their time and energies to suing one another have less time and energy left for innovation. A Silicon Valley entrepreneur commented that today a start-up company would need as many lawyers as engineers.

Several observers have spoken of other sources of a change in the prevailing culture of contemporary societies, however. Mrs. Thatcher's observation that people used to aspire to do something, not to reach some social station, strikes a chord. In the culture of social standing or celebrity, people struggle to get ahead of others, to rise in rank—to climb the greasy pole, but not to produce anything. Substantive achievement is not recognized. This culture depreciates the moral qualities that high-achieving people generally have—determination, judgment, and care—and puts a harsh light on the ways in which they are ordinary or worse—their everyday habits and their peccadilloes. In many recent biographies of some great figures, the pattern is to dwell on the subject's failings and transgressions. Biographies of Edwin Hubble, Edward Hopper, and Alfred Hitchcock are examples. More evidence of this can be seen in recent biographies of Thomas Jefferson that paint him as going along with slavery when in fact his hatred of slavery was a salient feature of his public life. Some reviewers devoted more space to the accusations than to the achievements for which their subjects had become recognized and admired. Ironically, reviews of the recent film biography of Mrs. Thatcher, *Iron Lady,* saw the film as about the "pathos of her personal life," not noticing that the film traced her entire career and was rich in scenes, speeches, and remarks on politics, political economy, and the society around her—including her withering remark about the desire to "do something."

The ethos of American society has declined to even lower lows, however. Recent decades saw the development of a *culture of self-importance* or *entitlement.* Many academics, once researchers endlessly testing ideas, now rate themselves so highly that they pontificate with no research at all. Cold callers and bulk emailers intrude as if their exigencies justified the disruption. Teenage girls have babies as pets to reinforce their importance. The growing sense of entitlement helps explain the ever-rising outlays for the safety net, which, in artificially raising economic independence beyond what people's private wealth would provide, makes it harder to obtain employee loyalty and employee engagement. The attitude of entitlement can only make it harder for a start-up firm to obtain employees who take initiative, give a hand to others, and lend the concentration and judgment on which success importantly depends. The culture of self-importance is another contributor to the litigiousness touched on above.

Many observers of America have commented on the rise of what is called an adolescent culture. What is being observed is not a lessened willingness to make bets. Adolescents are often drawn to taking a risk, and many of today's financial firms have been "betting the ranch," or the company. A lessened willingness to save *is* observed, but high saving in a nation is not an absolutely necessary condition for high innovation: some other nation may do the saving, or the effort required may come out of other investment activity. Yet developing creative, innovative products does require entrepreneurs with the willingness to dedicate themselves to a process that, whatever its fascinations, would be jeopardized if they paid themselves cash that the project may need. And, unfortunately, the willingness to accept austerity for a year or two or more in the quest for an achievement, which grown-ups routinely did in the 19th century, does appear to have dwindled. Peter Thiel, a venture capitalist in social media, noticed in his interviews of fledgling start-up CEOs that the young entrepreneurs were paying themselves more than 100,000 dollars a year (until he met Mark Zuckerberg at Facebook, who paid himself very little). Furthermore, originality requires being willing and able to intensely concentrate on a regular basis for a long period of time. And this ability seems also to have waned in recent decades. An educator told Elie Wiesel that Shakespeare's *Julius Caesar* could not be taught any longer in New York State high schools because students lacked the attention span to read it.

As has been widely noted, today's young people have, on average, less experience with solitude than those in previous generations. A large proportion of persons entering the labor force from the late 1940s to the mid-1960s were only children, so they learned when growing up to fantasize and think by themselves. Since then, only children have become more rare. Furthermore, people by themselves with some time to think are now offered the distractions of the social media—"the economy of internet self-gratification." The young generation today needs to be continually in contact through blogs, email, and Twitter. That leads to a decline in thinking, which reinforces conformism. More and more people accept the positions taken by their political party or religion or friends rather than working out their own positions. It would be surprising if this conformity did not weigh on innovation in the business economy.

With the rise of the group in the American economy, one might think that the support of the group has bolstered the sense of security, so that a person would feel safe enough to venture to innovate. However, the group may have operated instead to potentiate the importance of not losing position in the group, as measured by income and employment status.

Besides all these new values, there has appeared a resurgence of traditional values that has encroached on dynamism in another way. The movement for a new attention to family values has put pressure on companies to allow employees to work at home, as many, both men and women, are doing. The detachment of an appreciable part of a company's workforce from the company offices is bound to reduce the frequency of interaction among employees and thus reduce the innovativeness not only of the remote workers but also the innovativeness of the employees still in the office. This is not sheer speculation. A front page newspaper story describes the rise of home-workers to alarming proportions in recent years and the courageous move of one corporation, Yahoo and its new head, Marissa Mayer, in the past year to bring home-workers back to the office.[8]

In summary, modern values may well remain intact—that these nutrients of a life of richness and personal growth are not extinct is basic to this book's thesis that grassroots dynamism and the resulting indigenous innovation must be a goal of every nation that can reach it! And traditional values are not all bad—not all of them. Yet a society may allow some of its traditional values lying alongside its modern values to get in the way of its dynamism.

8. See "Yahoo Orders Home Workers Back to the Office," *New York Times,* February 25, 2013.

A Broader Nexus between the State and the Economy

Critics of the role played by the state on both the left and the right have pointed to ways in which governments have gone well beyond the classical role of stepping in to repair market failures and redress economic injustice. Politicians use their governmental power to dispense patronage in hope of electoral support, and political parties solicit or accept contributions from companies, unions, political funds, and wealthy individuals in return for support of their special interests. In the competition for votes and campaign funds, some economic inefficiencies and injustices are lost in the shuffle. It has not been considered, however, that the politicization of government costs a *modern* economy some of its *dynamism*—even if static inefficiency and injustice have not worsened.

There has always been some degree of corporatism of one variety or another—interrelations between the state on the one hand and capital and labor on the other. By now, though, there has been a considerable broadening of the nexus between the state and the business economy, much of it in the past decade. Chapter 6 recounted America's corporatist developments in the 1930s, when unions gained huge power. (Unions shrank in the private sector over the postwar decades with the Chandlerian transformation of companies into upper and middle managers and their assistants, but union coverage has since expanded into the public sector.) The chapter also recounted fresh corporatist developments that began in the 1950s when powerful companies exerted enormous influence on the government. This development in America was clear to Dwight Eisenhower, who referred to the "military-industrial complex" in his presidential valedictory in 1963.

Recently, a *congressional-banking* complex has developed far beyond what existed before. One would think that the government would be in an adversarial relationship to the banks in view of its duty to police their observance of regulatory restrictions and requirements. Yet banks and political interests have entered into new arrangements for their mutual benefit. One such relationship regards banks' holdings of U.S. government debt. A bank is generally required to hold equity against its holdings of assets, so it does not become insolvent at the slightest fall in their prices, and government debt is not exceptionally safe—governments can default without a bankruptcy court to look after the bondholders. But U.S. banks have been exempted from equity requirements on their holdings of U.S. sovereign debt (and multilateral agreements at the Bank for International Settlements exempt all banks from equity requirements on all sovereign debt). The benefit to the banks is that they are spared the capital cost of the equity. The benefit to the government is that it obtains higher prices on its bond offerings—thus lower interest rates—to the extent that the banks seize upon the decreased cost of holding government debt to acquire more government debt. The government in turn may seize upon the reduction in its interest cost to sell more public debt with which to finance larger or more prolonged budgetary deficits. The gain to the political parties from being able to borrow more cheaply and thus borrow more is obvious: The bailouts that a group of nations sent to Greece in its 2011/2012 fiscal crisis went straight to the banks that held Greek debt, to protect the banks' willingness and capacity to hold huge levels of sovereign debt. Yet society does not gain by privileging the debt of the state, since that makes it harder for businesses to finance capital expenditures and innovative projects.[9] And interventions to discourage or prevent governments from defaulting shuts down the credit market's function of curbing credit to nations that borrow so much as to destabilize their economies and those of commercial and financial partners, thus making the global economy more unstable, which is a deterrent to attempts at innovation, which are already quite risky.

Another such relationship regards residential mortgages. In 1970, two government-sponsored enterprises went into the banking business when Congress authorized the existing Federal National Mortgage Association, known as Fannie Mae, to purchase private mortgages not insured by other agencies and created the Federal Home Loan Mortgage Corporation, known as Freddie Mac, to compete with Fannie Mae. Legislation signed by George H. W. Bush in 1992 directed that these government sponsored enterprises (GSEs) extend their financing to "affordable housing" for "low- and moderate-income families." The Clinton administration in 1999 pushed Fannie Mae into subprime mortgages and into easing credit requirements on subprime borrowers. Congress in that year charged both GSEs with buying 30 percent of the mortgages on new dwellings in their respective markets, and banks were pressured to step up their purchases from the GSEs of mortgage-backed securities. By 2006, Fannie Mae and Freddie Mac had acquired mortgages costing 2 trillion dollars—one-seventh of the annual GDP. The role the government played here is not sufficient to explain the breadth of the speculative boom in housing that occurred: High-priced houses defaulted

---

9. See Amar Bhidé and Edmund Phelps, "More Harm Than Good: How the IMF's Business Model Sabotages Properly Functioning Capitalism."

with the same likelihood in 2008 as low-priced houses. Neither is that role sufficient to explain how housing prices rose 60 percent before falling to earth: There had to be a speculative fever, since stepping up homebuilding by 30 percent would not seem to require a 60 percent increase in prices.

These financial relationships are the tip of an iceberg—a corporatist *complex* between the government and the private sector. The pervasiveness was suggested by the inexorable accumulation of regulations cited in Chapters 7 and 9. Data from Unified Agenda report that from 1997 to 2006 there were about 80 new "significant" rules a year (each costing at least 100 million dollars annually).[10] Significant new rules per year went into an even steeper climb in 2007—reaching 150 a year in 2011. That is not only an ominous trend. The cumulative addition of new rules since 1996 may already be having perceptible effects on investment and on interest in innovation. Start-up firms may need more and more lawyers to navigate their way through an ever-larger thicket of regulation.

A parallel development concerns patents and copyrights. In 1704, when commissions of literary works by princes and the aristocracy could no longer slake the literate public's thirst for reading, Daniel Defoe, the novelist, economist, and foremost advocate of intellectual property of his day, complained that literary works were copied so fast that no one made a living from writing—a clear market failure. England introduced the first copyright protection with the 1709 Statute of Anne in the reign of Queen Anne. Parliament had already enacted patent protection with the 1623 Statute of Monopolies in the reign of James I. In that early time, patent protection almost certainly encouraged creating new methods or new products more than it discouraged creating them through fear of royalties owed others and the legal costs of disputing royalty claims. (For the first patent owner there was nothing but blue skies.) But now the economy is clogged with patents. In the high-tech industries, there is such a dark thicket of patents in force that a creator of a new method might well require as many lawyers as engineers to proceed. In the pharmaceutical industry, excessive patent protection is causing litigation and

10. The data are compiled semi-annually by the Regulatory Information Service Center at Unified Agenda. Note that the cumulative mounts up to non-negligible levels. If those costs are undiminished, the total cost per year of just those post-1996 rules must have mounted to *at least* 80 billion dollars a year by 2006; and if 80 such new rules continue to be written, the cost will mount to at least 160 billion by 2016 and 240 billion by 2026. The latter cost is 2 percent of a 10 trillion dollar GDP and 1.5 percent of a 15 trillion GDP. Very possibly each new significant rule will be subject to "increasing costs," as lawmakers run out of rules that meet little resistance.

the rise in pharmaceutical prices.[11] Copyright protection has only recently seen controversy. The industries producing literary and artistic products do not seem so clogged with copyright protection as to have driven away many working writers, artists, and designers. But it is important to recall that an innovation is greater, the wider its use. The passage by Congress in 1998 of the Sonny Bono Act lengthening copyright protection by 20 years—to author's life plus 70 years—prevents wider use of Walt Disney's creations and prevents wider use of performances copyrighted by the record companies. The length of the copyright term may also be deterring new innovations that would have had to draw on products at Disney and EMI. Members of Congress have a private interest in lengthening copyright and patent protections, since they can expect to share in the big gains of the few without paying for the small costs borne by the rest of society.

Industries in which the government has been an important regulator or protector are particularly liable, in view of their close contact, to become industries that seek more extensive government aid. As Luigi Zingales wrote, businesses took advantage of "a new opportunity: using political influence not just to reduce government influence but to mold it to companies' advantage."[12] That nicely sums up one of the important ways by which corporatism metastasized into a densely interconnected system of mutually beneficial relationships between private and public—a system that is virtually a parallel economy. It is a system its advocates call industrial policy; its critics, corporate welfare.

A subsidy is not inherently bad. But subsidies to industries (including the farm industry)—grants, loans, guarantees, and tax breaks—often masquerade as changes in the direction of the market economy when their real function is to benefit supporters and cronies of legislators. And not with small potatoes: the outlay for corporate welfare reached 92 billion dollars in fiscal year 2006. As could have been expected, a number of prominent subsidized programs became notorious for their disastrous losses: the Supersonic Transport and the Synthetic Fuels Corporation in the 1970s, the ethanol subsidy of the 1990s, and Fannie Mae and Freddie Mac in the past five years. Of

---

11. The pharmaceutical industry lays the diminished flow of new drugs to the longer time required for drug approval by the regulatory body and suggests that lengthening patent protection of new drugs would be a natural remedy. But the long time it takes the regulatory authority to license new drugs operates to reduce their number and to stretch out their expected lifetime, and the lengthy patent protection merely ensures that competing producers will not drive down the prices, causing the innovators to lose their monopoly rents.

12. Zingales, *A Capitalism for the People*.

course, many companies, notably Hollywood studios, have had their disasters too. The problem is that subsidies redirect the economy's innovation toward politicians, who lack deep specialized knowledge, and away from the private sphere, where judgments are made by idea men, entrepreneurs, financiers, and market people who consider whether there are not better initiatives to think about or develop.

The nexus between private and public, while pervasive, is far more invasive in a few targeted industries. The control of the government over the education and healthcare industries has attracted attention of late. It can no longer be described in terms of enumerated regulations, protections, and subsidies: it is organic and granular. A recent paper by Arnold Kling and Nick Schulz describes this government control:

> [H]ealth care and education are increasingly government-dominated industries. And this domination produces two ill effects that exacerbate the changes these sectors are already undergoing: Government influence artificially increases the demand for both health care and education (by significantly subsidizing both) and it makes both sectors even less efficient than they would be otherwise (by shielding them from market forces).[13]

Efficiency is not the only thing adversely affected. Some pathways of innovation have been blocked as well. There is little room now for entry into the industry of private schools and colleges or of private hospitals, which had spearheaded the 20th-century advances in American education and medicine; and little room for doctors to deviate from standard procedures and teachers to try out new courses and teaching methods.

It is easy to find a downside in virtually everything done by politicians—a "latent function" masquerading as benevolence. We forget that most regulations, protections, and effective nationalizations have benefits as well as costs, else it would have been hard to make a case for them. So one wonders: How large a toll does the corporatist trend take on dynamism? Fortunately, the spread of such corporatist relationships across the economy, if it is as deep and pervasive as suggested above, can be expected to leave evidence of various kinds. We know that corporatist governments find it more convenient to deal with an industry populated by a few giant corporations than one with a great many small enterprises: The government has the phone numbers of the corporate giants. And there is evidence of a huge rise in industrial concentration in the American economy over the past six decades. In the financial

13. Kling and Schulz, "The New Commanding Heights," p. 10.

sector, the big banks have become behemoths, while the small banks have shrunk. In the non-financial sector too, economic activity has moved dramatically away from small and medium-sized enterprises (on which innovation largely depends) to large corporations, as shown in official data compiled in 2011 by John Foster, Robert McChesney, and Jamil Jonna.[14] Gross profits of the 200 largest corporations as a percentage of gross profits in the economy went from about 15 percent in the early 1950s to 26 percent by the mid-1960s, a level around which it fluctuated until 1966; then it rose steeply to about 30 percent in the period 2004–2008. (About the same is true of the revenue.) The market share of the four largest firms in selected retail industries has— very roughly—doubled between 1992 and 2007, reaching astonishing levels, such as 71 percent in book stores and 73 percent in both computer/software stores and general merchandise stores. As a consequence of government regulations and union work rules, there are often routine delays in starting and completing urban office buildings—delays so long that some new ideas have to be passed up.

Furthermore, if the large companies that have spread in the past couple of decades are relatively secure, their exciting and unpredicted growth behind them, we should expect to find evidence that more and more of the economy, companies or industries, are zones of stability—zones not firing many and not hiring many either—and, nestled among such zones, fewer and fewer zones of development (these are the start-ups) or growth (these are the successful ones) or shrinkage (the ones that are failing). It is no surprise, therefore, to find in Figure 10.1 a downhill trend in *job destruction* from 1989 to 2007, as more and more workers are safe in the cocoons of the large established companies. The economy seems to be moving to a frozen state! Over the same span, a downward trend in *job creation* is visible too, as fewer and fewer of the working-age population are entering or leaving the start-ups, the growth companies, and the failing companies.[15] In short, the economy gives

14. Foster et al., "Monopoly and Competition in Twenty-First Century Capitalism."
15. It must be added that, since the former, relatively stable, zones, taken together, are the preponderant part of the economy, they are capable of providing a significant amount of creative, intellectual work in the aggregate while a small amount per worker; the other zones provide a disproportional amount of creative work, but they are a small part of the economy. When in the autumn of 2009 the large companies took fright at the fall-off in prices and sales, they terminated many of the forward-looking projects—projects building "organizational capital," in recent terminology—and terminated the employees who were at work on them. (The national statistics recorded the subsequent rise in output per employee, and most commentators called it a rise of "productivity," though no advance in methods of production or improvement in prices had occurred.)

Fewer new businesses are being started . . .

Business births (thousands)

2006   550   2009   400

. . . but start-ups play a crucial role in job creation . . .

Net job creation by type of company (millions)

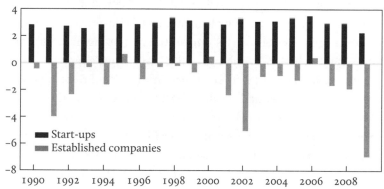

. . . which remains weak

U.S. private sector job creation and destruction (% of employment)

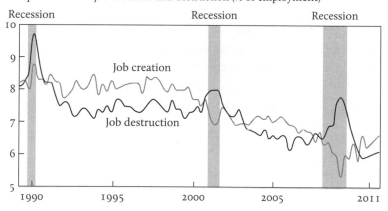

FIGURE 10.1 Start-ups in the United States, 1990–2009 (Source: *Financial Times.* © The Financial Times Limited 2013. All Rights Reserved.)

evidence of a relentless decline in *turnover,* which is one of the rather reliable signs of a decline in economic vitality and the fruit that can grow from it if properly tended: economic dynamism.

The abovementioned activities of government represent a corruption of the role of the state, once seen as advancing people's prosperity and achievement. From 1830 to 1930, federal government initiative and intervention were animated by a classical concern for *resources* and *productivity:* the canals, the Louisiana Purchase, the transcontinental railroad, public schools, and so forth; attention later widened to abuses in business, such as protection for workers, creditors, and investors. There was no initiative and intervention aimed at the direction and stability of consumption, such as social insurance programs that supplemented available private insurance. With the reemergence in Bismarck's time of the corporatist idea of government, that began to change. By the end of the 1940s, entitlements in the category of *social insurance* had been established in America, Britain, and elsewhere: insurance for the aged and the disabled (Social Security in the United States) and medical insurance (Medicare in the United States) as well as smaller programs, such as unemployment insurance. By the end of the 1960s, entitlements in the category of *social assistance* were widespread: help with medical needs of the poor (Medicaid in the United States), nutritional needs (Food Stamps), and housing needs. What Europe terms its "social model" socialized the provision of medical care with state-owned hospitals and state-employed doctors, while America's model totally corporatized medical care with programs that regulated services, set prices, and reimbursed the services of private doctors and private hospitals. Now all this is overgrown and bungled.

Few grasp the scale of these social welfare programs. It is true that America fell far behind Europe in social spending in the 1980s: By 1990 social expenditure by governments in the 21 nations of the European Union stood at 20.5 percent of GDP; the figure in the United States was 13.5 percent. But, slowly, the United States has been catching up to the Continent, while Germany and Sweden retrenched from 2003 to 2007: By 2000, the EU spending stood at 21.5 percent, the United States was at 14.5. By 2007 the European Union was at 22.0, while the United States reached 16.2. (All the 2012 figures are up, at 24.1 and 19.5, respectively, owing to unemployment relief.) That spending level in America is now large enough to be quite important. It approaches one-quarter of disposable income. That is in the neighborhood of the share of nonwage income in disposable income—dividends, interest income, proprietorship profits, and land rents. Thus the income of

Americans coming from what may be called *social wealth* is comparable to the income deriving from their private wealth. Moreover, few benefits of social wealth are taxed, while the income from private wealth is all taxable.

In America, as in France and, to a lesser extent, one or two other nations, social welfare outlays will soon have a mountain to climb. A mass of baby boomers working their way through the system will be adding hugely to the annual claims on Social Security and Medicare as they reach retirement. And the baby boomers will not be followed by a mass of replacements entering the labor force. So, sooner or later, additional tax revenues must be raised on both counts (to the extent that "discretionary" spending cannot or will not be cut). Hence, disposable income will be cut. Thus the world of entitlement will nearly swamp the world of work. A calculation by a New York financial economist, Mary Meeker, finds that the *present discounted value* of Americans' entitlements added up to 66 trillion dollars at the end of 2010—a sum that is 569 percent of Americans' disposable income; this dwarfs the U.S. public debt of about 10 trillion. That level of social wealth exceeds Americans' private wealth. (Official data put household net wealth at only 60 trillion dollars in mid-year 2011, or 517 percent of disposable income: assets were 74 trillion and liabilities 14 trillion.) Thus the system of social welfare in America, while commonly thought to be a pale reflection of what is offered by Europe's social model, is in fact quite a colossus.

In one theory of this surge, legislators enacted entitlements on this scale on the assumption that the economy would "grow out" of these entitlements before their deficit financing became onerous, which, as the Great Slowdown went on and on, could finally be seen to be a huge mistake. As Richard Ravitch, a warrior of political reform in both city and state governments, said:

> Politics in America has always been a matter of people running for office
> on the promises that they are going to confer more benefits. But all of a
> sudden, we can no longer afford to . . . pay for all the benefits we've . . .
> obligated ourselves to pay.[16]

But most of the entitlements created were calculated. Even in the past 10 years, new benefits have been enacted where their cost could start later or start small so that little or no tax increase was required. It helped that expansion of the colossus had bipartisan support from Nixon to Bush. The 2003 law signed by President Bush extending Medicare from hospital bills to

16. Quoted in Jacob Gershman, "Gotham's Savior, Beaten by Albany," *Wall Street Journal*, December 11–12, 2010, p. A13.

medicines, which added several trillion dollars to the present value of entitle-ments at a stroke, had the support of Democrats and Republicans alike. Many Republican legislators, finding that the working class had joined the party in the Reagan years, swallowed their distaste for entitlements. The Democratic party, finding in its midst middle class people who wanted to adopt Europe's social model as much as possible, presented no opposition.

Traditional values have had a more radical influence on the policymaking of Republicans as well as Democrats. Republicans are well known for their unwillingness to use the government's powers of taxation to redistribute—from nationals to foreigners, from profits to wages, and even from high-wage earners to low-wage earners. In their doctrine, revenues are to be reserved for the general interest. Yet, since the 1970s, Republicans from Richard Nixon to George W. Bush have interpreted various government benefit, from social insurance programs to subsidized access to mortgage credit and education loans to the middle class, as being in the general interest.

In another theory of the surge, growth of public benefits follows natu-rally with the growth of people's incomes—Wagner's Law. But income growth was slower from 1973 to 2007 than it had been in previous postwar decades. A quite different theory of the surge views the rise of the superstructure of entitlements—much like the rise of giant corporations—as a normal phe-nomenon in the development of organizations. They seek resources with which to achieve their goals and then to grow large enough to be able to sur-vive as long as they can. Once traditional limits on government were with-drawn, the growth of the public agencies was inexorable.

This colossus has had important consequences—and not just the obvi-ous sidelining of alternative government programs, such as addressing the nation's crumbling infrastructure or jobs and wages of the working poor. An effect of consumption entitlements (and public consumption in general) on the population's participation in the economy has long been identified in the classical economics of public finance. The familiar argument is that the higher tax rate imposed on income to pay for the benefit discourages work. (One's savings from the state's providing things free just pays one's tax, but by working a little less one can reduce the tax owed without affecting the benefits.)

Two other links between entitlements to employment, however, operate independently of tax rates. Recall that increased wealth has a "wealth effect," diminishing participation in the economy—the supply of labor—and thus contracting employment; of course, an increase in the after-tax *wage* (or "net wage") that employers offer would have the opposite effect, drawing people into participating in the economy and thus expanding employment. The *ratio* of the net wage to wealth is what matters (in many models), so equal percentage increases in wages and wealth offset one another. That ratio soared from the early 1950s to 1965–1975 with the resumption of fast productivity growth in the 1950s and 1960s, which largely explains the peak levels of employment reached in the 1960s. (See Figure 10.2.) The ratio subsided after the Great Productivity Slowdown brought about slower growth of wages, which partially explains the relatively low employment prevailing from 1979 to 2008. (The years of normal employment in 1995–1996 fit nicely with the normal level of the wage-wealth ratio. The sharp fluctuations of the late 1990s and mid-2000s are explained by the internet boom and the construction boom.) But if we add *social* wealth to the "wealth" in the wage-wealth ratio, fattening the denominator, we explain about half the difference between the high post-boom, post-crisis employment rates in 2011–2012 and the level in 1995–1996.

The other link operates through the demand for labor. If the government finances the future explosion of entitlement outlays mostly by an outpouring of government debt, raising taxes later to service that debt (the way governments finance wars), the effect is the prospect of increased interest rates in the future and thus even in the present, and perhaps increased tax rates on businesses at some point. Even today when savers are willing to lend at cheap interest rates, since they no longer are expecting bonanzas of future consumption, these prospects must weigh on share prices and the values placed on the business assets that companies require to produce—plants, employees, and overseas customers.[17]

These employment effects from new entitlements hinge on what might be called the Greek disease but could just as well be called the American disease. The "sound" response of fiscal policy would announce a period of revenue increases leading to a reduction of the public debt that would *decrease* people's *private* wealth by the amount that the new entitlement *increases* their

17. Edmund Phelps and Gylfi Zoega in "Portents of a Darkening Outlook: Falling Equities and a Weaker Dollar Herald Economic Slowdown," *Financial Times*, July 31, 2002, say that "the driving forces behind big swings in a nation's economic activity . . . are non-monetary fundamentals" and high up on the list of those are "workers' wealth and entitlements." The focus was narrowed to future entitlement outlays in Phelps, "The Way We Live Now," *Wall Street Journal*, December 28, 2004. It took readers through the consequences of a demographic time bomb when 15 to 20 years later the bond market will be flooded with public debt to cover the swelling size of Social Security and Medicare outlays. Both essays emphasized that expected future entitlement outlays contract present employment by weighing down share prices and the real exchange rate.

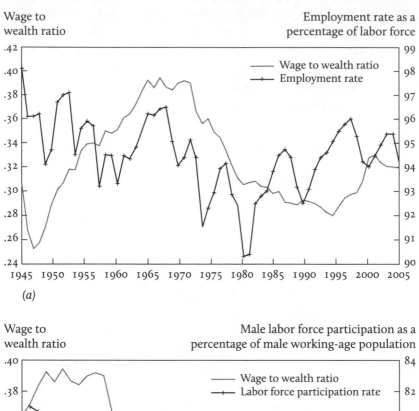

(a)

Wage to
wealth ratio

Male labor force participation as a
percentage of male working-age population

(b)

FIGURE 10.2 (a) Wage to wealth ratio and the employment rate. (b) Wage to wealth ratio and the labor force participation rate (males only). (Source: Gylfi Zoega.)

social wealth. In this way, the government would "neutralize" the wealth effect on employment and saving of the new government program, as first proposed in Phelps, *Fiscal Neutrality toward Economic Growth* (1965). Yet, under President George W. Bush, the government went the other way with the 2001 and 2003 tax reductions. In a February 2001 op-ed, "The Unproven Case for Tax Cuts," the present author protested:

> The tax cut would impose a burden on the future either in reduced public services or else a public debt much increased. This burden . . . makes the tax cut vulnerable to several objections. [One] is that, while the burden of the Bush tax cut would go on forever, its effectiveness [in providing a fillip to labor supply] would not. With time, the incentive effects would progressively weaken and the structural lift to employment would disappear, as workers and managers grew wealthier in response to their higher after-tax wages. . . . If public services are not to be cut back, tax rates must sooner or later go higher than they otherwise would have done in order to deal with the increased public debt. [And] for all we know, the future is as likely to get worse as to get better. . . . Bush's economic policy turns its back on Americans' traditional desire to leave the country better than they found it. In [the 1950s and] 1990s this ameliorist spirit was expressed in the policy of setting tax rates high enough to pay down the government's debts and to emerge with . . . the possibility of falling tax rates in the future. In Washington's lurch toward large tax cuts, and even large spending increases, there is a profound—indeed, disquieting—shift in economic philosophy.

It is not puzzling that legislators let taxes lag behind the entitlements they create, of course. If they had to raise taxes very visibly when enacting a new entitlement, the entitlement might fail to gather enough votes to pass. By cutting taxes they convey the impression that experts have advised that future tax increases are far from necessary: one explanation for under-taxation.

Here innovation finally comes in. We have seen that the welfare colossus shrinks the role of the market by reducing people's incentives to earn; it does that either by causing higher tax rates (with no increase in wealth) or causing higher wealth (with little or no tax increase). That in turn reduces the incentive of market enterprises to engage in innovative activity. The scale of innovation, as Smith would have put it, is limited by the *size of the market*. If, for example, everyone works 30 hours a week instead of 40, the stock of innovations will grow more slowly, as will the stock of capital.

A by-product of the sizeable increase in the scope and size of government in America has been a need for higher taxes. A political pact appears to have been reached in which the upper half of income earners propose to the poor, "we will take on your share of the taxes if you agree that we decide what you will receive in the form of education, public projects, and so on." The result is a bias against state expenditure for education and infrastructure: why would a taxpaying family want music classes for children if the taxpayers had to pay for their own two children plus the children of a nonpaying family? In effect, the lower half accepts a starved public sector in return for a reduction of take-home inequality—a somewhat illusory reduction at that.

It is no wonder, in view of the adverse developments in institutions, values, and economic policies, that America gives signs of a serious decline in economic dynamism and thus—most of the time—in resulting innovation. While the rate of innovation fluctuates, it has been subdued most of the time over most of the business sector since the early 1970s. It is also no wonder, in view of the rise of anti-modern values and policies, that the lower segments of the working population, whose modern values were relatively fragile and their disadvantages daunting to begin with, have suffered a costly decline in their rewards relative to others and in their upward mobility.

The Second Transformation

At this point, which is the end of the narrative and the climax of the book, it may be useful to recapitulate the main observations made and the inferences drawn.

The changes from the 1970s to the 2000s in the way America's economy works—most of which came earlier to the other great avatars of modern capitalism, Britain, France, and Germany—are momentous. The new reworking of the American economy constitutes a Second Transformation—a transformation a century and a half after the Great Transformation, 1820–1930, brought modern capitalism. That first incarnation of modern capitalism did not entail zero government. It could and did operate alongside activist governments that decided whether to purchase new lands, whether to provide infrastructure capital with or without user charges, and where taxation would best raise the revenue needed to function. That modern version of capitalism could have instituted low-wage work subsidies to companies to widen inclusion, without weakening its modern spirit. But while the government, of necessity, was making basic judgments in the political sphere, there was a private sphere in which individuals made the final decisions. Wealth owners—capitalists—got to judge how best to invest their wealth, drawing on the new ideas of imaginative business people and the zeal of resourceful entrepreneurs. This modern capitalism became a worldbeater when, in the 1800s, it acquired endemic, impressive capabilities for indigenous innovation. Those few societies willing and able to adopt it enjoyed unrivaled prosperity, widespread job satisfaction, productivity that was the marvel of the world, and the end of mass privation for the first time in human history.

The second transformation has injected a tacit and finely articulated form of corporatism into the American economy. Modern capitalism has been cordoned off (health and education are to some extent restricted areas) and constrained where it is still in place. The system is less primitive or blatant than that of Bismarck or Mussolini. But its political nature is similar: It draws no line between the state and the market, thus it creates a parallel economy that competes with the market economy and is another source of risk, scaring off innovations. Corporatism's managerial state has assumed responsibility for looking after everything from the incomes of the middle class to the profitability of large corporations to industrial advances. Corporatists, like the communists before them, assumed that all their wishful goals were possible without cost.

The economic performance of the economies that had so recently been exemplars of modern capitalism has recently been disastrous. Yet the fault lies not with the inevitable shortcomings of a well-maintained modern capitalism or even a "reckless" one allowed to operate with a "lack of regulation." It lies with the new corporatism:

> The new corporatism chokes off the dynamism that makes for engaging work, faster economic growth, and greater opportunity and inclusion. [It] does that by maintaining lethargic, wasteful, unproductive and well-connected firms at the expense of dynamic newcomers and outsiders; and by pursuing goals such as consumption, social insurance, and rescue of companies and industries over nourishing lives of engagement, creating, and exploring. Today, airlines, auto manufacturers, agricultural companies, media, investment banks, and much more have at some point been deemed too important to weather the free market on their own, receiving a helping hand in the name of the "public good."

> The costs of corporatism are all around us: dysfunctional corporations that survive despite their gross inability to serve their customers; sclerotic economies with slow output growth; a dearth of engaging work; scant opportunities for young people; governments bankrupted by their efforts to palliate these problems; and increasing concentration of wealth in the

hands of those connected enough to be on the right side of the corporatist deal.[18]

Tragically, this system in parts of the world, notably north Africa, is commonly called "capitalism" because the capital there is largely under private ownership, no matter that it is a system ruled by political power—by an alliance of leaders in the state and leaders in the state-backed corporations, generally coming from the same elite—not by private capital in the sense of faceless and friendless capitalists in a brutal competition to find profits before someone else does—"capital" in the sense of Marx. And, cynically, in America, Britain, and continental Western Europe, the corporatist system's apologists and beneficiaries have the temerity to blame all the recent failures on "recklessness," and "lack of regulation" and to suggest that "the future of capitalism" hangs on more oversight and regulation, which in reality means more corporatism.

In all the numerical data on the broadened nexus between government and society—between the state and the individual—there is no clear evidence on the degree to which corporations, banks, and individuals are the drivers of the new system and the extent to which politicians supply the impetus. A 2012 documentary film, *Heist: Who Stole the American Dream?* sees corporations and banks as the sole instigators:

> In 1978, Supreme Court Justice Lewis Powell . . . urged American corporations to take a stronger role in influencing politics and law. . . . While on the Supreme Court, he successfully argued for the right of corporations to make political contributions. . . . Starting in 1994, the North American Free Trade Agreement [NAFTA], which encouraged the outsourcing of cheap labor; the 1999 repeal of parts of the Glass-Steagall Act, which had separated commercial and investment banking; and the Commodity Futures Modernization Act of 2000, which deregulated over-the-counter derivatives, allowed financial institutions to run wild. Both major parties promoted deregulation fever.[19]

These charges are not contextualized. There is no mention that the Court was extending to corporations what it had granted in the spirit of corporatism to labor unions long ago—and with little complaint. NAFTA was a step toward free trade, which is much valued by a great portion of American and

18. Ammous and Phelps, "Blaming Capitalism for the Ills of Corporatism," *Project Syndicate,* January 31, 2012.

19. The summary is in the movie review by Stephen Holden, "Tracing the Great Recession to a Memo 40 Years Ago," *New York Times,* March 1, 2012.

European society. Neither is it mentioned that in legalizing over-the-counter derivatives, America was catching up to the structured financial products invented in Italy and analyzed by French mathematicians. Nor is it mentioned that it was the U.S. government that rigged the banking industry for sub-prime housing instead of focusing on innovation and financing government deficits; it was the government that enticed people into levels of consumption and leisure they could not afford.

But it hardly matters. Even if shareowners, lenders, and wealth owners generally have more political power now than in the Galbraithian 1950s and 1960s era—Galbraith thought that big business in those times ran the show, but the silver lining was its pro-social acts that Congress would not or could not legislate—the explosion of corporate welfare, self-serving regulations and deregulations, and a sea of social insurance have all depended upon a willingness or eagerness on the part of government officials and legislators to protect vested interest and to cater to special interests in return for electoral support and financial support. It is a *system* of interlocking parts: a corporatist system fluctuating between tripartism—government, organized business, and organized labor—and bipartism, in which labor is less well connected. What propels the system is ultimately the economic and political culture of self-importance and self-dealing. Sometimes labor is up and business down, and sometimes it is the other way around.

The success of the modern economy from the middle 1800s to the early 1970s raised human spirits as nothing had done in the millennia before. It was a triumph of modern morality and a vitalist spirit, mixed with a dose of ancient materialism. Yet, with the passage of time, it has suffered the predations of the political sector, the decay of its culture, and the betrayals by its managers. Though the world is "ruled by ideas," as Keynes said, modern capitalism was a new idea still not widely understood: Its ethical basis and moral foundation had not yet been developed. Corporatism was an old idea with which many were more comfortable. So the competition of ideas is not necessarily going to play out in the present century as it did in the past. We should have known that, after a spectacular run of more than 100 years, modern capitalism might be weakened and imperiled.

If we are to embark on reform we will need this time to expound our values and aims: to explain what sort of careers and economic life are most rewarding, what kind of economy would promote a good life, and how it can offer justice toward all.

CHAPTER ELEVEN

The Good Life:
Aristotle and the Moderns

It is undeniable that the exercise of a creative power, that a free creative activity, is the true function of man. It is proved to be so by man's finding in it his true happiness. But it is undeniable, also, that men may have the sense of exercising this free creative activity in other ways than in producing great works of literature or art; if it were not so, all but a very few men would be shut out from the true happiness of all men.

MATTHEW ARNOLD, "The Function of Criticism"

[S]omeday, not too long from now, you will gradually become old and be cleared away. . . . Your time is limited, so don't waste it living someone else's life. Don't be trapped by dogma, which is living with the results of other people's thinking. Don't let the noise of others' opinions drown out your own inner voice, heart and intuition. They somehow already know what you truly want to become.

STEVE JOBS, Stanford University commencement

CHAMPIONS OF CORPORATISM AND THE NEW CORPORATISM have all thought in materialist terms—in terms of inefficiencies in production, wasteful unemployment, and costly fluctuations. Conventional champions of capitalism did too. The corporatists argued that the corporatist system was superior in these terms to the modern-capitalist system. They said the system would generally deliver higher productivity, less waste from unemployment, and, thanks to job protection, greater stability in individuals' wealth, wages, and employment. In fact, the performances in these terms of the relatively well-functioning corporatist economies has proved at best roughly comparable to that of the relatively well-functioning modern capitalist economies in the last decades of the 20th century. To choose between the two systems we have to move on from the materialist perspective of classical political economy.

The many words of praise here for modern capitalism tend to emphasize nonmaterial rewards: the stir of challenges, the satisfactions of testing and exploring, and the thrill of success. Exemplars of a well-functioning modern capitalism are seen as offering participants opportunity to find lives of sufficient richness, self-expression, and personal development. Corporatism is seen as a chilling doctrine that, in protecting people from each other, would stifle creativity, block initiative, and penalize nonconformism.

It is the strong dynamism of a well-functioning modern economy that accounts for its distinctive rewards. The engagement in its processes is its own reward—the experience of mental stimulation, the challenge of new problems to solve, the chance to try the new, and the excitement of venturing into the unknown. Of course, there are by-products—the transience of the work, the precariousness of the profit, the likelihood of failed attempts and even ultimate failure; also, the possibility of being defrauded or conned. These rewards and hazards are the pluses and minuses of the modern economy.

Present-day corporatists can reply that their system also brings good feelings and experiences—solidarity, security, and industrial peace. They constantly suggest that these are basic to a good society. Hence, the human *significance* of the rewards and the hazards of the modern economy have to be understood and appreciated to have a sense of the desirability or appeal of the modern economy—relative to a corporatist economy or any other sort. (Some say—many Marxists, though not Marx himself—that the nonmaterial matters little, if at all.) There can be no justification of a well-functioning modern capitalism if people do not want what it is good at offering. So there are *fundamental* questions that are logically prior to questions of what could be done and would be worth doing in America to reverse the decline of dynamism, to which the decline of job satisfaction and other recent malfunctions are arguably linked—questions that must take precedence to matters of fine-tuning, such as banking reform and the income tax schedule.

This chapter takes up the question: Which of the two sorts of economic systems would a person want for himself or herself: the concerted system for solidarity and the rest or the individualist system for exploration and all that? The system for protection or the system for dynamism? Have people long wanted the modern life, since even the dawn of modernity, and before it? (Other fundamental questions having to do with diversity and equity are the subject of the next chapter.) Are there higher dimensions of performance— dimensions of a *good life*—in which an economy must perform well to be deemed a *good economy*?

Questions of the "good economy" and the "good life" it serves are not familiar ground in political economy. As others have complained, socialist thought—the left—does not convey a conception of the desirable economic life—a life that socialists believed their preferred system would be best suited to serve. It sees every economy as a sausage machine, simply linking the hours the workers put in to the sausage that comes out—with close attention paid to how the output is divided among the workers. Corporatist thought has no truck with the good life of the individual either, focusing instead on *national* output and *social* harmony through "concertation," social insurance for spreading wealth, and a cultivated spirit of solidarity.

The trouble with those latter perspectives on economic systems is that they overlook or deny the importance of the *means* to the ostensible ends—the processes and character of the economic system by which each day products are produced and jobs created. The means have consequences beyond the materialist results. Choosing one of the relatively modern economies spells differing pathways and resulting experiences, thus a string of modern rewards and hazards.

It may be asked what hope there is of arriving at a well-considered and widely agreed conception of the good life in view of the differences in what nations and generations chose. Nineteenth-century America drew boatloads of people with hopes of "making it" in new ventures and enterprises, while others chose to remain in Europe. By the end of the century the boatloads seemed more interested in corporatist and socialist practices, such as unionizing and raiding the profits. By the second half of the 20th century, people everywhere spoke of marshaling resources to solve the "real problems" of society. But changing choices do not necessarily signify changing values. It may be that the seemingly new wants are, in most cases, the creature of new conditions or a new capacity, as with those resulting from increased wealth or greater democracy. In recent decades, more and more people say they wish for a level of economic security not dreamt of a century ago. But these wishes have not taken into account a society's adopting a system that, intentionally or not, slows down change. In judging the rival economic systems in the "economically advanced" countries of the 21st century, the right criteria are people's fundamental, well-considered aspirations.

The humanities—especially philosophy and literature, but more recently psychology too—have things to say about the deepest desires and rewards. Over the millennia, humanists have thought about the ways of life that give the deepest, most lasting satisfaction, and they have accumulated several arresting insights. Their insights into the good life help us understand how an enterprising and innovative kind of economy began to sprout up once countries could afford it. (Just pointing to the falling away of restraints is not sufficient.) These insights take us a long way toward a justification for a society's support of an entrepreneurial, innovative economy. If political economy does not learn what the humanities have to teach, it will be the poorer for that: It will continue to be unequipped to deliver the winning argument in the re-emerging debate over the modern economy.

The Humanist Concept of a Good Life

The *concept* of the good life—the idea of such a thing—starts with Aristotle.[1] It means the sort of life that people, on reflection, would choose to the extent feasible—after non-elective goods such as food and shelter are obtained. In his book *Nicomachean Ethics,* which has a large readership to this day, he contrasts ways of life that are just *means* to an end with the *good life,* which is not a means to some end but rather an end in itself—lived for its own sake.[2] To paraphrase his argument: people need food (by producing it or trading domestic products to get foreign food) as a means to energy, need energy as a means to build shelter and sheds, need those as a means to protect oneself and one's produce against wet and cold, and so forth. Every *final* good—gourmet cuisine, haute couture, bel canto opera—is the end-point of a program or activity. Aristotle is interested in the *ranking* of the various "activities," each culminating in some kind of final good. Aristotle credits to thoughtful people a sense of what the "highest good" is. His aim is to explain, or interpret, the ranking—at least the ranking that thoughtful, serious people exhibit with the life choices they make.

Aristotle recognizes that a certain amount of "moneymaking" is "forced" on society (1096a). This recognition might suggest he believes the good life is affordable only to an elite. He implies that, in his time, it was not within the reach of the less fortunate. But he never says—nor is there any reason to believe—that the good life will never be accessible at the bottom rungs of

---

1. The next four sections grew out of a public lecture at Columbia in 2007. They were later the basis of my paper for the Festschrift collection *Arguments for a Better World: Essays in Honor of Amartya Sen,* K. Basu and R. Kanbur (eds.), Oxford: Oxford University Press, 2009. This chapter is a different development of the lecture, with departures, corrections, and deletions.

2. Following convention, page numbers refer to Immanuel Bekker's classic edition of Aristotle (1831). A helpful edition is Aristotle, *Nicomachean Ethics* (1999).

society. Aristotle also notes that slaves generally had slavery forced on them—his own teacher, Plato, might have been sold into slavery—so there is no basis for inferring that they lacked an innate desire or capacity for the highest good.

Aristotle implies that pursuit of the "good" by a person making his entire life on a deserted island, even a rich island, would not compare, generally speaking, to pursuit of the good "in cities"—in a society, in other words. Thus he recognizes the many interactions and complementarities *at the level of ideas* among people in a society. As a consequence, a society needs to decide what the good life consists of in choosing the economic institutions to support and the culture to transmit in school. Thus, "we should try to grasp, in outline at any rate, what the good is" (1094b). This insight exposes a weakness in the competing libertarian idea that the good life is one of freedom. There could be societies in which there is total freedom but a culture of crime, promiscuity, or drugs makes most if not all people unhappy.

Some of Aristotle's finest passages are about what the good life is *not*. It is *not* doing the politically correct thing. That may be the objective of politicians, he says, but "it appears to be too superficial to be what we are seeking, for it seems to depend more on those who honor than on the one honored, whereas we intuitively believe that the good is something of our own and hard to take from us." Next he argues that the good does not consist of virtues either. We require some virtues to pursue the good life successfully, but virtue is not sufficient in itself: you could be miserable being virtuous if you had no sense of the right track to be on—the one toward your happiness.

There is a way to live that is good for people, then. Whatever the particular conception of the good that a nation or people might have, the good life always means the inner condition, or state of mind and feeling, that people seek in the way they live their lives. (When referring to this state Aristotle uses the Greek word *eudaimonia* (1095b), the precise meaning of which comes up below.) This idea of the good life conveys a humanist spirit. This is *not* the idea of a godly life, such as the idea in some religions that men and women have the function of utilizing resources to survive and reproduce themselves in order that another generation might survive and reproduce, and so on over an indefinite future. The difference between the two concepts is the difference between a life of duty to god and a life of value to oneself. In this respect, Aristotle, writing in the 4th century BC, took a position very different from that of the Judaic scholars of the 1300s BC and later clerics.

Lest he be taken for a hedonist, Aristotle hastens to explain that, although the good life is something that humans strive for and find gratifying, a good life is *not* one of "amusement": "It would be absurd," he writes, "if [our] end were amusement and our lifelong efforts and sufferings aimed at amusing ourselves. . . . We amuse ourselves to relax . . . so that we can go back to do something serious" (1176b). Perhaps Aristotle is having a bit of fun with his student-age listeners. Surely we do not have to be slaves of the good life. We ought to allow ourselves a night at the opera or the movie house, even when it will not advance our life projects. Besides, you never know. As the work unfolds we may be struck with some insight for use in an as-yet-unknown future.

We see that Aristotle's subject is the nature of the paths that are *right* for people. He does *not* hold that the good life is a life of freedom, as if it does not matter what people do with that freedom. Neither does he constrain the good path to one of the paths that society has already left open to individuals, as if it did not matter to him whether freedom was narrow or wide. (Perhaps Aristotle would have approved every increase in freedom that can be shared by all—every increase that does not constrict anyone else's freedom. In any case, it was left to Rawls to write that book.)

Aristotle's Conception of the Good Life

What is Aristotle's own *conception* of the good life? In substantive terms, he characterizes it as the *pursuit of knowledge*. In his words, "[t]he best [thing] is understanding. . . . This activity is supreme, since understanding is the supreme element in us" (1177a). "*Eudaimonia*," he writes, "[derives] from some sort of study." Study is the "highest good," he argues, largely because it requires "reason," and reason is the main faculty that separates human beings from the other animals. He adds that this conception fits with his observation that *eudaimonia* is not felt by the other animals.[3]

The thrust of Aristotle's argument, animals aside, is that, with increases in the ability to understand and the wealth with which to afford it, a person reaches increasingly the more elevated kinds of satisfactions rather than just enjoying more and more of the old ones. The satisfactions from the knowledge accumulated and from the pursuit of knowledge are at the top of the hierarchy of final goods. The higher the income level, the larger is the

---

3. That last part could be questioned. Suppose that dogs, dolphins, or others *did* possess reason, as imagined in Gustav Mahler's *Songs of a Wayfarer*. That would not refute the proposition that knowledge is the "best [good]" and pursuit of it the "supreme activity." The claim that *eudaimonia* is felt only by humans is not obviously necessary to Aristotle's argument, though he appeared to think so.

proportion of expenditure on these elevated pursuits. In this sense, they are the highest good.

The narrowness of the knowledge that Aristotle appears to regard as the "highest good" and whose pursuit is the "supreme activity" is out of tune with modern values. He appears to envision that the knowledge sought by people is solely an end, as distinct from a means, and that the pursuit of knowledge is an ascetic activity, practiced in a cloistered setting, perhaps stimulated by the occasional study group or conversation with a friend—the sort of activity carried on by mathematicians, theoretical physicists, and scholars, such as philosophers and historians. No doubt these narrow views of Aristotle's derive from the narrowness of his background, having been confined to a world oriented around classical knowledge rather than practical knowledge, and around the classical way of acquiring it—by study.

There is another problem with the thesis in its original form. If the highest good is exclusively knowledge that is not used for anything, a society, as it becomes more and more productive or rich, will devote more and more time to the leisure activity of pursuing such knowledge, which has no commercial value in the marketplace. So the theory predicts that as hourly productivity increases in a country, we will observe at some point little or no further increases in the production and sale of goods—only steady further increases in leisure activity in the pursuit of knowledge. This is precisely the prediction made in the essay by John Maynard Keynes, "Economic Possibilities for Our Grandchildren" (1963)—an essay adorable to some and appalling to others. But we do not observe that outcome.[4] The puzzle is obviously resolved, though, once we take a broader view of knowledge, and the one or two other things people seek alongside it.

Here we must move on to subsequent thinkers, though Aristotle is never far away.

The Pragmatists and the Good Life

Succeeding philosophers and writers, with no sense of being out of tune with the Aristotelian perspective, have focused on other kinds of knowledge and other kinds of activities in pursuit of such knowledge while bearing in mind

---

4. Aristotle could not have been pleased with the finding of recent happiness researchers that, *after a point*, further increases in productivity do not add to reported happiness, a paradox I have discussed elsewhere. See, for example, Layard, *Happiness* (2007).

Aristotle's fundamental insights about the hierarchy of desires: the desire for knowledge and the place of knowledge as the most desirable good yet the last to be affordable.

Humanist writers and philosophers after Aristotle have introduced *practical* knowledge, a good that is definitely *not* valued just for itself—much of it *informal* knowledge, which does not make its way into documents. These humanists have also introduced the quite different kinds of activities that are carried on in gaining such knowledge and the worldly contexts in which such knowledge is pursued.

In one group there are the pragmatists—so named because they call attention to the ways that ends are pursued and the value that some ways may have and others may lack. (They are far from "pragmatic" about the pursuit of ends.) The pragmatists focus on knowledge acquired and used for the purposes of producing or acting in some way. People start their working life with a stock of knowledge, of course, and gain much new knowledge in solving the problems that typically arise. To succeed in their work or their business they have to be able to meet its technical demands: problem solving is a factor in one's success. The considerable knowledge acquired in the process is generally gratifying, no matter that it was not sought for its own sake. It provides a sense of mastery and of standing on one's own feet.

An early figure in this group is the poet Virgil, who was born of peasant stock in the Po Valley in 70 BC (some 300 years after Aristotle's birth) and settled in Rome in the age of the emperor Augustus. Virgil's well-known poem *Georgics* somehow came to be viewed as a primer on agriculture until fairly recently; but at a deeper level it is an ode to humanity and Roman culture.[5] It speaks at length and admiringly of the vast knowledge the farmer acquires and draws upon in plowing, planting trees, tending cattle, and keeping bees. It expresses the farmer's engagement in this work and his satisfaction at a successful harvest. This poem contains one of Virgil's immortal lines: *Felix qui potuit rerum cognoscere causas.* (Happy is he who knows the causes of things.)

Voltaire fits well in this group. Writing in late 18th-century France, when the feudal manors were shrinking and opportunities for careers in business were opening up, he conveys the importance of a life of action—of work. As he dramatizes in his apparently imperishable book *Candide,* the action need not be for social causes or to right wrongs; Voltaire advises us to forget all that. Instead,

---

5. The change of interpretation is credited to Roger Mynors. See his *Georgics by Virgil* (1990). The quote is from verse 490 in book 2 of the *Georgics.*

he suggests that business life could be meaningful and amply rewarding. The stirring and touching finale for sextet and chorus of the musical *Candide*, composed by Leonard Bernstein with words taken from Voltaire by Stephen Sondheim, manages to condense much of Voltaire's thought to four lines:

We're neither pure nor wise nor good.

We'll do the best we know.

We'll build our house, and chop our wood.

And make our garden grow.

Society, Voltaire is suggesting, lacks the wisdom, expertise, and benevolence to design, operate, and preserve the best of all possible economies. But although we know little about many important things, we can embark on careers, society permitting. All of us can have good lives building our own careers and businesses—and can thus end up with an economy that is good enough. Voltaire urges us to grasp that the knowledge and experiences we draw upon and the knowledge and experiences we gain along the way are likely to make such a life interesting and rewarding. (It is not surprising, then, that French economists were first to see a key role for the *entrepreneur*.)

In the middle decades of the 20th century closer attention was paid to the nature of the satisfactions deriving from the workplace and to the part played by the individual's *acquisition* and *use* of *private knowledge* in those satisfactions. A pioneer is John Dewey, the American pragmatist philosopher and one of the lions of Columbia for decades. Dewey, anticipating Hayek, understands that ordinary workers possess considerable specialized knowledge of use in the course of their work. He emphasizes the human need to exercise this knowledge in problem-solving activity.[6] Even the worker of ordinary education can be engaged in and can gain intellectual development from the formation of skills—a type of knowledge—arising from problems that are put to him or her in the workplace—or could be put to him or her if the workplace were desirably organized. Furthermore, Dewey seems also to grasp that each worker is apt to know things the others do not, so that there is a role for the workers sitting around a table working out for themselves the best solution to the problem of the day.[7]

---

6. His writings in this area run from his *Human Nature and Conduct* (1922) to *Experience and Education* (1938).

7. Dewey disapproved of Fordian mass production and hoped the workplace would be reformed again to provide the intellectual satisfactions of which it was capable. Of course, market forces have by now pretty much eliminated the assembly line—or, in many cases, moved it to Guangdong province.

The psychologist Abraham Maslow in a much-read 1943 paper drew up a hierarchy of human needs, starting with the most basic.[8] In this hierarchy, he gives a place to the need to acquire "mastery" of a trade or skill—typically after some apprenticeship. This need comes immediately after the physiological needs at the base and, next up the ladder, security needs. Maslow also recognizes the need for an ongoing *process* of problem-solving, a process of "self-actualization."

John Rawls, toward the end of his magisterial work on economic justice, sets out with great clarity the main theme of this literature on the good life— the "Aristotelian perspective," as he dubbed it.[9] One acquires knowledge over a career through the development of one's "talents," or "capacities," which is the essence of one's *self-realization*. And this self-realization, or as much of it as we obtain, is the central drive that every one of us has. Rawls's forcefulness and clarity are on full display in his exposition:

> [H]uman beings enjoy the exercise of their realized capacities (their innate or trained abilities) and this enjoyment increases the more the capacity is realized or the greater its complexity. . . . [It] is a principle of motivation. It accounts for many of our major desires . . . Moreover, it expresses a psychological law governing changes in the pattern of our desires. [It] implies that as a person's capacities increase over time . . . and as he trains these capacities and learns how to exercise them, he will in due course come to prefer the more complex activities he can now engage in which call upon his newly realized abilities. The simpler things he enjoyed before are no long sufficiently interesting or attractive. . . . Now accepting the Aristotelian Principle, it will generally be rational, in view of the other assumptions, to realize and train mature capacities. . . . A rational plan . . . allows a person to flourish, so far as circumstances permit, and to exercise his realized abilities as much as he can.[10]

A relatively recent contribution to this topic is that by Amartya Sen in his 1992 and 1999 books.[11] There is something fundamentally missing, Sen suggests, in present-day thinking about the good life in the sense of Aristotle. Neoclassical economic theory, which is still taught (whether or not exclusively), takes "utility," or happiness, to be a function of the bundle of

8. Maslow, "A Theory of Motivation."
9. Rawls, *A Theory of Justice* (1971, pp. 424–433).
10. Rawls, *A Theory of Justice* (1971, pp. 428–429).
11. Sen, *Inequality Reexamined* and *Commodities and Capabilities*.

consumer goods and leisure chosen, and this happiness could be seen as *indirectly* a function of the resources possessed. It is as if the economy's actors all participate in a comprehensive once-and-for-all auction in which they will contract their entire future. Sen objects. In his "capabilities approach," any fulfillment from one's life will require one to acquire "capabilities"— capabilities "to do things." And *choosing* which capabilities to try to acquire is part of the satisfaction. Thus he gives content to Marshall and Myrdal's suggestion (cited in Chapter 3) that the jobs absorb the mind:

> [Besides the *indirect* one there is a] connection between capability and well-being . . . making . . . well-being . . . depend [*directly*] on the *capability* to function. *Choosing* may itself be a valuable part of living, and a genuine choice with serious options may be seen to be—for that reason—richer. . . . [A]t least some types of capabilities contribute *directly* to well-being, making one's life richer with the opportunity of reflective choice.[12]

Sen is not imagining some joy of choosing. He is pointing to the deeper satisfaction from being competent at selecting a new route if conditions change. ("Having won the lottery, I'm going to make the smart decision to quit the mine and take voice lessons.")

There is another point, which may have been in the back of Sen's mind. Rawls tacitly postulates a neoclassical world. There may be random events, but their probabilities are known. They do not get in the way of the fact that the *prospect* of "self-realization" has a clear meaning: it is how far you, he, or she would expect to get in your development—how far on the average, with repeated rolls of the known dice. But in a modern economy, some basic change in the shape of the economy is almost certain to have occurred within a generation, but we have no foreknowledge of what it will be. In that sort of economy, the sort of "self" a person develops in one scenario, or evolution, may differ considerably from that developed in another scenario. What is "realized" as one goes through life is not only the distance of one's development but also the direction of one's development. In this world, the "self" is neither fixed nor subject to fixed laws of motion, so the concept of the self is of no explanatory value. In *Henry V,* Prince Hal gives voice to the intense fluctuations possible in personal development, when, two years after his coronation and girding for his great battle with the French, he remarks, "I have turned away my former self."

---

12. Sen, *Inequality Reexamined* (1992, p. 41), italics added. Sen cites Marx and Hayek among several precursors who placed a value on freedom independently of outcomes.

The Vitalists on the Good Life

The post Aristotelian literature of the pragmatists stops short of saying some of the most important things about a good life. This literature is almost arid in portraying life at its best as one long series of pragmatic exercises in problem solving, which serve to keep us engaged and yield the satisfactions of mastery. This conception of the good life, though it has merits, makes no room for the thrill of imagining new possibilities and new conquests and the satisfactions that result if the "dreams" are realized—and the (lesser) satisfactions if they are not. Life lived to the full has always been richer than the pragmatist description. But it was odd that so narrow a version of Aristotle's good life was being advanced at a time—from 1920 to 1970—when unprecedented numbers were having a much more colorful life. In the modern economics of that time, it hardly needs repeating, individuals were exercising their creativity in conceiving a new product and their imagination in forecasting its benefits to end-users; and teams were taking on the risks of attempting its development and its adoption.[13] Is there, then, some other perspective on the good life that conveys what it feels like to be an actor in such a world and expresses the value that the actors in the modern economy place on participating in its processes?

A quite different conception of the good life was growing up from ancient times in parallel with the pragmatist version. It is the conception to which Columbia's Jacques Barzun and Yale's Harold Bloom gave the name *vitalism.* Some key figures and ideas were touched on in Chapter 4, but a fuller account is called for here. Until not long ago, students in European high schools and American colleges were introduced in the core curriculum to the vitalist literature of the Western canon. The earliest vitalist may be Homer, the Greek poet of the 12th century BC and author of the *Iliad* and the *Odyssey.* These epic poems tell of ancient Greek heroes—their determination, courage, and patience.

Another early vitalist is the sculptor Benvenuto Cellini, a larger-than-life figure of the Renaissance (and the protagonist of the Berlioz opera named after him). In his *Autobiography* he frankly relishes his creativity and revels in

---

13. The transition from mercantile to modern is made by one man—Robinson Crusoe—in Defoe's 1719 novel. Jean-Jacques Rousseau in his 1762 book *Émile* views Crusoe as having allowed only "necessity" to determine what he tackled. But once Crusoe secured food supplies and shelter, he did not simply solve the problems he met on a predetermined path: he succeeded in making pottery and adopted a parrot, neither a necessity, using his creativity and imagination.

making it. Even today, a young reader could be taken aback by such powerful ambition.

In a slightly later period, Cervantes and Shakespeare dramatize the individual's quest. The message of Cervantes' novel *Don Quixote*—the "Man of La Mancha" with the "Impossible Dream"—is that a life of challenge and adventure is necessary for human fulfillment; and if the barren economy of the Spanish desert does not supply such challenges, one must somehow create them by one's self—*imagining* them, if necessary. In Shakespeare's *Hamlet*, the prince concludes he must act against the king if he is to be someone, aware that he may fail and may pay with his life. The play suggests an initial uncertainty over the king's responsibility. (As the columnist David Brooks remarked, it is rare now that anyone will show he knows that what he is saying may not be true.) It suggests too Hamlet's initial ambivalence about taking an action that would risk everything he has—his position and Ophelia. Bloom in his *Shakespeare: The Invention of the Human* lionizes Shakespeare as the complete vitalist—a "spacious mirror" in which we can all see ourselves.

In the 18th-century Enlightenment, such a view is reflected by some, though not all, of the key figures. David Hume, disputing the *rationalism* of the French, gives a crucial place to the "passions" in decision-making and to "imagination" in the growth of society's knowledge. (Hume may be the first modern philosopher.) As already mentioned, Voltaire urged people to look for satisfaction in individual pursuits, to "grow your own garden." Jefferson wrote of the "pursuit of happiness" and commented that people came to America "to make their fortune." The term "pursue" conveys that seeking a fortune is more valuable than *having* one. The journey is the end.

At the dawn of the first modern societies, the Romantics were wild about exploration and celebrated discovery as well as the determination and perseverance it often takes. We all recall the line of John Keats on the moment when Hernán Cortés "stared at the Pacific . . . silent upon a peak in Darien" and that fierce stanza in William Earnest Henley's *Invictus*: "It matters not how strait the gate/How charged with punishments the scroll/I am the master of my fate/I am the captain of my soul."

Next there were the philosophers of modernity. No American philosopher wrote of vitalism with more energy than William James did. He saw great vitality with his own eyes. Born in New York City in 1842, he was witness throughout his life to the transformation of the American economy from relatively slow paced to explosively innovative. In his ethic, the excitement of fresh problems and new experiences are at the heart of the good life.[14] If Walt Whitman is the poet of the American ethos, James is its philosopher.

At the turn of the century, the notion quietly arises that there is indeed a fixed self, but one does not start one's adult life knowing very well what the needs of that self are. The thesis is that the journey of life is not simply advances, one after the other, in self-realization. Rather it is a journey of *self-discovery*. Through a series of trials and experiences we discover "who we are," which may differ quite a lot from who we thought we were when we started. This approach to the good life is set out quite precisely by a successful singer-songwriter of our day:

> This new album [*Born This Way*] is about rebirth in every sense. . . . It's about being able to be reborn, over and over again throughout your life. . . . until you find the identity inside yourself that defines best who you are and that makes you most feel like a champion of life.[15]

The discovery of oneself (before one's career is over) does not mark an end of one's personal development. Maslow's self-actualization and Rawls's self-realization may well continue but will be better directed for having discovered oneself. That suggests that there is no need to postulate that the self remains fixed throughout all this discovery.

A raft of new ideas from Friedrich Nietzsche, the upstart German psychologist and philosopher, changed the way we think about motivation, even life itself. In a hundred aphorisms, he speaks of venturing into the unknown, overcoming obstacles, failing to overcome obstacles, and learning to persevere through adversity, and "what doesn't kill us makes us stronger." In particular, he crystallized the weakness of the pragmatist approach to the good life. We are not really sacrificing for a future gain when we diet before going on our next film shoot or when we tighten our belts to help finance our entrepreneurial project. We are happy to be in a project that offers us so much, no matter that it demands much from us. As Nietzsche sees it, our work on such

14. William James wrote somewhere, "My *flux*-philosophy may well have to do with my extremely impatient temperament. I am a motor, need change, and get very quickly bored." (Cited in Barzun, *A Stroll with William James*, 1983, p. 265.) By "motor" he did not mean anything like a mechanical device, as Barzun remarks.

15. Lady Gaga, interviewed in Fry, "Lady Gaga Takes Tea with Mr Fry" (2011, p. 12). The actor Alan Alda is also eloquent on this theme in his oft-quoted address at his daughter's commencement: "Be brave enough to live creatively. . . . You have to leave the city of your comfort and go into the wilderness of your intuition. . . . What you'll discover will be wonderful. What you'll discover will be yourself." Quoted in his autobiography, *Things I Overheard While Talking to Myself* (2007, p. 21).

projects meets an inner need, not a need for some cash. He explains that the hurdles encountered in our projects are not costs on the way to materialist payoffs. Instead, overcoming obstacles is itself the source of the satisfaction. The projects are their own reward—the highest reward.[16]

The French philosopher Henri Bergson, a friend of James and likewise a witness to the high modernity of the 19th century, was another champion of vitalism.[17] Picking up Nietzsche's notion of people's need for challenges, Bergson conceives of people energized by a current of life (*élan vital*) and organizing themselves for "creative evolution"—the title of his 1907 book. The theme with which he is now associated is that intense involvement in challenging projects transforms people, so that they are repeatedly in the process of *becoming*. The book *Creative Evolution* elevates this "becoming" far above mere "being." There are almost always precursors, though: not only Nietzsche but also Montaigne, Henrik Ibsen, and Søren Kierkegaard, who held that to exist we must create ourselves.

There is little on personal creativity in philosophy. Nietzsche wrote of a person as carving out his or her own values—the lines between good and evil. But he does not speak of the great satisfactions of creating a symphony or a book or any other product (though Nietzsche, a lover of Wagner's operas, was an amateur composer). Bergson clearly understands that creativity would no longer exist if we had reached a world of *determinism*. However, Bergson does not describe a creative life or show any appreciation of its interior rewards.

Some literary critics and biographers have seen creativity as a central subject of literary criticism. Lionel Trilling wrote of literature as the human activity "that takes the fullest and most precise account of variousness, possibility, complexity and difficulty." Matthew Arnold, quoted at the start of the chapter, spoke of "the sense of exercising . . . free creative activity in other

16. In Nietzsche's view, each day's advance with the project "must appear justified at every moment—or incapable of being evaluated, which amounts to the same thing." (This appears in his posthumous notebook *The Will to Power* (1883–1888), which is not about power over other people but is analogous to the will to win the ball game. See the illuminating treatment of Nietzsche in Richard Robb's 2009 paper, "Nietzsche and the Economics of Becoming."

17. Bergson rose to fame with his 1907 book published in Paris and wider fame with the 1911 English edition, *Creative Evolution.* He was appointed to the College de France and won the Nobel Prize in Literature in 1927. (Incidentally, Henrik Ibsen's dramatic poem *Peer Gynt* (1876) anticipates Bergson's theme when the Button Moulder says, "To be yourself is to slay yourself./But on you, that answer's sure to fail;/So let's say: To make your life evolve/From the Master's meaning to the last detail." The quote is from the 1980 English translation by Rolf Fjelde, p. 195.)

ways than in producing great works of literature or art."[18] Several writers have described the creative life and to varying degrees gotten inside the creators who were their subjects. It was a frequent subject of Arthur Koestler's books, such as *The Act of Creation* (1964) and *The Sleepwalkers* (1968) on the making of modern physics. Irving Stone's *Lust for Life* (1937) and Joyce Cary's *The Horse's Mouth* (1944) might be mentioned, both turned into films. Michael Leigh's screenplay *Topsy-Turvy* explored the lives of Gilbert and Sullivan.

Yet we often turn to writers of fiction in hopes of finding an insight into the forces driving individuals—especially when there is a sense of new forces at work or old forces newly empowered. The interwar decades were a turbulent time, full of tectonic shifts and upheavals. Far from showing any slowing down after the historic triumphs from 1870 to the eve of World War I in 1913, America resumed its stunning innovation in the 1920s. In the 1930s, undeterred by the Great Depression, it posted a record-breaking rate of innovation. A few writers sought to reflect the exhilaration and intoxication felt in the process of such creation and discovery. An over-the-top novelist of the time made the attempt to express the mystery and thrill of exploration:

> At length, sick with longing for those glittering sunset streets and cryptical hill lanes among ancient tiled roofs, nor able sleeping or waking to drive them from his mind, Carter resolved to go with bold entreaty whither no man had gone before, and dare the icy deserts through the dark to where unknown Kadath, veiled in cloud and crowned with unimagined stars, holds secret and nocturnal the onyx castle of the Great Ones.[19]

Three decades later the expression "to boldly go," thought to derive from this passage, became the mantra of NASA in the early years of the project to go to the moon.

The difference between the pragmatist take on the good life and the vitalist take is striking. The term "hurdle" is in the lexicon of both schools, but hurdles come up in contrasting ways. In the vitalist view, people are *looking for* hurdles to overcome, problems to solve: if you do not happen to meet any, you change your life so that you start meeting them. In the pragmatist view, people *encounter* hurdles in the course of being pragmatic—of working in an industry or profession that seems to offer the best prospects of success.

18. Respectively, Trilling, *The Liberal Imagination* (1950, p. xxi), and Arnold in his 1865 "The Function of Criticism at the Present Time," reprinted in Arnold, *The Function of Criticism* (1895, p. 9).

19. Lovecraft, *The Dream-Quest of Unknown Kadath* (1964, p. 291), written in 1927.

The pragmatists do not specify what humankind wants to succeed at. They only say that, whatever a person's career is aimed at, the person—unless very unlucky—will meet innumerable problems and solve a great many of them. Their *engagement* in problem solving is an intellectual side of the good life. The resulting mastery is another part of the good life: the part called *achievement.* The value of engagement and mastery could be seen as part of what Aristotle had in mind—just as Nietzschean overcoming and Bergsonian becoming could also be seen as having roots going back to Aristotle.

Vitalism—the doctrine of vitalism, regardless of the strength of vitalism in recently modern economies—is enjoying a revival, after decades of pragmatism. Early English translations of Aristotle's *Ethics* rendered *eudaimonia* as "happiness." That seemed right, since one would suppose that persons engaging in "study," as Aristotle recommended, would take pleasure in gaining more of the world's knowledge and feel delighted at knowing so much. And it diminished the human project to suggest that it was the way to "fun and laughter"—even if, in fact, it does cause jokes and smiles. However, some later scholars such as John Cooper have decided that a better rendering of the word is "flourishing," a suggestion later seconded by Thomas Nagel, although subsequent translators have gone on using "happiness." If we adopt that translation of *eudaimonia* as "flourishing," the *Nicomachean Ethics* is arguing that the good life is one of flourishing, while wryly recognizing that it is a fuzzy concept:

> What is the highest good in all matters of action? As to the name, there
> is almost complete agreement, for uneducated and educated alike call it
> flourishing, and make flourishing identical with the good life and success-
> ful living. They disagree, however, about the meaning of flourishing.[20]

If we translate *eudaimonia* as "flourishing," it broadens considerably what Aristotle meant by "study." He must have thought that people would feel excitement at reading the fierce debates and experience a frisson of suspense at uncovering new evidence for or against controversial ideas. He must also have thought that a life of questing for knowledge is deeply fulfilling. (The sober Thomas Jefferson must have thought the same thing when declaring that people had a right to "the pursuit of happiness.") So Aristotle must be reinterpreted. He is not so much an advocate of studying the physical world as he is a champion of searching, exploring, investigating, and experimenting in all areas—to the extent those things were possible in the 4th century BC. He emerges as the seminal thinker on mankind's desire to flourish.

20. *Nicomachean Ethics,* I.4 1095a14–20.

Some of the vitalist literature conjures up climbers and explorers interested in testing or proving things to a large public. Of course, a successful innovation is also a public thing. (A hermit's invention is not an innovation.) But there are other vitalist models. Sen's emphasis on "doing things" sounds a vitalist note. Another emphasis is found in recent work by the American sociologist Richard Sennett. He finds evidence in his interviews that many Americans want to feel embarked on a mission to "make a difference." He gives the example of a nurse who preferred the front line in the emergency room of the big city hospital to more lucrative work as a temporary nurse. Sennett suggests these people have a deep need for a "sense of agency"—"vocation" was an earlier way to put it.[21]

The latest book on the subject is *Flourish* by Martin Seligman.[22] He posits that mankind seeks "well-being." But well-being, like freedom, is constructed of several elements, and, like freedom, it cannot be measured—only the elements can. (Seligman comments that the *life satisfaction* reported in household surveys captures our current mood but barely reflects "how much meaning" there is in our lives and "how engaged we are in our work.") For Seligman, the elements are: satisfaction with life, engagement, personal relationships, meaningfulness, and an achieving life (that is, achievement for its own sake). Each element, he argues, contributes to well-being, is pursued for its own sake, and can be measured. This wide-ranging inventory of the ingredients of the good life is evidently the product of careful thought. However, it is missing the contribution of vitalism to "well-being" or whatever it is that humans want. Though Seligman enthusiastically uses the term flourishing, he does not recognize the high-level flourishing—testing, creating, exploring—that we associate with vitalism.

Is vitalism in fact a part of the prevailing ethic in the present age? Inferences based on people we know would not be reliable. The World Values Survey produced by the ethnographers Ronald Inglehardt and colleagues at the University of Michigan surveyed household attitudes and compiled the results in many countries during the years 1991–1993. "When you look for a job," they asked, "do you look for opportunities for initiative?" Fifty-two percent of the total respondents said yes in the United States and 54 percent in

21. Sennett, *The Culture of the New Capitalism* (2006, p. 36). His main thesis is that the unfortunate mutations in modern capitalism over the past two decades have caused these people to lose their sense of dedication and direction.
22. Seligman, *Flourish* (2011). Another entrant in the vitalist literature is Jamison, *Exuberance* (2004).

Canada. "Opportunities for taking responsibility?" Sixty-one percent in the United States and 65 percent in Canada said yes. (In France 38 percent said yes to initiative, 59 percent to interestingness, and 58 percent to responsibility.) The pragmatist version of the Aristotelian ethic is also found in those surveyed. "Opportunities for interesting work?" Sixty-nine percent said yes in the United States, 72 percent in Canada.

Such large nations may be different. Are small countries more communal, less success-driven, than the large countries? Asked in the mid-1990s what the attitude of the public toward Iceland's new entrepreneurs was, the economist Gylfi Zoega said, "They don't feel bad about it. They are thinking only about how to achieve their own success." So it is a live hypothesis that vitalism captures a crucial drive and its motivations importantly shape our experience and our resulting fulfillment in our society.

Aristotle, as noted, thought that the ethic named after him was a universal of human nature. Is the Aristotelian ethic—the vitalist and pragmatist versions included—predominant? It has never lacked rivals. Referring apparently to his country, the Italian economist Pasquale Lucio Scandizzo remarked that a life of contemplation also enjoys a following. There have always been people motivated by a desire to be of service to a group or to society, such as Doctors without Borders, or by a desire to express devotion, such as Bach with his cantatas. There are also lives of social entrepreneurship, such as the career of Florence Nightingale, and lives of sexual exploration or conquest, such as the Marquis de Sade and Casanova; but those lives are not counterexamples to vitalism's power, only distinctive directions of it. In the minds of most, however, the materialist conception of the good life is a serious contender against the Aristotelian perspective and may in some countries be more prevalent.

In the materialist perspective, most people are driven by the desire to earn or profit in order to accumulate wealth or power. Wealth is accumulated until it can sustain a high level of consumption or a high level of leisure or both. China's pivotal reformer, Deng Xiaoping, declared that "it is glorious to be rich." In Calvin's doctrine, earning wealth has God's blessing, and a person's attainment of wealth is a sign of God's favor—the more the wealth, the greater is the favor. In America, major wealth accumulation is widely thought to be motivated by the pro-social uses to which it can be put. Yet two of the most common examples invite the Aristotelian interpretation that they were driven by a desire for knowledge. After creating his fortune at Microsoft, Bill Gates founded a colossal philanthropy aimed at trying out new tools to advance economic development in poverty-stricken nations. The German businessman Heinrich Schliemann drove himself to earn a vast fortune expressly to fund his subsequent search for the ancient city of Troy. The fortune made by many an entrepreneur could be seen as a mere by-product of an obsession to test a quirky idea, such as Ray Kroc's McDonalds empire, in which each franchise was to have no scope for initiative—the antithesis of Hayek's idea of the benefit from openness to on-the-ground judgment and the stress here on grassroots creativity. (Kroc's successors backed away from the bee in Kroc's bonnet.) The careers of George Soros and Warren Buffett are perhaps driven by desires to show that their understanding of asset markets and business investment is superior. Yet most people's wealth accumulations, including outsize accumulations, may be aimed at un-Aristotelian goals: security, comfort, beauty, pride, respect, and the rest. In Freudian psychology there is the suggestion that careers of almost demonic intensity and huge ambition are a sign of some wound that the victim hopes to heal through achievement. Far worse off are those who, having made a great fortune, have no idea of how to use it in a rewarding way. The high suicide rate among present-day China's new multimillionaires may be an example.[23]

However one comes out of the tangled motivations of earning and learning, creating and accumulating, few would deny that lives of earning and wealth accumulation do not offer the gratification and pride that lives of creation and innovation offer. The particular conception of the "highest good" we find celebrated in Aristotle, Virgil, Cellini, Nietzsche, James, and Bergson—the experience of flourishing—better captures the sort of life we admire and aspire to than does the ethic of Weber and the subsequent economists who extolled economic progress.

The ethic of flourishing is alive even today in the West, the materialist ethic and other ethics notwithstanding. It flowered with the scientific revolution that began around 1675; England's Bill of Rights in 1689, which expanded rights against the king; and the Enlightenment inspired by Hume, Jefferson, and Voltaire in the mid-1700s. The prevalence of the Aristotelian ethic was necessary for the birth of the modern economies of the 19th century, whether or not it was the trigger or a further trigger. (The continuation of some modern economies could also be necessary for the survival of the Aristotelian ethic in other parts of the world.)

This chapter must not be read as implicitly suggesting that the arrival of a desire for flourishing lay behind the appearances of the modern economy

23. "Suicide: Wealth Leaves Many Unhappy," *China Daily News*, September 11, 2011, p. 1.

in the 19th century or that the ebbing of this ethic lies behind the decline of the modern economy—of economic dynamism—in one nation after another in the 20th century. Aristotle firmly held that the desire for flourishing was a universal of human nature, though the opportunity was not necessarily there for everyone or every country. Chapters 9 and 10 entertained the possibility that elements of the economic culture have weakened over recent decades. But those chapters *do not* propose that there has been somehow a loss in desire to have a life of flourishing. At most they prepare us for the possibility of an erosion of the workplace attitudes requisite or helpful to economic dynamism. These chapters *do* adduce evidence of a resurgence of competing values, such as a communitarian or corporatist ethic and family values, not a loss of the modern desires.

The prevailing culture(s) and the prevailing ethic(s) are not the same things. People may lose—perhaps out of social pressure—some of the right attitudes required for meeting "good" wants of theirs that remain intact.

Implications for a Good Economy

We may suppose, as Rawls supposed, that a society seeks and builds an economy to provide mutual benefits for its citizens. So, as a life in pursuit of the highest good, or benefit, is termed by Aristotle the "good life," an economy enabling people's mutual pursuit of the highest good may be termed a *good economy.* An economy is good if and only if it permits and fosters the good life.

Where flourishing is a prevalent conception of the good life, the economy, to be good, must serve people's urge to imagine and create the new, their quest to "act on the world," in Hegel's image, thus to seek to innovate, and their desire to pioneer new practice.

An economy that is good in this sense may be rife with injustices, of course. Many commentators and academics have recently suggested, though, that such a "good" economy is bound to create inequalities and cause deprivations for others preferring another sort of life. So this "good" economy is unjust. The next chapter sorts out and takes a position on the issues.

CHAPTER TWELVE

The Good and the Just

Ius est ars boni et aequi.
[Law is the art of the good and the equitable.]

PUBLIUS IUVENTIUS CELSUS

A society is a cooperative venture for mutual advantage. . . . There is an identity of interests, since social cooperation makes possible a better life for all than any would have if each were to live solely by his own efforts. There is a conflict of interests, since persons are not indifferent as to how the greater benefits produced by their collaboration are distributed, for in order to pursue their ends they each prefer a larger to a lesser share. A set of principles is required for choosing among the various social arrangements which determine this division of advantages and for underwriting an agreement on the proper distributive shares. These . . . are the principles of social justice.

JOHN RAWLS, A Theory of Justice

THE CLASSIC DEFENDERS OF CAPITALISM from mercantile days onward have sought an economy having fewer "interferences" with what they see to be the good in capitalism—the "freedoms" and the "growth"—without a thought for what a *just* economy is. In the premise of some of these classic defenders, each participant receives in pay the value of his or her contribution to national product, exactly as if each worked in isolation, so it is difficult if not impossible to see what moral claim one sort of participant might have to the pay of other sorts. But this premise is untenable. Seeing high earners (and their capital) working with low earners, we understand there is a *mutual* gain from the exchange of services. The Progressives of the early 1900s spoke of a "social surplus" from people's collaborative participation in a nation's economy: The productivity gains from exchange of heterogeneous inputs—labor, land, and capital—add to the pecuniary reward of virtually every kind of talent, every kind of soil, and every kind of capital employed in a market economy. In a modern economy, moreover, innovations result more frequently, and their average payoff is far greater when separate populations merge into an integrated national economy of large scale and variety. Bill Gates's new products could not have made him 50 billion dollars without millions of end-users. Thus high earners benefit from cooperating with others and could subsidize the others without going into the red. Yet it does not follow from this idea of a social surplus that, as egalitarian socialists concluded, everyone ought to be paid the same hourly wage. Equal wage rates would not be workable. (Is a would-be innovator to be paid for the hours spent in the garage?) Even if this equalitarian precept were workable, it would remove the pecuniary dividend that many potential innovators would need to induce them to quit their safe positions and make the extreme effort required for innovation.

Some others among the classic defenders, while conceding that the low earners benefit the high earners, jump to say that the high earners, through their capital investment and innovation, greatly benefit the low earners—pulling up their wages and employment. They see no reason why the high earners should dig into their pockets to pay subsidies aimed at further benefiting the low earners. But this view of a market economy is as mistaken as the previous one. The free market sets wages that send signals and present incentives serving *efficiency*—in some rough and ready way, at any rate—*not* any ideas of *equity*. There may be social or economic considerations that would call for modifying the market mechanism through subsidies and taxes to move some market wages and employment in the desired directions. The problem arising in recent decades is that there are so many considerations and so many conceptions of society's interests, from Jeremy Bentham's utilitarianism—the "greatest good"—to the socialist idea of a social dividend financed by the state's wealth or confiscations to corporatist subsidies for anything that special interests can induce lawmakers to legislate.

A breakthrough came with the 1971 treatise *A Theory of Justice* by John Rawls. A moral philosopher by training, he was responding to the absence of any known notion of what "just" means that is not either unclear or badly flawed. Writing in the turbulent 1960s, when university campuses in America were being torn apart by protests, he could not have missed the acute need for an understanding of justice that a consensus might build around.[1]

---

1. I shared with Rawls some of the turmoil. We had adjoining offices in 1969–1970 at the Center for Advanced Study in the Behavioral Sciences in Palo Alto, California. One winter day, looking down at the Stanford campus, we could see smoke rising from Encina Hall. Radicals had occupied it and set it on fire. Later they attacked the Center, burning the bank of offices where we worked. Rawls's manuscript survived, as did mine, though a nearby one was a total loss.

Obviously the context of Rawls's work in the 1960s—particularly the protests of black activists—has some parallels to the context in which the present book was written—particularly the Occupy Wall Street protests. Both protest groups had only the vaguest of visions and had little or no idea of how to translate it into an operational solution. Rawls supplied a clear vision of distributive justice and said enough to indicate that it could be realized. (It could be said that both the black activists and Rawls showed influences of American thought on work, earning, and opportunity going back to Lincoln and to Paine. Neither the voices of black pride nor Rawls were talking about handouts.)

Rawls starts by sketching general principles of justice based on the idea of a "social contract" in Locke, Rousseau, and Kant and reformulating it "so that it is no longer open to the more obvious objections." To decide what is just, a society's citizens, shedding their vested interests, imagine an *original position* in which they are to deliberate, with no one knowing whose shoes he will be in when their society and its economy begin operations; not even how many shoes there are of this size and that. In this way Rawls was breaking with Jeremy Bentham, whose idea of the "greatest good" had much influence, especially among economists. In the magisterial opening page Rawls writes:

> Each person possesses an inviolability founded on justice that even the
> welfare of society as a whole cannot override. For this reason justice
> denies that the loss of freedom of some is made right by a greater good
> shared by others. It does not allow that the sacrifices imposed on a few are
> outweighed by the larger sum of advantages enjoyed by many. . . . In a just
> society the rights secured by justice are not subject to political bargaining
> or to the calculus of social interests. (p. 3)

This theory, Rawls argues, leads to a precise conception of justice in the distribution of the rewards from work—an element of *economic justice* in the terminology here—*not* to a justification of the entitlements of the welfare state, about which he was silent. In this conception, economic justice demands the avoidance, where practicable, of economic inefficiency. So some sort of market economy is necessary for justice because other types of economy would cause serious inefficiencies—everyone's wages would be unnecessarily depressed. Furthermore, in a world of differing talents and backgrounds, some wage inequalities are necessary because a system of wage equality would be so inefficient as to lower all pay rates, not just high pay rates. (It would cause employers to be stuck with their round pegs in square holes and cause workers to work less or take less productive jobs they had spurned in favor of high-paying jobs, thus a loss of tax revenue out of which wage subsidies could be paid.) Then comes the famous conclusion in Rawls's argument: *inequality* in after-tax, after-subsidy wages is *just* to the extent it *serves* the working poor—the "least advantaged" working in the economy. The just amount of wage inequality—of the wage gap—is precisely wide enough to deliver the *maximum* remuneration of the lowest earners.

The new vision and new concepts in Rawls's book were electrifying and quickly altered the discourse in economics as well as moral philosophy, though the book was scorned by the right for supposedly neglecting freedom, notwithstanding that Rawls had stressed freedom as essential to justice, and criticized by the left, for whom inequality was worse than poverty. Rawls's attention to the wage may look soulless, compared to cries from the heart against exclusion and violence, but he sees a decent wage as the gateway to a person's "self-respect" and "self-realization." He writes poignantly that a higher wage may make it possible to take a son to the ballgame or to participate in school and town meetings, and thus to gain greater social inclusion. The present author's 1997 book *Rewarding Work* supplemented Rawls's argument for redistribution to the lowest-paid: Subsidizing companies' employment of low-wage workers, by increasing their employment in business, would widen their involvement in society's central project and open up a sense of the world of work in poor families and neighborhoods. The message applies as much to India as to America.[2]

Yet Rawls's book did not hold answers to some fundamental questions about the *modern* economy that we would like to address to him were he still among us. Though he refers often to "prospects" and "expectations," his market economy has no dynamism, and the future it brings is always foreseen. In this austere setting, the book has to adopt a view of the "good" that is—in his own words—so "thin" as to exclude the rich facets of the good life from the ancients to the moderns: Instead, the degree of good available to a person is reducible to the traditional things that his or her wage can buy. As a

---

2. A recent opinion column by Bharat Jhunjhunwala in *Tehelka: India's Independent Weekly Magazine* on May 7, 2012, condemns the unemployment compensation scheme proposed by Akhilesh Yadav, chief minister of Uttar Pradesh, and advocates employment subsidies instead:
> Phelps has suggested the government must give employment subsidy to the employed. ... People could benefit from the subsidy only by engaging in productive work ... That is precisely what Gandhi had said in *Young India* of 13 October 1921: "I must refuse to insult the naked by giving them clothes they do not need instead of work which they sorely need." Yadav should listen to Professor Phelps and Mahatma Gandhi. He should devise schemes that create demand for workers and provide relief to the poor through productive work.

consequence, Rawls did not think through the distinctive issues about economic justice that arise in a modern economy. And his theoretical framework did not help with the justification of that economy—of *modern* capitalism.

Justice in a Modern Economy

What if in a society everyone had a passion for the good life of Aristotle, Montaigne, and Nietzsche, and every young person hoped for a career in an economy structured for dynamism—thus the fullest opportunity to conceive new ideas and to develop, launch, and pioneer the new products they envision or inspire? For such a society, any good economy would have to be a well-functioning *modern* economy of some sort. Any economy *not* offering these would-be participants such opportunity, thus frustrating their aspirations for a good life, would be unjust in the sense of Rawls and many others. What, though, would a modern economy have to look like to be *just*?

To arrive at answers to questions of Rawlsian economic justice in this economy, a citizen could ask herself how she would decide a question from the viewpoint of the Rawlsian original position: she knows she would pursue the good life but does not know her chances of being gifted in imaginative powers, curiosity, intuition, pioneering spirit, and other capacities of value in that pursuit. In that original position, the argument goes, she would favor the broadest opportunity to start a business, the broadest access to capital from the financial sector, and the broadest access to legal protections. In short, she would favor equal opportunity: if it were unequal, *she* could be one of those shut out. (She would also favor affirmative action in anticipation she could be one of those not receiving as much access as some others.)

What in a modern economy would justice in income distribution involve? A modern economy is striking for the *extraordinary income*—oversize profits and capital gains in anticipation of profits—that accrues to those whose new idea or whose entrepreneurial development or marketing of a new idea led to a successful adoption in the marketplace. Since those working under the direction of an entrepreneur are paid wages in anticipation of the chance of commercial success, there are also losses and capital losses to deal with. Varying parts of these incomes would be spent or accumulated to pay for the use of others' new products and for helping to finance one's next innovative venture or finance someone else's new project. Thus there is a so-called circular flow. In this way, income and wealth would come to be highly valued, even if tangible capital is not going to be very important. A citizen who puts himself in Rawls's original position might, at first, be against taxing the winnings of the winners to cushion the losses of the losers. With more reflection, however, he might see that such redistribution would *encourage* risk taking by the private sector: the government, as a partner sharing in the gains and losses, is reducing the risk of the private parties. On still further thought, though, the citizen in the original position might wonder why society should encourage risk taking. Why would I want to see the state encouraging more high-risk investing and pure gambling when what I want is to participate in an economy of dynamism? And I might like the frisson of excitement that comes from a leap of faith, a voyage into the unknown. So a citizen, knowing what the good life is but not knowing his endowments, would not be interested in the government's taking a share of the profits to mitigate losses—and certainly not to mitigate losses on failed investments that had nothing to do with innovation.

Taxing profits is widely thought to be necessary to do justice to workers, not to finance cushions for failed innovators. While Rawls's book is about just wages, its focus is on the redistribution of *ordinary income*—in particular, the redistribution of *wage* income from high-wage to low-wage earners.[3] There is no profit income in the non-modern, even classical, economy that is the setting for Rawls's book and for the basic public finance literature—aside from profits arising from monopoly, which would be a distraction here. The subject of economic justice in an economy of *dynamism*, though, raises the question of taxing the *profits from innovation* to subsidize labor. (Note that any resulting increase in after-tax, after-subsidy wage income in the economy would in turn make feasible a higher general tax on labor from which to finance a higher employment subsidy to the disadvantaged.) But this pot of gold is chimerical. It is not established as an empirical matter that taxation of profits garners increased revenue for use in boosting pay of low-wage workers. It is theoretically possible that taxing profits ultimately lowers wages by dragging down future levels of productivity more than it raises wages by collecting more revenue at any given level of national product and national income. So we cannot conclude that

3. In the 1970s, the book prompted a spate of papers in academic journals that, building on analytics developed by James Mirrlees in 1971, created theoretical models of the effects of the structure of taxation on wage incomes and identified the structure that was theoretically optimal on Rawls's criterion of maximizing the lowest wage, known as the "maximin" criterion. One of these was Phelps, "Taxation of Wage Income for Economic Justice" (1973). Another paper studied whether Rawlsian justice required the taxation of interest income to subsidize labor.

just taxation, even from the Rawlsian perspective on wage rates, would call for taxing the profits of innovation.

Of more fundamental importance, it is not clear in the present setting, in which all persons aspire to the Aristotelian good life, that all tax revenues must be allocated to boosting through employment subsidies the *wage* of the least advantaged participants. It is possible that even they would rather see tax revenues used to lift the dynamism of the economy than to subsidize their employment. Even if the least advantaged care only about their wage, there may exist government projects that do more—dollar for dollar—to raise low-wage employment and thus pull up the lowest wage rates than employment subsidies would do. These would include government projects that would remove large blockages to efficiency or to dynamism. It is unfortunate, though, that the least-advantaged are seen to be part of what Marx dubbed the *lumpenproletariat,* in whom he evinced little interest, rather than humans in the normal range who are to a degree engaged in what they do and welcome the problems and opportunities that it may present. That view has led economic policymakers of a Rawlsian complexion to assume that for the least advantaged only the wage can be appreciated. That workers, even the least-paid among them, have *interests besides their pay* suggests that workers might not choose—in the original position or in the voting booth—to have the government spend all its tax revenues on their subsidization. They might take an interest in a national project that seizes their imagination. It is a little too narrow to view Rawlsian justice as fully met if there is an annual budget that clears away all the obstacles to efficiency and to dynamism that have arisen over the past year, then allots to employment subsidies what, if any, remains of the budget.

There are other topics of economic justice besides intervention through fiscal means in the life prospects of persons after their talents and capacities are already formed. A classic topic is early intervention in the education of children disadvantaged by their social circumstances—a subject of the economist James Heckman. It can be argued that justice in a modern economy requires the state to take action to address in the early schooling years the disadvantages among people that would impair their ability to compete on a level playing field against others engaged in attempting innovation. (It would be anomalous for the state to spend, say, 5 percent of national income on raising wages of the disadvantaged and not a penny on raising the potential wage of people with poor wage prospects.) Although most citizens already know that their children are normal or better than normal, they can mentally insert themselves into Rawls's original position to consider in an unbiased way what would be a just level to bring the least-advantaged children up to.[4]

Justice amidst Multiple Human Natures

A Theory of Justice gained simplicity in its treatment of the good by supposing that *all* members of the society seek the "primary goods" and they *all* understand that one's wage is the means to them. The section above on the modern economy, in its treatment of the good, gained simplicity by supposing that *all* members of society seek the good life as Aristotle and his humanist successors conceived it, and they *all* understand that having work that is interesting, challenging, and adventurous is necessary to that life. That premise was not as fantastic as might be assumed. In America from the 1870s to the 1960s—the high years of modern capitalism—humanities courses invited students in elite schools to sense and identify with the human condition and the set of values and beliefs that run through Western history. At Columbia College in the presidency of Nicholas Murray Butler, the required course Contemporary Civilization, a course in history and philosophy, was started by John Erskine in 1919, and the required Humanities A, or HumLit, in 1937 by Jacques Barzun and Lionel Trilling. At the University of Chicago, the Great Books program, developed by Mortimer Adler and instituted by president Robert Hutchens, started in 1942. At Amherst College, a humanities course from 1947 to 1968 led all freshmen through a pantheon of epic leaders, truth seekers, humanists, individualists, vitalists, and pragmatists—all to prepare them for former president Alexander Micklejohn's "life worth living." Anthony Kronman, a teacher of humanities and law at Yale, writes of the humanities course in America from Charles Eliot's rise to the presidency of Harvard in 1869 to the "watershed year" 1968:

---

4. If it is agreed by citizens in the original position that justice requires the greatest feasible prospects for the less advantaged, the citizens will also quickly agree that the state must raise its expenditure level on disadvantaged children to the point where the benefit of an additional billion would be less than the benefit of simply putting the billion into employment subsidies or into activities that raise dynamism, which would indirectly raise the prospects of the least advantaged. Rawls would have added that, as the principles of justice do not allow the wages of the more advantaged to be hammered down to the wage level of the less advantaged, so the same principles do not allow the state to slow the pace of education in the schools so that more of the less advantaged can keep up with more of the others. In any well-functioning economy, modern or not, the talents of the most-able people and the capacities of average people are a resource to be drawn on for mutual gain. If choked off, the working poor would be in a desperate plight.

There are patterns of life that have had a perennial attraction for human beings. . . . The humanities acquaint us with the core commitments of these patterns. . . . Understanding [them] can never eliminate [our] demand . . . to live a life that recognizes, honors and expresses our own uniqueness . . . [n]or can it ever by itself answer the question of what living is for. . . . But the humanities can give us guidance. . . . [The humanities course] . . . invited each student to see himself as a participant in a "great conversation" . . . to think of previous participants—poets, philosophers, novelists, historians and artists—as addressing each other in a long, unbroken conversation about the most important matters in life. . . . Shaped by its belief in the validity of the idea of human nature and by a confidence in the perennial significance of a limited number of exemplary types of human fulfillment, [the humanities] formed, for many years, the core of a program [on] the meaning of life.[5]

It appears that these humanities, while welcoming the diversity of talents and career preferences in any human society and recognizing the variety in the "forms" of human fulfillment that result, discern a "human nature," a nature that is universal from the time when humans used caves for flute concerts. This common nature includes—at the highest level—a desire to express creativity, a relish for challenge, an enjoyment of problem solving, a delight in novelty, and the restless need to explore and to tinker. The pursuit and experience of these "highest goods" is the way to human fulfillment—and to "becoming," which is a large part of it. This human nature and this human fulfillment is displayed by artists and scientists, for example, and by a wide range of less unusual people, including business people, engineers, physicians, and lawmakers. These people are often called "modern" because this way of life—this dealing in new ideas—and this human fulfillment became endemic only after the ideas of the late Renaissance, the Scientific Revolution, and the Enlightenment ushered in the modern societies with modern economies that arose in the 19th century. But the potential for this life and this fulfillment was always there, witness some of the impressive figures in the pre-modern societies, such as the incessantly questioning Socrates, the clever Cleopatra, the venturesome Leif Ericson, and the visionary Catherine the Great.

Yet there has always been another view. In the present day, there are dissenters to the humanities who suppose that there is not simply a variety of

5. Kronman, *Education's End* (2007, pp. 78–87).

"forms" of human fulfillment: There exists another *kind* of human fulfillment, which many are still finding. This movement points to those people,
even in today's relatively modern societies, who flock to callings that do not
promise human fulfillment as the humanities know it. In some of the more
traditional societies, such as southern Italy, the occupation of women is preponderantly in the home, where they take care of their children and their
husbands. In very traditional societies, the occupation of many men is often
in the church, where they serve as priests, ministers, rabbis, or imams. In all
societies, some men and women take up employment as caregivers in a nurs-
ing home or a hospice; some others prefer positions in nonprofit organizations aimed at a cause, such as the environment, to work in an organization
where the individual's own benefit is not the objective. In these lines of work,
there is relatively little prospect, if any, of experiencing exploration or creation. There is no one here like Cellini or Chanel.

The orientation of many people, even in the most modern economies,
toward family or community or country or religion—or, these days, the earth—
harks back to the traditions in Western societies until the modern revolution.
Today's traditionalism—a harkening back to the pre-modern traditions—
presents an opposition to modernism like the opposition between Platonic
"being" and the "becoming" of Montaigne, Nietzsche, and Bergson. Montaigne
associates the former with the transcendental and the divine. The preference
of some people for a traditional vocation such as caregiving in spite of its relatively static character may reflect a love of God or love of community that is
greater than their self-love, thus greater than any stirring to seek human fulfillment as Aristotle or Montaigne or Nietzsche or Bergson conceived it. (To speak
of that sort of satisfaction from such a traditional occupation as "human fulfillment," or "flourishing," would be to deny those terms their accustomed meaning. If fulfillment were so broadened, what activity by a free, healthy, and sane
adult would not be said to be a way to fulfillment?)

The question here is what we should understand Rawlsian justice to
entail in an economy in which people of a *different* human nature, thus apt to
pursue an *alternative* life if the terms are not prohibitive, coexist with people
having the nature portrayed in the humanities—the "human nature" that
Aristotle and the moderns had in mind when speaking of the good life. Certainly the freedom of people to act on their own human nature, no matter if
it deviates from the human nature central to the humanities, is basic to Rawlsian justice. But the just treatment of persons engaged in their very different
pursuits is less obvious.

Late in his career, Rawls finally underlined something that was implicit earlier in his book: His distributive justice, by its very definition, applies to those whose work contributes to the income generated by society's cooperative venture, its economy, not to hermits and others who stand outside it. Rawls stated bluntly, lest there be misunderstanding, that those who "surf all day" are not in his category of the least-advantaged contributors. "Surfers must somehow support themselves" without benefit of surfing subsidies.[6]

The activity of people in the home—managing the household or raising children—is essential to society as we know it. (A recent OECD study reports that the time spent by Australian men in cooking, cleaning, and childcare has risen to 3 hours a day and is still much higher among women.) And we are sensitive to the fact that, for some, this is a "lesser life," in Sylvia Ann Hewlett's striking characterization.[7] Yet this activity is also not to share in the Rawlsian redistributions of *income*. The redistributions in Rawls's theory are made from the economic surplus created by the contributions of paid labor, and it is redistributed to paid labor. Mothers, for example, have no claim to this surplus, since they have no hand in producing it; what they produce they produce for love. (Our intuition suggests there ought to be redistribution of the nonpecuniary benefits within the home, though that may be difficult.)

By this logic, it appears that those who, out of a sense of service or devotion, find an occupation in a *volunteer sector* where there are no receipts from which to pay them an income—volunteers at nonprofits caring for the environment, caregivers tending to the penniless, priests ministering to the faithful for only a bed and a meal, and so forth—would likewise have no just claim to receive a Rawlsian subsidy, since there is no income generated that could be redistributed, and nothing is left for them from the "social surplus" after it has all gone to the lower-paid among those who produced. If this sector *does* have receipts per worker from which to pay these workers a wage, say, the wage rate of the lowest paid in the economy, that would not alter the fact that they have no just claim against the social surplus produced by those pursuing the good life in the economy. That may seem counterintuitive. Wouldn't a citizen meditating in the original position and recognizing the possibility that *she* might be one of those persons of another nature, thus devoted to another life, decide that justice requires paying the Rawlsian subsidy to those

---

6. Rawls, *Justice as Fairness* (p. 179). Rawls then appears to suggest in further comments that one could not safely infer that the surfers are as badly off as the worst-paid workers, since the surfers rejected work and do so even after a subsidy pulls up the net wage of lowest earners.

7. Hewlett, *A Lesser Life* (1986).

whose *calling* is the cause of low wages just as much as to those whose *productivity* is the cause? But the Rawlsian subsidy is paid out of a calculation of equity, not need or deserts. To be eligible for the prizes one has to play the game. Not some other game.

There is also the issue of the thrust of the state beyond its responsibility for distributive justice and efficiency. What would Rawlsian justice allow? The section above observed that the state may take opportunities to repair dysfunctions in the economy that are a drain on its dynamism, just as it may take opportunities to address inefficiencies. Such activities are not unjust from a Rawlsian perspective if the benefits compensate the low-wage workers. But now we are acknowledging that some working-age members of society are active in pursuit of a radically different kind of life. The citizen in the original position might think it is in his self-interest to temper the state's promotion of dynamism in service of the good life and reallocate it in the service of the other kinds of life, since he must anticipate that *he* may turn out to be one of those who march to a different drummer. But he ought to think again: The state's programs and agencies in service of dynamism, while benefiting the working poor among others, come out of the pockets of the working poor. The unknown risk of being drawn to a different life is not a coherent justification for siphoning some of the rewards of the least advantaged in the economy to those who exit from the economy for another life, as if the latter were disadvantaged collaborators. They are not disadvantaged, just different, and they are not collaborators in the production of a redistributable social surplus.

A Liberating System Not Shown to Be Unjust

The discussion above has been about adjustments and extensions that a modern economy would require to be not simply well-functioning, meaning without major malfunctions, but functioning *justly*. That discussion leads to the final question: Whether the modern economy, when well and justly-functioning, would be a just system. Rawls's principle was that a just economy is one with a structure that would make the prospects of the least advantaged higher than they would be in any other system. In his elaborations toward the end of his book, Rawls, whose descriptions of market economies, capital and socialist, were basically classical, was unable to say which one was just: a pre-modern capitalism or a pre-modern socialism; the differences separating them were not decisive in his eyes. But a thoroughly *modern* society, in which modern values are broadly held, would see the modern-capitalist economy and the standard alternatives, such as market socialism and corporatism, as being worlds apart.

The present book, after comparing the main alternatives, sees reasons to believe that a modern economy, when functioning well and justly, is tailor-made to produce the flourishing and personal growth that are at the core of the good life. The book then finds a range of evidence that a modern-capitalist economy is outstanding in the prospects it offers ordinary people for the good life: The economies relatively strong in modern values and with relatively muted traditional values generally perform better in all the metrics of the good life—job satisfaction, unemployment, and wage level. With that evidence in hand, a member of a thoroughly modern society, placed in Rawls's original position and assuming that he might be among the least advantaged, would have good reason to decide that the modern-capitalist economy, if justly-functioning and well-functioning, was the right choice to make. (A member expecting to be the most advantaged might prefer a planned economy in hopes of being the czar.) It would offer the least advantaged better prospects for a good life than socialism's bureaucracies would or corporatism's cronies and clientele. (In a short while, however, a case of pluralism of values will be taken up.)

Of course, anyone making that defense or any other defense of the modern-capitalist economy must be conscious of the deep antipathy that many people have expressed for capitalism, modern or pre-modern. The antipathy for the great mounds of wealth in private hands and for the acquiring of great wealth is particularly strong. In some reflections following his exposition Rawls writes:

> What men want is meaningful work in free association with others, these
> associations regulating their relations to one another within a framework
> of just basic institutions. To achieve this state of things great wealth is not
> necessary. In fact, it is more likely to be a positive hindrance, a meaning-
> less distraction at best if not a temptation to indulgence and emptiness.[8]

It is true that exaggerated estimations of one's wealth lead to excessive demands for leisure and consumption, thus to reduced employment as well as reduced investment and innovation. Trying to justify modern capitalism as a machine for accumulating wealth could not be more crass. Yet, despite its ill effects, people's wealth is bound to soar in the event the product or method they work on turns out to be a highly profitable innovation. And, as remarked

8. *A Theory of Justice* (p. 257).

before, a chance of extraordinary pecuniary benefits helps motivate people to work on projects that may prove lucrative. So it is not inherently unjust that large inequalities of wealth emerge in modern capitalism; it is in traditional societies that the large wealth inequalities are apt to be neither inherent nor just. Furthermore, wealth has a positive side. It is unnecessary to say that if a person's wealth increases and others' wealth does not, that person will be able to live better in every way. But even if everyone's wealth is increased (by the same amount or in equal proportion), people will then be better able to afford to pursue their interests and express their personalities and their values.

Yet many a social critic speaks of an "injustice"—some inherent flaw that some other sort of system does not have—that renders a modern economy—even one outfitted for economic justice, such as economic inclusion—"unjust." There are at least three broad dimensions in which the modern economy might conceivably fall short. Some other sort of economy, perhaps only a variant of the modern economy, might offer *greater* prospects of the good life or offer those prospects to *more* participants than the modern-capitalist economy offered, or offer a *better life* than the good life in its various classic descriptions. And in the universe of potential alternative economies there must be some as yet unknown star that burns brighter than the modern one. It would not be feasible to sift through the whole litany of objections raised. But the claims that a modern economy is unjust, no matter how well-functioning and justly-functioning, has to be discussed.

Critics of modern capitalism, however, tend to argue that the modern-capitalist economies—and maybe all other economies—are unjust relative to some economic system that they *envision* but that is *not built*. Famously, socialists of the 19th century, before there was a socialist economy, supposed that it would offer wider prospects for employment and higher wages than the modern-capitalist economies could. Once built, however, the socialist economies were seen to offer poorer wages and lower employment than the modern-capitalist economies had—those that were left standing after the onslaught of socialism and corporatism.

The corporatists of the 20th century envisioned a state-led economy that served well the aspirations of a largely *traditional* society. Once corporatist France and Italy had a track record, however, it could be seen that state power had not generated the promised dynamism, so they could not sustain rapid productivity growth and low unemployment beyond the 1990s.

By 1970 social critics in the West envisioned a new sort of economy that would pay a lower price for the good life. The new economy was supposed to offer the prospect of substantial economic stability. But the economies that continental Western Europe claimed to be buffered against instability through heavy job protection and large public sectors, such as those in continental Western Europe, had nothing to show for it: They had low employment and major slumps. And they have paid a steep price: They have little or no dynamism and, as a consequence, underdevelopment, low employment, and not necessarily stable employment at that.

There are plenty of economies in human history that offer more stability and equality than any modern economy ever did. But observation over modern history does not turn up alternatives to the modern economy that deliver less inequality and less instability while delivering no less of the good life.

The modern economy has met new criticisms in recent decades: Portfolios must be balanced; growth must be balanced rather than running in one direction, as in the internet boom; and global imbalances in saving and investment must be corrected. These criticisms seem not to understand that the genius of a well-functioning modern economy is its deployment of the insights and judgment of people immersed in the economy in the economy's decisions about the directions in which a nation should best invest:

> The IMF claims a mandate to address "economic imbalances" . . . because
> it would be good for world stability. But what is the purpose of a private
> international credit market if not to permit a nation enjoying an invest-
> ment boom to borrow abroad and a nation in an investment slump to lend
> overseas? . . . Next, the IMF speaks of "crisis prevention." The zero tolerance
> for financial crisis suggests that the IMF has lost sight of the rationale for a
> well-functioning modern-capitalist economy. Several Western nations have
> sought to maintain it not because Stalin's Gosplan could not get the relative
> prices of nuts and bolts right but because the pluralism of entrepreneurs
> and investors, all with differentiated insights and experiences, is an inspired
> way to manage the uncertainties that creating new futures entails.[9]

To regard as a flaw the tendency to crash in an economy with the creativity of the American economy—during most of its history, at any rate—is like calling the tendency toward swings between mania and depression in deeply creative people a flaw. It is easy to understand that, in an economy possessing dynamism, a failure to work out new ideas or a dry spell without new ideas may bring on depression. (Of course, the loss of local and regional banks in the past

---

9. Edmund Phelps, "IMF Seems to Have Lost Sight of Rationale for Capitalism," *Financial Times,* letter to the editor, April 25, 2000.

decade and consequent loss of expertise in lending constitute a new dysfunction in economies that had been in the forefront of modern economies. But these pathologies do not represent an injustice in modern economies. The dysfunction can be corrected.)

A provocative critique has arisen in recent years: The good life has been conceived too narrowly. It requires a "balance" between work and home. And the modern economy, which is voracious, leaves not enough time and calm for domestic life and childcare. Here the critics do not want to take issue with the good life so much as to broaden it to the home. They suppose that a new economy can be created in which participants can "have it all"—the rich domestic life and close involvement with children that may have been a feature of the traditional societies centuries ago *without loss* of the dynamism of which a modern economy is capable and the flourishing that is its most important fruit. But talk of a "work-life balance," as if work were not integral to life, casts doubt on whether these critics have understood very well the good life and the conditions on which it depends. A flourishing life in the world of work can come only from an emotional commitment that leads to deep involvement in the work—it cannot be had on the cheap. If going to a four-day workweek or putting a nursery in the offices were found not to lessen employee engagement and effectiveness in many kinds of companies, such companies would have done so. Imposing those practices on companies (through a tax or a fine) would cost companies some employee engagement and thus some of their vibrancy and their dynamism. One company after another has learned that robotic production can be done by employees at home, but innovation requires an office for employee interactions.

A deeper point is that home life cannot be part of the good life unless it too is rich with challenges and hurdles. Some people may at some time find more challenge at home than in business, but they cannot expect to find more flourishing by cutting back on challenges and hurdles. The author Katie Roiphe makes the argument:

> Why is balance necessarily good? Isn't part of the skill or joy of life in the imbalance, in the craziness, in the bizarre or implausible intensity? . . . I am a single mother with three jobs. But I have come to see that there is a kind of exhilaration or happiness in the chaos itself. . . . [T]he human psyche is too complicated, too messy, too elusive, for problems to be solved by "balance," by "healthy environments," by the sheer stubborn physical presence.[10]

10. Katie Roiphe, "There Is No Such Thing as Having It All," *Financial Times*, June 30, 2012.

These visions of an alternative to the modern-capitalist economy all evoke magical thinking—a belief that for any worthy goal there is always a way. But modern thinking tells us that we have to choose among our ends—that we cannot have it all.

The question of the justice of a well and justly-functioning economy is quite different for a society in which one or more elements seek different kinds of life—a life of caring for others or a life of contemplation or a life devoted to family values. Such a pluralism of values—traditionalist ethics alongside modernist ethics—came up in the discussion above of the subsidies to the least-advantaged workers that are required by economic justice in a modern economic system; here we discuss the system required for justice. The crux of the matter is that in any modern society there exists an economy based on exchange, which the modern society supports for the mutual advantage of those who participate in it, while those from the one or more dissenting cultures want to opt out of that exchange system in quest of their dissenting goals. Some social critics appear to believe that it is an injustice of the modern-capitalist economy that it does not provide a space for participants motivated by traditionalist values. In the perspective of this book—the perspective of Kant, Rawls, and some others—justice requires that those who want to pursue a traditional life ought to be free to work and earn in a traditional sector, just as those who aspire to the good life in its classic descriptions must be free to work in the modern sector. (In this diverse society, resources in one economy would be remunerated from what it produces and resources in the other would work without compensation or be paid out of charitable contributions.) It would be a grotesque injustice to consign those with modern values to an unmodern economy relatively devoid of change, originality, and discovery.

Of course, the state will be called upon by people in the original position to protect the ideals of the various traditions, such as traditions of caring. Justice requires tolerance of other lifestyles and thinking, but it does not require those who would pursue the good life to engage in self-denial or to surrender to those styles. Justice does not allow the traditions of the others to so constrict the modern economy as to block the expression of its dynamism in innovative activity and thus modern life.

In this kind of pluralistic society, it might turn out that each ship floats on its own bottom, neither economy cross-subsidizing the other. However we may regard that, it is not an injustice. Justice in the sense of Rawls does not require the modern sector to transfer money to the traditional sector for work subsidies or for any other purpose, since Rawlsian justice in the modern sector is about equity in the distribution of the fruits of that sector. If, however, participants in the modern sector unanimously want the government to subsidize the traditional sector, it would be just to do so. And there is no injustice in individuals donating to that sector. In America, a sector of nonprofit corporations and charitable foundations has become large owing to philanthropy, though some philanthropists acknowledge that their contributions are encouraged by the tax benefits granted by the government, which are apt to lessen the revenue left for the working poor.

We have been discussing justice toward traditionalist elements in a modern society—a society in which modern values have prevailed and created an economy in which the modern sector predominates. Justice is done to those with heavily traditional values by permitting them to operate in a parallel economy and, since that does no harm to the modern economy, justice is done to those with modern values too. (The parallel economy might help the modern economy by drawing away those whose traditional values might make them costly employees and might demoralize the other employees.) It is worth touching on justice toward modernist elements in a heavily traditional society. The problem here is that, unless those with modern values are a tiny minority, allowing them to freely develop and operate a modern sector would have unwelcome impacts on the traditional majority. After all, the counter-revolution of the corporatists against the encroaching modern business economy was set off by the harms that the traditionals felt at the hands of the moderns. Responding to that problem, the state in some European nations—Italy and to a lesser extent France, for example—established penalties and barriers that put a curb on the vibrancy and the dynamism of the modern sector—the sector "parallel" to the sector containing rural industry, state enterprises, the central government, and the church. (And this "parallel" sector was so small in relation to the force of the traditional culture that the latter dragged down entrepreneurship and innovatorship.) The European nations did not generally allow a modern economy to flower, nor did they encourage their citizens to seek lives of nonconformity, creativity, and adventure. Prevailing attitudes and beliefs did serious injustice by blocking and even discouraging the moderns from their pursuit of the good life.

So, though one might think at first that the European nations having strong traditionalist values were perfectly just in installing highly corporatist or socialist economies, much as nations having modernist values were just in welcoming modern economies, the truth is that the traditionalist societies barred ordinary people from chances to pursue the good life—while the modern societies did not bar people from finding traditional lives in nongovernmental organizations, foundations, nonprofits, churches, and the home. And that was unjust.

We do not need to remind ourselves that *actual* modern-capitalist economies do exhibit injustices, as do actual corporatist economies. The most glaring one is the omission of sufficient measures to pull employment and wages of the lowest-paid employees up to much higher levels, though nations with corporatist economies have similarly failed. Another glaring injustice is the practice of inflating disposable incomes through undertaxation and enactment of entitlements that will not be paid, though private and social wealth are puffed up in the corporatist nations too. But these injustices could be corrected if only the beneficiaries understood the fallaciousness of their excuses. However, being neither inherent nor peculiar to a modern-capitalist economy, these injustices do not show that modern capitalism itself is unjustified. It is only marred.

If the argument of this book is right, then, a modern-capitalist economy *is* justified—in nations where it can function well and justly and where modern values are prevalent enough to operate it, at any rate. Of course, it is possible—perhaps likely—that, in the future, some subsequent system will come to be seen as the just system—until such time as it too gives way to another system.

To conclude: The advent of modern economies was a godsend for the fortunate nations to which they came. From the mid-1800s to the mid-1900s, the first modern economies—all of them more-or-less modern capitalist— were marvels of the Western world: They brought economic dynamism, a phenomenon never before seen or imagined, and they brought broad inclusion, which pre-modern capitalism had only begun to do. The new economic system got its dynamism and its inclusion by enlisting the imagination and energy of participants from the grassroots on up. The innovation they caused could not have been so extraordinary had it not engaged the mind and seized the imagination of participants down to craftsmen, day laborers, farmers, traders, and factory workers.

This book finds that, far from being a system of materialism, coarseness, Babbitry, Philistinism, and greed that stands in the way of the good life, the modern economy answered a widespread desire for the good life. It arose out of the modern movement for emancipation from traditional societies with their suffocating feudal economies and from the routine and desolation of mercantile capitalism—a system Smith found uninspiring. The mass engagement in innovation and the mass flourishing that resulted from the modern economy perfectly illustrated the Aristotelian perspective on the highest good and the Rawlsian perspective on justice. This system for mass flourishing was the treasure of the modern era—of the modernist values arising from Pico, Luther, and Voltaire to Hume and Nietzsche.

Yet the older myths of economic success have not gone away. They do not see the possibility of dynamism in private enterprise. In one such story, a nation's freedom relative to freedom in other nations determines its relative economic success. But while freedom is obviously necessary for innovation, it is not sufficient. Freeing people to do a thing may not prompt them to do it. Often one has to *make* one's freedom by taking the plunge. Another story lays economic success to the discoveries of science, not those of business. But this story fails to explain why some nations "took off" and other advanced economies did not, and why the take-offs began in a lackluster period for science. Yet another story says that fast innovation in a nation can be achieved by the public sector—faster than what, if any, the private sector can do. It is not seen as significant that no nation has done any such thing yet—unless we relabel Bismarck's German economy as state-driven rather than modern capitalist.

Getting our theories right is going to be crucial for the West and the East too in the next decades. America is unlikely to recover the dynamism and resulting prosperity it had up to the 1970s as long as it operates on the belief that freedom is sufficient to do so, and that freedom can always be dialed up by a downward adjustment of tax rates as required—this is a great mistake. Modern values and traditional values are both consequential. The modern values that fueled the dynamism of old may have declined—and the opposing values of traditionalism have surely surged—more than fiscal policy can manage to offset. The cry of politicians for a rebirth of traditional values is about as loud as their cry for a rebirth of economic dynamism. As a result, the political parties continue to talk as if prosperity will return once agreement has been reached on fiscal measures of sufficient strength.

Europe will not recover to the respectable levels of employment it had in the 1990s, let alone regain the high prosperity of the early 1900s, as long as it clings to the belief that a corporatist economy—with the right state control over private capital—can achieve the stability and harmony that capitalism cannot, and can do so without any loss of the dynamism it had when its economy was more modern. These beliefs have not met the test. Yet Europe continues to operate a stultifying corporatist economy under the tyranny of traditionalist values.

If modern values are so important for careers of creators, inquirers, and explorers in the economic sphere, thus for a good economy, it might be wondered whether they are also important elsewhere in society. De Tocqueville noticed that they were. He recognized that America, a nation most conspicuous for its broad and intense engagement in the economic system, was also remarkable for its broad and intense engagement in the political system. As a result, there was flourishing in both spheres. For flourishing to occur in the political sphere there had to be a grassroots democracy that was in many ways the counterpart of the grassroots dynamism.

Anyone living today may have noticed that, in this respect, Europe is in a bad way in its political sphere as much as in its economic sphere. As Amartya Sen writes in "The Crisis of European Democracy":

> Europe cannot hand itself over to the unilateral views—or good
> intentions—of experts without public reasoning and informed consent
> of its citizens. Both democracy and the chance of creating good policy are
> undermined . . . when ineffective policies are dictated by leaders.

Similar points apply to economic dynamism, some of which have been made in this book. Innovation and broad flourishing are undermined when many of the directions taken by business are set by economic policy, when the formation of new businesses looks increasingly limited and managers are selected from elites to negotiate with government and community, and when companies are so large and hierarchical that workers of ordinary skill have no way to express innovative ideas and no incentive to conceive them.

In a society capable of modernity, then, the standard for a good and just political system is the standard for a good and just economy. The requirement for the good and the just in a modern society is the same in both the political and economic spheres.

Regaining the Modern

Society's course will be changed only by a change of ideas.

FRIEDRICH HAYEK

The coming generation of leaders and creators will have to rekindle the spirit of risk. Real innovation is difficult and dangerous but living without it is impossible.

GARRY KASPAROV and PETER THIEL

I N THE WEST THERE IS A SENSE THAT THE "glorious history of desire and dreams" has wound down. Most Western economies have been nearly stagnant—America since the mid-1970s and much of Western Europe since the late 1990s. While advances in information and communications, largely made in America, have given many the impression that such advances are endemic, labor productivity in the economy as a whole plodded from 1972 until the rollout of the internet began in 1996 and plodded again after the rollout was over in 2004. Wide damage has resulted. Employee compensation has barely grown. The employment rate of white men fell from 80 percent of their working-age population in 1965 to 72 percent in 1995 and 70½ percent at the end of 2007; that of black men fell even more. Total output thus slowed on both counts—labor productivity and labor input. Investment-good output for enterprises, private and public, was hard hit—falling relative to the total from 16 percent in the 1960s to 14.7 percent in the 1990s and 14.3 percent in the 2000s. Output for consumers did better, but jobs are tied more to the former than to the latter.

What can be done to try to restart the system of desire and dreams? The question has barely been discussed. The crisis of the year gets all the attention. Yet the fiscal crises hovering over several of these nations, America, Italy, and France among them, are traceable to the stagnation. So are the financial crises at the banks that had the misjudgment to finance Europe's fiscal profligacy and America's officially promoted and subsidized housing boom.

Fiscal crises arose because economic growth, after picking up the pace somewhat for a few years, slowed again early in the past decade—returning, in America, to the pace of the 1970s and 1980s. This dimmed the prospects for steeply rising tax revenues on which governments had been counting to scale the mountain of social insurance entitlement claims by the bulge of baby boomers. Did governments then rush into the breach with tax hikes or spending cuts? No, they widened the breach. In America, George W. Bush's tax cuts of 2001 and 2003 removed 600 billion dollars from revenues per annum—5 percent of GDP—and "compassionate conservatism" extended Medicare to free pills, adding trillions of dollars to entitlements. In Europe, official fiscal deficits were allowed to rise from around 1.5 percent of GDP over 1999–2000 to around 4 percent over 2003–2005 in Italy and France. And the true deficits, which would take into account that the day of reckoning when benefits soar above revenues was fast approaching, were much higher. This pandering to voters by cutting revenue rather than starting it on the long climb needed to finance existing entitlements was stark fiscal irresponsibility. This irresponsibility was flagrant, since unemployment rates, often given as an excuse for deficits even in times of dire fiscal straits, though rising a bit after the internet boom, were not trending above the normal levels of the 1990s. This irresponsibility contributed to weak exchange rates, a reduced share of world exports (despite exchange depreciations), depressed stock markets, and weak business investment. Corporations have amassed reserves rather than invest. They fear undertaxation in the past will bring supertaxation in the future.

The *financial* crises arose out of the slow growth, the attendant unemployment, and the resulting fiscal deficits. Following the slowdown, several governments in Europe, rather than rein in their deficits, ran the deficits as long as European banks would buy them at low interest rates; and the banks were content to buy them so long as sovereign debt was rated AAA by credit agencies requiring banks to hold little capital against such debt. The U.S. government, while continuing to borrow, encouraged others to borrow as well. It coaxed government-sponsored enterprises (GSEs) in the home mortgage market and commercial banks to establish reduced interest rates on subprime mortgages. It also encouraged a huge volume of student loans. The GSEs, banks, and other lenders went on financing the resulting explosion of demand for loans by speculators and new buyers as long as home prices kept on rising—while failing to appreciate the risk.

After the 2008 crisis and the onset of panic, unemployment rose, eventually peaking and receding only very slowly. A huge debate began over why the unemployment rate, nearing 8 percent, was falling back so weakly and erratically that it looked unlikely to go below 7 percent—far above the "old normal" of 5½ percent in 1995–1996 and even farther above the older normal of 4½ percent in 1965. The standard theories of economics purported to explain the weakness of employment, aside from the brief booms, with no reference to the post-1970 stagnation. Crude Keynesians parroted "deficient aggregate demand," never squaring that "deficiency" with the absence of deflation that their textbooks said was a telltale sign of such a deficiency. Supply siders blamed "high" tax rates, never noting that employment failed to rise after George W. Bush's massive 2001 and 2003 tax cuts—it rose only with his housing boom. But it is odd to speak either of low spending by consumers or high tax rates on wages as the cause of the employment slump when so many other causes are operating: technology is doing less than usual to increase supply; retirements are decreasing the supply; households are bursting with social benefits and tax credits, present and prospective, that further reduce supply; and the fiscal crunch ahead will send interest rates skyward. The toll of all this on business confidence undoubtedly lies behind the depressed valuations put on a range of business assets, from machine to customer and employee, by enough to account for all or most of the present slump—though the prevailing trickle of innovation may well be strong enough to lower somewhat further the unemployment rate.

The crude Keynesians bent on keeping up spending and the crude supply siders bent on holding down tax rates would blithely create high fiscal deficits and thus ever-rising public debt (on top of the entitlements) as long as the stagnation of productivity and wages persisted. They do not worry for, in their models, there is no public debt level too high for the economy to "grow out of," since, for them, growth is forever: if it pauses, it will resume—it always does. They cannot comprehend that stagnation is not impossible. (They do not really comprehend that the opposite of stagnation—the flowering that comes from dynamism—is not impossible either.)

The standard theories offer no inkling of what policy initiatives might solve the stagnation of productivity and wages, thus their toll on employment. Their models were conceived to show how short-term fiscal interventions could shave off peaks and troughs of a short cycle around a rising trend path—not to address a sea change in dynamism bringing stagnation.

Thus the policy responses in Washington and other capitals have merely treated symptoms with make-work or offered palliatives with benefits and tax cuts. As Howard Stringer, head of Sony, in a March 2011 interview with

Fareed Zakaria, cried out, "It's fine to take care of the passengers and crew, but somebody has to save the ship!" There was nothing in the policy responses in America—in Bush's two terms or Obama's first term—or in Europe that could be seen as a transformational change intended to reverse the stubborn slowdown of innovation, hence productivity, that lay *behind* the drift of wages onto a lower path, the loss of jobs, and the sense of a setback in economic inclusion. Policy circles have not taken any steps they thought or said would restore the spirit of "desire and dreams" that animated the West's best economies in their best times.

If the Western nations are to regain their pre-stagnation levels of employment, inclusion, and job satisfaction, they will need to find ways to end their respective stagnations. The solution is indeed to step up "innovation," as some economists and others have said. But the term has a variety of meanings, and the discourse on how nations might go about increasing innovation (in the appropriate sense) has barely started. Finding policies to speed innovation will require nations to have a basic understanding of the roots of innovation over modern history.

I believe that the perspective of this book, which is new in its focus on grassroots innovation and the social values behind it and new also in its emphasis on the rewards of the working life to which it gives rise, can shed light on how we got into the state we are in. More importantly, it can show us paths back to the exploration, challenge, and expression—and the daily discoveries and innovations—that were the West's most profound achievement.

The book is at one level a narrative of the modern economies that sprang up in the 19th century and struggled in the 20th—economies possessing the grassroots dynamism to generate homegrown innovation. I first conceived the book as setting out an understanding of the core of the modern system that lay behind the torrent of innovation, believing that this understanding would help to preserve it where still functioning. During the writing, though, I came to see that the system had seriously deteriorated—putting itself in danger and the "glorious history" with it. So the resulting book had to tell not only the story of the rise of modern economies in the West nearly 200 years ago: their material progress, economic inclusion, and human flourishing. It had also to relate the decline of the modern economy. In America, that decline set in about 40 years ago: a stubborn slowdown of growth, a shrinkage of inclusion—first among the working class, then middle-income workers—and a loss of job satisfaction—the symptoms of a decrease of dynamism and thus of the average rate of innovation. In Europe the loss of indigenous innovation was earlier and more profound, though masked by technological transfer from overseas. Hence, the reduced innovation in America ultimately forced severe slowdowns, especially in Italy and France. Searching for causes, the book looks at both institutions that enable or disable dynamism and values that encourage or discourage it.

The dynamism of the modern economy drew on a set of modern institutions. In the private sector, the accrual of property law and company law enabled people wishing to be innovators to start up new companies and close them down as fast, unfettered by society's views, if it had any. Stock markets, banks, and patents were open to long-term visions, thus to innovations, large and small. In the public sector, the few institutions and policies it had were oriented toward the far future. A series of actions over several decades expanded the resources available for investment and innovation, from loans for visionary projects and land grants to pioneering settlers to freeing slaves and writing laws to protect investors and creditors. There was political pork and graft, but they did not hobble enterprise and choke innovation. All that changed.

Now there is much rot in the once-modern institutions. Short-termism is rife in business and finance—not just governments. In the private sector, CEOs have no long-term interest in their companies, and mutual funds have only a short-term interest in holding the shares. The result is that virtually all innovation can come only from outsiders—start-ups and angel investors—competing with established companies and industries. This short-termism reduces the *supply* of innovation—the innovatorship, risk capital, and venturesome end-users that innovation requires. In the public sector, corporatism has spread from Europe to America and metastasized into clientelism, cronyism, and pandering—graft is the least of it. Corporatism has also brought an explosion of regulations, grants, loans, guarantees, taxes, deductions, carve-outs, and patent extensions intended mainly to serve vested interests, political clients, and cronies. The protection of vested interests chokes off the opportunity that outsiders with new ideas would have to break into the market. All this has further reduced the supply of innovation. There is more. The corporatist government's contacts with political supporters and lobbyists shrink the size of the market left to innovators. In the past decade, large banks, large companies, and large government formed a nexus to pump up home mortgage debt in America and to create unchecked sovereign debt and unfunded entitlements in several nations in Europe. So America has joined Europe in having a parallel economy that draws its nourishment from the ideas of political elites, whatever their motives, rather than from new commercial ideas. All this reduces the rewards of innovation—the *demand* for innovation.

This book also sees the reprise of a surfeit of traditional values—restraining and suffocating attitudes and beliefs originating in pre-modern times. With the modern era, stretch version, a series of *modern* values arose from the 1500s onward that fueled grassroots dynamism by bringing out in people their need for the freedom to make a mark, create, explore, and pioneer: A good life is one lived to the fullest. People possess the imagination to create new things and the judgment to think for themselves. Advances in understanding are promoted if established ideas have to compete with new ideas. Economies work better if one has a right to own property. And everyone has a right to work for one's own gain, one's own property—not to be used as a means to the ends of others—of society or one's spouse. Advances in the economy are promoted if established companies and job holders have to compete with newcomers. The creativity and evolving desires of a modern world make its future indeterminate. So the modern world is open for us "to act on"! In a few nations, the modern notions prevailed over absolutism, determinism, antimaterialism, scientism, elitism, and the primacy of the family. These fortunate few supported modern-capitalist economies in the 19th century until their decline in the 20th. This too has changed.

Now, the balance between modern and traditional values appears on the whole to have swung back significantly. There may have been no loss in the intensity with which modern values are held nor in the prevalence of those holding them. Some scant survey evidence suggests that modern values gained or regained some ground between the decadal data wave of the early 1990s and the wave in the early 2000s, perhaps brought by the excitement of the internet boom. However, survey data record a strong increase of *traditional* values. These include family values and community values, of course, and some age-old ethical dogma: advance in lockstep, take no action (like competing) that would harm others, and the right to be compensated for every reversal at the hand of the market or the state.

There is also evidence that these values have won heightened influence over Western economies. The resurgence of family values and community values has drained companies of some of their innovative spirit and pressured them to serve community life and family life more and the bottom line less. With the rise of stakeholderism, anyone deciding to start up an innovative company would have to expect that its property rights would be diluted as it copes with an array of figures—its own workforce, interest groups, advocates, and community representatives—who ardently believe they have a legitimate "stake" in the company's results. Many employees feel they have the right to hold on to their jobs—no matter that many others would do the job for far less money—so long as they add something to profit or the company makes a profit from other divisions that can cover the loss. With the rise of solidarism, entrepreneurs seeking profits from successful innovations must expect that any profits will be shared through corporate profit taxes. The broad classes of income are to move in lockstep, so if upper incomes soar higher, the schedule of tax rates on high income is to be shifted up to share the wealth with the middle class—no matter if those tax rates become so high they lose more revenue than they gain. The backslide to a pre-modern fixation on wealth—which was harmless in Europe's corporatist societies, since their high tax rates effectively barred people from becoming rich—has poisoned America. It lured a generation away from voyages of creativity and discovery like those of their forebears to careers in banking or consulting. With the rise of a pre-modern culture of medieval entitlement, self-importance, conformism, and group dependence, there has been a palpable decline in vitalism—in "doing," as Thatcher or Sen might term it. Thus, even if modern values are intact, pre-modern notions have regained influence over business and the government. This accounts in part, if not in full, for how America and earlier Europe lost some of their dynamism and thus their indigenous innovation.

What can be done? Western societies will have to work on both their institutions and culture to restore their economic dynamism if they are to improve markedly their performance in employment, productivity, and, crucially, the work experience. While the universities and the press can help, many reforms and new forms will require governments at various levels—central, state, and local. Hayek said that no state could create a system for economic efficiency—though Lenin came pretty close. It is even truer that no state can create from scratch a set of institutions and values that would generate the dynamism for high indigenous innovation: In large part, our institutions and values evolved, then decayed, through the trial and error of entrepreneurs, financiers, and adopters. Yet governments in the past were at times activist in the formation of institutions and values—imperfect interventions resulting from inherently imperfect knowledge. So it will not be a widening of the scope of governments if, desiring to restore dynamism, they undertake *new* interventions and rescind *old* ones.

Governments will not act to restore dynamism until they become aware of the importance of the role played by dynamism in a modern-capitalist economy. At present, they are still in thrall to pre-modern notions that have been resurgent for several decades. In America, the Democratic Party voices a new corporatism well beyond Franklin Roosevelt's New Deal or Lyndon Johnson's Great Society. Geraldine Ferraro, the vice-presidential candidate in 1984, encapsulated it in what has become the party's mantra: "The promise of our country is that the rules are fair. If you work hard and play by the rules, you can earn your share of America's blessings." It suggests that America's century of mass flourishing was somehow the product of a pre-modern, mechanical economy in which people's wage rates could be relied on to rise in parallel, and all people had to do was put in the hours best for them. There was no such thing as particular individuals, enterprises, or industries, with their special insight, vision, and good fortune, driving up *their own* wages and profits disproportionately through innovations. And if perchance some industry or occupation did face wages falling off the pace, the government would award special projects to pull those wages up. The Republican Party has come just as deeply under the influence of traditional values. Bush's "compassionate conservatism" conceives the good economy as mercantile capitalism plus social protection and social insurance. Seeing the economy as a servomechanism pinged by shocks, the party has no thought of trying to guard and nourish dynamism in the economy and no desire to shape it for indigenous innovation. One can hardly believe this is the party of Lincoln. In Europe, birthplace of solidarity and security, there is a failure to grasp that most innovation, as in the past, must be indigenous either in Europe or America or both—little of it will be Schumpeterian manna from heaven or the state. They fail too to grasp that Europeans would have more engaging economies if they stopped depending on America to make their innovations for them.

The present crisis of the West can be laid to its leaders' unawareness of the importance of dynamism: A breadth of dynamism is the main source of innovative activity and its engaging jobs, and this activity—its extent, insights, and luck—is the main source of growth in productivity and income. Thus grassroots dynamism was crucial to the good economy of the past: to material progress, inclusion, and job satisfaction. And restoration of that dynamism will be crucial to the rebirth of the good economy. The parlous finances of most Western governments at the present time only make this restoration more urgent.

To take action—well-judged actions—governments must also have a sense of the way forward. They will have to have an elementary understanding of *how* the business sphere of a well-functioning modern economy generates dynamism. It is not mechanical: It is organic, in Bergson's and Barzun's terminology. It is not an ordered system: It is turned topsy-turvy by homegrown innovation and the crazy scramble to try to create innovation. Interventions will benefit from intuition and experience and will be dangerous without them. Now, however, Washington has little business background. Few regulators have worked much in business, and reportedly some have never been inside a business office! Few legislators have spent a substantial part of their careers in businesses other than in their own law firms. Washington's naïvete was demonstrated in 2012 when Congress estimated that expiration of the Bush tax cuts (worth about 500 billion dollars annually) would cost 800 billion dollars in annual domestic output if no tax cuts were put in their place. Without an estimate of how much the reckless deficits caused by the Bush cuts cost innovation and thus investment in the past, let alone how the resulting reduction of the deficits would boost innovation in the future, it is indeterminate whether expiration would weigh heavily on employment or whether jobs would soon be buoyed up by entrepreneurs' new confidence. "We simply don't know," as Keynes commented on a similar issue.

Orienting the state toward dynamism, then, is going to need personnel in government with some practical knowledge of how innovation is generated and how it is deterred in the various industries—from manufacturing and banking to health care and schooling. America's founders envisioned that Congress would consist primarily of persons pausing for an interlude from their private endeavors, primarily businesses ranging from large farms to urban factories, offices, and shops. Thus senators and representatives would come from the world of business and go back when their term was up.

But if that method is out of reach, another approach is needed. Consider regulators. It would be desirable to require them to have an internship in one or two industries or specialties. Such regulators, with training costs comparable to those of business experts, accountants, and similar professionals, would have to expect comparable income, otherwise few would enter the field. Interns would acquire experience and insight. Maybe they would not penetrate to the depths of dynamism, but they would gain a working understanding of the costs as well as the benefits various regulatory restrictions might bring.

Legislators could gain from interning too, but they need a more general background. If legislators are to be apt stewards in guiding the refitting of the business economy for high dynamism, they will have to have insight and judgment. This will require some sort of education. Keynes once remarked that one studies economics not because any particular theoretical result in the standard works has a great deal of substantive value but because it is the way that a practitioner learns to ask the right questions. Imaginably, something like France's *grande école* for politics and economics, Science Po, or China's postgraduate programs for its leaders could be instituted in other countries, including America. But there is something worrying about the prospect of legislative leaders under the spell of a guru of unknown insight. Better a system encouraging them to read and to discuss by themselves. Legislators can find a body of literature with which to start that will give them a feel for how innovation has worked in the past and, with little doubt, how it will have to work in the future. On the history of grand innovation they may read Harold Evans's *They Made America* and *The Dawn of Innovation* by Charles Morris. On the innovation system they may read Hayek's classic "Competition as a Discover Procedure," Richard Nelson's "How Medical Know-How Progresses," and *The Venturesome Economy* by Amar Bhidé. On corporatism they may start with *The Rise and Decline of Nations* by Mancur Olson. My book, while weighing in on these aspects, points to the cultural values behind dynamism and to the forces arrayed against it.

With a background in matters of innovation, legislators and regulators would have dynamism on their minds and could usefully ask of every bill and regulatory directive: How would it impact the dynamism of our economy? Legislators would not approve or let slide fiscal deficits as massive as the West has seen for a decade on the thinking that to act against them would cost jobs. Instead they would grasp that massive deficits over many years ultimately threaten increased costs of credit and depressed valuations of business assets and are thus bad for innovation and investment—hence bad for employment, productivity, and job satisfaction.

A background in innovation would contribute to improved governance over the economy. In America and in much of Europe the fall in the share of jobs in manufacturing has led many legislators to favor an industrial policy of stimulating some manufacturing industries through subsidies, mandates, or private-public partnerships, and GSEs in preference to other parts of the economy, reopening a fight over political economy—over the governance of the economy—that goes back to Colbert, Hamilton, List, Keynes, and Prebish. They make the discredited argument that subsidies in the directions proposed increase economic growth, and the harvest of additional tax revenue makes it safe for the government to engage in the practice. As a French businessman recently exclaimed, referring to the grandiose pretensions of French politicians, "they would create value from their ministries!" It is far better to leave the directions of the economy to the competition of the market, since the state does not have the knowledge or judgment to improve the efficiency of the market's allocation of investment. In fact, subsidies, mandates, and GSEs have a sorry record of unintended consequences in agriculture, construction, energy, and finance: subsidies for growing soy for biofuels, for the purchase of solar panels, for profitless green energy companies, and for the ventures of Fannie Mae and Freddie Mac. Legislators with innovation on their minds would shrink from extending these initiatives to manufacturing. They would grasp that more start-up companies will form and succeed in a country if the legislature does not handicap them by encouraging less-innovative companies and industries to use up fuel, land, labor, and finance capital— companies and industries that would not otherwise have gotten in the way.

In general, public policies and all the governmental institutions and practices of the corporatist economy must be shrunk and some of them terminated. A government is needed for a well-functioning modern economy, of course, and conceivably some circumstances might demand a large one. What is important to keep small is special interest legislation. To that end the government could be required to finance all special interest legislation through special funds earmarked for the purpose, while public expenditure in the general interest would come from general revenue. The requirement of special funds would serve to call attention to the outlay and to ensure that the benefit level is geared to what the beneficiaries are willing to pay. At present, much special interest legislation exists in the form of tax deductions, exemptions, and carveouts of which the public is not aware or in the form of general-interest legislation. My book argues that the provision of private benefits to special interest groups leads not simply to some inefficiency but to a culture that undermines the spirit of aspiration and discovery that is required for economic dynamism. Putting an end to a wanton disregard for the costliness of special interest legislation is likely to be a necessary condition for sustained dynamism. The relatively good performance of Sweden and Norway does not refute this proposition, since on most evidence they possess little dynamism and not a great deal of satisfaction either. I would add that my book is far from suggesting that government "limited" in this way is a *sufficient* condition for economic dynamism.

Once a nation has made it a goal to return to dynamism it will find a great deal of reform to undertake in the private sector too. The formerly dynamic economies will have to be refitted with some new institutions. Few changes are more needed than reforms to stop the corporate practice of paying CEOs very high salaries over a term expected to be very short, which induces them to disregard innovative projects that could pay off only in the long term. Company law could be amended to forbid corporations from using their capital to bestow golden parachute payments to CEOs every time they are dismissed, which similarly pushes CEOs to go for short-term gains rather than long-term gains from innovations that would be far more valuable to shareowners, since share prices reflect prospects over the whole of the company's future. (It may seem that making it harder for CEOs to select the directors on their corporate board would also serve to hold them to a higher standard, but while it might save society and the shareowners from CEO incompetence, it could also stimulate the CEOs to even more short termism before they are changed for another CEO.)

Also high on the list is reform of the mutual funds. They must be stopped from threatening a CEO with dumping her company's stock unless she fixes her attention on hitting the next quarter's earnings target. This extortion is legal at present, but it could be made an offense for mutual fund managers to threaten officials of a company with such financial damage and an offense for CEOs not to report them. (In some countries it is illegal to pay ransom to kidnappers.) Another problem is the rise of mutual funds that attract retail investors on the selling point that they offer minimum risk via a highly diversified portfolio of stocks. If all stocks were picked that way, new shares issues aimed at financing relatively unprofitable corporate expansions would receive as much financing as new issues aimed at profitable expansions.[1]

Restoration of grassroots innovation will require an overhaul of the banking industry. That will require a wealth of start-up companies with unfamiliar ideas, and such companies receive financing only from someone with the personal knowledge that comes from up-close observation and reflection. So the restoration of high dynamism will require the revival of financing the old-fashioned way—"relational banking" in which the lender or investor through accumulating experience comes to have a sense of the chances of the company it is financing that is about as good as the company does. Governments mindful of innovation could redraw the map of financial institutions so as to provide vastly more finance for innovative projects and start-ups.

To this end, governments in Europe and America could restructure some of the existing banks. To date, discussions of the banking industry since the

---

1. It is argued in reply that hedge fund managers do a reasonably good job of judging the worth of shares, so if the government will see to it that there is enough of them, the dynamism of the economy will not suffer from the mechanical diversification among the general public. But it is doubtful that there could be enough talented hedge fund managers for this task.

2008 crisis have been centered around correcting banking's tendency to instability, thus insolvency. Thus far, legislatures have enacted regulations largely intended to restrict risky practices, such as excessive short-term borrowing. But there is fear that the banks will be able to keep one step ahead of the regulators, thus exposing the economy yet again to the risks of financial crisis. A more reliable approach to instability seeks instead to restructure banks for a narrower mission, leaving risky assets to financial markets with the appropriate expertise. This route could also be an approach to the acute deficiency of risk capital, or angel finance, for start-up companies and innovative projects generally. If Europe and America begin restructuring the banking behemoths of the present day into smaller units with much less latitude, governments that are mindful of the need for dynamism can then seek to ensure that the new narrow banks are oriented toward lending to business, especially innovative business.

In addition, a government mindful of innovation will want to license and encourage formation of new financial companies designed for relational banking ("banks" if they do not take big equity positions, "merchant banks" if they do). The government will want to see the landscape of the economy dotted with local investors and lenders. (Never mind George Bailey, the small town mortgage banker in Frank Capra's film *It's A Wonderful Life.* He only lent to home buyers.) Imaginably, such a system might prove limited or slow to develop, though. In 2010, Leo Tilman and I proposed a national bank specializing in extending credit or equity capital to start-up firms. Our proposal was modeled after the highly successful Farm Credit System. Although it would entail only a modest investment by the U.S. government, with the rest of the capital being borrowed under government guarantees, the main worry with any such GSE is the moral hazard that officials will succumb to pressure from politicians to use it to supply patronage. The fact that some sovereign debt agencies have operated without charges of politicization is encouraging. Meanwhile, the market itself has come to the rescue with resources that, though not large, are very welcome: the super-angel funds formed in California.

Some other institutions in the private sector are overdue for a reexamination. Labor unions and professional associations are capable of raising uncertainties for anyone contemplating an innovative venture. In Europe, the medical and legal associations have great power. Union "manifestations" and wildcat actions are still awesome. In France, President François Hollande demanded in November 2012 that Lakshmi Mittal guarantee the long-term future of workers at his steel plant in Florange, France. Earlier, bands of workers took their managers hostage—a practice known as bossnapping. In America, the unions, now more important in the public sector than the private, are not thought to impair innovation. But the fact that unionized construction takes a year in New York to build office buildings that Shanghai builds in a few months puts that faith in doubt. The lawsuit of the U.S. government against Boeing for opening a plant in a right-to-work state must give pause to innovators. The financial reorganization of General Motors, which put the labor union's trust fund ahead of the claims of bondholders, must give pause to those lending to innovators. It is thought that the legal and medical associations serve to uphold quality. But, whatever their overall effects, the restrictions they impose on new entrants surely operate to reduce innovation. It would be of symbolic importance for the spirits of innovators and entrepreneurs generally if the powers of labor unions and professional associations entered into the public debate.

Though reform of the institutions of the private sector is of the greatest importance for the revival of its dynamism, it will also be important to strengthen the modern values—the desire for challenge, expression, and the rest—that nourish and enlist the human resources that go into dynamism, resources such as creativity, curiosity, and vitality. It was the heady mix of modern values that brought forth and continued to fuel the world's first modern economies. These economies launched a marvelous take-off of productivity, lifting wages and wealth in their train, in the process of transforming work from little more than a means of income to a fount of mental stimulus, challenge, and adventure for more and more people. The modern peoples wanted that modern kind of life. If the modern economies flowed from the values of the modern era, it is reasonable to think that a revival of the modern economy would benefit from a reaffirmation and wider spread of modern values. Once, entrepreneurs were wedded to seeing how far their companies could go. Would today's CEOs follow short-termist policies if they cared more about building companies than building their dream houses? Moreover, there is no compelling reason to suppose that the modern spirit will survive if the West does not go back repeatedly to its greatest expressions.

In *Lost in Transition,* Christian Smith finds evidence from his interviews with young adults that they have not found their way. Their difficulties arise not from any failure of their own but from society's failure to provide them the cultural resources to help them in their journey to adulthood and help them thrive. Asked about the consumerism around them, most are positive—some justifying it as good for the economy. Asked to talk about what sort of a life they would like to lead, they speak about working for the money—working to have "nice things," a family, and financial security. Very few spoke of the nature of the work they wanted to do. The words "challenge," "exploration," "adventure," and "passion" were not in their vocabulary. They are lost.

We must reintroduce the main ideas of modern thought, such as individualism and vitalism, into secondary and higher education both to refuel grassroots dynamism in the economy and to preserve the modern itself. Americans are now debating the Common Core State Standards recently introduced in most states into grades K-12. The English Standards reemphasize expository writing and "informational" texts like essays and biographies, which had been displaced by fiction aimed more at communicating feeling and compassion. The argument is that young people will need expository writing in their careers and the economy needs it too. But what a modern economy needs more than personnel with expository skills is people eager to exercise their creativity and venturesome spirit in ever-new and challenging environments. It needs people who when they were young read the intriguing and uplifting works of the imagination by the likes of Jack London, H. Rider Haggard, Jules Verne, Willa Cather, Laura Ingalls Wilder, Arthur Conan Doyle, and H. P. Lovecraft.

Can the nations of the West regain the high dynamism of their best times? A nation's corporate and financial institutions could be reformed to play the role they once did in the innovative process. The haze of regulation and pork barrel contracts could be curbed so that businesses across the economy would once again have the freedom and incentive to attempt innovation. Fiscal responsibility could be reestablished to allay business fears that profit from innovation would be taxed away. But without a supportive culture, these steps will not be sufficient; they will not even be taken. The genius of high dynamism was a restless spirit of conceiving, experimenting, and exploring throughout the economy from the bottom up—leading, with insight and luck, to innovation. This grassroots spirit was driven by the new attitudes and beliefs that defined the modern era, and a full return to high dynamism will require that those modern values prevail again over traditional ones: Nations will have to push back against the resurgence of traditional values that have been so suffocating in recent decades and revive the modern values that stirred people to go boldly forth toward lives of richness. Nations can hope to regain their past brilliance if they have the will do so. A future of mass flourishing depends on it.

TIMELINE: MODERNISM AND MODERNITY

Age of Antiquity

500,000 years ago   The construction of shelters spreads; fire used for cooking and heating

35,000 BC   Flutes made out of a vulture bone used in southern German cave

10,000 BC   Wooden knives set with flint blades used in Palestine

7500 BC   Jericho adopts weaving, fortification, cultivated cereals

6000 BC   Farming spreads through Macedonia

3300 BC   Writing, sailboats, wheeled vehicles, and animal-drawn ploughs begin to be used in Sumer

2400 BC   Sumerian king declares debt cancellation within his kingdom and makes the first political reference to "freedom"

1760 BC   Code of Hammurabi in Babylonia outlines laws on private property

ca. 1500 BC   Egypt develops glass technology and industry; Egyptian glass beads become a popular trading commodity

ca. 450 BC   Socrates founds Western philosophy and with his student, Plato, introduces the dialogue as a device for exploring questions in philosophy, politics, and management

385 BC	Plato founds the Academy in Athens, the West's first institution of higher learning
ca. 350 BC	Aristotle creates a comprehensive system of philosophy, covering ethics, aesthetics, logic, science, politics, and metaphysics
105 BC	Paper developed in ancient China

Early Middle Ages ca. 500–800

ca. 500	Greek mathematician Anthemius of Tralles uses camera obscura
ca. 800	Chinese alchemists discover gunpowder, but innovation does not follow

High Middle Ages ca. 800–1300

ca. 1088	Use of movable type system recorded in *Chinese Dream Pool Essays*
1215	King John of England issues the Magna Carta Libertatum outlining rights against the king
1282	Mechanization of papermaking (paper mill) in Xàtiva, Kingdom of Aragon

Late Middle Ages ca. 1300–1500

1400s	Trade spreads via Hanseatic routes and Silk Road
ca. 1444	Gutenberg's printing press first assembled
1455	Gutenberg's printing press is used for mass production of the Gutenberg Bible, enabling thousands to read it for the first time
1480s	Portuguese sailors use astrolabe to circumnavigate Africa
1486	Giovanni Pico della Mirandola publishes *Oration on the Dignity of Man,* a manifesto of the Renaissance, arguing that mankind possesses creativity
1492	Columbus opens sea routes to the Western hemisphere

Early Modern Age ca. 1500–1815

late 1400s–1500s	With Pico on human creativity, Erasmus on expanding possibilities, and Luther on the liberty of Christians to read

	and interpret the Bible for themselves, the modern era (1500–2000) begins
1500	Foreign trade extends via the Hanseatic routes, Silk Road, and ocean lanes
1509	*The Praise of Folly* by the humanist Erasmus is first published in Paris
1517	Luther posts the "95 Theses" demanding a wider role for the individual in the practice of religion
1540s	Calvinism views secular vocations as having religious value and extending God's providential governance
1553	In a setback to free thinking, Michael Servetus, first European to describe the circulation of the blood, is burned at the stake as a heretic by John Calvin and the Geneva council
1580	Michel de Montaigne's *Essais*, chronicling his own inner life and the personal growth he calls "becoming," first published in Paris
1600	Giordano Bruno, a precursor of the modern cosmologist, is similarly put to death by the Inquisition
1600–1760	Baroque composers develop the basic building blocks of tonal music
1603	Shakespeare publishes early text of *Hamlet*
1614	Miguel de Cervantes's *Don Quixote* is published
1620	Francis Bacon outlines a new logic in his *Novo Organum*, developing the modern scientific method
1628	William Harvey uses logic to deduce the circulation of the blood, ushering in Western medicine
1688	Glorious Revolution takes place in England, in which Parliamentarians unite with William of Orange to expel King James II
1689	English Bill of Rights puts the rights first proposed by the Magna Carta into actual effect
1698	John Castaing, a broker operating out of an Exchange Alley coffeehouse in London, begins posting lists of prices for stocks and commodities, constituting thereby the beginnings of the London Stock Exchange
1719	Daniel Defoe's *Robinson Crusoe* is published in London

1740	David Hume publishes *Treatise of Human Nature*
1748	David Hume publishes *An Enquiry Concerning Human Understanding* on how knowledge is increased
1750s	Neoclassical art is practiced by Jacques-Louis David, Thomas Gainsborough, and Joshua Reynolds
1750–1810	Wages in Britain fall
1759	Adam Smith's *Theory of Moral Sentiments* first published in London
1759	Voltaire's *Candide*, celebrating individual enterprise, first published in France
1760s	Adam Smith delivers what became *Lectures on Jurisprudence*
1776	James Watt installs first steam engine in a British factory
1776	Thomas Paine's *Common Sense* opposes British rule as an obstacle to America's prosperity
1776	America's Declaration of Independence proclaims the right of people to self-government and the "pursuit of happiness"
1776	Adam Smith's *Wealth of Nations* first published in London
1781	Immanuel Kant's *Critique of Pure Reason* argues for the intimate connection of reason and experience
1785	Immanuel Kant's *Foundations of the Metaphysics of Morals* rejects an older idea of liberty in Hobbes and Smith, in which men treat each other as means instead of ends
1780s	Pig iron frame is developed by the iron mill of Cort & Jellicoe
1787	Contracts Clause is added to the U.S. Constitution
1788	U.S. Constitution creates a House of Representatives and Senate and opens federal voting to all males with property qualifications
1789	French Revolution begins
1791	Polish-Lithuanian Constitution calls for political equality between townsfolk and nobility
1792	Wall Street's first crisis occurs
1792	Mary Wollstonecraft writes *A Vindication of the Rights of Woman*

1796–1797	Financial panic takes place in the United Kingdom and America
1803	Beethoven's Second Symphony expresses the experience of successive trials
1803	Jean-Baptiste Say, in his *Traité d'économie politique* in Paris, contrasts entrepreneurs with rent-seekers
1804	William Blake writes of "dark Satanic mills," of which there were then only very few
1812	U.S. vote is extended to white men without property
1814	Bourbon Restoration restores Kingdom of France after the First Empire under Napoleon

High Modern Age ca. 1815–1940

1815	The Napoleonic Wars and the War of 1812 end; the modern economy is born in Britain
1815	Output per worker begins its "take-off" in England, making it the first modern economy
1818	Mary Shelley's *Frankenstein; or, The Modern Prometheus* is published in London
1819	U.S. Supreme Court, in a suit with the Corporation of Dartmouth College, rules that all corporations have rights, including the right not to have their charter rewritten by new state laws
1819	Financial panic occurs in America
1820	Output per worker begins its "take-off" in America, making it the second modern economy
1820	Percy Bysshe Shelley's *Prometheus Unbound* is first published
1820–1840s	German wages decrease
1821	Hegel's *Grundlinien der Philosophie des Rechts* (*Elements of the Philosophy of Right*) is published in Berlin, arguing that rules are necessary to enable people to do the creative things for their self-actualization—to "act on the world"
1820s	In Britain, wages take off as innovation sweeps the country, while in Germany wages fall until 1848

1820s	French Romantic movement in painting begins
1823	Samuel Brown patents the first industrially used internal combustion engine
1824	Beethoven's Ninth Symphony, with passages of frenzy and near chaos, premiers in Vienna
1830s	France and Belgium, following Britain, begin sustained growth of output per head
1830–1860s	Britain's output per head rises markedly
1830	Massachusetts legislature extends charters beyond public works like canals and colleges
1830	July Revolution in France overthrows Bourbon King Charles X and instates Louis-Philippe
1830	Belgian Revolution establishes a parliamentary democracy
1830	Output per worker begins to "take-off" in France and Belgium
1832	The English Reform Act extends the vote for the House of Commons to men without reference to property qualifications and redistributes seats to urban areas
1833	The Slavery Abolition Act emancipates slaves in the British West Indies
1833	Federal imprisonment for debtors is abolished in America
1835	Alexis de Tocqueville's *Democracy in America* is first published in France
1836	A lithograph depicts nine firms on New York's Liberty Street, four of which will be bankrupt within five years
1836	Samuel Colt introduces the revolver
1836	Samuel Morse develops the electrical telegraph system and Morse code
1837	Connecticut permits companies to incorporate without a legislative act
1837	Financial panic occurs in America
1839	Dickens's *Oliver Twist* is published in London
1841	U.S. Bankruptcy Act of 1841 eases penalties of default; it is repealed in 1843

1842	Musikverein is founded to support the Vienna Philharmonic Orchestra
1842	Philharmonic Society of New York is founded to create a top orchestra
1843	Søren Kierkegaard publishes in Copenhagen under a pseudonym his *Either/Or* on the necessity of leaps of faith
1844	Joint Stock Companies Act in England permits incorporating though without limited liability
1844	J. M. W. Turner paints *Rail, Steam and Speed*
1846	Financial panic occurs in Europe
1847	Emily Brontë's *Wuthering Heights* is published under the pseudonym Ellis Bell
1848	Charlotte Brontë's *Jane Eyre* is published in London
1848	King Louis-Philippe of France is overthrown; popular uprisings sweep Europe
1848	Karl Marx and Friedrich Engels's *The Communist Manifesto* is published
1851	Herman Melville's *Moby-Dick* is published in New York
1852	Robert Schumann premiers *Manfred Overture* in Leipzig
1854	Franz Liszt premiers *Les preludes* in Weimar
1854	Charles Dickens's *Hard Times* is published in London
1856	Joint Stock Companies Act of 1856 in England grants corporations limited liability
1857	Herman Melville's *The Confidence-Man* is published in New York
1857	Financial panic occurs in Europe and America
1858	Charles Dickens's *David Copperfield* is published in London
1859	Samuel Smile's *Self-Help* is published in London
1859	*On the Origin of Species* by Charles Darwin describes the natural selection among variants of a species thrown up by "chance"
1863	Abraham Lincoln delivers the Emancipation Proclamation
1863	France allows companies to incorporate with limited liability

1864	Fyodor Dostoevsky's *Notes from the Underground* is published in Russia
1866	German states lose unification under the Austrian Empire
1867	U.S. Bankruptcy Act of 1867 eases penalties for default; it is repealed in 1878
1869	Debtors Act abolishes imprisonment for debt in England
1870	"High Modernism" begins in the arts and goes on to 1940
1870	U.S. vote is extended to non-white men
1870	Germany allows companies to incorporate with limited liability
1870	Western European output per head is up 63 percent over the 1820 level; the U.S. level is up by 95 percent
1870s–1940s	The period of high modernism in painting emerges
1871	Otto von Bismarck unifies German states and Prussia under Kaiser Wilhelm's Empire
1872	Nietzsche publishes *The Birth of Tragedy*
1873	Financial panic takes place in Europe and America
1876	Mark Twain's *The Adventures of Tom Sawyer* is published in America
1876	Richard Wagner premieres *Der Ring des Nibelungen* at the Bayreuth Festival
1880	Fyodor Dostoevsky publishes *The Brothers Karamazov*
1887	Sociologist Ferdinand Tönnies's *Community and Society* is published in Germany
1888	Vincent van Gogh paints *Sower with Setting Sun*, *The Painter on the Road to Tarascon*, and *Café Terrace on the Place du Forum*
1893	Financial panic occurs in Europe and America; unemployment in America is over 12 percent from 1893 to 1898
1894	Building off of Eadweard Muybridge's proto-film experiments, Thomas Edison undertakes the first commercial exhibition of films with his Kinetoscope parlors
1898	U.S. Bankruptcy Act of 1898 gives companies the option of being protected from creditors
1900	Fifty towns in Germany qualify as cities (up from four in 1800)

1901	Thomas Mann's *Buddenbrooks* is published in Germany
1902	Ransom Olds's Oldsmobile production-line manufactures affordable automobiles
1902	Arnold Schoenberg's *Verklärte Nacht* premieres in Vienna
1907	Henri Bergson's *L'évolution créatrice* is published in Paris, translated into English four years later as *Creative Evolution* and published to great acclaim
1910s	Franz Kafka writes *The Trial*, "In the Penal Colony," and *The Castle*, depicting the oppressiveness of totalitarianism and the hierarchical state
1912	Futurist Giacomo Balla paints *Dynamism of a Dog on a Leash*
1912	Joseph Schumpeter publishes in Leipzig his landmark book, *Theorie der wirtschaftlichen Entwicklung*, translated as *The Theory of Economic Development* in 1934
1913–1915	Ernst Ludwig Kirchner paints half a dozen paintings titled *Berlin Street Scene*
1913	Igor Stravinsky premieres *The Rite of Spring* in Paris
1914	Henry Ford's assembly line makes a Model T car in 1 hour 33 minutes
1919	Walter Gropius founds Bauhaus in Weimar
1919	Ludwig von Mises's *Nation, State, and Economy* is published in Vienna
1920	By this year, most Americans live in cities
1920	U.S. vote extends to women
1921	John Maynard Keynes publishes *A Treatise on Probability*
1921	Frank Knight's *Risk, Uncertainty and Profit* is published
1922	Le Corbusier presents his plan for Ville Contemporaine
1922	Max Weber's *Economy and Society* is published posthumously in Tübingen
1922	Ludwig von Mises's *Socialism: An Economic and Sociological Analysis* is published
1923	C. S. Peirce's *Chance, Love, and Logic: Philosophical Essays* is published

1927	Werner Heisenberg's "Über den anschaulichen Inhalt der quantentheoretischen Kinematik und Mechanik" ("On the Perceptual Content of Quantum Theoretical Kinematics and Mechanics") sets out the first version of the Uncertainty Principle
1927	First talkie film, *The Jazz Singer,* is released
1930	Sigmund Freud's *Civilization and Its Discontents* is published in Germany
1930	P. T. Farnsworth patents the television; World War II prevents its spread in the United States until 1948
1931	*M* directed by Fritz Lang is released
1933	George Balanchine and Lincoln Kirstein form the New York City Ballet
1935	Frank Lloyd Wright completes Fallingwater
1935–38	Alfred Hitchcock's *The 39 Steps* and *The Lady Vanishes* dramatize how little we understand of the world
1935	*Collectivist Economic Planning*, edited by Friedrich Hayek, is published in London
1935	Oskar Morgenstern's "Volkommene Voraussicht und Wirtschaftliches Gleichgewicht" ("Perfect Foresight and Economic Equilibrium") appears in *Zeitschrift für Nationalökonomie*
1936	John Maynard Keynes's *General Theory* is first published
1937	Charlie Chaplin's *Modern Times* satirizes the assembly line
1938	Jean-Paul Sartre's *Nausea* is published in Paris
1939	Raymond Chandler's *The Big Sleep* is published
1940s	Robert Merton introduces the law of unexpected consequences and the "latent function" a law may have
1940	Charles Ives' *The Unanswered Question*, drafted in 1906, is published and performed

Late Modern Age ca. 1941 to the present

1944	Friedrich Hayek's *The Road to Serfdom* is published in London
1945	Karl Popper's *The Open Society and Its Enemies* is published in London

1951	Ludwig Mies van der Rohe completes the Farnsworth House
1953	In *Waiting for Godot,* Samuel Beckett draws a surreal portrait of modern-day anxiety
1955	Former trucking company owner Malcom McLean designs the modern intermodal container with engineer Keith Tantlinger and gives the patented designs to industry
1957	Karl Popper's *The Poverty of Historicism* is published in London
1958	Michael Polanyí's *Personal Knowledge*, from the 1951–1952 Gifford Lectures, is published
1960s	Harold Pinter's play *A Slight Ache* dramatizes how little we know about the social world around us
1961	Friedrich Hayek's "The Non-Sequitur of the 'Dependence Effect'" is published
1961	Jane Jacobs's *The Death and Life of Great American Cities* is published in New York
1966	Tom Stoppard's play *Rosencrantz and Guildenstern Are Dead* suggests that each person is limited by his or her position
1968	Friedrich Hayek's "Competition as a Discovery Procedure" is published
1969	Jane Jacobs's *The Economy of Cities* is published
1970	*Microeconomic Foundations of Employment and Inflation Theory*, a volume from a conference organized by Edmund Phelps, introduces wage and price expectations into employment determination
1989	Thomas Nagel's *The View from Nowhere* is published
1991	Paul Johnson's *The Birth of the Modern: World Society 1815–1830* is published
1992	Following protocols agreed upon earlier in the 1990s, Netscape's initial public offering launches the internet into widespread use
2006	Edmund Phelps gives Nobel Prize Lecture on understanding economies of dynamism

2006	In a conference, *Perspectives on the Performance of the Continental Economies,* Edmund Phelps reports that the differences in nations' economic values largely account for differences in their productivity and employment.
2007	Roman Frydman and Michael Goldberg's *Imperfect Knowledge Economics* is published
2008	Amar Bhidé's *The Venturesome Economy* is published
2009	Mark C. Taylor's *Field Notes from Elsewhere* reflects on living in modern times
2011	Martin Seligman's *Flourish: A Visionary New Understanding of Happiness and Well-being* is published

BIBLIOGRAPHY

Abelshauser, Werner. "The First Post-Liberal Nation: Stages in the Development of Modern Corporatism in Germany." *European History Quarterly* 14, no. 3 (1984): 285–318.

Abramovitz, Moses. "Resource and Output Trends in the United States since 1870." *American Economic Review* 46 (1956): 1–23.

Aghion, Philippe, and Enisse Kharroubi. "Stabilization Policies and Economic Growth," in Roman Frydman and Edmund Phelps (eds.), *Rethinking Expectations: The Way Forward for Macroeconomics*. Princeton, N.J.: Princeton University Press, 2013.

Alda, Alan. *Things I Overheard While Talking to Myself*. New York: Random House, 2007.

Allen, Robert C. "The Great Divergence in European Wages and Prices." *Explorations in Economic History* 38 (2001): 411–447.

Ammous, Saifedean, and Edmund Phelps. "Climate Change, the Knowledge Problem and the Good Life." Working Paper 42, Center on Capitalism and Society, Columbia University, New York, September 2009.

――――. "Blaming Capitalism for the Ills of Corporatism," *Project Syndicate*, January 31, 2012. http://www.project-syndicate.org/commentary/blaming-capitalism-for-corporatism.

Andrews, Malcolm. *Dickens on England and the English*. Hassocks, Sussex: Harvester, 1979.

Aristotle. *Aristotle: Nicomachean Ethics*, edited by Terence Irwin. Indianapolis, Ind.: Hackett Publishing, 2nd edition, 1999.

Arnold, Matthew. *The Function of Criticism*. London: Macmillan, 1895.

Austen, Jane. *Sense and Sensibility*. London: Thomas Egerton, 1811.

――――. *Mansfield Park*. London: Thomas Egerton, 1814.

Bairoch, Paul. "Wages as an Indicator of Gross National Product," in Peter Scholliers (ed.), *Real Wages in 19th and 20th Century Europe: Historical and Comparative Perspectives*. New York: Berg, 1989.

Balas, Aron, Rafael La Porta, Florencio Lopez-de-Silanes, and Andre Shleifer. "The Divergence of Legal Procedures." *American Economic Journal: Economic Policy* 1, no. 2 (2009): 138–162.

Balleisen, Edward J. *Navigating Failure: Bankruptcy and Commercial Society in Antebellum America*. Chapel Hill: University of North Carolina, 2001.

Banfield, Edward C. *The Moral Basis of a Backward Society*. New York: Basic Books, 1958.

Barzun, Jacques. "From the Nineteenth Century to the Twentieth," in Contemporary Civilization Staff of Columbia College (eds.), *Chapters in Western Civilization*, vol. II. New York: Columbia University Press, 3rd edition, 1962.

———. *A Stroll with William James*. New York: Harper, 1983.

———. *From Dawn to Decadence: 500 Years of Western Cultural Life*. New York: Harper Perennial, 2001.

Bekker, Immanuel. *Aristotelis Opera edidit Academia Regia Borussica*. Berlin, 1831–1870.

Bentolila, Samuel, and Giuseppe Bertola. "Firing Costs and Labour Demand: How Bad Is Eurosclerosis?" *Review of Economic Studies* 57, no. 3 (1990): 381–402.

Berghahn, V. R. "Corporatism in Germany in Historical Perspective," in Andrew W. Cox and Noel O'Sullivan (eds.), *The Corporate State: Corporatism and the State Tradition in Western Europe*. Aldershot, U.K.: Edward Elgar, 1988.

Bergson, Henri. *Creative Evolution*. New York: Henry Holt, 1911.

Berle, Adolf, and Gardiner Means. *The Modern Corporation and Private Property*. New York: Transaction Publishers, 1932.

Bhidé, Amar. "The Hidden Costs of Stock Market Liquidity." *Journal of Financial Economics* 34 (1993): 31–51.

———. *The Venturesome Economy*. Princeton, N.J.: Princeton University Press, 2008.

Bhidé, Amar, and Edmund S. Phelps. "More Harm Than Good: How the IMF's Business Model Sabotages Properly Functioning Capitalism," *Newsweek International*, July 11, 2011, p. 18.

Blanchflower, David, and Andrew J. Oswald. "Well-Being, Insecurity and the Decline of American Job Satisfaction." Working Paper, National Bureau of Economic Research, Cambridge, Mass., 1999.

Bloom, Harold. *The Visionary Company: A Reading of English Romantic Poetry*. New York: Doubleday, 1961.

———. *The Western Canon: The Books and Schools of the Ages*. New York: Penguin Putnam, 1994.

———. *Shakespeare: The Invention of the Human*. New York: Riverhead Books, 1998.

Bodenhorn, Howard. *A History of Banking in Antebellum America: Financial Markets and Economic Development in an Era of Nation-Building*. Cambridge: Cambridge University Press, 2000.

Bojilov, Raicho, and Edmund S. Phelps. "Job Satisfaction: The Effects of Two Economic Cultures." Working Paper 78, Center on Capitalism and Society, Columbia University, New York, September 2012.

Boulding, Kenneth. *Beyond Economics: Essays on Society, Religion, and Ethics*. Ann Arbor: University of Michigan Press, 1968.

Bourguignon, Philippe. "Deux éducations, deux cultures," in Jean-Marie Chevalier and Jacques Mistral (eds.), *Le Cercle des economistes: L'Europe et les Etats-Unis*. Paris: Descartes et Cie, 2006.

Bradshaw, David J., and Suzanne Ozment. *The Voices of Toil: Nineteenth-Century British Writings about Work*. Athens, Ohio: Ohio University Press, 2000.

Brands, H. W. *American Colossus: The Triumph of Capitalism, 1865–1900*. New York: Doubleday, 2010.

Brass, Dick. "Microsoft's Creative Destruction." *New York Times,* February 4, 2010, p. A27.

Braudel, Fernand. *The Mediterranean and the Mediterranean World in the Age of Philip II,* vol. 2. New York: Harper and Row, 1972.

Brontë, Charlotte. *Jane Eyre.* London: Smith, Elder, and Company, 1847.

Brontë, Emily. *Wuthering Heights.* London: Thomas Cautley Newby, 1847.

Caldwell, Christopher. "The New Battle for the Old Soul of the Republican Party." *Financial Times,* February 24, 2012, p. 9.

Calvin, John. *Institutio Christianae Religionis (Institutes of Christian Religion).* Geneva: Robert Estienne, 1559.

Cantillon, Richard. *Essai sur la Nature du Commerce en Général.* London: Fletcher Gyles, 1755.

Caron, François. *An Economic History of Modern France,* translated by Barbara Bray. London: Methuen, 1979.

Cary, Joyce. *The Horse's Mouth.* New York: Harper, 1944.

Cassirer, Ernst. "Giovanni Pico della Mirandola: A Study in the History of Renaissance Ideas." *Journal of the History of Ideas* 3, no. 3 (1942): 319–346.

Casson, Mark. "Entrepreneurship," in Mark Casson (ed.), *International Library of Critical Writings in Economics,* vol. 13. Aldershot, U.K.: Edward Elgar, 1990.

Cather, Willa. *Death Comes for the Archbishop.* New York: Alfred A. Knopf, 1927.

Cellini, Benvenuto. *The Autobiography of Benvenuto Cellini.* New York: Alfred A. Knopf, 2010.

Cervantes, Miguel de. *Don Quixote.* Madrid: Juan de la Cuesta, 1605–1620.

Chandler, Alfred D., Jr. *Strategy and Structure: Chapters in the History of the American Industrial Enterprise.* Cambridge, Mass.: MIT Press, 1962.

——. *The Visible Hand: The Managerial Revolution in American Business.* Cambridge, Mass.: Harvard University Press, 1977.

——. *The Coming of Managerial Capitalism.* New York: Richard D. Irwin, 1985.

——. *Scale and Scope: The Dynamics of Industrial Capitalism.* Cambridge, Mass.: Harvard University Press, 1990.

Christiansen, G. B., and R. H. Haveman. "Government Regulations and Their Impact on the Economy." *Annals of the American Academy of Political and Social Science* 459, no. 1 (1982): 112–122.

Clark, Gregory. "The Long March of History: Population and Economic Growth." Working Paper 05-40, University of California, Davis, 2005.

——. *A Farewell to Alms: A Brief Economic History of the World.* Princeton, N.J.: Princeton University Press, 2007.

Coke, Edward. *The Second [Third and Fourth] Part[s] of the Institutes of the Laws of England.* London: Printed for E. and R. Brooke, 1797 (first written 1641).

Conard, Nicholas J., Maria Malina, and Susanne C. Münzel. "New Flutes Document the Earliest Musical Tradition in Southwestern Germany." *Nature* 460 (2009): 737–740.

Coolidge, Calvin. "Address to the American Society of Newspaper Editors, Washington, D.C.," January 17, 1925. Online by Gerhard Peters and John T. Woolley, The American Presidency Project. http://www.presidency.ucsb.edu/ws/?pid=24180.

Cooper, John M. *Reason and the Human Good in Aristotle.* Cambridge, Mass.: Harvard University Press, 1975.

Crafts, N.F.R. "British Economic Growth, 1700–1831: A Review of the Evidence." *Economic History Review* 36, no. 2 (1983): 177–199.

Crooks, Ed. "US 'Creative Destruction' out of Steam." *Financial Times,* December 12, 2011.

Dahlhaus, Carl. *Nineteenth-Century Music.* Berkeley: University of California, 1989.

David, Paul A. "The Growth of Real Product in the United States before 1840: New Evidence, Controlled Conjectures." *Journal of Economic History* 27, no. 2 (1967): 151–197.

Defoe, Daniel. *Robinson Crusoe.* London: W. Taylor, 1719.

——. *Moll Flanders.* London: W. Taylor, 1721.

Demsetz, Harold. "Toward a Theory of Property Rights II: The Competition between Private and Collective Ownership." *Journal of Legal Studies* (June 2002): 668.

Denning, Peter J., and Robert Dunham. *The Innovator's Way: Essential Practices for Successful Innovation.* Cambridge, Mass.: MIT Press, 2010.

Dewey, John. *Human Nature and Conduct.* New York: Holt, 1922.

——. "The House Divided against Itself." *New Republic,* April 24, 1929, pp. 270–271.

——. *Individualism Old and New.* New York: Minton, Balch, and Company, 1930.

——. *Experience and Education.* New York: Simon and Schuster, 1938.

Diamond, Jared M. *Guns, Germs, and Steel: The Fates of Human Societies.* New York: W. W. Norton, 1997.

Dickens, Charles. *Sketches by Boz.* London: John Macrone, 1836.

——. *Oliver Twist.* London: Richard Bentley, 1837.

——. *David Copperfield.* London: Bradbury and Evans, 1850.

——. *Hard Times.* London: Bradbury and Evans, 1854.

——. *Speeches, Letters and Sayings.* New York: Harper, 1870.

——. *The Uncommercial Traveler and Reprinted Pieces.* Philadelphia: John D. Morris, 1900.

Dods, Marcus. *Erasmus, and Other Essays.* Longdon: Hodder and Stoughton, 1891.

DuBois, Armand Budington. *The English Business Company after the Bubble Act, 1720–1800.* New York: Octagon, 1971.

Edlund, Lena. "Big Ideas." *Milken Institute Review* 13, no. 1 (2011): 89–94.

Eggertsson, Thrainn. *Imperfect Institutions: Possibilities and Limits for Reform.* Ann Arbor: University of Michigan Press, 2006.

Erhard, Ludwig. *Wohlstand für Alle.* Dusseldorf: Econ-Verlag, 1957.

——. *Prosperity through Competition.* New York: Praeger, 1958.

Evans, Harold. *They Made America.* New York: Little Brown, 2004.

——. "Eureka: A Lecture on Innovation." Lecture given at the Royal Society of Arts, London, March 2011.

Ferguson, Adam. *Essay on the History of Civil Society.* Dublin: Grierson, 1767.

Ferraro, Geraldine. "Inspiration from the Land Where Dreams Come True." Speech, San Francisco, July 19, 1984. Available at http://www.cnn.com/ALLPOLITICS/1996/conventions/chicago/facts/famous.speeches/ferraro.84.shtml.

Finley, M. I. *The Ancient Economy.* Berkeley: University of California Press, 1999.

Fitoussi, Jean-Paul, and Edmund S. Phelps. *The Slump in Europe.* Oxford: Blackwell, 1988.

Fogel, Robert William. *Railroads and American Economic Growth: Essays in Econometric History.* Baltimore: Johns Hopkins University Press, 1964.

Foster, John Bellamy, Robert W. McChesney, and Jamil Jonna. "Monopoly and Competition in Twenty-First Century Capitalism." *Monthly Review* 62, no. 11 (2011): 1–23.

Foster-Hahn, Francoise, Claude Keisch, Peter-Klaus Schuster, and Angelika Wesenberg. *Spirit of an Age: Nineteenth-Century Paintings from the Nationalgalerie, Berlin.* London: National Gallery, 2001.

Freud, Sigmund. *Das Unbehagen in der Kultur.* Vienna: Internationaler Psychoanalytischer Verlag, 1930.

——. *Civilization and Its Discontents,* translated by James Strachey. New York: W. W. Norton, 1989.

Fry, Stephen. "Lady Gaga Takes Tea with Mr Fry." *Financial Times* (London), May 27, 2011, p. 12.

Frydman, Roman, and Michael Goldberg. *Imperfect Knowledge Economics: Exchange Rates and Risk.* Princeton: Princeton University Press, 2007.

Frydman, Roman, Marek Hessel, and Andrzej Rapaczynski. "When Does Privatization Work?" *Quarterly Journal of Economics* (1999): 1153–1191.

Geddes, Rick, and Dean Lueck. "Gains from Self-Ownership and the Expansion of Women's Rights." *American Economic Review* 92, no. 4 (2002): 63–83.

Gibbon, Edward. *The History of the Decline and Fall of the Roman Empire.* London: Strahan and Cadell, 1776–1789.

Giffen, Robert. "The Material Progress of Great Britain." Address before the Economic Sector of the British Association, London, 1887.

Gombrich, E. H. *The Story of Art.* London: Phaidon, 4th edition, 1951.

Gordon, Robert J. "U.S. Productivity Growth over the Past Century with a View to the Future." Working Paper 15834, National Bureau of Economic Research, Cambridge, Mass., March 2010.

——. "Is U.S. Economic Growth Over? Faltering Innovation Confronts the Six Headwinds." Working Paper 18315, National Bureau of Economic Research, Cambridge, Mass., August 2012.

Gray, Henry. *Anatomy, Descriptive and Surgical.* Philadelphia: Blanchard and Lea, 2nd American edition, 1862.

Greenwald, Bruce C. N., and Judd Kahn. *Globalization: The Irrational Fear That Someone in China Will Take Your Job.* Hoboken, N.J.: John Wiley and Sons, 2009.

Groom, Brian. "War Hero Who Became Captain of British Industry." *Financial Times,* October 2–3, 2010, p. 7.

——. "Gloom and Boom." Books Section, *Financial Times,* October 2–3, 2010, p. 16.

Gwartney, James, Robert Lawson, and Joshua Hall. *Economic Freedom of the World: 2011 Annual Report.* Vancouver: Fraser Institute, 2011.

Hall, Robert, and Charles I. Jones. "Why Do Some Countries Produce So Much More Output per Worker Than Others?" *Quarterly Journal of Economics* 114, no. 1 (1999): 83–116.

Hansard, Thomas C. (ed.). *Hansard's Parliamentary Debates.* Third series, second volume of the session. London: Cornelius Buck, 1863

Hayek, Friedrich. "The Trend of Economic Thinking." *Economica* 13 (1933): 127–137.

——. "Socialist Calculation: The State of the Debate," in Friedrich Hayek (ed.), *Collectivist Economic Planning; Critical Studies on the Possibilities of Socialism.* London: Routledge, 1935.

——. *The Road to Serfdom.* London: Routledge, 1944.

——. *Individualism and Economic Order.* Chicago: University of Chicago Press, 1948.

Hayek, Friedrich. *The Counter-Revolution of Science; Studies on the Abuse of Reason.* Glencoe, Ill.: Free Press, 1952.

———. "The Non-Sequitur of the 'Dependence Effect.'" *Southern Economic Journal* 27 (1961): 346.

———. "Competition as a Discovery Procedure," in *New Studies in Philosophy, Politics, Economics and the History of Ideas.* Chicago: University of Chicago Press, 1978.

Heckman, James J., and Dimitriy V. Masterov. "The Productivity Argument for Investing in Young Children." *Applied Economic Perspectives and Policy* 29, no. 3 (2007): 446–493.

Henley, William Ernest. *Poems.* New York: Charles Scribner's Sons, 1898.

Hewlett, Sylvia Ann. *A Lesser Life: The Myth of Women's Liberation in America.* New York: Morrow, 1986.

Hicks, John. *A Theory of Economic History.* Oxford: Oxford University Press, 1969.

Hoon, Hian Teck, and Edmund Phelps. "Payroll Taxes and VAT in a Labor-Turnover Model of the 'Natural Rate.'" *International Tax and Public Finance* 3 (June 1996): 185–201.

———. "Growth, Wealth and the Natural Rate: Is Europe's Jobs Crisis a Growth Crisis?" *European Economic Review* 41 (April 1997): 549–557.

———. "Effects of Technological Improvement in the ICT-Producing Sector on Business Activity." Columbia University Department of Economics Discussion Paper 0506-21, February 2006.

Howard, Philip K. *The Death of Common Sense: How Law Is Suffocating America.* New York: Random House, 1995.

———. *The Collapse of the Common Good: How America's Lawsuit Culture Undermines Our Freedom.* New York: Ballantine, 2001.

Hume, David. *A Treatise on Human Nature.* London: John Noon, 1739–1740.

———. *Philosophical Essays Concerning Human Understanding.* London: A. Millar, 1748. Subsequently republished as *An Enquiry Concerning Human Understanding.*

Huppert, Felicia A., and Timothy T. C. So. "What Percentage of People in Europe Are Flourishing and What Characterises Them?" Retrieved January 4, 2013, from www.isqols2009.istitutodeglinnocenti.it/Content_en/Huppert.pdf.

Ibison, David. "The Monday Interview: Carl-Henric Svanberg." *Financial Times,* October 1, 2006, p. 11.

Ibsen, Henrik. *Peer Gynt,* translated by Rolf Fjelde. Minneapolis: University of Minnesota Press, 1980.

Inglehart, Ronald, and Christian Welzel. *Modernization, Cultural Change, and Democracy: The Human Development Sequence.* Cambridge: Cambridge University Press, 2005.

Irving, Washington. *The Sketch Book of Geoffrey Crayon, Gent.* London: John Murray, 1820.

Jackman, Richard, Richard Layard, and Stephen Nickell. *Unemployment: Macroeconomic Performance and the Labour Market.* Oxford: Oxford University Press, 1991.

Jackson, R. V. "The Structure of Pay in Nineteenth-Century Britain." *Economic History Review* 40, no. 4 (1987): 561–570.

Jacobs, Jane. *The Death and Life of Great American Cities.* New York: Random House, 1961.

———. *The Economy of Cities.* New York: Random House, 1969.

James, Harold. *Europe Reborn.* Princeton, N.J.: Princeton University Press, 2009.

Jamison, Kay Redfield. *Exuberance: The Passion for Life.* New York: Alfred A. Knopf, 2004.

Jefferson, Thomas. *The Works of Thomas Jefferson,* vol. 2. New York: G. P. Putnam and Sons, 1904.

Johnson, Paul. *The Birth of the Modern: World Society 1815–1830.* New York: Harper Collins, 1991.

Jones, Jonathan. "Other Artists Paint Pictures, Turner Brings Them to Life." *Guardian,* May 6, 2009. Available at www.guardian.co.uk.

Karakacili, E. "English Agrarian Labour Productivity Rates before the Black Death: A Case Study." *Journal of Economic History* 64 (March 2004): 24–60.

Keats, John. *The Poems of John Keats,* edited by Jack Stillinger. Cambridge, Mass.: Belknap Press of Harvard University Press, 1978.

Kellaway, Lucy. "Jobs, Motherhood and Varieties of Wrong." *Financial Times,* July 29, 2012, p. 16.

Kennedy, Maev. "British Library Publishes Online Archive of 19th Century Newspapers." *Guardian,* June 18, 2009, p. 18.

Keynes, John Maynard. *A Treatise on Probability.* London: Macmillan, 1921.

———. *General Theory of Employment, Interest and Money.* London: Palgrave Macmillan, 1936.

———. "Economic Possibilities for Our Grandchildren," in *Essays in Persuasion.* New York: W. W. Norton, 1963.

Kindleberger, Charles Poor. *A Financial History of Western Europe.* New York: Oxford University Press, 1993.

Kirby, William C. "China Unincorporated: Company Law and Business Enterprise in 20th Century China." *Journal of Asian Studies* 54 (February 1995): 43–46.

Kling, Arnold, and Nick Schulz. "The New Commanding Heights." *National Affairs* 8 (Summer 2011): 3–19.

Knight, Frank. *Risk, Uncertainty and Profit.* Boston: Hart, Schaffner and Marx; Houghton Mifflin, 1921.

Koestler, Arthur. *The Act of Creation.* New York: Macmillan, 1964.

———. *The Sleepwalkers.* New York: Macmillan, 1968.

Kronman, Anthony T. *Education's End: Why Our Colleges and Universities Have Given Up on the Meaning of Life.* New Haven, Conn.: Yale University Press, 2007.

Krugman, Paul R. *Geography and Trade.* Cambridge, Mass.: MIT Press, 1992.

Kuczynski, Jürgen. *Labour Conditions in Western Europe.* London: F. Muller, 1937.

———. *A Short History of Labour Conditions under Industrial Capitalism.* London: F. Muller, 1942–1945.

Kuznets, Simon. "Population Change and Aggregate Output," in *Demographic and Economic Change in Developed Countries, a Conference of the Universities–National Bureau Committee for Economic Research.* Princeton, N.J.: Princeton University Press, 1960.

Lange, Oskar. "On the Economic Theory of Socialism," in Oskar Lange, Benjamin E. Lippincott, and Frederick M. Taylor (eds.), *On the Economic Theory of Socialism.* Minneapolis: University of Minnesota Press, 1938.

Layard, Richard. *Happiness: Lessons from a New Science.* London: Penguin, 2007.

Layard, Richard, and Stephen Nickell. *Handbook of Labor Economics.* Amsterdam: North-Holland, 1999.

Leroux, Pierre. *De l'égalité; précédé de l'individualisme et du socialisme.* Paris: Slatkine, 1996.

Lincoln, Abraham. "Second Lecture on Discoveries and Inventions" (1859). In *Collected Works of Abraham Lincoln,* vol. 3. New Brunswick, N.J: Rutgers University Press, 1953, 356–363.

Lindert, Peter H., and Jeffrey G. Williamson. "English Workers' Living Standards during the Industrial Revolution: A New Look." *Economic History Review* 36, no. 1 (1983): 1–25.

Lippmann, Walter. *The Good Society.* New York: Little Brown, 1936.

Litan, Robert E., and Carl J. Schramm. *Better Capitalism: Renewing the Entrepreneurial Strength of the American Economy.* New Haven, Conn.: Yale University Press, 2012.

Loasby, Brian J. *The Mind and Method of the Economist: A Critical Appraisal of Major Economists in the 20th Century.* Aldershot, U.K.: Edward Elgar, 1989.

Lovecraft, H. P. *The Dream-Quest of Unknown Kadath* (1926), in *At the Mountains of Madness and Other Novels.* Sauk City, Wisc.: Arkham House, 1964.

Lowenstein, Louis. *The Investor's Dilemma: How Mutual Funds Are Betraying Your Trust and What to Do about It.* Hoboken, N.J.: John Wiley and Sons, 2008.

Lubasz, Heinz. *Fascism: Three Major Regimes.* New York: John Wiley and Sons, 1973.

Maddison, Angus. *The World Economy: Historical Statistics.* Paris: OECD, 2006: table 1b, p. 439, and table 8c, p. 642.

Mann, Thomas. *Buddenbrooks.* Berlin: S. Fischer Verlag, 1901.

Marr, Andrew. *The Making of Modern Britain.* London: Macmillan, 2009.

Marshall, Alfred. *Elements of Economics.* London: Macmillan, 1892.

——. *Principles of Economics: An Introductory Volume.* London: Macmillan, 1938.

Marx, Karl. *Grundrisse der Kritik der politischen Ökonomie* (1858). Frankfurt: Europäische Verlagsanstalt, 1939–1941.

——. *Critique of the Gotha Program* (1875). Moscow: Moscow Foreign Languages Publishing House, 1947.

Marx, Karl, and Friedrich Engels. *The Communist Manifesto.* London: 1848.

Maslow, Abraham. "A Theory of Motivation." *Psychological Review* 50 (1943): 370–396.

Maugham, W. Somerset. "The Man Who Made His Mark." *Cosmopolitan,* June 1929.

Melville, Herman. *Moby-Dick.* New York: Harper and Brothers, 1851.

——. *The Confidence-Man.* New York: Dix, Edwards, 1857.

Mickelthwait, John, and Adrian Wooldridge. *The Company: A Short History of a Revolutionary Idea.* New York: Modern Library, 2003.

Milanović, Branko. *Liberalization and Entrepreneurship: Dynamics of Reform in Socialism and Capitalism.* Armonk, N.Y.: M. E. Sharpe, 1989.

Mill, John Stuart. "The Law of Partnership" (1851), in John M. Robson (ed.), *Essays on Economics and Society Part II.* London: Routledge and Kegan Paul, 1967.

Mises, Ludwig von. "Die Wirtschaftsrechnung im sozialistischen Gemeinwesen." *Archiv für Sozialwissenschaften und Sozialpolitik* 47 (1920): 86–121.

——. *Die Gemeinwirtschaft: Untersuchungen über den Sozialismus.* Jena: Gustav Fischer Verlag, 1922.

——. "Economic Calculation in the Socialist Commonwealth," in Friedrich Hayek (ed.), *Collectivist Economic Planning; Critical Studies on the Possibilities of Socialism.* London: G. Routledge, 1935.

——. *Socialism: An Economic and Sociological Analysis,* translated by J. Kahane. London: Jonathan Cape, 1936.

Mokyr, Joel. "The Industrial Revolution and Modern Economic Growth." Max Weber Lecture given at the European University, San Domenico di Fiesole, Italy, March 2007. Revised June 2007.

——. "Intellectual Property Rights, the Industrial Revolution, and the Beginnings of Modern Economic Growth." *American Economic Review* 99, no. 2 (2009): 349–355.

Montaigne, Michel de. *Essais.* Paris: Garnier, 1962.

Morris, Charles. *The Dawn of Innovation: The First American Industrial Revolution.* New York: Public Affairs, 2012.

Muller, Jerry Z. *The Mind and the Market: Capitalism in Modern European Thought.* New York: Alfred A. Knopf, 2002.

Mussolini, Benito. *Quatro Discorsi sullo Stato Corporativo.* Rome: Laboremus, 1935.

——. *Four Speeches on the Corporate State.* Rome: Laboremus, 1935.

Mynors, R.A.B. *Georgics by Virgil.* Oxford: Clarendon Press, 1990.

Myrdal, Gunnar. *The Political Element in the Development of Economic Theory.* London: Routledge and Kegan Paul, 1953.

Nagel, Thomas. "Aristotle on Eudaimonia." *Phronesis* 17, no. 3 (1972): 252–259.

——. "What Is It Like to Be a Bat?" *Philosophical Review* 83, no. 4 (1974): 435–450.

——. *The Possibility of Altruism.* Oxford: Oxford University Press, 1978.

Nelson, Richard. "How Medical Know-How Progresses." Working Paper 23, Center on Capitalism and Society, Columbia University, New York, January 2008.

Nicholls, A. J. "Hitler's Success and Weimar's Failure," in *Weimar and the Rise of Hitler.* Houndmills, Basingstoke, U.K.: Palgrave Macmillan, 1968.

Nickell, Stephen. "Fundamental Changes in the UK Labour Market." *Oxford Bulletin of Economics and Statistics* 63 (2001): 715–736.

Nietzsche, Friedrich. *Der Wille zur Macht,* edited by Heinrich Köselitz, Ernst Horneffer, and August Horneffer. Leipzig: Naumann, 1901.

——. *The Will to Power,* translated by Walter Kaufmann. New York: Vintage, 1968.

Nocken, Ulrich. "Corporatism and Pluralism in Modern German History," in Dirk Stegmann et al. (eds.), *Industrielle Gesellschaft und politisches System.* Bonn: Verlag Neue Gesellschaft, 1978.

OECD (Organisation for Economic Co-operation and Development). *Historical Statistics 1960–81.* Paris, 1983.

——. *The OECD Jobs Study: Facts, Analysis, Strategies.* Paris, 1994.

OECD (Organisation for Economic Co-operation and Development) and Jean-Philippe Cotis. *Going for Growth: 2007.* Paris, 2007.

Olson, Mancur. *The Rise and Decline of Nations.* New Haven, Conn.: Yale University Press, 1982.

Paganetto, Luigi, and Edmund S. Phelps. *Finance, Research, Education, and Growth.* Houndmills, Basingstoke, U.K.: Palgrave Macmillan, 2005.

Paine, Thomas. *Common Sense.* London: H. D. Symonds, 1792.

Paxton, Robert. *The Anatomy of Fascism.* New York: Alfred A. Knopf, 2004.

PBS. "The Planning Debate in New York, 1955–1975." *American Experience: New York Disc 7; People & Events.* Television.

Phelps, Edmund S. *Fiscal Neutrality toward Economic Growth.* New York: McGraw-Hill, 1965.

——. "Population Increase." *Canadian Journal of Economics* 1 (1968): 497–518.

Phelps, Edmund S. "Taxation of Wage Income for Economic Justice." *Quarterly Journal of Economics* 87 (August 1973): 331–354.

—— (ed.). *Altruism, Morality and Economic Theory.* New York: Basic Books, 1975.

——. "Arguments for Private Ownership," in *Annual Economic Outlook*. London: European Bank for Reconstruction and Development, 1993.

——. *Structural Slumps: The Modern Equilibrium Theory of Employment, Interest and Assets.* Cambridge, Mass.: Harvard University Press, 1994.

——. *Rewarding Work: How to Restore Participation and Self-Support to Free Enterprise.* Cambridge, Mass.: Harvard University Press, 1997 (2nd printing 2007).

——. "Behind This Structural Boom: The Role of Asset Valuations." *American Economic Review (Papers and Proceedings)* 89, no. 2 (1999): 63–68.

Phelps, Edmund S. "The Importance of Inclusion and the Power of Job Subsidies to Increase It." *OECD Economic Studies* 31 (2000/2): 86–113.

——. "The Unproven Case for Tax Cuts." *Financial Times,* February 2, 2001, p. 13.

——. "Reflections on Parts III and IV," in Philippe Aghion, Joseph Stiglitz, Michael Woodford, and Roman Frydman (eds.), *Knowledge, Information, and Expectations in Modern Macroeconomics: In Honor of Edmund S. Phelps.* Princeton, N.J.: Princeton University Press, 2003.

——. "The Good Life and the Good Economy: The Humanist Perspective of Aristotle, the Pragmatists and Vitalists; And the Economic Justice of John Rawls," in Kaushik Basu and Ravi Kanbur (eds.), *Arguments for a Better World*: *Essays in Honor of Amartya Sen.* Oxford: Oxford University Press, 2008.

——. "Economic Culture and Economic Performance," in Hans-Werner Sinn and Edmund S. Phelps (eds.), *Perspectives on the Performance of the Continental Economies.* Cambridge, Mass.: MIT Press, 2011.

Phelps, Edmund S., and Richard R. Nelson. "Investment in Humans, Technological Diffusion, and Economic Growth." *American Economic Review* 56, no. 1–2 (1966): 69–75.

Phelps, Edmund S., and Robert Reich. Radio interview, National Public Radio, October 17, 2006.

Phelps, Edmund S., and Gylfi Zoega. "The Search for Routes to Better Economic Performance in Continental Europe: The European Labour Markets." *CESifo Forum* 5, no. 1 (2004): 3–11.

——. "Entrepreneurship, Culture and Openness," in D. B. Audretsch, Robert J. Strom, and Robert Litan (eds.), *Entrepreneurship and Openness.* Cheltenham, U.K.: Edward Elgar, 2009.

——. "Job Satisfaction: The Effect of Modern-Capitalist and Corporatist Institutions." Working Paper 77, Center on Capitalism and Society, Columbia University, New York, December 2012.

Phillips, A. W. "The Relationship between Unemployment and the Rate of Change of Money Wage Rates in the United Kingdom, 1861–1957." *Economica* 25 (1958): 283–299.

Polanyí, Karl. *The Great Transformation.* New York: Farrar and Rinehart, 1944.

Polanyí, Michael. *Personal Knowledge*: *Towards a Post-Critical Philosophy.* Chicago: University of Chicago Press, 1958.

Popper, Karl R. *The Poverty of Historicism.* London: Routledge and Kegan Paul, 1957.

Prescott, Edward, and Stephen Parente. *Barriers to Riches.* Cambridge, Mass.: MIT Press, 2000.

Rapaczynski, Andrzej. *Nature and Politics: Liberalism in the Philosophies of Hobbes, Locke and Rousseau.* Ithaca, N.Y.: Cornell University Press, 1987.

Rawls, John. *A Theory of Justice.* Cambridge, Mass.: Harvard University Press, 1971.

——. *Justice as Fairness: A Restatement,* edited by Erin Kelly. Cambridge, Mass.: Harvard University Press, 2001.

Razzell, Peter, and Christine Spence. "The History of Infant, Child and Adult Mortality in London, 1550–1850." *London Journal* 32, no. 3 (2007): 271–292.

Robb, Richard. "Nietzsche and the Economics of Becoming." *Capitalism and Society* 4, no. 1 (2009).

Roh, Franz. "After Expressionism: Magic Realism," in Lois Parkinson Zamora and Wendy B. Faris (eds.), *Magical Realism: Theory, History, Community.* Durham, N.C.: Duke University Press, 1995.

Roland, Gérard. "Understanding Institutional Change: Fast-Moving and Slow-Moving Institutions." *Studies in Comparative International Development* 38, no. 4 (2004): 109–131.

Rosenberg, Nathan, and L. E. Birdzell. *How the West Grew Rich: The Economic Transformation of the Industrial World.* New York: Basic Books, 1986.

Rostow, W. W. *The Process of Economic Growth.* Oxford: Clarendon, 1953.

——. *The Stages of Economic Growth, a Non-Communist Manifesto.* Cambridge: Cambridge University Press, 1960.

Rothschild, Emma. *Economic Sentiments: Adam Smith, Condorcet, and the Enlightenment.* Cambridge, Mass.: Harvard University Press, 2001.

Rousseau, Jean-Jacques. *Émile, ou de l'Education.* Paris: Garnier-Flammarion, 1966.

Rylance, Rick. "Getting on," in Heather Glen (ed.), *The Cambridge Companion to the Brontës.* Cambridge: Cambridge University Press, 2002.

Sadka, Efraim. "On Progressive Income Taxation." *American Economic Review* 66, no. 5 (1976): 931–935.

Saint-Simon, Henri de. *Lettres d'un habitant de Genève à ses contemporains.* Paris: Librairie Saint-Simonienne, 1803.

——. *Nouveau Christianisme.* Paris: Bossange, 1825.

Sassoon, Donald. "All Shout Together." *Times Literary Supplement,* December 6, 2002, p. 5.

Say, Jean-Baptiste. *Traité d'économie politique.* Paris: Rapilly, 1803.

Schlesinger, Arthur Meier. *The Coming of the New Deal: 1933–1935.* Boston: Houghton Mifflin, 2003.

Schlicke, Paul. *Oxford Reader's Companion to Dickens.* Oxford: Oxford University Press, 1999.

Schmitter, Philippe C. "Still the Century of Corporatism?" *Review of Politics* 36, no. 1, The New Corporatism: Social and Political Structures in the Iberian World (1974): 85–131.

Schumpeter, Joseph A. *Theorie der wirtschaftlichen Entwicklung.* Leipzig: Duncker and Humblot, 1912.

——. *The Theory of Economic Development.* Cambridge, Mass.: Harvard University Press, 1934.

——. *Capitalism, Socialism and Democracy.* New York: Harper and Brothers, 1942.

Seligman, Martin. *Flourish: A Visionary New Understanding of Happiness and Well-Being.* New York: Free Press, 2011.

Sen, Amartya. *Inequality Reexamined.* New York: W. W. Norton, 1992.

Sen, Amartya. *Commodities and Capabilities.* New York: Oxford University Press, 1999.

———. "The Crisis of European Democracy." *New York Times,* May 22, 2012.

Sennett, Richard. *The Culture of the New Capitalism.* New Haven, Conn.: Yale University Press, 2006.

Shelley, Mary Wollstonecraft. *Frankenstein; or, The Modern Prometheus.* London: Lackington, Hughes, Harding, Mavor and Jones, 1818.

Shelley, Percy Bysshe. *Prometheus Unbound: A Lyrical Drama with Other Poems.* London: C. and J. Ollier: 1820.

Sidorsky, David. "Modernism and the Emancipation of Literature from Morality." *New Literary History* 15 (1983): 137–153.

———. "The Uses of the Philosophy of G. E. Moore in the Works of E. M. Forster." *New Literary History* 38 (2007): 245–271.

Silver, Kenneth E. *Esprit de Corps: The Art of the Parisian Avant-Garde and the First World War, 1914–1925.* Princeton, N.J.: Princeton University Press, 1992.

———. *Chaos & Classicism: Art in France, Italy, and Germany 1918–1936 [published on the Occasion of the Exhibition Chaos and Classicism: Art in France, Italy, and Germany, 1918–1936].* New York: Guggenheim Museum, 2010.

Slaughter, Anne-Marie. "Why Women Still Can't Have It All." *Atlantic Monthly,* July/August 2012, pp. 85–90, 92–94, 96–98, 100–102.

Smiles, Samuel. *Self-Help with Illustrations of Character and Conduct.* London: John Murray, 1859.

Smith, Adam. *Inquiry into the Nature and Causes of the Wealth of Nations.* London: W. Strahan and T. Cadell, 1776.

———. *Lectures on Jurisprudence* (1762–1763). Oxford: Clarendon Press, 1978.

———. *The Theory of Moral Sentiments* (1759). New York: Penguin, 2009.

Smith, Christian (with Kari Christoffersen, Hilary Davidson, and Patricia Snell Herzog). *Lost in Transition: The Dark Side of Emerging Adulthood.* New York: Oxford University Press, 2011.

Snow, C. P. *The Two Cultures and the Scientific Revolution.* New York: Cambridge University Press, 1959.

Spengler, Oswald. *The Decline of the West.* New York: Alfred A. Knopf, 1926.

Spiegelman, Willard. "Revolutionary Romanticism: *The Raft of the Medusa.*" *Wall Street Journal,* August 15, 2009, p. W14.

Starr, Frederick S. "Rediscovering Central Asia." *Wilson Quarterly,* Summer 2009, pp. 33–43.

Stewart, Barbara. "Recall of the Wild: Fighting Boredom, Zoos Play to the Inmates' Instincts." *New York Times,* April 6, 2002, p. B1.

Stone, Irving. *Lust for Life.* New York: Doubleday, 1937.

Tanzi, Vito. *Government versus Markets: The Changing Economic Role of the State.* New York: Cambridge University Press, 2011.

Taylor, Mark C. *Field Notes from Elsewhere: Reflections on Dying and Living.* New York: Columbia University Press, 2009.

Theil, Stefan. "Europe's Philosophy of Failure." *Foreign Policy,* January–February 2008, pp. 55–60.

Thurm, Scott. "Companies Struggle to Pass on Knowledge That Workers Acquire." *Wall Street Journal,* January 23, 2006, p. B1.

Titmuss, Richard. *The Gift Relationship: From Human Blood to Social Policy.* New York: Pantheon Books, 1971.

Tocqueville, Alexis de. *Democracy in America.* London: Saunders and Otley, 1835.

——. "Letters from America," translated by Frederick Brown. *Hudson Review* 62, no. 3 (2009): 375–376.

Tönnies, Ferdinand. *Community and Civil Society,* translated by Jose Harris. Cambridge: Cambridge University Press, 2001.

Tooze, J. Adam. *The Wages of Destruction: The Making and Breaking of the Nazi Economy.* New York: Viking, 2007.

Toynbee, Arnold. *A Study of History.* New York: Oxford University Press, 1947–1957.

Trilling, Lionel. *The Liberal Imagination.* New York: Doubleday, 1950.

Twain, Mark. *The Adventures of Tom Sawyer.* Hartford, Conn.: American Publishing, 1876.

Van Gogh, Vincent. *The Letters: The Complete Illustrated Edition,* edited by Leo Jansen, Hans Luitjen, and Nienke Bakker. London: Thames and Hudson, 2009.

Vincenti, Walter G. "The Retractable Airplane Landing Gear and the Northrop 'Anomaly.'" *Technology and Culture* 35 (January 1994): 1–33.

Volpi, Giulio. "Soya Is Not the Solution to Climate Change." *Guardian,* March 16, 2006.

Voltaire. *Candide, ou l'optimisme.* Paris: Sirène, 1759.

Weber, Adna Ferrin. *The Growth of Cities in the Nineteenth Century: A Study in Statistics.* Ithaca, N.Y.: Cornell University Press, 1899.

Weber, Max. *Wirtschaft und Gesellschaft.* Tübingen, Germany: J.C.B. Mohr (P. Siebeck), 1922.

——. *The Protestant Ethic and the Spirit of Capitalism,* translated by Talcott Parsons. London: Unwin, 1930.

——. *Economy and Society,* edited by Guenther Roth and Claus Wittich. Berkeley: University of California Press, 1978.

Wells, David Ames. *Recent Economic Changes and Their Effect on the Production and Distribution of Wealth and the Well-being of Society.* New York: D. Appleton, 1899.

Wuthering Heights. Dir. William Wyler. Perf. Merle Oberon, Lawrence Olivier. Samuel Goldwyn. Film, 1939.

Zingales, Luigi. *A Capitalism for the People.* New York: Basic Books, 2012.

ACKNOWLEDGMENTS

I N MY CAREER I HAVE HAD many advantages—parents, teachers, colleagues, and a happy marriage with my wife Viviana. This book is dedicated to four giants who for decades inspired and influenced me: Paul Samuelson, William Fellner, John Rawls, and Robert Merton.

The book grew from several ideas, one of them being the importance of a nation's attitudes and beliefs. In the 1980s Viviana sometimes remarked to me in our travels that we shouldn't be surprised that people in other countries behave in ways different from my country of birth, America, and hers, Argentina. Nations differ in their attitudes and beliefs. This perspective stayed with me as we visit or work in countries overseas. I also remembered a fascinating dinner, probably in the 1990s, with the sociologist Seymour Martin Lipset at which he told me of his work on values in America that were less pronounced elsewhere. In a course I gave at Columbia from 1992 to 2006, World Economic Problems, I began to suggest that differences in values give rise to the differences in economic institutions and economic performance we observe in the West. Research on the hypothesis started in May 2006 when I had the good fortune to find two graduate students, Luminita Stevens and Raicho Bojilov, who were eager to test the hypothesis against data. They hit upon the World Values Survey, which proved in a 2006 report to be a gold mine.

(In 2010 I was delighted to be able to tell the WVS founder Ronald Inglehart about some of our statistical results.)

In that same course and a later seminar, two research assistants helped me by reading and distilling a range of materials that improved my book at many places: Eleanor Dillon and Valeria Zhavoronkina. More informally, three other students, Oren Ziv, Edward Fox, and Jonathan Krueger engaged me in discussion. My Chapter 1 quotes Jonathan's term paper. (I learned one day that the acuteness of his comments on my text came from reading scripts for a Hollywood studio. I was sad to see him die so young and talented.)

No work as different from standard texts as this one could have been written by a committee, but it could not have been written without numerous, often continuing, interactions with others. During the four years of writing, I benefitted enormously from the generous help on a range of issues of Richard Robb, Gylfi Zoega, Raicho Bojilov, Amar Bhidé, Roman Frydman, Saif Ammous, and Juan Vicente Sola—all colleagues of mine at Columbia's Center on Capitalism and Society. Richard and Saif kindly read chapters of the book. Jeff Sachs and Amartya Sen were there for me in times of need. Peter Jungen was a great supporter of my message in recent years, as was Luigi Paganetto from early days at the Consiglio Nazionale delle Ricerche. Esa Saarinen made me see how valuable it is to write with all the empathy and passion I feel. hConversations with Barnaby Marsh and Mark C. Berner of the Templeton Foundation and with Seth Ditchik of Princeton University Press were also a boost. I am also grateful to Robert J. Gordon for providing me with the calculations that made it possible to chart in Chapter 9 the slowdown of total factor productivity alongside his chart showing the lesser slowdown of labor productivity.

I am very grateful to the Kauffman Foundation, particularly to Carl Schramm, Robert Litan, and Robert Strom, for their consistent financial and intellectual support of my research on modern capitalism. I am glad too that Andrew Wylie took on the book and gave its publication the benefit of his advice.

I have been blessed with the help of an extraordinarily talented group who came out of Literature and Classics at Harvard. It was perfect. They knew much that I did not know. Miranda Featherstone, a writer, edited chapters in 2008 and 2009. Francesca Mari, also a writer, followed in 2010. Jeff Nagy, a poet, came in 2012. They not only did their work at a high level. They put their hearts into it. Their spirit made my years on the project a special pleasure.

INDEX

Page numbers for entries occurring in figures are followed by an *f,* those for entries in notes, by an *n,* and those for entries in tables, by a *t.*

attainments, in modern experience of work, 59–60

Austen, Jane, 65–66; *Mansfield Park,* 67; *Sense and Sensibility,* 66

Australia: corporatism in, measurement of, 181; economic performance of, recent, 171–73; hours spent on household chores in, 299

Austria: corporatism in, interwar, 151; corporatism in, measurement of, 180–82; corporatism in, performance of, 182–85; economic performance of, recent, 171–73, 182–85; infectious diseases in, decline of, 49; job satisfaction in, 207, 214; mercantile capitalism in, 5; in World War I, 144

Austrian Empire, 149

Austrian school of economics, 30, 121, 129–30

authoritarianism, loss of freedom under, 133

autocracy, vs. democracy, in formation of modern economies, 93–95

automobile industry, 32–33, 156, 160

Babbage, Charles, 27

baby boomers, 227, 259, 311

Babylonia: credit institutions in, 91; private property in, 84

Bach, Johann Sebastian, 13, 286

Bacon, Francis, *Novo Organum,* 10

Bairoch, Paul, 6n8, 45n3

Balanchine, George, 75

Balla, Giacomo, 71

Balleisen, Edward J., 91n10

ballet, 75

Balzac, Honoré de, 67

bank(s): concentration of industry, 256; government debt held by, 251–52; government relationship with, 251–52; Italian, bailouts of, 144; local and regional, decline of, 303–4; merchant, 91–92, 322; origins and rise of, 91–92; as partnerships vs. corporations, 244; reform of, for recovery of dynamism, 321–22; structural faults of, as source of post-1960s economic decline, 244–46; U.S. reform of, 154, 245, 321–22

bankruptcy, origins of, 91

Bankruptcy Acts (U.S.), 91

Baring family, 91

Baroque music, 72

Barre, Raymond, 157

Barres, Maurice, 151

Barzun, Jacques: *From Dawn to Decadence,* 98, 217; humanities courses taught by, 296; on James (William), 281n14; on modern era, 98,

203; on organic generation of innovation, 318; on vitalism, 99n13, 279

Becker, Gary, 208n16

Beethoven, Ludwig van, 72–73

Belgian Revolution, 96

Belgium: corporatism in, measurement of, 179–82; corporatism in, performance of, 182–86; democracy in, development of, 95–96; economic knowledge in, 11; economic performance of, recent, 174, 182–86; mercantile capitalism in, 5; output per worker in, 5, 6; population growth in, 107–8; real wages per worker in, 44; urbanization in, 108

Benedict, Ruth, 194

Bentham, Jeremy, 290, 291

Bentolila, Samuel, 201n6

Bergson, Henri, 318; *Creative Evolution,* 282, 282n17

Berle, Adolf, *The Modern Corporation and Private Property,* 243

Berlin (Germany), March Revolution in, 117

Berners-Lee, Tim, 27

Bernstein, Leonard, 276

Bertola, Giuseppe, 201n6

Beveridge, William, 132n15

Bhidé, Amar, 29n6, 244; *The Venturesome Economy,* 319

Bill of Rights (1689, England), 86, 287

biofuels, 130–31

Birth of the Modern (Johnson), 98

Bismarck, Otto von, 149, 157, 170

black activism, in 1960s, 291

Black Death, 3, 4

Blake, William, 51, 67

Blanchflower, David, 196, 231, 231n10

Bloom, Harold, 99n13, 279; *Shakespeare: The Invention of the Human,* 280

Blowup (film), 78n2

blue collar workers. *See* working class

Bodenhorn, Howard, 92, 92n11

Boeing, 323

Boer War, 53n15

Bojilov, Raicho, 212

Bolshevik revolution, 134

booms: construction, 234, 261; dot.com, 201, 226; housing, 226, 245, 252–53, 310, 312; internet, 219, 261, 303, 311, 315; in mercantile capitalism, 115

borrowing, short-term, by banks, 244–45, 322

bossnapping, 162–63, 323

Boulton, Matthew, 12, 13, 89

bourgeoisie: in mercantile economies, 97; in modern economies, 97, 114

Bourguignon, Philippe, 209, 210

Bradley, Harold, 32

Bradley, Owen, 32

Bradshaw, David J., 66

Brass, Dick, 242, 242n5

Braudel, Fernand, 1, 44, 44n2

Brazil, corporatism in, 151–52

bribery, in corporatism, 178

Britain: art depicting modern life in, 69–70; bankruptcy in, 91; commerce in, rise of, 96–97; common law in, 84, 85, 87n8; competition in, 195; corporatism in, interwar, 152, 155–56; corporatism in, measurement of, 179, 179–82; corporatism in, postwar, 163–64, 165; democracy in, development of, 95; economic culture of, 195; economic knowledge in, sources of, 11, 12; economic performance of, interwar, 155, 156; economic performance of, recent, 171–76; financial panics in, 115; formation of modern economy in, 79, 84, 95, 102; infectious diseases in, decline of, 49; intellectual property rights in, 85; inventions of First Industrial Revolution in, 12, 13, 14; job satisfaction in, 199, 233; joint-stock companies of, 89–90; literature on modern life in, 63–67; mercantile capitalism in, 2, 5, 115; output per worker in, 5–6, 7n9, 43; population growth in, 107–8; post-1960s economic decline in, 222, 233; poverty in, decline of, 48; productivity growth in, 19th-century, 5–8; property rights in, 85; public opinion in establishment of capitalism in, 113; real wages per worker in, 5, 6, 6n8, 44, 45, 46–47; rule of law in, 86–87; socialism in, 120, 132n15, 163; unemployment in, 50, 51, 222; urbanization in, 61, 108; wage-productivity ratio in, 44, 47; wars of, 53n15; working class wages in, 46–48. See also England; Ireland; Scotland

British Parliament. See Parliament, British

Brontë, Charlotte, Jane Eyre, 66

Brontë, Emily, Wuthering Heights, 64, 64n6

Brooks, David, 239, 280

bubbles, in mercantile capitalism, 115. See also booms

bubonic plague, 3, 4

Buddenbrooks (Mann), 67

Buffett, Warren, 287

Burckhardt, Jacob, 111

bureaucratic red tape, as measure of corporatism, 162, 162n26, 164, 180

Bush, George H. W., 226, 252

Bush, George W.: compassionate conservatism of, 311, 317; expansion of Medicare under, 259–60; policy response to stagnation, 313; tax cuts of, 226, 247, 263, 311, 312, 318

business knowledge: growth in, 34; in recovery of dynamism, 318–19

business sector. See companies; corporations

Butler, Nicholas Murray, 296

Byron, Lord, 63n5

Calmfors, Lars, 202n8

Calvin, John, 100, 286

Calvinism, and economic culture, 78

Cameron, David, 205

Canada: corporatism in, measurement of, 179–82, 180n6; economic performance of, recent, 171–74, 182–86; job satisfaction in, 198, 201, 214; modernization of economy of, 41–42

Candide (Voltaire), 101–2, 275–76

Cantillon, Richard, 106

capital: definition of, 7; of entrepreneurs, 25; vs. labor, in innovative activity, 23–24; 19th-century growth of, 7–8; physical, in value of companies, 187; population growth in returns on, 108n23; socialist approach to allocation of, 120

capital access index, and job satisfaction, 204

capital goods, vs. consumer goods, in post-1960s economic decline, 224, 224n4, 225n5, 228n7

capitalism: antipathy for, 301; competition in, repression of, 26; corporatism's critique of, 150; definition of, 41n1; introduction of innovation into, 26; mercantile (See mercantile capitalism); modern (See modern capitalism); mutual gain from exchange of services in, 289–90; origins of, 2, 108; scholarship on rise of, 77–78, 108–9; socialism's critique of, 117–20; use of term, 41n1, 266. See also specific countries

Capitalism, Socialism and Democracy (Schumpeter), 10, 10n12, 27n4, 207

careers. See employment; job(s); work

caregiving, fulfillment through, 298

Carlyle, Thomas, 67, 117n2

cartels, in corporatism, 143, 148, 151

Casanova, Giacomo, 286

Cassel, Gustav, 9n11

on copyright, 254; democracy in, 95; on mortgages, 252; reaction to post-1960s economic decline in, 226, 228–29

consensual corporatism, in Germany, 149–50

conservatism, compassionate, 311

Constable, John, 69n14, 71

constitution(s): German, 157; Italian, 156–57; lack of, in Europe, 144; in measurement of corporatism, 181–82; Polish-Lithuanian, 93; U.S., 87, 89

constitutional democracy, moral hazards in, 178

constitutional government, origins of, 86–87

construction boom, 234, 261

consumer goods, vs. capital goods, in post-1960s economic decline, 224, 224n4, 225n5, 228n7

contracts: enforcement of, 81; limitations of, 206; social, 140, 166, 166n29, 291; U.S. Constitution on, 87, 89

Coolidge, Calvin, 136

Cooper, John, 284

copyrights: origins of, 85, 253; problems caused by, 253–54

corporate welfare, 254, 267

corporations: concentration of sector in large, 256; culture of, 208; governance of, flaws in, 243; origins and development of, 89–90, 105; vs. partnerships, banks as, 244; short termism in, 243–44, 314, 320–21; structural faults of, as source of post-1960s economic decline, 241–46; U.S. Supreme Court on rights of, 89, 266

corporatism, 135–69; agenda of, 141–43, 166; classic, 166; competition in, 24, 26, 142–43, 168, 180; critique of modern economy in, 135–43, 150; current status of, 314; dark side of, 168–69; definition of, 26, 143n6; economic justice in, 186, 301, 302, 306–7; future of, 308–9, 320; the good life in, 269, 270; innovation in, lack of, 167–68, 186–92, 314; job satisfaction in (See job satisfaction); measurement of, approaches to, 159, 179–82, 180n6; modern elements in, suppression of, 306–7; moral hazards of, 178–79; new version of, 166–68, 265–66; origins of, 137–41; in post-1960s economic decline, 251–58, 265–66; postwar evolution of, 150, 157–65; as third way, 150; between world wars, 143–57. See also specific countries

corporatism, performance of: assumptions in scholarship on, 201–3; claims vs. evidence

on, 178–86, 268–69; interwar, 155–57; in new version, 265–66

corporazioni (ancient guilds), 145–46

corruption, as sign of corporatism, 181

Cort, Henry, 12

Cortés, Hernán, 280

Cotis, Jean-Philippe, 180n6

Counter-Revolution of Science, The (Hayek), 34n10

courage, in creation of ideas, 28

Craft, Robert, 30

crashes, in mercantile capitalism, 115

Creative Evolution (Bergson), 282, 282n17

creativity: in cities, 106–7, 107n21; drivers of, 26–36; in dynamism, 28, 35; in the good life, 282–83; imagination in, recognition of role of, 101

credit institutions, origins of, 91

Crimean War, 53n15

crises. See financial crises

critical mass, populations at, 108

Cubism, 71

culturalism, in corporatism, 142

culture(s): company, 208; in economics, lack of consideration of, 194–95; vs. institutions, 195n1; political, 194; significance of international differences among, 194

culture, economic, 96–104; definition of, 96, 194, 207–8; in economic performance, 103–4, 210–11; in formation of modern economies, 96–104, 109; international differences in, 103–4, 209–11; in job satisfaction, 194, 207–15, 213f, 214f; of mercantile capitalism, 97; modern values in, 98–104; in post-1960s economic decline, 246–50; Protestantism and, 78; in recovery of dynamism, 323–24; of socialism, 120; traditional vs. modern, corporatism on, 137–39. See also values; specific countries

curiosity, in creation of ideas, 28, 29

currency speculation, 144, 244

Dartmouth College, 89

Darwin, Charles, 38

Daumier, Honoré, 45

Dawn of Innovation, The (Morris), 319

Debtors Act of 1869 (Britain), 91

debtors' prisons, 91

Declaration of Independence, U.S., 93, 136

Decline and Fall of the Roman Empire (Gibbon), 79n3

Decline of the West, The (Spengler), 79n3

Decree of July 1926 (Italy), 146
deficits. *See* government deficits
Defoe, Daniel: *Moll Flanders,* 63; on need for
  copyrights, 253; *Robinson Crusoe,* 37, 39, 63,
  279n13
democracy: and corporatism, coexistence of,
  157; European, development of, 95–96; in
  formation of modern economies, 93–96, 105,
  109; grassroots, 309; modern values in origins
  of, x; moral hazards in, 178; scholarship on
  rise of, 77; U.S., development of, 94–95
Democracy in America (Tocqueville), 79n3
Democratic Party (U.S.): on social welfare, 260;
  traditional values in, 260, 317
Demsetz, Harold, 84–85, 85n6
Deng Xiaoping, 52, 195, 286
Denmark: corporatism in, measurement of,
  180–82; corporatism in, performance of,
  182–84; economic performance of, recent,
  171–73, 176, 182–84; job satisfaction in, 198,
  199, 213–14; mercantile capitalism in, 5
depressions, economic: of 1893–1898, 116; in
  Germany, 148; modern history of, 116. *See
  also* Great Depression
derivatives, 266, 267
desires, hierarchy of, 275
determinism: creativity and, 282; historical,
  9, 10, 37
Dewey, John, 58n3, 246–47, 276, 276n7
Diamond, Jared, 77, 79; *Guns, Germs and Steel,*
  78n1
Dickens, Charles: *David Copperfield,* 65–66; on
  debtors' prisons, 91; *Hard Times,* 64–65; on
  modern experience of work, 64–66, 66n10;
  Oliver Twist, 45, 64; *Sketches by Boz,* 65, 65n9;
  Speeches, Letters and Sayings, 65n9; *The
  Uncommercial Traveller,* 65n9
diet, effects of modern economies on, 49,
  49n13
difference, making a, 285
dignity, 52, 81, 118
diminishing returns, 3, 7
directedness, in corporatism, 138, 166
discoveries, in modern experience of work,
  59, 62
Discovery, Age of, 100
discovery procedure, 34, 34n9. *See also* Hayek,
  Friedrich
disease: effects of modern economies on, 48–
  50; population density in spread of, 106
distributive justice, 291–95, 299–300, 305–6. *See
  also* Rawls, John

diversity: of cities, 106–7, 116; in dynamism,
  38; of human nature, 297–98; and wage
  inequality, 186
division of labor, in innovation, 23
Doctors without Borders, 286
Doctrine of Fascism, The (Mussolini), 145
Dolfuss, Engelbert, 151
D1/D5 ratio, 186n12
Don Quixote (Cervantes), 63, 100, 280
Dornbusch, Rudi, 174
dot.com boom, 201, 226
Douthat, Ross, 238
Draghi, Mario, 174
due process, development of, 86–87, 87n8
Dupont, 241n4
Durkheim, Émile, 147
Duyckinck, Evert, 68n12
dynamism, 19–40; definition of, ix, 20, 194;
  in definition of modern economies, ix, 19;
  diversity in, role of, 38; drivers of creation
  of ideas in, 26–36; economic culture in,
  194, 323–24; economic freedoms in, x, 29,
  308; emergence of first economies with,
  14–15, 307; growth in relation to, 19–22;
  human resources needed for, 28, 29, 31, 35;
  measurement of, approaches to, 21–22;
  pecuniary and nonpecuniary motives in, 25,
  25n3, 29; recognition of role of, in modern
  capitalism, 317; recovery of, approaches to,
  316–24; recovery of, prospects for, 308–9, 316–
  17; rise of (*See* modern economies, formation
  of); selection mechanisms for ideas in, 24–26;
  social system in, 36–40; understanding of
  mechanisms of, need for, 317–19

Earned Income Tax Credit (EITC), 177n3, 206,
  228–29
East India Company, 89
eBay, 205
economic growth: in corporatism, 144–45,
  158–59, 161, 178; dynamism in relation to,
  19–22; in financial crises, origins of, 311; first
  economies with sustained, 6–15; postwar
  comparison of, 158–59, 159n23, 161. *See also*
  performance
"Economic Possibilities for Our
  Grandchildren" (Keynes), 274
Economic Reform of 1948 (Germany), 158
economics, Keynes on study of, 319
"Economics and Knowledge" (Hayek), 31n7
economies. *See specific countries and types of
  economies*

economies of scale, in 19th-century productivity growth, 7–8

Economy and Society (Weber), 78n2

Edison, Thomas, 33

education: in economic justice, 295–96, 296n4; government role in, 255, 295, 296n4; humanities courses in, 296–97; of legislators and regulators, 318–19; modern values in, 324; in socialist economies, 177

efficiency: economic freedoms and, 81; in economic justice, 291, 300; government role in, 316; in socialism, 121, 123, 129–30, 132–33

Einaudi, Luigi, 157

Einstein, Albert, 113

Eisenhower, Dwight, 251

EITC. *See* Earned Income Tax Credit

Eliot, Charles, 296

Elmeskov, Jørgen, 201n6

employee engagement, 58, 62, 304

employers' associations: in German corporatism, 149, 150, 160; in Italian corporatism, 145

employment protection, in corporatism, 180, 190–91, 190f, 191f, 201

employment protection legislation (EPL), 180, 191, 201, 201n6

employment rates: in corporatist economies, 188–91; entitlements' impact on, 260–63; growth as synonym for high, 222; innovation rate and, 188–91, 222–23; market-cap-to-output ratio as predictor of, 188–89, 189f; of men, decline in, 310; productivity growth rate and, 190n14. *See also* job(s); unemployment

enclosure movement, 108

end-users: adoption of innovation by, 29, 29n6; diversity among, 38; uncertainty about, 37

energy production, capital in, 24

engagement: employee, 58, 62, 304; in the good life, 284; political, 309

Engels, Friedrich, 117n2; *The Communist Manifesto*, 41n1, 109, 117, 119

England: Bill of Rights in, 86, 287; copyrights in, 253; economic knowledge in, 3–5; mercantile capitalism in, 2, 3–5; poverty in, decline of, 48

Enlightenment: definition of, 10; the good life in, 280, 287; headline inventions of, 12; origins of modernism in, 100–101; scientific advances in, 10–11

Enquiry Concerning Human Understanding, An (Hume), 28n5, 101

entitlement, culture of, 249

entitlements: employment affected by, 260–63; expansion of, 229–30, 258–60

entrepreneur(s): angel investors and, 35–36; definition of, 25; diversity among, 38; early recognition of value of, 100–101, 276; economic freedoms needed by, 29, 82; initiative taking by, 58–59, 98, 98n12; vs. innovators, 28; pecuniary vs. nonpecuniary returns for, 25, 25n3; pre-modern vs. modern, 28; scientific advances used by, ix, 9–10, 28; in selection process for ideas, 25; social, 25, 286; uncertainty of, 37

"entrepreneurial spirit," coining of term, 78n2

EPL. *See* employment protection legislation

equilibrium: in market economies, 9; punctuated, 22–23

equity, and wages in free market, 290. *See also* justice

Erasmus, Desiderius, 99–100

Erhard, Ludwig, *Prosperity through Competition*, 158

Ericson, Leif, 59, 297

Erskine, John, 296

ESOPs, 128–29

Espejo, Eugenio, 11

Essais (Montaigne), 100

ethics: Aristotelian, 286–88; modern, 211; vs. morality, 208; socialist, 118–20, 123; work, 123. *See also* values

ethnic diversity, and wage inequality, 186

ethnicity, in corporatism, 141n5

eudaimonia, 272, 273, 284, 288

Eurasia, specialization of labor in, 77

Europe: constitutions in, lack of, 144; debate over alternatives to capitalism in, 110; democracy in, development of, 95–96; distribution of modern economies in, 77–78; economic culture of, vs. U.S., 209; financial crises in, origins of, 310–11; financial panics in, 115; job satisfaction in, 232–33; music depicting modern life in, 72–74; political engagement in, 309; post-1960s economic decline in, 221–22, 232–33, 314; recovery of dynamism in, approaches to, 316–24; recovery of dynamism in, prospects for, 308–9, 317; revolutions of 1848 in, 116, 117; social welfare in, 258–59. *See also specific countries*

European Economic Commission, 158

European Union, establishment of, 158

Evans, Harold: "Eureka," 32–33; *They Made America*, 33, 319

Evans, Oliver, 33
evolution, theory of, 38
evolutionary socialism, 118
Expressionism, 55, 70–71

Fabian socialism, 118, 120
Facebook, 243, 249
factories: Dickens on, 64, 65; rise of, 51–52. *See also* manufacturing
"factory councils" movement, 146
failures, social value of, 38
family satisfaction, 197–98
family values, 250, 315
Fannie Mae, 252–53, 254
Farm Credit System, 322
farm workers, output of, 3–4, 3n3
Fascist Manifesto of 1919, 144
Fascist Party (Italy), 144, 146
February Revolution (1848), 117
Federal Register of Regulations, 164
Federal Reserve, U.S., 175
Ferguson, Adam, *Essay on the History of Civil Society,* 2n2
Ferraro, Geraldine, 317
feudal system: decline of, 80, 108; wealth accumulation in, 104
Feynman, Richard, 113
Field Notes from Elsewhere (Taylor), 71
50-10 ratio, 186n12, 227
financial crises: of 2007–2008, 185, 186, 311–12, 322; origins of, 310–11
financial institutions: in job satisfaction, 204–5; reform of, in recovery of dynamism, 321–22; rise of, 91–92. *See also* bank(s)
financial panics, 115
financiers: angel investors as, 35–36; pluralism of views among, 38
Finland: corporatism in, 180, 185; economic performance of, recent, 171–73, 176; job satisfaction in, 213–14
Finley, M. I., *The Ancient Economy,* 1
Fiscal Neutrality toward Economic Growth (Phelps), 263
Fitch, John, 12
Five-Year Plans, of France, 151
Fleming, Alexander, 33
Flexicurity, 198
Flourish (Seligman), 285
flourishing. *See* mass flourishing; personal flourishing
Fogel, Robert, 14
food production, labor vs. capital in, 23–24

Ford, Henry, 32–33
Ford Motor Company, 156
foreign trade. *See* trade
Forster, E. M., 136
Foster, John, 256
Four Speeches on the Corporate State (Mussolini), 145, 145n8, 146
Four-Year Plans, of Italy and Germany, 151
framework conditions, 81. *See also* institutions, economic
France: art depicting modern life in, 69; corporatism in (*See* French corporatism); democracy in, development of, 95; dynamism of, loss of, 41; economic culture of, 209–10, 246; economic knowledge in, 11; economic performance of, recent, 171–76, 182–87, 192; emigration from, 185; entrepreneurs in, recognition of value of, 100–101, 276; February Revolution in, 117; intellectual property rights in, 85; job satisfaction in, 199, 201, 214, 233; joint-stock companies of, 90; labor force participation in, 51; labor unions in, 162–63, 322–23; literature on modern life in, 67; mercantile capitalism in, 5, 115; music depicting modern life in, 74–75; output per worker in, 5–6; population growth in, 107; post-1960s economic decline in, 222, 233; productivity growth in, 19th-century, 5–8; property rights in, 85; real wages per worker in, 5, 6, 44, 45; socialism in, 134, 151; social welfare in, 259; tax code of, 165; unemployment in, 222; unemployment insurance in, 50; urbanization in, 61, 108; wage-productivity ratio in, 44–45, 47; wars of, 53n15
Franco, Francisco, 151
Frankenstein (film), 64
Frankenstein (Shelley), 63–64
Fraser Institute, 204, 204n14
Freddie Mac, 252–53, 254
freedom(s): in dynamism, x, 29, 308; in economic success, 308; in formation of modern economies, 81–85, 105; in the good life, 272, 273; international differences in, 104; in justice, 292; in modern experience of work, 59; in socialism, 133
free market, wages in, 290
French corporatism: measurement of, 179–82, 180n6; origins of, 151, 162; performance of, 182–87; postwar, 162–63
French Revolution of 1789–1799, 45, 85, 93, 95
French Revolution of 1830, 95

French Revolution of 1848, 95

Freud, Sigmund, 138, 138n3, 287; *Civilization and Its Discontents,* 139

Fromm, Erich, 194

frontier, U.S., economic role of, 102, 108n23

Fuggers, 91

future: in historicism, 9; unknowability of, 37–38

Futurist art, 71

Gainsborough, Thomas, 68

Galbraith, John Kenneth, 34, 129n12, 267

Gallup, 231, 233

Gandhi, Mahatma, 292n2

Gates, Bill, 193, 242, 286, 290

Gaulle, Charles de, 151

GDP: government outlays as percentage of, 162, 162n25, 164, 179–80; per employee, international comparison of, 182–83, 183f; per hour worked, international comparison of, 183–84, 184f; state-owned enterprises in, 171, 177

gender: barriers based on, effects of modern economies on, 74; and housework, 299; and human fulfillment, 298; and job satisfaction, 231, 231n10; and wage inequality, 227. *See also* men; women

General Motors, 241n4, 323

General Social Surveys, 62, 231, 232n11, 233

General Theory (Keynes), 37n14

Gentile, Giovanni, 145

Georgics (Virgil), 275

Géricault, Théodore, 69, 69n13

German corporatism: interwar, 141n5, 147–50, 155–57, 170; measurement of, 179–82, 180n6; origins of, 137; performance of, 182–87; postwar, 157–63, 162n25

German Historical School of Economics, 9–10, 9n11, 27

German Workers Party, 147. *See also* Nazi Germany

Germany: anti-Semitism in, 141n5, 147; art depicting modern life in, 70–71; constitution of, 157; corporatism in (*See* German corporatism); democracy in, development of, 96; dynamism of, loss of, 41; economic culture of, 209–10; economic growth in, postwar, 158–59, 161; economic knowledge in, 11; economic performance of, interwar, 155–57; economic performance of, recent, 171–76, 182–87, 192; job satisfaction in, 199, 201, 214, 233; joint-stock companies of, 90; literature on modern life in, 67; March Revolution in, 117; mercantile capitalism in, 5; music depicting modern life in, 72–74; Nazi (*See* Nazi Germany); output per worker in, 5–6; population growth in, 107; post-1960s economic decline in, 222, 233; productivity growth in, 19th-century, 5–8; real wages per worker in, 5, 6, 44, 45; socialism in, 118, 119n5, 134, 147; social welfare in, 258; unemployment in, 222; unification of (1871), 149; urbanization in, 60; wage-productivity ratio in, 45, 47; wars of, 53n15; women in labor force of, 195; World War I reparations by, 148

Gibbon, Edward, *Decline and Fall of the Roman Empire,* 79n3

Giersch, Herbert, 157

Giffen, Robert, 47, 47n7, 48

Giffen good, 47n7

Gilbert, W. S., 283

Gladstone, William Ewart, 46

Glass, Philip, 75

Glass-Steagall Banking Act of 1933 (U.S.), 154, 245

global economy: dynamism in rise of, 22; in "golden age" narratives, 238; internationalization of innovation in, 20; measurement of dynamism in, 21; money culture in, 247

Glorious Revolution of 1688, 86

Godwin, William, 63n5

Goethe, Johann Wolfgang von, 67

Gogh, Vincent van, 70

"golden age" narratives, 237–40

golden parachute payments, 321

gold standard, 175

Goldwyn, Samuel, 64n7

Gombrich, E. H., 69, 69n14

good, the, Aristotle on, 271, 272

good economy: Democrats' conception of, 317; dynamism in restoration of, 317; the good life in proper definition of, 269–70, 288; as modern economy, 293, 309; Republicans' conception of, 317

good life, the, 268–88; ancient concepts of, xi; Aristotle on, 271–75, 277, 284, 288; in corporatism, 269, 270; definition of, 271, 272; economic justice and, 293; humanism on, 270–73; in modern capitalism, 301; in modern economies, xi–xii, 307–8; pragmatists on, 274–79, 281, 283–84; in socialism, 270; universality of goal of, 296; vitalists on, 279–88; work-life balance and, 304

Gordon, Robert J., 220n1

Gotha Program, 119n5

government: constitutional, origins of, 86–87; expansion of powers of, 86; joint-stock companies chartered by, 89

government debt. *See* sovereign debt

government deficits: in financial crises, 311; lack of understanding of, 318; need for understanding of, 319; tax rates and, 226, 227n6, 311, 318

government institutions. *See* institutions

government outlays: and job satisfaction, 206–7, 207n15; as measure of corporatism, 161–62, 162n25, 163, 164, 179–80

government regulations: business knowledge underlying, lack of, 318–19; effects on innovation, 82–83; harm vs. benefits of, 82–83, 206; and job satisfaction, 206, 207; in new corporatism, 167; rise in number of, 253, 253n10

government (state) role: in efficiency, 316; in modernism, 136–37; in post-1960s economic decline, 251–64, 266–67; in recovery of dynamism, 316–24

grassroots democracy, 309

Great Books programs, 296

Great Depression: corporatism and, 150, 152, 153, 155; productivity growth in, 8, 222; recovery from, 235; Second, 175

Great Divergence, 11

Great Moderation, 116n1

Great Recession of 2008–2009, 235, 236

Great Transformation of 1820–1930, 264–65

Greece, ancient: infrequent innovation in, 1; rule of law in, 87

Greece, modern, bailout of, 252

Groom, Brian, 163–64

gross domestic product. *See* GDP

Grosz, George, 71

growth, as synonym for high employment, 222. *See also specific types*

guilds, 26, 140, 149

guild socialism, 118

Gutenberg, Johannes, 77

Hamburg (city-state), commercial economy of, 2

Hamlet (Shakespeare), 100, 280

Hammurabi, Code of, 84

happiness: Aristotle on, 284; in the good life, 277–78, 284; income in relation to, 52–53; literature on, 71–72; neoclassical economics

on, 277–78; productivity growth and, 274n4; pursuit of, in U.S., 101, 280, 284

Hard Times (Dickens), 64–65

Hargreaves, James, 12

Harris Interactive, 231n9

Hart, Lorenz, 153n16

Harvey, William, 10, 100

"having it all," 304–5

Haydn, Joseph, 72

Hayek, Friedrich, ix; on adaptations, 31; in Austrian school, 30, 121; counter-revolution of science, 34n10; "Dependence Effect," 34n9, 129n12; on discovery procedure, 34, 34n9, 37n14, 319; "Economics and Knowledge," 31n7; on efficiency, 316; on feasibility of socialism, 125–32, 133; on German corporatism, 149, 156n21; *Individualism and Economic Order*, 31n7; on laissez-faire, 132n15; Mises as teacher of, 121; on personal knowledge in innovation, 30–31, 31n7, 101; in recognition of indigenous innovation, 128, 129, 129n12; *The Road to Serfdom*, 129n12, 131–32, 132n15, 133, 149, 156n21; Schumpeter influenced by, 10n12; on social change, 310; on unknowns in innovation, 34; use of knowledge in society, 31n7

healthcare industry: government role in, 255, 258; improvements in, with rise of modern economies, 50; in U.S. vs. Europe, 258

Hecht, Ben, 64n7

Heckman, James, 295

hedge funds, 243–44, 321n1

Henley, William Ernest, *Invictus*, 280

Henry V (Shakespeare), 278

"heroic spirit," 2, 2n2, 15

Hewlett, Sylvia Ann, 299

Hicks, John, 7n10

historicism, 9, 10, 26, 37

Hitchcock, Alfred, 78n2, 224n4, 248

Hitler, Adolf, corporatism under, 147, 148, 155, 155n18, 156, 156n21, 170

Hobbes, Thomas, 37

Hockney, David, vii

holding companies, 88

Holland. *See* Netherlands

Hollande, François, 322

Holocaust, 141n5

home: balance between work and, 304; in the good life, 304; management of, 298, 299; working from, innovation impeded by, 39, 250, 304 home mortgages, government role in, 252–53, 311

Homer: *Iliad,* 279; *Odyssey,* 279

Hoon, Hian Teck, 222

Hoover, Herbert, 155, 175

Hopper, Edward, 248

hospital practice, improvements in, with rise of modern economies, 50

housework, 298, 299

housing, in recession of 2008–2009, 236, 311

housing boom, 226, 245, 252–53, 310, 312

Howard, Philip K., 165

"How Medical Know-How Progresses" (Nelson), 319

Hubble, Edwin, 248

Hudson's Bay Company, 89

Hugo, Victor, *Les Misérables,* 45

human fulfillment, 297–98

humanism: in economic culture of modern economies, 98; on the good life, 270–73; vs. socialism, 132, 133

humanities, in core curriculum, 296–97

human nature: economic justice and, 296–300; as universal vs. diverse, 297–98

Hume, David: *An Enquiry Concerning Human Understanding,* 28n5, 101; on the good life, 280; on imagination, 28, 28n5; on mercantile capitalism, 97; *Treatise on Human Nature,* 97

"hundred years' peace," 53n15

Hungary: job satisfaction vs. security in, 233; market socialism in, 125

Hutchens, Robert, 296

hygiene, effects of modern economies on, 49

Ibert, Jacques, 74–75

Ibsen, Henrik, 282

Iceland: corporatism in, measurement of, 181; job satisfaction in, 214; population density of, 105; vitalism in, 286

ICT. *See* information and communications technologies

ideas: competition of, 24; drivers of creation of, 26–36; failed, value of, 38; in modern economies, 23–27; population density in spread of, 106; science as source of, 26–27; selection mechanisms for, 24–26; society's role in, 36–40

ideas sector, 23

imaginarium, modern economy as, 27–28

imagination: in creativity, recognition of role of, 101; in dynamism, 28, 29, 32; in the good life, 280

IMF. *See* International Monetary Fund

imitation, vs. innovation, 20; in corporatist economies, 187; in global economy, 20, 21

immigration: economic performance and, 185–86; job satisfaction and, 201

importance of job, in job satisfaction, 199–201, 200t

incentives: in joint-stock companies, 90; short-term, at corporations, 243–44, 314, 320–21; in socialism, 122–26, 123n7

inclusion, economic: definition of, 173, 227; international decline of, 176; in modern capitalism, 307; in nineteenth-century London, 64n6; in post-1960s economic decline, 227–30; as social benefit of wage growth, 47; in socialism, 173, 176; subsidies for, 240, 292

income: control of, in corporatism, 159; extraordinary, 293; vs. flourishing, vii; and the good life, 271–72, 273–74; growth of, in expansion of social welfare, 260; happiness in relation to, 52–53; justice in distribution of, 291–95, 299–300, 305–6. *See also* wage(s)

income inequality. *See* wage inequality

income tax. *See* tax(es)

Index of Social Infrastructure, 181n8

India, employment subsidies in, 292n2

indigenous innovation: capacity for (*See* dynamism); in corporatism, evidence on lack of, 187–92; definition of, ix, 9; emergence of economies based on, 14–15; Hayek's role in recognition of, 128, 129, 129n12; as source of economic knowledge, 14–15

individualism: in corporatism, 147, 151, 166, 168; in modernism, 99–100, 135–36; origins and development of, 99–100; in socialism, 132–33

Individualism and Economic Order (Hayek), 31n7

industrialization: Dickens's views on, 65; as stage of modernization, 108–9

Industrial Revolution, First: dates of, 12, 13n13; headline inventions of, 12–14

Industrial Revolution, Second, 13n13

infectious diseases, effects of modern economies on, 48–50

informal sector, in socialist economies, 174

information and communications technologies (ICT), 180n6, 225n5, 228, 228n7

Inglehardt, Ronald, 285

initiative, taking, in modern vs. traditional economies, 58–59, 98, 98n12 innovation(s): vs. adaptation, 31–32; in ancient world, 1, 1n1; current status of, 313–16; definition of, vii, 1, 20, 20n1; development vs. adoption of, 20, 20n1; division of labor in, 23; employment in relation to, 188–91, 222–23; end-users' role in, 29, 29n6; indigenous (See indigenous innovation); international differences in distribution of, 77–78, 105; vs. invention, 20n1; mass, in modern economies, 53–54, 308; need for, to reverse stagnation, 313; in post-1960s economic decline, 225, 228, 263–64; public recognition of role of, vii–viii; during recessions, 235, 235n14; regulations' effects on, 82–83; Schumpeter's account of, ix, xi, 10, 10n12; vs. scientific discoveries, 11, 12–13; scientific discoveries as cause of, ix, xi, 9–12, 26–27; selection mechanisms for, 24–26; short termism and, 314; in socialist economies, lack of, 127–29, 130; as source of economic knowledge, 12–14; stages in process of, 23; understanding of mechanisms of, need for, 317–19; use of term, 20n1; variations in volume of, 20–21

innovation system, national economy as, 20

input. See productivity

insiders, in corporatism, 178–79

insight, in dynamism, 28, 29, 32

institutions: vs. culture, 195n1; financial (See financial institutions); German Historical School on role of, 9n11; political, 93–96, 142–43; in rise of innovation, vii, 79–80

institutions, economic: of capitalism, 204–7; in economic performance, 104; financial institutions as, 91–92; in formation of modern economies, 81–92, 314; freedoms as, 81–85; international differences in, 104; in job satisfaction, 201–7; private property as, 83–86, 204; in representative democracies, 93–94; of socialism, 120

insurance: social, 206–7, 258; unemployment, 50, 201–2

intellectual property rights: in formation of modern economies, 85–86; origins of protections for, 85–86, 253; problems caused by, 253–54

interactivity: in dynamism, 38–39; in modern experience of work, 58, 60–61

interchange, in modern experience of work, 58, 60–61

interest rates, expansion of entitlements and, 261

international differences: in economic culture, 103–4, 209–11; in economic knowledge, 11–12; in innovation, rise of, 77–78, 105; in job satisfaction (See job satisfaction); in modern values, 103–4, 285–86

International Monetary Fund (IMF), 303

International Social Survey Programme, 199

international trade. See trade

internet boom, 219, 261, 303, 311, 315

internet revolution, 188, 226

internships, for regulators and legislators, 318

inventions: accidental innovations, 33; characteristics of inventors, 12–13; headline, of First Industrial Revolution, 12–14; vs. innovation, 20n1; as source of scientific knowledge, 12–13

investment banks: and commercial banks, separation of, 154, 245; origins of, 92; as partnerships, 88; structural faults of, as source of post-1960s economic decline, 244–46

Ireland: corporatism in, interwar, 151; corporatism in, measurement of, 180–82; corporatism in, performance of, 182–86; economic performance of, recent, 182–86; job satisfaction in, 196, 198, 201, 214; pauperism in, 48

Irving, Washington: "The Legend of Sleepy Hollow," 68; The Sketch Book of Geoffrey Crayon, Gent., 68

isolation, innovation impeded by, 39

Israel, modernization of economy of, 42

Italian corporatism: interwar, 141–42, 143–47, 155–56; measurement of, 179–82, 180n6; performance of, 182–87; postwar, 160–63

Italy: art depicting modern life in, 71; authoritarianism in, 133; bribery in, 178; capitalism in, rejection of, 144–45; constitution of, 156–57; corporatism in (See Italian corporatism); dynamism in, 21; economic knowledge in, 12; economic performance of, interwar, 155–56; economic performance of, recent, 171–77, 182–87, 192; job satisfaction in, 199, 201, 214, 233; mercantile capitalism in, 5, 144; music depicting modern life in, 74; 19th-century productivity in, 8, 21; post-1960s economic decline in, 233; scientism in, 142; socialism in, 134, 144; in World War I, 144

Jacobs, Jane, 106–7, 107n21

James, William, 58n3, 280–81, 281n14, 282

Malthus, Thomas, 9

managerial revolution, 241

managers: professional, rise of, 241–43; socialist, incentives of, 124, 125; socialist, innovation by, 127–28

Mann, Thomas, *Buddenbrooks,* 67

manufacturing: in post-1960s economic decline, 234–35; in recovery of dynamism, 319–20

"Man Who Made His Mark, The" (Maugham), 29n6

March on Rome (1922), 144

March Revolution (1848), 117

marginal tax rates, 175, 247n7

market capitalization: definition of, 187; as indicator of innovation, 187–91, 188f, 189f, 190f, 191f; in measurement of job satisfaction, 204–5

market-cap-to-output ratio, 187–91, 188f

market economies: equilibrium in, 9; wage setting in, 290. *See also* capitalism; socialism

Marriage of Maria Braun, The (film), 174

Marshall, Alfred: career of, 56n1; *Elements of Economics,* 56n1; on experience of work, 56–57, 58, 278; *Principles,* 47n7

Martin, Peter, 90

Marx, Karl: *The Communist Manifesto,* 41n1, 109, 117, 119; on dignity of work, 118; on Gotha Program, 119n5; historical determinism of, 10, 37; on institutions, role of, 9n11; on *lumpenproletariat,* 295; on materialism, 97; on modernization, 108–9; on productivity growth, 41; Tönnies compared to, 137, 137n2; working class wages and, 46

Marxian socialism, 118, 120. *See also* communism

Mascagni, Pietro, 74, 137

Maslow, Abraham, 277, 281

mass flourishing (nationwide prosperity): definition of, vii; economic justice in, 308; history of rise and fall of, vii, ix; innovation in (*See* innovation); personal flourishing in, vii; political engagement and, 309; public memory of experience of, viii; public recognition of mechanisms of, vii–viii

mass innovation, in modern economies, 53–54, 308

mass production, 276n7

mastery, in the good life, 277, 279, 284

material effects of modern economies, 41–54; on disease and mortality, 48–50, 55; on

economic inclusion, 47; on living standards, 40, 43, 52; popular opinion on, 45–48, 51–52; on productivity growth, 40, 41, 42–43; on unemployment, 50–51, 115–16; on wage growth, 43–50, 52, 109, 114; on working class, 45–48

materialism: in commercial era, 97; corporatism's critique of, 139; and the good life, 286–87; in literature, 66–67

Maugham, Somerset, "The Man Who Made His Mark," 29n6

Maurras, Charles, 151

"maximin" criterion, 294n3

Mayer, Marissa, 250

McChesney, Robert, 256

McCloskey, Deirdre, 8

McDonalds, 287

McKinsey & Company (consulting firm), 24

Means, Gardiner, *The Modern Corporation and Private Property,* 243

means to an end: vs. the good life, 271; pragmatists on, 275

median wage, 114, 227–28

medical practice: government role in, 255, 258; improvements in, with rise of modern economies, 50; in U.S. vs. Europe, 258

Medicare, expansion of, 259–60

Medicis, 91

Meeker, Mary, 259

Meistersinger, Die (Wagner), 74, 137

Melville, Herman: *The Confidence-Man,* 67, 68n12; *Moby-Dick,* 67–68, 68n12

men: employment rates of, decline in, 310; wage inequality among, 227

mental stimulation, through work, 56–58, 61–62, 118

mercantile capitalism, 2–5; bubbles and crashes in, 115; chartered companies in, 89; contemporary critics of, 2, 2n2; culture of, 97; definition of, 2; economic knowledge in, 2–5; experience of work in, 36, 59, 60; vs. modern capitalism, 26, 41, 110; vs. modern economies, 36, 59, 60; origins and rise of, 2, 96–97

merchant banks, 91–92, 322

Merton, Robert, 167

Michelangelo, 99

Mickelthwait, John, *The Company,* 90n8

Micklejohn, Alexander, 296

Microsoft, 242, 286, 290

micro uncertainty, 37

middle class: music of, 72; rise of, 52

motherhood, 299
multiculturalism, and socialism, 173
multifactor productivity. *See* total factor
  productivity
music: diversity in, 38; experience of modern
  life depicted in, 72–75; innovation in, 72–73;
  interactivity in, 39; source of ideas in, 30
Mussolini, Benito: career of, 143–44;
  corporatism under, 142, 143–47, 170; *The
  Doctrine of Fascism*, 145; *Four Speeches on the
  Corporate State*, 145, 145n8, 146
mutual aid societies, 50
mutual funds: reform of, for recovery of
  dynamism, 321; structural faults of, as
  source of post-1960s economic decline,
  243–44
Mynors, Roger, 275n5
Myrdal, Gunnar, 56–57, 58, 278
myths: of economic success, 308; national, 80

NAFTA, 266–67
Nagel, Thomas, 99n13, 284; *The Possibility of
  Altruism*, 208
Napoleon, 95–96, 149
Napoleonic Code of 1804, 85
Napoleonic Wars, 115
National Economic Chamber (Germany), 148
National Economic Council (Germany), 149
national economies, as innovation system, 20.
  See also specific countries
nationalism, German, 147
National Labor Relations Act of 1935 (U.S.), 154
National Labor Relations Board (U.S.), 154
national mythologies, 80
National Opinion Research Center, 231n9
national prosperity. *See* mass flourishing
National Recovery Act of 1933 (U.S.), 152
National Recovery Administration (NRA),
  152–53
National Socialist German Workers Party
  (NSDAP), 147. *See also* Nazi Germany
"natural" monopolies, 241
natural resources, in innovation, 78–79
Nazi Germany: anti-Semitism in, 141n5, 147;
  authoritarianism in, 133; corporatism in,
  147–50, 155–57; economic performance of,
  155–57; Hayek's response to, 132n15, 133;
  women in labor force of, 195
needs, hierarchy of, 277
Nelson, Richard, 142; "How Medical Know-
  How Progresses," 319
Nelson-Phelps model, 29n6

neoclassical economics: happiness in, 277–78;
  welfarism of Keynes in, xi
neo-liberalism, 158, 203
neo-neoclassical economics, 11
Netherlands: chartered joint-stock companies
  of, 89; corporatism in, measurement of,
  179–82; corporatism in, performance
  of, 182–86; economic knowledge in, 12,
  economic performance of, recent, 171–73,
  176, 182–86; mercantile capitalism in, 5, 115;
  Wassenaar Agreement in, 161
net (after-tax) wage, 227n6, 260–61
new corporatism, 166–68, 265–66
New Deal, 152–54
New Orleans, jazz in, 75
Newton, Isaac, 11
New York, Philharmonic Society of, 72
New Zealand, corporatism in, 181
Nickell, Stephen, 180, 201n6
Nicomachean Ethics (Aristotle), 271, 271n2, 284
Nietzsche, Friedrich, 101, 281–82; *The Will to
  Power*, 282n16
Nightingale, Florence, 286
NIMBY, 83
Nocken, Ulrich, 149
nonmaterial effects: job satisfaction as (*See*
  job satisfaction); of modern economies (*See*
  modern life)
nonparticipants in economy, economic justice
  and, 298–300, 305–6
nonpecuniary motives, in dynamism, 25, 25n3,
  29
nonprofit sector, 298, 299, 306
"Non Sequitur of the 'Dependence Effect,' The"
  (Hayek), 34n9, 129n12
North American Free Trade Agreement
  (NAFTA), 266–67
Northrop, 34
Norway: corporatism in, measurement of,
  181–82; corporatism in, performance of,
  182–84; economic performance of, recent,
  171–73, 182–84, 320; job satisfaction in, 207;
  mercantile capitalism in, 5
Noyce, Robert, 27
NRA. *See* National Recovery Administration
NSDAP. *See* National Socialist German
  Workers Party
nutrition, effects of modern economies on,
  48, 49

Obama, Barack, 313
Oberton, Merle, 64n7

observations, in creation of ideas, 30

Occupy Wall Street protests, 291

OECD. *See* Organisation for Economic Co-operation and Development

OECD Jobs Study, The (OECD), 222

oligarchic economies, as type of corporatism, 26

Olson, Mancur, *The Rise and Decline of Nations,* 319

Omidyar, Pierre, 205

only children, 250

opera, 74–75, 137

opportunity costs, in socialism, 122, 126

Organisation for Economic Co-operation and Development (OECD), 161, 180, 182, 187, 229; *Economic Outlook,* 173; *The OECD Jobs Study,* 222

Organization of National Labor Act of 1934 (Germany), 148

Orwell, George, 65

Oswald, Andrew, 196, 231, 231n10

outliers, 198–99

output, of dynamism, measurement of, 21. *See also* productivity

output per unit of capital, 220

output per worker (labor productivity): in corporatism vs. capitalism, 156, 182–85, 184f; growth in, as material benefit of modern economies, 42–43; market cap in relation to, 187–88, 188f; in mercantile era, 3–5, 3n3, 4n4; 19th-century growth in, 5–8; in socialism vs. capitalism, 177; synonyms for, 42; 20th-century growth in, 8; wages in relation to, 44–45, 47. *See also specific countries*

outsiders, in corporatism, 178–79

Ozment, Suzanne, 66

Paine, Thomas, *Common Sense,* 136

paintings, experience of modern life depicted in, 68–72

Pajama Putsch, 152n15

panics, financial, 115

parallel economies, 306

Paris (France): February Revolution in, 117; wages in, 45, 45n3

Parliament, British: on chartered companies, 89; democracy in, 95; in Glorious Revolution, 86; on patents and copyrights, 253

Parliament, Italian, 144

partnerships, 88, 244

Patent Act (U.S.), 85

patents: origins of, 85, 253; pharmaceutical, 254n11; problems caused by, 253–54

pauperism, reduction in, as social benefit of wage growth, 48

peace, during rise of modern economies, 53n15

Pecora, Ferdinand, 245

Pecora Commission, 154

pecuniary motives, in dynamism, 25, 25n3, 29

Peirce, Charles, 58n3

penicillin, 33

performance, economic: of corporatism (*See* corporatism, performance of); economic culture in, 103–4, 210–11; in good economy, 269–70; of socialism, claims vs. evidence on, 170–78. *See also specific countries*

Perón, Juan, 152

Perry, Claire, 55

personal achievements: in the good life, 284, 285; in modern experience of work, 59

personal flourishing: definition of, vii, 15; desire for, 287–88; *eudaimonia* as, 284; in the good life, 284–85, 287–88; in mass flourishing, vii

personal growth: careers as means to, 65–66; as modern value, 99; in socialism vs. capitalism, 119; in vitalism, 99n13

personal hygiene, effects of modern economies on, 49

personal knowledge: in creation of ideas, 30–31, 31n7, 101; in the good life, 273–77, 284

Petipa, Marius, 75

pharmaceutical industry, 254, 254n11

Phelps, Edmund S., 106n20, 167n30, 177n3, 198n4, 204, 205, 206, 208n16, 212, 222, 224n4, 247n7, 252n9, 261n17, 322; *Fiscal Neutrality toward Economic Growth,* 263; *Rewarding Work,* 240, 292; "The Unproven Case for Tax Cuts," 263

Philharmonic Society of New York, 72

Phillips, A. W., 51

physical capital, in value of companies, 187

Picasso, Pablo, 139

Pico della Mirandola, Giovanni, 99

Pigou, Arthur Cecil, 56n1

Pius XI (pope), 139

Pixar, 33

plague, bubonic, 3, 4

Plato, 37n14, 272

pluralism: in dynamism, 38; of values, and economic justice, 305–6

poems, symphonic, 73–74

public sector: innovation within, 38, 308; labor unions in, 323; as measure of corporatism, 159, 161–63, 164, 178, 179; in recovery of dynamism, 316–20

public works, chartered companies in, 89

Puccini, Giacomo, 74

punctuated equilibrium, 22–23

Quadragesimo Anno (Pius XI), 139

quests, viii, 74, 136, 280, 288

racial diversity, and wage inequality, 186

Raft of the Medusa, The (Géricault), 69, 69n13

railroads: art depicting, 69–70, 71; European, 116; U.S., 14, 33

Rand, Ayn, 82

rational behavior, in socialism, 122

rational-humanism, 63n5

rationalism, 280

Ravel, Maurice, 74–75

Ravitch, Richard, 259

Rawls, John: on justice, 228, 290–95, 299–300, 305–6; on self-realization, viii, 277, 278, 281, 292; student protests of 1960s and, 290, 290n1; *A Theory of Justice*, 228, 289, 290–96; on wealth accumulation, 301

Razzell, Peter, 48n9

Reagan, Ronald, 164, 226, 229, 247

real wages per worker: definition of, 4; economic knowledge and, 4; effects of modern economies on, 43–50; in mercantile era, 4–5, 4n4; 19th-century growth in, 5–8; 20th-century growth in, 8

reason: in the good life, 273; in humans vs. animals, 273, 273n3

recessions: of 2008–2009, 175, 235, 236; innovation during, 235, 235n14; job security in, 234; in mercantile capitalism, 115; in post-1960s economic decline, 235–36; recoveries from, 235–36

redistribution, of income, 292, 293–95, 299–300

Red Scare, 134

red tape, bureaucratic, as measure of corporatism, 162, 162n26, 164, 180

Reform Act of 1832 (Britain), 95

regional banks, decline of, 303–4

regulations. *See* government regulations

Reich, Robert, 62

Reichstag, 148, 149

Reiss, Diana, 61

relational banking, 321, 322

religion, and economic culture, 78

Renaissance: commerce and foreign trade in, 2; origins of modernism in, 99–100; sparse innovation in, 1

representative democracy, in formation of modern economies, 93–96, 105, 109

Republican Party (U.S.): on social welfare, 260; traditional values in, 260, 317

Rerum Novarum (Leo XIII), 139

resource allocation: in socialism, 119–20, 125–26; in U.S., corporatist influence on, 164–65

responsibility: obligations of, in modernism, 136–37; social, in corporatism, 139

retirement, mental stimulation after, 62

revolutions of 1848, 116, 117

Rewarding Work (Phelps), 240, 292

Reynolds, Joshua, 68

Ricardo, David, 9, 194

Richberg, Donald, 153

Riefenstahl, Leni, 139

Riesman, David, *The Lonely Crowd,* 238

rights against the king, 86–87

Ring of the Niebelung, The (Wagner), 74, 119, 141

Rise and Decline of Nations, The (Olson), 319

Risk, Uncertainty and Profit (Knight), 37n13

Road to Serfdom, The (Hayek), 129n12, 131–32, 132n15, 133, 149, 156n21

Robb, Richard, 68n12

Robertson, Dennis H., 56n1, 185

Robinson Crusoe (Defoe), 37, 39, 63, 279n13

Rocco Laws. *See* Sindical Laws

Rodgers, Richard, 153n16

Rodin, Auguste, *The Thinker,* 71

Roiphe, Katie, 304

Romanticism: art of, 68–70; conception of the good life in, 280; literature of, 63–64

Rome, ancient: innovation in, 1; legal system of, 84–85, 137, 202; private property in, 84–85

Rome, March on (1922), 144

Roosevelt, Franklin, 152–55

Roosevelt, Theodore, 154

Rorty, Richard, 58n3

Roscher, Wilhelm, 9n11

Rostow, Walt W., 6, 6n7, 7, 8, 78

Rothschild family, 91

Rousseau, Jean-Jacques, *Émile,* 279n13

Royce, Josiah, 58n3

ruinous competition, 245–46

rule of law: in democracies, 94; development of, 86–87; role in capitalism, 87, 94

rural areas: creativity in, vs. cities, 107, 107n21; depopulation of (*See* urbanization)

Ruskin, John, 69

Russia: Bolshevik revolution in, 134; factories of, 52; music depicting modern life in, 75. *See also* Soviet Union

Rylance, Rick, 66n11

Saalfeld, Diedrich, 6n8
Saarinen, Esa, 39
Sade, Marquis de, 286
Sadka, Efraim, 247n7
Saint-Simon, Henri de, 117, 117n2
Salazar, Antonio, 151
Salgado, Plínio, 151–52, 152n15
Samuelson, Paul, 80, 244
Sandberg, Sheryl, 243
Sarbanes-Oxley law (U.S.), 164
Sardinia, Statuto Albertino of, 144n7
Sassoon, Donald, 117–18
saving: in economic culture, 78; productivity growth and, 223–25; in socialist economies, 174
Say, Jean-Baptiste, 101, 207
Scandizzo, Pasquale Lucio, 286
Schechter v. United States, 153
Schliemann, Heinrich, 287
Schmitter, Philippe, 143n6
Schröder, Gerhard, 161
Schulz, Nick, 255
Schumann, Robert: *Manfred,* 73; piano quartet in E flat major, 73
Schumpeter, Joseph: *Capitalism, Socialism and Democracy,* 10n12, 27n4, 207; on capitalism as culture, 207; on definition of innovation, 20n1; on entrepreneurs, need for, 9–10, 28, 98n12; in German Historical School, 9–10, 9n11; on nonpecuniary returns for entrepreneurs, 25n3; on punctuated equilibrium, 22–23; on science in innovation, ix, xi, 9–12, 10n12, 27; *The Theory of Economic Development,* 10n12; on vibrancy, 20; Weber's influence on, 78n2
science: corporatist view of advances in, 142; in dynamism, x; in economic success, 308; entrepreneurs' use of, ix, 9–10; innovations as separate from discoveries in, 11, 12–13; innovations attributed to discoveries in, ix, xi, 9 12, 26 27; material benefits of modern economies and, 53; publication of findings in, 11; as source of economic knowledge, 9–12
Scientific Revolution, 10–11, 100, 287
scientism, 10–13, 26–27, 142
Scotland: mercantile capitalism in, 2; poverty in, decline of, 48

sculpture, experience of modern life depicted in, 71
Second Great Depression, **175**
Second Industrial Revolution, 13n13
Second Transformation, of U.S. economy, 264–65
Securities Act of 1933 (U.S.), 154
Securities and Exchange Commission, 154
Securities Exchange Act of 1934 (U.S.), 154
Seipel, Ignaz, 151
selection mechanisms, for ideas in modern economies, 24–26
self-actualization: in the good life, 277, 281; in modern experience of work, 58
self-affirmation, in modern experience of work, 58–59
self-discovery: in the good life, 281; in modern experience of work, 59; as modern value, 99; in vitalism, 99n13, 281
self-expression, in modern experience of work, 58–59
self-importance, culture of, 249
self-interest: in corporatism, 148, 152n15; in mercantile economies, 97
self-ownership, 81–82
self-realization: in the good life, 277, 278, 281; in modern experience of work, 58; Rawls on, viii, 277, 278, 281, 292
self-respect, 81
Seligman, Martin, *Flourish,* 285
Sen, Amartya, 58n3, 132n15, 133, 277–78, 278n12, 285, 309
Sennett, Richard, 285, 285n21
Severini, Gino, 71
shadow price, in socialism, 122
Shakespeare, William: *Hamlet,* 100, 280; *Henry V,* 278; *King Lear,* 100
shareowning: in formation of modern economies, 83; structural faults of, in post-1960s economic decline, 243–44
Shaw, George Bernard, 147
Shelley, Mary, *Frankenstein,* 63–64
Shelley, Percy Bysshe, 64; *Prometheus Unbound,* 63n5
short-term borrowing, by banks, 244–45, 322
short termism, in management of companies, 243–44, 314, 320–21
Simon, Julian, 106n20
Sindical Laws of 1926 (Italy), 145
Sinn Féin, 151
skilled workers, vs. unskilled workers, wages of, 46, 47

total factor productivity (multifactor productivity): in corporatist economies, 184n11; definition of, 177, 220–21; in post-1960s decline in U.S., 220–21, 221f, 225, 226; in socialist economies, 177

total satisfaction, 198n4

Toynbee, Arnold, 79; *A Study of History,* 79n3

trade, foreign: in early economies, spread of, 2, 77; and job satisfaction, 204n14; postwar expansion of, 158; and smallpox, 48

trademarks, origins of, 85

traditional economics, on productivity growth in 19th century, 7–8

traditional economies: definition of, xii; economic justice in, xii, 302, 305–6; experience of work in, vs. modern economies, 57–59, 109; initiative taking in, 58–59, 98, 98n12; wage inequality in, 302

traditional societies: human fulfillment in, 298; modern elements in, suppression of, 306–7

traditional values: and economic justice for nonparticipants in economy, 298–300, 305–6; economies based on (*See* traditional economies); examples of, 99; and job satisfaction, 211–15, 213f; measurement of, 212–13, 215t; in policymaking, 260; resurgence of, 250, 308, 315–16; struggle between modern values and, viii, x–xi, 211–12, 308, 315–16; in U.S. political parties, 260, 317

Traviata, La (Verdi), 74, 137

Treatise on Human Nature (Hume), 97

trilateralism, of corporatism, 160–61

Trilling, Lionel, 282, 296

tripartism, of corporatism, 147, 148, 160–61, 267

trust, in economic culture, 208–9

tulip mania, 115

Turner, J. M. W., 69–70

Twain, Mark, 91n10

typhoid fever, 49

typhus, 49

tyranny of the majority, 93

uncertainty, economic, 37, 37n13, 318

underground economy, 174

unemployment: in depressions, 116; effects of modern economies on, 50–51, 115–16; in financial crisis of 2007–2008, 311–12; in post-1960s economic decline, 221–24, 226–27, 231–32, 235; postwar corporatism and, 161; in socialist economies, 171–74; in socialist ethic, 118; tax rates and, 226, 227, 227n6; urbanization and, 50–51

unemployment insurance, 50, 201–2

Unified Agenda, 253, 253n10

unions. *See* labor unions

United Kingdom. *See* Britain; England; Ireland; Scotland

United States: banking reform in, 154, 245, 321–22; bankruptcy in, 91; banks in, types of, 92; chartered joint-stock companies of, 89; corporatism in (*See* United States corporatism); democracy in, development of, 94–95; economic culture of, 101–3, 209, 246–50, 309; economic knowledge in, sources of, 11–12; economic performance of, interwar, 155–56; economic performance of, recent, 171–76, 182–86, 192; entrepreneurs in, recognition of value of, 101; financial crises in, origins of, 310–11; financial panics in, 115; formation of modern economy in, 78–79, 94–95, 102–3; frontier of, 102, 108n23; "golden age" narratives of, 237–40; infectious diseases in, decline of, 49; intellectual property rights in, 85; inventions of First Industrial Revolution in, 12; job satisfaction in, 62, 198, 199, 201, 213–14; job security in, 116n1; labor unions in, 323; literature on modern life in, 67–68; mercantile capitalism in, 5; middle class in, rise of, 52; modern values in, 101–3, 136; music depicting modern life in, 72; natural resources of, 78–79; output per worker in, 5–6, 6n6, 7, 7n9, 43; political engagement in, 309; population growth in, 107–8; poverty in, decline of, 48; productivity growth in, 19th-century, 5–8; public opinion in establishment of capitalism in, 113; public sector of, size of, 179; railroads of, 14, 33; real wages per worker in, 5, 6; recessions in, history of, 235–36; recovery of dynamism in, approaches to, 316–24; recovery of dynamism in, prospects for, 308, 317; Second Transformation in, 264–65; social welfare in, 258–60; sovereign debt of, 251–52, 261–63, 312; taxes in (*See* tax); urbanization in, 60, 108; wars of, 53n15

United States, post-1960s economic decline in, 219–67; corporatism in, 251–58, 265–66; culture as source of, 246–50; early data on, 219–27; European impact of, 221–22, 232–33; "golden age" narratives on, 237–40; government role in, 251–64, 266–67; inclusion affected by, 227–30; innovation in, decline of, 225, 228, 263–64; job satisfaction affected by, 230–33, 231n9, 232f; job security affected by, 233–34, 234n12; origins of, 219–20, 313–14; policy reactions to, 225–27, 228–30; productivity slowdown in, 192, 219–25, 220f, 221f; recessions in, 235–36; structural faults as source of, 241–46; structural shifts during, 234–35; unemployment in, 221–24, 226–27, 231–32, 235; wage inequality affected by, 227–30

United States corporatism: current status of, 317; interwar, 152–56; measurement of, 179–82, 180n6; and post-1960s economic decline, 251–58, 265–66; postwar, 164–65; in Second Transformation, 265–66

universal banks, 92

University of Chicago, 296

unknown unknowns, 28, 33–34

"Unproven Case for Tax Cuts, The" (Phelps), 263

unskilled workers: in Dickens's novels, 64–65; vs. skilled workers, wages of, 46, 47

urban areas. *See* cities

urbanization: emergence of big cities in, 108; and experience of work in modern economies, 60–61; in formation of modern economies, 104–8; and innovativeness, 39–40, 39n16; and unemployment, 50–51

"Use of Knowledge in Society, The" (Hayek), 31n7

users. *See* end-users

utilitarianism, 290

Valois, Georges, 135

value-added tax, 202

values: corporatist, 159; in the good life, 285–86; in job satisfaction, 208–15; socialist, 118–20, 132–33. *See also* culture; modern values; traditional values

Van de Velde, Willem, the Younger, 69

van Gogh, Vincent, 70

Vargas, Getúlio, 151, 152n15

Vargas Llosa, Mario, 62

Veblen, Thorstein, 66–67, 194

Velasquez, Diego, 68

Venice (city-state), commercial economy of, 2

Venter, J. Craig, 113

Venturesome Economy, The (Bhidé), 319

Verdi, Giuseppe, 74, 137

Vertigo (film), 78n2

vibrancy: definition of, 20, 194; vs. dynamism, 20, 21, 22; economic culture in, 194

Vichy regime, 151

Vienna (Austria): infectious diseases in, decline of, 49; Philharmonic Orchestra of, 72

Vincent, Walter, 32

Viner, Jacob, 39n16

Virgil, *Georgics,* 275

virtues, vs. the good life, 272

Visconti, Luchino, 154

visual arts, experience of modern life depicted in, 68–72

vitalism: decline of, 316; definition of, 99n13; in formation of modern economies, 102–4, 105; on the good life, 279–88; origins and rise of, 100, 279–81; revival of, 284

Vittorio Emanuele III (king of Italy), 144

Volcker, Paul, 175

Volkswagen, 160

Voltaire: *Candide,* 101–2, 275–76; on the good life, 275–76, 280

voluntary corporatism, in Germany, 149–50

volunteer sector, 299

voodoo economics, 226

wage(s): after-tax (net), 227n6, 260–61; in corporatism, 142–43, 186; effects of modern economies on, 43–50, 52, 109, 114; equal, impossibility of, 290, 291–92; happiness in relation to, 52–53; job satisfaction in relation to, 196, 199, 201; justice in distribution of, 291–95, 299–300, 305–6; median, 114, 227–28; output per worker in relation to, 44–45, 47; ratio of wealth to, 223–24, 223n3, 261, 262f; real (*See* real wages); in relationship between innovation and employment, 222–23, 223n3; social benefits of growth in, 47–50; in socialism, 119–25

wage inequality: in corporatism, 186; justice of, 290, 291–92, 302; in modern capitalism, 302; in post-1960s economic decline, 227–30; rise of, 114–15, 227–28; in socialism, 176–77

wage-productivity ratio, 44–45, 47

wage-wealth ratio, 223–24, 223n3, 261, 262f

Wagner, Richard, 72–73; *Die Meistersinger,* 74, 137; *Ring of the Niebelung, The,* 74, 119, 141

Wagner Act of 1935 (U.S.), 154

Wagner's Law, 260

Wallonia (Belgium), 96

Walt Disney, 254

wars: booms and recessions caused by, 115; during rise of modern economies, 53n15

Wassenaar Agreement (1982), 161

Watt, James, 12, 13, 89

wealth: job satisfaction in relation to, 196, 201; and labor force participation, 260–61, 262f; in money culture, 246–48; ratio of wage to, 223–24, 223n3, 261, 262f; in relationship between innovation and employment, 223, 223n3; social vs. private, 259, 261–63

wealth accumulation: antipathy for, 301; in capitalism, rise of, 108; democratization of, 115; disparities in, rise of, 114–15; in economic culture, 104; as economic freedom, 83–84; in economic justice, 301–2; and the good life, 286–87; motivations for, 286–87; in socialism, 119

wealth effect, 260–63

Wealth of Nations, The (Smith), 2n2, 97

wealthy: income of, vs. working class wages, 47; infectious diseases among, decline of, 49

Webb, James Watson, 91n10

Weber, Max: on economic culture, 78, 97, 194; on economic freedoms, 82; *Economy and Society,* 78n2; on formation of modern economies, 79, 97; in German Historical School, 9n11; on modernization, 108–9; *The Protestant Ethic and the Spirit of Capitalism,* 78n2

Wedgwood, Eli, 89

Weimar Germany, 148, 150, 157

welfare: corporate, 254, 267; social (*See* social welfare)

welfarism, neoclassical, xi

well-being: in the good life, 285; Smith's conception of, xi

Wells, David, 48, 48n8, 49, 49n13

Wen Jiabao, 130

West Germany, corporatism in, 157–62

Whale, James, 64

Whitman, Walt, 281

Wiesel, Elie, 249

Wilde, Oscar, 136

Wilhelm (emperor of Germany), 149

William II (king of England), 86

Williamson, Jeffrey, 6n8

Will to Power, The (Nietzsche), 282n16

Wilson, Woodrow, 154

wisdom, in creation of ideas, 28

Wollstonecraft, Mary, 67

women: labor force participation by, 195; self-ownership of, 81–82

Wooldridge, Adrian, *The Company,* 90n8

work: balance between home and, 304; devaluation of, 229–30; in the good life, 275–78, 304

work, experience of: effects of modern economies on, 55–62; mental stimulation through, 56–58, 118; in mercantile vs. modern economy, 36, 59, 60; modern literature on, 62–68; modern paintings on, 68–72; in traditional vs. modern economy, 57–59, 109. *See also* job satisfaction

workers, in socialism: incentives of, 122–26, 123n7; rights of, 118

work ethic, in socialism, 123

working class: diet of, 49; effects of modern economies on wages of, 45–48, 114; in Italian corporatism, 145–46; job satisfaction among, 62; music of, 72

Works Project Administration, 153

World Bank, *Bureaucrats in Business,* 171

World Economy, The (Maddison), 3

World Values Surveys (WVS), 103, 196, 197–98, 199, 210, 211, 212–13, 233, 285–86

World War I: German reparations for, 148; Italy in, 144

World War II: corporatism after, 156–57; Holocaust in, 141n5

writing, expository, 324

Wullschlager, Jackie, 55

Wuthering Heights (Emily Brontë), 64, 64n6

Wuthering Heights (film), 64, 64n7

WVS. *See* World Values Surveys

Wyler, William, 64n7

Yahoo, 250

zaibatsu, 152

Zakaria, Fareed, 313

Zingales, Luigi, 254

Zoega, Gylfi, 198n4, 204, 205, 206, 261n17, 286

Zola, Émile, 67

zoology, modern views in, 61

Zuckerberg, Mark, 243, 249